# 797,885 Books
are available to read at

www.ForgottenBooks.com

Forgotten Books' App
Available for mobile, tablet & eReader

ISBN 978-1-332-71255-7
PIBN 10534020

This book is a reproduction of an important historical work. Forgotten Books uses
state-of-the-art technology to digitally reconstruct the work, preserving the original format
whilst repairing imperfections present in the aged copy. In rare cases, an imperfection in
the original, such as a blemish or missing page, may be replicated in our edition. We do,
however, repair the vast majority of imperfections successfully; any imperfections that
remain are intentionally left to preserve the state of such historical works.

Forgotten Books is a registered trademark of FB &c Ltd.
Copyright © 2015 FB &c Ltd.
FB &c Ltd, Dalton House, 60 Windsor Avenue, London, SW19 2RR.
Company number 08720141. Registered in England and Wales.

For support please visit www.forgottenbooks.com

# 1 MONTH OF FREE READING

## at
## www.ForgottenBooks.com

By purchasing this book you are eligible for one month membership to ForgottenBooks.com, giving you unlimited access to our entire collection of over 700,000 titles via our web site and mobile apps.

To claim your free month visit:
www.forgottenbooks.com/free534020

\* Offer is valid for 45 days from date of purchase. Terms and conditions apply.

English
Français
Deutsche
Italiano
Español
Português

# www.forgottenbooks.com

**Mythology** Photography **Fiction**
Fishing Christianity **Art** Cooking
Essays Buddhism Freemasonry
Medicine **Biology** Music **Ancient Egypt** Evolution Carpentry Physics
Dance Geology **Mathematics** Fitness
Shakespeare **Folklore** Yoga Marketing
**Confidence** Immortality Biographies
Poetry **Psychology** Witchcraft
Electronics Chemistry History **Law**
Accounting **Philosophy** Anthropology
Alchemy Drama Quantum Mechanics
Atheism Sexual Health **Ancient History**
**Entrepreneurship** Languages Sport
Paleontology Needlework Islam
**Metaphysics** Investment Archaeology
Parenting Statistics Criminology
**Motivational**

# A COLLECTION
## OF
# SERMONS AND TRACTS:
## IN TWO VOLUMES.
### CONTAINING,

| VOL. I. | VOL. II. |
|---|---|
| I. ANNUAL SERMONS. | I. ORDINATION SERMONS. |
| II. OCCASIONAL SERMONS. | II. POLEMICAL TRACTS. |
| III. FUNERAL SERMONS. | III. DISSERTATIONS. |

Several of which were never before PRINTED.

By the late REVEREND and LEARNED

# JOHN GILL, *D. D.*

To which are Prefixed,

# MEMOIRS
## OF THE
LIFE, WRITINGS, and CHARACTER of the AUTHOR.

---

## VOL. II.

---

LONDON:
Printed for GEORGE KEITH in Gracechurch-Street.
M DCC LXXIII.

# ADVERTISEMENT.

IT may be neceſſary to appriſe the Reader, that ſeveral of the Doctor's Tracts are not included in this collection: namely, His "Diſſertation concerning the Antiquity of the Hebrew Language, Letters, Vowel-Points and Accents; The Doctrine of the Trinity ſtated and vindicated; The Doctrine of the Reſurrection ſtated and defended; The Doctrine of Juſtification by the Righteouſneſs of Chriſt, ſtated and maintained; The Doctrine of God's everlaſting Love to his Elect, and their eternal Union with Chriſt; together with ſome other Truths, ſtated and defended, againſt Dr Taylor; The Doctrine of the Saints' final Perſeverance, aſſerted and vindicated; The Doctrine of Predeſtination ſtated, and ſet in a Scripture-Light, againſt Mr Weſley; The Prophecies of the Old Teſtament reſpecting the Meſſiah conſidered, and proved to be literally fulfilled in Jeſus; containing an Anſwer to the Author of The Scheme of Literal Prophecy, &c. Two annual Diſcourſes on the Duty of Prayer and Singing of Pſalms; An Eſſay on the Original of Funeral Sermons, Orations and Odes; A brief Confeſſion of Faith," &c. The reaſon why theſe Tracts are omitted, is, becauſe moſt of thoſe ſubjects are fully treated of in his *Body of Divinity*. Either of the above Tracts may be had ſeparately, and if encouraged, will be collected into a volume, like the two already publiſhed.

The Editor takes, likewiſe, this opportunity of requeſting the candor of the learned Reader to excuſe any literary miſtakes, which may occur in any of the quotations from the dead languages: an apology, which there would have been no reaſon for offering, had theſe two volumes undergone the Doctor's laſt reviſal.

# THE CONTENTS.

## VOLUME II.

| | Page |
|---|---|
| I. A Sermon at the Ordination of the Rev. George Braithwaite, M. A. | 1 |
| II. A Sermon at the Ordination of several Ministers, | 14 |
| III. A Sermon at the Ordination of the Reverend Mr John Davis, | 30 |
| IV. A Sermon at the Ordination of the Reverend Mr John Reynolds, | 49 |
| V. Truth Defended: in Answer to a Pamphlet on the Supralapsarian Scheme, | 65 |
| VI. An Answer to the Birmingham Dialogue-Writer, Part I. | 107 |
| VII. An Answer to the Birmingham Dialogue-Writer, Part II. | 135 |
| VIII. The Moral Nature and Fitness of Things, Considered, | 162 |
| IX. The Necessity of Good Works unto Salvation, Considered, | 181 |
| X. The Ancient Mode of Baptizing, Maintained and Vindicated, | 196 |
| XI. A Defence of ditto, | 238 |
| XII. The Divine Right of Infant-Baptism, Examined and Disproved, | 259 |
| XIII. The Argument from Apostolic Tradition, in favour of Infant-Baptism, with others advanced in a Pamphlet, called, The Baptism of Infants a reasonable Service, &c. Considered; and also An Answer to a Welch Clergyman's Twenty Arguments for Infant-Baptism. To which are added, The Dissenters Reasons for separating from the Church of England, | 317 |
| XIV. Antip.edobaptism; or, Infant-Baptism an Innovation, | 382 |
| XV. A Reply to a Defence of the Divine Right of Infant-Baptism; with Strictures on Mr Bostwick's Vindication of Infant-Baptism, | 407 |
| XVI. The Scriptures the only Guide in Matters of Religion, | 479 |
| XVII. Baptism a Divine Commandment, | 497 |
| XVIII. Infant-Baptism, a Part and Pillar of Popery, | 511 |
| XIX. A Dissertation on the Eternal Sonship of Christ, | 534 |
| XX. A Dissertation on the Rise and Progress of Popery, | 565 |
| XXI. Dying Thoughts, | 585 |

## ERRATA.

Page 264. Line 1. administration ordinances, read of ordinances.
324. 11. instead of aaffirm, r. affirm.
389. 12. for hut, r. but.
413. 8. for being imminent, r. being immanent.
462. 14. for thidg, r. thing.

# ORDINATION SERMONS.

## SERMON XXXVII.

*The Duty of a Pastor to his People.*

Preached at the ORDINATION of the Reverend GEORGE BRAITHWAITE, M.A. March 28, 1734.

2 TIMOTHY IV. 16.

*Take heed unto thyself, and unto thy doctrine; for in doing this, thou shalt both save thyself, and them that hear thee.*

THE part of the work of this day assigned to me, is to give a word of exhortation to you, my Brother; who have been at this time solemnly ordained a pastor or overseer of this church. Your long standing, and usefulness in the ministry, might justly excuse every thing of this kind, did not custom, and the nature of this day's service, seem to require it. You will therefore suffer a word of exhortation, though it comes from a junior minister, since you know in what situation we are; our senior ministers are gone off the stage of this world, who used to fill up this place, and whose years best became it: *Our fathers, where are they? and the prophets, do they live for ever?* Give me leave to address you in the words of the great apostle of the Gentiles to *Timothy, Take heed unto thyself, and unto thy doctrine; for in doing this, thou shalt both save thyself, and them that hear thee;* since this epistle was written, not for his sake only, but for the use and service also of other ministers of the gospel in succeeding ages; that they might *know how they ought to behave themselves in the house of God, which is the church of the living God, the pillar and ground of truth.* In it the apostle gives a large account of the proper qualifications of the officers of churches, bishops, and deacons; and in this chapter descends to some particular advice and directions to *Timothy*, and which are designed for the benefit and advantage of other preachers of the word, and pastors of churches. I shall not take any notice of them here, seeing I shall have occasion to make use of them in some parts of the following discourse; and shall therefore immediately attend to the words of my text, in which may be observed,

I. A charge or exhortation given to *Timothy*.
II. Some reasons to support it, and engage his regard unto it.

I. Here is a charge or exhortation given, which consists of three parts.
*First*, To take heed to himself.
*Secondly*, To take heed to his doctrine.
*Thirdly*, To continue therein.

*First*, The apostle exhorts *Timothy* to *take heed to himself*. This is not to be understood of him merely as a man, that he should take care of his bodily health, his outward concerns of life, or make provision for his family, if he had any; not but that these things are to be equally regarded by a minister of the gospel, as by any other person. Though he ought to be diligent in his studies, laborious in his work, and preach the gospel *in season and out of season*; yet he ought to be careful of the health of his body, and not destroy his natural constitution. The words of the wise man are applicable to our present purpose, *be not righteous over-much, neither make thyself over-wise, why shouldest thou destroy thyself*[a]? The apostle *Paul*, in this epistle, advises *Timothy* to take care of himself in this sense, seeing he had much work upon his hands, and but of a weakly constitution; he exhorts him, that he would *drink no longer water, but use a little wine, for his stomach's sake, and his often infirmities*[b]; and it is alike true of a minister as of any other man, what is elsewhere said, *If any provide not for his own, and especially for those of his own house, he hath denied the faith, and is worse than an infidel*[c]. But this is not what the apostle has here in view, when he says *take heed to thyself*.

Nor is this exhortation given to *Timothy* under the character of a believer, or private christian. There are some things which are common to ministers, and private christians; their cases, in some respects, are alike, and cautions to them are equally necessary: they have the same corruptions, are subject to the same temptations, and liable to the same daily failings and infirmities; and therefore such, whether ministers or people, who think they stand, should *take heed lest they fall*. Unbelief, and distrust of divine providence, presence, power, and assistance,

---
[a] Eccles. vii. 16.   [b] 1 Tim. v. 23.   [c] 1 Tim. v. 8.

aſſiſtance, have a place in the hearts of miniſters as well as others, and ſometimes riſe to a conſiderable pitch, and do very much prevail; when ſuch advice as this muſt be needful, *take heed, brethren, leſt there be in any of you an evil heart of unbelief, in departing from the living God*. There are many inſtances which might be produced, in which this exhortation would appear to be ſuitable to *Timothy*, and ſo to any other goſpel miniſter, conſidered as a believer and a chriſtian.

But I apprehend, that the apoſtle regards him in his miniſterial capacity, as a preacher of the word; and is deſirous, that he would take heed to himſelf, as a miniſter, and *to the miniſtry which* he had *received in the Lord, that he fulfil it*. It becomes a miniſter of the goſpel to take heed to his gifts beſtowed upon him, by which he is qualified for his work, that he does not loſe, but uſe and improve them; to his time, that he ſpends it aright, and does not ſquander it away; of the errors and hereſies which are in the world, that he is not infected by them; to his ſpirit, temper, and paſſions, that he is not governed by them; to his life and converſation, that it be exemplary, becoming his office, and makes for the glory of God; and to the flock committed to his care, which is the other part of himſelf.

1. A miniſter ought to take heed to his gifts beſtowed upon him, whereby he is qualified for the work of the miniſtry. Jeſus Chriſt, when he aſcended on high, received gifts for men, ſuch as were proper to furniſh, and fit them for miniſterial ſervice; and he has given them to men, *he gave ſome apoſtles, and ſome prophets, and ſome evangeliſts, and ſome paſtors, and teachers*[e]: that is, he gave gifts, to qualify them for theſe ſeveral offices; and he ſtill continues to give gifts to ſome, by which they become capable of diſcharging the work and office of paſtors of churches; and where theſe are given, they ought to be taken care of.

Now, a miniſter of the goſpel ſhould take heed to his gifts, that he does not loſe them. *The gifts and calling of God are without repentance*[f]. Gifts of ſpecial and ſaving grace are irreverſible; God never repents of them, or revokes them, or calls them in; where they are once beſtowed, they are never taken away; but gifts fitting men for public work and uſefulneſs, as they may be where true grace is not, ſo they may be removed, when ſaving grace never will. This we may learn from the parable of the talents, where our Lord ſays, *Take therefore the talent from him, and give it to him which hath ten talents. For unto every one that hath ſhall be given, and he ſhall have abundance: But from him that hath not ſhall be taken away even that which he hath*[g]. Wo therefore *to the Idol Shepherd*

[d] Heb. iii. 12. [e] Epheſ. iv. 11. [f] Rom. xi. 29. [g] Matt. xxv. 29, 30.

## A SERMON AT THE ORDINATION

*Shepherd*[h], the shepherd of no account, who is good for nothing; for *an idol is nothing in the world*; who *leaveth the flock*, makes no use of his gifts, deserts his station, forsakes the flock; *the sword shall be upon his arm, and upon his right eye; his arm shall be clean dried up, and his right eye shall be utterly darkened.* All his light and knowledge, his abilities and usefulness, shall be taken from him. Hence the apostle exhorts *Timothy, to keep by the holy Ghost the good thing which was committed to him*; by which he means, not grace, but either the gospel, or the gift of preaching it; grace cannot, gifts may be lost.

Moreover, a gospel minister should take heed to his gifts, that he uses them: *Neglect not the gift that is in thee*, says the apostle to *Timothy*; *which was given thee by prophecy, with the laying on of the hands of the presbytery*[k]. A minister may be tempted to neglect, lay aside, and disuse his gifts, for want of success in his work, or because of the slight and contempt which may be cast upon him, or by reason of the rage, fury, and persecutions of men; something of this nature was discouraging to *Timothy* in the exercise of his gifts, which occasioned the apostle to *put him in remembrance, that*, says he, *thou stir up the gift of God which is in thee, by the putting on of my hands; for God hath not given us the spirit of fear, but of power, of love, and of a sound mind. Be not thou therefore ashamed of the testimony of our Lord, nor of me his prisoner; but be thou partaker of the afflictions of the gospel, according to the power of God*[l]. As if he should say, "Let not that gift which God has bestowed upon thee lie dormant, and be neglected by thee, through a timorous and cowardly spirit; but boldly and bravely preach the gospel of the grace of God, though thou art sure to endure much affliction and persecution." Wo to that man, who, from any consideration whatever, wraps up his talent in a napkin, and hides it in the earth; such an one Christ, at the great day of account, will call *wicked and slothful*; and give orders to *cast* such *an unprofitable servant into outer darkness, where shall be weeping and gnashing of teeth*[m].

Besides, a minister ought not only to take heed that he uses his gifts, but also that he improves them; and, indeed, they are generally improved by using. Gifts, like pieces of armour, through disuse, grow rusty[n], but the more they are worn the brighter they are. There are several things which have a tendency to improve, and, with the blessing of God, do improve spiritual gifts, such as prayer, meditation, and reading. These the apostle directed *Timothy* to, for the improvement of his mind: *Till I come*, says he, *give attendance.*

---

[h] Zech. xi. 17.   [i] 2 Tim. i. 14.   [k] 1 Tim. iv. 14.
[l] 2 Tim. i. 6—8.   [m] Matt. xxv. 26, 30.
[n] Adde, quod ingenium longa rubigine laesum
Torpet.———       OVID.

*ance to reading, to exhortation, to doctrine* °; *meditate upon these things, give thyself wholly to them* ᴾ, or, be thou in them; be constantly intent upon them, *that thy profiting may appear to all* ᑫ, or in all things, that is, in all parts of useful knowledge. It is the duty of ministers to *stir up the gift of God which is in them* ʳ. Gifts are sometimes like coals of fire, covered and buried in ashes, to which there is an allusion in this passage ˢ, which must be stirred up, or blown off, that they may revive and be re-inflamed, and so communicate more light and heat. It is true, ministers cannot procure gifts for themselves, nor increase them of themselves; but God is pleased to give to his servants greater abilities, more light and knowledge, in the diligent use of means, *for unto every one that hath*, that is, that has gifts, and makes use of all proper methods to improve them, *shall be given, and he shall have abundance*.

2. A minister ought to take heed to his time, that he spends it aright, and does not squander it away. Time is precious, and ought to be redeemed, and diligently improved, by all sorts of men; but by none more than the ministers of the gospel, who should spend it in frequent prayer, constant meditation, and in daily reading the scriptures, and the writings of good men; which are transmitted to posterity for the benefit and advantage of the churches of Christ. They should give themselves up wholly to these things, and daily and diligently *study to shew* themselves *approved unto God, workmen that need not be ashamed, rightly dividing the word of truth* ᵗ. They ought not to spend their time in an unprofitable manner, or in needless and unnecessary visits. It is a mistake which prevails among church-members, that they must be visited, and that very often: if ministers are not continually calling on them they think themselves neglected, and are much displeased; not considering, that such a frequency of visits, as is desired by them, must be the bane and ruin of what might otherwise be a very valuable ministry; and at the same time furnishes an idle and lazy preacher with a good excuse to neglect his studies, and that with a great deal of peace and quietness of conscience, whilst he fancies he is about his ministerial work. I would not be understood, as though I thought that visits were needless things, and that they are no part of a minister's work: I am sensible, that he ought to *be diligent to know the state of his flock*; and that it is his business to visit the members of the church, at proper times, and on proper occasions; what I complain of, is the too great frequency of visits as is desired, and when they are unnecessary.

° 1 Tim. iv. 15.    ᴾ Εν τουτοις ισθι.    ᑫ Εν πασιν.    ʳ 2 Tim. i. 6.
ˢ Verbum αναζωπυρειν etiam modeste eum officii admonet. Significat autem ignem cineribus tectum excitare, sopitam favillam in flammam proferre. Aretius in 2 Tim. i. 6. In the same sense as here is the word used in Marc. Antonin. de seipso. l. 7. f. 2. Vid. Gataker. Annotat. in ibid.    ᵗ 2 Tim. ii. 15.

3. A minister ought to take heed to himself, that he is not infected with the errors and heresies which are in the world. There always have been, and still are, heresies among men, and there must be; *that they which are approved*, are faithful and approved ministers of Christ, might *be made manifest*, to the churches, and the world, by their zeal for truth, and against error. And whereas ministers, as well as others, are liable to have their *minds corrupted from the simplicity that is in Christ*, and to be *led away with the error of the wicked*, and so *fall from their own stedfastness*; it becomes them therefore, to take heed to themselves. This was the reason of the apostle's advice to the elders of the church at *Ephesus*, at his taking his leave of them; when he said to them, *take heed to yourselves, and to all the flock:—for*, says he, *I know this, that after my departing, shall grievous wolves enter in among you, not sparing the flock; also of your own selves shall men arise, speaking perverse things, to draw away disciples after them*. Take heed, beware therefore, of these perverse men and things, lest you also be drawn after them, and be carried away by them. Our Lord Jesus Christ thought it necessary to exhort his own disciples, to *beware of the doctrine of the Pharisees and Sadducees*; and to take heed, that they were not deceived by false Christs, and false prophets. Ministers, of all men, ought to be most careful to shun error, and avoid false doctrines; since their seduction may be the means of a greater spread of them, and of the ruin of multitudes of souls.

4. A minister ought to take heed to his spirit, his temper, and his passions, that he is not governed by them. The preachers of the gospel are men of like passions with others: Some of Christ's disciples were very hot, fiery, and passionate; they were for calling for *fire from heaven to* consume such who had displeased them; hence our Lord said unto them, *Ye know not what manner of spirit ye are of* [w]. One that has the government of his passions, and can rule his own spirit and temper, is very fit to rule in the church of God. *He that is slow to anger, is better than the mighty; and he that ruleth his spirit, than he that taketh a city* [x]. But if a man is influenced and governed by his passions, he will be led by them to take indirect and imprudent steps; and to manage affairs with partiality, to the prejudice of the church, and members of it.

5. A minister ought to take heed to his life and conversation, that it be exemplary to those who are under his care. Private christians may, and ought to be examples one to another; they should be *careful to maintain* [y], or go before each other in *good works*; but more especially, ministers ought to be *examples to the flock*. This is the advice the apostle gave *Timothy*; *be thou an example of the believers, in word, in conversation, in charity, in spirit, in faith, in purity* [z].

They

[u] Acts xx. 28—30. [w] Luke ix. 55. [x] Prov. xvi. 32. [y] Προΐστασθαι, Tit. iii. 8.
[z] 1 Tim. iv. 12.

They ought to be careful how they behave themselves in their families, in the church, and in the world; that they give *no offence in any thing, that the ministry be not blamed,* and so become useless and unprofitable. This was what the apostle *Paul* was careful of, with respect to himself, and his ministry; *I keep under my body, and bring it into subjection*[a]; I do not indulge, but deny myself all carnal lusts and pleasures, *lest that by any means, when I have preached to others, I myself should be a cast-away;* that is, not one rejected of God, or a reprobate; for he knew whom he had believed, and was *persuaded, that nothing could separate him from the love of God;* he had no fearful apprehensions of this kind; though he was jealous and cautious, lest he should be guilty of misconduct in his outward conversation among men; and so become αδοκιμος, rejected, and and disapproved of by men, and be useless in his ministry. Every christian ought to *adorn the doctrine of God our Saviour,* but more especially the preachers of it; their *lights* should *so shine before men, that they seeing their good works, may glorify their father which is in heaven* The name of God, the ways of Christ, and the truths of the gospel, are blasphemed, and spoken evil of, through the scandalous lives of professors, and especially ministers. Nothing is more abominable[b] than that one, whose business it is to instruct and reprove others, is himself notoriously culpable; to such a person and case, the words of the apostle are very applicable, *Thou therefore that teachest another, teachest thou not thyself? Thou that preachest, a man should not steal, dost thou steal? Thou that sayest, a man should not commit adultery, dost thou commit adultery? Thou that abhorrest idols, dost thou commit sacrilege? Thou that makest thy boast of the law, through breaking the law dishonourest thou God? for the name of God is blasphemed among the Gentiles through you*[c].

6. A minister ought to take heed to the flock committed to his care; which is but the other part of himself. There is a mutual relation, a close union, between a pastor and a church; they are in some sense one, and their interests are one; so that a pastor, by *taking heed to himself,* takes heed to his flock, and by *taking heed to his flock* takes heed to himself. Hence these two are joined together in the apostle's advice to the elders of the church at *Ephesus, Take heed to yourselves, and to all the flock, over the which the holy Ghost hath made you overseers, to feed the church*[d]. Pastors of churches should be careful that they feed the saints with knowledge and understanding; that they feed the flock, and not themselves; that they perform the whole office of faithful shepherds to them; that they strengthen the diseased, heal the sick, bind up the broken, bring again that

---
[a] 1 Cor. ix. 27.
[b] Quæ culpare soles, ea tu ne feceris ipse;
Turpe est doctori, cum culpa redarguit ipsum. CATO.
[c] Rom. ii. 21—24.   [d] Acts xx. 28.

that which was driven away, and seek up that which was lost; all which they should take diligent heed unto, since they must be accountable to the great Shepherd and Bishop of souls, for all those who are under their care. But so much for the *first* branch of the exhortation; I proceed to consider,

*Secondly*, The *second* part of the charge, which is *to take heed to his doctrine*, that is, to the doctrine to which he has attained, which he has a knowledge of, and ought to preach to others; otherwise the doctrine is not his own but another's; as Christ says of himself as man, *My doctrine is not mine, but his that sent me*[e]. Christ received his doctrine from his Father, and his ministers receive it from him, and deliver it to the people. The doctrine which a gospel minister preaches, is in the same sense his, in which the apostle *Paul* calls the gospel, *my gospel*, or *our gospel*; not that it was a system of doctrines drawn up, and composed by him; but what was given him by the revelation of Christ, was committed to his trust, what he ought to preach, and in which he was made useful to the souls of many.

Now a minister ought to take heed to his doctrine, that it be according to the scriptures, *all scripture is given by inspiration of God, and is profitable for doctrine*[f]. True doctrine springs from it, is agreeable to it, and may be confirmed and established by it; therefore *if any man speak, let him speak as the oracles of God*. He should be careful, that his doctrine has a place in the word of God, that it takes its rise from it, is consonant to it, and capable of being proved by it: *To the law, and to the testimony; if they speak not according to this word, it is because there is no light in them*[h]. Whatever doctrines do not spring from these fountains of light and truth, or are disagreeable to them, must be accounted *divers and strange doctrines*.

Care should also be taken by a minister of the gospel, that his doctrine be the doctrine of Christ; that is, such as Christ himself preached, which he has delivered out by revelation to others, and of which he is the sum and substance. *We preach Christ crucified, to the Jews a stumbling-block, and to the Greeks foolishness*[i]. This doctrine is most likely to be useful for the conversion of sinners, and comfort of saints; and a man that does not bring this with him is to be discouraged and rejected: *Whosoever transgresseth, and abideth not in the doctrine of Christ, hath not God: He that abideth in the doctrine of Christ, he hath both the Father and the Son. If there come any unto you, and bring not this doctrine, receive him not into your house, neither bid him God:-speed*[k].

Moreover, a minister should take heed that his doctrine be the same with that of the apostles. It was the glory of the primitive christians, that *they continued stedfastly*

---

[e] John vii. 16.  [f] 2 Tim. iii. 16.  [g] 1 Peter iv. 11.
[h] Isai. viii. 20.  [i] 1 Cor. i. 23.  [k] 2 John 9, 10.

*stedfastly in the apostles doctrine*; and it must be the excellency of a man's ministry, that it is agreeable to *that faith which was once delivered to the saints*. Jesus Christ received his doctrine from his Father, which he delivered to his apostles: *I have given unto them* says he, *the words which thou gavest me, and they have received them* [1]; who also were guided by the spirit of truth into all truth, as it is in Jesus; and under the inspiration of the same spirit have left the whole of it in writing to the churches of Christ; which should be the standard of a gospel-ministry throughout all generations.

Besides, it becomes a preacher of the Word to be careful that the doctrine he teaches be *according to godliness*; that it is not contrary to the moral perfections of God, or has a tendency to promote a loose and licentious life; but that it is agreeable to, and may be a mean of increasing, both internal and external holiness. Sin, as it is a transgression of the law, so it is *contrary to sound doctrine*; which sound doctrine is *according to the glorious gospel of the blessed God* [m]. The gospel no more countenances sin, than the law does; the *grace of God*, the doctrine of the grace of God, *that bringeth salvation*, the news of it to sinners, *hath appeared to all men, Gentiles as well as Jews; teaching us, that denying ungodliness and worldly lusts, we should live soberly, righteously, and godly in this present world*. Whatever doctrines are subversive of true piety, or strike at the life and power of godliness, are to be rejected: *if any man teach otherwise, and consent not to wholesom words, even the words of our Lord Jesus Christ, and to the doctrine which is according to godliness; he is proud, knowing nothing, but doting about questions, and strife of words, whereof cometh envy, strifes, railings, evil surmisings*, &c [o].

Again, it is highly necessary, that a pastor of a church should be careful that his doctrine be such as makes for the edification of the people; it ought to be solid and substantial, suited to their capacities, and what is food convenient for them; he should not, therefore, *give heed to fables, and endless genealogies*; he ought, in his ministry, to *shun prophane and vain bablings, and oppositions of science, falsly so called*. He should *not strive about words to no profit, but to the subverting of the hearers*; and should carefully and diligently *avoid foolish and unlearned questions, knowing that they do gender strifes* [p].

In a word, he should take heed, that his doctrine be sound and incorrupt; pure and unmixed, and that it be all of a piece, and consistent with itself. He ought to *speak the things which become sound doctrine*; that is, such things as are agreeable to it, and consistent with it, and which are wholesom and healthful to the souls of men. In his doctrine he ought to shew *uncorruptness, gravity, sincerity*, and use *sound speech, which cannot be condemned* [q]; he should not teach for *doctrines the commandments of men*, or join, or mix divine truths with human inventions.

[1] John xvii. 8.    [m] 1 Tim. i. 10, 11.    [n] Titus ii. 11, 12.
[o] 1 Tim. vi. 3—5.    [p] 1 Tim. i. 4. & vi. 20. 2 Tim. ii. 14, 16, 23.    [q] Tit. ii. 1, 7, 8.

inventions. The chaff and the wheat should be kept separate; nor should he blend law and gospel, grace and works together; and so be like them that *corrupt the word of God*, καπηλευοντες τον λογον τυ Θευ, "adulterate it, by mixing it with " their own fancies;" as unfair dealers in liquors, mix water with them, which is the sense of the word here used; *but as of sincerity, but as of God, in the sight of God*[r], should a gospel-minister *speak in Christ*. He ought to take heed that what he preaches is consistent with itself; that it has no *yea and nay*, no contradiction in it, and does not destroy itself; and so bring a reproach upon him, and he become useless to his hearers; *for if the trumpet give an uncertain sound, who shall prepare himself for the battle*[s]? consistence, harmony, and connection of things with each other, are the beauty and glory of a man's ministry; which must needs recommend it, and make it most useful, profitable and pleasant.

It is also very adviseable that he take heed that he express his doctrine in the best manner, and to the best advantage. He ought to be careful about the manner as well as the matter of his ministry; that he speak plainly, intelligibly, and boldly, the gospel, as it ought to be spoken: Elocution, which is a gift of utterance, a freedom of expression, with propriety of language, is one of the gifts fitting for public usefulness in the work of the ministry; and which may be improved by the use of proper means. The example of the royal preacher is worthy of our imitation, *because the preacher was wise he still taught the people knowledge; yea, he gave good heed, and sought out, and set in order many proverbs: the preacher sought to find out acceptable words; and that which was written was upright, even words of truth*[t]: he not only sought for proper and agreeable truths, but was careful to express them in the most acceptable manner.

To conclude this head; when a minister has used his care and diligence about his doctrine, that it be according to the scriptures, agreeable to the doctrine of Christ and his apostles; that it be according to godliness, and makes for the use of edifying; that it be sound and incorrupt, pure and unmixed, and consistent with itself; and that it be expressed in the best manner, and to the best advantage, he ought to take heed to defend it whenever opposed; for ministers are not only set to preach the gospel, but for the defence of it; they should *by sound doctrine both exhort and convince gainsayers*[u]; for which purpose, they should use the two-edged sword, *the sword of the spirit, which is the word of God*; and is both an offensive and defensive weapon, by which, at once, error is refuted, and truth established. I go on to consider,

Thirdly,

---

[r] 2 Cor. ii. 17. καπηλευοντες, cauponantes sermonem Dei. Metaphora sumpta est ab hospitibus & cauponantibus, quibus in more est, vinum aqua corrumpere. Sic Græci interpretantur, καπηλευειν, μαξιυειν τον οινον, hoc est, vinum corrumpere, & πηλον dicant olim significavisse οινον vinum. Aretius in loc. [s] 1 Cor. xiv. 8. [t] Eccles. xii. 9, 10. [u] Tit. i. 9.

*Thirdly,* The *third* part of this exhortation, which is, *to continue in them.* Some read the words, *Continue with them*[w], that is, with the people at *Ephesus*, where *Timothy* was, and where the apostle would have him remain; as appears from what he says to him at the beginning of this epistle, *I besought thee to abide still at Ephesus*[x]. But I chuse rather to consider them as they are in our translation rendered, *continue in them*; that is, in the doctrines which thou dost well to take heed unto. Much such advice does the apostle give to *Timothy*, in his second epistle to him, *continue thou,* says he, *in the things which thou hast learned, and hast been assured of, knowing of whom thou hast learned them.* It is very unbecoming ministers of the word, to be *like children tossed to and fro with every wind of doctrine;* daily shifting sides, and changing sentiments.

He that would be a preacher of the gospel to others, ought so to study the scriptures, and learn the doctrines of grace, as to be assured of them, to be at a point, at a certainty concerning them; that he may be able to speak them boldly, as they ought to be spoken; and when he has so done, he ought to adhere to them, abide by them, and continue in them; even though a majority may be against them, for we are not to *follow a multitude to do evil*[y]. Truth is not to be judged of by the number of its admirers; if this was a sure and safe rule to go by, the church of *Rome* would have the best pretensions to the truth of doctrine, discipline, and worship; for *all the world wondered after the beast*[a]. It should be no discouragement to a gospel-minister to observe, that there are but few that receive the doctrines of grace. Yea, he should abide by them, though they are opposed by men of learning and reputation. Truth does not always lie among men of that character; God is pleased to hide the mysteries of the gospel from *the wise and prudent,* and reveal them unto *babes;* and *by the foolishness of preaching* confound the wise, *and save them that believe.* It was an objection to our Lord's ministry, that not *any of the rulers or of the Pharisees believed on him; but this people who knoweth not the law are cursed*[b]. Ministers of the gospel should abide by, and continue in the doctrines of it, though it is only received by the poor and ignorant, and opposed by the rich and wise: Nay, they ought to do so, though there are some things in them which cannot be comprehended by corrupt and carnal reason; this should be no objection to a reception of them, or continuance in them. There are some things in the gospel which *eye hath not seen, nor ear heard, neither have entered into the heart of man,* that is, a natural man, to conceive of; wherefore it is no wonder, that the *natural man receiveth not the things of the spirit of God, for they are foolishness unto him, neither can he know them, because they are spiritually discerned*[c].

[w] Επιμενε αυτοις.   [x] Chap. i. 3.   [y] Chap. iii. 14.   [a] Exod. xxiii. 2.
[a] Rev. xiii. 3.   [b] John vii. 48, 49.   [c] 1 Cor. ii. 9—14.

Nor should the charges and imputations of novelty and licentiousness frighten and deter the ministers of Christ from abiding by the doctrines of grace, since these were the very reproaches and calumnies that the doctrines of Christ and his apostles were loaded with, *What thing is this? What new doctrine is this?* Say some concerning Christ's ministry[d]; and so the Athenians to *Paul, May we know what this new doctrine whereof thou speakest is?* They looked upon the more substantial truths of the gospel as novelties, upstart notions, such as were never heard of before; nay, they were accounted by some as having a tendency to open a door to all manner of wickedness and looseness of life; which occasioned the apostle to say, *And not rather, as we be slanderously reported, and as some affirm, that we say, Let us do evil that good may come; whose damnation is just*[e].

In a word, it becomes Christ's ministers to abide by, and continue in the doctrines of grace, though they risk their good name, credit, and reputation, are in danger of losing their outward maintenance, or worldly substance, yea, life itself; *for whosoever will save his life, shall lose it; but whosoever shall lose his life for my sake and the gospel's, the same shall save it*[f]. I now hasten briefly to consider,

II. The reasons given by the apostle to support the whole of this charge or exhortation; and to engage *Timothy's*, and so every other gospel-minister's, regard unto it.

*First*, His first reason is, *For in doing this thou shalt save thyself.* Jesus Christ is the only efficient and procuring cause of salvation: *There is no salvation in any other; for there is none other name under heaven given among men, whereby we must be saved*[g]. Ministers cannot save themselves. by any *works of righteousness done* by them; no, not by their ministerial services; it is in vain to expect salvation by any, or from any other than Christ Jesus: But ministers, by taking heed to themselves, may, through a divine blessing, and the influences of the Spirit of God, *save themselves from an untoward generation*, and be preserved from the *pollutions of the world*; may *keep* their *garments*, their outward conversation garments, so that they do not *walk* naked, and others *see* their *shame*. By taking heed to their doctrine they may save themselves from being infected with false doctrines, errors and heresies; those *roots of bitterness*, which springing up in churches, *trouble* some, and *defile* others. And by continuing in their doctrines, may save themselves from *the blood of all men*, with whom they are concerned. The work of a minister is an awful, solemn, and weighty one; if he does not warn and instruct both the righteous and the wicked, their blood will be required at his hand; but if he performs his office faithfully, he *delivers his*

---

[d] Mark i. 27. Acts xvii. 19.    [e] Rom. iii. 8.    [f] Mark viii. 35.    [g] Acts iv. 12.

*his soul*, that is, he saves himself from such a charge against him; as did the apostle *Paul*, who could say, *I am pure from the blood of all men; for I have not shunned to declare unto you all the counsel of God* [h]. Thus, by a minister's taking heed to himself and to his doctrine, and continuing therein, he saves himself from all just blame in his character and office; and may be truly accounted *a good minister of Jesus Christ, nourished up in the words of faith, and of good doctrine, whereunto he hath attained* [i].

Secondly, His other reason is, thou shalt also *save them that hear thee*; that is, by being an example to them both in word and conversation, thou shalt be the means of preserving them both from erroneous principles and immoral practices; or, thou shalt be instrumental in their eternal salvation. Ministers are instruments by whom souls believe, and so are saved; the word preached by them being, by the grace of the spirit, an *engrafted word, is able to save them*; and the gospel being attended *with the demonstration of the spirit, is the power of God unto salvation*. What can, or does, more strongly engage ministers to take heed to themselves, to their doctrine, and abide therein, than this? That they may be useful in the conversion, and so in the salvation of precious and immortal souls, which are of more worth than a world: *He that converteth a sinner from the error of his way, shall save a soul from death, and shall hide a multitude of sins* [k]. A hopeful view of this supports ministers in their work, and carries them chearfully through many difficulties that attend it; for such souls whom they have been useful to, will be their *joy, and crown of rejoicing*, in the great day of the Lord. These reasons, I trust, will engage you, my Brother, who have been this day set apart to the pastoral office in this church, to take heed to yourself, your gifts, time, temper, life and conversation, and to the flock now committed to your care: And I conclude, that these will also engage you to take heed to your doctrine; that it be according to the scriptures, the doctrine of Christ, his apostles, and true godliness; and such as will be profitable to them that hear it; that it be sound and incorrupt, pure and unmixed, and consistent with itself; that it be delivered out in the best manner you are able, and defended to the utmost of your ability, by which you will abide, and in which you will continue: In doing this you will be most likely to be instrumental in the conversion of sinners, and edification of saints. God give success to all your ministrations.

[h] Acts xx. 26, 27.  [i] 1 Tim. iii. 6.  [k] James v. 20.

SERMON

## SERMON XXXVIII.

*The Work of a Gospel-Minister recommended to Confideration.*

A CHARGE delivered at the ORDINATIONS of the Reverend
Mr JOHN GILL, Mr BONNER STONE,
Mr JAMES LARWILL, AND
Mr ISAAC GOULD, Mr WALTER RICHARDS.

2 TIMOTHY II. 7.

*Confider what I fay, and the Lord give thee underftanding in all things.*

THAT part of the fervice of this day, which is affigned to me, being to give a word of exhortation to the paftor of this church, now appointed and ordained to that office, and invefted with it; I have chofen to do it in the words read; in which may be obferved,

I. An exhortation of the apoftle *Paul* to *Timothy*, to confider what he had said, was faying, or about to fay to him; to attend to it, revolve it in his mind, and lay it up in his memory.

II. A prayer, or wifh for him, that the Lord would give him underftanding, in all that was, or fhould be faid; and in every thing elfe that might be ferviceable and ufeful to him.

I. An exhortation to confider well what had been, or fhould be said unto him; for it may refer both to what goes before, and to what follows after; to what goes before, to the advice given to *be ftrong in the grace that is in Chrift Jefus*; to have recourfe to Chrift for gifts and grace to fit him more and more for his work, and carry him through it; and ftrongly to believe that there is a fulnefs of them in Chrift, and that he fhould receive a fufficient fupply from him to help him in every time of need; and alfo to the inftructions delivered to him, to commit the doctrines of the gofpel he had heard of him to faithful men, and fuch as were of capacity to teach others; and likewife to the characters he himfelf bore, as a fol-
dier,

dier, a soldier of Jesus Christ, a good soldier of his; and therefore should patiently and constantly endure hardships, reproaches, and persecution, for the sake of him and his gospel; and should not unnecessarily entangle himself with the affairs of this life, but attend to military ones, that so he might please him that had chosen him to be a soldier; and as he was a combatant, that he must not expect the crown, unless he strove lawfully; and as a husbandman, bearing the precious seed of the word, that he must labour before he could partake of the fruits of it: or this may have respect to what follows after; that he would consider the sum and substance of the gospel he was to preach, and for which the apostle suffered, which was a risen Saviour, and includes his incarnation, obedience, sufferings, and death, with all the doctrines of grace in connection with them; as also that it became him to be very studious and diligent in the use of means, that he might acquit himself with honour in the discharge of his ministerial work; that he might appear approved of God, a workman not to be ashamed of his work, at all times rightly dividing the word of truth, shunning every thing contrary to faith and holiness; likewise, that he ought to *flee youthful lusts*, his age inclined unto, and *follow righteousness, faith, charity and peace*; and *meekly to instruct* those who contradicted themselves and their profession, that, if it was possible, they might be recovered out of the snare they were fallen into; to these this exhortation may refer, with other things that may be observed in the context. What farther improvement I shall make of it, will be to lay before you, the pastor of this church, for your consideration, various things relative to the work you have been chosen, and called unto, and the office you have been invested with.

'First, Consider the work itself, and what a work it is you are engaged in: It is a *work*, and not a *sine-cure*, but a service; there is business to be done, and a great deal of business too; it is called *the work of the ministry* [a], from the subject-matter of it, the ministry of the word, and the administration of ordinances; and the *work of the Lord* and *of Christ* [b], from the concern the Lord Jesus Christ has in it; he is the sum and substance of it, he calls unto it, and qualifies for it, assists in it, and when it is rightly done, it makes for his glory. Consider that it is a laborious work; ministers of Christ are not to be loiterers, but labourers in his vineyard; it requires much reading of the scriptures, frequent prayer; constant meditation, and study to prepare for it; *and much study is a weariness to the flesh* [c]: and in the performance of this service, with that zeal, fervour, and affection, which are necessary to it, a man, to use the apostle's phrase, *may spend and be spent* [d]; spend his animal spirits until they are quite exhausted

[a] Ephes. iv. 12.    [b] 1 Cor. xvi. 10. Phil. ii. 30.    [c] Eccles. xii. 12.
[d] 2 Cor. xii. 15.

exhausted and gone; for this work, followed with close application, will try the best constitution in the world, and at length waste and consume it: *Epaphroditus*, a faithful and laborious minister of the word, was *nigh unto death, for, or through the work of Christ*[a]: but then consider, for your encouragement, it is an honourable work; *if a man desire the office of a bishop, he desireth a good work*[f]; which is pleasantly, profitably, and honourably good; for what is more honourable than to be the servants of the most high God, and to be employed in such service of his, as *to shew unto men the way of salvation?* Than to be the ambassadors of Christ, and stand in his stead, and *beseech men to be reconciled to God?* Than to be *stewards of the mysteries of Christ, and of the manifold grace of God?* Than to be the lights of the world, stars in Christ's right hand, the messengers or angels of the churches, and the glory of Christ? Moreover, consider that this work well performed, is deserving of esteem from men; *they that labour in the word and doctrine are worthy of double honour*[g], of an honourable maintenance, and of honourable respect; they are to be received with gladness, and had in reputation; and to be known, owned, and acknowledged by those over whom they are as fathers, guides, and governors: and to be highly esteemed for their works sake: add to all this, that this is a work in which God is with his ministers, and they with him; for, says the apostle[h], *we are labourers together with God, ye are God's husbandry, ye are God's building*; the churches are God's husbandry, and to be manured and cultivated, planted and watered; which is a laborious work, and constantly to be attended to; and nothing can be done to any purpose, and with any effect, but through the presence and blessing of God; *neither is he that planteth any thing, neither he that watereth*, which to do is the work of gospel-ministers, but *God that giveth the increase*[i]; and as the people of God, in a church-state, are his building, and who are to be edified and built upon their most holy faith; *except the Lord build the house, they labour in vain that build it*[k]; but when his ministers go forth in his name and strength, preaching his gospel, and he grants his gracious presence and assistance, and he, *the Lord*, is *working with them*[l], they go on in their work with chearfulness and success.

Secondly, Consider the several parts of this work you are called unto and engaged in, which are to be performed by you, and are as follow;

1. The ministration of the word, which is a principal part of the work of a minister of Christ; the apostles, and first preachers of the gospel, besides the spiritual, had the secular affairs of the church upon their hands; which lying too heavy on them, they desired to be eased, by appointing proper persons to take

---

[a] Phil. ii. 30.  [f] 1 Tim. iii. 1.  [g] 1 Tim. v. 17.  [h] 1 Cor. iii. 9.
[i] 1 Cor. iii. 7.  [k] Psalm cxxvii. 1.  [l] Mark xvi. 20.

take care of the latter; that so they might give themselves up wholly and constantly *to prayer, and to the ministry of the word* ᵐ: Now consider what that is, that is to be ministered, it is the word of God, and not man; which, as it demands the attention of the hearer, so the assiduous application of the preacher: it is the gospel that is to be preached, the good news and glad tidings of peace, pardon, righteousness, and salvation by Christ; it is the gospel, which is given in commission to preach; it is the glorious gospel of the blessed God, which ministers are entrusted with; and there is a wo upon them, if they preach it not; they are appointed ministers of the new testament; not of the law, the killing letter, the ministration of condemnation and death; but of the gospel, the quickening spirit, the ministration of the spirit, of righteousness and of life: consider, that only the pure unmixed gospel of Christ is to be preached, the sincere milk of the word, unadulterated, and clear of all human mixtures; it is not to be blended and corrupted with the doctrines of men: the word of God is not to be handled craftily; the hidden things of dishonesty are to be renounced, and the manifestation of the truth is to be made to every man's conscience, in the sight of God: and the whole of the gospel is to be delivered; no truth of it is to be dropped, concealed, or kept back, upon any pretence whatsoever, though it may be displeasing to some; such a question is never to be admitted and reasoned upon one moment in your private studies and preparations, whether such a truth you are meditating upon will be pleasing or displeasing? for if you seek to please men, you will not be the servant of Christ; the only thing to be considered is, is it truth? if it is, speak it out, without fear of man; and though it may be traduced as irrational, or licentious, and be loaded with reproach, and charged with dangerous consequences; yea, it may be urged, that admitting it to be truth, since an ill use may be made of it, it should not be preached; but let none of these things move you; preach truth, every truth, and leave it with the God of truth, who will take care of it, and use it to his own ends and purposes. Consider, that Christ is the sum and substance of the gospel-ministry; and that he, as to his person, offices, and grace, is chiefly to be insisted upon; *we preach not ourselves, but Christ Jesus the Lord* ⁿ; as the anointed prophet, priest, and king; as Jesus the alone Saviour; as the Lord our righteousness, even *Christ crucified*, and slain for the sins of men; though such preaching may be *a stumbling-block* to some, and *foolishness to others* ᵒ. The great apostle *Paul*, who well understood the nature and import of the gospel-ministry, declares, that *he determined not to know any thing*, that is, not to make known, or preach any thing, *save Jesus Christ, and him crucified* ᵖ; and as Christ is the alpha and omega of the scriptures, so he should be of all your discourses and sermons; whatever subject you are upon, keep Christ in your eye,

Vol. II.　　　　　　　　D

ᵐ Acts vi. 4.　　ⁿ 2 Cor. iv. 5.　　ᵒ 1 Cor. i. 23.　　ᵖ 1 Cor. ii 2.

eye, and let it appear, some way or other, it has a connection with him, and centers in him. The gospel to be preached, is the gospel of the grace of God; and it is sometimes called the grace of God itself; the doctrines of it are the doctrines of free grace, and declare, that the salvation of men, from first to last, and in all the parts of it, is of grace, and not of works; and these are to be faithfully dispensed, as that the first step to the salvation of men, the choice of them to it, is of grace, and not of works; that men are justified freely by the grace of God, through the redemption that is in Christ Jesus, and not by the works of the law; that the full forgiveness of sins, though by the blood of Christ, is according to the riches of God's grace; and that eternal life is the free gift of God, through Jesus Christ our Lord: Yea, every truth that is contained in the scriptures, and is agreeable to them, is to be preached; for *all scripture is profitable for doctrine* [q]; from thence it is to be fetched, and by it to be supported and maintained; this is the standard of faith and practice; and as it is by this the hearers of the word are to try what they hear, and judge whether things are right or wrong, they hear; so this should be the rule to ministers to preach by; *to the law and to the testimony, if they speak not according to this word, it is because there is no light in them* [r]. The doctrinal part of the scripture is more especially to be attended to, because that is the food with which the flock and church of God is to be fed, by those who are the pastors and overseers of it; and therefore, as they should take heed to themselves, and to the flock under their care, so to their doctrine; that it be found doctrine, pure, and incorrupt; that it be intirely agreeable to the sacred writings; that it be the doctrine of Christ, which comes from him, and is concerning him; that it be such as was preached by his apostles, and is contained in their discourses and epistles; and that it be according to godliness: though not the doctrines of the gospel only are to be preached, but the duties of religion are also to be inculcated in their proper place and course, and to be pressed on believers upon gospel-principles and motives; the churches are to be taught to observe all things which Christ has commanded, every ordinance of his, and every duty enjoined, both with respect to God and men; saints are to be put in mind to be ready to every good work; and those that have believed in God, are to be charged to be careful to maintain good works for necessary uses; every doctrine and every duty, in their turns, are to be insisted on, throughout the circle of the evangelic ministry.

Let controversy, as little as may be, be brought into the pulpit; controversial sermons, when best managed, are generally unedifying ones to the people in common; tend to damp the true spirit of religion and devotion, which it is the design of preaching the word to excite; and serve to entangle, perplex, and confound.

[q] 2 Tim. iii 16.     [r] Isai. viii. 20.

confound weak minds; objections are often started to be solved, which are not easily done; by which means captious persons, and such as are disinclined to receive the truth, are furnished with them, who otherwise would not; and sometimes the solutions of such objections are not quite satisfactory to the friends of truth, and so rather tend to stagger than to establish: Upon the whole, it is best to preach the pure truths of the gospel in the plainest manner, and endeavour to illustrate and confirm them by scripture-testimonies, and by reasonings drawn from thence, and leave them with their native evidence upon the minds of men.

Now consider, that all this is to be done compleatly, constantly, and consistently; the gospel is to be preached *fully*, as it was by the apostle *Paul*[*], according to the measure of the gift of grace given; and when a man preaches the whole gospel of Christ, and delivers out all the doctrines of it, and urges to all the duties relative to it, and declares the whole counsel of God; then may he be said to do the work of an evangelist, and to make full proof of his ministry, and to fulfil the ministry which he has received of Christ: and this is to be done constantly; *these things*, says the apostle, *I will that thou affirm constantly*[t]; the truths, before spoken of, concerning the state of God's people in unregeneracy, the loving-kindness of God to them in their redemption by Christ, the saving them by the washing of regeneration, the justification of them by the free grace of God, and their heirship and title to eternal life, upon that; the word must be preached in season, and out of season, as often as opportunity offers; and the ministers of Christ must be *stedfast, unmoveable, always abounding in the work of the Lord, knowing their labour is not in vain in the Lord:* and care should be taken, that this work is done consistently; that the ministry is uniform, and all of a piece; that there is no contradiction, no yea and nay in it; otherwise great confusion will be created in the minds of hearers, and they will be thrown into the utmost perplexity, not knowing what to believe, or receive; *for if the trumpet gives an uncertain sound, who shall prepare himself to the battle*[u]?

'2. Another part of the work to be performed by you, is the administration of gospel-ordinances, and they are principally Baptism and the Lord's supper: the administration of baptism goes along with the ministry of the word; such, who have a commission from Christ to *teach* and *instruct* men in divine things, have a commission also to *baptize* those who are taught and instructed by them, *in the name of the Father, of the Son, and of the holy Ghost*; nor have any other a right to do it: some have thought that *Philip* who baptized the eunuch and others, was *Philip* the deacon; but be it so, he was an evangelist also, a preacher of the gospel, as it is plain he was; and therefore he baptized, not by virtue

[*] Rom. xv. 19.     [t] Titus iii. 8.     [u] 1 Cor. xiv. 8.

tue of his office as a deacon, but as a teacher and a preacher of the word of God. The apostle *Paul* indeed says, *Christ sent me not to baptize, but to preach the gospel* [w]; but then his meaning is, that he was not sent only to baptize, or this was not the principal part of his ministry; it was chiefly to preach the gospel, though not to the exclusion of the administration of ordinances; nor does he say this, as thinking, or speaking meanly of the ordinance of baptism; but because some persons had made an ill use of their being baptized by him; and were ready to boast of it, as if they were baptized in his name. It is incumbent on you, to administer this ordinance to the persons which are described in the word of God, and of which there are examples in it, and in the manner therein directed to, and practised. The ordinance of the Lord's supper, being an ordinance in the church, is to be administered by the pastor of it; such who break the bread of life in the ministry of the word, are to break the bread in the ordinance of the supper: the apostle *Paul* broke bread to the disciples, to whom he preached; and this ordinance is to be administered frequently, as is suggested in those words, *as often as ye eat this bread*, &c. [x]; in it the sufferings of Christ should be described, and his love set forth in the most moving and pathetic strains; and he be represented as crucified and slain, in as lively a manner, as the administrator is capable of.

3. Another part of your work, is to take care of the discipline of the house of God; for though every thing is to be done by the vote and suffrage of the church, the power of discipline being lodged in it by Christ, the head of it; yet the executive part of it will lie chiefly upon you; though none are to be admitted to, or excluded from the communion of the church, but according to its voice, and with its consent: yet it should be greatly your concern, to examine things closely, whether the persons are fit to be received or rejected; and to take care, that nothing be done through favour or affection, and with partiality. Pastors of churches have a rule and government committed to them; they are set over others in the Lord; they are not indeed to lord it over God's heritage, to rule them in an haughty and imperious manner, but according to the laws of Christ; which they are carefully to observe, and point out to the church, and see that they are put in execution; in doing which their government chiefly lies; you are therefore to take care, that every thing in the church be done decently, and in order, and according to the rule of the divine word: particularly, care should be taken that no case in difference, of a private nature, be brought into the church, before the rule is observed, which Christ has given in reference to such a case; that the offended brother should first tell the offender of his fault alone, and endeavour to convince him of it; and if he should not

succeed,

[w] 1 Cor. i. 17.     [x] 1 Cor. xi. 26.

succeed, then to take one or two more, and try by them to bring him to an acknowledgment of it; but, if after all he is obstinate and incorrigible, then bring it to the church [y]. But as for those that *sin openly*, that are guilty of notorious and scandalous crimes, in a public manner, to the great disgrace of religion, as well as grief of the church, these are to be *rebuked before all*, without any more to do, that *others may fear* [z] : the several rules to be attended to, with respect to church-discipline, you are to inculcate to the church, at proper times, and on proper occasions; as to admonish persons guilty of immorality and error, to withdraw from those that *walk disorderly*, after all methods taken to reclaim them are vain and fruitless; and *to reject an heretic, after the first and second admonition* [a], when without effect.

4. Another part of your work, is to visit the several members of the church, as their cases may require, especially when distressed, either in body or mind; then to pray with them, and for them, to speak a word of comfort to them, and give them your best counsel and advice; and this will introduce you into divers families; but take care not to meddle with family-affairs; what you hear and see in one family report it not in another; this may be attended with bad consequences: and whatever differences may arise between one and another, interfere as little as possible; chuse rather that differences between members be composed by other persons, the officers of the church, than by you, that no prejudices be entertained against your ministry; and particularly be careful to avoid that scandalous practice, the disgrace of the pulpit, bringing matters of difference into it, whether between yourself or others, or whether between one member and another, one side of which you may incline to take; for why should the peace and edification of a whole community be destroyed, through the noise and din of private quarrels? As this is a practice exceeding mean, it is very unbecoming the gospel of peace, and the ministers of it. Moreover, you will be called upon sometimes to visit sick persons, who are not members of the church; and who may be strangers to the grace of God, and the way of salvation by Christ; and who have been either profane persons, or resting upon their civility and morality, pleasing themselves, that they have wronged no man, and have done that which is right between man and man; and now in dying circumstances, hope, on this account, things will be well with them; and whose relatives may be afraid of your saying any thing to interrupt this carnal peace; yet, be faithful, labour to shew the one and the other their wretched and undone state by nature; the necessity of repentance towards God, and faith in our Lord Jesus Christ, in his blood, righteousness, and atoning sacrifice, for peace, pardon, justification, and salvation. This is a case, I assure you, will require a

good

Matt. xviii. 15—17.   [z] 1 Tim. v. 20.   [a] 2 Thess. iii. 6. Tit. iii. 10.

## A CHARGE AT THE ORDINATION.

good deal of care, judgment, and faithfulness. And now, I doubt not, but by this time you will be ready to say, *who is sufficient for these things* [b]? Wherefore,

*Thirdly*, Consider the qualifications necessary to the performance of the ministerial work; and what things are requisite and useful for the due discharge of it: and here let it be observed, that there are some things which are serviceable and useful in it, which, properly speaking, are not the qualifications for it; as for instance, the grace of God is a pre-requisite to this work; it is highly proper that those who are engaged in it, should be partakers of it in truth: yet grace is not the ministerial qualification; for this is what all the saints have in common, the graces of the spirit, faith, hope, and love; they all obtain like precious faith, for nature, kind, and object, though not to the same degree, one as another; they are all called in one hope of their calling, by the same grace, to the same glory; and they are all taught of God to love God, Christ, and one another; yet this does not qualify them for ministers of the word; if grace was a ministerial qualification, all the Lord's people would be what *Moses* wished they were, even all of them *prophets*. Human learning is very useful and serviceable to a minister of the gospel; to have such a share of it, as to be capable of reading the scriptures in the original tongues in which they were written; and by means of knowledge of languages, to be able to read the writings of many excellent good men, written therein, to their profit and advantage; as well as to know the use of words, and the propriety of speech: and such who are called to the work of the ministry, who have not had a liberal education, and yet have time and leisure, are not easily to be excused, if they do not make use of their time, and those means that may be had, to improve themselves in useful knowledge; and yet, after all, the highest attainments in human literature are not ministerial qualifications; for a man may be able to read the Bible in the languages in which it was written, and yet not understand the things contained in it; for it is a sealed book, which when put into the hands of a learned man to read and interpret, he cannot, *because it is sealed*. Good natural parts are of great service and use to a minister of the word; as to have a clear understanding, a solid judgment, a lively fancy, a fruitful invention, and a retentive memory; but these a man may have, and yet not be fit to be a minister of the gospel; yea, men may have all the above things, grace, learning, and natural parts, and not be qualified for this work. The apostle *Paul* had all of them; he was a man of good natural parts, which his adversaries perceived and owned; *his letters*, say they; *are mighty and powerful* [c], wrote in a masculine style, and full of strong reasonings, and nervous arguments; he had a large share of human literature, being brought up at the feet of *Gamaliel*, in all

---

[b] 2 Cor. ii. 16.  [c] 2 Cor. x. 12.

all the learning of the Jews, and of other nations; and he also was called by the grace of God; yet he does not ascribe his being a minister of the gospel to either, or all of these, but to a *gift* which he had received; a peculiar gift, fitting and qualifying him for this important work; for, speaking of the gospel, he says, *whereof I was made a minister according to the gift of the grace of God given unto me* [d]; with which agree the words of the apostle *Peter*, *as every one has received the gift, even so minister the same one to another* [e]: in some this gift may be greater, in others less; but in all where it is, it more or less qualifies for the service of the ministry: *having then gifts, differing according to the grace that is given unto us, whether prophecy, let us prophesy according to the proportion* or analogy *of faith* [f]; that is, let us interpret the scriptures, or preach the word, agreeable to the tenor of it: Now this gift lies in a competent knowledge of the scriptures, and of the things contained in them, and of a faculty of interpreting them to the edification of others; for the work of evangelical pastors or teachers, is to *feed the churches with knowledge and understanding* [g]; which, unless they have a considerable share of themselves, they will not be able to do with any profit and advantage to others: these are spiritual men, who having spiritual gifts, are capable of making judgment of all things necessary to be known unto salvation; of this knowledge and of this gift the apostle is speaking, when he says, *whereby when ye read ye may understand my knowledge in the mystery of Christ* [h]. But now, besides this share of knowledge and furniture of the mind, there must be a capacity of expressing it to others, to make up the ministerial qualification; a man must not only have wherewith to teach others, or matter to instruct them in, but he must be capable of doing it in an apt and suitable manner, that tends to edification; which the apostle means by *utterance*, which is a gift, and by mens being *able to teach others also*, and by being *apt to teach* [i]; for it signifies little what a man knows, or how great soever is the furniture of his mind, or the largeness of his ideas, and the compass of his knowledge, if he is not capable of clothing his ideas with apt and suitable words to convey them to the understanding of others. So then this gift consists of knowledge and elocution; and on whomsoever this gift is bestowed, whether on a gracious or a graceless person, on a *John* or a *Judas* [k]; or whether on a learned or unlearned man, on a *Paul* or

---

[d] Ephes. iii. 7.  [e] 1 Peter iv. 10.  [f] Rom. xii. 6.  [g] Jer. iii. 15.
[h] Ephes. iii. 4.  [i] Ephes. vi. 19.  2 Tim. ii. 2.  1 Tim. iii. 2.
[k] Judas had the same call and mission from Christ to preach the gospel with the rest of the apostles; and had the same gifts ordinary and extraordinary qualifying for it; and behaved so well in his office, that the rest of the disciples rather distrusted themselves than him, on Christ's declaring, one of them should betray him, saying each, *Is it I?* Matt. x. 1—8. and xxvi 21, 22 And, though I am of opinion, that for the most part, God gives special grace to those on whom he bestows gifts for the ministry, yet not always; as the instances in Matt. vii. 22, 23. Phil. i 15, 16. shew, and is a case the apostle supposes, 1 Cor. ix. 27. and xiii. 1, 2. and such may be the means of the conversion and edification of men: the reason of which is, it is the word of God they preach, and God can and does make use of his own word, to such purposes, by what instruments he pleases.

or a *Peter*; on a man of good natural parts or one of a meaner capacity; that is it that qualifies for the miniſtry; where indeed grace, learning, and natural parts all meet together in a man with this gift, they make him a very conſiderable and diſtinguiſhed man. Now, there are various things that are requiſite, in order to the due and regular exerciſe of this gift to uſefulneſs.

1. There muſt be a call to the exerciſe of it: beſides the inward call or diſpoſition of the mind to ſuch ſervice, and which muſt be ſubmitted to others; *for the ſpirit of the prophets is ſubject to the prophets* [k]; there muſt be an outward call by the church: it being notified to it by ſome means or another, that ſuch an one is thought to have a gift for the miniſtry, the church calls him to the exerciſe of it, tries his gift, and judges of it; and upon approbation, ſuch are ſeparated and ſent forth into the miniſtry, as *Saul* and *Barnabas* were; for no modeſt man will take this honour to himſelf, or thruſt himſelf into this work, unleſs he is called to it; though in this rambling age of ours, there are many run who were never ſent, and take upon them this work, without having a gift qualifying them for it, or a call from God or men unto it.

2. Where there is a gift, diligence and induſtry muſt be uſed to improve it; for otherwiſe it may decline, become leſs, and in length of time uſeleſs; yea, may be entirely loſt or taken away; for gifts are not like grace; grace, though it may decline as to exerciſe, can never be loſt; but gifts may, as appears from the parable of the *talents*, by which I underſtand miniſterial gifts; the man that had one talent wrapped it up in a napkin, and hid it in the earth, that is, he neglected it, and made no uſe of it; wherefore orders are given to take it from him, and give it to others; for *unto every one that hath ſhall be given, and he ſhall have abundance*; every one that hath a gift, and is diligent and conſtant in the uſe of it, that ſhall increaſe; but from him *that hath not*, who, though he has a gift, is as if he had none, neglecting to cultivate it, and make uſe of it, *ſhall be taken away even that which he hath* [l]. Gifts, like ſome metals, unleſs frequently uſed, become ruſty and good for nothing; hence the exhortation of the apoſtle to *Timothy*, not to neglect, but *to ſtir* up the gift of God that was in him [m], as you ſtir up coals of fire, that they may give more light and heat; ſo gifts by uſe become brighter and brighter, and more beneficial.

3. Faithfulneſs is neceſſary to the due exerciſe of this gift; thoſe that have it, are, or ſhould be, *good ſtewards of the manifold grace of God*; and now *it is required in ſtewards that a man be found faithful* [n]; to diſpenſe the myſteries of God, of which they are ſtewards, unto others; and *when God has counted* a man *faithful, putting* him *into the miniſtry* [o], he ought to continue faithful to him that has

---

[k] 1 Cor. xiv. 32.     [l] Matt xxv. 29.     [m] Tim. iv. 14.   2 Tim. i. 6.
[n] 1 Pet iv. 10.   1 Cor. iv. 2.     [o] 1 Tim. i. 12.

SERM. 38.   OF SEVERAL MINISTERS.

has put him into it, to the fouls of men committed to his care, and to the gospel, and the truths of it he is entrusted with. For *he that hath my word, let him speak my word faithfully: what is the chaff to the wheat? faith the Lord of hosts* [p].

4. Wifdom and prudence are alfo very requifite in the exercife of this gift, both in the choice of fubjects, and in the manner of treating them; a man that is a *steward* muft be *wife* as well as *faithful*, *to give* to every one of the houfhold *their portion of meat in due feafon* [q]; and a man that labours in the word and doctrine fhould be fkilful in the fcriptures, that *he may rightly divide the word of truth* [r]; and he that has to do with perfons in various cafes, and different circumftances, had need to have the underftanding and *tongue of the learned to fpeak a word in feafon to him that is weary* [s].

5. Minifters of the word ought to be careful of their lives and converfations; or otherwife, let their gifts be what they may, they will become ufelefs and unprofitable; they therefore fhould *take heed to themfelves* [t], to conduct and behave becoming their work and office; and fo to walk as to be *an example of the believers, in word, in converfation, in charity, in fpirit, in faith, in purity* [u]; and to take care they give no offence to the church, nor to the world, *that the miniftry be not blamed* [w]; for it is a moft fhameful thing, that they which teach others not to fin, but to guard againft it, fhould be guilty of the fame themfelves; fee *Rom.* ii. 23, 24. where the apoftle enlarges on this fubject.

*Fourthly*, Confider the means that are to be made ufe of for the cultivation and improvement of the minifterial gift; and for the better difcharge of the work and office to which you have been called and ordained. The directions the apoftle gives to *Timothy* on this head, are well worthy of your notice, and fhould be clofely purfued; *give attendance to reading; to exhortation, to doctrine.—Meditate on thefe things, give thyfelf wholly to them, that thy profiting may appear to all* [x]: in the firft and chief place ftudy the Bible, read that attentively, compare one paffage with another, fpiritual things with fpiritual, parallel places together; and particularly thofe that are more dark and obfcure with thofe that are more clear and plain; that thereby you may know more of the mind of the Spirit of God and Chrift in the facred pages; for the infpired writings are *profitable for doctrine, for reproof, for correction, for inftruction in righteoufnefs, that the man of God may be perfect, thoroughly furnifhed unto all good works* [y]; for thefe will furnifh out fufficient matter, both for things doctrinal and practical, to be infifted on in the miniftry of the word; and with whatfoever may be neceffary for the difcharge of the minifterial office. Read alfo the writings of good men, for

p Jer. xxiii. 28.   q Luke xii. 42.   r 2 Tim. ii. 15.   s Ifai i. 4.
t Acts xx. 28.   u 1 Tim. iv. 12.   w 2 Cor. vi. 3.   x 1 Tim. iv. 13, 15.
y 2 Tim. iii. 16, 17.

for these are not preserved and transmitted to posterity for nothing, but for use; but then read them with care and caution, as human writings, liable to mistakes, and having their imperfections; compare them with the word of God, and so far as they agree with that, and are consistent with themselves, regard them, and not otherwise. Meditate much on divine things, on the scriptures, and the doctrines contained in them: it is the character of every good man, that he *meditates in the law* ª, or doctrine of the Lord continually; and he finds his account in it; his *meditation* of God, of Christ, and of spiritual things, is *sweet* ᵃ, and delightful to him; and much more should it be the constant work and employment of a minister of the word. *Luther*, as I remember, it is said of him, that he used to say, " Meditation, temptation, and prayer, make a " divine." For prayer is also very necessary to be frequently repeated, since this goes along with the ministry of the word, and is so very useful in respect of it. The apostles desired to be eased of the worldly concerns of the church, that they might give up themselves to *prayer*, as well as to *the ministry of the word* ᵇ; and to the former in order to the latter. Ministers of the gospel should pray often, not only in public, but in private; not only for others, but for themselves; that they might be more qualified for their work, as well as be more successful in it; that they might have more spiritual light, knowledge, and understanding, and be more capable of instructing and feeding the people under their care; that they might have the eyes of their understandings more enlightened, to behold the wonderful things that are in the law, or doctrine of the Lord; and be better able to point them out to others.

*Fifthly*, Consider on the one hand the difficulties and discouragements that attend the ministerial work; and on the other hand, the encouragements to proceed on in it.

1. The difficulties and discouragements that attend it; these, I would observe, not to distress you in, or deter you from your work; but that, when you meet with them, they may not seem as though some strange or uncommon thing had happened unto you. There are some, which come from within a man's self; from in-dwelling sin, from *a law in the members warring against the law of the mind*; you will find when you would do good, evil is present with you, as particularly to hinder you in the pursuit of your studies; you will find a kind of slothfulness and disinclination to the work; nay, sometimes when the *spirit is willing* the flesh will be weak ᶜ, and will make excuses to put off preparation for it to another time. Sometimes you will be in darkness, and under divine desertions, and be in very uncomfortable frames; yet still you must go on, and prepare, in the best manner that you can, for instructing and comforting

---

ª Psalm i. 2.   ᵃ Psalm civ. 34.   ᵇ Acts vi. 4.   ᶜ Matt. xxvi. 41.

ing others; this is hard and difficult work, but it muſt be done: and difficulties and diſcouragements ſometimes ariſe from Satan's temptations, who is very buſy with all good men, eſpecially with miniſters of the goſpel: he deſired to have *Peter* in his hands; he buffeted the apoſtle *Paul*; he levels his arrows at thoſe who are the moſt fruitful, flouriſhing, and uſeful; as the archers that ſhot at *Joſeph*, that *fruitful bough by a well*, and grieved him, though *his bow abode in ſtrength, the arms of his hands being made ſtrong by the mighty God of Jacob*. You muſt expect Satan's temptations; he will tempt you to that which is unbecoming your character and office; he will tempt you perhaps to entertain groundleſs jealouſies of one or other of the members of the church; he will tempt you to drop your miniſtry, or however, in this place, and to do it in a pet and humour: theſe, and ſuch like temptations, ſhould be guarded againſt. Other diſcouragements will ariſe from the world, and the men of it, from their revilings and reproaches, wrath, rage, and perſecutions in one ſhape or other; but none of theſe things ſhould move you from your work, or cauſe you to deſert it. Remember you are choſen, and called to be a ſoldier of Jeſus Chriſt; and, as a good one, ſhould endure hardneſs, hard words, and hard uſage, for his ſake: yea, the difficulties and diſcouragements of goſpel-miniſters are increaſed by profeſſors of religion themſelves; not only by thoſe of other communities, who may traduce and ſpeak ill of ſuch, who are not altogether of the ſame principles with themſelves, but by the members of the churches over which they are paſtors; ſome of which are very weak and imprudent, and oftentimes make a miniſter very uncomfortable and uneaſy by their words and actions; though theſe things ſhould be conſidered as their weakneſſes and infirmities, and to be bore with; *for we that are ſtrong ought to bear the infirmities of the weak, and not pleaſe ourſelves* [d]; yet theſe muſt be reckoned among a miniſter's difficulties and diſcouragements; but,

2. You are to conſider the encouragements to go on in your work, notwithſtanding what may be met with in it which is difficult and diſcouraging; and which is a ſuperabundant counterbalance to that. Remember the gracious promiſes Chriſt has made of his preſence with his miniſters, and of his protection of them, and of his aſſiſtance in their work, and of a reward, though not of debt, yet of grace, that ſhall be given them: he has promiſed he will be with his miniſters in ſucceſſive generations, unto the end of the world, to ſupply and ſupport them; he holds them in his right hand, and will not ſuffer any to ſet upon them, to hurt them, until they have done the work he has called them to, and is deſigned to be done by them; his power and grace are ſufficient to bear them

[d] Rom. xv. 1.

them up in, and carry them through whatever service he engages them in; his strength is made perfect in their weakness, and as their day is, their strength is; so he has promised, and so he performs. Remember and consider, that they that be *wise*, and teach and instruct others, shall *shine as the brightness of the* firmament in the kingdom-state; *and they that turn many to righteousness*, or justify many, by teaching the doctrine of justification, or directing souls to the righteousness of Christ alone for it, *shall be as the stars for ever and ever* [d]; that those who have taken good heed to their flocks, over which the Holy Ghost hath made them overseers, and have faithfully fed them, and carefully watched over them, *when the chief shepherd shall appear, shall receive a crown of glory that fadeth not away* [e]; and will hear from Christ, *well done, good and faithful servant, enter thou into the joy of thy Lord* [f]. But I proceed to observe,

II. The prayer or wish of the apostle for *Timothy*, that *the Lord would give him understanding in all things*; and upon this I shall be very short; only drop a few things by way of explanation of it: and by *all things*, in which he desires he might have an understanding, he does not mean all things natural and civil; indeed the understanding of all such things comes from God; *every good and perfect gift* in nature, or in providence, as well as in grace, comes *from the Father of lights* [g]; all the wisdom and knowledge which *Bezaleel* and *Aholiab* had for devising and working curious works for the tabernacle, were of God; he put it into their hearts, and filled them with wisdom, knowledge, and understanding in these things; yea, even all the understanding the ploughman has in ploughing the ground, and breaking the clods, and harrowing them, and in sowing his seed, is all from God; he instructs him *to discretion*; this comes from him *who is wonderful in counsel, and excellent in working* [h]; and so the same may be said of knowledge of all natural and civil things, of all arts and sciences, liberal and mechanic: and indeed a minister of the word had need to be acquainted with all things in nature and civil life, thoroughly to understand all things contained in the scriptures of truth; since there are such a variety of metaphors, and so many allusions to things natural and civil; and such an adorable fulness in them, as *Tertullian* expresses it. But the apostle, no doubt, means understanding in spiritual things, in the scriptures, in the doctrines and mysteries of grace. The understanding of man is naturally dark as to those things; it is the Lord that gives men an understanding to know them, that opens their hearts, and enlightens their minds by the spirit of wisdom and revelation, in the knowledge of them; for whatever understanding natural men may have of natural things, they have none of spiritual ones; *there is none that understandeth*,

[d] Dan. xii. 4. [e] 1 Pet. v. 4. [f] Matt. xxv. 21. [g] Jam. i. 17.
[h] Isai. xxviii. 26, 29.

*derstandeth, there is none that seeketh after God*[1]. Now, besides the understanding of spiritual things, which God gives in common to his people, he gives to his ministers a larger understanding of divine things, and of the scriptures and the truths of them; he opens their understandings, as Christ did his disciples, that they may understand the scriptures; he gives unto them to know the mysteries of the kingdom of heaven, to a greater degree than he does to others; and he enlarges their understandings, and increases their gifts, their light, and knowledge; which is what the apostle in a more especial manner prays for here, on the account of *Timothy*; that he might be better instructed in every thing relative to his office, as an evangelist and minister of the word, and know how to behave in the church of God, which is the house of God, the pillar and ground of truth; and which is the principal end of his writing this; and the former epistle to him[k]. I have only one observation more to make, and that is, that the clause may be considered as an assertion, or a promise, *and the Lord will give thee understanding in all things*; and so is used as an encouragement to consider well what had been said, and to expect a richer furniture of knowledge, and a larger measure of spiritual light and understanding; and as Christ gives more light to his people, who are made light by him; and there is such a thing as growing in grace, and in the knowledge of Christ, and of all spiritual things, in common christians; and the path of the just is as the shining light that shines more and more unto the perfect day; so faithful ministers of the word, who are diligent and industrious in their work, may expect, and be assured, that God will give them an enlarged knowledge and understanding of divine truths, and of every thing necessary to the due performance of that sacred work they are called unto, and holy office they are invested with. I shall close, as I begun, with the words of my text, *Consider what I say*, or have been saying; consider the work of the ministry, that it is a work, and a laborious one, yet honourable and deserving of esteem from men; and that God will never leave his servants in it: consider the several parts of it, as the ministration of the gospel, the administration of ordinances, the care of the discipline of Christ's house, and visiting the afflicted and distressed: consider the necessary qualifications for it, and the things that are useful to the performance of it: consider the means to be made use of to enable for the better and more regular exercise of spiritual gifts; and the difficulties and discouragements that, on the one hand, attend this work; and, on the other, the encouragements to go on in it; *and the Lord give thee understanding in all things*; in all divine and spiritual things, in the truths of the gospel, and in every thing relative to your office, and the due discharge of it, you have this day been invested with. May the blessing of God rest upon you, and may you have success in your work.

SERMON

---

[1] Rom. iii. 12.     [k] 1 Tim. iii. 14, 15.

## SERMON XXXIX.

*The Doctrine of the Cherubim Opened and Explained.*

A SERMON at the ORDINATION of the Reverend Mr JOHN DAVIS, at *Waltham-Abbey.* Preached *August* 15, 1764.

---

EZEKIEL X. 20.

*This* is *the living creature, that I saw under the God of Israel, by the river of Chebar; and I knew that they* were *the Cherubim.*

BEING defired to fay fomething to you, my Brother, on this occafion, relative to the minifterial character you bear, and to the work you have been called to, and to the office you have been at this time invefted with; my thoughts have been led to this paffage of fcripture. *This is the living creature;* or creatures, the fingular for the plural; for there were four living creatures which Ezekiel faw in the vifion he refers to; thefe he *faw under the God of Israel,* under a firmament over the heads of thefe creatures; above which was the appearance of a man in a moft glorious and illuftrious form; and who was no other than the Son of God, who was to be incarnate, and here called *the God of Israel*; and which is no inconfiderable proof of our Lord's proper Deity, for *the God of Israel* muft be the true God: this vifion the prophet had *by the river of Chebar*; a river in *Chaldea,* where the captive Jews affembled, and *Ezekiel* with them; and when he had the vifion, as now repeated to him, the objects in it became more familiar to him; and he more wiftly looked at them, and perceived and was well affured, that the living creatures he faw were the cherubim; or were of the fame form and figure with the cherubim in the tabernacle of *Mofes* and temple of *Solomon*; for though he was not an high prieft, only a common prieft, and fo could never have feen the cherubim in the moft holy place himfelf, yet he might have had an account of them from an high prieft who had feen them; and befides there were figures of the cherubim carved upon the walls of the temple all around, and upon the doors of it; which, as his bufinefs was to be

fre-

frequently in the temple, he muſt have often ſeen, and full well knew them. See alſo *ver.* 15. where the ſame is affirmed as here.

It may ſeem ſtrange to you at firſt, that I ſhould read ſuch a paſſage of ſcripture on ſuch an occaſion; but it will not appear ſo long, when I inform you that my intention is, by opening and explaining the emblems of the cherubim, to lay before you the qualifications, duties, work, and uſefulneſs of the miniſters of the goſpel; to make way for which, it will be proper to inquire what the cherubim were, and what they ſignified; in order to which we muſt look both backwards and forwards, to the account of them in ſcripture, both before and after theſe viſions of *Ezekiel.* The account begins early, proceeds gradually, and by degrees becomes more clear, diſtinct, and perfect. The firſt mention of the cherubim is in *Gen.* iii. 24. quickly after the fall of man, and at his expulſion from the garden of *Eden*; when *Jehovah placed at the eaſt of the garden of Eden, cherubim, and a flaming ſword which turned every way, to keep the way of the tree of life*; but we are not told what theſe cherubim were, whether real creatures or only figures, nor what their form, nor their number ᵃ, only their poſition at the eaſt of the garden of *Eden*, and their uſe, *to keep the way of the tree of life*, the meaning of which will be given hereafter; only it may be obſerved, that *Moſes* calls them *the cherubim* ᵇ, for the word in the original has the prepoſitive and emphatic article; as if they were well known, as they were to *Moſes*, and might be to the people of *Iſrael* through him, who could inform them of them; for the book of *Geneſis* was written after *Moſes* had the order to make the cherubim, and place them with the mercy-ſeat over the ark in the holy of holies, as related in *Exodus* xxv. 18—22. from whence we learn, that the cherubim were figures of winged creatures; that they were in number two; that they were made of gold, of the ſame maſs with the mercy-ſeat; that they ſtood at both ends of it, looking to one another and to that, and overſhadowed it with their wings; and were ſo placed as to make a ſeat for the divine Majeſty, who took up his reſidence here, and therefore afterwards is often deſcribed by him *that dwelleth between the cherubim.* The ſame figures were ſet in the moſt holy place in *Solomon*'s temple; and where alſo were two others of a larger ſize, made not of gold, but of olive-wood gilded, and whoſe wings extended, and touching each other, reached from one ſide of the holy of holies to the other; but ſtill we are at a loſs for the exact form of theſe figures: this is ſupplied in the viſions of *Ezekiel*, related in this and in the firſt chapter; in which, four living creatures, he aſſerts to be the cherubim, are particularly deſcribed by their faces, their wings, their hands, and their feet, and by the

ſhining

---

ᵃ In the Targums of Jonathan and Jeruſalem on the place, they are ſaid to be two.

ᵇ את הכרבים.

shining appearance of the whole; but still we are left in the dark what these creatures were emblems of, until the gospel-dispensation took place, which brings dark things into light; when *John* had a vision similar to those of *Ezekiel*, with a very little variation, in which he had a more perfect view of the living creatures, and which gives a more exact description of them, of their situation and employment; that they were round about the throne of God, were rational creatures, and spiritual and constant worshippers of the divine Being, or however, emblems of such; with other marks and circumstances, by which it may be known with some certainty, who they were, or who are intended by them. The vision is related in *Rev.* iv. 6—9. and is the key to the interpretation of the cherubim. From whence it appears,

*First*, That these were not emblems of the divine persons in the Godhead. It is a fancy that some of late have embraced, and are greatly elated with it, as a wonderful discovery; that the cherubim are an hieroglyphic, the three faces of the ox, lion, and eagle, of the Trinity of persons in the Deity, and the face of a man joined to them, of the incarnation of the Son of God; and would have the word *cherubim* pronounced *ce-rubbim*, and translated *as the mighty ones*; but this is a mere fancy and false notion: For,

1. *John*'s four beasts, or rather *living creatures*, as the word should be rendered, for that of *beasts* is an uncomely translation, the same with *Ezekiel*'s living creatures, and which he affirms to be the cherubim, are represented as worshippers of the divine Being, and therefore cannot be emblems of the object of worship. They are said not only to be about the throne of God, and to admire and adore the attribute of holiness, and ascribe it to the almighty Being; but to give glory, honour, and thanks to him; to fall down and worship God, yea, to fall down before the Lamb in a worshipping posture, and to give the lead to others in divine worship. See *Rev.* iv. 8—10. and v. 8, 14. and xix. 4.

2. The cherubim are in many places most manifestly distinguished from the divine Being; they are represented as the seat or throne on which he sits, and as a vehicle in which he rides; so they are described at the first mention of them in *Gen.* iii. 24. where the words may be rendered *he*, Jehovah, *inhabited the cherubim*, or dwelt with, over, or between them [e]; and so he did in the cherubim over the mercy-seat, from between which he promised to commune with *Moses*; and therefore, as before observed, is often described as dwelling between the cherubim, and on which he is said to ride. See *Exodus* xxv. 22. *Psalm* lxxx. 1. and xviii. 10. and here the living creatures in my text are said to be *under the God of Israel*, and so distinct from him; and in *John*'s vision are described as about the throne of God, and as distinct from him that sat upon it;

[e] Vide Texelii Phœnix, l. 3. c. 7. p. 256, 257.

it; and the *seraphim* in *Isaiah*'s vision, the same with the *cherubim* here, are also distinguished from the Lord *sitting on a throne high and lifted up*; and are represented as attendants on him, and worshippers of him, *Isai.* vi. 1—3.

3. If the cherubim could be thought to be emblems of a plurality in the Deity, they would be emblems, not of a trinity of persons, but rather of a quaternity, since the cherubim had four faces, each distinct from one another; yea, *John*'s four living creatures were four distinct animals, each having a distinct head and face; and the face of a man, both in his and *Ezekiel*'s living creatures, is as distinct a face as any of the rest; and if they were emblems of persons, that must be so too; whereas the human nature of Christ, this is said to be an emblem of, is no person; Christ did not take an human person, but an human nature into union with his divine person, for reasons that might be given; much less is it a person in the Godhead, as this supposed emblem would make it to be. Besides, the human nature in Christ is his inferior nature, whereas the face of the man in the cherubim is the superior face, the rest being faces of irrational animals.

4. If the cherubim were an hieroglyphic of the Trinity, this would give a similitude of the divine Being, and of that in him which is the most incomprehensible to us, a Trinity of persons in the Deity; and would furnish with an answer to such a question, suggested as unanswerable, *To whom then will ye liken God? or what likeness will ye compare with him?* Isai. xl. 18, 25. and xlvi. 5. for then it might be replied, To the cherubim: but there is no likeness of God, nor any to be made of him; though the Son of God often appeared in an human form, and in the fulness of time became incarnate; and the holy Ghost once descended as a dove; yet the Father's shape was never seen at any time, *John* v. 37. This notion also is repugnant to the second command, which forbids the making any likeness of any thing that is in heaven above, *Exod.* xx. 4. and then most certainly forbids the making of any likeness of the divine Being. Supposing the cherubim at the garden of *Eden* were made by God himself, as those in the tabernacle and temple were made by his order; yet he would never make nor order to be made such as he forbid, which he must, if they bore the similitude of him; but the truth is, the cherubim were not a likeness of any thing above in heaven, nor of any thing on earth; there never having been seen nor known by any man on earth, as *Josephus* [a] affirms, any such creature whom they describe; and a certain Jewish writer observes [b], the making of them came not under the interdict or prohibition of the second command; which if made in the likeness of God it would.

5. To

---

[a] Antiq. l. 3. c.6. §.5.  [b] R. Isaac Mosaides apud Selden. de Jure Nat. & Gent. c. 6. p. 183.

5. To all which may be added, if the cherubim were known emblems of the Trinity, it can hardly be thought that any man would take the name of Cherub to himself, or impose it upon any of his family, or should be so called by others; yet we find a man with his family of this name, *Ezra* ii 59. *Neh.* vii. 61. and still less would it be given as it is, to Antichrist, the antitype of the king of *Tyre*, the man of sin and son of perdition, *Ezek.* xxviii. 14. where he is called *the anointed cherub*; which can never be in allusion to the divine Being, and the persons in the Godhead; but may be in allusion to the ministers of the word, the cherubim are the emblems of, as will be presently seen; since he is an ecclesiastical person, calls himself a Bishop, an universal Bishop, Christ's anointed Vicar, and Head of the church, the sole and infallible interpreter of the sacred scriptures. Nor,

*Secondly,* Are the angels meant by the cherubim; though this is a much better sense than the former, and has been generally received by Jews and Christians; and what has led many to embrace this sense is, the supposed allusion to the cherubim looking to the mercy-seat, 1 *Pet.* i. 12. where mention is made of angels being desirous to look into the mysteries of grace; though it may be observed that ministers of the word are sometimes so called, and may be there meant: however, *John's* four living creatures cannot be angels, since they are so often distinguished from them; not only by their names, the one being called *angels*, and the other *living creatures* in the same place; but also by their situation, the living creatures are represented as nearest to the throne of God, and round about it, then the four and twenty elders next to them, and round about them, and then the angels as round about both; but what puts it out of all doubt is, that these living creatures are by themselves owned to be *redeemed to God by the blood of the Lamb, out of every kindred and tongue, people and nation*: which cannot be said of angels; for as they never sinned, they never stood in need of the blood of Christ to redeem them. See *Rev.* v. 8, 9, 11. and vii. 11. and xv. 7. Wherefore,

*Thirdly,* Since the four and twenty elders in the visions of *John* are the representatives of gospel-churches, so called in allusion to the twenty-four courses of the priests, and the twenty-four stations of the Levites, fixed in the times of *David*; who, as they in turn attended the service of the temple, represented the whole body of the people of *Israel*; so these twenty-four elders before the throne, and in the temple of God, represent the whole *Israel* of God, all the members of the gospel-church-state from first to last; and since the four living creatures are clearly distinguished from them both by name and by situation, and by giving the lead to them in divine worship, as ministers of the word do to the churches; it remains, that the ministers of the gospel only can be meant

by

by *the living creatures*, or *the cherubim*[f]. See *Rev*. iv. 4, 6, 9, 10 and v. 8, 11, 14. and vii 11. and by confidering the feveral places where they are made mention of, this will appear to be the truth of the matter. As,

1. *Gen.* iii. 24. where they are firft fpoken of, and are faid to be placed *at the eaft of the garden of Eden*, with a flaming fword, *to keep the way of the tree of life*; I am quite content to have the phrafe rendered, *to obferve the way of the tree of life*, as the word is often tranflated by us[g]. The flaming fword may be an emblem of the fword of the Spirit, which is the word of God, and which is fharper than a two-edged fword, and has itfelf two edges, *law* and *gofpel*; by the one, when it enters and cuts deep, is the knowledge of fin, and of the fad confequences of it, and leaves a fenfe of wrath and fiery indignation; and by the other, the knowledge of Chrift and falvation by him, and is called the gofpel of falvation; and the flame of it may denote the light, heat and glory, which are in the word, when accompanied with a divine influence; fo the cherubim may be an hieroglyphic of the minifters of it; and it is the fenfe of fome, both Jews and Chriftians[h], that the miniftry of the word is referred to and intended by the whole. When *Adam* had finned, he was driven out of the garden of *Eden*, to prevent his eating of the tree of life, left he fhould imagine that by that action of his, his life was preferved and continued, and would be for ever; teaching him thereby, that he was not to expect falvation and eternal life by any acts and works of his own, nor by any creature, nor by any outward means: and cherubim were placed without the garden, not to guard the way of the tree of life, literally underftood, or to prevent *Adam*'s accefs unto it; that was fufficiently done by his being driven out of it; but to obferve and point out to him, for his comfort and relief, the way to a nobler tree of life than that in the garden; to the true antitypical tree of life, Jefus Chrift, that tree of life that ftands in the midft of the paradife of God, the church, of which every overcomer of fin, Satan and the world, may take and eat, *Rev*. ii. 7. Chrift, the Wifdom and Word of God, who is a tree of life, the author and giver of life eternal to all thofe that lay hold by faith upon him; and happy is every one that fo doing retains him, *Prov.* iii. 18. even Chrift the way, the truth, and the life, the true way to eternal life. Now the cherubim were in this emblems

---

[f] I am not alone in this fentiment; Dr Lightfoot is of the fame opinion, *Profpect of the Temple*, c. 38. Pfeiffer. Dub. Vexat. cent. 4. loc. 4. p 407. Ofiander in ibid. and fo Vitringa on Ifa vi. 2. though of another mind are, Witfius in Ægyptiac. l. 2. c. 13. §. 35. and Oecon. Fœder. l. 4. c. 6. §. 44. and Marckius, Fafcic. Differtat. dif. 24. §. 17, &c. bot Dr Goodwin. in his expofition of the Revelation, p. 5, 6. takes *John*'s four living creatures to be the officers of the chriftian church.

[g] לשמר See Pfalm cvii. 48. Eccles. xi. 4. Ifai. xlii. 20. Jonah ii. 8.

[h] Vide Fagium in loc.

of ministers of the gospel, *the servants of the most high God; whose work it is to shew unto men the way of life and salvation by Jesus Christ.*

And this is the business that you, my Brother, should be constantly employed in, in instructing men that they are not to be saved by their own works, duties and services; that God saves and calls men, not according to their works, but according to his purpose and grace; that men are to expect the pardon of sin, not on the account of their repentance and humiliation, but through the blood of Christ, and according to the riches of God's grace; that *by the deeds of the law no flesh living can be justified* in the sight of God; but that a man is justified *by faith in the righteousness of Christ, without the deeds of the law*; that men are not saved by the best works of righteousness done by them, but by the abundant mercy and free grace of God, through Christ. You are to acquaint all that you are concerned with, that salvation is by Christ alone; that God has chosen and appointed him to be his salvation to the ends of the earth; and that he has appointed men to salvation alone by him; that he has sent him into the world to be the Saviour of them; this is the *faithful saying, and worthy of all acceptation,* you are to publish and proclaim, that Christ *came into the world to save the chief of sinners;* and that by his obedience, sufferings and death, he is *become the author of eternal salvation* to them; and that there is salvation in him, and in no other; and that *there is no other name given under heaven among men whereby they can be saved.* Souls sensible of sin and danger, and who are crying out, *What shall we do to be saved?* you are to observe, and point out Christ the tree of life unto them; and say, as some of the cherubs did to one in such circumstances, *Believe on the Lord Jesus Christ, and thou shalt be saved,* Acts xvi. 31. Your work is to lead men, under a sense of sin and guilt, to the blood of Christ, shed for many for the remission of sin; and in his name you are to preach the forgiveness of it to them; you are to direct believers, under your care, to go by faith daily to Christ the mediator, and deal with the blood of sprinkling for the remission of their sins, and the cleansing of their souls; which sprinkled on them speaks peace and pardon, purges the conscience from dead works, and cleanses from all sin. You are to point out the righteousness of Christ, as the only justifying righteousness of men, by whose obedience only men are made righteous; the ministration of the gospel is a ministration of righteousness, even of the righteousness of Christ, which is revealed in it from faith to faith; and such should be your ministration. You are to acquaint men, that this righteousness is unto all, and upon all that believe; and that such are justified from all things by it, *from which they could not be justified by the law of Moses;* and that the acceptance of men with God, is only in Christ the beloved. You are to observe to men the atoning sacrifice of the Son of God, and to direct

them,

them, as one of the cherubs did, pointing to him, and saying, *Behold the Lamb of God, which taketh away the sin of the world!* John i. 29. to bid them view the sin-bearing and sin-atoning Saviour, and look to the Lamb in the midst of the throne as though he had been slain; by whose slain sacrifice sin is put away, and they perfected for ever that are sanctified. But more of this may be observed,

2. In the account of the cherubim over the mercy-seat in *Exod.* xxv. 18, &c. there they are said to be *two*, and were emblems of the prophets of the Old Testament, and of the apostles of the New, with their successors, the ministers of the word in all generations; between whom there is an entire harmony and agreement; the prophets spoke of the sufferings of Christ, and the glory that should follow; and the apostle *Paul*, and the other apostles, said no other things than what *Moses* and the prophets did say, that Christ should suffer, and be the first that should rise from the dead; they both agreed in laying ministerially Christ as the foundation, and in directing men to build their faith and hope upon him, as well as they themselves were laid on him; and therefore he is called *the foundation of the apostles and prophets*, Ephes. ii. 20. even as the mercy-seat was the basis on which the two cherubim stood, and by which they were supported: and it may be observed, in agreement with the number of the cherubim, that the seventy disciples of Christ were sent forth by him *two* by *two* to preach his gospel; and the ministers of the word that prophesy in sackcloth during the reign of antichrist, are called the *two* witnesses, Luke x. 1. Rev. xi. 3. and the addition of two other cherubim of a larger size in *Solomon*'s temple, may signify the greater perfection of the gospel-ministry, and the larger number of gospel-ministers, in the gospel-church of the New Testament, of which *Solomon*'s temple was a type. The matter of which the cherubim over the mercy-seat were made, was pure *gold*, and of the same mass with the mercy-seat; denoting the rich gifts and graces of the Spirit, with which ministers of the gospel are qualified for their work; and which are of the same kind and nature with those of Christ, as man; only in measure, his without; and the rich treasure put into these earthen vessels, and the precious truths of the gospel, comparable to gold, silver and precious stones, committed to their trust to minister. The use of the cherubim was to overshadow the mercy-seat, and therefore they are called *the cherubim of glory shadowing the mercy-seat*, Heb. ix. 5. which they did with their wings; denoting in ministers their ministrations, the readiness and chearfulness of them; the cherubim looked towards one another, and towards the mercy-seat, and pointed to that.

And this, my Brother, is a principal part of your work, as one of the cherubs, to direct to Christ the mercy-seat, the channel of the grace and mercy of God to the souls of men; as God *set forth Christ* in his eternal purposes and decrees *to be a propitiation,* ἱλαστήριον, *Rom.* iii. 25. the same word the Greek interpreters use for the mercy-seat in *Exodus* xxv. so you are to set him forth in your ministrations as the propitiation, propitiatory, and mercy-seat: let the mercy-seat be ever in view; keep in sight in all your ministrations the doctrine of atonement and satisfaction by the blood and sacrifice of Christ; let this be the pole-star by which you steer the course of your ministry; direct souls to the throne of grace, to the mercy-seat, to God in Christ, where they may hope to find grace and mercy to help them in time of need: and, for your encouragement, observe the situation of the cherubim, they were upon the mercy-seat, at the ends of it, being beaten out of the same mass of gold with that; denoting the nearness of ministers to Christ, their union to him, and dependence on him, and support by him, who holds the stars in his right hand: and also his presence with them; for between the cherubim, the *shekinah,* or glorious majesty of God, dwelt; and Christ has promised to be with his ministers unto the end of the world. But I go on,

3. To consider the *living creatures* in the visions of *Ezekiel* and *John,* called the *cherubim;* and who will appear to be proper emblems of the ministers of the gospel, by considering their names and number, their form in general, and the several parts by which they are described in particular.

*1st,* Their names and number.

(1.) What both *John* and *Ezekiel* saw are called *living creatures;* for the ζωα in *John's* vision exactly answer to the חיות in *Ezekiel's,* and both signify animals that have life and breath: ministers of the word are *creatures,* both as men and as ministers; as men they are the creatures of God, as others; though they are the ambassadors of God, and stand in his stead, yet they are men and not gods, frail, mortal men; *the prophets, do they live for ever?* no: they are also sinful men, as the apostle *Peter,* one of the cherubs, owned himself to be; and men of like passions with others, as the apostle *Paul,* another of the cherubs, acknowledges; and therefore allowances must be made for their weaknesses and infirmities: and they are creatures as ministers, they are made so, not by themselves nor by other men: *Paul an apostle, not of men, neither by man, but by Jesus Christ, and God the Father,* Gal. i. 1. he did not thrust himself into the ministry, but God put him into it; nor did he become a minister of the word by his own attainments, not by all the learning he acquired at the feet of *Gamaliel,* or elsewhere; but he was *made a minister,* as he himself says, *according to the gift of the grace of God given unto him,* Ephes. iii. 6, 7. and so all that are *made able ministers of the New Testament,* are made so of God; for they are not sufficient of themselves, but *their sufficiency is of God,* 2 Cor. iii. 5, 6. And they are *living* creatures, they are regenerated, quickened, and have spiritual life in them; and so say the things which they have seen, and heard, and felt; which,

which, if unregenerate, they would not be able to do: and it is requisite they should be lively in their ministrations; it is most comfortable to themselves, and best for those to whom they minister, when they are lively in their frames, lively in the exercise of grace, and in the discharge of duty; when *they are fervent in spirit*, while they are *serving the Lord* their God; and under a divine influence, they are *the savour of life unto life*; the instruments and means of quickening dead sinners, and of reviving and refreshing drooping saints; and happy are those that fit under the ministry of the living creatures, regenerate men, the living and lively ministers of the gospel.

(2.) These living creatures are called *cherubim*. *Ezekiel* affirms they were the cherubim, and he knew them to be so. Many are the etymologies given of this word, and it is difficult to come at the true meaning of it. I shall not trouble you with every thing that is said [i], only what may seem proper, suitable, and pertinent. And, 1. *Philo* the Jew says [k], the cherubim signify *much knowledge*; and in which sense he is followed by many ancient writers [l], who interpret the word of *large knowledge*; and *fulness* of it; but for what reason, I must own, I cannot see; but be it so, this I am sure of, the ministers of the gospel have need of a large share of knowledge, both of things natural and spiritual; knowledge of themselves, and of their state by nature and by grace, and an experience of the work of the spirit of God upon their hearts; knowledge of Christ, his person, offices, and grace; knowledge of the scriptures, which *Timothy knew from a child, which are able to make men wise to salvation, are profitable for doctrine and instruction,* and to fit and furnish ministers for the work they are employed in; knowledge of the mysteries of grace, of God, and of Christ; all which are quite necessary for them, since their business is to feed men with knowledge and understanding, and to train them up in it, till they come to the unity of the faith, to a perfect knowledge of the Son of God, and *to the measure of the stature of the fulness of Christ* —2. Others think the word has the signification of *might, power, and strength*; in which sense the root of it is used in the Syriac language [m]: the ministers of the gospel are called strong; *we that are strong*, Rom. xv. 1. and they have need of all the strength they have, as to bear the infirmities of weak saints, so the insults, indignities, reproaches and persecutions of sinful men;

---

[i] The Talmudists in Chagigah, fol. 13. 2. & Succah fol. 5. 2. say, the Cherub is as if it was Ce-rubya, as a young man; in which form it was commonly supposed the Cherubim were; others as Ce-rab, as a master; others as Ce-rub, as a multitude, one being as a large multitude See Pfeiffer. Dubia Vexat. cent 1. loc. 10. p. 27. Hillerus in Onomastic. Sacr. derives it from a word which signifies to cover, and interprets Cherub covering. See Ezek. xxviii. 14.

[k] De Vita Mosis, l 3. p. 668.

[l] Clement. Alex. Stromat. l. 5. p. 563. Suidas in voce χερουβιμ. Hieron. Paulino, T. 3. fol 3. F. de Nom. Heb. in Exod. fol. 98. F. & Comment. in Esaiam. c. 6. 2. Isidor. Origin l. 7. c. 5. Vide Fromme Dissert. de Cherubim. §. 3.

[m] Vide Castel. Lexic. Heptaglott. in rad כרב.

## 40  A SERMON AT THE ORDINATION

men; they have need to be strong in the grace that is in Christ, that they may be able to do the duties of their office, and to endure hardness as good soldiers of Christ; they have need to *be strong in the Lord, and in the power of his might*; that they may be able to *wrestle against principalities and powers, the rulers of the darkness of this world*; they ought to be strong to labour in the word and doctrine, to do the work of the Lord as it should be done : but *who is sufficient for these things?*—3. Others [n] observe that the word *Cherub*, by a transposition of letters, is the same with *recub*, which signifies a *chariot*; in which form the cherubim are supposed to be, hence we read of *the chariot of the cherubim*, 1 Chron. xxviii. 18. and nothing is more common in Jewish writers than the *mercavah*, the chariot of *Ezekiel*, meaning the cherubim; and the living creatures, and the wheels might be in such a form as to resemble a chariot; and those who plead for angels being meant by them, with pertinency enough to their hypothesis, apply the words in *Psalm* lxviii. 17. *The chariots of God are twenty thousand, even thousands of angels, the Lord is among them as in Sinai.* But why may not the cherubim, admitting this sense of the word, be applied to the ministers of the gospel; since they are represented as vehicles, as chosen vessels to bear the name of Christ, to carry and spread his gospel in the world? and, which conveys the same sentiment, are signified by the white horse on which Christ is said to sit, and go *forth conquering and to conquer.* See *Acts* ix.15. *Rev.* vi. 2.—But, 4. What I am most inclined to give into is, that the word cherubim is derived from *Carab*, which in some of the eastern languages signifies[o] to *plow*; and in plowing, oxen were used formerly, and so they are in some places at this day : now not only one of the faces of the cherubim is the face of an ox, but that face particularly is called the face of the cherub, as may be observed by comparing *Ezek.* i.10. with chap. x.14. See also 1 *Kings* vii.29. So that the cherubim seem to have their denomination from this particular face of theirs: and that oxen were emblems of ministers of Christ, as will be considered more particularly hereafter, is evident from the apostle *Paul*, who having quoted the law concerning not muzzling the ox when it treads out the corn, adds, *Doth God take care for oxen? or saith he it altogether for our sakes?* for the sake of us ministers? *for our sakes, no doubt, this is written:* and from oxen he catches at once the idea of plowing, and applies it to ministers, *that he that ploweth should plow in hope,* that is, of enjoying the fruit of his labour, 1 *Cor.* ix. 9, 10. There is a prophecy of gospel-times, and of ministers in them, which runs thus, *Strangers shall stand and feed your flocks, and the sons of the alien shall be your plowmen*; that is, Gentiles should be pastors of christian churches, and feed them as flocks are fed; and that some of such who are aliens from
the

---

[n] De Dieu in Gen. iii. 24. Gusset. Comment. Ebr. p. 401.
[o] Chald. Syr. & Ar. vide Castel. ut supra.

the commonwealth of *Israel* should be employed in the Lord's husbandry, and be instruments in breaking up the fallow ground of mens hearts, and of sowing the seed of the word in them, *Isai.* lxi. 5.

(3.) To these names of the living creatures, the *cherubim*, may be added that of *seraphim* in *Isaiah* vi. 2. The Jewish writers[p] are generally agreed that the visions of *Isaiah* and *Ezekiel* relate to the same thing; and whoever closely compares them, will see a likeness between them; and have no doubt remain, but that the Cherubim and Seraphim design the same persons: the ministers of the gospel may be called by the latter name, which signifies *burning*, because of their ministerial gifts, comparable to coals of fire; and because of their fervent love to Christ and the souls of men, and because of their flaming zeal for the cause and interest of their Master.

(4.) The number of the living creatures, both in the visions of *Ezekiel* and *John*, being four, as the four chariots and the four spirits of the heavens, in the visions of *Zechariah*, chap. vi. 1, 5. may have respect to the four parts of the world; the commission of gospel-ministers being *to go into all the world, and preach the gospel to every creature*.

2dly, The form of the living creatures, and the several parts by which they are described, agree with the ministers of the word. The general form is not agreed upon on all hands: some think that it inclined mostly to that of the ox or calf[q]; to which they are induced by what has been observed, the face of the ox and of the cherub being the same; and some[r] suppose that the golden calf made by *Aaron*, and the calves of *Jeroboam*, were made after the model of the cherubim upon the mercy-seat; but this is without foundation. Others suppose[s] them of a mixed form, and that their faces are not to be understood of their faces strictly taken, but of their general forms and appearances; as that they had the face of a man, the breasts and mane of a lion, the shoulders and wings of an eagle, and the feet of an ox or calf; which seems not probable: rather the general form of them was human, and most resembled that, except in the parts which are otherwise described; for it is expressly said, *they had the likeness of a man*, Ezek. i. 5. and the ministers of the gospel are men; they are redeemed from among men; their business lies with men; they are sent to teach all nations of men, to preach the gospel to every human creature, and to and among the Gentiles *the unsearchable riches of Christ*. But this will more appear by considering the several parts by which the living creatures or cherubim are described.

Vol. II.          G          (1.) By

[p] T. Bab. Chagigah, fol. 13. 2. Maimon. Moreh Nevochim, par. 3. c. 6.
[q] Bochart. Hierozoic. par. 1. col. 412.    [r] Moncæus de Vitulo aureo, l. 1. c. 4. Gaffarel's unheard-of Curiosities, part 1. c. 1. §. 6, 7.    [s] Pradus and Villalpand. on Ezekiel.

(1.) By their faces, which are four. 1. *The face of a man*; intimating, that the ministers of the word should be humane, courteous, and civil to all men they are concerned with; pitiful and compassionate to wounded consciences, tempted souls, troubled and distressed minds, as well as to backsliders, in restoring them; and be men in understanding, knowing, rational, wise and prudent; and be manly and courageous, quit themselves like men, and be strong and valiant in the cause and interest of their Master.—2. *The face of a lion*, the *strongest among beasts*, Prov. xxx. 30. the strength of ministers has been hinted at already; the lion is remarkable for its boldness and intrepidity; *the righteous are* said to be *bold as a lion*, Prov. xxviii. 1. to be bold and intrepid, and not fear the faces of men, is a proper qualification of the ministers of the gospel; such were *John* and *Peter*, and the apostle *Paul* was not inferior to them in boldness and courage; though to shew how necessary such a qualification was, he desires the *Ephesians* to pray for him, that utterance might be given him, that he might *open his mouth boldly to make known the mystery of the gospel, and therein speak boldly, as he ought to speak*, Ephes. vi. 19, 20. Yet this was not wanting in him; for he elsewhere says, *We were bold in our God to speak the gospel of God with much contention*, 1 Thess. ii. 2. — 3. *The face of an ox*; a creature made for labour, and when in good state and plight, fit and strong for labour, and used to be employed in plowing the ground and treading out the corn; and is a fit emblem of gospel-ministers, employed in tilling God's husbandry, plowing the fallow ground of mens hearts, and treading out the corn of the word for their use, labouring in the word and doctrine: and, it may be, an emblem of them not only in labour but in patience; the ox that is accustomed to the yoke, patiently bears it; and which is seen not only in bearing the yoke of the ministry, but the weaknesses of the saints, and the reproaches of wicked men; in *meekly instructing those that oppose themselves*, and in waiting for the fruit and success of their labours.—4. *The face of an eagle*; a creature that soars high, has a strong and clear sight, and can look stedfastly on the sun; it espies its prey at a great distance, scents the carcass where it is, and gathers itself and its young to it; *for wheresoever the carcass is, there will the eagles be gathered also*, Matt. xxiv. 28. and fitly represents gospel-ministers, who have a clear sight into the sublime mysteries of grace, and see things which eye has not seen, the vulture's eye, the most sharp-sighted among carnal men; and who make it their business to preach a slain crucified Christ, and direct souls to him to feed by faith upon him; *we preach Christ crucified, &c.* 1 Cor. i. 23. and ii. 2—5. These faces were stretched upwards, for so the words may be rendered in *Ezek.* i. 11. *thus their faces and their wings were stretched upwards*, towards heaven; signifying that ministers of the gospel look upwards to Christ in heaven for fresh supplies of gifts and grace, an increase of light and knowledge, of wisdom and strength, to fit them more for their work,

and

and to enable them to perform it; being fenfible that without him, his grace and ftrength, they can do nothing; but through him ftrengthening them they can do all things, *Phil.* iv. 13.

(2.) The living creatures, who are the cherubim, are defcribed by their eyes; particularly in *John*'s vifion of them, where they are faid to be *full of eyes, before and behind, and within*, Rev. iv. 6, 8. fee alfo *Ezek.* x. 12. The eye is the light of the body; and what the eye is to the natural body, the minifters are to the church, the body of Chrift; yea they are *the light of the world*; and *if the eye be fingle*, if minifters be fincere, and have a fingle view to the glory of Chrift and the good of fouls, *the whole body will be full of light*, the church will be illuminated by them, *Matt.* v. 14. and vi. 22. they are *Argos*-like, have many eyes; and they have need of all they have to look into the facred fcriptures, which are a fealed book to learned and unlearned men, deftitute of the Spirit of Chrift; only to be looked into fo as to be underftood by fuch who have their eyes enlightened, their underftandings opened by Chrift, as were the difciples; the fcriptures are to be diligently fearched into, and explored for the rich treafure that is in them; and thofe that fearch into them, as for hid treafure, fhall find knowledge of great and excellent things; but thefe efcape the fight of all but thofe who have fpiritual eyes to fee. Minifters of the gofpel had need to be full of eyes, to look to themfelves, and to the flocks committed to them; to take the overfight of them, and feed them with the words of faith and found doctrine; to take heed to themfelves and to their doctrine, that it be wholefom, pure and incorrupt; and to their lives and converfations, that they give no offence to Jew nor Gentile, nor to the church of God, that the miniftry may not be blamed and rendered ufelefs; and alfo to efpy dangers, and give warning and notice of them, arifing whether from without or from within; to look diligently left any *root of bitternefs*, of error or herefy, or of immorality and profanenefs, fpring up in the churches, and trouble fome and defile others; and to watch againft falfe teachers, and to be careful to keep up the difcipline of Chrift's houfe. They have, as they fhould have, eyes *before* and *behind*; eyes *behind*, to obferve things paft, the fulfilment of prophecies, promifes, and types in Chrift; *before*, to look to predictions yet to be fulfilled relating to the church and kingdom of God; *behind* them, to watch againft Satan, who *goes about feeking whom he may devour*, and who comes upon the back of them at unawares; and *before* them, to watch over the flocks they have the overfight of; *behind* them, to the twenty-four elders, the members of the churches to whom they minifter, fo fituated with refpect to the four living creatures; and *before* them, to the throne of God and the Lamb, on whom is their dependence, from whom they expect fupplies, and whofe glory they are concerned for: and they have alfo eyes *within*, to look into the finfulnefs and corruption of their nature, and which is a means of keeping them humble under all their attainments, gifts and usefulness; and into the state and case of their own souls, and their inward experience; which qualifies them to speak to the cases of others, and by which they can make better judgment of the truth of doctrines, having a witness of them within themselves; and to look into the treasure that is put into them, in order to bring forth from thence things new and old, both for the profit and pleasure of those that hear them.

(3.) The living creatures, or cherubim, are described by their wings. The cherubim over the mercy-seat had wings, but how many is not expressed; but it is the opinion of some¹, both ancient and modern, that they had six, and so many had the Seraphim in *Isaiah*'s vision, chap. vi. 2. and the same number had the living creatures in *Ezekiel*'s vision; for though they are said to have four, chap. i. 6. yet not four only; from *ver.* 11, 23. it seems as if they had two more, and it is certain the living creatures in *John*'s vision had six, *Rev.* iv. 8. and, 1. With two of them particularly they flew, as *Isaiah*'s Seraphim did; which in ministers, denote their swiftness, readiness and chearfulness to do the work of God, to minister the word, and to administer ordinances, to visit the members of churches when needful, and do all good offices for the saints, that lay in their power. The Greek version of *Ezek.* i. 7. is, *their feet were winged;* expressive of the same thing, particularly of their readiness to preach the gospel, their feet *being shod with the preparation of the gospel of peace*; and for the same reason, a sett of gospel-ministers are represented by an angel flying in the midst of heaven, having the everlasting gospel to preach to all nations, *Rev.* xiv. 6.— 2. With other two wings they covered their faces; ministers, sensible of the purity and holiness of God, and the spirituality of his law, in comparison of which they see themselves unholy, carnal and sold under sin, blush at their sins and imperfections, and are conscious of their unworthiness to be employed in such service, looking upon themselves to be less than the least of all saints, the chief of sinners, and unfit to be ministers of the word; and are ashamed of their poor performances, and acknowledge that they have nothing but what they have received, and therefore have nothing to glory of at best.— 3. With other two wings the living creatures covered their feet: however beautiful the feet of gospel ministers may appear to others, to whom they come running with the good tidings of peace, life, righteousness, and salvation by Christ; yet they, sensible of their deficiencies, confess, that having done all they can, and in the best manner they could, they are but unprofitable servants. So *Isaiah*'s Seraphim covered their feet with two of their wings, but *Ezekiel*'s living creatures covered their bodies with them, and seem to have made use of four for that purpose, *chap.* i. 11, 23.— 4. Their wings were stretched upwards, *ver.* 11. so ministers
look

---

¹ Clement. Alex. Stromat. l. 5. p. 563. Fortunat. Scacchi Eleochrysm. par. 2. c. 36. p. 474.

look towards heaven, up towards Chrift, from whence are all their expectations of grace to help them to perform their work, and of all fuccefs in it: and their wings were alfo *joined one to another*; that is, the wings of one living creature to that of another; denoting minifters affection to each other, their giving mutual affiftance to one another, their concern in the fame work of the Lord, preaching the fame truths, and adminiftering the fame ordinances, having the fame zeal for the glory of God, love to Chrift and to the fouls of men, and being of the fame mind and judgment; and efpecially they will be fo in the latter day, when they fhall *fee eye to eye*, Ifai. lii. 8.— 5. The found of their wings is worthy of notice, and is repeated once and again, that it might be obferved, faid to be *like the noife of great waters; as the voice of the almighty, when he fpeaketh*, chap. i. 24. iii. 13. and x. 5. which is no other than the gofpel miniftered by them, a joyful found, a found of love, grace and mercy, peace, righteoufnefs and falvation; and which, like the found of waters, was heard at a diftance, when by the miniftry of the apoftles it went into all the earth; the voice of Chrift, and which is the gofpel alfo, is compared to the fame, *Rev.* i. 15. for its rapidity and force, under a divine influence; and which is not the voice, found and word of man, but of God himfelf; which appears by its powerful effects on the hearts of faints and finners, when attended with a divine energy; and indeed it is the Lord God almighty that fpeaks in minifters, and fpeaks powerfully by them, 1 *Thefs.* ii. 13. 2 *Cor.* xiii. 3.

(4.) Thefe living creatures, or the cherubim, are defcribed by having *the hands of a man under their wings on their four fides*, Ezek. i. 8. and x. 8. this denotes the activity of gofpel-minifters, who have not only the theory and knowledge of things, but are men of practice and bufinefs; they have much work to do all around them, on every fide; preaching the gofpel, adminiftering ordinances, vifiting their people, praying with them, and giving them counfel and advice, inftruction and exhortation, when needful; and they have hands to work with and ftrength given them, and which they employ, and are *ftedfaft and immoveable, always abounding in the work of the Lord*; and they do it with judgment, acting like men of underftanding and reafon: and their hands being *under their wings*, fhew, that befides their public work they do much in private, in their ftudies and clofets, in meditation and prayer, where no eye fees them but the eye of God; and alfo in private houfes where they pray, inftruct, counfel and advife, as the nature of cafes that prefent require; and whatever they do, whether in private or public, they do it not to be feen of men; or in an oftentatious way, as the Scribes and Pharifees; they boaft not of their own performances, they afcribe all to the grace of God which is with them, and own that it is by that they are what they are, and do what they do; fuch is their modefty and humility, which this phrafe is expreffive of.

(5.) The

(5.) The living creatures, or cherubim, are described by their *feet*, which are said to *be straight*; and with them *they went every one straight forward, and they turned not when they went*, Ezek. i. 7, 9, 12. they made straight paths for their feet, and went not into crooked paths; they turned not, neither to the right hand nor the left; their eyes looked right on, and their eyelids right before them, and steered their course accordingly: thus faithful ministers of the word walk uprightly, according to the truth of the gospel, and go in the paths of truth and righteousness; and neither turn to error on the one hand, nor to immorality on the other; and having put their hand to the plough of the gospel, neither look back nor turn back; for such that do so, are not fit for the kingdom of God, *Luke* ix. 62. Moreover, it is said of the living creatures, the cherubim, that *the sole of their feet was like the sole of a calf's foot*; round, the hoof divided, and fit for treading out the corn, and which is more firm and sure than the sole of a man's foot, which is apt to slip and turn aside; and so may denote the firmness, steadiness, and constancy of faithful ministers in their work, particularly in treading out the corn of the word for the nourishment of souls to whom they minister: and it is also added of the cherubim, that their feet *sparkled like the colour of burnished brass*; which may not only signify the strength and firmness of ministers to support under all the weight of work and sufferings, expressed by brass; so Christ's *feet* are said to be *like unto fine brass, as if they burned in a furnace*, Rev. i. 15. but also the brightness of their conversations, and the shining purity and holiness of their lives; and when the light of their works, as well as of their doctrines, shine before men, they look as bright as polished brass, and become *examples of the believer, in word, in conversation, in charity, in spirit, in faith, in purity*, 1 Tim. iv. 12. Moreover, the living creatures were directed by the Spirit, *whither the Spirit was to go, they went*, Ezek. i. 12, 20. so, as the prophets of the Old Testament spake as they were moved by the holy Ghost, the ministers of the New Testament are led by the Spirit, and guided by him in their ministrations into all truth as it is in Jesus; as well as they are influenced by him in their conversations, to walk as becomes the gospel of Christ; and as they are qualified by him with his gifts and graces for the work of the ministry, so he disposes of them where he pleases, and makes them overseers of such and such flocks in such and such places, according to his will; and they go as they are led by him, where he has a work for them to do. A remarkable instance of this see in *Acts* xvi. 6—10 where the apostles were forbid by the holy Ghost preaching in one country; and, assaying to go into another, the Spirit suffered them not; but they were directed to steer their course another way, and to another place, where souls were to be converted, and a gospel-church planted. Once more, when and where the living creatures went, the wheels went; and according to the motion and position of the one, were the

motion

motion and position of the other: *when the living creatures went, the wheels went by them; and when the living creatures were lift up from the earth, the wheels were lift up; when those went, these went, and when those stood, these stood,* Ezek. i. 19, 21. and x. 16, 17. the wheels signify the churches; and where there is the ministry of the word by the living creatures, the ministers of the gospel, there generally churches are raised and formed by them; and as the ministry of the word is continued or removed, so is a church-state fixed or changed; it is in this way and by this means that the candlestick is either continued or removed out of its place: and it may be observed in *John's* vision, agreeably to this, that when the four living creatures gave glory to God, the four and twenty elders fell down before him and worshipped him, *Rev.* iv. 9, 10. and v. 14. Ministers begin the worship of God, move first in acts of devotion, and then the churches and the members of them follow and join with them; and as they receive their doctrine, and are guided by them in matters of worship, so they copy after them in their conversations: and, generally speaking, as ministers be, churches are; if ministers have raised affections and elevated frames, so it often is with the churches, and the members of them, that sit under their ministrations; if ministers are active and lively, the churches are so too; but if dull, indolent, and inactive, so are church-members; if ministers are evangelical in their preaching, so are the people that hear them; but if they minister in a legal manner, of the same complexion, spirit and temper, will the members and hearers be

(6.) The living creatures, or cherubim, are described by the appearance of them, *like burning coals,* and *like lamps,* Ezek. i. 13, 14. Ministers of the gospel may be thus described, because of their ministerial gifts; the extraordinary gifts of the spirit are signified by *cloven tongues as of fire,* Acts ii. 3. and ordinary gifts for the ministry are represented as *coals of fire,* which are to be stirred up and enflamed, and not lie neglected, disused, or quenched, 2 *Tim.* i. 6. 1 *Thess.* v. 19. And the cherubim or ministers may be set forth hereby, because of the clear light of truth that shines in them, and because of their ardent love to Christ and the souls of men, which is one qualification for the ministry; hence says Christ to *Peter,* when he had affirmed once and again that he loved him, and appealed to his omniscience for the truth of it, *Feed my lambs, feed my sheep,* John xxi. 15—17. intimating, that such a lover of him was a fit person to feed the flock or church of God; even one whose love is so ardent that *the coals thereof are coals of fire, which hath a most vehement flame, that many waters cannot quench*; even waters of afflictions, reproaches, persecutions, and sufferings for the sake of Christ and his gospel: and by coals of fire may they be described, because of their burning zeal for the glory of God and the interest of a Redeemer; hence they

are

are called Seraphim, fiery or burning, as before obferved; and it is not unufual for minifters of the gofpel to be compared to *lamps*; the apoftles are called the lights or lamps of the world; and *John* the Baptift was *a fhining and burning light* or lamp; and fo others have been, holding forth the word of light and life to men: and whereas it is faid that *it*, the fire, *went up and down among the living creatures*; this is true of the word of God, compared to fire, *Jer.* xx. 9. and xxiii. 29. by which the minds of minifters are enlightened, their hearts warmed, and are filled with zeal for God, and become the means of enlightening and warming others; which *fire was bright*, clear, as the word of God is; and *out of the fire went forth lightening*; denoting the quick and penetrating efficacy of the word, and the fudden increafe of the kingdom and intereft of Chrift by it, which, like lightening, has been fpread from eaft to weft. Thus I have opened and explained the doctrine of the cherubim in the beft manner I could, and have fhewn the agreement between them and the minifters of the gofpel.

And now, my Brother, from thefe emblems you may difcern what is your principal work and bufinefs as a minifter of the gofpel; that it is to preach falvation by Chrift, the doctrines of pardon by his blood, of juftification by his righteoufnefs, and of atonement and fatisfaction for fin by his facrifice, with other truths of the gofpel; that you are to be laborious in this work, diligent and induftrious, conftant and immoveable in it; that you are to be bold and intrepid in it, not fearing the faces of men; and to be watchful over yourfelf and others that are your charge; to be tender and compaffionate to all in diftrefs, whether of body, mind or eftate, and to be humane in your deportment to all; that you are to walk uprightly, and be an example to the flock in your life and converfation; that you are to look up to heaven for frefh fupplies of grace to carry you through your miniftrations in all the branches of it; and through the whole exprefs fervent love to Chrift and the fouls of men, and a zeal for his glory: and may you be a fhining and burning light in your day and generation, and fuccefsful in the work of the Lord, and have many to be your joy and crown of rejoicing at the coming of Chrift.

SERMON

# SERMON XL.

*The Form of sound Words to be held fast.*

A CHARGE delivered at the ORDINATION of the Rev. Mr JOHN REYNOLDS.

2 TIMOTHY I. 13.

*Hold fast the form of sound words, which thou hast heard of me, in faith and love, which is in Christ Jesus.*

THAT part of the work of this day, which I have been desired to take, is to give the Charge to you, my Brother, who have been at this time ordained pastor of this church; and which I have chose to do in the above words of the apostle *Paul* to *Timothy*, to whom this epistle is directed.

The connection between the apostle and *Timothy* was such, that besides his being an apostle, and an inspired one, it gave him a just claim to use the authority and freedom he does in giving him this charge; and was such as laid *Timothy* under an obligation to pay a regard unto it; which was this, he had been an hearer of the apostle; and it is observed in the charge itself, *which thou hast heard of me*; and is used as a reason and argument why he should attend unto it; he had been instructed by him in the mysteries of grace and doctrines of the gospel; and besides, was a son of his after *the common faith*. Now, though, my Brother, there is no such connection between you and me, to give me a like claim, and lay you under a like obligation; yet, what is here urged and pressed, being an incumbent duty on every one that is engaged in the sacred work of the ministry, you will suffer this exhortation kindly, and take it in good part: in which may be observed,

I. The principal thing it is concerned about, *the form of sound words*.
II. The exhortation respecting it, to *hold it fast*.
III. The manner in which it is to be held, unless it should be rather a reason why it should be held fast, *which thou hast heard of me, in faith and love, which is in Christ Jesus*.

I. The principal thing this charge is about, *the form of sound words*. By *words* are not meant mere words, of these we should not be tenacious, when one may as well be used as another, to express the sense and meaning of any doctrine; when words are synonymous, signify the same thing, and convey the same idea, to wrangle and dispute about them would be vain and trifling; such mere logomachies and strivings about words to no profit, are condemned and dissuaded from, by our apostle [a]. Yet when words and phrases have long obtained in the churches of Christ, and among the faithful dispensers of the word; the sense of which is determinate and established, and well known, and they fitly express the meaning of those that use them; they should not be easily parted with, and especially unless others and better are substituted in their room; for there is often truth in that maxim, *qui fingit nova verba, nova gignit dogmata*, " he that coins new words, coins new doctrines." Should any man require of me to drop certain words and phrases in treating of divine truths, without offering to place others and better in their room; I could consider such a man in no other view, than that he had an intention to rob me, to rob me of what is more precious than gold and silver, that is, truth. There are certain words and phrases excepted to by the adversaries of truth, because they are not, as said, syllabically expressed in scripture; but be it so, if what they signify is contained in scripture, they may be lawfully and with propriety used, and retained in use: some concern the doctrine of the divine Being, and others the work of Christ; some relate to the divine Being, as essence, unity, trinity in unity, and person. *Essence* is no other than that by which a thing or person is what it is, and may with great propriety be attributed to God, who is το ον, the being, who is, exists, and which his glorious name JEHOVAH is expressive of, deciphered by the apostle *John, who is, and was, and is to come* [b]. Nor need we scruple the use of the word *unity* with respect to him, since our Lord says, *I and my Father are one* [c]; one in nature and essence, though not in person; nor the phrase *trinity in unity*, since the apostle *John* says, *there are three that bear record in heaven, the Father, the Word, and the holy Ghost; and these three are one* [d]: as for the word *person*, that is used in scripture both of the Father and of the Son; the Son is said to be *the express image of his person* [e]; that is, of the person of God the Father; and the Son must be a person too, or he would not be the express image of his Father's person; besides, the word is used of him also, for we read of *the light of the knowledge of the glory of God in the face of Jesus Christ* [f]; or in the person of Christ, and so the phrase is rendered in the same epistle, chap. ii. 10. *for your sakes forgave I it in the person of Christ*. Such phrases

---

[a] 1 Tim. vi. 4. 2 Tim. ii. 14.   [b] Rev. i. 4.   [c] John x. 30.
[d] 1 John v. 7.   [e] Heb. i. 3.   [f] 2 Cor. iv. 6.

phrases as concern the work of Christ objected to, are the imputation of his righteousness to his people, and the imputation of their sins to him, and the satisfaction made by him for them; as for imputed righteousness, that is nearly syllabically expressed, *even as David also describeth the blessedness of the man, unto whom God imputeth righteousness without works*[g]; and as for the imputation of sin to Christ, though it is not in so many syllables expressed, the thing itself is plain and clear: *he hath made him to be sin for us, who knew no sin*[h]; that is, God made him sin by imputing sin to him, for in no other way could he be made sin, since no sin was inherent in him; and this agrees with the language of the Old Testament, *the Lord hath laid on him*, or *made to meet on him, the iniquity of us all*[i]; that is, by imputing it to him. And though the word *satisfaction* is not used of the work of Christ in scripture, yet what is meant by it is plentifully declared in it; as that Christ has done and suffered in the room and stead of his people, every thing with well-pleasedness to God, and to the full content of law and justice; as when it is said, *the Lord is well-pleased for his righteousness sake*[k]; the reason follows, *he will magnify the law, and make it honourable*; *and also Christ hath given himself for us, an offering and a sacrifice to God for a sweet smelling savour*[l]; so that it may be truly said, God is fully satisfied with the obedience, righteousness, sufferings, death and sacrifice of Christ.

But after all, the apostle in the charge given does not design mere words but doctrines; so *the words of our Lord Jesus Christ*[m], he somewhere speaks of, are no other than the doctrines preached by Christ, or the doctrines concerning his person, offices and grace; and the words of the apostles of Christ, are no other than their doctrines; *their sound went into all the earth, and their words*, that is, their doctrines, *unto the ends of the world*[n]: and these are *the words of faith and good doctrine*, in which Timothy was *nourished*[o]: and these are *sound* words or doctrines; so we often read of *sound* doctrine, as, *if there be any other thing, that is contrary to sound doctrine*; and *the time will come, when they will not endure sound doctrine*; and *that he may be able by sound doctrine to exhort*, &c. *and speak thou the things which become sound doctrine*[p]: and which may be called *sound*, in opposition to the doctrines of false teachers, *the perverse disputings of men of corrupt minds, destitute of the truth, and reprobate concerning the faith*[q]; whose words or doctrines *eat as doth a canker*[r], prey upon the vitals of religion; and are said to be *pernicious*, ruinous, and destructive to the souls of men; and some of which the apostle, without any breach of charity, bestows the epithet of *damnable* upon[s]: and good doctrines may be called *sound*, because they are in themselves

salutary

---

[g] Rom. iv. 6.    [h] 2 Cor. v. 21.    [i] Isai. liii. 6    [k] Isai. xlii. 21.
[l] Ephes. v. 2.    [m] 1 Tim. vi. 3.    [n] Rom. x. 18.    [o] 1 Tim iv. 6.
[p] 1 Tim. i. 10. 2 Tim. iv. 3. Tit. i. 9. and ii. 1.    [q] 1 Tim. vi. 5. 2 Tim. iii. 8.
[r] 2 Tim. ii. 17.    [s] 2 Pet. ii. 1, 2.

salutary and healthful; *pleasant words*, as the wise man says [*], and such evangelical doctrines be; they *are as an honey-comb, sweet to the soul, and health to the bones*: the words or doctrines of our Lord Jesus Christ and his apostles are *wholesom* ones, salubrious and nourishing; the words of faith and good doctrine have a nutritive virtue in them, under a divine blessing, to nourish persons up unto eternal life; they contain milk for babes, the sincere milk of the word, which they desire that they may grow thereby; and meat for strong men, who have their spiritual senses exercised, to discern between good and evil; and these being found by believing souls, are eaten, and prove to be the joy and rejoicing of their hearts, and are more esteemed of by them than their necessary food.

Now there is a *form* of these sound words or doctrines: by which may be meant the form or manner of teaching them; as the Jew, who was an instructor of others, had his *form of knowledge and of truth in the law* [t], a method of instructing in the knowledge of it, and of teaching the truths contained in it; so a christian teacher has *the form of godliness* [u], a form of knowledge of it, and a method of teaching the mysteries of godliness, though sometimes without the *power* of it: or rather, here it signifies a brief summary or compendium of truths; the Jew had his creed, which contained the six principles, the beginning of the doctrine of Christ, the author of the epistle to the Hebrews speaks of; which the believing christian was not to stop at and stick in, but to go on to perfection; to embrace and profess doctrines more sublime and perfect [v]. The apostle *Paul*, that compleat, exact, and accurate preacher of the gospel, reduced the subject of his ministry and the doctrine he preached, to two heads, *repentance toward God, and faith toward our Lord Jesus Christ* [x]; he gives a most excellent form of sound words, and a summary of the gospel in *Rom.* viii. 29, 30. *Whom he did foreknow, he also did predestinate: — moreover, whom he did predestinate, them he also called; and whom he called, them he also justified; and whom he justified, them he also glorified*; and which some, not improperly, have called the golden chain of man's salvation; every link in it is precious, and not to be parted, and the whole is not to be departed from: the word ὑποτύπωσις, here used, may signify *a pattern*, and so it is rendered *1 Tim.* i. 16. the allusion is thought to be to painters, who first form a rough draught, or draw the outlines of their portrait, which is as a pattern to them, within the compass of which they always keep, and beyond which they never go. A scheme, a system of gospel-truths may be extracted from the scriptures, and used as a pattern for ministers to preach by, and for hearers to form their judgments by, of what they hear; which seems to be what the apostle calls the analogy or *proportion of faith*,

---

* Prov. xvi. 24.   t Rom. ii. 20.   u 2 Tim. iii. 5.
v See my Comment on Hebrews vi. 1.   x Acts xx. 21.

*faith* [r], which should not be deviated from : *if any man teach otherwise, and consent not to wholesom words, even the words of our Lord Jesus Christ, and to the doctrine which is according to godliness; he is proud, knowing nothing* [z] : and again, says the apostle, *though we, or an angel from heaven, preach any other gospel unto you, than that which we have preached unto you,* and he adds, *than that ye have received, let him be accursed* [a]; and this is the τυπος, or *form of doctrine* [b], which is delivered to the saints, or into which they are delivered, as into a form or mold, and become evangelized by it; and according to this they are to form their judgment of preachers, and shape their conduct and behaviour towards them; for if they bring not *the doctrine of Christ* with them, they are not to receive them, nor bid them *God-speed* [c] : if ministers, when they have formed and digested from the scriptures a scheme and system of gospel-truths, would be careful to say nothing contradictory to it; there would not be that want of consistency so justly complained of, in the present ministry in common, nor that confusion in the minds of hearers.

I have hitherto dealt chiefly in generals, I shall now descend to the particulars of this form of sound words or doctrines, which you, my Brother, should hold fast; and shall begin,

*First,* With the doctrine of the Trinity of persons in one God; which is the foundation of revelation, and of the economy of man's salvation; it is what enters into every truth of the gospel, and without which no truth can be truly understood, nor rightly explained : it consists of various branches; as that there is but one God, and that there are three distinct persons in the Godhead, Father, Son and holy Spirit, and that these are equally and truly God. There is but one God; this is the voice both of reason and revelation; it is the doctrine of the Old and of the New Testament; it is the doctrine of *Moses* and the prophets; *hear O Israel, the Lord our God is one Lord* [d] : and it is the doctrine of Christ and his apostles; of Christ, who calls the above words, *the first of all the commandments* [e]; and of the apostles, who declare, there is *one God and one Mediator* [f]; to believe and profess this truth is right and well, *thou believest that there is one God, thou dost well* [g] : all professing christianity are Unitarians in a sense, but not in the same sense; some are Unitarians in opposition to a trinity of persons in one God; others are Unitarians in perfect consistence with that doctrine. Those of the former sort stand ranked in very bad company; for a Deist who rejects divine revelation in general, is an Unitarian; a Jew that rejects the writings of the New Testament, and Jesus of *Nazareth* being the Messiah, is an Unitarian; a Mahometan is an Unitarian, who believes in one God, and

in

[r] Rom. xii. 6.    [z] 1 Tim. vi. 3.    [a] Gal. i. 9, 10.    [b] Rom. vi. 17.    [c] 2 John 10.
[d] Deut. vi. 4.    [e] Mark xii. 39.    [f] 1 Tim. ii. 5.    [g] James ii. 19.

in his prophet *Mahomet*; a Sabellian is an Unitarian, who denies a diſtinction of perſons in the Godhead; a Socinian is an Unitarian, who aſſerts that Chriſt did not exiſt before he was born of the virgin, and that he is God, not by nature, but by office; an Arian may be ſaid, in a ſenſe, to be an Unitarian, becauſe he holds one ſupreme God; though rather he may be reckoned a Tritheiſt, ſince along with the one ſupreme God, he holds two ſubordinate ones. Thoſe only are Unitarians in a true and ſound ſenſe, who hold a trinity of diſtinct perſons in one God. This is the doctrine of divine Revelation, the doctrine of the Old and of the New Teſtament, the doctrine of that famous text before mentioned, *hear O Iſrael, the Lord our God is one Lord*; the word for *our God* is plural, the word uſed is *Elohim*, a word of the plural number, and expreſſive of a plurality of perſons; and the ſenſe of the words is, and it is the ſenſe of the ancient Jews [h], our God, *Elohenu*, the three divine perſons are one *Jehovah*, one Lord; and with this perfectly agrees what the apoſtle *John* ſays, *there are three that bear record in heaven, the Father, the Word, and the Holy Ghoſt; and theſe three are one* [i], are one God. The authenticity of this paſſage has been diſputed, but not diſproved; the knowledge and uſe of it may be traced up to the times of *Tertullian*, who lived within a hundred years or thereabouts of the writing of the autograph itſelf by the apoſtle *John*; but could it be diſproved, the doctrine is to be defended without it, as it was by the antient chriſtians againſt the Arians: the proof of it is abundant; not to take notice of any other but the baptiſm of Chriſt, and the form of the adminiſtration of baptiſm preſcribed by him; at the baptiſm of Chriſt, all the three divine perſons appeared; there was the Son of God clothed in human nature, ſubmitting in that nature to the ordinance of baptiſm, being baptized of *John* in *Jordan*'s river; and there was the Father, who by a voice from heaven declared, ſaying, *this is my beloved Son, in whom I am well pleaſed* [k]; and there was the Spirit of God, who deſcended upon him as a dove; this was reckoned ſo clear a proof of a trinity of perſons, that the ancients uſed to ſay, "Go to *Jordan*, and there learn the "doctrine of the trinity:" and the form of the adminiſtration of baptiſm preſcribed by our Lord, which was to baptize *in the name of the Father, of the Son, and of the Holy Ghoſt* [l]; is ſuch a teſtimony of a trinity of perſons in unity, that the whole herd of *Antitrinitarians*, of whatſoever name, are not able to deſtroy; a proof this of the divinity of each perſon, ſince baptiſm adminiſtered in their name, is a ſolemn act of religious worſhip, and which otherwiſe would be idolatry; and of the equality of each perſon, ſince it is ordered to be adminiſtered equally in the name of the one, as in the name of the other; not in the name of one ſupreme God, and in the name of two inferior ones; and of the diſtinc-

tion

---

[h] Zohar in Gen. fol. 1. 3. and in Exod. fol. 18. 3. 4. and in Numb. fol. 67. 3.
[i] 1 John v. 7.　　[k] Matt. iii. 17.　　[l] Matt. xxviii. 19.

tion of thefe by the relative properties in the divine nature, paternity, filiation and fpiration; and of their unity as the one God, fince the order is to adminifter baptifm not in the *names*, but in the *name* of Father, Son and Spirit. And now it is to be believed and to be held faft, that thefe are equally and truly God: of the Father there is no difpute; and of the deity of the Son there need be no queftion, fince of the Son of God it is exprefsly faid, *this is the true God and eternal life* [m]; and again, *unto the Son, he faith, Thy throne, O God, is for ever and ever* [n]; the divine names he bears, and the divine nature and perfections, and the fulnefs of them he is poffeffed of; the divine works which are attributed to him, and the divine worfhip paid him, are full proofs of his true and proper deity: and that the holy Spirit is truly and properly God, is manifeft in that, lying to him is called *lying to God*: the name *Jehovah* is given him which belongs only to the moft High; he is defcribed as a perfon, having underftanding and will, and to whom perfonal actions are afcribed, and as a divine perfon, poffeffed of eternity, immenfity, omniprefence, omnifcience, &c. and the doctrine of the deity of thefe perfons fhould be held faft, fince this has an influence on the works afcribed to them, and without which they could not have been performed by them: and along with this is to be taken the doctrine of the eternal generation of the Son of God, and which, with the reft, my Brother, you are to hold faft; fince this is the hinge on which the doctrine of the trinity depends, without this it cannot be fupported; take away this, and it falls to the ground; this the Antitrinitarians of every name are fenfible of, and therefore bend all their force and fpite againft it, and is a reafon why it fhould be held faft by us: that Chrift is the Son of God, is attefted by the divine perfons themfelves; and has been acknowledged by angels and men, good and bad; but the thing is, in what fenfe he is fo: not in any of the Socinian fenfes; I fay, not in any of them, becaufe they are many, which fhows the wretched puzzle and uncertainty they are at about it; for there can be but one true fenfe in which Chrift is the Son of God: he is not called the Son of God, becaufe of fome likenefs in him to God, as they fometimes fay; nor becaufe of the affection of God to him, as at other times; nor is he fo by adoption; nor on account of his miraculous incarnation; nor of his refurrection from the dead; nor of his mediatorial office: but fince he is faid to be the begotten Son of God, and to be the only begotten of the Father, and the Father is faid to be his own Father, his proper Father, and fo not in an improper, figurative and metaphorical fenfe, he appears to be the Son of God by the generation of him, who faid, *Thou art my Son, this day have I begotten thee* [o]: how and in what manner the Son is be-

gotten

[m] 1 John v. 20.     [n] Heb. i. 8.     [o] Pfalm ii. 7.

gotten of the Father, I do not pretend to explain, nor ought any; but I firmly believe he is, and that for this very good reason, because the scripture asserts it; *we beheld his glory, the glory as of the only begotten of the Father* ᵖ.; we know but little of our own nature, and still less of the nature of God, and should be content with the account which he himself has given of it, who best understands it. For *what is his name?* that is, his nature, *and what is his Son's name, if thou canst tell* ᵠ*?* I have said, that "the doctrine of a trinity of persons in the "unity of the divine essence, depends upon the article of the son's generation, "and therefore if this cannot be maintained, the other must fall of course;" and for my own part, could I be prevailed upon to part with this article of faith, I would at once give up the doctrine of the trinity, as quite indefensible; and indeed it would be the height of folly ʳ to talk of a distinction of persons in the Deity, when the foundation of such distinction is removed; for we pretend to no other distinction in it, but what arises from the internal relative properties in God, as paternity, filiation and spiration, the ground of which is, the eternal generation of the Son; for without that there can be neither Father, nor Son, nor Spirit. The works of God done by him, such as those of creation, redemption and grace, and offices bore, serve to illustrate the distinction made, but could never make any: the works of God are *ad extra*, and are common to the three persons, and therefore do not distinguish them; for though some works are more peculiarly attributed to one than to another, each has a concern in them all: besides they come too late, they are wrought in time, whereas the nature of God, be it what it may, is eternal; and if there is any distinction in it, it must be natural, original and eternal; and indeed the Father was never without the Son, nor the Son without the Father, but was the eternal Son of the eternal Father; and neither of them without their breath or spirit, the Spirit which proceedeth from the Father, and is the Spirit of the Son: besides, as what God is, and he is what he always was, he is, and was so necessarily; and if there is any distinction in his nature, it is of necessity, and not of will; whereas the works of God are arbitrary things, which might or might not have been, according to the will and pleasure of the divine Being; but God would have been what he is, and if there is any distinction in him, it must have been, if these had

never

---

ᵖ John i. 14.    ᵠ Prov. xxx. 4.

ʳ Of such absurdity and inconsistence the late Dr Ridgley was guilty; exploding the doctrine of the generation of the Son of God, and adopting the Socinian notion of Sonship by office; and yet at the same time declaring for a distinction of three divine persons in the Godhead. A strange paradox this! and it is a disgrace to that body of men of whose denomination the Doctor was, that none of his brethren attempted to refute him, though they in general disliked his opinion and dissented from him; perhaps they thought the contradiction was so glaring, that his own notions confuted themselves; this is the best apology I can make for them.

never had been; if there never had been an angel created, nor a man redeemed, nor a finner fanctified, nor any office fuftained by Chrift as mediator, which is arbitrary alfo. This then being the cafe, if the article of the Son's generation cannot be maintained, as then there can be no diftinction of perfons, we muft unavoidably fink into the Sabellian folly; therefore, my Brother, hold faft this part and branch of the form of found words.

*Secondly*, Another part of this form of found words to be held faft, is the doctrine of the everlafting love of the three perfons to the elect; the love of the Father in chufing them in Chrift, providing a Saviour for them, and fending him in the fulnefs of time to work out their falvation; the love of the Son in becoming a furety for them, in the affumption of their nature, and in fuffering and dying in their room and ftead, to obtain their eternal redemption; and the love of the Spirit in applying grace unto them, implanting it in them, in being their Comforter, the Spirit of adoption to them, and the earneft of their inheritance, and the fealer of them up unto the day of redemption: this love is to be held, and held faft, as being foveveign and free; not arifing from any caufe or caufes in men, from any motives and conditions in them; not from their lovelinefs, being defiled and lothefom as others, and by nature children of wrath; nor from their love to God, fince he loved them firft, and when they did not love him; nor from their obedience and good works, fince while they were foolifh and difobedient, the love and kindnefs of God the Saviour towards man appeared; but from the will and pleafure of God, who loved them becaufe he would love them. And this doctrine of the love of God is to be held, and held faft, as being fpecial and difcriminating; not as a love of all, but of fome only; for though the earth is full of the goodnefs of the Lord, and all the inhabitants of it partake thereof, and fhare the bounties of his providence; his tender mercies are over all his works, and he caufes his fun to fhine, and rain to defcend on the juft and unjuft; yet he has a peculiar people whom he has chofen for himfelf, and to whom he bears a peculiar love; hence *David* defired [1], that he would *remember* him *with the favour* he bore to his *own* people. This fhould be held, and held faft, as being what commenced from everlafting, and continues to everlafting; it was taken up in the heart of God before the world was, and he refts and abides in his love, and nothing is able to feparate from it: it is as immutable and invariable as himfelf; as he is the Lord that changes not fuch is his love, yea, he himfelf is love, *God is love* [2]; the ftates and conditions of men are various, but the love of God is the fame in all; he may change his difpenfations, but he never changes his love; when he hides his face, he ftill loves; and when he chides, chaftifes and corrects, he does not utterly take away

nor

[1] Pfalm cvi. 4.     [2] 1 John iv. 16.

nor at all take away his loving-kindness. This doctrine in this light is to be held fast, because the everlasting love of God is the bond of union to him, and is the source and spring of all the blessings of grace, which are exhibited and held forth in the several doctrines of grace.

*Thirdly*, The doctrine of eternal, personal, and particular election, is another part of the form of sound words to be held fast; as that election is eternal, was *from the beginning*, as the apostle tells the Thessalonians [u]; not from the beginning of the gospel coming unto them, or from the beginning of their conversion and faith, but from the beginning of time, or before time: for the phrases, *from the beginning*, and *from everlasting*, are the same, as appears from *Prov.* viii. 23. Besides, the apostle expressly says, this choice was made *before the foundation of the world*, Eph. i. 4. It is also personal and particular; not a choice of propositions and characters, but of persons, he *hath chosen us*, as in the same place; not a choice of whole bodies of men, of nations, and churches, but of particular persons, known to the Lord by name; *the Lord knows them, that are his* [w]; *I know whom I have chosen*, says Christ [x]: they are as if they were particularly named: hence their *names* are said [y] to be *written in the Lamb's book of life*. This choice is of pure grace; not on the foresight of faith; for faith is the fruit of it, flows from it, and is secured by it; *as many as were ordained unto eternal life, believed* [z]: nor on the foresight of holiness, or on account of that; for God chose his people, not because they were holy, but that they might be so: he chose them through sanctification before time, and therefore calls them to holiness in time: nor because of their good works; for *the children not being yet born, neither having done any good or evil, that the purpose of God, according to election, might stand, not of works, but of him that calleth* [a]. And here it is called the *election of grace* [b], and strongly argued not to be of works, but of the pure sovereign grace of God: and it is both to grace and glory, to special blessings of grace, of faith, and holiness, to conformity to the image of Christ now, and to eternal glory and happiness hereafter, which is ensured by it; for, *whom he predestinates, he also glorifies*. Now, this part of the form of sound words is to be held fast, because it stands foremost in the blessings of grace, and is the standard and rule according to which God proceeds in dispensing the rest; for he blesses his people with *all spiritual blessings in Christ, according as he hath chosen them in him* [c]

*Fourthly*, The doctrine of the covenant of grace is to be held fast, made between the eternal three, when there were none in being but themselves; no creature,

---

[u] 2 Thess. ii. 13.   [w] 2 Tim. ii. 19.   [x] John xiii. 18.   [y] Phil. iv. 3. Rev. xiii. 8. and xvii. 8. and xx. 15.   [z] Acts xiii. 48.   [a] Rom. ix. 11.   [b] Rom. xi. 5, 6.   [c] Ephes. i. 3, 4.

ture, neither an angel, nor a man, nor the foul of a man; none but God, Father, Son and Spirit, between whom and them alone the covenant-transactions were; even before the world was, or any creature whatever in being; hence it is called an *everlafting covenant* [b], being from everlafting; as well as it will continue to everlafting; which appears from Chrift's being fet up fo early as the mediator of it, from the provifion of bleffings of grace in it fo early, which were given to the elect in Chrift, and they were bleffed with them in him before the world was; and from promifes made in it fo early, particularly the promife of *eternal life, which God, that cannot lie, promifed before the world began* [c]. It is abfolute and unconditional; no conditions in it but what were engaged to be performed, and have been and are performed by the Son of God, and by the Spirit of God: with refpect to the perfons on whofe account the covenant was made; all the promifes run in this ftile, " I *will* be their God, and they *fhall* be
" my people; I *will* put my fear in their hearts, and they *fhall* not depart from
" me: I *will* take away the ftony heart, and give them an heart of flefh; a new
" heart and a new fpirit *will* I give them, and I *will* put my fpirit within them,
" and *caufe* them to walk in my ftatutes; and they *fhall* keep my judgments, and
" do them [d]." It is a covenant of pure grace to the elect, and is fure, firm, and inviolable: it is *ordered in all things and fure*; its bleffings are the *fure* mercies of *David*, and its promifes are all yea and amen in Chrift [e]. It is a covenant God will not break, and men cannot: it is immoveable, and more fo than rocks and mountains; the mountains fhall depart, and the hills be removed; but the covenant of peace fhall never be removed [f]. Now the doctrine concerning this is to be held faft, becaufe it is the bafis of the works done by the Son and Spirit of God; of the Son's work in redemption, according to his furetyfhip-engagements in this covenant; and of the Spirit's work in fanctification, according to his own agreement in it.

*Fifthly*, The doctrine of original fin, which opens and defcribes the ftate and condition of men by nature, is another part of the form of found words to be held faft; as that all men finned in *Adam*, in whom they were federally as their covenant-head; in which refpect he was the *figure* or type of *him that was to come* [g]; that is, of Chrift. Hence the apoftle gives the parallel between thefe two covenant-heads; the one, as conveying grace, righteoufnefs, and life, to his feed; and the other, as conveying fin, condemnation, and death, to all his pofterity. Befides, all men were in *Adam* feminally, in like fenfe as *Levi* was in the loins of *Abraham*, when he paid tithes to *Melchizedek* [h]: fo all men were

I 2                                                                              in

[b] 2 Sam. xxiii. 5.      [c] Titus i. 2.         [d] Jer. xxxii. 38—40. Ezek. xxxvi. 26, 27.
[e] 2 Sam. xxiii. 5.   Ifai. lv. 3.   2 Cor. i. 20.      [f] Ifai. liv. 10.      [g] Rom. v. 14.
[h] Heb. vii. 9, 10.

in the loins of their firſt father, and when he ſinned, ſinned in him, and were made, conſtituted, reckoned, and accounted ſinners, by his diſobedience. The guilt of his ſin is imputed to them, ſo as that judgment comes upon them all to condemnation; and death reigns over them, and all die in him, and a corrupt nature is propagated from him to them: they are all, like *David, ſhapen in iniquity, and conceived in ſin:* and indeed how can it otherwiſe be? for *who can bring a clean thing out of an unclean? not one*[1]. There never was but one inſtance of *Adam*'s race free from his ſin, and that was the human nature of Chriſt: but then that did not deſcend from him by ordinary generation, but was brought into the world in a ſupernatural way, and ſo eſcaped the contagion of ſin. Now it is neceſſary that this doctrine ſhould be held faſt, ſince it accounts for the corruption of human nature; ſhews the reaſon of mens being ſo prone to ſin, and biaſed to it; ſo impotent to that which is good, and ſo averſe to it: and alſo ſhews the neceſſity of redemption, regeneration, and ſanctification.

*Sixthly,* The doctrine of redemption by Chriſt, is another part of the form of ſound words to be held faſt; as that it is ſpecial and particular; though Chriſt gave his life a ranſom for many, yet not for all: thoſe that are redeemed by him are redeemed from among men, *out of every kindred, tongue, people, and nation:* they are Chriſt's ſpecial people he came to ſave: his ſheep the Father gave him, and he undertook the care of, he laid down his life for: the children of God, that were ſcattered abroad, he came to gather together by his ſufferings and death; and his church he gave himſelf for, even *the general aſſembly and church of the firſt-born, which are written in heaven:* and that this redemption is procured by way of ſatisfaction to the juſtice of God; he redeemed his people by paying a price for it, even his precious blood. Redemption was obtained by Chriſt through his ſufferings, the juſt for the unjuſt; by his being wounded, bruiſed, and ſtricken, for the tranſgreſſions of his people; by bearing their iniquities, and the puniſhment of them; by his being made ſin and a curſe for them, thereby redeeming them from ſin and the curſes of the law; and this doctrine of redemption by the blood of Chriſt, and atonement by his ſacrifice, ſhould be held faſt, it being the foundation of a ſinner's peace, joy, and comfort.

*Seventhly,* The doctrine of juſtification by the imputed righteouſneſs of Chriſt, is another branch of the form of ſound words to be held faſt: this proceeds from the free grace of God, through the redemption that is in Chriſt; the matter of it is what is commonly called the active and paſſive obedience of Chriſt, which, with the holineſs of his nature, are imputed for juſtification, being what
is

---

[1] Job xiv. 4.

is required to it by the holy law of God; and hence sometimes men are said to be *made righteous by the obedience* of Christ, and sometimes to be *justified by his blood*[k], which is put for his whole sufferings and death; by the one Christ has fulfilled the preceptive part of the law; and by the other has bore the penalty of it; and by both has given full satisfaction to it: the form of it is the imputation of righteousness without works, by an act of God's grace: this righteousness is revealed in the gospel from faith to faith; and faith is wrought in the soul, to lay hold on it, receive it, and plead it as its justifying righteousness, from whence much peace and comfort flow. Justification may be considered as a sentence conceived in the divine mind from eternity; and as pronounced on Christ, the head and surety of his people, when he rose from the dead, and upon them in him; and as it is again pronounced in the conscience of a believer, when the righteousness of Christ is revealed to him, and received by him; and as it will be notified, and be openly and publicly pronounced before angels and men, when all the seed of *Israel*, or the whole elect in a body, shall be justified and shall glory. This is to be held fast; for, as *Luther* called it, it is *articulus stantis vel cadentis ecclesiæ*, "the article by which the church stands or falls."

*Eighthly*, The doctrines of pardon, peace, and reconciliation by the blood of Christ, are parts of this form of sound words to be held fast; that the pardon of sin is through the blood of Christ, which, as it was shed for the remission of sin, through it we have it, and through that only, and not on account of repentance, humiliation and confession, as meritorious or procuring causes of it; and that peace is made by the blood of Christ, from whence peace of conscience flows; and that both reconciliation for our sins, and reconciliation of our persons to God, is made by the death of Christ; hence the gospel which publishes this is called the *word of reconciliation*, and the *gospel of peace*[l], which therefore should be held fast.

*Ninthly*, The doctrines of regeneration, effectual calling, conversion, and sanctification by the spirit, power, and grace of God, are parts of the same form and system; the necessity of regeneration, without which there is no seeing nor entering into the kingdom of God, must be asserted; and that it is not of man, of the power and will of man, but of the power and will of God: that effectual vocation is by the grace of God, and not according to the works of men; that conversion is not of him that willeth nor runneth, but of the mighty power of God, who works in men both to will and to do; that sanctification is absolutely necessary to salvation, for without holiness no man shall see the Lord; that this is the work of the Spirit of God, and is therefore called the *sanctifica-*

*tion:*

---

[k] Rom. v. 9, 19.  [l] 2 Cor. v. 19. Ephes. vi. 15.

*tion of the Spirit* [m], and which he gradually carries on, and will perform until the day of Chrift. Wherefore,

*Tenthly* and *laftly*, and which bring up the rear, the doctrine of the faints final perfeverance is a part of this form of found words to be held faft; even that all that are chofen by the Father, and redeemed by the Son, and fanctified by the Spirit, fhall perfevere in faith and holinefs to the end; being incircled in the arms of everlafting love, fecured in the everlafting covenant, united to Chrift their head, furety, and faviour, built on him the rock of ages, againft which the gates of hell cannot prevail, and fo are like mount *Zion,* which can never be removed; and being in the hands of Chrift, out of whofe hands none can pluck, and who is able to keep them from falling; and being kept by the power of God through faith unto falvation. Thefe are at leaft fome of the principal things which make up the form of found words, which you, my Brother, are to hold faft, maintain and publifh in your miniftry.

What remains now to be confidered are the exhortation to hold it faft, and the manner in which it is to be done, on which I fhall not long dwell.

II. The exhortation refpecting the form of found words, *hold faft.* This fuppofes a man to have it, as all fuch exhortations fuppofe perfons to have what they are exhorted to hold, and hold faft; and which is fometimes expreffed; as, *that which ye have already, hold faft till I come*; and again, *hold that faft which thou haft, that no man take thy crown* [n]: and *Timothy,* to whom the exhortation in the text is given, was in poffeffion of the form of found words; it was a facred depofitum committed to his truft. Hence it follows, *that good thing, which was committed unto thee, keep by the holy Ghoft which dwelleth in us;* it was in his hand, in his head, and in his heart; *the word is nigh thee, even in thy mouth and in thy heart; that is, the word of faith which we preach* [o]; and what is had fhould be held; it fhould be held forth, *holding forth the word of life* [p], and the word of light. Minifters are lights, and have light communicated to them, which fhould fhine forth, and not be put under a bufhel; what they have freely received they fhould freely give; what is told them in private in their ftudies, they fhould publicly declare, and affirm thofe things conftantly; they fhould hold faft the faithful word, as they have been taught, and have taught others, and tenacioufly abide by it; fo *Timothy* was exhorted to do, and which will ferve more fully to confirm and explain the exhortation here, *continue thou in the things* which thou haft *learned, and haft been affured of, knowing of whom thou haft learned them* [q].

This exhortation to *hold faft the form of found words,* is oppofed to dropping or departing from it, which may be done by thofe who have had it; men may

*receive*

[m] 1 Pet. i. 2.   [n] Rev. ii. 25. and iii. 11.   [o] Rom. x. 8.   [p] Phil. ii. 16.   [q] 2 Tim. iii. 14.

*receive the grace of God in vain*; that is, the doctrine of the grace of God; they may first receive it with seeming pleasure and satisfaction, and afterwards reject it; they may fail of the grace of God in this sense, and fall from it partially or totally; so such that seek for and hold justification by the law, *are fallen from grace*[1]; from the doctrine of grace, and particularly from the doctrine of justification by the grace of God through the righteousness of Christ: and as private professors may drop and depart from the doctrines of the gospel formerly received and held by them, so may ministers of the word drop and depart from sound words and doctrines they have formerly professed and preached. And it is opposed to wavering about the form of sound words, and instability in it; and suggests, that such who have it should not be like children, toss'd about with every wind of doctrine, nor be carried about, like meteors in the air, with divers and strange doctrines, doctrines various in themselves and foreign to the word of God; but should affirm constantly with boldness, confidence and courage, the truths of the gospel; for this also stands opposed to timidity, cowardice and pusillanimity; when they should be valiant for the truth, stand fast in the faith, quit themselves like men, and be strong; and not give way, no not for an hour, that the truth of the gospel might continue with the saints.

Moreover this exhortation, considered in this light, supposes that *Timothy*, and so other gospel-ministers, may at times be under temptations to let go the form of sound words, or drop the truths of the gospel, through fear of men, and because of the obloquy, reproaches and persecutions of men, see v. 7, 8, 12. they may be tempted hereunto, as on the one hand to escape being censured as bigots, enthusiasts, narrow-spirited men, and void of common-sense and reason; and on the other hand to obtain the characters of men of sense, of moderate principles, of candor and ingenuity, and of being polite and rational preachers. And it also suggests that there might be such persons who sought every opportunity to wring this form of sound words out of the hands of *Timothy*, and so of any other minister of the word, as well as of those under their ministry; men that lie in wait to deceive, to beguile and corrupt the minds of men from the simplicity in Christ, and therefore to be guarded against.

III. The manner in which the form of sound words is to be held fast; *in faith and love, which is in Christ Jesus:* which words may be connected with the phrase *which thou hast heard of me.* *Timothy* had heard the apostle preach those sound doctrines with great faithfulness; for he was a faithful minister of the gospel, who *kept back nothing that was profitable, and shunned not to declare the whole counsel of God*; he had heard him speak the truth in love, with great warmth of affection,

[1] 2 Cor. vi. 1. Heb. xii. 15. Gal. v. 4.

affection, with much vehemence and fervency of spirit; and he himself had heard and received the word preached in faith, and had mixed it with faith, and digested it by it, and was nourished with it; he had received the love of the truth, and the truth in the love of it: and the phrase, viewed in this light, contains a reason why therefore he should hold fast the form of sound words he had received in such a manner: or they may be considered as connected with *the form of sound words*; as if faith and love were the subjects of it; that it lay in things to be believed, as the gospel does; and therefore called the word of faith, the faith of the gospel, and the faith once delivered to the saints; and in duties and ordinances to be observed from love to God and Christ; and so is a reason as before, why it should be held fast: or else it is to be connected with the exhortation *hold fast*; and so directs to the manner in which it is to be held; the faithful word, the word to be believed, is to be held, held forth, and held fast in faithfulness; *he that hath my word*, this form of sound words in his head, and in his mouth and heart, *let him speak my word faithfully; what is the chaff to the wheat? faith the Lord*[s]; and this word of truth is to be held fast and spoken in love; in love to God, to Christ, to the word, and to the souls of men. It follows, *which is in Christ Jesus*; either the form of sound words is in him; all truth is in him, he is full of that as well as of grace; *all the treasures of wisdom and knowledge*, of the mysteries of grace, *are hid in him*[t], and they come from him; the words or doctrines of wisdom and knowledge *are given from one shepherd*[u], Christ, to his under shepherds, to feed his churches with knowledge and understanding: or else this is to be understood of the graces of faith and love, in the exercise of which the word is to be preached, heard and held fast; these are originally in Christ, and come from him; *the grace of our Lord was exceeding abundant with faith and love, which is in Christ Jesus*[v]; as well as they are exercised on him as the object of them.

Thus have I considered this charge of the apostle to *Timothy*, in the method proposed; and you, my Brother, should receive it as if it had been delivered to you, it being what concerns and is obligatory upon every minister of the gospel: I shall close with some other branches of the apostle's charge, to *Timothy*, which you would do well also to advert unto; *Be thou an example of the believers, in word, in conversation, in charity, in spirit, in faith, in purity.—Give attendance to reading, to exhortation, to doctrine—neglect not the gift that is in thee—meditate upon these things, give thyself wholly to them, that thy profiting may appear to all.— Take heed unto thyself, and unto the doctrine, continue in them; for in doing this, thou shalt both save thyself and them that hear thee*[x]. I have done; God give success to your ministrations.

TRUTH

[s] Jer. xviii. 28.    [t] Colos. ii. 3.    [u] Eccles. xii. 11.    [v] 1 Tim. i. 14.
[x] 1 Tim. iv. 12—16.

# TRUTH DEFENDED.

Being an ANSWER to an ANONYMOUS PAMPHLET, intitled, *Some Doctrines in the Supralapsarian Scheme impartially examined by the Word of God.*

LATELY came to my hands an anonymous pamphlet, intitled, *Some Doctrines in the Supralapsarian Scheme impartially examined by the Word of God.* The author of it is right, in making the word of God the rule and standard by which doctrines and schemes are to be tried and examined. *To the law and to the testimony; if men speak not according to this word, it is because there is no light in them* [a]. He sets out with large declarations of his regard to the sacred writings, which to swell the performance are too often repeated, even *ad nauseam*; and yet, in his very first paragraph, drops a sentence not very agreeable to them, if any sense can be made of it: "All opinions and maxims, he says, that cor-"respond not with this divine rule, we should either entirely reject, or *at least* "refuse to admit as articles of our faith [b]." But why not entirely reject them, without any hesitation? why this disjunctive proposition? why this softening clause added? If it can be thought to be so, or to convey a different idea from the former, as it is designed it should; though I should think, to refuse to admit doctrines and maxims as articles of faith, that do not correspond with the divine rule, is the same thing as to reject them as articles of faith. The man seems to write in the midst of hurry and surprise. Since he has met with schemes and opinions so exceedingly shocking and stunning, it would have been adviseable for him to have sat down and waited until he was better come to, and more composed, before he put pen to paper, and committed his frightful apprehensions to writing. And indeed one would have thought he has had time enough to have recovered himself from the surprise he has met with, seeing it is near *four* years ago, since the more modern pieces he has taken notice of were published to the world.

I. The examination begins with the foundation-principle of the Supralapsarians, as he calls it, that "God chose his people without considering them as "fallen creatures [c]." He does well to begin with their foundation-doctrine; for if he can demolish the foundation, the superstructure must fall; if he can pluck up what he supposes to be the root of many false opinions, the branches which

[a] Isai. viii. 20.   [b] Supralapsarian Scheme, p. 1.   [c] Id. Ibid. p. 3.

which grow from it will die in courſe. But though this received opinion of theirs, as our author ſtiles it, is a denomination one, or that from which they are called Supralapſarians; yet it is far from being a foundation-principle, or a fundamental article of faith with them; nor do they conſider this point, in which they differ from others, as the principal one in the doctrine of election They and the Sublapſarians are agreed in the main points reſpecting that doctrine; as, that it is an eternal act of God; that it is of certain particular perſons; that it is unconditional, irreſpective of faith, holineſs, and good works, as cauſes and conditions of it; and that it entirely ſprings from the good-will and pleaſure of God. The Contra-Remonſtrants were not all of a mind concerning the object of predeſtination, but did not think it worth their while to divide upon that account. Nay, ſome [d] of them were of opinion that it was not neceſſary to be determined, whether God, in chooſing men, conſidered them as fallen, or as not yet fallen; provided it was but allowed that God in chooſing conſidered men in an equal ſtate, ſo as that he that is choſen was not conſidered by God either of himſelf, or by his own merit, or by any gracious eſtimation, more worthy than he who is not choſen. That famous Supralapſarian, Dr *Twiſs* [e], declares, that "as for the ordering of God's decrees, upon which only ariſe " the " different opinions touching the object of predeſtination, it is merely *apex logicus*, " a point of logic." The decrees of God may be diſtinguiſhed into the decree of the end, and the decree of the means, that they may the better be conceived of by our finite underſtandings; which are not able to conſider all things at once, and together, as they lie in the divine mind, but of one thing after another; and that without dividing and ſeparating of God's decrees, or ſuppoſing any priority or poſteriority in him. Now the decree of the end muſt be conſidered before the decree of the means; and that what is firſt in intention, is laſt in execution, and ſo *vice verſa*. Let then eternal life and glory, or a ſtate of everlaſting communion with God, be the end of election, as it is with reſpect to man, then the creation, permiſſion of *Adam*'s fall, and the recovery out of it, are the means in order to that end. It follows, that, in the decree of the end, man could not be conſidered as a fallen creature, but as yet not created; becauſe the creation and the permiſſion of the fall belong to the decree of the means, which is in order of nature after the decree of the end. For if God firſt decreed to create man, and to permit him to fall, and then decreed to bring him to a ſtate of eternal life and happineſs; according to this known rule, that what is firſt in intention is laſt in execution, this ſtrange abſurdity will follow, that man will be firſt brought into a ſtate of eternal life and happineſs, and then created and permitted to fall. Let the end be the manifeſtation of God's glory, which certainly

[d] Vid. Act. Synod. Dordr. par. 2. p. 48.
[e] Riches of God's Love, againſt Hord, par. 1. p. 35.

tainly is the supreme end of election, then the means are creation, permission of sin, redemption, sanctification, and, in a word, compleat salvation; which, though they are materially many, yet make up but one formal decree, called the decree of the means. Now according to the former rule, the intention of the end must be first, and then the intention of the means; and, consequently, man cannot be considered in the decree of the end, the manifestation of God's glory, as yet created and fallen; because the creation and permission of sin belong to the decree of the means, which in order of nature is after the decree of the end. But if, on the contrary, God first decreed to create man and permit him to fall, and then decreed to manifest the glory of his grace and mercy, in his eternal salvation; according to the above rule, that what is first in intention is last in execution, and so *vice versa*, it will follow, that the glory of God's grace and mercy are first manifested in the eternal salvation of man, and then he is created and suffered to fall. Likewise it is to be observed, that the several things mentioned in the decree of the means, creation, permission of sin, and salvation, are not to be considered as subordinate, but as co-ordinate means, or as making up an entire, compleat medium. We are not to suppose that God decreed to create man that he might permit him to fall, or that he decreed to permit him to fall, that he might save him; but that he decreed to create him, permit him to fall, and to save him notwithstanding his fall, that he might glorify his grace and mercy. Nor are we to conceive of them after this manner, that God first decreed to create man, and then decreed to permit him to fall; for it would follow that man, in the execution of these decrees, is first permitted to fall, and then he is created: Nor thus, that God first decreed to create man, and permit him to fall, and then decreed to save him; for, according to the former rule, man would first be saved, and then created and permitted to fall. These are some of the reasonings of the Supralapsarians; particularly of Dr *Twiss*, as may be seen in his *Vindiciæ*, and in his *Riches of God's love, against* Hord. This poor man, that takes upon him to write against the Supralapsarians, would do well to try his skill in unravelling and destroying this kind of reasoning: But alas! his capacity will never reach it. I am afraid the very mention of these things will increase his surprise and fright. However, since he has taken upon him to object to this opinion of the Supralapsarians, it will be proper to hear what he has to say. And,

1. He proposes to shew, that this doctrine is destitute of support from the scripture, and tells us [f], he has *often wondered* what part of sacred writ can be produced to support it; and that he has been searching and trying to know the language of the divine word concerning election; and shall therefore mention, and, in a few words, comment upon those scriptures, which, says he, *I judge,*

[f] Supralapsarian Scheme, p. 4.

*are only neceſſary* to be confidered in this difpute; and thefe are, 1 *Peter* i. 2. *Eph.* i. 3, 4. *Rom.* viii. 29. If the man is really ignorant, as I am inclined to think he is, and does not know what parts of facred writ the Supralapfarians have produced to fupport their doctrine, he has acted a weak part in meddling with the controverfy; if he does know, he has acted a worfe in concealing of them. He promifes to mention and comment on thofe fcriptures which *he judges* are *only* neceſſary to be confidered in this difpute; but he ought to have mentioned the fcriptures, which the men he oppofes judge neceſſary to be confidered in this difpute; and to have fhewn the mifapplication of them, and that they are not pertinent to their purpofe: is this impartially to try and examine, by the word of God, the Supralapfarian fcheme, as his title promifes? every one knows, that knows any thing of this controverfy, that the fcriptural part of it is about the fenfe of the *ninth* chapter of the epiftle to the *Romans*; and the queftion is, whether the Sublapfarian, or the Supralapfarian fcheme, concerning the objects of election and reprobation, is moft agreeable to the fenfe of the apoftle in that chapter; particularly, whether the Supralapfarian fcheme, of God's chufing fome, and leaving others, confidered as unfallen, as having done neither good nor evil, does not beft agree with the account the apoftle gives in *ver.* 11—13. of the election of *Jacob*, and rejection of *Efau*; and more efpecially whether it does not beft agree with the fame apoftle's account, in *ver.* 21. of the potter's making *of the fame lump one veſſel unto honour, and another unto diſhonour?* This author fhould have mentioned thefe fcriptures, and commented upon them, and anfwered the arguments of the Supralapfarians from them; in particular, thofe of that eminent Supralapfarian, *Theodore Beza*, in his *notes* upon the laſt of thefe *texts*, which I fhall tranfcribe for this man's fake; and he may try whether he is capable of anfwering of them. " Thofe who, by the mafs,
" or lump, fays this great man, underftand mankind corrupted, do not fatisfy
" me in the explanation of this place: for firft, it feems to me, that the phrafe
" of informed matter, neither fufficiently agrees with mankind, either made
" or corrupted. Moreover, if the apoftle had confidered mankind as corrupted,
" he would not have faid, that fome veffels were made to honour, and fome to
" difhonour; but rather, that feeing all the veffels would be fit for difhonour,
" fome were left in that difhonour, and others tranflated from that difhonour to
" honour. Laftly, if *Paul* had not rofe to the higheft degree, he had not fatisfied
" the queftion objected; for it would always have been queried, whether that
" corruption came by chance, or whether indeed, according to the purpofe of
" God, and therefore the fame difficulty would recur. I fay, therefore, *Paul*
" ufing this moft elegant fimile, alludes to the creation of *Adam*, and rifes up
" to the eternal purpofe of God, who, before he created mankind, decreed of
" his

"his own mere will and pleasure, to manifest his glory, both in saving of some "whom he knew, in a way of mercy, and in destroying others, whom he also "knew, in righteous judgment. And verily, unless we judge this to be the "case, God will be greatly injured; because he will not be sufficiently wise, "who first creates men, and looks upon them corrupt, and then appoints to "what purpose he has created them: nor sufficiently powerful, if, when he "has taken up a purpose concerning them, he is hindered by another, so that "he obtains not what he willed; nor sufficiently constant, if, willingly and "freely he takes up a new purpose, after his workmanship is corrupted."

As for the scriptures mentioned by our author, as opposing the Supralapsarian scheme, I shall not trouble the reader, by observing the mangled work he makes with them, and the low and mean comments he makes upon them; I shall only say, that it will be readily owned, that sanctification, obedience, and conformity to the image of God and Christ, are things included in the decree of election: but do these things necessarily suppose, that the persons whom they concern, were, in that decree, considered as impure, unholy, disobedient, and in a want of conformity to the image of God and Christ? were not the elect angels chosen to sanctification, obedience, and conformity to the image of God? will any one say, that these things supposed them to be, or that in the decree of election, they were considered as impure, unholy, disobedient, and in a want of conformity to the image of God? But, admitting that these things, with respect to men, suppose them in such a case; it should be observed, that they belong to the decree of the means, and therefore fall short of proving that God, in the decree of the end, or in decreeing men to eternal life and happiness, for the glorifying of himself, considered them in such a state; since the decree of the end, in order of nature, is before the decree of the means; unless we can suppose the all-wise being to act in such a manner as no wise man would, namely, first fix upon the means, and then appoint the end. Now if God first decreed to create man, permit his fall, and then sanctify and conform him to the image of his Son, before he decreed to glorify himself in his salvation, the consequence will be, that God is first glorified in the salvation of man; and after that, man is created, suffered to fall, is sanctified, and conformed to the image of Christ; because, what is first in intention, is last in execution. There is one thing more I would observe, and that is, that this author ‡ delivers it as the settled opinion of the Supralapsarians, "that we were not elected as holy and obe-"dient beings, but to the end we might be such:" And I am much mistaken, if this is not the settled opinion of all Sublapsarians, except such as are in the Arminian scheme. But what is this mentioned for? why, to shew that the Supralapsarians

‡ Supralapsarian Scheme, p. 5.

pralapsarians are inconsistent with themselves, and guilty of so flagrant a contradiction, as is not to be reconciled by any. But where does it lie? "why, where-as they affirm, that we were not the almighty's choice, because we were holy; but that he did chuse us to be made holy, and yet, in that choice, beheld us free from all defilements and deformity." But this author must be told, if he does not know it, that the Supralapsarians, in considering men not yet created, and so not fallen, as the objects of election, suppose them neither good nor bad, righteous or wicked, holy or unholy, but in the pure, that is, in the mere mass of creatureship, not yet made, much less corrupted, and as having done neither good nor evil; now is this such a flagrant contradiction, never to be reconciled, that men considered neither as holy or unholy, as obedient or disobedient, should be chosen to holiness and obedience?

2. This author [h] proceeds to shew, that "the doctrine of the Supralapsarians is repugnant to their own opinion of God's eternal foreknowledge, according to which he was pleased to make his choice." To which I reply; that the Supralapsarians will readily own, that the omniscient Jehovah did, at one view, see, and perfectly behold, whatsoever would come to pass, throughout all ages of time; and that he has an universal prescience of all creatures and things, in their different states and circumstances; but then they will deny that election proceeds upon, or that God has been pleased to make his choice according to this his general and eternal prescience. It is true, that those who are elected, are elected according to the *foreknowledge of God the Father* [i]; *and whom he did foreknow, he also did predestinate to be conformed to the image of his Son.* But these passages are not to be understood of the universal prescience and foreknowledge of God; for then all men would be elected and predestinated, for *whom he did foreknow, he also did predestinate*; but all men are neither conformed to the image of Christ, nor predestinated to be so: it remains, that the foreknowledge, according to which election and predestination proceed, is God's special foreknowledge of his own people, and which is no other than his everlasting love to them, which is the source and spring of his choice of them; and the meaning is, that *whom he foreknew*, that is, in his eternal mind knew, owned, approved of, loved with an everlasting love; *he chose* them to salvation, *and predestinated* them to be conformed to the image of his Son.

3. This writer [k] goes on to observe, that "this doctrine of God's choosing his people without considering them as fallen creatures, tends to lessen the infinite grace and mercy of God in their election." I reply; that though it has been a matter of controversy between the Supralapsarians, and others, whether

[h] Supralapsarian Scheme, p. 7.
[k] Supralapsarian Scheme, p. 8.
[i] 1 Pet. i. 2. Rom. viii. 29.

ther election is an act of mercy, yet not whether it is an act of grace; they, with the scriptures [l], affirm, that election is *of grace,* springs from the sovereign grace and good pleasure of God, and is not influenced by, or to be ascribed to the works of men; but then they cannot observe, that it is ever said to be of mercy. Regeneration is ascribed to the mercy of God, 1 *Pet.* i. 3. so is forgiveness of sins, *Luke* i. 77. yea, our whole salvation, *Titus* iii. 5. but never election; not that, but *salvation is* said to be *of God, that sheweth mercy,* Rom. ix 15. Their reasons, among many others [m], too many to mention, why it cannot be an act of mercy, are, because the angels are elected, but not of mercy; the human nature of Christ is elected, but not of mercy. They argue, that supposing it should be admitted, that election is an act of mercy, it must either be *actus elicitus,* an actual will of being merciful, or *actus imperatus,* the act of shewing mercy itself: not the latter, because that supposes persons not merely foreknown as miserable, but in actual being, and in real misery, and is a transient act upon them; whereas election puts nothing in the persons chosen : if it is an act of mercy, it must be the former, God's actual will of being merciful; but this does not necessarily presuppose misery, or miserable objects, it being internal, and immanent in God, and the same with his mercy itself; and would have been the same, nor would God have been the less merciful, if the world had not been, and there had never been a miserable object on whom to display it. The act of election does not presuppose men sinners and miserable, nor indeed can it; for should it presuppose sin, it would presuppose the decree of the permission of sin; and the permission of sin would be first in God's intention, than man's salvation of God's mercy, and consequently would be last in execution; than which, nothing can be thought of more absurd. Besides, though election is not an act of mercy, yet it is far from having any tendency to lessen the mercy of God, and does, even according to the Supralapsarian scheme, abundantly provide for the glorifying of it; since, according to that, the decree of the end is, the glorifying of the grace and mercy of God, tempered with justice : The decree of the means provides for the bringing about of this end, which includes creation, the permission of sin, the mission of Christ, sanctification, and compleat salvation ; so that the elect of God may well be called *vessels of mercy*; since through such means, they are brought to eternal life and glory; though, in the decree of the end, they are considered as not yet created and fallen, than which, nothing can more tend to advance the free grace and mercy of God.

4. This author [n] urges, that "this way of stating election strikes severely "against the justice of God, in passing by the rest of mankind, not included
in

[l] Rom. xi. 5, 6.  [m] Vid. Twiss. Vindiciæ, l. 1. p. 1. D'gr. iv. c. 1 & Digr. ix. c. 1—4.
[n] Supralapsarian Scheme, p. 9.

"in this decree; for hereby they are rejected as creatures only, and not as sinful creatures." It is very strange, that election should severely strike against the justice of God, when, according to this way of stating it, it is a choice of persons to eternal life and happiness for the glorifying of the grace and mercy of God, mixed with his justice; and so as much provides in end and means, for the honour of divine justice, as for the glory of grace and mercy: and it is stranger still, that election should be a passing by the rest of mankind, not included in this decree: I suppose he means reprobation; for he has an extraordinary hand at putting one thing for another. Now let it be observed, that though the Supralapsarians do not consider reprobation as an act of justice, but of sovereignty, yet not of injustice; nor does their way of stating it at all strike at the justice of God. They suppose, that God, in the act of preterition, considered the objects of it, as not yet created and fallen; and determined, when created, to leave them to their own will, and deny them that grace which he is not obliged to give: and where is the injustice of all this? But then, though they do not premise sin to the consideration of the act of preterition, yet they always premise it to the decree of damnation; which this author, as is generally done, confounds together. They say, that as God damns no man, but for sin, so he decreed to damn no man, but for sin: and surely this cannot be thought to strike severely against the justice of God. It is true, they do not look upon sin to be the cause of the decree of reprobation, *quoad actum volentis*, which can only be the will of God; but *quoad res volitas*, the cause of the thing willed, damnation. Besides, this way of stating the decrees of election and reprobation, respecting men, can no more strike at the justice of God, than the way of stating these decrees, respecting angels, does; which cannot be done in another way: for the elect angels could never be considered as fallen; and therefore the other angels, who were passed by, and rejected at the same time, must be rejected as creatures only, and not as sinful creatures; unless it can be thought that the angels were not chosen and passed by at the same time, nor then considered in a like state; and that God chose some of them upon their foreseen holiness and obedience, and rejected the rest upon their foreseen rebellion and disobedience; and if so, why may not the election and rejection of men, be thought to proceed upon the same foot? which none, that I know of, will come into, but such that are in the Arminian scheme. This theme, our author says, he has been always cautious of meddling with, lest he should *darken counsel for want of knowledge*; and it is pity he meddled with it now, since he discovers so much ignorance of it: who can forbear thinking of the common proverb? Thus having considered what he calls the foundation doctrine of the Supralapsarians, he proceeds,

II. To

II. To examine some of the doctrines º which grow from this root, as the natural offspring of it, and appear with the same complection; and begins,

1. With their doctrine of eternal justification. What this author says, I am persuaded, will never meet with general credit, "that eternal justification is the "natural offspring of the Supralapsarian doctrine, respecting the objects of elec-"tion, not considered as fallen creatures." He goes all along, I observe, upon a false notion, that whatever is thought, or said to be done in eternity, is a Supralapsarian doctrine: whereas, the Sublapsarians themselves allow election to be from eternity, before the foundation of the world, and so before the fall of *Adam*, though not without the consideration of it; and in this they differ from the Supralapsarians. I know a reverend Divine, now living in this city of *London*, who, if I mistake not, reckons himself among the Supralapsarians, and says, that they dig deepest into the gospel; and yet is a strenuous opposer of justification from eternity, and even before faith: on the other hand, there have been some who have thought, that the object of election is man fallen, and yet have been for justification before faith. For my own part, I must confess, I never considered justification from eternity, any other than a Sublapsarian doctrine, proceeding upon the suretyship-engagements of Christ, and his future satisfaction and righteousness; upon which foot the Old-Testament-saints were openly justified, and went to heaven long before the satisfaction was really made or the justifying righteousness brought in; and, indeed, if the objects of justification are *the ungodly*, as the scripture represents them to be, they must be considered as fallen creatures. However, if the doctrine of eternal justification is the natural offspring of the former, and appears with the same complection, and is to be maintained with equal force of argument, we have no reason to be ashamed of it; and I am sure we have no reason to be in any pain on the account of the opposition this doughty writer makes unto it: he says, we have exceeded all the bounds of revelation in our inquiries after it, and then barely mentions three or four places of scriptures, which speak of justification *by* faith; and concludes, that therefore there is no justification *before* it; an extraordinary way of arguing indeed! When justification by faith no ways contradicts justification before it; nay, justification perceived, known, enjoyed by faith, supposes justification before it; for how should any have that sense, perception, and comfort of their justification by it, if there was no justification before it? He proceeds ᵖ to observe the order or chain of salvation, in *Romans* viii. 30. where calling is represented as prior to justification; an objection I have formerly answered in my *Doctrine of Justification* ᵠ, to which I refer the reader, and take the opportunity of

observing

---

º Supra'apsarian Scheme, p. 10.　　ᵖ Ibid. p. 11.　　ᵠ Page 70.

obſerving, that neither this author, nor any other, have attempted to anſwer the arguments there made uſe of in favour of juſtification before faith: I will not ſay they are *unanſwerable*; but I may ſay, that as yet they are *unanſwered*: this author, if he pleaſes, may try what he can do with them, and it might have been expected in this his performance; but inſtead of this, he ſets himſelf, with all his might, againſt ſome other doctrines, which he repreſents as Supralapſarian, as calculated to favour the ſcheme of eternal juſtification, and as branches of it; as,

1. "That God was eternally reconciled to the elect; and that no ſcripture "can be produced to prove that the Lord Jeſus did come to procure reconcili- "ation for them; and that wherever Chriſt is ſaid to make peace by his blood, "it is to be underſtood only of his reconciling the ſinner to God*." Whether he refers to any thing that has been publiſhed, or dropped in private converſation, or who the perſons are, that affirm this, I know not: I greatly fear he has both miſrepreſented their words and meaning. I muſt own, I never heard of any ſuch thing as an eternal reconciliation of God to the elect. Reconciliation ſuppoſes former friendſhip, a breach of it, and a conciliation of it again; which is inconſiſtent with the everlaſting, invariable and unchangeable love of God to them. *God was* indeed from everlaſting *reconciling*, not himſelf to the world, but *the world* of his elect *to himſelf*; that is, drawing the ſcheme and model of their reconciliation by Chriſt, or ſettling the way and manner in which reconciliation, atonement, and ſatisfaction for their ſins, ſhould be made; and accordingly made a *covenant of peace* with his Son, appointed him to be their *peace*, and in the fulneſs of time ſent him to make *peace by the blood of his croſs*, and laid upon him *the chaſtiſement* of their *peace*; and who has actually *made reconciliation for* their ſins; and ſo they, even when enemies, were actually *reconciled*; that is, their ſins were actually expiated and atoned for *to God, by the death of his Son*. This is the doctrine of reconciliation the ſcriptures ſpeak of, and which I never knew before was ever reckoned a Supralapſarian doctrine: for ſurely reconciliation, atonement, or ſatisfaction for ſin, which are ſynonymous terms, expreſſive of the ſame thing, muſt ſuppoſe perſons ſinners herein concerned. Let it be farther obſerved, that God from all eternity loved his elect with an invariable love; that he never entertained any hatred of them, or was at enmity with them; that there is no ſuch thing as a change in God from hatred to love, any more than from love to hatred; that our Lord Jeſus Chriſt did not by his atoning ſacrifice procure his Father's love to the elect, ſeeing his being a propitiation for ſin was a fruit, effect, and evidence of that love. Agreeably, the ſcriptures never ſpeak of God's being reconciled to his elect either in eternity or in time, but of their being reconciled to him; and not ſo much of the reconciliation of

their

---

*r* Supralapſarian Scheme, p. 12.    *s* 2 Cor. v. 19.

their persons, as of a reconciliation for their sins; whereby their persons are reconciled, not to the *love* and affections of God, which they always shared in, but to the *justice* of God, which insisted upon a satisfaction to a broken law; which being given, both love and justice are reconciled together, *righteousness and peace kiss each other*, in the affair of their salvation. Now there is nothing in this doctrine of reconciliation that is opposite,.

(1.) To the sin-offerings and peace-offerings under the law; since these were made to the God of *Israel* for the people of *Israel*, whom God loved above all people that were upon the face of the earth, and were typical of that atoning sacrifice, in which indeed were discovered the severest resentment of justice against sin, and yet the clearest evidence of strong love and affections to persons then enemies, and destitute of love to God: *Herein is love, not that we loved God, but that he loved us, and sent his Son to be the propitiation for our sins*[t]. In this both type and antitype agree, that the reconciliation is not of God to men, but for men to God; though this author says, "it is past all dispute, that the party to be reconciled is God";" when it is the very thing in dispute between us. It is no where said of the sacrifices of the law, that God was reconciled by them to the people of *Israel*; and it is no where said of the sacrifice of Christ, the antitype of them, that God is by it reconciled to his elect; though I am content that God should be said to be reconciled to his elect by the death of Christ, provided no more is meant by it than satisfying of his justice, not a conciliating or procuring his love and favour. The author's reasoning on the denial of this, that the reconciliation must be made to the house of *Israel*, or for the God of *Israel*, or with the sinner or the sin, is so stupid and senseless, that it deserves no consideration.

(2.) Nor does this doctrine, which denies that Christ came to reconcile God to sinners, oppose, as is suggested ", what is prophesied of him in the Old Testament, or what is affirmed of his performance in the New; since though it was prophesied of him, that God should *make his soul an offering for sin*[x]; and it is affirmed of him, that *he gave himself for us, an offering and a sacrifice to God*[y]; yet it is neither said that he should, or that he did do this for the elect, to remove any enmity in the heart of God against them, or to turn any hatred of his into love towards them, or to purchase and procure the love and affections of God for them: so far from this, that because they had a peculiar share in the love and affections both of the Father and the Son, the Father made the soul of his Son an offering for them, and the Son gave himself an offering unto God on their account. The Old Testament says, that *the Lord is well-pleased for his righteousness sake; he will magnify the law, and make it honourable*[z]; and

the

---

[t] 1 John iv. 10.    " Supralapsarian Scheme, p. 15.    " Ibid. p. 15.
[x] Isai. liii. 10.    [y] Ephes. v. 2.    [z] Isai. xlii. 21.

the New Testament says, that Christ has so *loved* his, that he *has given himself for* them, *an offering and a sacrifice to God, for a sweet-smelling savour* [a]; but neither the one nor the other say, that either God was to be, or that he is hereby reconciled to his elect, or they hereby ingratiated into his affections. What is written in *Colos.* i. 20. 1 *Cor.* xv. 3. *Heb.* ii. 17. *Colos.* ii. 14. *Ephes.* i. 7. perfectly agree with the doctrine of reconciliation I am now contending for; nor does this oppose that plain scripture, *Rom.* v. 1. *Therefore being justified by faith, we have peace with God, through our Lord Jesus.* We have no need to remove the stop in the text; though how this author dare venture to alter the reading of it, and render the words *peace in God*, or what is his reason for it, I know not. The peace the text speaks of, does not design the peace, reconciliation, and atonement made by the blood of Christ, but the effect of it; even an inward conscience peace, which believers have with God, or God-ward, through Christ the donor of it, springing and arising from faith's apprehending an interest in the justifying righteousness of the Son of God.

(3.) Nor does this doctrine lessen, or tend to frustrate the great and important ends of our Saviour's sufferings and death, as this author attempts to prove [b]. The ends of his sufferings and death were to *bring* the elect *to God*, to *make reconciliation* for their *sins*, to *reconcile* them to God; and accordingly they *were, even when enemies, reconciled to God by the death of his Son* [c]. Where does the scripture ever represent the end of Christ's sufferings and death to be to reconcile God to his elect; that is, to remove any enmity in his heart against them, or to procure for them his love and favour? but on the contrary, it represents the sufferings and death of Christ as fruits and evidences of his matchless and surprising love to them. *God commendeth his love towards us, in that while we were yet sinners, Christ died for us* [d]. The doctrines of reconciliation and justification, thus viewed in the light of scripture, can never clash with the satisfaction of Christ, nor tend to lessen and frustrate it; since reconciliation is no other than satisfaction and atonement to the justice of God, and justification proceeds upon the foot of satisfaction, and everlasting righteousness. Nor is there room or reason for that stupid inference and conclusion, that because Christ came to reconcile sinners to God, therefore he became an offering to the sinner, and not to God. There is a twofold reconciliation the scriptures speak of; the one is obtained by the price of Christ's blood, the other by the power of his grace; you have them both in one text, *Rom.* v. 10. *For if when we were enemies, we were reconciled to God by the death of his Son, much more being reconciled, we shall be saved by his life.* The meaning of which is; that if, when the elect of God were in a state of nature, and so of enmity to God, atonement was made for their

---

[a] Ephes. v. 2.     [b] Supralapsarian Scheme, p. 19.
[c] 1 Pet. iii. 18. Dan. ix. 24. Heb. ii. 17. Rom. v. 10.     [d] Rom. v. 8.

their fins by the facrifice and death of Chrift, which is ftrongly expreffive of the amazing love of God to them; then much more being by the Spirit and grace of God reconciled to this way of peace, pardon, atonement, life and falvation, they fhall be faved, through the interceding life of their Redeemer.

(4.) This doctrine, as it has been ftated, does not render the offices of Chrift, as mediator, interceffor and high prieft, needlefs, yea, of none effect; unlefs this author can imagine, according to his own fcheme, that it is the *fole* work of the mediator, interceffor and high prieft, to reconcile God to the elect. This we indeed fay is *no* part of his work, in fuch fenfe, as to conciliate the love and favour of God to them; but does it follow, from hence, that his office is needlefs, and of none effect? Is it not needful, to reconcile the elect to God, to make reconciliation for their fins? Is he not ufeful, as mediator, to be their advocate and interceffor, their way of accefs to God, and acceptance with him, and of conveyance of all the bleffings of the covenant of grace to them, whence he is called the mediator of it? I would alfo afk this author, if he thinks when God is reconciled to the elect by the death of his Son, or rather when they believe; for it feems there is no reconciliation before faith in Chrift, the blood, facrifice and death of Chrift will not effect it, according to thefe men, till faith has given the finifhing ftroke: I fay, I afk this author, whether he thinks that the office of Chrift, as mediator, ceafes? for, according to his way of reafoning, it fhould ceafe, when reconciliation is really made. Whereas Chrift, after believing as well as before, is *the mediator between God and man*, and *ever lives to make interceffion for us* [e]. We are able to prove that Chrift was fet up as mediator from everlafting; that his mediation was always neceffary, and ever will be; that as he is the medium of all grace now to us, he will be the medium of all glory to all eternity. To conclude this head; our [f] author feems to be convinced that *John* iii. 16. expreffes the love of God to his elect, antecedent to his giving and fending of his Son to be the propitiatory facrifice; fince he does not attempt to offer any thing againft the expofition, or to give another fenfe of it.

2. "Another branch of their (the Supralapfarians) eternal juftification, is faid [g] to be their refufing to pray for the pardon of fin, any otherwife than the manifeftation of it to their confciences." Strange! that pardon of fin fhould be a *branch* of eternal juftification, when it is a diftinct bleffing from it; as, I think, I have fufficiently made to appear in my treatife [h] concerning it: ftranger ftill! that *refufing to pray* for it fhould be deemed a branch of it: and what is of all moft wonderful, is, that this fhould be reckoned a Supralapfarian point,

---

[e] 1 Tim. ii. 5. Heb. vii. 25.    [f] Supralapfarian Scheme. p. 24.
[g] Ibid. p. 25.    [h] Doctrine of Juftification, p. 2—5,

point, when pardon of sin supposes sin, and sin supposes the fall; and whether it is to be conceived of as in the divine mind, from eternity, or as passing into successive acts in time, as men sin, or as manifested to their consciences, the objects of it cannot be considered otherwise than as sinners, fallen creatures; and therefore is a Sublapsarian, and not a Supralapsarian doctrine. Is this man qualified to examine the Supralapsarian scheme? He proceeds to try this practice of refusing to pray for the pardon of sin, any otherwise than the manifestation of it to the conscience, by the example of the holy men of God, and by the advice and direction of our blessed Lord and Saviour. He might have spared the pains he has taken in collecting the instances of praying for the pardon of sin, since the question is not, whether the saints, in any sense, should pray for it; for we allow, that they have done it, that they are directed to it, and should do it; but the question is, in what sense they have done it, and should do it? Now we apprehend, that when believers pray for the pardon of sin, that their sense and meaning is not, nor should it be, as if the blood of Christ should be shed again for the remission of sin, or as if compleat pardon was not procured by it, or as though this was to be obtained by their praying, tears, humiliation, and repentance, or that any new act of pardon should arise in the mind of God, and be afresh passed; but when they pray in this manner, their meaning is, either that God would, in a providential way, deliver them out of present distress, or avert those troubles and sorrows they might justly fear; or, that they might have the sense and manifestation of pardon to their souls, fresh sprinklings of the blood of Jesus, and renewed applications of it to their consciences; and this, we believe, is both their duty and interest to do daily, since they are daily sinning against God, grieving his Spirit, and wounding their own consciences [i]. The instance of the apostle's advising *Simon Magus* to pray, is not to pray particularly for the pardon of sin, or that the evil thought of his heart might be forgiven him, as this author suggests [k]; but to repent and pray in general; and this is added by way of encouragement, *If perhaps the thought of thine heart may be forgiven thee.* However, I will not contend with him about it, since nothing in this controversy depends upon it. He goes [l] on to observe, that,

3. "The third branch of their eternal justification is, that God loved and de-
" lighted in the elect as much while in their sinful state, and in the height of their
" rebellion against his laws, as when they are converted, and made obedient to
" his ways." That God loves his elect, and delights in them, as considered in Christ, and so as justified in him before the foundation of the world, I firmly believe; and which is far from being a licentious way of talking, or from being any contradiction to the holiness of God: but that his love to them, and
delight

[i] See my Discourse on Prayer, p. 27, 28.   [k] Page 27.   [l] Page 28.

delight in them as such, should be *a branch of their eternal justification*, is what I confess I never was acquainted with before; and what is more news still, is, that this *spurious tenet*, as this author in his great wisdom and modesty calls it, is built upon eternal union with Christ, which he represents as a false and sandy foundation; whereas the persons he opposes, consider the everlasting love of God to his elect as the foundation, yea, the bond of their eternal union. Of this one would think he could not be ignorant; but really every page, and almost every line, discover such stupidity and ignorance, that it is not at all to be marvelled at. He goes on, in his former way, to consider this tenet of God's loving and delighting in his elect, while in their unconverted estate with the rest, as a Supralapsarian point; and which he calls a common maxim of the Supralapsarians. I intreat this author, that he would never more attempt to write about Supralapsarian principles, or to try and examine the Supralapsarian scheme, until some of his friends, patrons, or editors, have better informed him concerning them. What, is this a Supralapsarian tenet, that God loves and delights in his elect while in their sinful state, and in the height of their rebellion? Surely these persons must be considered as sinners, as fallen creatures; and therefore as this author has stated the point, it must be a Sublapsarian, and not a Supralapsarian one. Had he indeed represented it as our sense, that God loved and delighted in his elect, as in Christ from all eternity, above the fall, and without any consideration of it, he had done us more justice; and this would have bid fair to have been deemed a Supralapsarian point: but this would not have answered his *wicked* design; I can call it no other, which is, to suggest to weak minds "that God loves and delights in the sins and rebel- "lions of his elect, or loves and delights in them considered as sinners, and "rebellious persons;" things we abhor, as much as he: for what else can reflect dishonour on the Christian religion, or strike at the doctrine of God's holiness, or stand diametrically opposite to all practical godliness, or oppose those scriptures which speak of God as hating sin, and abhorring the workers of iniquity? Not the doctrine of God's loving and delighting in his elect, as considered in Christ, in whom they cannot be considered otherwise than as holy and righteous. We know that men in an unconverted state cannot please God, that is, do those things which are well-pleasing to him; and yet their persons may be acceptable in his sight, not as considered in themselves; for so they cannot be, even after conversion, notwithstanding all their humiliations, repentance, tears, prayers, and services; but as considered in Christ, in whom, and in whom alone, they are the objects of God's love and delight. But it seems we are to hear of this again; and therefore at present I shall take my leave of it, till we know what he has farther to object.

4. He-

4. He proceeds ᵐ to prove, "that these authors (the Supralapsarians) in "order to support their doctrine of eternal justification, have very unjustly "affirmed that our blessed Saviour was by imputation a sinner; yea, that he "became *very* sin." I shall content myself in making some general observations upon his long harangue on this head, which will serve to discover his weakness and ignorance.

(1.) I observe, that as his title-page promises an examination of some doctrines in the Supralapsarian scheme, and his assurance leads him on; so, according to his usual way, he affirms that the doctrine of Christ's being made sin, or a sinner by imputation, or of the imputation of sin to Christ, is a doctrine in the Supralapsarian scheme, or a Supralapsarian notion: whereas imputation of sin supposes sin, and that supposes the fall; wherefore the persons whose sins were imputed to Christ, and in whose room and stead he bore them, must be considered as sinners and fallen creatures. And hence it appears to be a Sublapsarian, and not a Supralapsarian doctrine.

(2.) I take notice of the unfair and disingenuous dealing of this writer. He first proposes to prove, that it is unjustly affirmed that Christ was *by imputation* a sinner, and immediately alters the state of the question, and represents it as the notion of the Supralapsarians, that Christ was *really* the sinner, and made *truly* and *properly* sin, and made sin, or a sinner, in a *proper* sense ⁿ; whereas though, with Dr *Crisp*, we affirm, that there was a *real* transaction, a *real* imputation of sin to Christ, and that he *really* bore the sins of his people in the Protestant sense, as opposed to that of the Papists, who sneeringly call every thing imputed, putative, fantastic and imaginary, with whom our author seems to join: but then we say that Christ is only the sinner by imputation, or was only made sin this way; not that sin was inherently in him, or that it was committed by him; in which sense only he can be truly, properly, and really the sinner. And this is what Dr *Crisp* himself says, and that in the very passage this man takes upon him to confute: "Christ, says he, stands a sinner in God's "eyes; though not as the actor of transgressions, yet as he was the surety." This observation alone is sufficient to set aside all the trifling and impertinent reasonings of this writer on this head. We are not afraid, nor ashamed to say, that Christ was made original and actual sin in this sense; that is to say, that original sin, and the actual sins of God's people, were imputed to Christ, and he bore them and made satisfaction to justice for them: Nor can we observe any absurdity in descending to particulars, and saying that the swearing, the lying, blasphemy, *&c.* of God's elect, were laid upon him, imputed to him, and he took them upon him, and bore them away. Nor does this reflect upon the holiness of God, as

this

---

ᵐ Supralapsarian Scheme, p. 31, 32.    ⁿ Ibid. p. 33, 37, 48.

this man suggests[o], in making his Son by imputation the worst thing that ever was in the world; since there never was any one thing in the world which so much discovers the holiness of God, and strictness of his justice, than his giving his Son to be the propitiation for our sins; which could not be done without the imputation of them to him: Nor does this act of imputation make God the author of sin, any more than the imputation of the righteousness of Christ makes the Father the author of that righteousness; nor does this reflect dishonour, either on the divine or human nature of Christ, since neither of them can be defiled with sin; but, on the other hand, serves much to express the wonderous love, grace, and condescension of Christ, that *he who knew no sin, should be made sin for us.*

(3.) I observe the rudeness of the man, in representing the doctrine of the imputation of sin to Christ, or his being made sin by imputation, "as vile and "ridiculous, and equally as pernicious as Transubstantiation[p]; a scheme not "to be freed from inexplicable perplexities, and vile nonsense[q]; calling it "ridiculous doctrine, spurious stuff, yea, blasphemy[r];" when it is the doctrine of our reformers, of all sound Protestant divines, never denied by any but Socinians and Arminians, or such as are inclined to them: Wherefore had he thought fit to have rejected it, yet for the sake of so many valuable men who have espoused it, he ought to have treated it with decency. Nor can I pass by his rude treatment of Dr *Crisp* and Mr *Hussey*; the one he represents as guilty of blasphemy, or something like it, and an addle-headed man, that *knew not what he wrote*[s]; and the other, as a *ridiculous writer*[t]; when they were both, in their day and generation, men of great piety and learning, of long standing and much usefulness in the church of Christ; whose name and memory will be dear and precious to the saints, when this writer, and his pamphlet, will be remembered no more.

(4.) I observe, this author treats the doctrine of Christ's being a sinner by imputation, as a novel doctrine[u], and embraced by men of a vehement thirst after novelty. I have already hinted, that this was the doctrine of the first reformers, and all sound Protestant divines, that our sins were imputed to Christ, and Christ's righteousness imputed to us. This was the faith of the ancient church, in the first ages of christianity, as appears from a passage of *Justin Martyr*[w], one of the most early christian writers extant: "What else, "says he, speaking of Christ, could cover our sins, but his righteousness? In "whom could we, transgressors and ungodly, be justified, than in the only

Vol. II.  M  Son

---

[o] Supralapsarian Scheme. p. 39, 40.  [p] Ibid. p. 37, 39, 55.  [q] Page 46.
[r] Page 47—49.  [s] Supralapsarian Scheme, p. 38, 47, 50.  [t] Ibid. p. 52.
[u] Ibid. p. 37, 49.  [w] Epist. ad Diognet. p. 500.

"Son of God? Ω της γλυκειας ανταλλαγης, "O sweet change!" O unsearchable
"performance! O unexpected benefits! Ινα ανομια μεν πολλων εν δικαιω ενι κρυβη;
"that the transgression of many should be hid in one righteous person; and
"the righteousness of one justify many transgressors." Yea, some of the ancient writers have expressed themselves in terms full as exceptionable as what
Dr *Crisp* has made use of: so *Chrysostom* [x]; "Τον γαρ δικαιον εποιησεν αμαρτωλον;
"for he hath made that righteous one a sinner, that he might make sinners
"righteous:" indeed he does not only say so, Αλλ' ο πολλω μειζον ην, "but what
"was much more;" for he does not express the habit, but the quality; he
"does not say, he made him a sinner, but sin itself; that we might be made,
"he does not say righteous, but righteousness, even the righteousness of God."
So *Oecumenius* [y]; "Christ, says he, Ην σφοδρα αμαρτωλος, "was the great sinner,"
"seeing he took upon him the sins of the whole world, and made them *his own*."
So *Austin* [z]; "He, that is, Christ, is sin, as we are righteousness; not our
"own, but God's; not in ourselves, but in him; *sicut ipse peccatum, non suum*
"*sed nostrum*, even as he himself is sin; not his own, but ours; not in himself,
"but in us." Some of them have been very express, as to Christ's bearing
the filth of sin; particularly *Gregory* of *Nyssa*; "For, says he [a], speaking of
"Christ, Μεταθεις γαρ προς εαυτον τον των εμων αμαρτων ρυπον, having translated to
"himself the filth of my sins, he imparted to me his own purity, and made me
"a partaker of his beauty." And in another place [b], says he, "the pure and
"harmless one, Τον της ανθρωπινης φυσεως καταδεχεται ρυπον, took upon him, or
"received the filth of human nature; and passing through all our poverty,
"came to the trial of death itself." And elsewhere he says [c], "purity was,
"εν τω ημετερω ρυπω, in our filth; but the filth did not touch that purity;"
meaning, that the holy nature of Christ was not defiled by it. I shall not now
take notice of some later writers; perhaps I may hereafter: I hope this will be
sufficient to clear the doctrine from the charge of novelty.

(5.) I cannot overlook the wretched vanity and ignorance of the man about
tropes and figures. Though I cannot but think his learned friend, or friends,
who had the supervisal of his performance, have been far from acting the kind,
faithful, and friendly part, in suffering him to expose himself as he has done;
he tells us [d], that " it is very evident, that all the scriptures that they (Dr *Crisp*,
" and others) depend upon as plain proofs that Christ was made very sin for us,
" are *metonomies*, which is a figure frequently to be met with in the Bible;"
and

---

[x] In 2 Cor. Homil. 11.　　[y] In Heb. ix. p. 845.　　[z] Enchirid. c. 41.
[a] In Cant. Homil. 2. p. 491.　　[b] De Beatitud. Orat. 1. p. 767.
[c] In Diem. Nat. Christ. p. 787. Vol. II.　　[d] Supralapsarian Scheme, p. 35, 36.

and then by an asterisk, we are directed to the margin, where, for the sake of the poor, illiterate Supralapsarians, a definition is given of a metonymy, which is this; "a metonomy is a changing, or putting one thing, or more, for an-"other:" "and, says he, in the body of his work, sometimes you have the "cause for the effect, and sometimes the effect put for the cause;" and among the instances, he produces this is one, that *unbelief is put for faith*. Now, not to take notice that a metonymy is a trope, and not a figure, nor of his miscalling it *metonomy*, instead of *metonymy*, which might have been thought to have been an error of the press, but that it is so often repeated; I say, not to take notice of these things; he says, "a metonomy is a changing, or putting one "thing, or more, for another;" but surely it is not a changing, or putting *any* one thing for another; it looks as if he thought so, seeing, among his examples, he makes *unbelief to be put for faith*. There is a metonymy of the cause and effect, subject and adjunct, but never of contraries; as grace and sin, vice and virtue, faith and unbelief are: this looks more like the figure *antiphrasis*, than the trope *metonymy*. Our author, by his new figure in *rhetoric*, will be able, in a very beautiful manner, to bring off the vilest of creatures, *that call evil good, and good evil; that put darkness for light, and light for darkness; that put bitter for sweet, and sweet for bitter*[a]. Let me ask this author, since he has put this instance among his examples of a metonymy of the cause for the effect, and of the effect for the cause; let me, I say, ask him, whether he thinks unbelief is the cause of faith, or faith the cause of unbelief; and seeing he has got such a good hand at metonymies, we will try what use he can make of them in explaining the scriptures in this controversy.

(6.) The scriptures made use of to prove the imputation of sin to Christ, or that Christ was made sin by imputation, are, 2 *Cor.* v. 21. *Isai.* liii. 6. Now our [f] author "hopes to make it plain, that these scriptures are as truly figura- "tive texts as those are that represent Christ to be a lion, a star, a door, a rock, "a vine," &c. and observes, that "all the scriptures depended on as plain "proofs, that Christ was made very sin for us, are *metonomies*." But he should have observed, that the scriptures which speak of Christ as a lion, a star, a door, a rock, a vine, &c. are metaphors, and not metonymies; and could he produce any, where Christ is said to be *made* a lion, a star, a door, a rock, a vine, &c. there would appear a greater likeness between them, and such a text which says, he was *made sin for us:* he fancies [g] the doctrine of transubstantiation is as well supported by scripture as this doctrine; that the constructions we put upon the texts in dispute about it, are as gross as those the Papists put on such as they produce in favour of theirs; which is not very surprising, since he seems to have

[a] Isai, v. 20.     [f] Supra'apsarian Scheme, p. 35.     [g] Ibid. p. 37.

an opinion of popish doctrines, and to be verging that way; for in one [l] part of this performance of his, he frankly acknowledges, that he has no *high* opinion of popish doctrines, which *supposes* that he has *an* opinion of them, and begins, at least, to think a little favourably of them, though not very highly. But let us attend to the texts in dispute; the first is, 2 *Cor.* v. 21. *For he hath made him* to be *sin for us, who knew no sin, that we might be made the righteousness of God in him*; which, he says, has been notoriously wrested, and observes [k], that " this text, in both parts of it, is *metonomically* spoken, and is the cause put " for the effect; and the native language of it is, that God made his dear Son " a sin-offering for us, that we might partake of the promised blessings, or the " righteousness of God in him." Admitting the words are to be taken in a metonymical sense, yea, that the meaning is, that Christ was made an offering for sin; they are not a metonymy of the cause for the effect; for sin is not the cause, though the occasion of a sin-offering; there might have been sin and no offering for it: offering for sin is not an effect necessarily arising from it, but what purely depended on the will and pleasure of God; but taking the words in the sense of a sin-offering, it is, as *Piscator* [l] observes, *Per metonymiam subjecti occupantis in veteri Testamento usitatam*. Besides, this sense of the words is so far from destroying the doctrine of the imputation of sin to Christ, that it serves to confirm it: for as the typical sin-offerings under the law, had first the sins of the people put upon them by the priest, and typically imputed to them, and were bore by them, *Lev.* x. 17. before they could be offered for them; so our Lord Jesus was first made sin, or had the sins of his people imputed to him, or he could never have been made an offering for them. I deny, that *salva justitia Dei*, consistent with the justice of God, Christ, an innocent person, could ever bear even the punishment of our sins, or be made a sacrifice for them, or die for them, as he did, according to the scriptures, if they had not been imputed to him; punishment could never have been inflicted on him, if sin had not been reckoned to him. Though I see no reason why *sin*, in one and the same sentence here, should have two different meanings, as it must have, according to this sense of them, *he hath made him to be sin for us, who knew no sin:* the word *sin*, last mentioned, cannot be meant of an offering for sin; for it is not true, that Christ knew no sin-offering, when multitudes had been offered up under the law; but the meaning is, that he never was guilty of sin; and yet he who never was guilty of sin, was made so by imputation, that is, had the guilt of our sins imputed to him; which well agrees with, and may be confirmed by the latter part of the text, *that we might be made the righteousness of God in him.* Now in the same way that we are made the righteousness of God,

was

[l] Supralapsarian Scheme, p. 125.   [k] Ibid. p. 37, 38.   [l] In loc.

was Chrift made fin: we are made the righteoufnefs of God by imputation, that is, the righteoufnefs of Chrift, who is both God and man, is imputed to us; fo Chrift was made fin by imputation, that is, our fins were imputed to him. What this author fays ᵐ concerning our being made the effects of God's righteoufnefs or faithfulnefs, I own, I cannot, for my life, form any idea of; and though he has attempted to explain it, he has left it inexplicable; I choofe not to ufe his own phrafe, *inexplicable nonfenfe*. Before I difmifs this text, I would take notice of one very extraordinary obfervation of this author's ⁿ; which is, that this way of reafoning to prove Chrift a finner, will prove that all men, that have the righteoufnefs of Chrift imputed to them, are their own faviours; his argument is this: " If by the imputation of our condemning fins to Chrift " he was made a finner, then, by the imputation of his faving righteoufnefs, " we are made faviours." But, with his leave, this does not follow; but the truth and force of the reafoning ftands thus: If by the imputation of our condemning fins to Chrift, he was made a finner, and condemned as fuch, then, by the imputation of his righteoufnefs, we are made righteous, and faved as fuch; for not finner and faviour, but finner and righteous, falvation and condemnation, are the antithefes. Give me leave to fubjoin the fenfe of two or three of our principal reformers, and found Proteftant divines, of this paffage of fcripture, who wrote long before Dr *Crifp*'s time. *Calvin* upon the text fays; How are we righteous before God? namely, as Chrift was a *finner*; for, in fome refpects, he fuftained our perfon, that he might become *guilty* in our " name; and, as a finner, be condemned, not for his own, but the offences " of others; feeing he was pure, and free from all fault, and underwent punifhment due, not to himfelf, but to us:" which agrees with what he fays on *Gal.* iii. 13. " Becaufe he fuftained our perfon, therefore he was a *finner*, and " deferving of the curfe; not as in himfelf, but as in us." *Beza* on the place, has thefe words; that " the *antithefis* requires, that rather Chrift fhould be " faid to be made fin for us, that is, *a finner*, not in himfelf, but on the ac- " count of the *guilt* of all our fins, *imputed* to him; of which the two goats " were a figure, mentioned *Lev.* xvi." *Pifcator*, as well as *Beza*, having mentioned the other fenfe of Chrift's being made a fin-offering, adds, " rather fin here, by a metonymy of the adjunct, fignifies *fummum peccatorem*," " the chief finner; " inafmuch as all the fins of all the elect were imputed to Chrift; which expofition the following antithefis favours, that *we might be made the righteoufnefs of God in him*; that is, " righteous before God; namely, by a " righteoufnefs obtained by the facrifice of Chrift, imputed to us by God." So that though the words may be taken in a metonymical fenfe; yet they are

not

ᵐ Supralapfarian Scheme, p. 41, 43.    ⁿ Ibid. p. 49.

not a metonymy of the cause for the effect, but a metonymy of the adjunct: so *scelus* is put for *scelestus*, by Latin authors, as here sin for the sinner.

I now proceed to what our author has to say to *Isai*. liii. 6. *The Lord hath laid on him the iniquity of us all*. This text, he says °, Dr *Crisp* makes the foundation of his several sermons, to prove that our blessed Lord was made a sinner; and says, that he very injudiciously affirms, that it is the very fault, or transgression itself, that the Lord laid upon Christ; but he purposes to make it plain, that he is mistaken in his opinion about this text, and that it was not the crime or fault, but the punishment due to us for our sins, that was laid upon Christ, which, he thinks, is evident from *ver*. 5, 7. To which I reply; that the punishment due to us for sin, could not have been laid upon Christ, nor could he have been wounded for our transgressions, or bruised for our sins, or have been oppressed and afflicted, had he not had our sins laid upon him, that is, imputed to him: nor is it inconsistent with the holiness of God, to take either original sin, or our actual sins and transgressions, even particular sins, and lay them upon Christ; since this was done in order to shew his infinite holiness, his indignation against sin, and the strictness and severity of his justice in the punishment of it; nor is this inconsistent with the nature of sin, nor any rude and extravagant way of thinking of it, which surely may as truly and properly be put, or laid upon Christ, as the iniquities and transgressions of the children of *Israel* in all their sins, which mean their very crimes, were typically put and laid upon the scape-goat. This writer ᴾ goes on to observe, that the prophecy in *Isaiah* liii. 4. *Surely he hath borne our griefs, and carried our sorrows*, was fulfilled by our Lord's healing the diseases of the people, *Matt*. viii. 16, 17. and argues, that if the text in *Isai*. liii. 4. is to be construed in the same method as the sixth and eleventh verses are, the consequence will be, that our Lord bore the palsy of the Centurion's servant, and the fever of *Peter*'s wife's mother: this, he thinks, will greatly hamper our scheme, so that we shall not be able to produce any thing consistent with it, free from inexplicable perplexities and vile nonsense. But what reason can be given, why the expressions in the several places, should be interpreted in the same way? What though our Lord, in his state of incarnation, being a *man of sorrows and acquainted with griefs*, is said to *bear the griefs, and carry the sorrows* of men, because he had compassion on them, and sympathized with them in their sickness, which put him upon healing of them; and in such sense, bore them as a parent bears the sicknesses of a child, or a husband bears the infirmities of a wife; *for we have not an high priest which cannot be touched with the feeling of our infirmities*: does it therefore follow, that this must be the sense of Christ's bearing our sins, when he suffered for them as our
surety?

° *Supralapsarian Scheme*, p 44.      ᴾ Ibid. p. 46.

surety? Can it be thought that he sympathized with our sins, or with us on the account of them, which put him upon suffering for them, as he is said to bear or sympathize with mens sicknesses and diseases, or with them upon the account of them, which put him upon healing of them?

(7.) The imputation of the filth of sin to Christ, and his bearing of it, would come next to be considered; but our author has not thought fit to make use of any arguments against it, and therefore I do not think myself obliged to enlarge upon it; only would observe, that filth and guilt are inseparable from sin; and therefore, if sin is laid upon Christ, and imputed to him, guilt and filth must be likewise: nor can I see how we can expect to be cleared of the one and cleansed from the other, unless Christ bore them both, when his soul was made an offering for sin, and his blood was shed to cleanse from it. This writer would, indeed, be nibbling at it, but knows not how to go about it; and only cavils at some expressions of Mr *Hussey*'s concerning it. Whether, in *Psalm* c. 7. there is any allusion to the brook *Cedron*, or *Kidron*, over which our Lord went into the garden, I will not say; but I see not why that black and unclean brook, or common-sewer, may not be an emblem of the pollutions and defilements of sin; which being laid on Christ when he passed over that brook, made him so heavy and sore amazed in his human nature, as to desire the cup might pass from him. As to what Mr *Hussey* says of our iniquities being put into this bitter cup, and of his drinking of it, and of the torrent of our sins and blacknesses running into his soul with that wrath; this is not to be understood of sin being inherent in him, or of his being defiled with it, the contrary to which he solidly proves; but only of the imputation of them to him, and of his susception of them; for he says [q], "It was not pain or torture abstractly in the bitter draught, but pollu-
" tion, the dregs of our sins, sin being the only impure thing in God's account,
" and so the spot of sin, the filth and pollutions of sin, were *imputed* to him by
" his Father, and put upon Christ's account, and mingled with his wormwood
" cup, that it made his holy soul to tremble." Nor is the simile he makes use of a foolish one, of a drop of ink, or poison, falling upon a fiery globe of brass, without leaving any sullying mark upon it, or receiving any stain or pollution by it; nor does it tend to extenuate the flood of the filthiness of sin, that has been running ever since *Adam*; nor is it unsuitable to the imputation and susception of it; which is all he means by his drinking of it; but is designed to set forth the infiniteness of Christ, and of his power to resist the infection and stain of sin; as may be seen at large in this valuable writer; who himself frankly owns [r], "that the similitude is imperfect, to set out the matter in the
" deep mysteries of this *gold tried in the fire*, or the person of Christ in his suf-
ferings;

[q] The glory of Christ unveiled, p. 491.     [r] Ibid. p. 498.

"ferings; the greateſt of which was, the Father's imputation of our ſins to
"him." What our author further obſerves concerning ſome texts of ſcripture,
engaged by the Supralapſarians, to ſpeak for their opinions of eternal juſtifi‑
cation and adoption, being what is introduced by him, with reference to a
living author, I leave it to him to anſwer for himſelf; who, I doubt not, will
make a proper and ſuitable reply. I proceed,

*Secondly*, To defend the doctrine of *eternal union*, which this author calls ᵗ "a
"branch which grows from the fruitful root of the Supralapſarian tree; which,
"ſays he, they ſtile eternal, actual, union." As this author particularly refers
to myſelf, throughout his performance on the head of union, I take leave to
aſk him, Where has he found eternal union in any writings of mine, ſtiled eter‑
nal, *actual* union? I have carefully avoided calling juſtification, or union from
eternity, actual; though for no other reaſon than this, leſt any ſhould imagine,
that I conſidered them as tranſient acts of God upon the elect, which require
their perſonal and actual exiſtence; for otherwiſe, as I believe, that eternal
election is actual, and eternal reprobation is actual, as they are immanent acts
in God; ſo, I believe, eternal juſtification is actual, as it is an immanent act
in God that juſtifies; and eternal union is actual, as it is an act of God's ever‑
laſting love to his elect, whereby he has knit and united them to himſelf. I go
on to aſk, where have I ſaid, or who has told this man, that a non-entity was
united to an exiſtence? The language with which this expreſſion is cloathed,
manifeſtly ſhews it to be of his own ſhaping. The elect of God, though they
have not an *eſſe actu*, an actual being from eternity; yet they have an *eſſe repre‑
ſentativum*, a repreſentative being in Chriſt from everlaſting, which is more than
other creatures have, whoſe future exiſtence is certain; and therefore at leaſt
capable of a repreſentative union from eternity, and which has been readily
owned by ſome divines, who are not altogether in the ſame way of thinking
with myſelf. However, it ſeems eternal union is a branch which grows from
the fruitful root (not from the body) of the Supralapſarian tree. Poor crea‑
ture! it is plain he knows nothing of the Supralapſarian tree, as he calls it, ei‑
ther root, body, or branch; for as he is pleaſed to explain the meaning of
eternal, actual, union, it is this, "that they (I ſuppoſe he means the elect) had
"actual union with Chriſt, whilſt they were in their ſins;" and if ſo, they muſt
be conſidered in their union with Chriſt, as fallen creatures; and then it will
follow, that this is a branch which grows from the Sublapſarian, and not the
Supralapſarian tree. But paſſing theſe things, I ſhall now attend to what he
has to object to what I have written ᵘ on the ſubject of union. And,

(1.) Whereas

---

ᵗ Supralapſarian Scheme, p. 74.   ᵘ In a Letter to Mr Abraham Taylor, p. 29. &c.

# TRUTH DEFENDED.

(1.) Whereas I have undertaken to prove that it is not the Spirit on Chrift's part, that is the bond of union to him, I endeavoured to do it by obferving that the Spirit is fent down, and given to God's elect, in confequence of an antecedent union of them to Chrift; and that he, in his perfonal inhabitation, operations and influences of grace in them, is the evidence, and not the efficient caufe of their union. That an elect perfon is firft united to Chrift, and then receives the fpirit in meafure from him, and becomes one fpirit with him, I thought was pretty evident from 1 *Cor.* vi. 17. *He that is joined unto the Lord, is one fpirit.* From whence I concluded, and ftill conclude, that a perfon's becoming one fpirit with Chrift, or receiving the fame fpirit Chrift has, though in meafure, is in confequence of his being joined or united to him; and not that he firft becomes one fpirit, or receives the fame fpirit from Chrift, and then is joined or united to him. The fenfe of the text is evident, and admits of no difficulty: But, fays " this writer, " it evidently proves that the Spirit of Chrift dwells in all that are united to him." I grant it, that the Spirit of Chrift dwells in all that are united to him, fooner or later; but the queftion is, whether the indwelling of the Spirit is antecedent to their union, or in confequence of it? If it is in confequence of it, then that is not the bond of union: If it is antecedent to it, it muft be before faith; for, according to this man's fcheme, union is by faith, and there is none before it: and fo the abfurdity he would fain leave with me, follows himfelf; "that the holy Spirit dwells with unbelievers." To illuftrate this matter, of a perfon's receiving the Spirit from Chrift, in confequence of union to him, I made ufe of a fimile taken from the head and members of an human body, and the communication of the animal fpirits from the one to the other, in confequence of the union between them. This author, though in his great modefty he owns that he is poorly fkilled in philofophy, a conceffion he needed not have given himfelf the trouble to make; yet thinks himfelf capable to make it appear, that I am not a little wanting in the application of my argument: I fuppofe he means *fimile*; for I am often obliged to guefs at his meaning. But what is it he fancies is wanting? In what is it inapplicable? Does it not exactly tally with what I am fpeaking of? But inftead of fhewing the want of application, or any difparity in the cafe, which he does not attempt, he puts me upon proving *, "that there is any life in the head of " a body natural, when the members are all dead; or that the life of the natu- " ral body is all extinct before the head dies, or that the head can fubfift with- " out any living members, or that the body natural is deftitute of natural life, " when united to a living head;" things I have no concern with, and which are no part of the fimile I make ufe of; and which is made ufe of by me only to fhew, that as the animal fpirits from the head are communicated to the members

" Supralapfarian Scheme, p. 76.    * Ibid. p. 77.

bers of the body, not antecedent to union between them, or in order to effect it, but in consequence of it: so the Spirit of Christ is communicated from him the head to the members of his body, not antecedent to their union, or in order to effect it, but in consequence of it: whence it follows, that he cannot be the bond of this union; and by this I abide. For the proof of the Spirit's being the evidence of communion, and so of union, and therefore not the bond of it, I produced 1 *John* iii. 24 and chap. iv. 13. Only the first of these scriptures is taken notice of by this writer[x]; who fancies that the former part of this text was disagreeable to me, and therefore left out by me. I declare I was far from thinking it to be so; and am well content it should be transcribed at large, it being a witness for, and not against my new notion, as he is pleased to call it: *And he that keepeth his commandments dwelleth in him, and he in him; and hereby we know that he abideth in us, by the Spirit which he hath given us.* The meaning of which is, that those persons, who under the influences of the Spirit of God are enabled to keep the commandments of God, dwell in him, and he in them; that is, they have communion with him, as the effect of union to him; for these acts of indwelling are not uniting acts, but acts of communion, in consequence of union; of which the Spirit being given them, is an evidence. Now could it be proved that Christ dwells in his people by his Spirit, though the scripture no where says so, but that he *dwells in* their *hearts by faith*; yet it does not follow that he is united to them by his Spirit, because this act of indwelling is an act of communion: not this, but his everlasting love, which is the foundation of his dwelling in them, is the bond of union. That the Spirit is the seal of covenant-love and of union with Christ, will not be denied: But then his being a seal, is no other than his being a certifying evidence and witness of these things. Now from the Spirit's being a witness and seal of union, this man suggests[y] that he must be the bond of it; because the party that seals, is *the principal of the bond:* where his poor wandering head is running upon a *pecuniary bond*, a bond in writing, by which a man is bound to another; and in which he most miserably blunders; seeing it is not the principal, or he to whom the bond is made, but the debtor, or he who obliges himself to the other, that signs and seals: Whereas the thing in dispute is, a bond of union between persons, by which they are united to each other. Nor will it be denied that the Spirit quickens and regenerates us, begets and maintains spiritual life in us; but then all this is in consequence of union to Christ: nor is it by this spiritual life which he begets and maintains, that we have union with our living head, but we have this spiritual life as the effect of that union, and thereby have communion with him; and though the elect of God, whilst dead in trespasses and sins, have no communion with Christ, yet there is a sense in which they are united to him then; which union is the ground and foundation of their being quickened.

(2.) I have

[x] Supralapsarian Scheme, p. 79.    [y] Ibid. p. 81.

(2.) I have also affirmed that faith is not the bond of union to Christ, and desired those who plead for union by faith, to tell us whether we are united to Christ by the habit or act of faith; and since there are different acts of it, whether our union is by the first, second, third, &c. acts of believing? To which our author has not thought fit to return any answer. I go on to argue, that if union is by faith as an habit, it is not by faith on our part, because faith, as such, is the gift of God; and if it be by faith as an act of ours, it is by a work, for faith, as such, is a work; and then not by grace, since works and grace cannot be blended. To which this author [a] replies: " what if we have union " with Christ in that part which lies on our side the question, by acts of ours, " unto which we are enabled by the Spirit of God, who works faith in us; does " this tend to lessen the exceeding grace of God?" I answer, that what he says of the Spirit's working faith in us, is right, but that regards faith as an habit; though that there is a part lying on our side the question, to bring about our union to Christ by an act of ours, I utterly deny: Strange! that an uniting act, or a bond of union, must be *parted*, that there should be a *part* belong to us, and another to the Spirit of God? But to his question I answer, that to ascribe our union to Christ in part to acts of ours, though enabled to them by the Spirit of God, does lessen the grace of God: and I argue thus, that if to ascribe election in part to works, to any acts of ours as to faith, though enabled to it by the Spirit of God, would tend to lessen the glory of grace in it; so to ascribe our union to Christ to any acts of ours, to faith as such, though enabled to it by the Spirit of God, would tend to lessen the glory of that grace and love of Christ, which is the alone bond of it. This writer [a] farther suggests, that I incline to admit the grace of love to be the union-bond; and argues, that that being an act of ours, it must consequently be esteemed a work, and so be liable to the same difficulty: whereas, though I observe, that had our divines fixed upon the grace of love as the bond of union, it would have been more plausible and feasible than their fixing upon faith; yet I am far from an inclination to admit of it, when I affirm, in so many words, that " it is not our love to Christ, but his love to us, which is alone the real bond of our union to him."

I proceed to observe, that " faith is no uniting grace, nor are any of its acts of a cementing nature." This man [b] fancies I am guilty of such a flagrant contradiction, as is not to be produced in any book besides; because I add, " faith indeed looks to Christ, lays hold on him, embraces him, and cleaves " unto him; it expects and receives all from Christ, and gives him all the glory." These sentences, it seems, are closely united; and yet an agreement between them cannot be proved. I own, I am not so quick-sighted as to see any contradiction,

[a] Supralapsarian Scheme, p. 82.     [a] Ibid. p. 83.     [b] Ibid. p. 83.

tradition, much less a flagrant one, in them. Was I sensible of it, I should be thankful for the discovery. I perceive that the acts of laying hold on, embracing and cleaving to, are thought to be uniting acts. I confess I never thought that whatever my hand lays hold on, is united to it, or one with it. I now lay hold on my pen, and hold it in my hand, make use of it, take it up, and lay it down at pleasure; I do not find they are one, but two distinct things; my pen is not one with my hand, nor my hand with my pen, nor do they both make one third thing. I never knew that one person's embracing another was an uniting their persons together, or that any union or relation between them commenced upon such an act. When the apostles exhorted such who were partakers of the grace of God, *to cleave to the Lord with purpose of heart*, it can never be thought that their exhortation was to unite themselves to the Lord with purpose of heart, since these were persons already united to him. All these acts of looking to Christ, laying hold upon him, embracing of him, and cleaving to him, are acts of faith performed under the influences of the Spirit, in consequence of union to Christ; and are such, in which believers have communion with him. He seems displeased with what I say, that " a soul can no more " be said to be united to Christ by these acts, than a beggar may be said to be " united to a person, to whom he applies, of whom he expects alms, to whom " he keeps close, from whom he receives, and to whom he is thankful." This, he says [c], deserves no answer. The reason I guess is, because he can give none. However, I will take his own instance, of a distressed beloved child's looking to, embracing of, cleaving to, and hanging about its tender father, with intreaties and expectations of supply; and deny that these are uniting acts, or such as unite the father to the child, or the child to the father; but are all in consequence of a relation, a relative union, that subsisted between them, antecedent to these acts.

I farther observe, that union to Christ is the foundation of faith, and of all the acts of believing, or seeing, walking, receiving, &c. That faith is the fruit and effect of union, even of what is commonly called vital union: for as there must first be an union of the soul and body of man, before he can be said to live, and there must be life, before there can be reason; so there must be a union of the soul to Christ, before it can spiritually live: and there must be a principle of spiritual life, before there can be faith. This I thought also was fully and fitly exemplified in the simile of the vine and branches, which must first be in the vine, before they bear fruit; and may be illustrated by the ingrafture of the wild olive-tree into a good one; and concluded, that union to Christ is before faith, and therefore faith cannot be the bond of union. The substance of what is replied [d] to this is, " that though we cannot produce good
" fruit

[c] Supralapsarian Scheme, p. 84.   [d] Ibid. p. 85, 86.

# TRUTH DEFENDED.

"fruit until we are in union with Christ the living head, yet there is no absurdity in saying, that there is life produced in the soul, previous to our union
with him;—and that a spiritual work (an aukward way of talking; why not
the Spirit?) which begets a spiritual life in us, is necessary to meten (meeten)
us for union to him the living head." And though he approves the argument,
yet does not believe the application of it agreeable to truth; namely, that because
there is an union of the soul and body of man before he can be said to live, that
therefore the soul of man must be united to Christ before he has spiritual life.
In a word, though he agrees that there must be a principle of life, before there
is any exercise of faith, yet denies that there was union to Christ, before this
principle was wrought. Now let it be observed, that the union I am here speaking of, is what is commonly called vital union; an union in time, at conversion,
which is no other than *Christ formed in us*; upon which a principle of spiritual
life is immediately produced: for *he that hath the Son, hath life*; and then follow faith, and the exercise of it. Therefore this union cannot be by faith, nor
faith be the bond of it, since it follows upon it: for though, as upon the union
of the soul and body, life is immediately produced; yet the union, in order of
nature, must be considered previous to life. So though, upon the formation of
Christ in us, called the vital union, the principle of spiritual life is immediately
produced; yet the formation of Christ, or the union of him to us, must be considered antecedent to this life. No, says this man; there is life produced in the
soul, previous to our union with Christ, in order to it; yea, to meeten for it:
whence it must unavoidably follow, that a man may have a principle of spiritual life, and yet be *without Christ*; be separate from him, and without union
to him; contrary to the express words of the apostle, *He that hath not the Son
of God, hath not life*[e]. Besides, does this doctrine give honour to the glorious
head of influence, Christ Jesus, which teaches that a man may have a principle
of spiritual life, without union to him, the living head; and in order to meeten
for it, and consequently elsewhere, from another quarter? What appears most
plausible, at first view, in favour of this preposterous notion, is the instance[f] of
the scion, that must have life previous to its ingrafture. But pray what kind
of life is it, that the scion of the wild olive-tree lives, before its ingrafture into
the good olive-tree? it is a life agreeable to its nature; it is the life of the wild
olive-tree, not of the good olive-tree. So men before conversion, before Christ
is formed in them, live, not a spiritual life, a life of grace, but a life of sin;
there is no principle of spiritual life, before Christ is formed in the soul. The
simile of the vine and branches, in *John* xv. 4, 5. he thinks[g] is of no service to
me, but rather against me; since there would be no need of the exhortation,
*abide in me*, if no act or acts of ours are concerned about maintaining union with
Christ:

[e] 1 John v. 12.     [f] Supralapsarian Scheme, p. 89.     [g] Ibid. p. 86, 88.

Chrift: and obferves, that abiding in Chrift is by faith, and the fame with ftanding by faith, *Rom.* xi. 20. and argues, that if our ftanding and abiding in Chrift are by faith, then do we hold union thereby; and whatfoever holds us to union, is the bond of it. To which I need only reply, that the phrafes of abiding in Chrift, and ftanding by faith, regard the perfeverance of the faints, in confequence of their union to Chrift. Now though perfeverance is by faith, or faith is the means of perfeverance, under the powerful influence of grace; yet it does not follow that it is the bond of union; fince both perfeverance, and faith, by which we perfevere, are the effects of it. I obferved, from the above paffage, that "faith is a fruit of the Spirit, which grows upon the branches that are in "Chrift the vine; and that thefe branches muft be firft in the vine, before they "bear this fruit." This author wonders [h] who will attempt to deny it. Very well; if no body will attempt to deny it, the caufe is given up, the point is gained: for if perfons muft be firft in Chrift the vine, that is, united to him, before they bear the fruit of faith, that is, believe in him; it follows, that union is before faith, and that faith is the fruit and effect, and not the bond of it. The fimile of the wild and good olive-trees, he fays [i], I have borrowed piece-meal, and have omitted to quote it (the text) in the margin. I own, I borrowed the fimile from *Rom.* xi. 17, *&c.* as being an appofite one; but never thought, nor do I think now, that the paffage has any reference to the ingrafture of fouls into Chrift, but into a vifible church-ftate: For if ingrafture into Chrift is intended, it will follow, that perfons may be ingrafted into him, that is, united to him, and yet be broken off from him; which fuppofes their intire apoftacy from him; which none will give into, unlefs they are far gone into Arminian principles. The plain meaning of the paffage is, that the Jews, who rejected the Meffiah, were broken off from their vifible church-ftate, or from being the vifible church of God; and the Gentiles, that believed, were taken into it; and that the Jews, when they believed, would be again grafted, or taken into a vifible church-ftate. Hence the whole of our author's reafoning, about the neceffity of faith, and the removal of unbelief, antecedent to an ingrafture into Chrift, as founded upon this fcripture, comes to nothing.

(3.) Having proved that neither the Spirit on Chrift's part, nor faith on ours, is the bond of union, I proceeded to fhew that the everlafting love of the Father, Son and Spirit, is the bond of the union of the elect unto them. To this, not one fyllable is replied: But whereas I obferve that there are feveral things which arife from, and are branches of this everlafting love-union, and which I apprehend make it appear that the elect are united to Chrift before faith; this author has thought fit to make fome remarks upon them.

I obferve,

[h] Supralapfarian Scheme, p 88.     [i] Ibid. p. 90.

I observe, from *Ephes.* i. 4. that there is an election-union in Christ from everlasting: my meaning is, that election is an act of God's everlasting love, in which the objects of it were considered in Christ; and how they could be considered in Christ, without union to him, is, what I say, is hard to conceive. So that I apprehend, that as eternal election is a display of God's everlasting love to his people, it is an instance also of their eternal union to Christ. No, says [k] this man; election is a fore-appointing persons to an union; as the choice of stones for a building, or of a branch for ingrafture. Had the text in *Ephes.* i. 4. run thus, *according as he hath chosen us to be in him*, or *that we might*, or *should be in him*; this sense of election would have appeared plausible: but the words in connection with the preceding verse run thus, *who hath blessed us with all spiritual blessings in heavenly places in Christ, according as he hath chosen us in him*; and therefore will not admit of such an interpretation as this, "that it was according to the eternal design of God, to bestow divine and special favours upon them, *when in Christ*; or that they were chosen to divine and special blessings, *through* Christ;" but that they were blessed with these divine and special blessings *in* Christ, according as they were chosen in him. I do not say that election is the uniting act, that is, the everlasting love of God; nor do I see any absurdity, in supposing union previous to this choice, though I think they go together; but this I say, that in election men are considered *in Christ*, and so is a proof of eternal union to him; and by this I abide, until something else is offered to confront it.

I have also said, that there is a legal union between Christ and the elect from everlasting, the bond of which, is the suretyship of Christ, and so he and they are one, in a law-sense, as surety and debtor are one: and likewise, that there is a federal union between them from everlasting; Christ being considered as head, and they as members with him in the covenant of grace. This [l] writer is of opinion, that the legal and federal union is one and the same; I am content they should be thought so: my design hereby is not to multiply unions, or as though I thought there were so many distinct ones, believing that God's everlasting love is the grand original bond of union, and that these are so many displays of it, proving it; and particularly, that it is before faith, the main thing I had in view. The relations of surety and debtor, head and members, conveying different ideas, I thought it proper to consider them apart; however, I am willing they should go together, provided neither of them is lost: but I observe, the former of these is entirely sunk by this author, and no notice taken of it: for though they both relate to one and the same covenant, yet are to be distinctly considered; and if Christ is not to be considered as the surety of his people, as one with them, in a law-

sense,

[k] Supralapsarian Scheme, p. 79, 92—95.     [l] Ibid. p. 78, 92, 95.

sense, as surety and debtor are one; what foundation is there for his satisfaction for them? nay, not only so, but even the relation of head and members is dropped by this author, under a pretence that it has been already proved, that there is no being in Christ before faith, as members of his body; and goes on to consider the relation of husband and wife, which is not at all mentioned by me; and calls ᵐ upon the men of the Supralapsarian scheme, to produce any text of scripture that informs us that God, in either of the persons of the Godhead, calls any of the children of men his spouse, or wife, or bride, before they are made so by a mutual covenant. The reader will be apt to conclude, from a large citation out of Dr *Goodwin*, that it was made by me under the present head; whereas it stands in another part of my book, and made, together with some others, from Dr *Witsius*, and Mr *Richard Taylor*, with no other view than to observe to the Gentleman I wrote the *Letter* to, that there was no reason why the assertors of eternal union should be treated as ignorant and enthusiastic preachers, when men of such characters as above, had, in some sense, asserted it. Now, though I do not think myself obliged to take any further notice of this citation, not being made to vindicate my sense of union, yet I cannot but observe the rudeness and pertness of the man, in treating so great a man as Dr *Goodwin* was, in the manner he does; and at once pronounce, that what is said by him, is not worthy to be esteemed either good divinity, or good argument. He next falls ⁿ foul upon a passage of mine in another part of my book, and upon another subject, where I say that the gift of God himself to his people, in the everlasting covenant, is a gift and instance of his love to them before conversion. This he denies, and says, the scriptures which mention this gift, evidently prove the contrary; the scripture he produces, is *Heb.* viii. 10. from *Jer.* xxxi. 33. and observes, that this covenant is a mutual agreement between God and converted people; for you read here, says he °, that the laws of God were to be written upon their hearts, and in their minds, before God is their God, and they are his people. To which I reply; that there is not the least evidence from any of these passages, that this covenant is a mutual agreement between God and any people, converted or unconverted; nor is there any such thing as a mutual covenant between God and fallen creatures; the mutual covenant talked of at conversion, is all a dream and fancy. The covenant here spoken of, is wholly and entirely on the part of God, and seems rather to respect unconverted than converted persons; since one branch of it regards the writing and putting of the laws of God in their hearts and minds, which converted ones have already; nor is this mentioned as the cause or condition of his being their God, but rather, his being their God in covenant, is

the

ᵐ Supralapsarian Scheme, p. 96.   ⁿ Ibid p. 99.   ° Ibid. p. 100.

the ground and foundation of this; since this is mentioned in *Jer.* xxxii. 38. previous to his promise of giving one heart, and one way, and putting his fear into them; all which suppose them unconverted. In a word, our author thinks [p], that the covenant of grace is not a uniting covenant, no relation arising from it between God and his people, between Christ and his members; it is only a settling the conditions, and laying a sure foundation for a federal union with his people, that is, upon the conditions of faith and repentance; so that the covenant of grace from eternity, is only a foundation for a covenant. I am content he should enjoy his own sentiments, without reproaching him with inexplicable nonsense. But since he has called upon the Supralapsarians to produce a text, wherein any of the children of men are called by God, in either of the persons of the Godhead, his spouse, wife, or bride, before they are made so by a mutual covenant, I propose to his consideration, *Isaiah* liv. 1, 5, 6. where Christ is called *the husband* of the Gentile church, and she *his wife*, long before it was in being: and even in the text he himself mentions, *Ephes.* v. 23. Christ is said to be the head of the church, even as the husband is the head of the wife; which includes the whole general assembly and church of the first-born, even all the elect, converted or unconverted.

The next union I mention, is the natural union that is between Christ and his people; in this, our author says [q], is nothing but what agrees with the holy scriptures, and so it passes without a censure. The last I take notice of, is a representative one, both from everlasting and in time. This man imagines [r] I have given away the cause, by acknowledging that the natural union was not in eternity, since hereby the notion of an eternal representative union is entirely destroyed; for, adds he, it is exceeding remote from all the rules of argument, to suppose that Jesus Christ represented the elect people as members in him, when he had no meaner nature than divine. This writer is, no doubt, acquainted with all the rules of argument: but what does the man mean, when he talks of Christ's having *no meaner* nature than divine? I hope the reader will excuse my warmth, when such a horrid reflection is made upon the divine nature of the Son of God; no *meaner* nature! This supposes, indeed, the human nature to be meaner, but implies the divine nature to be mean; or, where is the degree of comparison? he suggests [s], that Christ could not represent the elect in eternity unless he had human nature from eternity; and that there could not be a real union of the persons of the elect in eternity, without their real existence. I reply; that it was not necessary, in order to Christ's being the Mediator, Head, and Representative of the elect in eternity, that he should be then actually man; only that he should certainly be so in time: besides, there was a federal union of the human nature to the Son of God from eternity, or the human nature had

a co-

[p] Supralapsarian Scheme, p. 101.    [q] Ibid. p. 102.    [r] Ibid. p. 102.    [s] Ibid. p. 103.

venant subsistence in the second person from everlasting. Nor was the real existence of the persons of the elect necessary to their real union to Christ, only that
they should certainly exist: I call their union real, in opposition to that which
is imaginary; for surely the love of Christ to the elect, from everlasting, was
real, which is the bond of union, though their persons, soul and body, did not
really, or actually exist. He proceeds [t] to consider the import of some other
*texts* of scripture, which, he says, we are subject to imagine favour our fond
notion of eternal union; though he considers but *one*, and that is 2 *Tim.* i. 9.
*Who hath saved us, and called us with an holy calling ; not according to our works,
but according to his own purpose and grace, which was given us in Christ Jesus, before
the world began.* This grace he sometimes takes for a promise of grace, sometimes for grace in the covenant itself; yea, he says, it evidently intends our calling; so that, according to him, our calling must be before the world began.
But be it what it will, whether a promise of grace, or a purpose of grace, or
grace itself, it was given *to us in* Christ, *before the world began*, and on that our
argument depends: if we were *in* Christ when this grace, or promise of grace,
was given, we were united to him; for how we could be considered *in him*,
without union to him, he would do well to acquaint us.

I must, in justice to this author, before I conclude this head, acquaint my
reader, that he has quoted "some, what he calls plain texts of scripture, to
shew that the sacred book does most evidently set aside the opinion of eternal
union, yea, or of union before faith: the scriptures are, *Rom.* viii. 9. and xvi. 7.
2 *Cor.* v. 17. all which I have before taken notice of in the *Letter* he refers to ;
and all that he remarks is, that I will needs have it, that these scriptures intend
only the evidence of union with Christ from everlasting; which sense he does
not attempt to set aside; only that the phrase, *If a man is in Christ, he is a new
creature*, he says, supposes that none but new-born souls are united to him;
whereas the meaning is, that whoever professes himself to be in Christ, ought
to appear to be so: and yet, after all this, this man has the front to say ", that
men are not united to Christ until they believe, has been proved by *almost innumerable scriptures and arguments*; when he only produces *three* scriptures, and
not *one* argument from them. This man is resolved to carry his point at any
rate, right or wrong; he sticks at nothing.

*Thirdly*, We are now come to a point this author discovers a great itch, and
eager desire to be at, namely, the doctrine of God's love and delight in his elect
before conversion. He has been two or three times nibbling at it before, and
I have already exposed his folly in placing it in the Supralapsarian scheme, when
it can be no other than a Sublapsarian doctrine.

1. In

---

t Supralapsarian Scheme, p. 104.  u Ibid. p. 77.  * Ibid. p. 128.

1. In my *Letter* above referred to, I write concerning the invariable, unchangeable, and everlasting love of God to his elect, and give instances of his love to them, not only in eternity, but in time, and that even while they are in an unconverted estate, from *Rom.* v. 6, 8, 10. 1 *John* iv. 10. *Ephes.* ii. 4, 5. *Titus* iii 3—6. which this writer thinks fit to pass by in silence. I then mention three gifts of God, which are instances of his love to his people before conversion, not to be matched by any after it; namely, the gift of *Himself*, the gift of his *Son*, and the gift of his *Spirit*. This man denies that either of these are given to the elect before conversion. As to the first, he says, " God never " gives himself to any of the children of men until they believe[x];" and suggests, that the scripture I produce, *I will be their God, and they shall be my people,* proves it; being, as he thinks, a mutual covenant between God and converted people: but I have shewn already, that it is not a mutual covenant between God and others; and that the promises of it suppose the persons it concerns unconverted; and, indeed, God's being the God of his people, is the first ground and foundation-blessing of the covenant; and the reason why any covenant-blessing, and among the rest, conversion, is bestowed upon any of the sons of men, is, because he is their covenant-God and Father; so that, consequently, he must stand in this relation to them before conversion. Besides, if they are his people before conversion, though not openly to themselves and others, 1 *Pet.* ii. 10. yet secretly to him, *Psalm* cx. 3. *Matt.* i. 21. he must be their God before conversion; for these two relate unto, and suppose each other. He does not deny that Christ was a gift of God's love before conversion; but fancies that I have receded from what I proposed; since, as it is expressed by me, he is only given *for* them. I answer; My proposition is, to shew that there are such gifts of God before conversion, as are instances of his love *to* his people then; and surely Christ being given *for* them, is an instance of God's love *to* them, *John* iii. 16. He seems to triumph upon this, and says[y], " could he have proved " his proposition, he had certainly laid a strong, if not an improveable (I suppose it should be immoveable) foundation for his doctrine." Well, if this will do, I am able to prove that Christ was given *to* his people in his incarnation, before he was given *for* them in his sufferings and death; *To us a child is born, to us a son is given,* Isai. ix. 6. and I hope it will be allowed, that the gift of Christ, in his incarnation, extended not only to the believers of that age in which he was born, but to all the elect, to all the children, for whose sake he partook of flesh and blood. As to the third and last of these gifts, he judges[z], " that the Spirit is not given to any of the children of men till they are converted, " or at that very instant;" and gives broad intimations, as if he thought he was

not

[x] Supralapsarian Scheme, p. 110, 100.   [y] Ibid. p. 111.   [z] Ibid. p. 112.

not given at all, until he is given as a comforter. The text in *John* xvi. 8. which my expressions refer to, he seems to intimate, does not regard the conviction and conversion of men, but the reproving of the world. I will not contend with him abour the sense of the text; it is enough to my purpose, if it will be but allowed, that the Spirit of God is the author of real conviction and conversion; who therefore must be considered as sent, and given, antecedent to conviction and conversion, in order to begin, carry on, and finish the work of grace, when he finds men dead in sin, devoid of all grace, in a state of nature; and therefore, surely, must be a gift and instance of God's love to them, whilst in that state

2. In order to prove that the love of God to his elect, from everlasting, is a love of complacency and delight, I observe, that his love to his Son, as Mediator, is such a love; and that whereas God loves his people with the same kind of love he loves his Son, which I prove from *John* xvii. 23. it must needs follow, that the love he bears to them, is a love of complacency and delight. This author [a] thinks I have strained and forced the text I mention beyond its real meaning; and that my notion is unfairly inferred from it; he believes I know the word *as* is of the comparative degree, and rarely intends equality: if I do not know, I am sure he cannot tell me; it is only his ignorance of the comparative degree, that will excuse him from designed blasphemy against the Son of God. His learned reviser and editor should have informed him, that *as*, of itself, is of no degree, but is according to the word to which it is joined; it is used in forming comparisons, and is an adverb of likeness and equality. He seems to be conscious, that it sometimes, though rarely, intends equality, and gives himself a needless trouble to collect together several texts, where it signifies likeness: I could easily produce others, where it is expressive of equality; see *John* i. 14. and x. 15. *Phil.* ii. 8. 2 *Cor.* x. 7. However, I am content it should signify likeness, and not equality, in the text mentioned; let it be a likeness of a very minute or small degree, I hope it will be allowed to be of the same kind; and if this is granted, my argument stands good; "that if God has loved his Son with a love of complacency and delight from everlasting, and he has loved his elect with the same kind of love from everlasting, with a like love, though not to the same degree; then he must have loved them from everlasting, with a love of complacency and delight."

3. I go on to observe, that Jesus Christ loved the elect from everlasting with a love of complacency and delight, as they were presented to him in the glass of his Father's purposes and decrees; my meaning is, as they were presented to him in all that glory his Father designed to bring them to; which I prove from *Prov.* viii. 31. and see no reason why the Father's love should not be the same.

[a] Supralapsarian Scheme, p. 114, 115.

This man thinks [b], that the text in *Proverbs* refers to the delight Chrift had in the fore-views of his people, having his own, and his Father's beautiful image impreffed upon them; or rather, that it refers to a farther view which the Son of God took of the moft perfect ftate of his members upon earth, in the kingdom-glory. And why may not the thought be carried a little farther, that Chrift was not only *rejoicing in the habitable part of his earth*, in the fore-views of his people dwelling with him, and he with them, here on earth; but that his *delights were with the fons of men*, as fore-viewed by him in all that ultimate glory they are to enjoy to all eternity; and then we are agreed? Now let it be obferved, that this complacency and delight in them, was taken up from everlafting, as abundantly appears from the context; nor could any intermediate ftate, as that of nature, make any alteration in this love of delight. Chrift loved them before they were in a ftate of nature, and while they were in it, though not as confidered as unregenerate and rebellious finners, or becaufe they were fo; which is the vile infinuation all along made; but as the whole election of grace ftood prefented to him *a glorious church, without fpot or wrinkle, or any fuch thing*; juft fuch as he will prefent them to himfelf another day.

4. I farther obferve, that God's choofing his people in Chrift before the foundation of the world, is an act of love fpringing from delight in them, even as his choice of the people of *Ifrael* (which was an emblem of the choice of the true and fpiritual *Ifrael*) was owing to the delight he had in them; to prove which, I cite *Deut.* x. 15. and add, that all the favours and bleffings God beftows upon his people in time, fuch as bringing them out of a ftate of nature, or out of any diftrefs or difficulty, in a word, their whole falvation, arife from his delight in them; for the proof of which, I mention *Pfalm* xviii. 19. and cxlix. 4. *Jer.* xxxii. 41. *Zeph.* iii. 17. This writer [c] is of opinion, that what I have afferted, that God's choice of his people in Chrift, as an act of love fpringing from delight, requires more proof than I have produced, or than any man is able to produce. I fuppofe, he will not deny that God's eternal choice of his people in Chrift is an act of love; if he does, let him confider 2 *Thefs*. ii. 13. though he may as well deny it to be an act of love, for the fame reafon that he denies it fprings from delight, namely, that God has chofe them to *be holy, and without blame before him in love*; and from thence conclude, that this early choice was not the effect of his love to them, any more than of his delight in them; but that they might be objects of his love, as of his delight, when united to his Son: But furely, if they were *chofen in Chrift*, they muft be confidered in union with him, and muft be the objects both of love and delight; fince Chrift is the beloved Son of God, in whom he always was, is, and ever will be well pleafed,

and

[b] Supralapfarian Scheme, p. 117, 118.  [c] Ibid. p. 118.  [d] Ibid. p. 119.

and with all thofe that are in him. To illuftrate this matter, I mention the choice of the people of *Ifrael*, as a reprefentation of the choice of the people of God, which is owned to be thus far right : but when I affirm that this was owing to previous delight in them ; it is faid ᵈ, this requires more proof than *Deut*. x. 15. for it is not faid, that the Lord delighted in this people, and therefore he chofe them ; but that he delighted in their fathers to love them, and chofe their feed after them. I anfwer ; that the love with which the Lord loved the people of *Ifrael*, was the fame love with which he loved their fathers ; and therefore if he loved their fathers with a love of complacency, fo he loved them the children ; which is the ground and foundation of his choofing them ; fee *Deut*. vii. 6, 7. God's bringing his elect out of a ftate of nature, is owing to his *great love*, Ephes. ii. 4, 5. which, furely, it would not be called, was it feparate from delight ; and as that, fo all after-bleffings and favours fpring from the fame kind of love, for which I produce the above fcriptures. Though my defign there is not to prove by them, that God loves his elect with a love of complacency and delight while in a ftate of nature ; my readers will not be at a lofs about my defign in producing of them, nor think themfelves remarkably trifled with ; when they cannot but obferve, that my view is apparently this, that as electing and regenerating grace fpring from God's love of delight in his people, fo all the after-bleffings of grace and glory, in one continued chain, arife from the fame : whence it will appear, that God's love of complacency in his people, is invariably the fame, through every ftate, of nature, grace and glory.

5. I have obferved, that the diftinction of a love of pity and benevolence, and of complacency and delight, is made by fome popifh fchoolmen, and is fubverfive of the nature and perfections of God ; and reprefents him fuch an one as ourfelves, fubject to change ; that his love, like ours, alters, and by degrees increafes, and, from a love of pity and benevolence, paffes into a love of complacency and delight. This author feems difpleafed ᵉ that this diftinction fhould be afcribed to popifh fchoolmen, fince he is apt to believe, that there *is* (it fhould be *are*) very few of that pretended church (of *Rome*, I fuppofe he means) fo remote from the groffeft tenets of Arminianifm, as to allow of it. I can tell him there have been many in that church, more remote from Arminianifm by far, than he himfelf is ; and fhould I tell him, that fome of them have been Supralapfarians, it would have equal credit with him : however, be it fo, that this diftinction came from them, though he has no *high* opinion of popifh notions, which, as I obferved before, fuppofes that he has *an* opinion of them, yet he fhall not very willingly part with it ; much good may it do him, I do not envy

his

---

ᵈ Supralapfarian Scheme, p. 119.   ᵉ Ibid. p. 124, 125.

his poſſeſſion of it; let him make the beſt uſe of it he can. He fancies[f] that what I have ſaid concerning Chriſt being "the object of his Father's love and wrath, at one and the ſame time; that as he was the Son of God, he was always the object of his love and delight; but as he was the ſinner's ſurety, and while bearing the ſins of his people in his own body on the tree, he was the object of his diſpleaſure and wrath," is as ſubverſive of the nature and perfections of God, and repreſents him as liable to change as this diſtinction does; ſince here is a change from delight to the greateſt diſpleaſure, and from that to delight again. I anſwer, for the farther explanation of what I have ſaid, let it be obſerved, that I conceive that Chriſt was in no other ſenſe the object of divine wrath and diſpleaſure, as the ſinner's ſurety, than as he had the effects of wrath, that is, puniſhment due to ſin, inflicted on him, which he ſenſibly felt; but then, at the ſame inſtant, God took the utmoſt delight and pleaſure in him even as the ſinner's ſurety, viewing him ſtanding in the room and ſtead of his elect, with patience, courage, and greatneſs of ſoul, bearing all that was laid upon him, and giving full ſatisfaction to law and juſtice. *It pleaſed the Lord to bruiſe him*, Iſai. liii. 10. *Therefore doth my Father love me*, ſays Chriſt, *becauſe I lay down my life*, John x. 17. So that here was no change from delight to diſpleaſure, even when and while he bore the effects of that wrath, or that itſelf, which was due to others.

6. I cite a paſſage from *Ariſtotle*, in which that philoſopher affirms, that benevolence is properly neither friendſhip nor love; and that no man can be ſaid to love, who is not firſt delighted with the form or idea of the object: and, for my own part, I add, I cannot ſee that that can be love, which is without any delight in the object ſaid to be loved; and inſtance in ſome expreſſions of a man to his wife, and a parent to a child, declaring love without delight; which ſeem contradictory. This man at once falls[g] foul upon the poor philoſopher, as having aſſerted what is contrary to reaſon and experience; and then turning himſelf to me, ſays, "I would aſk this gentleman if he never ſaw an object, whoſe miſerable eſtate engaged his compaſſion, and diſpoſed him to ſhew friendſhip, by affording ſome relief to the miſerable creature, though there was no delightful form in the object, nor any thing but miſery to engage his kindneſs? What, is not that love, which diſpoſes one man to relieve another in miſery and neceſſity?" But it ſhould be obſerved, that the philoſopher is ſpeaking of one thing, and this man of another. *Ariſtotle* is not ſpeaking of ευεργεσια, benefaction, beneficence, or *doing well*, relieving a miſerable creature; but of ευνοια, benevolence, *wiſhing well* to another: And I hope this will ſerve to cool his reſentment againſt him. Let me, in my turn, aſk

this

---

[f] Supralapſarian Scheme, p. 125, 126.    [g] Ibid. p. 128.

this man, if, upon the fight of a miferable object, my pity is engaged fo far as to wifh him well, but give him nothing, whether this wifhing well, this bene‑volence of mine, is either love or friendfhip? Nay, fuppofing it is carried farther, and my benevolence paffes into beneficence, I relieve the poor object; fhould not this be confidered rather as an act of humanity, than either properly of friendfhip or love? I confefs I never thought, when I have given alms to a poor object, I did it to fhew an affection of love, or as any act of friendfhip to him; I little thought that a relation of friendfhip between us arofe from fuch an act, or that the poor creature and I commenced friends upon it. Upon the inftances of love without delight, I afk what kind of love would this be thought to be? He anfwers[h], why, probably, a love of compaffion and benevolence: and, as things will be circumftanced, great love too; that is, when the wife is leud, and the fon rebellious. I reply, that it is very poffible, and fometimes fo it is, when either of thefe is the cafe, that delight in the object continues; fo that love appears to be great indeed, real, and hearty: But when things are come to fuch a pafs, that there is no delight in the object, I cannot but be of opinion, that real, hearty love and affection, is gone too. And what may be faid or done that looks like love, arifes from the relation which ftill fubfifts, and a fenfe of duty which that obliges to, and not from real love and affection. But what he thinks is the ftrongeft evidence againft the notion of love being attended with delight in the object loved, is the advice of Chrift to his difciples, faying, *Love your enemies; blefs them that curfe you; do good to them that hate you; and pray for them which defpitefully ufe you, and perfecute you*[i]: And I do not know but it may, and yet fall fhort of proving what it is brought for. I ap‑prehend, the love with which Chrift exhorts his people to love their enemies, is not to be underftood *quoad affectus*, as refpecting the internal affection of love: I cannot believe that Chrift requires of me that I fhould love a perfecutor as I do my wife, my children, my real friend, or brother in Chrift; but *quoad effectus*, as to the effects; that is, I am required to do thofe things as they lie in my way, and according to my ability, as a man would do to his neighbour, whom he loves; that is, feed him when hungry, and give him drink when thirfty. And fo are we taught to underftand this advice of Chrift by the apoftle *Paul*, in *Romans* xii. 19—21. But after all, fuppofing it could be proved that there is a founda‑tion for fuch a diftinction among men, as a love of pity and benevolence, and a love of complacency and delight, I would not be over-confident about thefe things. Though I muft confefs I cannot fee how mere pity can be love, or barely benevolence, or wifhing well, is love; yet I fay, fuppofing this, it does not follow that there is fuch a diftinction in the love of God, efpecially towards

the

---

[h] Supralapfarian Scheme, p. 129.   [i] Matt. v. 44.

the same persons, as they pass into different estates; which is to make the love of God to change by degrees, as the love of mutable creatures; and from one kind of love to pass into another, and from a lower to an higher degree: A thought to be abhorred by all those who know and believe what he says to be true; *I am the Lord, I change not.* This author next reverts [k] to the instance which I mention of a man's saying to his wife, "I love you well, though I can "take no delight in your person, nor pleasure in your company;" as a contradiction to his expressions of love; and observes, that I have wounded my notion of God's delighting in his elect, whilst in a state of nature, unless I can prove that he dwells with, and takes pleasure in the company of these his enemies. I reply, that I do not think that God loves or delights either in the persons, or in the company of his people, considered as sinners, as unconverted persons, as in a state of nature, as enemies to him; but as considered in Christ, and viewed in all that glory he designs to bring them to. And thus as the *delights* of the Son, so the delights of the Father, from everlasting, before the earth was, were not only *in*, but *with* them: They were not only rejoicing *in* them, but delighting themselves *with* them, in the fore-views of their dwelling with each other, and enjoying each other's company to all eternity.

And thus I have gone as far in my answer, as this author has in examining the Supralapsarian doctrines. It is much, when his hand was in, that he did not take under his examination some other doctrines handled in the *letter* he refers to; such as God's seeing no sin in his people, the non-necessity of good works to salvation, mortification, and the like; which he might as well have forced into the Supralapsarian scheme, as some others. He has indeed a fling or two at the doctrine of repentance, seems greatly concerned [l] that legal repentance is not to be valued and regarded, and thinks that this reflects upon the preaching of *John* the Baptist, Christ, and his apostles; whereas it was an evangelical repentance, and fruits meet for the same, which were preached up by them. He concludes [m], that the repentance which I allow sinners may be exhorted to, stands more remote from the power of the creature than legal repentance; as though I thought sinners were to be exhorted to it, as within the compass of their own power: whereas my express words are, "To exhort even to evan- "gelical repentance, as within the compass of the power of man's will, and as "a condition of the covenant of grace, and a term of acceptance with God; "and in order to make peace with God, and gain the divine favour, which is "the rant of some mens ministry; I say, to exhort to repentance with such "views, and on such considerations as these, is low and mean stuff; too mean

Vol. II.   P   for,

[k] Supralapsarian Scheme, p. 131.    [l] Ibid. p. 133, 134.    [m] Page 137.

"for, below and unworthy of a minister of the gospel." One vile reflection upon the doctrine of forgiveness of sins, through the blood of Christ, I cannot omit taking notice of, when he says [a], "I am ready to believe that God, in in- "finite wisdom, does require it (legal repentance) as *necessary to forgiveness*, in "all capable beings." What! is not the blood of Christ, which was shed for the remission of sin, sufficient to procure it, without legal repentance being necessary to it? I observe this author is very fond of this way of preaching, and is very desirous that others would engage in it. Was I thought worthy, or capable of giving advice, my advice to him would be not only to preach repentance towards God upon the gospel-scheme, but faith in our Lord Jesus Christ; only I should be afraid the man will put *unbelief for faith*. I should advise him to content himself in making use of what talents he has in preaching the word, and not scribble in the manner he does: But if he must needs be an author, let him write upon *moral* subjects, against the prevailing *vices* of the age, open profaneness, and impiety, things he may be better acquainted with, than evangelical truths, or Supralapsarian principles.

[a] Page 136.

# AN ANSWER

TO THE

BIRMINGHAM DIALOGUE WRITER,

Upon the following SUBJECTS:

| THE DIVINITY OF CHRIST, | IRRESISTIBLE GRACE, |
| ELECTION, | IMPUTED RIGHTEOUSNESS, |
| ORIGINAL SIN, | PERSEVERANCE, AND |
| FREE-WILL, | BAPTISM. |

HAVING lately met with a pamphlet, intitled, *A Dialogue between a Baptist and a* Churchman, *occasioned by the Baptists opening a new Meeting-house for reviving old Calvinistical doctrines, and spreading Antinomian, and other errors, at* Birmingham *in* Warwickshire, Part I. *by a* Consistent Christian; I prevailed upon myself to give it a reading, and make some remarks upon it. The author of it has thought fit to write in a *dialogue*-way, probably for this reason, that he might have the opportunity of making the *Baptist* speak what he pleases, and what he thought he was best able to reply to: So far he has acted wisely, that he has not made him say such things, he was conscious to himself, he was not able to answer. However, this must be acknowledged, that though he has represented the *Baptist* in the debate as a very weak man; yet, as very mild, calm, and good-natured, and by far a better christian, and of a more christian spirit and temper than himself; who, notwithstanding all his pretences to a calm and charitable religion, casts *firebrands, arrows, and death* [a]; reproaching, in a very mean and scandalous manner, both men and doctrines that are not agreeable to his own sentiments. One would think his Baptist never attended upon, at least, must not have received any ill impression, from the wild, furious, and uncharitable preachers at *Birmingham*; or else that the preachers that come there are not such persons this writer would have them thought to be.

I observe,

[a] Prov. xxvi. 18.

I observe, that in his running title in page 3. he calls his *dialogue*, *A Dialogue between a new Baptist and a Churchman*; what he means by a *new Baptist*, I am pretty much at a loss to know, since the Baptist, in this dispute, does not appear to have entertained any different notions about Baptism than what the Baptists have always held, nor any other doctrines but what the greater part of the Baptist churches have always asserted, as is manifest from their printed confessions of faith, published many years ago. Perhaps he calls him so, because he is one that has been lately baptized, or because the Baptists have opened a *new* Meeting-house at *Birmingham*; which, it seems, is the occasion of our author's writing this *dialogue*; at which he is very uneasy, and with the preachers that come thither; it being opened, as he says, for reviving *old Calvinistical* doctrines; by which, if any judgment is to be made by the dialogue, he means the doctrines of Christ's Divinity, Election, Original Sin, Efficacious Grace, Imputed Righteousness, and the Saints Perseverance; doctrines which our first reformers from Popery set out with, and the reformed churches embraced; and which also the established church of *England*, of which this writer would be thought to be a member, in her *Articles* maintains; doctrines which no church, community, or set of men under any denomination, have reason to be ashamed of; and it is the glory of the *Particular Baptists*, and, what is greatly to their honour, that they are so zealously affected to those truths, and to the utmost of their abilities defend them, in an age, when there are so many apostates from the faith once delivered to the saints. But, it seems, this new meeting at *Birmingham* is opened also for spreading Antinomian, and other errors; what those Antinomian, and other errors are, he does not tell us. He cannot mean the above doctrines, since they are distinguished from them, and besides were never reckoned Antinomian ones; perhaps we shall hear of them in the *next part*, for at present we are only entertained with the *first part* of this mighty work, consisting of *forty-four pages*. We are to have a *second part*, and I know not whether a *third*, *fourth*, and *fifth*, or how many more. If this writer goes on at this rate, we may expect proposals for printing by subscription *The Works of the Consistent Christian, in Folio*. This puts me in mind of what I formerly have seen, *The History of Tom Thumb, in Folio*, with Dr *Wagstaff*'s notes upon it.

Our author stiles himself *a Consistent Christian*; for my own part, I cannot help being so uncharitable (if it must be reckoned so) as to call in question his Christianity; I take him to be a *Heathen*, and not a *Christian*, much less a *consistent* one; since he gives strong intimation of his belief of a supreme and subordinate Deity, a superior God, and an inferior one; and both as the objects of religious worship. He says [b] that God the Father is *the supreme and most high*

---
[b] Dialogue p. 11.

*high* God, and that Jesus Christ the Son of God is *not* so; but yet he is *a God*, and such an one as all men are commanded to worship; and, in consequence, there must be two different Gods, two distinct Deities, the one superior, the other inferior, which are to be worshipped; and if we may worship two Gods, we may worship two hundred: and if this is not heathenism, and downright idolatry, I know not what is. But let him be admitted a *Christian*, if it can be, is he a *consistent* one? No; does the mild, calm and gentle spirit of christianity appear in him? His *dialogue* is a standing proof against it. Are his notions consistent with the doctrines of christianity? This is easily determined; for if there are any doctrines peculiar to christianity, they are those he militates against. Is he consistent with his character as a *churchman*? Far from it, he contradicts and opposes the Articles of the Church of *England*; he is no true son of the church, but a degenerate plant, and ought to be rejected as such: though I am informed, it is greatly suspected that he is a *Presbyterian* preacher; and if so, he has shewn much insincerity and unfaithfulness, things not consistent with a Christian, by taking upon him the name of a *Churchman*, and talking of *our Church* and *you Dissenters*[c]: But be he what he will, a Churchman or a Dissenter, to me he appears to be a *Posture* or *Dancing-master*; he sets up for a judge of gesture and action; he can tell you what motion is proper or is not for the pulpit or the stage, and no doubt elsewhere. The gestures of the *Baptist* preachers at *Birmingham*, it seems, are not agreeable; they do not behave *secundum artem*; he represents them as very ridiculous and antic. One would imagine, from his account of them, that they have got into the way of the *Quakers*; yea, that their preachers are women preachers, nay, even that the old *Sybils*, *Pythonesses*, and *Dæmon Prophetesses* of the Heathens, were risen out of their graves, and were come to *Birmingham*, and there playing their old pranks. How easy is it for persons to put others in an odd and aukward dress, and then laugh at them?

But, to leave him possessed of his *little* diversions, I proceed to consider what is more serious, and ought to be treated with more regard and decency than this author has thought fit to shew, namely, the doctrines which these preachers assert, and he opposes. But before he brings them into the debate, he is pleased to give us his sense of *Orthodoxy*, and to explain some passages of scripture, which by the help of his *Concordance* he has collected together, where the word *sound* is used, as applied to *doctrine*, *speech* and *faith*. As to orthodoxy, I can assure this writer, that the Baptists do not make any confession, catechism, articles, or any writings of men, as he suggests[d], the standard of it, but the Bible only; and though soundness of doctrine and uprightness of conversation ought

to

[c] Dialogue, p. 16.     [d] Ibid. p. 7.

to go together, and the former has a tendency to promote the latter, yet they are two different things, which this author seems to confound; nor will the text in *Psalm* cxi. 10. prove them to be the same: *a good understanding have all they that do his commandments.* Doing the commandments of God according to his will, from a principle of love and gratitude, with a view to his glory, and without any dependence upon what is done for salvation, is indeed a proof of a man's having a good understanding of the will of God, of the way of salvation by Christ, and of the doctrine of grace, which teaches men to *deny ungodliness and worldly lusts,* and to *live soberly, righteously and godly in this present world.* But then, doctrine and practice, knowledge and obedience, are distinct things; and it is possible for a man to have a considerable share of speculative knowledge of gospel-truths, and yet not live uprightly in his life and conversation; and, on the other hand, to perform acts of morality as to outward appearance, and to be externally upright, sincere and good, and have no good understanding of the truths and doctrines of the gospel.

The passages of scripture cited [e] out of the epistles of the apostle *Paul* to *Timothy* and *Titus,* which speak of *sound doctrine, speech and faith,* are to be understood of such doctrinal truths as are to be found in and gathered out of the word of God, which have a tendency to influence and promote, and, when attended with the Spirit of God, do really and powerfully influence and promote practical religion; but then they are distinct from that practical religion which they serve. *Sound doctrine,* in 1 *Tim.* i. 10. is the same with *the glorious gospel of the blessed God,* which, though it no ways countenances, but is as contrary to whoring and lewdness, lying and stealing, malice and murder, as the law which is made for and lies against such as commit these things; yet it is distinct from the law which forbids these things, and condemns persons that are guilty of them. *A sound mind,* or rather *the spirit of a sound mind,* in 2 *Tim.* i. 7. is such a mind or spirit, that he who is possessed of it, is *not ashamed of the testimony of our Lord,* ver. 8. and particularly of that glorious part of it, *ver.* 9. where our salvation and vocation of God are said to be *not according to our works, but according to his own purpose and grace, which was given us in Christ Jesus before the world began.* The *form of sound words,* in ver. 13. is distinct from *faith and love,* and the exercise of these graces, in which it was either heard, or to be held fast. It does not, indeed, mean the *Assemblies Catechism,* nor any *Church Articles,* nor any words which man's wisdom teacheth; yet the *Articles* of the Church of *England* and the *Assemblies Catechism,* so far as they agree with the words of scripture, the words which the Holy-Ghost hath taught, ought each of them to be esteemed a form of sound words, and to be abode by against all opposition; though this author rudely suggests, that they are what *man's folly* have taught;

when,

[e] *Dialogue,* p. 8, 9.

when, it is well known they were both of them drawn up by men of great learning and judgment, gravity and piety. A fine *Churchman*, or a pretty *Presbyterian* parson this! *Sound doctrine*, in 2 *Tim.* iv. 3. is *the word* of the gospel, which the apostle exhorts *Timothy* to preach constantly, *ver.* 2. the same with *the truth*, and stands opposed to *fables*, ver. 4. by the constant preaching of which, watching in it, and abiding by it, *Timothy* would *do the work of an evangelist, and make full proof of his ministry*, ver. 5. *Sound doctrine*, in *Titus* i. 9. is *the faithful word* of salvation alone by Christ and his righteousness, which is to be *held fast* in spite of all *gainsayers, unruly and vain talkers*, such as our author declares himself to be. To be *sound in the faith*, ver. 13. is opposed to giving heed to *Jewish fables and commandments of men*, ver. 14. to infidelity, and a mind and conscience defiled with bad principles, *ver.* 15. which it is no wonder should be attended with bad practices, notwithstanding their profession of knowing God when they have no regard to the Lord Jesus Christ, *ver.* 16. *Sound doctrine*, in *Titus* ii. 1. is distinct from the practice of virtue and morality, and the rules thereof, given to both sexes, to young and old, in the following verses: these are not the sound doctrine itself, but *the things which become* it, as this author might have learnt from the text itself. To be *sound in faith*, ver. 2. is firmly to believe the doctrine of faith; to be *sound in charity*, is to love the Lord, his people, truths and ordinances, with all the heart and soul; and to be *sound in patience*, is chearfully and constantly to bear whatever we are called to suffer for Christ's sake and his gospel. *Sound speech*, ver. 9. is the doctrine of grace delivered in the wholesom words of our Lord Jesus, without corrupting the word of God; speaking it with all faithfulness, integrity and sincerity, as in the sight of God. Upon the whole, it is easy to observe that the contexts of these several texts do not countenance the exposition this writer has given of them. I shall now attend to what he has to object to those doctrines which he undertakes to oppose and refute; as,

I. The doctrine of Christ's deity and equality with the Father. In his debate on this subject, I observe the following things:

1. That he holds *f* that Jesus Christ is *a God*, but not *the most high God*. The reason why he believes him to be *a God*, is, because the Father has given him divine perfections, universal dominion or headship, authority to judge, and has commanded all men to worship him; but he thinks he cannot be the most high God, because there is but one most high God, who is the God and Father of Christ; for both to be so, appears to him a contradiction, and he cannot believe two contradictory propositions; and besides Christ, before he became man,

came

*f* Dialogue, p. 11.

came from the Father, was sent and employed by him, he observes; which would be a thought absurd and blasphemous, and to be abhorred, if he was the supreme God. To all which I reply; if the Father has given to Christ divine perfections, for which reason he is God, or a God; he has either given him only some divine perfections, or all divine perfections; if he has only given him some divine perfections, then he is imperfectly God, or an imperfect one; if he has given him all divine perfections, then he must be equal to him; and, indeed, *all that the Father hath are* his ᵍ; not by his gift, or as arising from and depending upon his will and pleasure, but by necessity of nature, as being his own and only begotten Son. Universal dominion, or headship and authority to judge, are indeed given to him, not as the Son of God, but as the Son of man. Again; if the Father only is the most high God, and Christ is a God, that is, a God inferior to him, whom he has commanded all men to worship; then there are two distinct Gods, objects of religious worship, directly contrary to the express words of the first command, *Thou shalt have no other Gods before me* ʰ. Moreover, if the most High over all the earth is He whose name alone is *Jehovah*, and Christ's name is *Jehovah*; if the same things which prove the Father to be the most high God, are said of the Son, as they are, why may he not be thought to be the most high God equally with the Father? To say, indeed, that there are two supreme or most high Gods would be a contradiction; or to say that the Father is one most high God, and the Son is another most high God, would be two contradictory propositions. But who says so? We say, that Father, Son and Spirit are the one most high God; and to say and believe this, is not to say and believe two contradictory propositions, for there is but one proposition, and no contradiction in it. Once more; though Christ, before his incarnation, came from and was sent by the Father as the angel of his presence, to redeem *Israel* out of *Egypt*, to lead them through the Red sea and wilderness into *Canaan*'s land, yet this no ways contradicts his proper deity and equality with the Father; for though he agreed to be sent, as an equal may by agreement be sent by another, and which may be thought and said of the divine persons in the Godhead, without absurdity and blasphemy; and though he condescended to take upon him an office for the good of the people of *Israel*; yet he appeared with full proof of proper deity, of his equality with the Father, from whom he came, and of his being with him the one most high God; for he calls himself *the God of Abraham, the God of Isaac, and the God of Jacob*, Exod. iii. 6. and I AM THAT I AM, ver. 14. and Jehovah says of him, that his *name* was *in him*, chap. xxiii. 21. and intimates that he could, though he would not, pardon iniquity, which none can do but the most high God.

2. I

ᵍ John xvi. 15.      ʰ Exod. xx 3.

2. I observe, that he seems to be aware that the passage of scripture, *Phil.* ii. 6. where it is said, that Christ *being in the form of God, thought it not robbery to be equal with God*, stands in his way, since it expresly asserts Christ's equality with God; and therefore he attempts to remove it, by saying [l], that that translation, he thinks, is given up by most learned men, because it corresponds not to the *original Greek*. Who those learned men are that have given it up he does not tell us, nor point out in what it does not correspond to the *original Greek*. Arians and Socinians have quarrelled with it, but learned Trinitarians have stiffly defended it: however, this *dialogue-writer* [k] "thinks it must be wrong,"

(1.) Because it no way suits the context, which speaks of "the same person "in the same image or likeness of God, as obedient to God and exalted by him." But what this author observes, is a reason why it should be right, and not wrong; for if Christ was *in the form of God*, εν μορφη Θεου, in the essential form of God, for no other can be intended; if he existed in the nature and essence of God, was arrayed with the same glory and majesty, and possessed of the same perfections, he must be equal to him; nor could it be thought by Christ, nor should it by any other, a robbery, to assert his equality with him; for, as to be in *the form of a servant*, is to be really and truly a servant; to be *in the likeness of a man*, and to be *in fashion as a man*, is to be really and truly man; so to be in *the form of God*, is to be really and truly God: and if Christ is really and truly God, he is equal with the Father. And whereas in the context he is represented as *obedient unto death*, not unto God, as this author inadvertently expresseth it, and exalted by God; these things are evidently said of him as man, and express both his humiliation and exaltation in the human nature; and no ways contradict his equality with the Father in the divine nature.

(2.) Another reason why this translation is thought to be wrong, is, "because "it is contradictory to the reason God has given us, as our highest guide, to "conceive that the Son, who was begotten by the Father, came from him, "has his life, power, dominion, glory, as a gift and reward from him, should "be equal to him." I take no farther notice of this man's great encomium of reason, than just to observe, that whatever guide reason is to us in things natural and civil, it is a very poor one in religious affairs, in things which concern our spiritual and eternal welfare, being so wretchedly corrupted by sin: however, one would think, in matters of revelation, the revelation itself, the scriptures of truth, should be a higher guide to us than reason, especially the Spirit of God, who in them is promised to *guide us into all truth*. But what contradiction is it even to reason, to conceive that the Son, begotten by the Father, should be equal to him? Was such a thing never known in nature, that a Son was equal to

[l] Dialogue, p. 11.  [k] Ibid. p. 12.

to a Father? And why should it be thought contradictory to reason, that *the only begotten Son of God, who is the brightness of his Father's glory, the express image of his person, in whom the fulness of the Godhead dwells,* should be equal to God? His coming from God, and having his life, power, dominion and glory from him, as a gift and reward, and all those scriptures which speak of them as such, are to be understood of him in his office-capacity and relation, as he is man and mediator; and not of him as a divine person, as God over all, blessed for ever; who, as such, does not derive his being, life and glory from another, but equally enjoys them with his Father, without derivation.

(3.) A *third* reason given is, " because it is a sense contrary to all those plain " texts which speak of Christ as the express image of the Father, as commissioned " by him, as doing his will, *&c*." I reply, that this sense is not at all contrary to those scriptures which speak of Christ as the image of God, but perfectly accords with them; since Christ is the essential image of God, and as such partakes of the same nature, essence, perfections and glory with his Father, and therefore must be equal to him. As for those scriptures which speak of him as commissioned by the Father, doing his will, seeking his glory, praying to him for his original glory; and, as appointed by him universal head and judge, these are to be understood of him as Man and Mediator, and so are no contradiction to his equality with God in the divine nature. This writer sets himself, with all his might, against this great truth of the Son's equality with the Father; but is it to be wondered at, when he even postpones Jesus Christ to the apostles *Peter* and *Paul*, and that more than once in this *dialogue*? Speaking of the fruits of the Spirit: " they are, says he¹, such as we find in the life and sermons of " St *Paul* and of his master Jesus Christ." And in another place ᵐ, " the Jews " did so, that is, set up their judgment against their teachers, in following *Peter* " and *Paul*, and Jesus Christ."

3. Whereas it is observed to him what Christ says, *John* x. 30. *I and the Father are one:* he replies ⁿ, " would you have Christ contradict himself in the " same breath, by saying, we two persons are one person, one Being, one God? " The easy, natural and just sense, he says, is, that he and the Father were " one, as he did the Father's will and acted by commission from him, and pur- " sued the same end and design; and not to be understood of his unity of essence, " for he cannot think that a begotten and an unbegotten essence are the same." To which I answer, that though there are two persons spoken of in this ⁿ text as being in some sense one, *I*, as one Person, *and* MY FATHER as another Person; yet we do not say that the meaning is, that these two Persons are one Person, this would be a contradiction; but that these two Persons are of one and the

same

¹ Dialogue, p. 6, 7.   ᵐ Ibid. p. 16.   ⁿ Ibid. p. 12, 13.

same nature, which is no contradiction. This writer thinks, that to understand the words of unity of will, or rather of doing the Father's will, best suits the context; whereas Christ, in the context, is speaking not of unity of will, but of sameness of operation, and of his having the same power the Father has, to keep his sheep from perishing, which he proves from their being ONE; and from whence should sameness of power arise, but from sameness of nature? Nor is the essence of the Son begotten, and the essence of the Father, as distinct from that of the Son, unbegotten, none ever thought or said so, that I know of. The Father, as a divine Person, begets; the Son, as a divine Person, is begotten in the divine nature and essence; but that nature or essence is not begotten, but in both the same. This man calls himself a *Churchman*; did he pay any regard, as he does none, to the *Articles* of the *Established Church*, he might observe this doctrine, he is militating against, fully expressed in them: in the *first Article* are these words, " in unity of this Godhead there be three Persons *of one substance*,

power and eternity, the Father, the Son, and the Holy Ghost." The beginning of the *second Article* runs thus: " the Son, which is the word of the Father, " begotten from everlasting of the Father, the very and eternal God, *of one sub-* " *stance with the Father*, took man's nature in the womb of the blessed virgin, " of her substance."

4. This writer seems ᵒ very desirous, that " persons, under a notion of speak- " ing honourably of the Son, would be careful of eclipsing the glory of the " Father, and of dishonouring him, by setting up a rival with him in supreme " empire, and of affronting and displeasing the Son, by belying him, as the " Jews did, when they said he made himself equal with God." But what danger can there be of lessening or sullying the Father's glory by asserting the Son's equality with the Father? Nothing is taken from the Father and given to the Son; the same things are said of the one as of the other; the same nature, perfections and glory are ascribed to the one as to the other; nor need we fear affronting and displeasing either the Father or the Son, by giving equal honour to them; since as the Son has *thought it not robbery to be equal with God* ᵖ, God has declared it is his will, *that all men should honour the Son as they honour the Father* ᵍ; which is done by asserting that they are of one and the same essence, substance and eternity; and are what may be understood by the words *co-essential, con-substantial, co-eternal*: though this writer calls them great swelling words, hard and unintelligible names ʳ. That the Jews *belied* Christ, when they said he made himself equal with God, does not appear; our Lord never charged them with belying him, nor did he go about to convince them of a lie or a mistake;

ᵒ Dialogue, p. 13.    ᵖ Phil. ii. 6.
ᵍ John v. 23.    ʳ Dialogue, p. 14.

mistake; but afterwards said those things which were enough to confirm them, and any one else, in the truth of his equality with the Father.

5. This man laughs, as those of his complection generally do, at mysteries in religion, and at this doctrine being a mystery, though revealed, and as being above, though not contrary, to reason: he says [1], that " if any doctrine was a " mystery before, revealing it has made it no longer a mystery." It is true, that when a thing is revealed, it is no longer a mystery *that it is*, but may still remain a mystery *how it is, what it is*: as in the case before us, it is no longer a mystery, now revealed, that the three persons, Father, Son and Spirit, are one God; but *how* they are so, is still a mystery. The incarnation of Christ, God manifest in the flesh, is not a thing hidden from us, being revealed; but *how* the word was made flesh, will ever continue a mystery to us. It is no longer a mystery, that the living will be changed at Christ's second coming; but *how* they will be changed, is a mystery to us. So the resurrection from the dead is a certain part of revelation; nevertheless, it is mysterious to us *how* it will be brought about; and our ideas of rising from the dead, and living again, must be greatly short of the things themselves: though this author says [2], he " very " well understands what rising from the dead and living again means, as well " as he does rising from sleep and living again." I suppose he would have said, being awake again, means; for I hope he does not think that men are dead when asleep, and come to life again when they rise out of it. These doctrines instanced in are above our reason, and seem as contrary to our ideas of things, and the dictates of reason, as what we have been considering may be thought to be. I go on,

II. To consider what he has to say to the doctrine of eternal Election, though he chiefly militates against that of Reprobation. Our author's harangue upon this head is mere plagiarism, being stolen out of Dr *Whitby upon the Five Points*, as any one may easily observe, by comparing it with the *second chapter* of his *first discourse* concerning *Election* and *Reprobation*, and many other passages in that performance; and since I have lately considered the arguments and reasonings of that writer, I might at once dismiss this subject, by referring the reader to the answer I have already given; but as that may not be in the hands of every one to whom this may come. I choose to take some notice of what is here advanced. The sum of the charge against this doctrine is, that " it is " unmerciful, unjust, insincere, and uncomfortable."

1. It is charged with cruelty and unmercifulness; God is said to be [3], according to this doctrine, " a most cruel Being, and more hard-hearted than *Pharaoh*;"
but

---

[1] Dialogue, p. 15.  [2] Ibid. p. 15.  [3] Ibid. p. 19, 20.

but I hope it carries no mark of cruelty and unmercifulness in it to the elect, who are *vessels of mercy afore prepared unto glory*: it can only be thought to do so to the rest, for whom God has ordained no help; and to raise the idea of cruelty towards them, they are represented * under the lovely characters of God's offspring, his creatures, and his children; but not a word said of their rebellions, sins and transgressions, or of their being " the children of wrath, the chil-
" dren of hell, and the children of the Devil;" and to increase this idea, they are considered ˣ as in distress and misery, in a perishing condition, through some misfortune, and not upon the account of any sin or iniquity they have been guilty of. With the same view their number is taken notice of; " the human
" race is said to be *infinite*, and *help* decreed only for a very few; whilst God
" has resolved *not* to help millions of undone creatures, and to torment them
" millions of years and ages, for what they could not help; and this only to
" shew what his power and wrath can do, or from *pure ill nature*." But supposing God had decreed help for *none* of the *infinite* race of his fallen offspring, as this author calls them, but had determined to leave them *all*, being fallen to the perversity of their hearts and ways, and to punish them for their sins and transgressions committed against his righteous law; would this have been deemed cruelty and unmercifulness? Has he not proceeded in such a manner with the whole body of the apostate angels, those millions of undone perishing creatures, whom he has resolved not to help, and who are equally his offspring, his creatures, and his children, as the fallen race of *Adam*, so considered? And is this ever esteemed *cruelty*, and *pure ill nature*? Now if it was not acting the cruel and unmerciful part, not to ordain help for any of the fallen angels, it would not have been acting such a part, had God resolved not to help any of the fallen race of *Adam*; and if it would not have been an act of cruelty to have determined not to help *any* of the race of mankind, surely it can be no act of cruelty or unmercifulness to ordain help for *some* of them, when he could in justice have condemned all. The doctrine of Election is no unmerciful one, yea, it is more merciful than the contrary scheme, since it infallibly secures the salvation of *some*; whereas the other does not ascertain the salvation of *any* single person, but leaves it uncertain, to the precarious and fickle will of man.

2. This doctrine is charged ʸ with *injustice*, and God is represented as " a most
" unrighteous Being; since, according to it, he threatens a severer damnation,
" if men accept not his offer, which he knows they cannot accept; has decreed
" to damn millions of men for being fallen in *Adam*; a decree, it is said ᶻ,
" which *none but a Devil* could make; and a thousand times more unjust than
" the decree of *Pharaoh* to drown all the male children, because they were born
" of

* Dialogue, p. 17.   ˣ Ibid. p. 18—20.   ʸ Ibid. p. 19.   ᶻ Ibid. p. 22.

"of *Israelitish* parents, or were born males; and also has decreed to damn men "for not believing in a Christ who never died for them, and for not being con- "verted, when he has decreed not to convert them." To all which I reply, that God's act of election does no injustice either to the elect or non-elect; not to the elect, to whom it secures both grace and glory; nor to the non-elect, or to the rest who are left out of it: for as God condemns no man but for sin, so he has decreed to condemn no man but for sin. And where is the unrighteous- ness of such a decree? It would have been no unrighteousness in God to have con- demned all mankind for sin, and would have been none in him, if he had decreed to condemn them all for sin. If therefore it would have been no injustice in him to have decreed to condemn all mankind for sin, it can be none in him to decree to condemn some of them for sin, when he could have decreed to have condemned them all. Herein he shews both his clemency and his justice; his clemency to some, his justice to others. As to the things particularly instanced in, I answer, that when this author points out any offers of help in a saving way God has made to all mankind, or to any to whom he has decreed no saving help, and then threatens them with a severer damnation for non-acceptance of them, I shall attend to the charge of unrighteousness. That *all men sinned in Adam*, and that by his *offence judgment came upon all men to condemnation*, the scriptures declare [a]; and therefore to say that God condemns men, or has de- creed to condemn them for the offence of *Adam*, or for their sinning in him, and being fallen with him in his first transgression, cannot be disagreeable to them; though we do not say that any of the sons of *Adam*, who live to riper years, are condemned only for the sin of *Adam*, but for their numerous actual sins and transgressions. And as for infants dying in infancy, their case is a secret to us; yet inasmuch as they come into the world *children of wrath*, should they go out as such, would there be any unrighteousness in God? Again; as God will not condemn the heathens, who never heard of Christ, for not believing in him, but for their sins against the law and light of nature; nor such as have heard of him, for not believing that he died for them, nor for not being con- verted, but for their transgressions of God's law; of which condemnation, their disbelief and contempt of Christ and his gospel will be an aggravation, of which they had the opportunity of being informed: so we do not say that God has de- creed to condemn or damn men for the things mentioned by this writer.

3. The doctrine of God's chusing some, and leaving others, is charged [b] with insincerity, and with representing God as "the most *deceitful* and insincere *Being*; "yea, as *the greatest of all cheats*, when he offers to sinners a salvation never pur- "chased for them, and which he has absolutely decreed never to give them; "and when he offers it upon conditions they cannot comply with, without irre- "sistible

[a] Rom. v. 12, 18. [b] Dialogue, p. 19, 22, 23.

" fiftible grace, and he has decreed never to give them that grace; and when
" he threatens a heavier damnation if they do not believe and obey the gofpel,
" which he knows they cannot do." To which I anfwer, that falvation is not
offered at all by God, upon any condition whatfoever, to any of the fons of men,
no, not to the elect: they are *chofen* to it, Chrift has procured it for them, the
gofpel publifhes and reveals it, and the Spirit of God applies it to them; much
lefs to the non-elect, or to all mankind; and confequently this doctrine, or God
according to it, is not chargeable with *delufion* and *infult*. When this author
goes about to prove any fuch offers, I fhall attend to them; and if he can prove
them, I own, I muft be obliged to think again.

4. This doctrine is reprefented [c] as " very *uncomfortable*, becaufe it leaves
" the reft of thefe children, and millions of his creatures, in helplefs mifery for
" ever; and makes it a hundred to one to a man that he is not elected, but
" muft be for ever damned." But when it is confidered that thofe children are
rebellious ones, and thofe creatures vile and wicked, who are thus left, it can
give no unlovely and horrid image of God to fuch who know that he is *righteous in all his ways, and holy in all his works* [d]. Should it be faid, that *fuch* are
alfo the men that are chofen; it is very true, and therefore they admire and
adore electing grace, and receive abundance of fpiritual comfort from it: nor
is it fuch a chance matter or uncertain thing to a man, as a hundred to one,
whether he is elected or no, to whom *the gofpel* is *come not in word only, but alfo
in power, and in the holy Ghoft*; who from hence may truly know and be comfortably affured of his *election of God* [e]. What true and folid comfort can arife
from the univerfal fcheme, or from God's univerfal love? When notwithftanding that, and redemption by Chrift, and the general offers of mercy, yea, grace
itfelf beftowed, a man may be loft and damned.

One would think, that fince this writer takes upon him the name of a *Churchman*, he might have been more fparing of, and lefs fevere in, his reflections
upon this doctrine, feeing it is fo exprefsly and in fuch ftrong terms afferted in
the feventeenth *Article* of the *Church of England*, and there reprefented as a very
*comfortable* doctrine. The Article runs thus: " Predeftination to life is the
" everlafting purpofe of God, whereby (before the foundations of the world
" were laid) he hath conftantly decreed, by his counfel, fecret to us, to deliver
" from curfe and damnation thofe whom he hath chofen in Chrift out of man-
" kind, and to bring them by Chrift to everlafting falvation, as veffels made
" to honour. Wherefore they which be endued with fo excellent a benefit of
" God, be called according to God's purpofe, by his Spirit working in due
" feafon; they through grace obey the calling; they be juftified freely; they
" be made fons of God by adoption; they be made like the image of his only
" begotten.

[c] Dialogue, p. 22, 23.    [d] Pfalm cxlv. 17.    [e] 1 Theff. i. 4, 5.

" begotten Son Jesus Christ; they walk religiously in good works; and at
" length, by God's mercy, they attain to everlasting felicity." And then it is
afterwards observed, that " the godly consideration of predestination, and our
" election in Christ, is full of sweet, pleasant and unspeakable *comfort* to godly
" persons, and such as feel in themselves the working of the Spirit of Christ,
" mortifying the works of the flesh, and their earthly members, and drawing
" up their minds to high and heavenly things; as well because it doth greatly
" establish and confirm their faith of eternal salvation to be enjoyed through
" Christ, as because it doth fervently kindle their love towards God."

5. Before I quit this subject, I would just remark the sense this author gives of several texts, which plainly assert a predestination and election, in the epistles of *Paul* and *Peter*; by which, I suppose, are meant, *Rom.* viii. 29, 30. and ix. 11, 23. and xi. 5—7. *Ephes.* i. 4, 5. 2 *Thess.* ii. 13. 1 *Pet.* i. 2. The sense of them, according to his reading and judgment, and according to others, whom he esteems the best writers and preachers, is this[f]; " Those texts, says he,
" are to be understood of God's first electing and adopting the seed of *Abra-*
" *ham*; and then, upon their crucifying the Son of God, and rejecting his
" gospel, God's choosing, electing or adopting all the spiritual seed of *Abraham*,
" though amongst the Gentiles; all virtuous and good men, all who believed
" the gospel; and this agreeable to his ancient designs, before he laid the foun-
" dation of the Jewish ages." But these passages of scripture have not one word, one syllable, one jot nor tittle in them of God's electing and adopting the seed of *Abraham*, the natural seed of *Abraham*, or the Jewish nation, as such; but of some persons only from among that nation, and from among the Gentiles; and that not upon the Jews' crucifying Christ, and rejecting his gospel, or before the foundation of the Jewish ages were laid; but before the foundation of the world, from the beginning, even from eternity: and though all the spiritual seed of *Abraham*, whether among Jews or Gentiles, all good men, all who believe in Christ, are elected; yet they were not elected as such, or because they were so, but that they might be so; for such who are chosen in Christ, are chosen, not because they *were*, or *are*, but that they *should be*, holy, and without blame before God in love.

III. The doctrine of original sin, and the concern which the posterity of *Adam* have in it, is greatly found fault with; it is not, indeed, separately and distinctly considered, but dragged into the debate about Election and Reprobation. And,

1. The *Baptist*, in this *Dialogue*, is made to say[g], that men lost their ability to repent, to believe and obey the gospel in *Adam*, and by and at the fall; upon which,

[f] Dialogue, p. 26, 27.   [g] Ibid. p. 24.

which, this writer makes this wife fuppofition : "I fuppofe the women loft it "in *Eve*, and the men in *Adam*." This little piece of drollery Dr *Whitby* [b] has fuggefted to him, from whom he has *borrowed*, or rather *ftolen*, a great many of his beautiful and mafterly ftrokes in this performance. *Adam*, in his ftate of innocence, had a power of doing what is truly good and righteous; but by finning, loft it. God made him upright, but he finned, and loft the uprightnefs, the rectitude of his nature; and this lofs is fuftained by all his pofterity: for *there is none righteous, no not one; there is none that underftandeth, there is none that feeketh after God; they are all gone out of the way, they are together become unprofitable, there is none that doeth good, no not one* [i]. This man owns [k], that " we fuffer lofs through *Adam*'s fall, and have an hereditary difeafe con- " veyed to us which worketh death;" which hereditary difeafe cannot be any one particular corporal difeafe, becaufe no fuch difeafe is hereditary to all mankind, or conveyed to every individual of human nature. No difeafe but the difeafe of fin is hereditary, and conveyed to *Adam*'s whole pofterity, and this worketh death; *the wages of fin is death*, not only corporal, but eternal; as the antithefis in the following words declares, *but the gift of God is eternal life through Jefus Chrift our Lord* [l].

2. This writer thinks [m], "God is not at all angry with us for what *Adam* did, " nor that it is juft to condemn his pofterity for what was done by him fo long " ago." To which I anfwer, that all men are *by nature children of wrath* [n], that is, deferving of the wrath and difpleafure of God, becaufe they bring a corrupt nature into the world with them, derived from *Adam*, and conveyed unto them by natural generation; they are *fhapen in iniquity and conceived in fin* [o], and as fuch, muft be difpleafing to God; *whatfoever is born of the flefh is flefh* [p]; that is, is carnal and corrupt; and whatfoever is fo, cannot be agreeable to God: and fince this is the confequence of *Adam*'s tranfgreffion, why may not God be thought to be angry and difpleafed with men on that account, and even punifh them for it, fince he threatens to *vifit the iniquities of the fathers upon the children* [q] ? It is true, indeed, that in general that rule holds good, that *the fon fhall not bear the iniquity of the father* [r]; though this is not without exceptions to it, and only holds in fuch cafes in which children have no concern with their parents; whereas the pofterity of *Adam* were not only concerned with him as their natural, but as their federal and reprefentative head; they ftood in him, and fell with him in his tranfgreffion. The apoftle exprefsly fays, that *in him all have finned*; and gives this as a reafon why *death hath paffed upon all men* [s].

Befides,

[h] Difcourfe of Election, p. 79. Ed. 2. 78.    [i] Rom. iii. 10—12.    [k] Dialogue, p. 24.
[l] Rom. vi. 23.    [m] Dialogue p. 24.    [n] Ephes. ii. 3.    [o] Pfalm li. 5.
[p] John iii. 6.    [q] Exod. xx. 5.    [r] Ezek. xviii. 20.    [s] Rom. v. 12.

Besides, he further observes[t], that *by the offence of one, judgment came upon all men to condemnation*. The plain and obvious meaning of which is, that all men are condemned through the offence of the first man, being made sinners by his sin: which is expresly asserted by the apostle, when he says[u], *by the disobedience of one many were made sinners*. But, says our author[w], "that St *Paul*, by *sinners*, "means *sufferers*, is plain, not only from reason, for no other sense can be true, "but from his own explication, *in Adam all die*." This sense he has learned from Dr *Whitby*[x]; but does not pretend to give us one instance in which this word is ever so used. Αμαρτωλοι always signifies persons criminal, guilty of a fault, and frequently such who are notoriously so. The sense he gives is contrary to the apostle's design in the context, to the distinction he all along makes between sin and death, the one being the cause, the other the effect; and is to be disproved by the following part of the text, *by the obedience of one shall many be made righteous*: where *the obedience* of Christ is opposed to *Adam's disobedience, righteous* to *sinners*; and a being *made righteous* by the one, to a being *made sinners* by the other. Now, by the rule of opposition, as to be *made righteous* by Christ's *obedience*, is to be constituted and accounted so for the sake of his obedience; so to be made *sinners* by *Adam's* disobedience, is to be constituted and reckoned so on the account of it: and, after all, how is it reconcileable with the justice of God, that men should die in *Adam*, suffer for his disobedience, if they are in no sense guilty of it, or chargeable with it? But,

3. The imputation of *Adam's* sin, the ground of which is the covenant God made with him as a federal head, is represented[y] as "an absurd and unrighteous "scheme of divinity; and what men must quit their understandings, and give "up all the principles of reason, truth and justice, to give into." But where is the absurdity or injustice of God's setting up *Adam* as a federal head to all his posterity, to stand or fall together, who were all naturally in his loins, as *Levi* was in the loins of *Abraham*? Had we been in being, had we been admitted principals, given out our own orders, and made our own choice, could we have made a better choice than God did for us? And since, had he stood, we should have enjoyed the advantages arising from his standing, why should we think it any hardship or injustice done us, that we share in the consequences of his fall? Was it never known, even among men, that posterity unborn have been obliged by covenants, which could not be made by their order, of which they could have no knowledge, and to which they gave no consent? Nay, have not children been involved in the crimes of parents, and been subject to penalties, and have endured them on the account of them, as in the case of treason? And have such procedures been reckoned absurd and unrighteous?

4. This

---

[t] Rom. v. 18.  [u] Verse 19.  [w] Dialogue, p. 25.
[x] Discourse of Election, p. 85. Ed. 2. 84.  [y] Dialogue, p. 25.

4. This author seems to have no other notion of original sin, but as it is an approbation or imitation of *Adam*'s transgression; " if we approve of, says he ᶻ, " and imitate *Adam*'s transgression, we may be punished for such approbation " and imitation, but not for his transgression:" which was the vain opinion of the *P*elagians, condemned by that church, to which he would be thought to belong, in her ninth Article, and in which she represents original sin as deserv. of God's wrath and damnation: it begins thus, " Original Sin standeth not in " the following of *Adam*, (as the Pelagians do vainly talk) but it is the fault " and corruption of the nature of every man that naturally is engendered of " the offspring of *Adam*, whereby man is very far gone from original righte- " ousness, and is, of his own nature, inclined to evil; so that the flesh lusteth " always contrary to the spirit; and therefore in every person born into this " world it deserveth God's wrath and damnation "

IV. The doctrine of man's free-will, and the irresistible grace of God in conversion, is next considered. And under this head our author,

1. Most bitterly exclaims ᵃ against the preachers of free grace, and affirms, that they are the greatest enemies to it in the world, upon their scheme of predestination, particular redemption, and the ministry of the gospel; and asks if this and that, and the other thing, are grace in God, some of which are suppositions of his own, and were never articles of our faith. And pray let me ask this writer, upon the foot of the universal scheme, " what grace is that in God, " to decree to save all men conditionally, to send his Son to redeem all man- " kind; and yet to millions, even to whole nations, and that for many hundred " years together, never so much as to afford the means of grace, the means of " knowing the way of salvation and redemption by Christ; and to multitudes, " who enjoy the outward ministry of the word, he does not vouchsafe his spirit " to convince of sin, righteousness, and judgment, or to make application of " salvation, but leaves them to go on in sin, and at last eternally damns them?" Whereas, according to the particular scheme, God chooses some peremptorily to eternal salvation, sends his Son to obtain eternal redemption for them, calls them effectually by his grace, and at last brings them safe to eternal glory; in doing which, are shewn forth the exceeding riches of his grace, in his kindness towards them.

2. He next proceeds to state the notion of free-will, which he himself gives into: " If, says he ᵇ, by *free-will*, you mean a faculty or power in man to turn " his thoughts to this subject or another, to do good or ill actions, to choose " the way of life or death, when both are set before him, to receive or reject

" the

ᶻ Dialogue, p. 24.   ᵃ Ibid. p. 28.   ᵇ Ibid. p. 29, 30.

"the offers of Chrift, when fairly made; I cannot but think every man hath "this fort of *free-will*." And further obferves <sup>c</sup>, that fuch who "declaim "againſt *free agency*, act upon this principle as much as other men—exhort "and perfuade to religion and good works, and act and live upon the prin- "ciple of *free agency*, while in words they deny it." I hope, then, fuch perfons are not Antinomians; and yet this poor inconfiftent man, though he ſtiles himſelf a *confiftent Chriftian*, immediately obferves: "Thus do Antinomian "notions in divinity turn mens heads, and quite intoxicate their brains." We own, that there is a power of free-will in man to perform the natural and civil actions of life, yea, the external parts of religion, but not any thing that is fpiritually good; fuch as to convert and regenerate himſelf, to believe in Chriſt, and repent of fin in an evangelic manner. God made man at firſt upright, with a power to do that which is truly good, and under no co-active neceffity of finning; his prefent cafe is not owing to his original make, but to his fin and fall. Men in an unregenerate ſtate, are only free to do evil, without a power to do good; which is no felf-contradiction; as appears from the cafe of the devils, who have no power to do good, are wholly bent upon evil, and yet do it freely. This freedom, indeed, is no other than fervitude; men are overcome by fin, are brought into bondage through it, and are flaves unto it. This may be thought, indeed, contrary to the notion of man's prefent ſtate, being a ſtate of *trial*, and to fome mens way of preaching; but does not contradict man's obligation to duty, nor overthrow the doctrine of a future judgment. Regenerate perfons are free to do that which is good; but this freedom they have not naturally, but from the grace of God, by which they are made a *willing people in the day* of its *power* upon them. No man is or can be truly converted unto God, but by his powerful, efficacious and irrefiftible grace. But,

3. To fay a man cannot turn to God without his almighty and irrefiftible grace, is reprefented <sup>e</sup> as making the gofpel not only an ufelefs, but a deceitful inftitution. This muft be denied; it is not hereby made a deceitful one, fince that fully and clearly holds forth and expreffes this truth, that no man can come to Chriſt except the Father draw him; nor is it made an ufelefs one, feeing it is *the power of God unto falvation* to many fouls, agreeable to this doctrine. But if no man can come to God or Chriſt unlefs irrefiftible grace draw him, it is urged <sup>d</sup>, that "then he cannot help turning, then there can be no fault in not "turning, and no virtue in turning to God." This argument, as well as fome others, is borrowed from Dr *Whitby* <sup>e</sup>. And to it I anfwer, that not to turn to
God,

<sup>c</sup> Dialogue, p. 31.     <sup>d</sup> Ibid.     <sup>e</sup> Ibid.
<sup>f</sup> Difcourfe of Election, p. 260, 261. Ed. 2. 252.

God, or to be in an unconverted state, is to be in a sinful one, and to live in sin is blameworthy: and though man, by sinning, has involved himself in a state out of which he cannot extricate himself; yet is he not the less culpable on that score for living in it, though none will be punished for not being elected or converted, but as sinners. And when a man is turned or converted to God, this is, indeed, no natural virtue in him; nor is it to be ascribed to any such virtue; but all the praise and glory of it are to be given to the powerful and efficacious grace of God, who will follow his own work of grace with glory, and not to the free-will of man; for, as it is expressed in the *tenth* Article of the *Church of England*, which I would recommend to the perusal and consideration of our *Churchman*; " The condition of man, after the fall of *Adam*, is such, that he can-
" not turn and prepare himself, by his own natural strength and good works,
" to faith and calling upon God: wherefore we have no power to do good works
" pleasant and acceptable to God, without the grace of God by Christ prevent-
" ing us; that we may have a good-will, and working with us when we have
" that good-will."

4. This man observes [f], that " men resist the holy Ghost, and when God would " heal them, will not be healed, nor come to Christ for Life." I reply, men may indeed resist the holy Ghost, as the Jews did, *Acts* vii. 51; which is what I suppose is referred to: but this is to be understood of resisting the holy Ghost in the external ministry of the word, of the Jews contempt, rejection and persecution of the prophets and apostles; as appears from the following words, and not of a resisting the internal operations of his grace; though we do not deny that these may be resisted, yet not so, as to be overcome, frustrated and brought to nothing: this is our sense of irresistible grace. As for God's willingness to heal persons when they would not be healed, I know no such expression in scripture, especially as referring to spiritual healing; it is said in *Jer.* li. 9. *We would have healed Babylon, but she is not healed*. But this designs not the willingness of God, but of the Jews, or some other people to heal her. This mistake Dr *Whitby* [g] is guilty of: It is not always safe to follow him. It is true, indeed, the Jews *would not* come to Christ for life, which is an argument not *for*, but *against* free-will; and shews the weakness, wickedness and obstinacy of the will of man.

V. Another doctrine militated against by this *Dialogue*-writer, is, that of the insufficiency of man's righteousness to justify him before God, and the imputation of the righteousness of Christ for that purpose. And,

1. He

---

[f] Dialogue, p. 32.    [g] Discourse of Election, p. 204, 477. Ed. 2. 199, 457.

1. He allows [h], that the false deceitful outside and ceremonial righteousness of the scribes and Pharisees, of Jewish and Christian hypocrites, — may well enough be compared to *filthy rags*; but not the righteousness of the saints. But pray, who were the persons that acknowledged their righteousness to be *as filthy rags* in *Isai* lxiv. 6. the only place of scripture where this phrase is used? Were these scribes or Pharisees, Jewish or Christian hypocrites, who made such an ingenuous and hearty confession of the pollution both of their nature and actions? No, they were the church of God, a set of godly persons in *Isaiah*'s time, whose minds were impressed with a sense of the awfulness of the divine Majesty, and of their own vileness and unworthiness; they were men truly humbled before God, in a view of the impurity of their nature, the imperfection of their services, and their coldness and backwardness to things divine and spiritual; as the context manifestly shews. Can it be thought that such words as these should be spoken by hypocrites, *we are all as an unclean thing?* How strong and full is the following expression? *And all our righteousnesses are as filthy rags:* not only some part of our obedience, but all our performances, even the best of them, every thing done by us, that can come under the name of righteousness, are so, being attended with so much sin and imperfection. What righteousness was that which the apostle *Paul* renounced, *Phil.* iii. 9. and desired not to be found in? Says [i] this man, his Jewish righteousness, or conformity to the ceremonial law; but this he had renounced before, in *ver.* 4—7. and then adds, *ver.* 8. *Yea, doubtless, I count all things but loss for the excellency of the knowledge of Christ Jesus my Lord.* Now, by *all things*, he must mean something else, over and above, and besides what he had before renounced, and which at least, in part, he explains of his *own righteousness, which is of the law*, his moral righteousness; yea, all the obedience he had been enabled, by the grace of God, to perform, since his conversion; for to understand it of his ceremonial righteousness, is to make him guilty of a very great tautology.

2. The *imputed righteousness of Christ*, this author says [k], is a phrase no where to be found in God's book, nor is it easy to be understood; wherefore he calls it unscriptural and unintelligible doctrine. Imputed righteousness is a phrase neither unscriptural nor unintelligible, nor is the imputed righteousness of Christ so. *David* describes *the blessedness of the man to whom God imputeth righteousness without works* [l]. Now what righteousness is that which is imputed without works? not a man's own righteousness, that cannot possibly be imputed without works; it must be the righteousness of Christ, which is imputed without the works of men being joined unto it to make it perfect. Again: *Abraham believed God, and it was imputed to him for righteousness* [m]. Not *Abraham*'s own faith, or faithful

[h] Dialogue, p. 33.    [i] Ibid.    [k] Ibid. p. 34, 35.    [l] Rom iv. 6.
[m] Verse 3.

ful obedience, as says [a] this man; but the object of his faith, the righteousness of the *Messiah*, in whom he believed; for that which was imputed to *Abraham*, was not imputed to him only, but to others, even to believers under the gospel dispensation. *Now it was not written*, says the apostle, *for his sake alone, that it was imputed to him; but for us also, to whom it shall be imputed, if we believe on him that raised up Jesus our Lord from the dead* [o]. So Christ is *made unto us righteousness* [p], by the imputation of it, not to himself, but to us; nor is the meaning, as this author [q] would have it, that the doctrine, example, life and death of Christ, are the means of making men righteous; but he himself *is made unto them righteousness*, and they are *made the righteousness of God in him*, through the imputation of his righteousness to them, as he is *made sin for them*, through the imputation of their sins to him [r]. Add to all this, that in the same way that we are *made sinners by the disobedience of one*, which is by the imputation of his disobedience to us, are we *made righteous by the obedience of one*, of Christ, namely, by the imputation of his obedience or righteousness to us [s].

3. This writer suggests [t], that the " doctrine of Justification, by the imputed " righteousness of Christ, is a poisonous doctrine; and asserts it to be an encou- " ragement to bad men and loose women to go on in sin, and a discouragement " to good men to perform duty." To which I need only say, with the apostle [u], *Do we make void the law through faith?* that is, by the doctrine of justification by faith in the righteousness of Christ, which is the doctrine he was speaking of? *God forbid! yea, we establish the law.* Nothing can lay men and women under a greater obligation to *live soberly, righteously and godly*, or has a greater ten-dency to make them *careful to maintain good works*, than this doctrine of grace, or the consideration of this, that *being justified by grace*, they *are made heirs according to the hope of eternal life* [w]. In this, as in other doctrines, our author shews himself to be no true *Churchman*; and, for the future, ought to drop that character. The doctrine of Justification is thus expressed in the *eleventh Article* of the *Church of England:* " We are accounted righteous before God only for the merit " of our Lord and Saviour Jesus Christ by faith, and not for our own works or " deservings; wherefore, that we are justified by faith only, is a most wholesom " doctrine, and very full of comfort; as more largely is expressed in the *Homily* of " *Justification*." Nor did the compilers of this Article reckon this doctrine a licentious one, or a discouragement to *good works*, as appears by the Article concerning them, which follows upon this.

VI. The

[a] Dialogue, p. 35.  [o] Rom. iv. 23, 24.  [p] 1 Cor. i. 30.
[q] Dialogue, p. 35.  [r] 2 Cor. v. 21.  [s] Rom. v. 19.  [t] Dialogue, p. 34, 35.
[u] Rom. iii. 31.  [w] Tit. ii. 11, 12. and iii. 7, 8.

VI. The doctrine of *Perseverance* is next introduced into the *dialogue*; and the writer of it,

1. Hopes " that every truly good man will persevere in his goodness; but " cannot say it is impossible for a righteous man to turn from his righteousness, " or for one *that has tasted the heavenly gift, and has partook of the holy Ghost, to* " *to fall away*; else, what need of so many cautions given to persons and " churches: besides, *David* and *Peter* did apostatize and fall away as well as " *Judas*ˢ." To which I answer; it is well this author has entertained any hope of a truly good man's persevering in his goodness; but why not believe it? since it is promised, that *the righteous shall hold on his way, and he that hath clean hands shall be stronger and stronger*ʸ. The apostle *Paul* was *confident of this very thing*, and so may we, that *he which hath begun a good work in* the saints, *will perform it until the day of Christ*ᶻ. A righteous man, one that is only so before men, and in his own apprehensions, who trusts to and depends upon his own righteousness for justification before God, such an one as is described in the xviiiᵗʰ and xxxiiiᵈ chapters of *Ezekiel*; such a righteous man, I say, may indeed turn from his own legal righteousness to an open course of sin, and die and perish eternally. But this is no proof of a truly righteous man, one that is made so by the obedience of Christ, who has a principle of grace wrought in him, in consequence of which, he lives *soberly, righteously and godly*, turning from his righteousness, and falling into sin, so as to be lost for ever. For, should this be, how could the righteousness by which he is justified be called an *everlasting* one, as it is in *Dan.* ix. 24 ? Nor could it be said, with truth, that *whom God justified, them he also glorified,* Rom. viii. 30. So, a man who has only a taste, a superficial knowledge of the *heavenly gift*, and has partook of the holy Ghost, either of the ordinary or extraordinary gifts of the Spirit, may fall away, so as not to be renewed again to repentance; but this is no instance of a man's falling away, who has truly eat the flesh and drank the blood of Christ by faith, and has been made a partaker of the special and internal grace of the Spirit of God. The cautions given to persons and churches to *watch and pray, lest they enter into temptation, to hold fast, to continue in well doing, &c.* are not arguments against, but means which the Spirit of God makes use of to secure the perseverance of the saints. Besides, though true believers cannot fall from grace totally and finally; yet inasmuch as they may fall so as to wound their own consciences, stumble others, and dishonour the name of God, there is room and reason for such cautions. Though *David* and *Peter* fell, yet not as *Judas* did, which is suggested; otherwise, why are they put together? *Judas* fell from a profession of Christ, and from his apostleship,

but

---

ˢ Dialogue, p. 36.    ʸ Job xvii. 9.    ᶻ Phil. i. 6.

but not from the grace of God, which he never had. *David* and *Peter* fell into great sins, but not totally and finally; there was a principle of true grace still in them, which was revived and excited by the Spirit of God, whereby they were enabled to turn from their iniquity, and do that which was right. " But, says this man [a], as it was possible for them to fall into sin, *mortal sin*; so it was possible for them to have died in the sin they had sinned, and how they would have fared in that case, he leaves us to judge." One would be tempted to conclude from this passage, that our *Churchman* is rather a member of the church of *Rome*, than of the church of *England*; since he seems to give into the popish distinction of sin, into *mortal* and *venial*, otherwise, why should he be so careful to explain sin, by *mortal* sin? Is not every sin mortal, that is to say, deserving of death? And though it was possible for *David* and *Peter* to fall into mortal sins, sins deserving of death, as they did; yet it was not possible they should die in them, since it is the will of God that none of his beloved ones, as *David* and *Peter* were, *should perish, but should come to repentance*; and since Christ undertook to die for their sins, and their sins were actually pardoned for Christ's sake.

2. Under this head, is brought in the doctrine of God's *seeing no sin in his people*, as he looks upon them through Christ, and as clothed with his righteousness; which is represented as "a doctrine immoral and absurd, unworthy of " God, and shocking to a pious mind [b]." But why should it be thought to be so, when it is expressly asserted in the sacred writings? *He hath not beheld iniquity in Jacob, neither hath he seen perverseness in Israel* [c]. With respect to the attribute of God's omniscience, it is freely allowed, that God sees all persons and things just as they are; he sees the sins of *David* and *Peter*, and he sees the sins of all professors of religion, even of his own people; and, in a providential way resents them, and chastises them for them, though he does not impute them to them, or punish them for them. But with respect to the article of Justification by Christ's righteousness, and pardon by his blood, God sees no sin in his people; their sins are covered from the sight of justice, they are all discharged, forgiven, blotted out, and done away; so that *when they are sought for, there shall be none, and they shall not be found* [d]. Now, as this doctrine does not impeach the omniscience of God, and perfectly accords with his justice, which is satisfied by the blood and righteousness of Christ, it cannot be absurd and unworthy of God; and since it leaves room for, and supposes God's resentment of sin in his people, and his chastisement for it, it cannot be an immoral one, or shocking to a pious mind.

3. The

[a] Dialogue, p. 36, 37.    [b] Ibid. p. 37.
[c] Numb. xxiii. 21.    [d] Jer. l. 20.

3. The absolute and unconditional promises of the covenant, mentioned in *Jer.* xxxi. 32, 33. and *Ezek.* xxxvi. 26. are produced in favour of the saints perseverance; whereas they belong to the doctrine of efficacious grace in conversion, and under that head should have been placed and considered: but this author is pleased to make his *Baptist* say any thing which he thinks fit, that he may make him appear weak and ridiculous, and himself a match for him. Of this conduct, his whole *Dialogue* is a proof. The prophetic texts usually brought in favour of the final perseverance of the saints, are, *Isai.* liv. 10. and chap. lix. 21. *Jer.* xxxii. 38—40. *Hos.* ii. 19. which this writer was either ignorant of, or perhaps did not care to mention them, nor meddle with them, as furnishing out arguments in proof of this doctrine beyond his capacity to reply to.

VII. The last thing considered in this debate is, the ordinance of *Baptism*; and it would have been writing out of character, indeed, to have attacked a *Baptist*, and not have meddled with his denomination principle. And,

1. I observe, "that the controversy about the time and mode of baptism, appears to him of no great moment; seeing baptism itself is an outward ordinance, or a mere ceremony, though of Christ's institution: nor is it mentioned in the commission given to St *Paul*, who was the apostle of the Gentiles[e]." But pray, were not all the apostles sent to the Gentiles, *into all the world, to teach all nations?* And was not the ordinance of baptism in the commission given to them all? What, though baptism is an outward ordinance; yet, since it is of Christ's institution, it must be of considerable moment to know and be satisfied, who are the proper subjects of it, and in what manner it should be performed. An ordinance of Christ should not be treated as an indifferent thing, to whom, or how it is administered; or whether it is attended to or not.

2. This man has many wise reasonings upon the mode of baptism: "I allow, says he[f], that if baptism with water be *efficacious*, and does operate to the purifying of the conscience, and cleansing of the heart, then the *more water the better*" I do not transcribe the sentence that follows, to avoid defiling of paper with the indecency of his expressions, since they add no force to his argument: would he be concluded by his own reasoning, he, and the rest of the *Pædobaptists*, ought to be the last that should drop the practice of immersion; for who are they that say that baptism is efficacious to internal purposes? Not the *Baptists*, who insist upon persons making a profession, and giving proof of their repentance towards God, and faith in Christ; of their being regenerated, and having their hearts and consciences cleansed and purified by faith in the blood of Christ, before they are admitted to this ordinance: But those

who

[e] Dialogue, p. 41.  [f] Ibid.

who say, that "by baptism original sin is taken away, persons are regenerated, "made members of Christ, and inheritors of the kingdom of heaven;" who behave as though they thought there could be no salvation without baptism; when, upon the least indisposition of a new-born infant, they are in a hurry to fetch the minister to sprinkle it; these, according to this man's reasonings, and his own principles, ought to plunge it. He goes on: "but if baptism "be only *declarative* and *significative*, then a handful of water, poured or sprin- "kled on the face (the chief part of the body, and the seat of the soul) may an- "swer this purpose as well, if a serious profession of christianity go along with "it, as well as sprinkling the whole congregation of *Israel*, Exod. xxiv." Here our author entertains us with considerable hints: not the heart, as some; nor the brain, as others; nor the *glandula pinealis*, but the face is the seat of the soul. He does not, indeed, tell us what part of the face; but leaves us to conclude it must be the forehead, since there the sign of the cross is made in baptism: but be it so, that the face is the chief part of the body, and the seat of the soul; and that baptism is declarative and significative, as it is of the suf- ferings, death, burial and resurrection of Christ, see *Rom.* vi. 3—5. *Coloss.* ii. 12. Not sprinkling or pouring a handful of water upon the face, but immersion or covering the whole body in water, only can be declarative and significative of these things; and therefore the former cannot as well answer the purposes of baptism as the latter. But, says this man, "it may do as well as sprinkling "the whole congregation of *Israel*." Very right, provided it was done by the same authority, and for a like end; but then, this is no instance of a *part* being put for the *whole*, or of the *sign* put for the *thing* signified. This our author, upon a review of his work when printed off, saw; and therefore, in his *table of the errors of the press*, one big enough for a *folio* volume, and which might have been still made larger, he has corrected this passage; and would have it read thus, "as well as sprinkling the twelve pillars, served instead of sprink- "ling the whole congregation of *Israel*." But how does it appear, that not the people, but the twelve pillars, were sprinkled instead of them? not one syllable is said of sprinkling the pillars in *Exod.* xxiv. only the people; for it is expressly said, that *Moses took the blood and sprinkled it on the people*; and the au- thor of the epistle to the *Hebrews* confirms it, by saying, *that he sprinkled both the book and all the people* ‡. However, if sprinkling water on the face in bap- tism will not do as well as this, it will "as well, says this writer, as eating one "morsel of bread and tasting wine may signify and declare a person's faith in "the death, and the second coming of Christ, to as good purpose, as eating a "meal or drinking a full cup in remembrance of him." I answer, the case is

‡ Heb. ix. 19.

not parallel, for baptism does not merely signify and declare a person's faith in the sufferings, death, burial and resurrection of Christ, but the things themselves; and therefore, though eating a morsel of bread and tasting the wine may, in the Lord's Supper, answer the purpose of that ordinance, as well as a full meal or cup; yet sprinkling or pouring water on the face in baptism will not answer the end of that ordinance, as well as immersion or covering the body in water. After all, a clogging clause is put into this argument, which is, that this may do as well, "if a serious profession of christianity go along with it." And of the same kind is the following paragraph, "if there be the answer of a good conscience, " or a sincere profession of christianity, and a hearty resolution to serve Christ, " which is the *moral*, or spiritual part of baptism, I do not think our Lord and " Master will be so scrupulous as some of his disciples are about the mode." But where is *the answer of a good conscience*, or a sincere profession of christianity, or a hearty resolution to serve Christ, in infants, for that of others for them can be of no avail, when water is sprinkled or poured upon their faces? We are obliged to this man, that he will vouchsafe to own us to be the disciples of Christ, we desire to be followers of him in every ordinance, and in this; the mode of which he has taught us, without any scruple, by his own example. Our author goes on, and observes, that "if the washing the principal part, instead of the " whole, be a more safe way for health, and a more decent way upon the rules " of chastity, I think it the better way; and that there is room to apply that sacred proverb, which our Lord applied on another occasion, *God will have* " *mercy, not sacrifice*; for he always prefers *morals* to *rituals*." This is the old rant, that has been answered over and over; and must be despised and treated as mere calumny, by all that know the safety and healthfulness of cold bathing, which now generally obtains; or have seen with what decency this ordinance is performed by us. He adds, " If St *Paul* made so little account of the external " part of baptism, 1 *Cor.* i. 13—17. what would he have said to a controversy " about the mode of using it?" It seems from hence, that baptism has an internal part as well as an external one; though before it is called an *outward ordinance*, and a *mere ceremony*. But what was the little account the apostle *Paul* made of it? Though he was not sent *only* or *chiefly* and principally to baptize, but to preach the gospel; and he thanks God, that he had baptized no more of the Corinthians, since they made such an ill use of it: yet it does not appear, that he at any time, or in any respect, made light or little account of it; since no sooner had he any intimation of it, as his duty, but he submitted to it; as did *Lydia* and the Jailor, with their housholds, and many of the Corinthians, if not as administered by him, yet by his order, and with his knowledge and consent; and, was he now on the spot, would soon put an end to the controversy
about

about the mode of it, could he be attended to, though I fear he would be little regarded by persons of this man's complexion; for since so little regard is had to his doctrines, there would be very little shewn to his sense, either of the mode or subjects of an ordinance.

3. The *time* of baptism is next considered, which, with this writer, is but another word for *the subjects* of it; for we have no controversy about the precise time of baptism, the question with us, is not whether an infant is to be baptized as soon as born, or at eight days, or when a month old; but whether it is to be baptized at all or no; nor whether adult persons are to be baptized at thirty years of age, or whether at *Whitsuntide*, or any other time of the year; but whether believers, and such that profess themselves, and are judged to be so, and they *only*, are to be baptized. This author says, that " it is certainly " very proper that parents devote their children to God; which they may do " by prayer, without baptizing, for which they have no warrant; and that they " enter them as infant-disciples in the school of Christ, in order to become his " actual scholars as soon as capable" But this is beginning wrong, and perverting the order which Christ has fixed, that persons should first be taught and made disciples, and then baptized; and not first baptized, and then made disciples. He asks, " Is it not as proper that this be done by the visible ceremony " of baptism, as for the Jewish children to be entered into their church by cir- " cumcision?" He ought first to prove, that Jewish children were entered into their church by circumcision; and then that it is the will of God, or appointment of Christ, that infants should be entered into the christian church by baptism; and that baptism succeeds circumcision, and for such a purpose; neither of which can ever be made good. He further asks, " If parents make a " profession of the christian faith at the baptism of their children, and also " enter into public engagements to give them a christian education, are not " *as good ends*, as to practical religion, answered by the baptism of christians " children, as by the baptism of adult persons?" I answer, that parents may do these things if they please, without baptizing their infants; nor were these ever designed as ends to be answered by baptism in any; a profession of faith should be made by the party baptized, and that before baptism. After a little harangue upon the virtue of washing the body with water, intimating, that this cannot make a person one jot holier, or secure from sin in future life, which no body ever affirmed, he owns, that " penitent confession of sin, profession of " faith in Christ, and engagement to a new life, were the conditions of baptism " to all Jews and Gentiles;" which, as we believe they are, we desire to have them continued so; for this we contend.

This Dialogue is concluded with some distinctions about *zeal*, and some censures upon the *Particular Baptists*, and their preachers, for their blind, bodily,
immodest

immodest and uncharitable zeal; which, if guilty of, this man is a very improper person to be a rebuker, since he has shewn so much intemperate heat against men, whom he himself owns to be the disciples of Christ; and against doctrines held by all the reformed churches. I wish he may appear of another spirit in his *second part*, which he has given us reason to expect.

I would fain persuade this author, to leave this pamphleteering way of writing, and appear undisguised. He seems to be fond of engaging in a controversy with the *Baptists* upon the above points, which require a larger compass duly to consider, than he has taken. I am a *Baptist*, he may call me, if he pleases, a *new Baptist*, or an *old Calvinistical* one, or an *Antinomian*; it is a very trifle to me, by what name I go. I have published a *treatise* upon the doctrine of the *Trinity*, another upon the doctrine of *Justification* by the imputed righteousness of Christ; and lately *three volumes* against the *Arminians*, and particularly Dr *Whitby*; in which are considered the arguments, both from scripture and reason, on both sides of the question; and am now preparing a *fourth*, in which the sense of the christian writers before *Austin* will be given upon the points in debate: if this Gentleman thinks it worth his while to attend to any, or all of them, and enter into a sober controversy on these subjects, I shall readily join him; and, in the mean time, bid him farewel, till his *second part* is made public.

# AN ANSWER

TO THE

BIRMINGHAM Dialogue-Writer's Second Part,

Upon the following Subjects:

| | |
|---|---|
| The Divinity of CHRIST, | Free-Will, |
| Election, | Imputed Righteousness, |
| Original Sin, | Perseverance, and |
| Free-Grace, | Baptism. |

THE *Birmingham* Dialogue-writer has, at length, thought fit to publish the *second part* of his Dialogue between a *Baptist* and a *Churchman.* Never was such a medley of things, such a parcel of rambling stuff, collected together; he is resolved to be voluminous at any rate: If he thus proceeds, we may indeed expect to see the works of the *Consistent Christian* in *folio.* I could wish he had answered to his *motto* in the *title-page*, taken from an *apocryphal* writer [a], *Blessed is the man that doth meditate honest* (good) *things by* (in) *his wisdom, and that reasoneth of holy things by his understanding;* for the things he has meditated are neither *good*, nor *honest*, nor *holy*; unless things contrary to the divine perfections, to the honour and dignity of Christ, and the doctrine of the inspired writings; unless to misrepresent an argument, which he frequently does, and misquote an author, as he has Mr *Millar* [b] particularly, can be thought to be so. I shall not disturb him in his vain mirth, but let him have his laugh out, at the theatrical behaviour, as he calls it, and gestures of preachers, and at mysteries in religion; only let him take care, lest he should find by experience the truth of that saying of the wise man, *As the crackling of thorns under a pot, so is the laughter of the fool: this also is vanity* [c]. A man of no faith, or whose faith is worse than none, or good for nothing, may go on to despise Creeds, Catechisms, Confessions and Articles of Faith: the Right of private Judgment will not be disputed; both ministers

---

[a] Eccles. xiv. 20.  [b] Page 65, 101.  [c] Eccles. vii. 6.

ministers and people have undoubtedly a liberty of speaking and writing what they believe to be truth, provided they do not abuse this liberty to the dishonour of God, the gratification of their own passions, and the injury of their neighbours.

What I shall attend unto, will be the following things; the Divinity of Christ, Election, Original Sin, Free-will, and Free grace, Imputed Righteousness, Perseverance, and Baptism; things that were the subjects of the *former part*, and are now brought on the carpet again, and re-considered in this. I begin,

I. With the Deity of Christ. This writer very wrongly distinguishes between *true, real,* and *proper* Deity, and *absolutely supreme* Deity; as if there could be true, real, and proper Deity, and yet that not be absolutely supreme; whereas Deity is either fictitious or true, nominal or real, proper or metaphorical. There are many who are called gods, that are not really so; there are such who by nature are no gods, fictitious deities, the idols of the heathens; and there are such who are so only in an improper sense, as civil magistrates: Now none of these are truly, really and properly gods; there is but one that is truly, really and properly God, and who is the only absolutely supreme God, Father, Son, and Spirit. To say, there are more gods than one, who are really, truly, and properly so, is to introduce the *Polytheism* of the Gentiles. To assert that the Father is the absolutely supreme God; that the Son is truly, really, and properly God, but not the absolutely supreme God; and that the holy Spirit is also really, truly, and properly God, but not the absolutely supreme God; is to assert one absolutely supreme God, and two subordinate Gods, who yet are truly really, and properly so. The arguments for and against the supreme Deity of Christ, and his equality with the Father, are as follow.

1. This writer having asserted in his *first part* [c], that Christ is God, or a God, because the Father hath *given* him divine perfections, the following argument was formed in answer to it: "If the Father has given to Christ divine perfections, "for which reason he is God, or a God, he has either given him only some "divine perfections, or all divine perfections; if he has only given him some "divine perfections, then he is imperfectly God, or an imperfect one; if he "has given him all divine perfections, then he must be equal to him [d]." Now this was *argumentum ad hominem*, an argument formed on his own principles, and not mine, as any one who has the least share of common sense and understanding will easily observe; and yet this man, either ignorantly or wilfully represents it as an argument proceeding upon my own principles; whereas it is he, and not I, that says, the Father has *given* to Christ divine perfections. I affirm, that all the Father hath are his; he possesses and enjoys all divine perfections,

[c] Page 11.  [d] Answer, p. 13, 14.

fections, *not by gift*, but in right, and by necessity of nature: that no divine perfection is given him as the Son of God; though all power, dominion, and authority to judge, are given him as the son of man. Hence the absurdity of communicating any thing to the self-existent supreme God, and the self-contradiction of necessity and gift, are impertinently alledged, and the argument, as formed on his own principles, stands unanswered; which has brought him into a dilemma, out of which he knows not how to extricate himself: For if the Father has *given* him divine perfections, it must be either some, or all; if only some, then the *fulness of the godhead* does not dwell in him, nor can he be truly, really, and properly God; if all, and so no perfection of Deity is wanting in him, then he must be equal to the Father.

2. Another argument against the subordinate Deity of Christ, and in favour of his equality with the Father, is this: " If the Father only is the most high " God, and Christ is *a God*, that is, a God inferior to him, whom he has com- " manded all men to worship; then there are two distinct Gods, objects of religi- " ous worship; directly contrary to the express words of the first command, *Thou* " *shalt have no other gods before me*[e]." This is an argument reducing to a manifest absurdity, and the Dialogue-writer's replies to it shew him to be in the utmost distress; he is confounded, and knows not what to say. *First*, he says [f], that " if there be any absurdity, any contradiction here to the first command, " it falls not directly on *him*, but on Christ and his gospel, from whence he " borrowed these truths." But does Christ in his gospel ever teach, that the Father is the most high God, or even the only true God, distinct from, and exclusive of the Son; and that the Son of God is *a God*, inferior and subordinate to the Father? Next, he observes [g], that the first command speaks of one person only to be worshipped as God supreme, and not of more persons than one. Be it so. Since then, according to this man's principles, Christ is a God inferior and subordinate to the most high God, he must be a distinct person from him, and consequently stands excluded from divine worship by the first command; wherefore the gospel-doctrine of worshipping the Son, cannot be taken in consistency with that: and, on the other hand, if Christ, a subordinate God, is one person with the supreme God, this would destroy his subordination, and give him supremacy, contrary to this author's notions. If this will not do, he goes on and tells [h] you, " You may suppose that God himself, in commanding men " to honour his Son, has repealed so much of the first command as is inconsistent " with the New-Testament-command to honour or worship his Son." This is cutting the *Gordian* knot indeed! This man, I suppose, would not care to be called an Antinomian; and yet the grossest Antinomian that ever lived upon

Vol. II.　　　　　　　　T　　　　　　　　　the

[e] Answer, p. 14.　　[f] Dialogue-writer, Part II. p. 28.　　[g] Page 29.　　[h] Ibid.

the face of the earth, never ventured upon what this man does, namely, to assert, or suppose, that any law, or part of a law, relating to the object of religious worship, was ever repealed or abrogated. *Lastly*, He adds [i], "that in *the ho-nour* paid to Jesus Christ, God the Father is ultimately honoured, as *this is paid to the glory* of God the Father." Now not to take notice of the blunder, the nonsense of this passage, in talking of *honour* being *paid to glory*; if the Father is ultimately honoured by that same honour which is given to the Son, as to himself, then I hope "the charge of robbing God the Father of his peerless majesty, or of ungodding him [k]," by asserting the Son's equality to him, is weak and groundless.

3. A *third* argument, proving Christ to be the most high God, stands [l] thus: "If the Most High over all the earth is he whose name alone is *Jehovah*, and Christ's name is *Jehovah*; if the same things which prove the Father to be the most high God, are said of the Son, as they are; why may he not be thought to be the most high God equally with the Father?" To which is replied, that [m] when the Son personates *Jehovah*, he may be called *Jehovah*, as an angel that sometimes speaks in the person of God; it being usual for such as deliver messages from others, to speak after the same manner those persons would have done, in whose name they come: So that no argument can thence be drawn for his supreme Deity; since that name is given to an angel, when speaking in *Jehovah*'s name. But it should be observed, that it cannot be proved that ever any created angel, speaking in the name of God, ever calls himself *Jehovah*, or is so called; all the places referred to by this writer, where an angel is called *Jehovah*, are to be understood of the uncreated angel, the Son of God, as will clearly appear at first sight, to any who will take the pains to inspect them. The passages are *Gen.* xviii. 13. and xix. 24. and xxii. 15, 16. *Exod.* xxiii. 20, 21. *Isai.* lxiii. 9. *Mal.* iii. 1. All which are so many firm and standing proofs of the truth of the observation, that Christ is called *Jehovah*; a name peculiar to the most high God, *Psal.* lxxxiii. 18. and therefore must conclude his supreme Deity, and the argument for it from hence, stands unshaken and unanswered. It may be usual with messengers to speak after the manner of the persons in whose name they come; but do they ever call themselves by their names? or are they ever so called by others? Did ever any ambassador of the king of *Great Britain*, when sent to a foreign court with an ambassy, stile himself the king of *Great Britain*? or call himself by the name of king *George*? or was he ever so called by others?

The doctrine, "that Father, Son, and Spirit, are the one most high God, is charged [n] with being a contradiction to reason, to the whole Bible; to be "a

---
[i] Dialogue-writer, Part II. p. 29.    [k] Page 43.    [l] Answer, p. 14.
[m] Dialogue, Part II. p. 29, 30.    [n] Ibid. p. 30, 31.

"a self-contradiction; yea, to have many contradictions in it." To which I answer: Though reason, unassisted by revelation, tells us there is but one self-existent, intelligent Creator and Ruler of the universe, the Bible makes a clearer and further discovery of this matter, and acquaints us that more than one person were concerned in creation and government. *Let us make man*, Gen. i. 26. *Let us go down and confound their language*, Gen. xi. 7. *Remember thy creators*, Eccles. xii. 1. *Thy makers are thy husbands*, Isai. liv. 5. Revelation speaks of three persons as concerned herein; and of these, not as making one person, but as being one God. *There are three that bear record in heaven, the Father, the Word, and the holy Ghost, and these three are one*, 1 John v. 7. that is, one God. Now if it is no contradiction to the Bible, which every where speaks conformable to the voice of right reason, to say that Father, Son and Spirit, are one God; then it is no contradiction to reason, or to the Bible, nor is it any self-contradiction, or big with others, to say, that Father, Son and Spirit, are the one most high God. But, in confutation of this, we are recommended,

4. To an argument which this writer has borrowed from another person, drawn up in the following form [o]: "He who is alone the supreme governor of
" the universe, is alone the supreme God; but the Father is alone the supreme
" governor of the universe." *This latter proposition proved.* "He who never
" acts in subjection to the will of any other person, and every other person
" whatsoever always acts in subjection to his will, is alone the supreme governor
" of the universe: But the Father never acts in subjection to the will of another
" person, and every other person whatsoever always acts in subjection to his
" will; therefore the Father alone is the supreme governor of the universe."
To which I answer, by denying the *minor* proposition, that the Father is alone the supreme governor of the universe; for the Son is with the Father the supreme governor of the world: *the kingdom is the Lord's*, that is, the Lord Christ's, for he is spoken of throughout that whole psalm [p]; *and he is the governor among the nations*. *My Father*, says Christ, *worketh hitherto* [q]; that is, in the government of the universe, in the administration of providence: *and I work*; I am jointly concerned with him in these things: which made the Jews rightly conclude that he made himself *equal* with *God*, an equal governor of the universe with him. Hence it is clear, that the Father is not *alone* the supreme governor of the universe. Moreover, the *minor* proposition of the argument brought in proof of this, that the Father is alone the governor of the universe, must also be denied; I mean that part of it on which the proof depends, that "every other person whatsoever always acts in subjection to his, the Father's will:" For though the Son of God always acts in *agreement*, yet not always in *subjection* to his Father's will;

[o] Dialogue, Part II. p. 30, 31.    [p] Psalm xxii. 28.    [q] John v. 17.

will; though he always acted in subjection to his Father's will in the human nature, yet not in the divine nature; particularly in the works of creation and providence; in these there is an agreement with, but not a subjection to his Father's will; *all things were made by him* in agreement, but not in subjection to the will of the Father; by *him all things consist*, and he *upholds all things by the word of his power*[r]; agreeable to his Father's will, but not obliged as by any power or authority superior to him.

5. This writer, in his *first part*[s], argues against the supreme deity of Christ, in this manner: "Before the Lord Jesus Christ became man, he came from the Father, was sent and employed by him; therefore it is impossible he should be the supreme God." It is readily granted, that Christ before his incarnation *came*, though he is not expressly said to be *sent*, to redeem *Israel*, lead them through the Red sea and wilderness, and bring them to *Canaan*. And it has been observed[t], that he appeared with full proof of his equality with the Father, since he calls himself the God of *Abraham*, *Isaac*, and *Jacob*, and, *I am that I am*, Exod. iii. 6, 14. And *Jehovah* says of him, *My name is in him*; and that he could, though he would not, pardon iniquity; all which this author takes no notice of, but catches at the phrases of *sending*, and being *sent*, which he thinks suppose superiority and inferiority; though it has been observed to him, that of two equals, by agreement one may be sent by the other: But this he thinks, as applied to two persons, who are the one most high God, is chargeable with absurdity and blasphemy. Not with absurdity; for though *he that is sent is not greater than he that sent him*[u], he may be equally as great. Nor did he appear at all inferior to the most high God when he came to redeem *Israel*; and even when he was sent to redeem mankind, though the glory of his Deity was greatly vailed and hid from the eyes of men in his state of humiliation, yet he did not lay aside his authority, or give up his supremacy and government; he was then in heaven, and as much one with the Father, and as greatly concerned with him in the government of the world, as before; see *John* i. 18. and iii. 13. and v. 17. Nor is it chargeable with blasphemy; it is indeed great condescension, a wonderful stoop of Deity; and the higher the Deity of Christ is carried, the more wonderful his condescension appears, whether in coming to redeem *Israel* before his incarnation, or for the salvation of his people at it. And here give me leave to correct a mistake of this author's in another place[w], in which he represents us as supposing that Christ was *begotten*, *sent*, *came* forth from the Father *as man*, before he was man: Whereas, as man, he never was *begotten* at all; and might be said to be *sent*, and *come* before he was man, in order to be

so,

---

[r] John i. 3. Coloss. i. 16, 17. Heb. i. 3.　[s] Page 11.　[t] Answer, p. 15, 16.
[u] John xiii. 16.　[w] Dialogue, Part II. p. 39.

so, with respect to his office-capacity, which he voluntarily, and in the most condescending manner, took upon him for the good of men.

6. Whereas the equality of Christ with the Father is pleaded for, as being strongly afserted in *Phil.* ii. 6. *John* x. 30. these passages are objected to. The first of these, at it stands in our Bibles, is so glaring a proof of the Son's equality with the Father, that the adversaries of it are not able to withstand it; wherefore they employ all their wit and learning to destroy the commonly received translation, and to establish another; and instead of *thought it not robbery to be equal with God*, render it, *did not affect, greedily catch at*, or *assume divinity*, or to appear *like a God*. The first after *Arius*, who embraced and contended for this version, was *Enjedinus* [x] the Socinian; and most of those this author mentions as giving up our translation, are such who gave into the Arian or Socinian schemes, or were inclinable thereunto, contrary to the sense of the far greater number of learned writers, ancient and modern. I perceive this *Dialogue-writer* is acquainted with a book intitled *Fortuita Sacra*, written by a person of worth and learning; he would do well to consult that learned writer upon this passage, who has refuted the translation and sense this author seems fond of, and has established the commonly received one, in agreement with the context, where Christ is said to *be in the form of God*; which he shews to be the essential form of God, all that is great and glorious in him, his very nature and Deity, in which Christ existed, and therefore must be equal to him. This use of the word μορφη, he proves from ancient writers [y]. Nor is this sense of it contradictory to right reason; for since in nature a son may be equal to a father, why not in the divine essence, for any thing this author has said to the contrary? Begotten, and not derived, is no contradiction, considered in different respects. Christ is begotten, as a Son, but underived, as God over all: He is not αυτουιος, *Son of himself*, though αυτοθεος, *God of himself*: He is Son of the Father, but God of himself; his personality and sonship he has of the Father, his being and perfections of himself: there is no foundation for a distinction between a begotten and unbegotten essence; not essence, but person is begotten: And false it is, to say that this is not taken notice of in the *Answer* to the *Dialogue* [z]. Moreover, the sense of the passage before us we contend for, is no ways contrary to those scriptures which speak of Christ as commissioned by the Father, doing his will, and nothing of himself; as not knowing the day of judgment; and that the Father is greater than he, and he is glorified by him; since these are spoken of him in his office-capacity, and as man and mediator. This phrase, *as man and mediator*, is greatly found fault with by this writer [a], as having, by joining these

---

[x] Explicat. Loc. Vet. & Nov. Test. p. 323, 324.   [y] Fortuita Sacra, p. 178, &c.
[z] See p. 20, 21.   [a] Dialogue, Part II. p. 38.

these words together, a mean fallacy in it, whereas the idea of a mediator comprehends the whole person of Christ as God-man, together with his office. But why may not these two be joined together without a fallacy, when the scripture says, that *there is one mediator between God and men, the man Christ Jesus* [b]? True indeed, Christ is mediator in both natures, human and divine, he having these united in one person as God-man; so that what is done in, or belongs to any of these natures, may, by virtue of this union, be predicated of his person; and yet these things must be attributed to the distinct natures to which they belong; as for instance, omnipotence and omniscience may be predicated of the person of Christ, and yet these belong only to him as considered in his divine nature: So doing nothing of himself, and not knowing the day of judgment, may be predicated of the Son, when these manifestly belong to him as considered in the human nature. This observation attended to, will unravel and destroy all that this author has wrote upon this head.

The passage in *John* x. 30. is a clear proof of the Son's equality with the Father; where Christ says, *I and my Father are one*; not one person, but one God, of one and the same nature: By which we mean the same divine essence and perfections; for the Son partakes of the same divine nature, and possesses the same divine perfections the Father does; he has all the fulness of the Godhead in him, and so is equal to him. In this sense the Jews understood him; upon which they charge him with blasphemy, because he made himself God; and to vindicate himself, he first argues from his inferior character, as being in office; that if magistrates without blasphemy might be called *gods*, much more might he, who was sanctified and sent into the world by the Father: But he does not let the stress of the proof of his deity rest here, but proceeds to prove that he was truly and properly God, by doing the same works his Father did. So that the Jews were not mistaken in his sense, nor did they belie him; though they wronged him, in charging him with blasphemy on this account. As for *John* xvii. 21. where Christ prays that believers may be one, *as* he and his Father are one, it is impertinently alledged, since the *as* there does not express equality, but likeness; for none will venture to say, not even this author himself, that believers are, or will be one with the Father and Son, in that self-same sense, as *they* are one with another; there is not the sameness of power, action or operation, which is acknowledged in the Father and the Son. Upon the whole, the text in *John* x. 3. stands fully against the subordination of the Son to the Father, and is a firm proof of his equality with him in nature and perfections; by which doctrine no dishonour is done to the Father, or affront given him; since no perfection of deity, or any branch of honour and worship, are denied him, or

given

[b] 1 Tim. ii. 5.

given to a creature; and since it is perfectly agreeable to him, that all men *should honour the Son, as they honour the Father.* I proceed,

II. To the doctrine of election and reprobation. The sum of the charge against this doctrine in the *first part*, is, that it is unmerciful, unjust, insincere, and uncomfortable; and this is the amount of the whole harangue upon it in *this part*. What I shall attend unto, will be the exceptions to what has been advanced, in order to clear it from this charge. And,

1. Whereas it is charged with cruelty and unmercifulness; it has been observed[c] that it carries no marks of cruelty and unmercifulness in it to the elect, who are *vessels of mercy afore-prepared unto glory*; which mercy this writer calls [d] "unwise and partial mercy, such as we are sure, says he, God can never be "guilty of." But pray, does not God say, *I will have mercy on whom I will have mercy?* Upon which the apostle observes, *So then it is not of him that willeth, nor of him that runneth, but of God that sheweth mercy.—Therefore hath he mercy on whom he will have mercy, and whom he will he hardeneth*[e]. And will this man call this mercy, shewn only to some, as influenced not by their will and works, but as arising from the sovereign will and pleasure of God, unwise and partial mercy? This man himself owns, that God's decreeing help for a few, is not an objection to the mercifulness of God; but the question is, he says[f], "where "is the pity of God, his grace, the founding of his bowels over them, for whom "he decreed no help?" I answer, there is pity, mercy and goodness shewn to these, in a general way of providence; and though none in a special way of grace, yet no cruelty, since God is not obliged to help them; and it is no cruelty in him to punish for sin. It has been further observed[g], in order to remove this charge, that if it was not acting the cruel and unmerciful part not to ordain help for any of the fallen angels, it would not have been acting such a part, had God resolved not to help *any* of the fallen race of *Adam*, much less to ordain help for *some*, when he could in justice have condemned *all*. This representation of the case is said[h] to be unfair in itself, inconsistent with our principles, and the illustration of it evasive; and it is asked, "amongst the fallen an- "gels did God shew mercy to some, everlasting mercy, while he decreed others "to hell, who were no more guilty than the rest?" I answer, no; he shewed mercy to none of them, but consigned them all over to ruin and destruction; and yet he is not chargeable with cruelty. But supposing he had shewn mercy to some, and not to others, as in the case of man; would he have appeared less merciful, by shewing of mercy to some, than by shewing none to any? And as for all the other questions put, whether God sent a proclamation of pardon

to

[c] Answer, p. 24.  [d] Dialogue, Part II. p. 56.  [e] Rom. ix. 15, 16, 18.
[f] Part II. p. 57.  [g] Answer, p. 26.  [h] Part II. p. 56.

to them that were fore-ordained to misery, or offered one on conditions not to be complied with, or exhorted to accept a salvation never purchased for them, or condemned to a heavier damnation for not believing a falshood, or for not doing an impossibility; these are all impertinent, and are no more applicable to men, upon our principles, than to angels. The fallen angels are, indeed, as is observed, personal, voluntary sinners, and are, and will be treated according to their own share of guilt; and so are all the adult posterity of *Adam*, who are and will be so treated either in themselves or surety; and, as many of them as will be condemned, will be condemned, not merely for the sin of *Adam*, and for their share of guilt therein, but for their own actual, personal, voluntary sins and transgressions; and as for the infant posterity of *Adam*, their case is a secret to us, and therefore, we choose to be silent about it.

Once more, it has been observed [r], that "the doctrne of election is more merciful than the contrary scheme, since it infallibly secures the salvation of some; whereas, the other does not ascertain the salvation of any single person, but leaves it uncertain, to the precarious and fickle will of man." The reply to this is by asking [k], which is more honourable to God, and more for the comfort of men? whereas the question is, which shews most mercy? Though one should think, that doctrine which ensures the salvation of *some*, should be more honourable to God, and more comfortable to man, than that which does not ascertain the salvation of *any* single man. This author does not attempt to disprove the doctrine of election infallibly securing the salvation of some; and, in a very feeble manner does he argue, for the ascertaining of salvation to man in the contrary doctrine; he asks, "is not the salvation of man sufficiently ascertained by the gospel's setting life and death before men, and offering them all needful assistance in the way of life?" he would have said, surely, *by the law's setting life and death*, since that is the proper business of the law, and not the gospel; can that be good news which sets death before men? But to leave this, Is moral suasion sufficient to ascertain man's salvation? Is the bare ministration even of the gospel itself, enough for this purpose? Is this the way God foresaw salvation would be ascertained to men, and the only one in which Christ and men could desire it should be ensured to them? when, where it is used in its utmost strength, it fails in innumerable instances, and was never sufficient, of itself, in one; and besides, is at most made use of but with a few, who are so in comparison of the far greater part of the world, who know nothing of the gospel, and the ministration of it: how then is salvation ascertained to them this way?

2. Another charge against this doctrine, is injustice, and that it represents God as an unrighteous Being: to which has been answered [l], that "the decree

"of

---

[r] Answer, p. 13, 14.　　[k] Part II. p. 77.　　[l] Answer, p. 27.

"of election does no injustice either to the elect or non-elect; not to the "former, since it secures to them both grace and glory; nor to the latter, since "as God condemns no man but for sin, so he has decreed to condemn no man "but for sin; and if it would have been no injustice in him, to have decreed "to condemn all men for sin, it can be none to him, to decree to condemn "some for sin." The reply to which is [m], that this answer is evasive and ambiguous, in regard it does not tell us, whether God condemns and decrees to condemn men for their own sin, or for the sin of *Adam*. But where is the evasion or shift in the answer? If it is for sin, and for sin only, with which men are chargeable, that God condemns, and has decreed to condemn, let it be what sin it will, the observation is full to the purpose, and sufficiently clears God from the charge of unrighteousness; nor is it ambiguous, since in a following paragraph it is plainly intimated and fully proved, that God condemns both for the sin of *Adam*, and for man's own personal iniquities; as the latter will not be denied, the former stands supported by those words of the apostle, *By the offence of one, judgment came upon all men to condemnation* [n]; which this writer takes no notice of, and makes no return unto; and yet the cry of unrighteousness entirely proceeds upon this point; though we do not say that any of the sons of *Adam* who live to adult age, are condemned only for the sin of *Adam*, but for their many actual sins and transgressions; and as for infants dying in infancy, it has been observed, their case is a secret to us; yet inasmuch as they come into the world *children of wrath*, should they go out as such, would there be any unrighteousness in God? All which, this author has passed over in silence: perhaps we may hear more of it under the article of Original Sin. This man has been told [o], that as God will not condemn the heathen for not believing in Christ, of whom they never heard, so neither will he condemn such who have heard of him, for not believing spiritually and savingly in him, or that he died for them, or for not being converted: and yet he says [p], not a word is produced to vindicate God from the charge our scheme fixes upon him, of damning men for not believing falshoods, and for not doing impossibilities. Men who have had the advantage of a divine revelation, may be condemned, not for not believing that Christ died for them, but for disbelieving that Jesus is the Messiah, and other things, which in the revelation are said of him; they may be condemned for their disobedience to the gospel, not for their being not converted by it, but for their contempt and rejection of it, as an imposture and a false report; and consequently, not for not believing falshoods, and for not doing impossibilities.

[m] Part II. p. 59.
[o] Answer, p. 28.
[n] Rom v. 18.
[p] Part II. p. 66.

3. This doctrine is farther charged with infincerity, or as reprefenting God as an infincere and deceitful Being; fince he offers to finners a falvation never purchafed for them, and on conditions not to be complied with. The anfwer to this is [q], that falvation is not offered at all by God, upon any condition whatfoever, to any of the fons of men, elect or non-elect; and therefore God, according to this doctrine, is not chargeable with infincerity and deceit. This occafions a terrible outcry [r] of *myftery of iniquity*, an *abominable tenet, horrid fcheme*, which has *the image of the devil* and the *mark of the beaft upon it*, and other fuch like language, which breathe out the fpirit, the very life and foul of *modern charity*, and is a true picture of it. This author owns, that hereby we are confiftent, in preaching and writing, with ourfelves and fcheme, and fo not chargeable with felf-contradiction; and fince it is of a piece with the reft of our tenets, and is likely to fhare the fame fate with them, we need not be in much pain about the confequences of it. But this tenet, that there is no offer of falvation to men in the miniftry of the gofpel, is faid to be inconfiftent with all the dictates of reafon, our ideas of God, and the whole fyftem of the gofpel: not furely with all the dictates of reafon; for how irrational is it, for minifters to ftand offering Chrift, and falvation by him to man, when, on the one hand, they have neither power nor right to give; and, on the other hand, the perfons they offer to, have neither power nor will to receive? What this author's ideas of God are, I know not, but this I fay, it is not confiftent with our ideas of God, that he fhould fend minifters to offer falvation to man, to whom he himfelf never intended to give it, which the minifters have not power to beftow, nor the men to receive: but, it feems, denying offers of falvation, is inconfiftent with the whole fyftem of the gofpel; the Bible is hereby knocked down at once, and made to be the moft delufive, and cheating book in the world; when the whole Bible is one ftanding offer of mercy to a guilty world. What! the *whole* Bible? the Bible may be diftinguifhed into thefe two parts, *hiftorical* and *doctrinal*; the hiftorical part of the Bible is furely no offer of mercy to a guilty world; the account of the creation of the heavens and the earth, in the firft *verfe* of it, can hardly be thought to be fo. The doctrinal part of it may be diftinguifhed into *law* and *gofpel*; the law, which is the killing letter, and the miniftration of condemnation and death to a guilty world, can be no ftanding offer of mercy to it: if any part of the Bible is fo, it muft be the gofpel; but the gofpel is a declaration of falvation already wrought out by Chrift, and not an offer of it on conditions to be performed by man. The minifters of the gofpel are fent to *preach the gofpel to every creature* [s]; that is, not to offer, but to preach Chrift, and falvation by him; to publifh peace and pardon as things already obtained

by

[q] Anfwer, p. 29.  [r] Part II. p. 61, 65.  [s] Mark xvi. 15.

by-him. The ministers are κηρυκες, *criers* or *heralds*; their business is κηρυσσειν, to *proclaim* aloud, to publish facts, to declare things that are done, and not to offer them to be done on conditions; as when a peace is concluded and finished, the herald's business, and in which he is employed, is to proclaim the peace, and not to offer it; of this nature is the gospel, and the whole system of it; which preaches, not offers peace by Christ, who is Lord of all. As for the texts of scripture produced by this writer, several have nothing in them respecting pardon, life and salvation, and much less contain an offer of either; as I have shewn at large in my *first part* of *The Cause of God and Truth*; whither I refer the reader; such as *Gen.* iv. 7. *Deut.* v. 29. *Prov.* i. 23. *Ezek.* xxxiii. 18. *Acts* iii. 19. others are gracious invitations to the means of grace, and promises of pardon and grace to poor sensible sinners; as *Isai.* lv. 1, 7. *Rev.* xxii. 17. *Acts* ii. 38. others, exhortations to duty with encouragements to it; as *Psalm* l. 23. *Mal.* iii. 7. *Matt.* vi. 5, 6, 15. and vii. 21. 1 *Tim.* iv. 8. 2 *Cor.* vii. 1. *Rev* xxii. 14.

4. This doctrine is represented as a very uncomfortable one; since it makes it a hundred to one to a man that he is not elected, but must be for ever damned. To which answer has been made ', it is not such a chance matter, or uncertain thing to a man, as a hundred to one, whether he is elected or no; to whom *the gospel is come, not in word only, but also in power and in the holy Ghost*; who from hence may truly know, and be comfortably assured of his *election of God* This man has now lowered his number, and made it *ten to one*, whether a man is elected or no, to whom the gospel is preached; but it is no odds at all to a man whether he is elected or no, to whom the gospel is preached; and to whom that is made *the power of God unto salvation*, or who is converted by it, which is the instance given. To which this writer replies ", "then the gospel is glad tidings "to no sinner in the world, unless he is actually converted." Why, truly, it is not glad tidings to such persons, nor is it judged so by them. It is so far from being good news to unconverted sinners, that it is disputed, despised, hated and abhorred by them; just as it is by this Dialogue-writer. There is no doctrine of the gospel that is really comfortable and truly delightful to a man in a state of nature: the doctrine of regeneration, delivered by Christ in these words ", *except a man be born again, he cannot see the kingdom of God*, can never be comfortable to an unregenerate man: nor can even any doctrine in which such as call themselves christians, are agreed; as for instance, the doctrine of an universal judgment, when all men must appear before God, and be accountable to him for the actions of their lives: this is a doctrine, to use this author's words, that all the world have reason to be affrighted at, and which no soul can possibly take any comfort from, till he does actually love God, and is irresistibly drawn to him;

but

' Answer, p. 30. " Part II. p. 67. " John iii. 3.

but it is not a whit the less true because it is uncomfortable to such persons, any more than the doctrine of election, which, however frightful it be to unconverted sinners, yields true peace and comfort to those who are born again, and have the *faith of God's elect*; though they take no pleasure in the rejection of others, but wisely leave it to the sovereignty of that God, who does whatsoever he pleases. Nor can the universal scheme afford such comfort to a converted man, as that of special grace does; since, according to the former, he may be lost and perish, when the latter secures certain salvation to him.

To close this head; it seems, according to this writer [x], that as the *nation* of the Jews are called *God's elect*, in like manner, the kingdom of Christ, converted ones, have the same title applied to them, not in their *personal*, but *social* capacity, as christian churches: so the whole church at *Thessalonica* are called *God's elect*, not with respect to single persons, but on the account of their being called by the gospel. But, surely, the calling of the Thessalonians by the gospel, must be *personal*, and not *social*, or as a christian church; and therefore their election must be personal too, of which their calling was an effect, fruit and evidence. And though the nation of the Jews are called *God's elect*, or *chosen*, as such, and were distinguished by many favours, as a nation, from the rest of the world; yet there was a special, personal and particular election among them, *a remnant, according to the election of grace* [y]: nor are all that bare that name under the gospel, or in the kingdom of the Messiah, churches, but particular persons: the *few*, Christ said, were *chosen*, when *many* were externally called by the gospel, were persons, and not nations or churches; these are *the elect*, for whose sake the days of tribulation will be shortened, whom false prophets cannot deceive, and whom the angels *will gather from the four winds*: not churches, nor all the members of churches, are the *poor of this world, whom God has chosen*, and made *rich in faith, and heirs of a kingdom*: the *elect Lady*, and her sister, and *Rufus*, chosen in the Lord, and the *elect strangers*, were persons chosen before the foundation of the world in Christ, to be holy and happy [z]. I go on to consider,

III. The doctrine of *Adam's* fall, and original sin. Under this head our author endeavours,

1. To prove the entire innocence of infants from scripture [a]. The passages he produces or refers to, are *Jer*. ii. 30. and xix. 4. *Matt*. xviii. 3, 4. the two first of these seem rather to be understood of the prophets, as they are by several

---

[x] Part II. p. 60, 67.   [y] See Rom. ix. 6, 7, 8, 27, 29. and xi. 5, 7.
[z] Matt. xx. 16. and xxiv. 22, 24, 31. Jam. ii. 5. 2 John i. 13. Rom. xvi. 13. 1 Pet. i. 1, 2. Ephes. i. 4.   [a] Part II, p. 73.

ral expositors, than of infants; the former of them has no apparent reference to children, and the latter of them distinguishes innocents from the sons, or the children that were burnt with fire, for burnt-offerings to *Baal*; and both seem rather to regard the prophets; who, though not free from sin, yet were innocent as to any crime for which they suffered, and their blood was shed. And supposing infants were intended, they are only called so in a comparative sense, in comparison of others, who have added to their original guilt and corruption many actual sins and transgressions; and as for the words of our Lord in *Matt.* xviii. 3, 4. the meaning is not, that men must be perfectly innocent, and entirely free from sin, or there can be no expectation of entering the kingdom of heaven; for then no man could hope to enter there; but that men must be *born again*, and appear to be so, and, in a comparative sense, must be holy, and harmless, free from pride, ambition, malice and envy. And even his learned *Cicero*, to whom he has recourse, helps him off but very lamely; for in the very citation he makes from him, he says, " We are no sooner born, but we fall into " a wretched depravity and corruption of manners and opinions; so that we " seem almost to suck in error with our mother's milk."

2. This writer endeavours [b] to set aside the proof of the imputation of *Adam*'s sin to his posterity, and the corruption of human nature by it, taken from *Psalm* li. 5. *Rom.* v. 19. *Ephes.* ii. 3. by giving different turns to, and false glosses on these passages: As to *Psalm* li. 5. he insinuates, that *David* might be base born, or unlawfully begotten, and so shapen in iniquity; and asks, is this a proof that other men are so, or that all men are so [c]? This is a gloss which is formed at the expence of the characters of *David*'s parents, of whom there is not the least suggestion of this nature in the word of God, but the reverse; for they are represented as holy and religious persons: this sense of them makes *David* illegitimate, who, therefore, must have been excluded from the congregation of *Israel*; whereas we have no intimation of any such exclusion; but, on the contrary, that he frequently went into the house of God with company; besides, he is not speaking of any sin his parents were guilty of, when he was conceived and shapen, but of sin and iniquity, in which he was conceived and shapen; nor would it have been agreeable to his design and view, to expose the sins of his parents, whilst he was lamenting his own. Our sense of *Romans* v. 19. that all mankind are made sinners by the imputation of *Adam*'s disobedience, is [c] said to be " contrary to reason, to the context, to known truths, to other more plain " scriptures, to be injurious to God, and abusive to mankind." It is not contrary to reason; imputation is not used by us in a moral sense, as when a man's own personal action, good or bad, is accounted to himself; but in a forensic

sense,

[b] Part II. p. 74, &c.      [c] Ibid. p. 76.

sense, as when the debts of one man are, in a legal way, transferred and placed to the account of another; which is neither contrary to reason, nor the practice of men: nor is it contrary to the context, which, this writer says, leads us, by *sinners* to understand *sufferers*, mortal men liable to die, as *ver.* 12, *&c.* but this is to make the apostle a most miserable reasoner, and guilty of proving the same thing by the same; the sense of whose words, *death passed upon all men, for that all have sinned*, must be, according to this interpretation, all men die because they die, or all men are sufferers because they are sufferers; whereas the apostle in these words, and throughout the context, shews, why death passed on all men, why many were dead, why death reigned as it did, why judgment came upon all men to condemnation; because all sinned in *Adam*, and by his disobedience were made, reckoned, and accounted sinners. Nor is this sense contrary to known truths, and other more plain scriptures; as to the latter, this author does not pretend to mention any to which it is contrary; and as for the former, though nothing can act personally before it has an actual personal being; yet as men may have a representative being, before they have an actual one, so they may act in their representative, as *Levi* paid tithes in *Abraham* before he was born; and though sin is a personal act, and a transgression of a law, yet it may be transferred to another, by imputation, not in a moral way, but in a judicial one: nor is our sense injurious to God, his being and perfections, or contrary to his methods of proceeding, who, in many cases, has *visited the iniquities of the fathers upon the children:* nor does it abuse mankind, but only represents how mankind are abused by sin; to which is owing all the miseries and calamities endured by man in this, or the other world. On the whole, our sense of the passage before us stands firm, without giving up any plain rule of interpretation of scripture, and which is further confirmed by the other clause in the text; for as men are made righteous in a forensick sense, or are justified, and have a right to life, through the righteousness or obedience of Christ, which this author owns, so they are made sinners in a forensick sense, by the disobedience of *Adam*, that is, by imputation; and this gives light to another passage of the apostle's [d], *in Adam all die*; and shews a reason for it, because *all sinned* in him, or were made sinners by his disobedience. The text in *Ephes.* ii. 3. *And were by nature children of wrath, even as others*; is not forgotten by us to be understood of God's elect; who, consistent with their being beloved in Christ with an everlasting love, may, considered as the guilty and polluted descendents of *Adam*, be called *children of wrath*; that is, deserving of it; for so they are by *nature*, guilty through the imputation of sin unto them, being the natural posterity of *Adam*, and filthy through a corrupt depraved nature, propagated and

communicated

[d] 1 Cor. xv. 20.

communicated to them by natural generation; for *whatsoever is born of the flesh is flesh*, carnal and corrupt, and not by custom or habits of sin, which become *second nature*.

3. We are called upon to prove that God made a covenant with *Adam* and all his posterity, which is the ground of his imputing sin unto them. That there was a covenant made with *Adam*, I suppose, will not be denied, since a promise of *life* was made to him upon his obedience, and *death* was threatened in case of disobedience, to which he agreed in his state of innocence; all which formally constitutes a covenant, and is so called, *Hos.* vi. 7. *They, like men*, or *Adam, have transgressed the covenant.* That this covenant was made with *Adam* and his posterity, in which he was their federal head and representative, appears from his being called *the figure of him that was to come* [e]; which is to be understood either of all mankind, who were to spring from him, or of the Lord Jesus Christ, who was to come in the fulness of time; if of the former, it proves that *Adam* was a type or figure of all his posterity, that he personated them all, and that they were all represented in him and by him, which is the very thing it is brought to prove; if of the latter, that is, of Christ, *Adam* could only be a type or figure of him, as a public person and a covenant-head; and the parallel between them, as such, is clearly run by the apostle in the context, and in another place [f]; shewing that as the one conveys sin and death to all his posterity, the other conveys grace, righteousness and life to all his. Without allowing such a covenant made with *Adam* and his posterity, in which they were to stand or fall with him; and without considering him as a covenant-head, and representative of them, in whom they sinned and fell, it cannot be accounted for, how *Adam*'s sin should " bring death on many, or render them liable to be treated as sinners, " or make them more liable to both sin and death, or that they should share " in the fatal consequences of his disobedience;" all which is acknowledged by this writer [g]

IV. Free grace and free-will come next into debate.

1. This man's notion of *free grace* is, that it is free and common to all men; upon which scheme he is asked [h], what grace is that in God to decree to save all men conditionally, to send his Son to redeem all mankind; and yet to whole nations, and that for many hundred years together, does not so much as afford the means of grace, of the knowledge of salvation, nor vouchsafes his Spirit to make application of it to them, but leaves them in their sin, and eternally damns them? To which he answers [i], " When we are upon the nature of the
" gospel

[e] Rom. v. 14.    [f] 1 Cor. xv.    [g] Part II. p. 77, 78.    [h] Answer, p. 39, 40.
[i] Part II. p. 81.

" gospel and the universality of its offers, there is no need to evade the argu-
" ment, by transferring the scene to the heathen world." I am at a loss to
know what argument is evaded by putting the question; for, if grace is free
and common to all men, if God's decree of salvation is universal, and reaches
to all the individuals of mankind, and Christ has died for them all, then, surely,
the heathen world has a concern in these things; and it must seem strange, if
all this is true, that the knowledge of salvation, and the means of it, should
not be afforded them, and they left in their sins to perish without law. Where
is the grace of this scheme? What is now become of free, common, and universal grace? And an idle thing it is, to talk of the universality of the offers of
the gospel, when the gospel is not preached to a *tenth* part of the world, nor
any thing like it; when multitudes, millions, whole nations know nothing of
it. What this man means by saying that this is equally a difficulty against God's
government of the world, I know not; since this argument does not concern
God's government of the world, but the administration of his grace to the sons
of men.

2. That there is a free-will in man, and that man is a free agent, is not denied by us; the natural liberty of the will, and the power of man to perform
the natural and civil actions of life, and the external parts of religion, are owned
by us. We assert, indeed, that there is no free-will in man of himself to do that
which is spiritually good, nor any power in him to perform it. This is the account of free-will which we have [k] already given, though this author suggests,
that we have given no other than he has done, and dare not define it [l]: he
thinks that man cannot be free who is under a *necessitating decree* to sin; and,
that if man has no power to do any thing spiritually good, and yet obliged to
do it, then he is obliged to impossibilities, and damned for not performing them.
To which may be replied, that whatever concern the decree of God has in the
sins of men, it does not necessitate or force them to do them; it does not at all
infringe the freedom of their will, or destroy their free agency; as appears in
the cases of *Joseph's* being sold into *Egypt*, and the crucifixion of Christ; which
were both according to the decree and counsel of God; and yet *Joseph's* brethren
and the crucifiers of Christ, acted as free agents, and with the full liberty of
their wills. The things spiritually good which man cannot do, have been instanced in [m]; as to convert and regenerate himself, to believe in Christ, and to
repent of sin in an evangelical manner; and these are things which he is not
obliged to do of himself, and will not be damned for not performing of them.
There are indeed things which man is obliged to, which he now cannot do, as
to keep the whole law; which impotency of his is owing to his sin and fall, by
which

[k] Answer, p. 41.    [l] Part II. p. 84.    [m] Answer, p. 41.

which we mean the sin and fall of *Adam*, and of all mankind in him; and this author may make what use he pleases of it.

3. An *O yes* is cried, and all men are desired to attend ⁿ; to what? to this; "Writers on your side have not the courage and honesty plainly to deny that that men are in a *state of trial*, though a consequence of their principles; yet now and then they craftily insinuate this article of their dark and hideous scheme." That the saints whilst in this life, are in a state of trial, that is of their graces by afflictions, temptations, &c. is readily owned; but then all mankind are not in such a state, only converted persons, who only have grace to be tried; but if by a state of trial is meant, as I suppose it is, that men are upon probation of their good or ill behaviour towards God, according to which their state will be fixed as to happiness or misery, that being as yet unfixed, so that whilst this life lasts it is uncertain whether they will be saved or lost: if this, I say is meant, I have had courage and honesty, as this man calls it, plainly to deny it years ago, and have published ᵒ my arguments and reasons against it, which this writer, if he pleases, may try if he can answer.

4. This writer thinks ᵖ that the *drawings* of God are necessary to conversion; but that these are only by moral suasion, and not by any powerful influence of divine grace, and so not irresistible. He owns irresistible evidence, illuminations and convictions; but such as may be resisted, and stifled, and come to nothing: how then are they irresistible? to use his own words, "If they may be resisted, then they are not irresistible ᑫ." We own, indeed, that the grace of God may be resisted, but not so as to be stifled, and come to nothing, to be overcome, and entirely frustrated. The instances given of God's grace being frustrated, and of resisting internal operations, are not at all to the purpose; since the passages alledged, *Hos*. vii. 1. *Luke* xiii. 34. and xix. 42. *Acts* xxviii. 24—27. regard not special grace, and internal operations, but external, temporal things, or the outward ministry of the word. It has been urged ʳ, that if no man can come to Christ unless irresistible grace draw him, then there can be no fault in not turning to him. To which it has been answered ˢ, that "to live in sin, is blame-worthy; and though man, by sinning, has involved himself in a state out of which he cannot extricate himself, yet is he not the less culpable on that score, for living in it:" which answer stands good, for any thing this man has replied to it ᵗ; since men are involved in this state not merely by another's, but by their own sin, and their continuance in it is of their own free-will. The argument from the offer of help has been set aside already, by denying there is any. The instance of a man's drinking himself into a fever, and

*continuing*

ⁿ Part II. p. 35.  ᵒ The Cause of God and Truth, part I.  ᵖ Dialogue, part II. p. 87.
ᑫ Ibid. p. 89.    ʳ Part I. p. 31.    ˢ Answer, p. 42, 43.    ᵗ Part II. p. 88.

continuing in it, notwithstanding commands of recovery, and offers of remedy, is stupidly impertinent; since not continuing in a fever, the consequence of his drinking, but in the sin itself, of which such an habit may be acquired he cannot break, can only have any shew of agreement with the case before us. We readily allow, that no internal operations are employed, as to thousands who hear the gospel. But then, says this writer\*, such cannot believe and obey, and therefore cannot be justly punished for not believing and obeying. I reply, that such indeed cannot believe with the faith which is of the operation of God, nor perform new and spiritual obedience, to which the Spirit of God is necessary, and for which he is promised in the covenant, and therefore will never be punished for not believing and obeying, in this sense: but then, without internal operations, or special grace, such as are favoured with an external revelation, are capable of believing the outward report of the gospel, and of yielding obedience to it; that is, of attending on the ministry of the word, and performing the external parts of religion; and in failure of these, may be justly punished for their unbelief and disobedience. I take no notice of our scheme being called by this man *Antichristian* and *Diabolical*; I am now pretty well used to such language, and indeed expect no other from men of *modern charity*.

V. The doctrine of justification, by the imputed righteousness of Christ, comes next under consideration. And,

1. Some passages of scripture, as *Isai*. lxiv. 6. *Phil*. iii. 9 which represent the insufficiency of man's righteousness to justify him before God, are brought under examination. As to *Isai*. lxiv. 6. our author seems to be at a loss whether he should follow the interpretation of *Grotius*, or *Henry* ⍏. However, that the prophet speaks of a hypocritical people, he thinks is a clear point, for this wise reason; because it is said, at the end of the verse, *we all do fade as a leaf, and our iniquities like the wind have taken us away*: whereas hypocrites are not so free to own their declensions and transgressions, and to confess the impurity of their hearts, and the imperfection of their obedience; they generally make the least of their sins, and the most they can of their righteousness: So that these words are a reason against, and not for, his sense of the passage. St *Paul*, in *Phil*. iii. 8, 9. he says, only renounced his ceremonial, not his moral righteousness. But it is not the righteousness of the ceremonial, but of the moral law, which the apostle continually opposes to the righteousness of faith; see *Romans* iii. 20—22. and iv. 13. and ix. 30, 31. and x. 5, 6. And when we say, that he renounced this righteousness, he knows very well our meaning is, not that he renounced doing it, or objected to the performance of it; but that he disclaimed all dependence upon it for justification before God; and, in respect

to

---

\* Part II. p. 89.  ⍏ Ibid. p. 91.

to that, defired only to be found in Chrift: which is not to reprefent the apoftle falfly and abfurdly, but perfectly agreeable with himfelf, and his principles.

2. This man has no other notion of imputation, but of accounting that to a man which is done by himfelf, and not what may be done, or contracted by another; contrary to the apoftle's fentiments, *Romans* iv. 6, 11, 23, 24. *Philem.* ver. 18. He argues againft the imputation of Chrift's righteoufnefs in this manner *; if no one fingle act of the righteoufnefs of Chrift is imputed to us, then the whole of it is not. Very right; for how indeed fhould the whole be imputed, if no one part of it is? But what are the particular acts of Chrift's righteoufnefs? His Incarnation, Baptifm, Poverty, Fafting, his Victory over Satan, Preaching, Miracles, his Confeffion before *Pilate*, Obedience to death, giving a Commiffion to his apoftles, his Interceffion, and governing and judging the World. All falfe. Not thefe, but the feveral acts of his *obedience* to the moral law, are the righteoufnefs of Chrift, by which men are *made righteous*, and by which they can only be made fo, by the imputation of it to them; the ground of which imputation is Chrift's being their head, furety, and reprefentative; fo that the righteoufnefs of the law being fulfilled by him, in their room and ftead, it is all one as if it was fulfilled by them, and is faid indeed to be *fulfilled in* them: which does not exempt them from fervice to God, or obedience to his law, but lays them under greater obligation in point of gratitude to an obfervance of it, though not in order to juftification by it.

3. It is ftill infifted on, that there is no text of fcripture to be found, proving the imputation of the righteoufnefs of Chrift. As for *Romans* iv. 3. he ftands to it, that it muft be underftood of *Abraham*'s faithful obedience, or obeying faith, and not the object of it; which, he fays ʸ, was the promife of God that he fhould have a fon, that was imputed to him for righteoufnefs. Now whatever may be faid for the imputation of *Abraham*'s act of faith to himfelf for righteoufnefs, nothing can be faid in favour of the imputation of the act of faith, that he fhould have a fon, to us, for righteoufnefs, *if we believe on him that raifed up Jefus our Lord from the dead*; where the apoftle clearly afferts that that *it*, which was imputed to *Abraham* for righteoufnefs, is alfo imputed to all them that believe. To which this man makes no reply. Nor does he take any notice of *Romans* iv. 6. 1 *Cor.* i. 30. 2 *Cor.* v. 21. which were produced as proofs of the imputation of Chrift's righteoufnefs to his people. He allows that we are made righteous by the obedience of Chrift, in the fame fenfe we are made finners by the difobedience of *Adam*; and fince he owns before ᶻ, that we are made righteous by the obedience of Chrift, in a *forenfic fenfe*, it muft be by the imputation of it to us.

4. This

ˣ Part II. p. 95.    ʸ Ibid. p. 98.    ᶻ Ibid. p. 78.

4. This author having suggested that the doctrine of imputed righteousness was a poisonous one, and tended to licentiousness; the contrary was proved from *Romans* iii. 31. *Titus* ii. 11, 12. and iii. 7, 8. which he has passed in silence; and instead of offering any thing in support of his former suggestion, he runs to the doctrine of Reprobation, of God's seeing no sin in his elect, and of irresistible grace; to which he adds a testimony of Bishop *Burnet*'s, concerning some persons in King *Edward* the VIth's time, who made an ill use of the doctrine of predestination. This is no new thing with this writer; nothing is more common with him, than to jumble doctrines together; never was such a lumbering, immethodical piece of work published to the world. It would be easy to exculpate the above doctrines, as well as this of justification, from the charge of licentiousness; and I have done it already [a], to which I refer the reader. I go on to consider,

VI. The doctrine of the saints perseverance. Under which article,

1. Some passages of scripture, made use of in favour of this doctrine, are represented [b] as a sandy foundation to build it upon. It seems that *Job* xvii. 9. is not a promise of God, but only the sentiment of *Job*. Be it so: Since it is a good one, and God has testified of him that he spake the thing that was right, it should be abode by. Moreover, since *Job* spake under divine inspiration, why should not these words be esteemed a promise of God by the mouth of *Job*? The *good work*, mentioned in *Phil*. i. 6. which the apostle was confidently persuaded, not barely *hoped*, would be performed until the day of Christ, he intimates, was either planting the church at *Philippi*, or an inclination to liberality; he does not know which. What should induce him to propose the latter sense, I cannot imagine; since there is not the least hint, in the text or context, of the liberality of these persons: And as for the former, that can never be intended; since planting of a church was a good work external and visible among them, and not a good work begun in them, in their hearts, and that in each of them singly and separately, as this was; for the apostle says, *even as it is meet for me to think this of you all*. The *everlasting righteousness*, said to be brought in by Christ, *Dan.* ix. 24. is suggested to be a covenant, whose terms of acceptance are unalterable. But the covenant of grace never goes by this name; and was it so called, it must be with respect to the everlasting righteousness of Christ, which always continues a justifying one to those interested in it; and therefore they shall never enter into condemnation, or finally and totally perish. Besides, the covenant confirmed by Christ, is spoken of ver. 26.

as

---

[a] In a Sermon, called, The Doctrine of Grace cleared from the Charge of Licentiousness; and in another, intitled, The Law established by the Gospel.    [b] Part II. p. 101, 102.

as diſtinct from this righteouſneſs. Once more: If the juſtification and glorification of converted Gentiles are inſeparably connected together, *Rom.* viii. 30. then thoſe who are truly converted, and are juſtified by the righteouſneſs of Chriſt, ſhall certainly be ſaved; and which is a doctrine to be defended, without eſtabliſhing the principle of fatality, or ſtoical enthuſiaſm. The prophetic texts in *Iſai.* liv. 10. and lix. 21. *Jer.* xxxii. 38—40. *Hoſ.* ii. 19. in favour of the ſaints final perſeverance, are left untouched, and are not meddled with by this writer.

2. Such paſſages of ſcripture as ſeem to militate againſt the perſeverance of the ſaints, are brought upon the carpet [c]; particularly, we are charged with giving an abſurd and contradictory turn to *Ezek.* xviii. 24—26. in ſuppoſing that the prophet, by a *righteous man's turning from his righteouſneſs*, means a hypocrite's turning from his hypocriſy, from his feigned righteouſneſs. But this is to give a perverſe turn to our words and ſenſe; for we ſay not, that the prophet means an hypocrite turning from a counterfeit and hypocritical righteouſneſs to a real one, but a man's turning from an external moral righteouſneſs to an open, ſhameful courſe of ſinning: All mere outward righteouſneſs is not hypocriſy, as the caſe of *Paul* before converſion ſhews, *Acts* xxiii. 1. *Phil.* iii. 6. which a man may have, deſtitute of the true grace of God, and may turn from into open ſin; and is no inſtance of the apoſtacy of a real ſaint, or a *truly juſt* man; which this man is not ſaid to be, in the paſſage referred to; and is elſewhere deſcribed as one that *truſts to his own righteouſneſs, and committeth iniquity* [d]. The text in *Heb.* vi. 4—6. is only tranſcribed at large, and the reader left to judge of the meaning of it. The ſpiritual meat and drink, 1 *Cor.* x. 3—5. the Iſraelites partook of in the wilderneſs, were the typical manna, and the water out of the rock; which they might do, and not partake of the ſpiritual bleſſings of grace ſignified by them: though, no doubt, many of them did; for the temporal calamities that befel them in the wilderneſs, are no proofs that they periſhed eternally. See *Pſalm* xcix. 8. To perſevere in grace and holineſs, is a bleſſing of grace beſtowed upon truly converted perſons; to make uſe of means of enjoying this bleſſing, is a duty, ſuch as to be *ſtrong in the Lord*, to *watch in prayer, &c.* Ephes. vi. 10, 19. and which the apoſtle *Paul* himſelf made uſe of: Though, when he ſays, *Leſt I myſelf ſhould be a caſt-away* [e], the word ἀδόκιμος, which he uſes, does not ſignify a reprobate, or one rejected of God, but one rejected and diſapproved of by men; his concern was not leſt he ſhould fall from the divine favour, or come ſhort of happineſs, of both which he was fully perſuaded, *Rom.* viii. 38, 39. 2 *Tim.* i. 12. which perſuaſion was not built upon his own reſolution and watchfulneſs, but upon the nature of God's love, and

[c] Part II. p. 102, 103.  [d] Ezek. xxxiii. 13.  [e] 1 Cor. ix. 27.

and the power of Christ; but left by any conduct of his, his ministry should be rendered useless among men. The instances of *David* and *Peter* are no proofs of the final and total apostacy of saints, since they were both recovered from their falls by divine grace. *Judas*, indeed, fell from his election to an office, but not from election to grace and glory, in which he never had any interest; and also from his ministry and apostleship, which is never denied to be an outward favour, though no inward special grace, and so nothing to the purpose. The chapters referred to, 1 *Cor.* x. *Heb.* vi. and x. *Rev.* ii. and iii. *Ezek* xviii. 2 *Peter* ii. I have largely considered elsewhere [f], and have shewn that they have nothing in them repugnant to the saints final perseverance; where I have also considered the several cautions and exhortations given to the saints respecting this matter; and have shewn the nature and use of them; to which I refer the reader.

3. Under this head is again introduced [g] the doctrine of God's *seeing no sin* in his people. In order to set this doctrine in a proper light, we distinguish between God's eye of omniscience and of justice; with the one he does, and with the other he does not behold the sins of his people, being justified by the righteousness of his Son: we also distinguish between the correction or chastisement of a father, and the punishment of a judge; which distinction we think might be allowed, and thought sufficient to keep the door shut, and not to open it to all manner and degrees of immorality, falshood and lewdness, as this man suggests [h]; though we do not distinguish, as he foolishly insinuates [i], between being *chastened* and *punished* in hell fire: who ever talked of fatherly chastisements in hell? The text in *Numb.* xxiii. 21. *He hath not beheld iniquity in Jacob*, &c. he says [k], is spoken of the whole body of *Israel*, all the posterity of *Jacob*, who apostatized, rebelled, fell, and were cut off through unbelief, and so no ways serves our cause. I answer, that that whole body of people were a typical people, typical of all God's elect, or his spiritual *Israel*, and what is spoken typically of them, is really true of the other; and as all that people were, on the day of atonement, typically cleansed from all their sins and transgressions, hence God, in respect to that, beheld no iniquity in them; so the whole spiritual *Israel* of God, or all God's elect, being cleansed from their sins, and having them all really expiated by the blood and sacrifice of Christ, God sees no iniquity in them to take vengeance on them for it. But if this will not do, this man has more to say, and that is, that learned men say, for he is no judge himself, that the *Hebrew* original will justify another reading, namely, *he doth not approve of outrage against the posterity of Jacob, nor vexation against Israel*. I reply, that as our version

agrees

---

[f] The Cause of God and Truth, Part I.     [g] Part II. p. 106.
[h] Part II. p. 107.     [i] Ibid. p. 106.     [k] Page 107, 108.

agrees with the context and design of the writer, so it entirely accords with the original *Hebrew*[1], and much more so than this other reading does; and is confirmed by the *Samaritan*, *Syriac* and *Arabic* versions, and by such learned men as *Vatablus*, *Pagnine*, *Arias Montanus*, *Junius* and *Tremellius*, *Drusius*, *Fagius*, *Ainsworth*, &c. and could this new translation, though it is wholly borrowed from *Gataker*, be justified, it would be so far from militating against, that it would rather establish the doctrine we contend for; for, if God disapproves of outrage and vexation against his people by others, he himself will give them none; or, in other words, he sees no sin in them so as to punish them himself: moreover, if this text was out of the question, the doctrine we plead for will stand its ground, we are not in such poverty and distress; for besides *Jer*. l. 20. which has been produced already, though this writer takes no notice of it, we have many others which contain the same truth; see *Psalm* xxxii. 1. and lxxxv. 2. and l. 2. and li. 7. 1 *John* i. 7. *Cant*. iv. 7. *Ezek*. xvi. 14. *Isai*. xliii. 25. and xliv. 22. *Col*. i. 21, 22. and ii. 10. *Rev*. iii. 18. and xiv. 5.

VII. We are now come to the last thing in the debate, the ordinance of Baptism. What is said upon this point may be reduced to these two heads, the subjects and the mode.

1. The subjects. The *probability* of the Jews baptizing the children of Gentile proselytes; of the apostles understanding and executing their commission, in conformity to their Jewish notions and customs; and of the early baptism of infants in the christian church, this writer thinks is ground sufficient for the practice[m], that is, of infant-baptism. But is it *probable* that there was such a practice among the Jews, before the coming of Christ, to baptize their proselytes and their children? since there is not the least hint of it, nor any allusion to it in the writings of the Old Testament, in which dispensation this practice is said to obtain; nor in the apocryphal writings of the Jews; nor in the writings of the New Testament; nor in those of *Philo* and *Josephus*, both Jews, and well versed in the customs of their nation; nor even in the *Misna* itself, a collection of their traditions; the authors and compilers of that have not the least syllable of this practice in it. This man, therefore, has either mistook his authors, or they have misled him: the truth of the matter is, this rite is first mentioned, not in the *Misna*, but the *Gemara*, a work later than the other, of some hundred years after Christ: and was this custom probable, is the *probability* of it a sufficient ground to establish such a practice upon, as a New-Testament-ordinance? Is it probable that the apostles understood and executed their commission according to their Jewish notions and customs, though it does not appear, nor is it probable

[1] לא הביט און ביעקב ולא ראה עמל בישראל  [m] Part II. p. 110.

bable that they had any such as this; and not rather according to the plain mind and meaning of their Lord and Master, who by his example and doctrine had taught them both how, or in what manner, and whom they should baptize? what probability is there of the early baptism of infants in the christian church? and, if there was, is that a sufficient foundation? Should there not be a plain proof for what claims the name of an ordinance, a positive institution, a part of religious worship? does it appear that any one infant was baptized by *John*, by Christ, or his orders, or by his apostles, or in the two first centuries? There was a talk about infant-baptism in the *third* century, but it will be difficult to prove a single fact, even in that; and if it could be proved, would this justify a practice that has neither precept nor precedent in the word of God? But it seems it was agreeable to the Jewish customs, to admit proselytes and their children by circumcision, and as soon as capable, to instruct them in religion ⁿ; and that the Jewish children were entered into their church by circumcision, and so baptism is the only sign of admission into the christian church. To which I answer, as to Jewish customs, we have seen already what foundation there is for them, or probability of them; and as for the Jewish church, it was national, and the children of the Jews, as soon as born, before they were circumcised, belonged unto it, and therefore were not entered by circumcision. The instance produced by this man clearly proves it; for the little children represented in *Deut.* xxix. 11, 12. as entering into God's covenant, and belonging to the congregation of *Israel*, were not as yet circumcised, see *Joshua* v. 5. and consequently could not be entered this way. Nor is baptism any admission, or a sign of admission of persons, infants, or adult, into a visible church of Christ; persons may be baptized, and yet not admitted into a church: what visible church of Christ was the eunuch admitted into, when he was baptized, or his baptism a sign of his admission into?

2. The mode of it. That there is any *efficacy* in baptism, to regenerate persons, take away sin, or make men more holy, is what is never asserted by us; nor do we think that a quantity of water is of any consequence on that account: we affirm it to be *declarative* and *significative* of the death, burial, and resurrection of Christ; for which reason we contend for the mode of immersion, as being so, and only so. The washing a part, the principal part of the body, this author thinks ° may stand for the whole. The instance with which he supports this, is in *Exod.* xxiv. 8. His sense of that passage is, that not the people, but the pillars were sprinkled; which, he imagines, must appear to every man in his senses: though, according to his own account, it did not so appear to some, who thought the twelve young men were sprinkled, instead of the people; and

though

ⁿ Part II. p. 113. ° Ibid. p. 110, 111.

though rejected by the learned *Rivet*, and others; yea, though *Moses*, and the author of the epistle to the *Hebrews*, say not a word of sprinkling the pillars, but affirm that the people were sprinkled. And if this man was in his senses, he would have seen which of these senses would have served his purpose best; for if not the people, but the pillars were sprinkled in their stead, then not a part, a principal part, nor any part of them, were sprinkled; and so no instance of sprinkling or washing a part of the body for the whole. He is now brought to allow that sprinkling, or washing the face, does not signify the death, burial, and resurrection of Christ; though dipping the face or head in water, may do it. But why not go further, and rather say, dipping the whole body in water does it? since we are said to be *buried with* Christ *in baptism*, Rom. vi. 1. Col. ii. 12. which men of sense and learning allow to refer to the ancient mode of baptizing by immersion. Baptism is never called *circumcision*; nor are persons in baptism said to be *crucified with* Christ, but to be *baptized into his death*, and to be *buried with him*; and which can be represented by no other mode than that of immersion, or covering the whole body in water. But, after all, this way must still be insinuated to be unsafe, and indecent; and the old rant and calumny continued, against the clearest evidence, and fullest convictions to the contrary.

Thus have I considered and replied to the material things objected to the doctrines before in debate. One might have expected, that, in this *Second Part*, the author would have proceeded on some new subjects. This, to be sure, cannot be the *Second Part* he formerly intended. Perhaps his long harangue on the freedom of speech, and liberty of writing, is to pave the way for what he has farther to communicate. I am very desirous he should speak out freely, and write all he has to say. What it is he has farther in design, does not yet appear: we must wait patiently, and in the mean time bid him adieu, until he obliges us with his *Third Part*.

[ *Note*, The pages in the foregoing marginal Notes in general refer to the Octavo Edition. ]

# THE MORAL NATURE AND FITNESS OF THINGS CONSIDERED.

#### Occasioned by

Some Passages in the Reverend Mr Samuel Chandler's Sermon, lately preached to the *Societies for the Reformation of Manners.*

NOTHING is more frequently talked of in this enlightened age, this age of politeness, reason and good sense, than *the nature and fitness of things*; or, *the reason and nature of things*; phrases, which to many, at least, that use them, are unmeaning and unintelligible sounds; and serve only as a retreat, when they have been fairly beaten out of an argument by the superior force and evidence of divine revelation. It may easily be observed, how glibly, and with what volubility of speech, with what a sagacious look, and an air of wisdom, these words are pronounced by some, who, when asked, what *things* are meant? what the *nature* of them? and, what the *fitness* which arises from them? are at once silenced and confounded. This must be understood of your lower-sized folks, who take up these sayings from others, and use them as parrots, by rote. It must be presumed, that their learned masters, from whom they have received them, better understand them, and are capable of explaining the meaning of them; among these, the Reverend Mr *Samuel Chandler* makes a very considerable figure; whose Sermon, lately preached to the *Societies for the Reformation of Manners*, lies before me; upon which I shall take leave to make some few strictures. This Gentleman, not content to assert, that the difference between moral good and evil is certain and immutable, which will be readily granted; further affirms, that "this arises from the nature of things; is strictly and pro-
" perly eternal; is prior to the will of God, and independent of it; is the inva-
" tiable and eternal rule of the divine conduct, by which God himself regulates
" and determines his own will and conduct to his creatures; the great reason and
" measure of all his actions towards them, and is the supreme original, univer-
" sal, and most perfect rule of action to all reasonable beings whatsoever; and
" that

"that there are certain fitnesses and unfitnesses of things arising from hence, which are of the same nature with this distinction; and that this difference, and these fitnesses and unfitnesses are as easily discerned by mankind, as the differences between any natural and sensible objects whatever."

One would be tempted to think, if all this is true, that this same nature and fitness of things is Deity, and rather deserves the name of God, than he whom we call so; since it is prior to, and independent of his will; is the unerring rule of action to him, and the supreme, universal, and most perfect rule to all reasonable beings whatsoever; and that itself is not directed and influenced by any rule or law from any other. Surely that must be God, which is possessed of such perfections, as necessary existence, eternity, independence, supreme power and authority over all reasonable beings. And if this is the case, we ought to worship and give homage to this Deity; this should we invoke, bless and adore; and not him, who, under the Old-Testament-dispensation, went by the name of the God of *Israel*, or the God of *Abraham*, *Isaac*, and *Jacob*; and who, in the New Testament, is stiled the *God and Father of our Lord Jesus Christ*. To this eternal and invariable rule should we yield a chearful and universal obedience, and not to the law and will of God; unless that shall appear to be directed and conducted by this supreme and most perfect rule of action. But before we fall down, and prostrate ourselves to this *new deity*, and pay our devoits to it, it will be proper, first to examine the several magnificent things which are predicated of it; and begin with,

1. The original of it. The moral nature and fitness of things is represented as something to be considered abstracted from God, and independent of his will, and so consequently as necessarily existing; for whatever exists independent of the divine will, necessarily exists, or exists by necessity of nature: and could this be made out, that the moral nature and fitness of things necessarily exists independent of the will of God, it must be allowed to be a deity indeed; for nothing exists by necessity of nature, independent of the will of God, but the being and perfections of God: either therefore this nature and fitness of things is something in God, or something without him; if it is something in him, it must be a perfection of his nature, it must be himself; and therefore ought not to be considered as abstracted from him, if it is something without him, apart from him, which exists independent of his will, that is, necessarily; then there must be two necessarily existing beings, that is, two Gods. It is said [a], that "the difference between moral good and evil, virtue and vice, as between darkness and light, and bitter and sweet, is a difference not accidental to, but *founded in the nature of the things* themselves; not merely the result of the determination and arbitrary will of another, but which

"the

[a] Sermon, p. 5.

" the very ideas of the things themselves do really and necessarily include." Or, as it is elsewhere expressed [b], " the distinction between moral good and evil doth " so *arise out of the nature of the things themselves*, as not to be originally and " properly the mere effect of the divine order and will, so as that it never would " have been, had not God willed and commanded it to be." But from whence do things morally good proceed? Do they not come from *God, from whom is every good and perfect gift?* As all natural and supernatural good comes from him, the fountain of all goodness; so all moral good takes its rise from him, and the moral perfections of his nature; which, and not the nature of things, are the rule of his will, determinations and actions. Who puts this nature into things, by which they are morally good, but the God of nature, of his own will and pleasure; and, what settles the difference between those things, and what are morally evil, but the nature and will of God? Or the will of God, which moves not in an arbitrary way, but agreeable to the moral perfections of his nature. As for things morally evil, which lie in a defect of moral good, are a privation of it, and an opposition to it, though they are not of God, nor does he put that evil nature into them that is in them, for he cannot be the author of any thing that is sinful; yet these things become so by being contrary to his nature and will. The difference between moral good and evil lies in, and the fitnesses and unfitnesses of these things are no other than, the agreement and disagreement of them with the nature and will of God; and whatsoever ideas we have of these things, and of their different natures, fitnesses and unfitnesses, we have from God; who of his own will and pleasure has implanted them in us, and in which we are greatly assisted in this present state of things by his revealed will; consisting of doctrines and instructions, rules and precepts, founded in, and agreeable to the perfections of his own nature. Besides, if the difference between moral good and evil is founded in, and arises from the nature of the things themselves, and is not originally and properly the effect of the divine order and will, then it cannot be said to be, as it is [c],

2. Strictly and properly eternal; for these things must exist, and this nature must be in them, from whence this difference arises, ere there can be this difference; wherefore if the things themselves are not strictly and properly eternal, then the nature of them is not strictly and properly eternal; and consequently the difference which is founded in, and arises from that nature, is not strictly and properly eternal. Moreover, nothing is strictly and properly eternal but God. If the nature and fitness of things is eternal; if there are eternal, everlasting, and unchangeable fitnesses of things, those fitnesses must be God. Should it be said, as it is [d], that " supposing the eternal and immutable existence of
" God

[b] Sermon, p. 10.  [c] Sermon, p. 6.  [d] Ibid. p. 10.

" God, the ideas of thefe things (good and evil, virtue and vice) muft have
" been the fame in his all-perfect mind from eternity, as they now are; and have
" appeared to his underftanding with the fame oppofition and contrariety of
" nature to each other, as they do now—and of confequence, the diftinction
" between moral good and evil is as eternal as the knowledge of God himfelf,
" that is, ftrictly and abfolutely eternal*;—and that before ever any created
" being received its exiftence, God had within himfelf the ideas of all *poffible*
" *futurities*; of the nature of all beings that fhould afterwards have life; of their
" feveral relations to himfelf, and one another; and faw what fitneffes, obliga-
" tions and duties, would, and muft refult from, and belong to creatures thus
" formed and conftituted ᶠ; – which fitneffes or unfitneffes were eternally prefent
" to the all-comprehenfive mind of God, and as clearly difcerned by him, as the
" natural differences of the things themfelves, from whence they flow ᵍ." It will
be allowed, that there is in God an eternal knowledge of all things poffible and
future; he knows all things poffible in the perfection of his almighty power,
who could, if he would, bring them into being; but then this knowledge of his
does not arife from, and depend upon the nature of the things themfelves, which
may be, or may not be; but it arifes from his own all-fufficiency. *Poffible
futurities*, or *poffible fhall-be*'s, I do not underftand. What foever is poffible may
be, and it may not be; but what is future fhall be, and fo not barely poffible,
but certain. A poffible futurity feems to be a contradiction. God knows what.
ever is poffible for himfelf to do; that is, he knows what his power can do;
and alfo what his will determined to do, or fhall be done: the former is called
*poffible*, the latter *future*. God's knowledge reaches to both, but then every
thing that is poffible is not future. All that God knows might be accomplifhed
by his power, he has not determined that it fhall be; and whatfoever he has determined fhall be, is future, and ceafes to be barely poffible. God fees and
knows all things future, in his own will, purpofes and decrees; for as it is the
power of God that gives poffibility to things poffible; it is the will of God that
gives futurity to things that fhall be. So God faw, knew, and had within himfelf the ideas of the nature of all beings that fhould afterwards have life; their
feveral relations to himfelf, and one another; and all fitneffes, obligations, and
duties belonging to them; becaufe he had determined within himfelf to bring
fuch creatures into being, beftow fuch natures upon them, put them into fuch
a relation to himfelf, and others; and make fuch and fuch duties fitting for them,
and obligatory upon them. In this fenfe it will be readily granted, that the
ideas of all things that come to pafs in time, were in his all-perfect mind from
eternity, as they now are; becaufe he determined within himfelf they fhould

come

* Sermon, p. 7.   ᶠ Ibid. p. 8.   ᵍ Ibid. p. 14.

come to pass in the manner they now do. The fitnesses and unfitnesses of things were eternally present to his all-comprehensive mind, because he willed they should be, either by his efficacious or permissive will. But then the eternity of these things in this sense, or the eternal difference of good and evil, as founded upon the eternal knowledge of God, arising from, and depending upon his own will, strongly militates against what is further said of this nature and fitness of things, or of the difference between moral good and evil, as that it is [h],

3. Prior to the will of God, and independent of it. By the will of God is meant either his will of purpose, and is what the scripture calls, *The counsel of his will* [i]; or will of precept, which is that system of moral laws, God has given to rational creatures as the rule of their actions. The Gentleman I am attending to, uses the phrase sometimes in one sense, and sometimes in another; and sometimes takes in both in one and the same paragraph; and plainly suggests, that this difference is prior to the will of God, and independent of it, taken in either sense; his words are these [k]; "this difference did originally and eternally subsist in the mind of God, as certainly as the difference between light and darkness; and was in idea ever present with him, before ever it became *the law of his creatures*, and appeared to them as the matter of his *command and will*; and is itself that necessary and invariable rule, by which God himself regulates and *determines his own will* and conduct to his creatures; and which, therefore, as a rule of action to himself, must be supposed to be independent of, and prior to, not the existence of God, which is absolutely eternal, but *to the will* of the eternal God, and to be, indeed, the great reason and measure of all his actions towards his creatures." Now, though it should be admitted, that things are fit and proper, just and good, antecedent to the revealed will of God, or his will of command; and that God wills these things, that is, commands them, because they are fit and proper, just and good; and not that they are so because he commands them; though one should think, whatever God commands must be fit and proper, just and good, for that very reason, whether we can discern any other reason or no, because he commands it; since he can command nothing contrary to his nature, and the moral perfections of it; yet, nevertheless, these must be subsequent to the secret will of God, or the counsel of his will, as that is within himself determining, settling, constituting, or permitting the order and situation of things, their natures, beings, and relations to himself and others; from whence the fitnesses and unfitnesses of things, and the difference of moral good and evil are said to arise. Whatever may be said for the independency of these things on the will of God, they can never be prior to it: For if the production of creatures into being is owing to the will

of

[h] Sermon, p. 11.   [i] Ephes. i. 11.   [k] Sermon, p. 10, 11.

of God, and follows upon it; if the several relations they stand in to one another are solely of his appointment and forming, then surely what is fit, or not fit to be done, in such a situation, must be fixed by, and be the result of his own will, as determining them according to the moral perfections of his nature; which determinations of his secret will being revealed, become the law of his creatures; and being so, this law is the surest rule of judgment to them, with respect to the difference of moral good and evil; what lays the strongest obligation upon them to do the one and avoid the other; and so must be the best rule of action to them. Mr *Chandler* himself owns[l], that "God might have "formed other creatures than what he hath; or produced some, or all of those "which now exist, in a different manner from what he actually hath done; he "might, for instance, have stocked our earth with inhabitants at once, and "formed them in the same manner as he did our first parents. And of conse- "quence, as the present frame of things is owing to the wisdom, the good plea- "sure and will of God, so the fitnesses of things which now actually take place, "and that particular system of moral virtue which mankind are obliged to re- "gard, and conform themselves to, must, as far as it is a constitution of things "actually existing, be resolved into the same good pleasure and will of God." Now, as the formation of creatures, and their production in this or the other manner, entirely depends on the will of God, and according to the variations of them the fitnesses of things must have altered; there would not have been the same fitnesses and unfitnesses, obligations and duties; so it wholly depended on the will of God whether he would create any or no; and if he had never formed any creature, in any manner whatever, as he might not have done, if he would, where had been this eternal nature and fitness of things? As therefore the formation of creatures follows upon, and is owing to the will of God, the nature and fitness of things, with respect to these creatures, cannot be prior, but must be subsequent to the will of God. Yea, this same Gentleman says[m], that "the will of God is not any thing distinct from the everlasting fitnesses of "things, but included in them, and indeed a necessary and essential branch "of them." If therefore the will of God is not distinct from them, is included in them, and a necessary and essential branch of them; then the nature and fitness of things is not without the will of God, is not prior to it, and independent of it. And though this same writer boldly asserts in one place[n], that the certain and immutable difference of things is entirely independent of the will of God; yet in other places he seems to stagger a little, and says[o], that this distinction is not originally and properly *the mere* effect of the divine order and will, and is not *merely* the result of the determination and arbitrary will of another;

23

[l] Sermon, p. 15.    [m] Ibid. p. 22.    [n] Ibid. p. 9.    [o] Ibid. p. 10, 5.

as if it was so in part, or in some sense, though not wholly and entirely so. He seems to be fearful, that if the distinction of moral good and evil, and the fitnesses and unfitnesses of things, are placed to the will of God, and made to depend upon it, the consequence may be, that these things will not continue the same[p]; vice may be virtue, and virtue vice; "impiety, injustice, and cruelty, " may be substituted in the room of piety, justice, and charity;" and, "that " there can be no possible certainty that God shall always will that which is now " good, in opposition to what is now called evil; but the one or the other, as " *caprice and humour shall direct him*, which immediately becomes either good " or evil; and on the contrary, evil or good, for no other reason, but because " he, *without reason*, wills them to be so." Not to take notice of the indecency, and irreverence of these expressions; the insinuations and suggestions of instability and change in the divine will, are groundless and unreasonable, since the will of God is as immutable as himself; and though it is not determined by the intrinsic difference of things without him, yet it is determined invariably by the rectitude of his nature; he cannot determine, or do any thing contrary to his moral perfections; he cannot deny himself. There is much more reason to fear these things may change, if the distinction between them lies in the nature and fitness of things, of which not only fallible men, but sinful men, men prone to vice, are the only judges; who being either led into a false way of reasoning, or influenced by their interests and passions, may put "evil for " good, and good for evil." Moreover, why should not the distinction of moral good and evil be attributed to, and considered as dependent upon the unalterable will of God, since all moral good flows from him as the fountain of it? Nor could there have been any moral evil without his permissive will; even as the productions of light and darkness, of bitter and sweet, are the effects of his will and pleasure. Light and darkness are his own formation; *I form the light, and create darkness; I make peace, and create evil; I the Lord do all these things*[q]. It was he that said, by his almighty power, and according to his own will, *Let there be light, and there was light*. What difference should we have been capable of discerning between light and darkness, if God, of his own pleasure, had not *divided the light from the darkness*, as he did? Nor have we any idea of the distinction of these things, but what that God of his will has given to us, who *called the light day, and the darkness night*[r]. As natural light and darkness are of God, and the division between them is made by him; so moral light and moral darkness are, the one by his effective, the other by his permissive will; and the difference between them settled by the determinations of his unchangeable mind, agreeable to the perfections of his nature. It is he that

[p] Sermon, p. 13, 14.   [q] Isai. xlv. 7.   [r] Gen. i. 3, 4.

that has made bitter and sweet, and of his own will and pleasure has put these different qualities in things; the fitnesses and unfitnesses of which are their agreement and disagreement with those laws and rules of nature, which God, of his own will, has placed in sensitive beings; and even so moral fitnesses and unfitnesses are their agreement and disagreement with those moral laws, which are the determinations of God's will, according to the rectitude of his nature; which of his own pleasure he inscribed on the heart of man in his creation, and has since delivered in writing, as the rule of his actions. To all which I only add, in opposition to this notion, that if this distinction of moral good and evil, this moral nature and fitness of things, is prior to, and independent of the will of God, it must be *prior* to the *first* cause, which is a contradiction in terms; for the will of God is the first cause of all things; nothing in the whole compass of being exists without the will of God, but his own being and perfections; and if this is co-eternal with God, and is as independent of his order or will as his own being, perfection, and happiness; it must, as has been already observed, necessarily exist, and consequently, must be God; yea, superior to him whom we call so; since,

4. It is said [s], that this "is itself that necessary, invariable, and eternal rule, "by which God himself regulates and determines his own will and conduct to "his creatures,—is the great reason and measure of all his actions towards his "creatures,—is the one certain and unerring rule of God himself [t];" than which nothing is more contrary to divine revelation, which assures us, that *our God is in the heavens; he hath done whatsoever he pleased* [u]; that he *works all things after the counsel of his own will* [x]; and, that he *does according to his will in the army of the heavens, and among the inhabitants of the earth* [y]. Whereas, according to this notion, not the will of God, but something prior to it, and independent of it, is the necessary, eternal, invariable, unerring rule, reason, and measure of all his actions, towards his creatures. This seems something like the Stoical fate and necessity, which give laws to God and man, and equally bind and oblige both [z]; though sometimes the Stoics [a] indeed consider fate, and the nature of things, not as things distinct from God, but as being himself, his own will; in which their notion is greatly to be preferred to what is now advanced. Be it so that the moral nature and fitness of things is a rule of action to men; that which is a rule to them cannot in every thing be thought to be so to God; for instance, let it be admitted, that it is agreeable to the nature and fitness of things, and to the original difference between moral good and evil, that one man should

not

[s] Sermon, p. 11.    [t] Ibid. p. 19.    [u] Psalm cxv. 3.    [x] Ephes. i. 11.
[y] Dan. iv. 35.    [z] Vid. Lips. Physiolog. Stoic. Dissert. 12. p. 62.
[a] Ibid. Dissert. 5. p. 23, 24. & Manuduct. ad Stoic. Philos. Dissert. 16. p 186, 187.

not take away the life of another, and that law, *Thou shalt not kill*, is established upon this certain and immutable distinction and fitness, and so is a rule of action to men; yet this is no rule to God, nor any measure of his actions; who, as he gives, and has power over, the lives of men, can take them away at his pleasure; as well by ordering one man to slay another, as *Abraham* to sacrifice his son [b], and the *Israelites* to slay "every man his brother, every man his com-"panion, and every man his neighbour [c], when there fell that day, and in that "manner, about three thousand men;" as by sending a fever, a dropsy, or any other distemper. Again, let it be allowed, that it is one branch of this moral nature and fitness of things, that one man should not take away the property of another; and that that law is founded upon it, *Thou shalt not steal:* yet God is not bound by this law; for, as *the earth is the Lord's, and the fulness thereof* [d], he disposes of it as he pleases, and takes away that which was one man's property, and gives it to another; which he has done in ten thousand instances of providence; and what is more, and full to our purpose, he could, and did order the Israelites to "borrow of the Egyptians jewels of silver and of gold, and "raiment," whereby they were spoiled [e], and plundered of their property. To say no more, if this nature and fitness of things is a rule of action to God, it must be something both before him, and above him; it must be his superior; since it must be considered as giving laws for the regulation and determination of his will and conduct to his creatures; though, as this writer well says [f], "he hath "no superior, can receive laws from none, nor have any external power to "oblige and constrain him." And what he further adds is right, "that he "hath a reason and rule of action within himself, is as evident as that he ever "acts at all; and as certain, as that he will always act wisely and well." Upon which I would observe then, not any thing without him is a rule unto him; not the nature and fitness of things, as of an abstract consideration from him; as prior to, and independent of his will; nor is it, as is suggested, his all-comprehensive knowledge of the nature of things, the relation beings stand in to him and one another, the fitnesses and unfitnesses which belong to them, the measure and degree of their powers and faculties, and all the several circumstances of their being; since these are the determinations of his will, and his knowledge of them arises from thence; he knows all these things will be, because he has determined that they shall be. It remains then, that nothing can be a rule to God but himself, his own nature, and the perfections of it. In all things of a moral nature his moral perfections within himself are the rule of his will and conduct. But,

5. Let

[b] Gen. xxii. 2.   [c] Exod. xxxii. 27.   [d] Psalm xxiv. 1.   [e] Exod. xii. 36.
[f] Sermon, p. 19.

5. Let us next examine, whether this diſtinction of moral good and evil, as founded in the nature of things, together with the original and unalterable fitneſſes ariſing from it, is the ſupreme, original, univerſal, and moſt perfect rule of action to all reaſonable beings whatſoever, as is aſſerted [t]. If this be true, all laws of God and men are to be diſregarded; and indeed, they are all plainly ſuperſeded by it; for if this is the ſupreme, original, and univerſal rule to all reaſonable beings, then all inferior, ſubordinate, and particular laws, as all the after-laws of God and men muſt be thought to be, merit no regard; at leaſt are no further to be regarded than as they may be thought to agree with, and are reducible to this grand one; and if it is *the moſt perfect rule*, then certainly there is no need of another. Yea, it is affirmed, that " it is impoſſible that " there can be any rule of action *more excellent* in itſelf, or more worthy the " regard of reaſonable beings." What need then have we of the law of God? This may lead us to queſtion, whether indeed there is any law binding upon us; at leaſt it tends to weaken our obligation to duty, as ariſing from the will of God. Indeed we are told [h], that " *the will* of God is a real and *immutable* " *obligation* upon us, to which we ſhould always pay the higheſt deference and " ſubmiſſion." What, the *higheſt* deference and ſubmiſſion? No ſurely, that muſt be paid to the *moſt perfect rule*, that rule which regulates and determines the will of God itſelf. And truly, this real and immutable obligation of the will of God upon us, is immediately brought under the general notion of the original fitneſſes of things, and is not allowed to be an obligation of a diſtinct nature and kind from them. So that as all morality is founded in the nature and fitneſs of things, our obligation to it ariſes from the ſame, and our obedience and diſobedience to be conſidered as an agreement or diſagreement with that ſcheme of things. Sin was therefore wrongly defined by our forefathers [i], who, in anſwer to that queſtion, " What is ſin?" ſay, " Sin is any want of conformity " unto, or tranſgreſſion of any law of God given as a rule to the reaſonable " creature." They ſhould have ſaid, Sin is any want of conformity unto, or tranſgreſſion of the nature and fitneſs of things, which is the unerring rule of God himſelf, and the moſt perfect one to all reaſonable creatures. How the apoſtle *John* himſelf will come off, I ſee not, who ſays, that *ſin is the tranſgreſſion of the law* [k], unleſs, by ſome dextrous management, inſtead of the law, ſhould be put the nature and fitneſs of things. But ſurely, to derive moral obligation from the will of God, muſt be of more uſe and ſervice to engage perſons in the practice of moral virtue, than to derive it from the nature and fitneſs of things, of which men themſelves muſt be judges. A rule of fitneſs may be a guide

[t] Sermon. p. 19, 20.    [h] Ibid. p. 21.
[i] The Aſſembly's larger Catechiſm, Queſt. 24.    [k] 1 John iii. 4.

guide in some cases; but the law of a superior, who has a right and power of enforcing it by sanctions, properly obliges. In the other case, there is nothing to hope for in consequence of agreement with it, and nothing to fear by straying from it; so that this immutable, and eternal obligation of moral virtue, will be found to be very little, if any at all, as derived from the nature and fitness of things; at most cannot rise higher than mens perception of the nature and fitness of things; for the nature and fitness of things can be no further a guide unto men, or obliging upon them, than as known by them; and if God had not made some notification of his will, with respect to moral good and evil, by giving us laws as the rule of moral conduct, our perception of these things would, in many cases, have been very deficient in the present state of things; and consequently moral fitness, as perceivable by us, would have been a defective rule, and not that universal and most perfect rule of action it is affirmed to be. But we are told [1],

6. That " this difference between moral good and evil, and the fitnesses and " unfitnesses which they necessarily infer, is as easily and certainly to be dis- " cerned by mankind, as the differences between any natural or sensible object " whatever." The natural and sensible objects particularly referred to, are light and darkness, bitter and sweet; which suppose natural and sensible capacities and powers, suited to the discernment of such natural and sensible objects; otherwise they cannot be easily and certainly discerned: A man blind from his birth, will not be able to distinguish between light and darkness; and one whose natural taste is vitiated, will not easily and certainly discern between sweet and bitter. So likewise there must be moral capacities and powers in men, suited to the discernment of moral good and evil; if these should be wanting, or impaired and corrupted, the difference between moral good and evil will not be so easily and certainly discerned. Now the moral capacity of man is greatly impaired and corrupted in the present state of things; men destitute of the light of grace, are *darkness itself*[m]; the *understanding* of men, even in things moral, is greatly *darkened* by sin, and they are *alienated from the life of God*; averse to living soberly, righteously and godly, *through the ignorance that is in them, because of the blindness of their hearts*[n]. The moral light of nature is very dim, and has shone out very faintly even in those who have made the greatest advances in moral science, destitute of a divine revelation, and without the assistance of God's grace. The moral taste of man is vitiated; he favours the things of the flesh; relishes sin, which he rolls in his mouth, and hides under his tongue, as a sweet morsel; so that through the blindness of his heart, and the viciosity of his taste, he is far from a clear discerning of the difference of moral good and

evil,

[1] Sermon, p. 22.    m Ephes. v. 8.    n Ephes. iv. 18.

evil, of the fitnesses and unfitnesses of things; of the amiableness of virtue, and the ugliness of vice. But, man is represented in a quite different light, as far from having his moral powers and capacity in the least impaired or corrupted by sin. It is said °, that " nature itself hath seemed to have been friendly to " mankind in this respect, which hath implanted a kind of *constitutional abhor-* " *rence* of vice in their minds, an *instinctive prejudice* against it, and fear to com- " mit it." Who is designed by nature, whether God, or the nature and fitness of things, I shall not stay to inquire; but go on to observe, that unless this is to be understood of man, as he was created by God, as he was in his state of innocence before his fall, the contrary to it is true; for though the God of nature has not implanted it, yet there is in the minds of men, in consequence of the corruption of human nature by sin, to use this author's phrases, a kind of constitutional abhorrence of good, and an instinctive prejudice against it; or rather a natural and habitual abhorrence of good and prejudice to it. Man is *shapen in iniquity, and conceived in sin* ᴾ; he is a *transgressor from the womb* ᑫ; the *carnal mind is enmity against God*, and all that is good; and *is not subject to the law of God, nor can it be* ʳ; *there is none that doeth good, no not one*; nor is there any *fear of God before their eyes* ˢ. In how many instances has it appeared, that the *imagination of the thought of man's heart is evil, and that continually* ᵗ? Such who are renewed by the grace of God, and are enabled to live sober and religious lives, yet *were sometimes foolish, disobedient, deceived; serving divers lusts and pleasures; living in malice and envy, hateful, and hating one another* ᵘ. Before their conversion, they *walked according to the course of this world, according to the prince of the power of the air, the spirit that now worketh in the children of disobedience; among whom* they *all had their conversation in times past, in the lusts of their flesh, fulfilling the desires of the flesh, and of the mind; and were by nature children of wrath, even as others* ˣ. Their conversion from darkness to light, from the power of Satan to God, from sin to holiness, from ungodliness to godliness, does not arise from any internal principle in themselves, from any natural will or power in them; nor is it brought about by the force of moral suasion, but is effected by the exceeding greatness of God's power, and the energy of his grace; which only gives them the mastery of their corruptions, puts down *the old man with his deeds*, dethrones sin, so as that it shall not have dominion over them. These same persons, after conversion, find in them a proneness to sin, and are, as *Israel* of old was, *bent to backsliding* ʸ; and are only preserved from a total one by the power of divine grace. The whole of

this

° Sermon, p. 26.     ᴾ Psalm li. 5.     ᑫ Isai. xlviii. 8.
ʳ Rom. viii. 7.     ˢ Rom. iii. 12, 18.     ᵗ Gen. vi. 5.
ᵘ Titus iii. 3.     ˣ Ephes. ii. 2, 3.     ʸ Hos. xi. 7.

this is so clear a point, that he must be a stranger to himself, to human nature, and to divine revelation, who will attempt a confutation of it. We are indeed told [z], that "vice is really a kind of art that requires some length of time to "become dextrous, and grow any considerable proficients in." *Ethic*, or morality, is indeed by some defined [a], "an art of living well and happily." But that vice or immorality should be an art, or a kind of art, to be learned, as arts usually are, by a collection of rules, a train of reasoning, with application of thought, and in length of time, I am inclined to believe, was never heard of before: it looks as if it required sagacity and good sense, some considerable abilities of mind, penetration of thought, diligence and industry, as well as time, to be wicked, at least to be dextrous proficients in sin; whereas persons may be sottish and foolish to every thing else, and yet wise enough to do evil. It is easy to see with what view such expressions are used; that they are calculated to encourage and support the old *Pelagian* notion, "that sin is only by ". imitation."

After all, supposing that the moral powers and capacities of men are not so corrupted and impaired, as they are by some thought to be; yet notwithstanding the difference of moral good and evil, with all their fitnesses and unfitnesses, may not be so easily and certainly discerned, as the difference between light and darkness, which is done at once, with a glance of the bodily eye; or as the distinction between sweet and bitter, which is discerned immediately; for moral science, like other sciences, is not to be learned at once, but by degrees; it takes in a very large compass, it consists of various rules, precepts, and instructions, concerning different virtues, which must be considered and examined with their contrary vices, ere the true distinction between them can be clearly seen. In order to have a clear and certain discernment of the difference of moral good and evil, with all their fitnesses and unfitnesses, we ought to have a knowledge of the several beings, God, and the creatures we stand related to, and of the several relations we stand in to them; all which require time, application of thought, and a train of reasoning; but if the discernment of these things is as easy and certain, as that of light and darkness, bitter and sweet, what need of all that care and pains in the moral education of children? why so much solicitude to instil the notions of virtue into them, and give them an abhorrence of vice? Since, as they grow up, the perception of the moral nature, fitness and unfitness of these things, will be as easy and as certain as their sight and taste of natural and sensible objects. What need also either of the laws of God or of men? And indeed, it is said [b], that "as they (men) need no command, or "law, to enable them to discern the natural difference in these things (moral "good

[z] Sermon, p. 26.    [a] Vid. Mori Enchirid. Ethic. l. 1. c. 1. p. 1.    [b] Sermon, p. 25, 26.

" good and evil) they as little need them to help them to pass a true judgment
" concerning them, or to teach them which, upon the whole, is fittest for
" them to chuse and refuse." Moreover, what need is there of moral preaching, or the continuance of a moral ministry? Why so much needless time and pains spent, in opening, inculcating, and enforcing moral duties, and exposing contrary vices? Since without all this men cannot fail of observing the difference of, and of giving the preference to the one above the other? One should think, that gentlemen who have been concerned in supporting readers of morality, should, upon such a principle as this, put their hands in their pockets, and at once pay off and discharge these moral preachers, as useless men. Such moral guides may easily be spared; since it is affirmed [c], that as nature and experience are *infallible rules* of judgment in natural things; they " are *equally sure guides* in
" things of a moral nature." But to proceed,

That the difference of moral good and evil, with the fitnesses and unfitnesses of things, has not in fact been so easily discerned as is contended for, will appear from the different sentiments men have entertained of these things, in different ages and dispensations. The moral philosophers among the heathens, as no one of them ever drew up a compleat system of morality, nor is such an one to be collected out of all their writings put together; nor was Mr *Woolaston's* celebrated performance, called, *The Religion of Nature delineated*, drawn up without the assistance of divine revelation; and, perhaps, is not without its defects. So what one of these philosophers inculcated, another neglected, and what one denied, another affirmed. Some of them taught, that there was no sin in incest and sodomy; and thought it was lawful for buyers and sellers to circumvent each other. *Plato*, a philosopher that made a considerable figure in moral science, commended community of wives, and brought it into his commonwealth [d]. The Stoics, a grave and stiff sett of moralists, were of opinion, not only that it became a wise man, but in some cases it was his duty, to destroy himself [e]; and, perhaps, many of those unhappy creatures who have been guilty of this sin, have not so clearly seen the evil of it; but have been ready to think, that they have a greater power over their own lives, than over others; and though they may not take away another man's life, may take away their own. The apostle *Paul* condemns *fornication*, *filthiness*, or obscene language, *foolish talking* or *jesting*, as very unbecoming, inconvenient, not fit to be practised; yea, as criminal, and highly displeasing to God. Whereas fornication was thought lawful by many; and *Cicero* asks [g], " When was not this
" done?

[c] Sermon, p. 25.
[f] Ephes. v. 3, 4.
[d] Vid. Grotium in Ephes. v. 6. Chrysippus allowed of incest. Laertius in vita ejus.
[e] Lipf. Manuduct. ad Stoic. Philos. Dissert. 22. p. 365.
[g] Verum siquis est, qui etiam meretriciis amoribus interdictum juventuti putet, est ille quidem valde severus—quando enim hoc non factum est? quando reprehensum? quando non permissum? Ciceron. orat. 34. pro M. Cœlio, p. 940. Ed. Gothofred.

"done? when reproved? when not permitted?" The Stoics [h] not only allowed, but pleaded for the use of obscene words; and ευτεαπλια, which is translated *jesting*, is reckoned by *Aristotle* [i] among moral virtues. Poligamy, or having more wives than one, was always a moral evil, and is generally understood to be so; yet some have pleaded for it, as not being criminal; and it was certainly practised by good men under the Old-Testament-dispensation, who do not appear to have had any notion of the immorality of it. To come nearer to our own times, the morality of the fourth command, especially that part of it which regards the time of worship, has been, for many years, disputed, and is still a subject of controversy; and the persons on both sides of the question are men of religion, seriousness and morality; and to come nearer still, Mr *Chandler* and I have different sentiments about some things, whether they are strictly criminal or not. " The many methods that are daily taking to debauch " the principles, and corrupt the manners of our youth, to inspire them with a " love of diversion and pleasure, to lead them into excessive expences, and " costly luxuries; and, in a word, to prejudice them not only against the " principles of religion, but the plain duties of virtue and social life;" such as the entertainments of the theatre, diversions of music, like those of *Israel* of old, *Isai*. v. 12. when his vices had almost brought him to his final ruin, cards, and fashionable games [k]; these, and the like entertainments, Mr *Chandler* says [l], may not be *strictly criminal* in themselves; though he owns they tend to corrupt the manners, and destroy the diligence, integrity, and virtue of the nation, and to be a sensual kind of life. I, for my part, on the other hand, think these things are strictly criminal. Mr *Chandler*, doubtless, has many on his side of the question, in his way of thinking, men of superior genius, and who are the more polite part of mankind; and I do not at all question, but that there are many of the same mind with myself; and though they may be of a lower size than the others, I will venture to say, they are at least equally as serious, sober, religious, and of as good morals. I shall not dispute the point who is in the right or wrong; it is enough to my purpose, and for which I take notice of it, that the moral nature and fitness of things is not of so easy and certain a discernment.

I had almost like to have forgot what this author tells us [m], " That this no-
" tion of the immutable and eternal obligation of moral virtue, is not one of
" the *peculiar discoveries* of the reason and good sense of the present age, but is
" plainly

[h] Vid Ciceron. Epistol. l. 9. ep. 22. Papirio Pæto, p. 1266.
[i] Ethic. l. 4. c. 14. p. 32. tom. 2. & magn. moral. l. 1. p 96.
[k] Of this sort, I suppose, is the game called Faro, lately advertised in the public papers, as a scandalous practice. and contrary to Act of Parliament.
[l] Sermon, p. 46—48.  [m] Ibid. p. 21.

"plainly taught both in the records of the Old and New Testament." The passages in the Old Testament are, *Psalm* cxix. 142. *Thy righteousness is an everlasting righteousness*, or, *is a righteousness* לעולם *for ever*; that is, it endures for ever; *and thy law is the truth.* Ver. 144. *The righteousness of thy testimonies is everlasting* לעולם *is for ever.* Ver. 152. *Concerning thy testimonies I have known of old*; or, as Mr *Chandler* says the words should be rendered, which I do not dislike, *I have known of old* כעדתיך *from thy testimonies, that thou hast founded them for ever.* Ver. 160. *Thy word is true from the beginning*; or as the words ראש דברך אמת may be rendered, *The beginning of thy word is truth, and every one of thy righteous judgments is for ever.* All which indeed clearly prove the perpetuity of the moral law, its immutable obligation upon us, the veracity and justice of God; which appear in it, and will abide by it, and continue with it, to defend the rights, and secure the honours of it; but, what is all this to the nature and fitness of things? or, How do these passages prove the eternal and immutable obligation of moral virtue, as prior to, and independent of the will of God? When the Psalmist is only speaking of the will of God as revealed in his law and testimonies; from whence, and not from the nature and fitness of things, he had learned of old, many years ago, the truth, righteousness, and continuance of them. The only single passage in the New Testament that is produced, is, *Phil.* iv. 8. *Whatsoever things are true, whatsoever things are honest, whatsoever things are just, whatsoever things are pure, whatsoever things are lovely, whatsoever things are of good report*; *if there be any virtue, and if there be any praise; think on these things.* That these expressions necessarily suppose, and infer, that truth, honesty, justice, and purity, are essentially different from their contrary vices, are lovely in their nature, praise-worthy in their practice, and which both God and man will approve and commend, will be easily granted; but still the question returns, what is all this to the nature and fitness of things? To the immutable and eternal obligation of moral virtue, as prior to, and independent of the will of God? Does the apostle make moral fitness, in this sense, the rule of action, or of judgment, with respect to truth, honesty, justice, and purity, and not rather the revealed will and law of God? The latter seems to be manifestly his sense, since he adds, *those things which ye have both learned and received, and heard, and seen in me, do, and the God of peace shall be with you.* Whence it appears, that the things he advises them to were such as he had taught them, according to the will of God, and which they had received upon that foot, and had seen practised by himself, in obedience to it.

I conclude with observing, that this notion of the moral nature and fitness of things, as prior to, and independent of the will of God, seems to have a tendency to introduce and establish among us, *Polytheism, Deism, Antinomianism,* and *Libertinism.*

1. *Polytheifm*, or the having more gods than one. It feems to favour the diftinction of a fuperior and inferior deity; for, as has been obferved, if the moral nature and fitnefs of things is eternal, does neceffarily exift, is prior to, and independent of the will of God, and is the fupreme rule of action to all reafonable creatures whatever, it muft be God; yea, fince it is the unerring rule of God himfelf, by which he regulates and determines his own will, it muft be both before, and above him; it muft be fuperior to him; he can enact no law but what that is the rule and meafure of; his will is no obligation of a diftinct kind from it; he appears to have no power or authority but what is derived from it. I am forry to obferve, agreeable to this notion, how diminutively Mr *Chandler* fpeaks of the divine being. You read nothing throughout the whole difcourfe of God being a *legiflator*, enacting laws of his own will and pleafure, agreeable to the perfections of his nature; as armed with power and authority to enforce them, and as claiming obedience from his creatures to them, as being his will, and founded in the rectitude of his nature; but on the other hand, he is thruft down into the place of a *reformer:* He is indeed called ⁿ the *great reformer* of mankind, and has the honour to be accounted *the Head of the Societies for the Reformation of Manners in England*°; though no more is allowed him in this work of reforming mankind, than what the Societies themfelves do; namely an " *endeavouring* to promote their happinefs by methods difcouraging their " vices, and exciting them to the love and practice of univerfal virtue ᴾ." After this it is no wonder it fhould be fuggefted, that the great defign of our bleffed Saviour's coming into the world, and the miffion of his apoftles into it, were only the reformation and amendment of mankind; and that there can be no other valuable end of a ftanding miniftry in the chriftian church, than to carry on the fame defign. This ftrengthens my apprehenfion, that this notion has a tendency to introduce,

2. *Deifm*, or to explode divine revelation, with all the doctrines and ordinances of it. And indeed, if this nature and fitnefs of things is *the univerfal and moft perfect* rule of action to all reafonable creatures whatever, then what neceffity is there, or can there poffibly be, of a divine revelation? This is *univerfal*, and comprehends every thing fit to be known and practifed; it is *moft perfect*, and therefore nothing can be added to it; it is as eafily difcerned as the diftinction between light and darknefs, fweet and bitter, and therefore needs no revelation to explain and enforce it. Admitting a revelation; the things contained in it muft be brought to this teft and ftandard, the nature and fitnefs of things, to be tried by, and judged of. Let the revelation come ever fo well fupported, and the evidence of things, as they ftand in it, be ever fo

clear;

---

ⁿ Sermon, p. 40.   ° Ibid. p. 42.   ᴾ Ibid. p. 40.

clear; yet if poor, fallible, short-sighted men, cannot see the fitness of them, they must be at once rejected, and consequently the revelation itself. So if *Baptism* and the *Lord's Supper*, the peculiar ordinances of the christian revelation; if the doctrines of the divine persons in the godhead; of the decrees of God; of the union of the two natures in Christ; of the expiation of sin, in a way of satisfaction; of justification by the imputed righteousness of Christ; of the resurrection of the same body, or any other doctrines of the christian religion, how clearly soever they may be revealed; yet if men do but once take it into their heads, that they do not agree with the nature and fitness of things, they must be exploded; and the next that follows, is revelation itself. Whether the abettors of this notion really design to encourage and establish Deism, I know not; but this I am sure of, the Deists are capable of improving it greatly to their purpose.

3. *Antinomianism*, or the setting aside of the law of God as a rule of action, seems to be the necessary and certain consequence of this principle. For if the moral nature and fitness of things is the *supreme, original, universal, and most perfect rule* of action to all reasonable beings whatsoever, prior to, and independent of the will of God, then what need is there of the law of God? or, what regard should be paid to it? Since, as it is said ¶, "It is impossible that there can be a rule of action *more excellent* in itself, or more worthy the regard of reasonable beings." Now, to set aside, and disregard the law of God, as a rule of life and conversation, or action, is strictly and properly *Antinomianism*. For my part, I have been traduced as an *Antinomian*, for innocently asserting, that the essence of justification lies in the eternal will of God; my meaning is, that God in his all-perfect and comprehensive mind, had from all eternity, at once, a full view of all his elect; of all their sins and transgressions; of his holy and righteous law, as broken by them, and of the compleat and perfect righteousness of his Son, who had engaged to be a surety for them; and in this view of things he willed them to be righteous, through the suretiship-righteousness of his Son, and accordingly esteemed, and accounted them so in him; in which will, esteem, and account, their justification lies, as it is an immanent act in God. By this way of thinking and speaking I no ways set aside, nor in the least oppose, the doctrine of justification by faith; I assert, that there is no knowledge of justification, no comfort from it, nor any claim of interest in it, until a man believes. I abhor the thoughts of setting the law of God aside as the rule of walk and conversation; and constantly affirm, that all that believe in Christ for righteousness, should be careful to maintain good works, for necessary uses. The cry of *Antinomianism*, upon such a principle as this, must be mere noise and stupidity. But here is a Gentleman that talks of something prior

¶ Sermon, p. 20.

prior to, and independent of the will of God, and antecedent to any law of his, as the supreme, original, universal, and most perfect rule of action to reasonable beings; as the immutable and eternal obligation of moral virtue, or from whence moral obligation is derived; whereby all authority on God's part, and all obedience on ours, are at once entirely destroyed. One should think, for the future, that not *John Gill*, but *Samuel Chandler*, must be reckoned the Antinomian.

4. *Libertinism* is another consequence, which, it may be justly feared, will follow upon this notion; for if men can once establish such a principle, that something prior to, and independent of the will of God, is the rule of action to them, called *the nature and fitness of things*, of which they themselves are the sole judges, as they may in consequence hereof be led on to explode divine revelation, and set aside the law of God as a rule of action; so what through a false way of reasoning, and the prevalence of their lusts, passions and interests, they may persuade themselves, that it is most fitting and agreeable to the nature of things, that they should do what makes most for their own pleasure and profit. This seems to be the source of all that wickedness and licentiousness acted by the Jews in the times of *Isaiah*, which occasioned the words, the subject of Mr *Chandler*'s discourse. They were not the meaner sort of the people, the refuse of the nation; they were the politer sort among them, that were *wise in their own eyes, and prudent in their own sight* [\*]; men of reason and good sense, as such vain mortals love to flatter one another; they were men of bold and strong spirits, as men of atheistical and deistical principles delight to be called; in a haughty and daring manner, they said [\*], *let him make speed and hasten his work, that we may see it; and let the counsel of the holy One of Israel draw nigh and come, that we may know it*. They were indeed the Deists of that generation, the contemners of revelation; *who cast away the law of the Lord*, set up something else as prior to it, *and despised the word of the holy One of Israel*; and so being guided by the false reasonings of their minds, and influenced by their own lusts, called *evil good, and good evil*.

I would be far from suggesting any charge of libertinism against Mr *Chandler*, or any others, who are in the same way of thinking with him; or that he or they are abettors of any of the above consequences; for though principles may be charged, persons must not on that account. I judge it most unreasonable to charge persons with holding consequences which they themselves deny, though these consequences may follow never so clearly from principles held by them. But I cannot forbear saying, that for Mr *Chandler* to represent stage-plays, cards, and other fashionable games and diversions, by which the nation is

---

[\*] Isai. v. 21. [\*] Verse 19.

is so much debauched, as not *strictly criminal in themselves*, is acting out of character as a moral preacher; unsuitable to a *Reformation* Sermon; unserviceable to the design of the *Societies* to whom he preached; and if these can be thought to be agreeable to the *nature and fitness of things*, from all such fitnesses the Lord deliver us!

## THE NECESSITY OF GOOD WORKS UNTO SALVATION, CONSIDERED·

OCCASIONED BY SOME

Reflections and Misrepresentations of Dr *Abraham Taylor*, in a Pamphlet of his lately published, called, *An Address to young Students in Divinity, by way of Caution against some Paradoxes, which lead to Doctrinal Antinomianism.*

ABOVE *six years* ago I sent a printed letter to the Gentleman whose name stands in the *title-page* to this, on account of some ill usage of myself, and contemptuous treatment of some doctrines of grace; to which he never thought fit to return an answer. The impression of that letter quickly went off, and I have frequently been solicited by my friends to reprint that, and my *Discourses on Justification*; but could never be prevailed upon to do any thing of that kind till now: for no other reason but this; I saw that he and his friends were not inclined to enter into a controversy about these things, and I did not choose to move it afresh, or appear forward to it, which I thought re-printing would look like, or might be so interpreted; and therefore I determined to sit still, and only defend myself when any attacks were made upon me. In this resolution I have persisted, notwithstanding the little, mean, and *disingenuous methods* this Gentleman has made use of, to render my character odious among men. The letter above mentioned was not written with any design to provoke to

wrath

wrath and anger; nor is there a single sentence, that I can remember, in it, that has any tendency that way: But it seems a grudge was conceived, which has been broiling upon his heart ever since, and now at this distance of time he takes up a single phrase, and inveighs against it with the utmost wrath and fury; whereby he has most sadly verified that observation of the wise man, that *anger resteth in the bosom of fools.*

A controversy has of late been moved, or at least revived, by some ministers of the *Independent denomination,* about the duty of unconverted persons to believe in Christ, or about the nature of that faith which such are obliged to; a controversy in which I have had no immediate concern: And whereas it has been given out, that a book published not long ago, called, *A further Enquiry after Truth,* is of my writing, though another man's name stands to it; I take this opportunity of declaring to the world, in justice to the worthy author of it whose name it bears, and that I may not take the credit of another man's labours, that there is not one single sentence of mine in it; nor did I see the author when he came to town to print, nor his performance, until it was in the press; who I doubt not will give a proper reply to the notice taken of him. The Gentleman I am now concerned with, has thought fit to nibble at this controversy; and which he might have done without meddling with me, since what he has broke his gall about, has no relation to that. He tells [b] the society to whom he dedicates this *miserable* pamphlet, that he " was glad that an oppor-
" tunity offered to declare against tenets, which can answer no purpose, but to
" weaken mens obligation to duty and holiness, and to lead to gross *Antino-*
" *mianism.*" But had he not an opportunity *six* or *seven* years ago of declaring against, not only this single tenet he has now taken notice of, but several others which he imagines has the same tendency, and of attempting a confutation of them, had he either a head or a heart for such a service? For some months past, we have been alarmed of this mighty work, that a *learned doctor* had conceived, and that in a short time the mountain would bring forth. But while we were waiting for, and expecting to see the wondrous birth, out turns a *silly mouse,* according to the poet's words;

*Parturient montes, nascetur ridiculus mus.*

The particular tenet, or principle struck at, is, " that good works are not
" necessary to salvation, not in any sense; no, not as the antecedent to the
" consequent." This is called " a filthy dream, a dangerous paradox, an un-
" scriptural absurdity [c], an extravagant position [d], a dangerous tenet, big with
" absurdity; a horrible blasphemy [e], the senseless paradox [f], rude and ignorant
blasphemy;

[b] Dedication, p. 3, 4.   [c] Address, &c. p. 5.   [d] Page 6.
[e] Page 7.   [f] Page 9.

"blasphemy[e]; the blasphemy invented by one of the vilest and lewdest heretics[h]; the draff of those who turned the grace of God into wantonness; and, to close all, an Antinomian paradox[i]." When these ill names and hard words are taken out, there is very little left for me to reply unto. And whether the doctrine opposed deserves such ill language, will be better judged of, when the terms of this proposition, "Good works are not necessary to salvation," and the sense of it, are explained.

By *good works* are meant, not the work of sanctification, a principle of grace or internal holiness, which though it is sometimes stiled *the good work*[k], yet is not the work of man, but the work of the Spirit of God, and is therefore called *the sanctification of the Spirit*[l]. This I firmly believe is absolutely necessary to eternal happiness, both in infants and adult persons, and that without it neither the one nor the other can ever see the Lord; sanctifying grace being an essential and initial part of salvation, or that branch of grace and salvation which the elect of God and redeemed of the Lamb are first made actually partakers of in their own persons, in order to their enjoyment of the heavenly glory. This man must be conscious to himself that I have expressed myself to this purpose in my letter to him; and yet he most basely insinuates that I hold, and represents me as saying, that "A conformity to him (Christ) in holiness, is not antecedently necessary to our reigning with him in light and glory[m]." If by conformity to holiness, is meant that internal conformity of the soul to Christ, the produce of divine grace in regeneration and sanctification; it is a thought that never entered into my head nor heart, and which I abhor. Passive holiness, or that holiness of heart which makes a soul like to Christ, and is no other than Christ formed in it, or his image instamped upon it, in the production of which it is entirely passive, is absolutely necessary to the everlasting enjoyment of him; yea, I believe that an outward conformity to Christ in conversation, or active holiness, external holiness of life, is absolutely necessary to evidence the truth of holiness of heart in all that are saved, who are either capable, or have an opportunity of performing it, and shewing it forth. This writer almost all along takes the liberty of altering the state of the question before us, and instead of *good works* puts *holiness*; thereby to suggest to his readers that I deny the necessity of sanctification to complete happiness; which as it is an iniquitous proceeding, so it gives us a specimen of his skill in the management of a *regular controversy* he prates about. Nor by *good works* are to be understood the internal acts and exercises of grace, as faith, hope, and love; for though these are our acts, under the influence of divine grace, and so may be called our works,

though

[g] Page 10.    [h] Page 12.    [i] Page 13.    [k] Phil. i. 6.
[l] 1 Pet. i. 2.   2 Thess. ii. 13.    [m] Address, &c. p. 13.

though not with much propriety, and as such good ones; yet these do not usually go by the name of good works, either in scripture, or in the writings of good men, or in our common way of speaking. This I mention to stop the mouths of some silly cavillers, who I perceive are fond of objecting these things. Though even these acts and exercises of grace cannot be thought to be so absolutely necessary to salvation, as that it cannot possibly be without them; since infants, as soon as born, though they may be capable of having the principles of faith, hope and love, implanted in them, yet I apprehend they cannot be capable of acting or exercising these graces: If therefore without these acts and exercises of grace persons cannot be saved, these must stand excluded from the kingdom of heaven. By *good works*, I understand a series of external holiness; not a single action or two, but a course of living soberly, righteously, and godly; a constant performance of religious duties and exercises, in the outward life and conversation: In this sense, and in this only, am I to be understood in the proposition before us, and in all that I have said, or shall say concerning it.

It may be proper next to inquire what is the meaning of the word *necessary*, and in what sense good works are so. That they are necessary to be done, or ought to be done, by all that hope to be saved by the grace of our Lord Jesus Christ, is readily granted; but not in point of salvation, in order to that, or with a view to obtain it. Good works are necessary to be done, on account of the divine ordination and appointment; for such as are the *workmanship* of God, are *created in Christ Jesus unto good works, which God hath before ordained, that they should walk in them*[a]. They are necessary, *necessitate precepti & debiti*, on account of the will and command of God, and of that obedience we owe to God, both as creatures, and as new creatures. They are necessary upon the score of obligation we lie under to him, and in point of gratitude for the numerous mercies we receive from him, and that by them both we and others may glorify him our Father which is in heaven. They are necessary to adorn the doctrine of God our Saviour, to recommend religion to others, to testify the truth of our faith, and give evidence of the reality of internal holiness. They are necessary for the good of our neighbours, and for the stopping of the mouths of our enemies. These things I have more largely observed and asserted in my letter to this man; all which he conceals from his readers, and most vilely suggests to them, that I have vented the same notion, and am of the same opinion with *Simon Magus, Carpocrates*, and their followers; who held that salvation was through faith and love, but that other good works were not necessary; but were to be looked upon by men as indifferent in their own nature, being neither good nor evil; nothing being naturally

[a] Ephesians ii. 10.

rally evil, and so might or might not be done: Things I never thought of, and of which I have the utmost abhorrence and detestation. With what face or conscience could he insinuate any thing of this kind, when I have so fully expressed myself upon the necessity of doing good works? But what will not a man say, intoxicated with passion? True indeed, I cannot say that good works are necessary to salvation, that is, to obtain it; which is the only sense in which they can be said with any propriety to be necessary to it, or in which such a proposition can be understood; and which I charge as a Popish and Socinian tenet, and hope I shall ever oppose, as long as I have a tongue to speak, or a pen to write with, and am capable of using either.

*Salvation* may be considered, either in the contrivance of it from eternity, in the mind and counsel of God; and the designation of persons to it; or in the impetration of it in time by Christ; or in the application of it in effectual vocation by the Spirit of God; or in the entire consummate enjoyment of it in heaven. In every of these views of it, good works are not necessary to it: Not to the contrivance of it, and designation of persons to it. God, when in his infinite wisdom he drew the scheme of salvation in Christ, fixed upon him to be the author of it, and appointed men unto it by him, was not moved hereunto by any works of his creatures, or by any foresight of them; they were then no moving causes with God, no conditions of salvation fixed by him, nor were as the antecedent to the consequent; no, not in the prescience or fore-knowledge of God: As they could not go before, so they were not fore-viewed by God, as any cause, condition, motive, or reason of his chusing one to salvation, and not another; *For the children being not yet born, neither having done any good or evil, that the purpose of God according to election might stand, not of works, but of him that calleth*[o]. Good works are the consequents and fruits of election to salvation, not antecedent to it. Nor are they necessary to the *impetration* or obtaining of it in time by Christ: These did not move Christ to engage in this work, they were no ways assisting to him in it; they did not help it forward, or in the least contribute to the performance of it, which was done entirely and compleatly without them.

Nor was it effected by him on condition of mens performing good works, nor were they necessary to it, as the antecedent to the consequent; they did not antecede or go before it, no, not in the divine mind or consideration, and in the view of Christ; for men were then considered, not as having done good works, but as evil and wicked; for *while we were yet sinners, Christ died for us*, and obtained eternal redemption by his blood; and *when we were enemies, we were reconciled to God by the death of his Son*[p]. Good works do not go before, but follow after redeeming grace: Christ *gave himself* for his people, *that he might re-*

[o] Rom. ix. 11.     [p] Rom. v. 8, 10.

deem them *from all iniquity, and purify unto himself a peculiar people, zealous of good works* [q].

Nor are they necessary to the *application* of salvation by the Spirit of God in effectual calling, neither as causes or conditions, or as the antecedent to the consequent; they can be no moving causes to it, nor do they come into consideration in the divine mind, as the reason or condition of it; they are not the rule and measure of God's proceedure in this affair; he *saves and calls with an holy calling, not according to our works, but according to his own purpose and grace* [r], Besides, before regeneration, before effectual vocation, before a principle of grace is wrought in the soul, before the new-creation-work is formed, which is the initial part of salvation, or that branch of it which God's elect are first actually made partakers of in their own persons, there are properly speaking no good works done by them, or can be done by them; and therefore cannot possibly be antecedent to salvation viewed in this light, but must be consequent to it: *We are his workmanship, created in Christ Jesus unto good works* [s]. Nor, lastly, are they necessary to the *consummate enjoyment* of salvation in heaven, no, not as the antecedent to the consequent; that is, as an antecedent cause to a consequent effect, which is the easy, common, and natural sense of the phrase; for who can hear of an antecedent to a consequent, unless by way of illation, but must at once conceive of that consequent as an effect depending upon the antecedent as a cause? Wherefore if good works are antecedent to glorification as a consequent, then glorification must be, and will be considered as an effect depending upon good works as its cause.

And as it will be difficult to fix any other sense upon the phrase, and persons are and will be naturally led so to conceive of it, this, and this alone, is a sufficient reason why it ought to be rejected and disused. This man himself will not say that good works are necessary as antecedent causes, or as antecedent conditions of salvation or glorification: Let him then tell us in what sense they are necessary, as the antecedent to the consequent. His performance is *An address to young students in divinity*, and he takes upon him to be a tutor and director of them in their studies; but leaves them in the dark, and does not offer to inform them in what sense good works are necessary, as the antecedent to the consequent. Will he say they are necessary as antecedent means of salvation? This is all one as to say they are necessary as antecedent causes, for every mean is a cause of that of which it is a mean. Will he assert that they are necessary, as an antecedent meetness or fitness for heaven? This must be denied. How can our poor, impure and imperfect works, our righteousnesses, which are as *filthy rags*, make us meet and fit for the heavenly glory? No, it

is

[q] Titus ii. 14.  [r] 2 Tim. i. 9.  [s] Ephes. ii. 10.

is not works of righteousness done by us, but the Spirit's work of grace within us, which will be performed until the day of Christ, which is the saints meetness for eternal happiness. Will he say that good works are such necessary antecedents to salvation, though he does not choose to say or cannot say what, as that salvationn cannot possibly be enjoyed where they do not go before? I have, in my letter to him, given instances to the contrary; proving that salvation is, where good works do not go before; as in the case of elect infants, and of persons called by grace in their last hours, when just ready to launch into eternity.

If this doctrine is true, that good works are so absolutely necessary to salvation, that there can be no possibility of any, where they do not go before; what an horrible scene must this open to parents of children, who lose by death many, or most or all of them in their infancy? since, upon this principle, they must for ever despair of their eternal happiness. One should think that such a man as this I am concerned with, would have took care to put in a saving clause in favour of infants, especially when suggested to him; who supposes that all the infants of believers are interested in the covenant of grace, and consequently must be saved, at least those who die in their infancy; and if saved, they must be saved without good works, which they neither do, nor are capable of doing.

*Martesius*[t], I observe, when treating of the necessity of doing good works, for such ends and uses as have been already mentioned, and which nobody denies, adds; "But this necessity is to be restrained to adult believers, who are able to perform outward good works; for *the infants of believers are saved without them* (even as they were sinners without any properly personal act of their own) though not without an inclination to them, by the grace and spirit of regeneration." Moreover, upon this principle, what hope can surviving relations entertain of their adult deceased friends; who though they have appeared to have had full convictions of their lost and miserable state by nature, clear views of the exceeding sinfulness of sin, an abhorrence of it, and repentance for it; to have seen the insufficiency of any works of the creature to justify before God, and render acceptable to him; the necessity of salvation alone by Christ; and to express some degree of faith in him, and hope of the heavenly inheritance; yet because they have not lived a regular life in time of health, have not gone through a course of good works, have not lived *soberly, righteously and godly in this present world*, must be therefore everlastingly banished from the realms of light?

---

t Hæc vero necessitas restringenda est ad fideles adultos, qui bona opera externa præstare possunt; infantes enim fidelium absque illis servantur (ut sine suo ullo actu proprie pe sonali erant peccatores) & si non absque inclinatione ad illa per gratiam & spiritum regenerationis. Maref, Colleg. Theolog. loc. 12. S. 12. p. 315.

light? What comfort can a man of this principle be a means of administering? or what comfortable words can he speak to a poor creature become truly sensible of sin, and his lost estate, of his need of Christ, and salvation by him, on a death-bed? Can he, though he is satisfied he has a true and thorough sense of things, encourage him to believe in Christ, and hope in him for everlasting life and salvation? No, he cannot; he must be obliged to tell him that it is too late to think or talk of these things, there is no hope for him; for since he has lived a vicious life, hell must be his portion; for where good works, a religious life and conversation, do not go before, there can be no consequent happiness. Whereas, on the other hand, according to our principle, parents may hope for the salvation of their infants that die in infancy; there is at least a possibility of it, whereas there is none in the other scheme; surviving relatives may rejoice, in hope of their deceased friends being gone to glory, who they have reason to believe have been called by grace, though at the last hour; ministers and others are capable of speaking words of peace and consolation to distressed minds, whose hearts are pricked and and become contrite on their dying beds: All which is a full confutation of what this writer asserts [u], that "it is absolutely impossible "that it" (this tenet, that good works are not necessary to salvation) "should "do good to any person whatsoever." I readily own, that good works are necessary to be performed by all that are walking in the way to heaven, and expect to be saved by Christ, and glorified with him, who are either capable, or have an opportunity of performing them; but then they are not necessary as causes, conditions, or means of procuring glory and happiness for them; nor are they necessary as the antecedent to the consequent, to pave their way to heaven, to prepare and make them meet for it; or to put them into the possession of it: they do not go before in any such sense, or for any such use; they follow after: *Blessed are the dead which die in the Lord, from henceforth; yea, saith the Spirit, that they may rest from their labours, and their works do follow them* [w].

It is said [x], that it cannot possibly be for the advantage of a saint or a sinner, to be told that good works are in no sense necessary to salvation, not as the antecedent to the consequent; and that it may do a great deal of harm and mischief to the one and the other. I have already shewn it may be for the advantage, use, peace, and comfort of poor sensible sinners on their death-beds, and of surviving saints: Nor do I see what harm or mischief it can do to saints, lively or declining ones, or to profane sinners; not to lively judicious christians, who are taught and encouraged by this doctrine to continue zealous of good works, and diligently to perform them, for many valuable, necessary uses,

though

[u] Address, &c. p. 7.    [w] Rev. xiv. 13.    [x] Address, &c. p. 6.

though not in order to falvation. What, will no motive induce a lively chriftian to do good works, but what is taken and urged from the neceffity of them unto falvation? Or can he be a judicious one, that acts from such a principle? Cannot a declining chriftian be induced to do his *first works*, unless he is told they are abfolutely neceffary to his falvation? Cannot it be thought that arguments, taken from the command and will of God, from the glory of God, the honour of Chrift, religion and truth, a man's own and his neighbour's good, demonftrating the neceffity of doing good works, may be made ufe of as means to quicken his diligence, to caft off his fpiritual floth and carnal fecurity, without infifting upon the neceffity of them to falvation? Nor can it tend to harden finners in fin, or put them upon running into greater tranfgreffions, or induce them to harbour fuch a conceit, that they may get to heaven, let them live as they pleafe; when they are told, that though good works cannot fave them, their evil works may damn them, or be the caufe of damnation to them.

As for the texts of fcripture produced by this writer, they are all of them impertinently alledged, and none of them at all to the purpofe. Some of them do not relate to good works, but to internal holinefs, the fanctification of the Spirit, as 2 *Thefs.* ii. 13, 14. *Heb.* xii. 14. which is that grace God chufes his people to, in order to their enjoyment of glory; and without which, and that as perfect, for fo it will be made by the Spirit of God, they cannot fee or enjoy the Lord; and therefore it becomes them, by conftant application at the throne of grace, to follow after a daily increafe of it, and by their lives and converfations to evidence the truth and reality of it. Others only exprefs the neceffity of doing good works to teftify the truth of faith, or contain motives in them to the performance of them; taken partly from the grace of God beftowed upon the faints here, and from the confideration of that happinefs and glory they fhall enjoy hereafter, as the fruits of grace, and not as the fruits and confequents of their works; as *James* ii. 17, &c. 2 *Peter* iii. 10—14. *Jude* 20, 21. 1 *John* iii. 1—3. And it is eafy to obferve, that the whole current of fcripture, and efpecially the Epiftles, run this way, to exclude works entirely from having any hand or concern in the juftification and falvation of men. The paffage out of *Clement*, I fuppofe, is chiefly produced to grace his margin with a large citation in *Greek*; fince it only fets forth the duty of thofe to perform good works, who would be found among the number of fuch who wait for God, and defire to partake of his promifed gifts: for certain it is, that *Clement* did not think that good works were neceffary to juftification or glorification; feeing he exprefsly excludes them from either, when he fays [r], "All are glorified and magnified, not by themselves,

or

---

[r] Παντες μη εδοξασθησαν κȷ εμεγαλυνθησαν, ȣ δι αυτων, ε των εργων αυτων, η της δικαιοπραγιας ης κατειργασαντο.

" or by their works or righteous actions which they have done, but by his own
" will: So we also, being called by his will in Chrift Jefus, are juftified; not
" by ourselves, nor by our wifdom, or underftanding, or piety, or works, which
" we have done in holinefs of heart; but by that faith, by which the Almighty
" God hath juftified all from the beginning, to whom be glory for ever and
" ever. *Amen.*"

We are next entertained with the rife and original of this tenet, that " good
" works are not neceffary to falvation." And it feems, according to our learned
author [*], that *Simon Magus* was the firft broacher of it: And we are expofed as
his difciples and followers; and fome pains are taken to tell an idle, filthy ftory,
of *Simon*'s picking up a whore in a baudy-houfe at *Tyre*, and committing fornication with her; no doubt with a view to infinuate to his readers, that our
principles being alike, our practice muft be fo too; or, at leaft, that our principles have the fame tendency. But if it fhould appear that *Simon*'s tenets and
ours are not the fame, what will become of this little fhow of reading, and the
mean artifice made ufe of to expofe us to fcorn and contempt? As for *Simon*'s
faying that falvation is by grace, and not by works, this was a doctrine he had
from the apoftles themfelves; which he turned into wantonnefs, and abufed to
vile purpofes; and is in itfelf never the worfe, nor is it to be thought the worfe
of, for his ill ufe of it: And as for the inference made from this doctrine, that
therefore good works are not neceffary; this is none of ours, we difclaim it;
there is no agreement between *Simon*'s tenet and ours, about good works; he
urged they were not neceffary to be done, we plead for the neceffity of doing
them, for the ends before mentioned, and which need not be repeated. *Simon*,
*Carpocrates*, and their followers, who are reprefented as being in the fame fentiments, held that every thing, befides faith and love, were things indifferent,
neither good nor bad in their own nature, and fo might be done or omitted.
But can this man, with any face or confcience, fay that thefe are our fentiments? We affirm that good works are in themfelves good, cannot be dif-
penfed with, but ought to be performed by all men; the tenet of thefe men
was, that good works were not neceffary at all in any fenfe, not neceffary to be
done. Where is the likenefs, the agreement?

Give me leave, on this occafion, to inquire into the rife and original, and
to point out the authors, abetters, and maintainers of the contrary tenet, that
*good works are neceffary to falvation.* The falfe apoftles in *Judea*, and other
judaizing

κατειργασατο, αλλα δια τυ θεληματος αυτυ κ̀ ημεις υπ δια θεληματος αυτυ εν Χριςυ Ιησυ κληθεν-
τες. υ δι εαυτων δικαιωμιθα, υδε δια της εμης σοφιας, η συνεσεως, η ευσεβειας, η εργων ων κατειρ-
γασαμεθα εν οσιοτητι καρδιας, αλλα δια της πιςεως, δι ης παντας τυς απ' αιωνος ο παντοκρατωρ θεος
εδικαιωσεν, ω εςω δοξα εις τυς αιωνας των αιωνων. Αμην. Clement. Rom. ad Corinth. epift 1. p. 72.
Ed. Oxon. [*] Addrefs, &c. p. 11.

judaizing profeſſors, were the firſt broachers of this notion; who taught the brethren, not only that circumciſion, but that obedience to the law of *Moſes*, the moral as well as ceremonial law, was neceſſary to ſalvation: ſee *Acts* xv. 1, 5. which gave the true apoſtles and primitive churches a great deal of trouble. To confute which, the apoſtle *Paul* eſpecially greatly laboured in all his writings, and particularly in his Epiſtles to the *Romans* and *Galatians*. The Papiſts, the followers of the man of ſin, have always been the abetters and maintainers of this principle; and ſo has *Socinus*, and his wretched adherents. The firſt among the reformed divines that vented it, was *George Major*, cotemporary and familiar with *Luther* and *Melancthon*: He has been repreſented by ſome, from whom one ſhould not have expected to have had ſuch a character of him on this account, as *ſatelles Romani Pontificis*, a perſon employed by the Pope of *Rome*; a tool of the Popiſh party, to create diviſions and diſturbances among the Reformed. The Papiſts finding they could not maintain with ſucceſs their notion, that *good works were meritorious of ſalvation*, inſtead of the phraſe, *meritorious of ſalvation*, ſubſtituted the other phraſe, *neceſſary to ſalvation*, as being a ſofter one, in order to gain upon incautious minds; when one and the ſame thing were deſigned by both: And this man was thought to be the inſtrument they made uſe of for this purpoſe. But however this be; certain it is, that the broaching of this doctrine by him gave great offence, and occaſioned much diſturbance. The writer of his Life intimates, that the conſequences of it gave *Major* himſelf ſome concern[*]; and that he declared, in ſo many words, that " whereas he ſaw that ſome were offended, for the future he would no more " make uſe of that propoſition." Among the chief of his oppoſers was *Nicolaus Amſdorfius*, who in great heat and zeal aſſerted, in contradiction to *Major*'s notion, that " good works were hurtful and dangerous to ſalvation;" a poſition not to be defended; unleſs when good works are put in the room of Chriſt, and are truſted to for ſalvation: But it is not doing of them, that is, or can be hurtful to ſalvation, but depending on them when done. This controverſy raiſed great troubles in the churches, and gave *Melancthon* a good deal of uneaſineſs; who at firſt was enſnared into the uſe of the phraſe, though he afterwards rejected it, as improper and dangerous. *Amſdorfius* did not deny that good works were *to be done*, but could not be prevailed upon to own that they were *neceſſary*. *Melancthon* at length allowed that " good works were not neceſſary " to ſalvation;" nor did he dare to aſſert it: " For theſe reaſons, ſays he, we " teach that good works, or new obedience, are neceſſary; yet this muſt not " by any means be tacked to it, that *good works are neceſſary to obtain ſalvation* " *and eternal life*." In his anſwer to the paſtors of *Saxony*, he has theſe words:
" Never-

---

[*] Quinimo diſerte teſtatus eſt, ſe propoſitione illa, qua videret aliquos offendi, deinceps non uſurum. Melchior. Adam. Vita Georg. Major. p. 470.

" Nevertheless, let us not use this phrase, *good works are necessary to salvation*." And, in another place, " Verily I say, that I do not make use of this phrase, *good works are necessary to salvation*; but I affirm, that these propositions are true, and properly and without sophistry thus to be declared; *new obedience is necessary*, or *good works are necessary*; because obedience is due to God, according to that saying, *Debtors we are*[b]." Now these were the sentiments, and which are exactly ours, of the great *Melanfthon*, that peaceable man, who never was charged with running into extremes in controversy; his greatest fault, and which has been complained of by some of his friends, who have had a great regard to him and his memory, was, that he was for composing differences, almost at any rate, sometimes, as was thought, to the injury of truth, and with the hazard of losing it.

I could easily produce a large number of learned and holy men, who have asserted the same thing: I shall content myself with transcribing *twelve* arguments, shewing that good works are not necessary to salvation, drawn up by that learned and judicious divine *Abraham Calovius*; who has deserved much of all men of learning and true christianity, for his learned animadversions on *Grotius*'s Annotations on several passages in the *Psalms* and *Prophets*, relating to the Messiah; and for his laborious confutation of *Socinus* and his followers, and his excellent defence of the orthodox faith against them. They are as follow. The question put is, " *Whether good works are necessary to salvation?* " The Socinians, says he [c], affirm this; but this opinion is deservedly rejected.

1. Because no such thing is ever to be found in the scriptures, namely, that *good works are necessary to salvation*. But if this was so principal a part of evangelic truth, as the adversaries plead, it should, upon the foot of the Socinian hypothesis, be contained in express words in the scriptures; since they assert, that all things necessary to be known for salvation, are contained expressly in the scriptures.

2. The

[b] Propter has causas docemus, necessaria esse bona opera, seu novam obedientiam, nequaquam tamen assuendum est, bona opera ad salutem & vitam æternam consequendam necessaria esse. In responso ad Pastores Saxonicos: Tamen hac phrasi non utamur, bona opera sunt necessaria ad salutem. Alibi. Plane dico, me non uti hac phrasi, bona opera sunt necessaria ad salutem; sed has propositiones affirmo veras esse, & proprie & sine sophistica sic dici: nova obedientia est necessaria, vel bona opera sunt necessaria, quia Deo debetur obedientia, juxta dictum, debitores sumus. Melancthon apud Hoornbeck. Summ. Controv. l. 9. de Lutheranis, p. 523, 524.

[c] Utrum bona opera necessaria sunt ad salutem? Affirmant hoc Sociniani: at sententia illa me ito reprobatur,

1. Qua nuspiam tale quid in scripturis habetur, bona sc. opera ad salutem necessaria esse. Si autem hæc tam præcipua esset evangelicæ veritatis pars, ut contendunt adversarii, expressis verbis eam in scripturis in contineri oporteret, vi hypotheseωs Socinianæ, qua omnia scitu necessaria ad salu em expresse in scripturis contineri asserant, &c. Calov. Socinismus Profligatus, Sect. 7. Art. 8. de bonis Operibus, Controv. 1. p. 787, 788, &c.

2. The apostle treating of the causes of our salvation, removes good works, and entirely excludes them; and teaches, that he only has blessedness, to whom God imputeth righteousness without works, *Rom.* iv. 6. Compare *Ephes.* ii. 8. *Titus* iii. 5. If therefore good works are entirely excluded from the causes of salvation, how will the same be necessary to salvation?

3. That which is not necessary to our justification, that is not necessary to salvation; because there are no other causes of salvation than of justification: But good works are not necessary to justification. *Ergo*,

4. If we are saved by grace, then good works are not necessary to salvation; for the antithesis remains firm, *If of grace, then not of works, otherwise grace is not grace*, Rom. xi. 6. But the former is true, *Rom.* vi. 23. *Ephes.* ii. 8, 9. therefore the latter also.

5. If by the obedience of one Christ we all obtain justification of life and salvation, then we are not saved by our own proper obedience: But the former is true, *Rom.* v. 17—19. therefore also the latter.

6. What is ascribed to faith alone, as it is contradistinguished from works, that is not to be attributed to works: But eternal salvation is ascribed to faith alone, *John* iii. 16. *Mark* xvi. 16. *Rom.* i. 17. and iv. 6. *Gal.* iii. 11. *Ephes.* ii. 8. *Titus* iii. 5. *Heb.* x. 38. *Ergo*,

7. What is necessary to salvation, that, as much as it is necessary, is prescribed and required in the evangelic doctrine, *Rom.* i. 16. and iii. 27. But good works, as necessary to salvation, are not prescribed in the gospel, which is not conversant about works, but only about faith in Christ, *John* iii. 16. and vi. 40. *Rom.* i. 17. and iv. 6. seeing the law is the doctrine of works, the gospel the doctrine of faith, *Rom.* iii. 27. *Gal.* iii. 12.

8. Add to this, that this assertion concerning the necessity of good works to salvation, has been already rejected as false, in the false apostles, *Acts* xv. 5. where an opposition is formed to the sentiment of the apostles, that we are saved by the grace of Jesus Christ, and that we are saved by the keeping of the law, or works, and that the keeping of the law is necessary to salvation.

9. If good works were necessary to salvation, we should have whereof to glory; but the holy Spirit takes away all glorying from us, and for this very reason excludes good works from hence, *Ephes.* ii. 8, 9. *Rom.* iii. 27. and iv. 1, 2.

10. If our election to salvation is of grace, and not of works, as the apostle teaches, *Ephes.* i. 4—6. 2 *Tim.* i. 9. good works cannot be asserted to be necessary to salvation; for as we are chosen from eternity, so we are saved in time.

11. By whatsoever doctrine the certainty of our salvation is weakened or destroyed, that ought to be rejected: But such is this doctrine of the Socinians. Ergo,

12. Wherever the scripture produces reasons for which good works are necessary, it mentions quite others, than that they are necessary to salvation; namely, that we ought diligently to perform good works, because of God, because of Christ, because of the holy Spirit, because of the holy angels, because of our neighbour, because of ourselves, yea, even because of the devil."

Thus this excellent writer, confuting the Socinian error, that *good works are necessary to salvation*, strongly defends the contrary; which our Theologaster calls a *filthy dream, horrible blasphemy*, &c. This, it seems, is one of the paradoxes which lead to doctrinal Antinomianism. But why a *paradox?* A paradox, in the antient use of the word, signified a most certain truth, at least, embraced as such by men of wisdom and learning, though contrary to the opinion of the vulgar; which being unusual, struck them with surprise; whence such verities were sometimes called παράδοξα, and sometimes *admirabilia* [d]. This use of the word, I suppose, will not be allowed to be applicable to this tenet. A paradox, in the modern use of the word, or in common acceptation, designs a proposition that carries in it either a real or seeming self-contradiction. Now the proposition, *good works are not necessary to salvation*, is plain and easy to be understood; and is either true or false, but no paradox. We need not go far for instances of paradoxes, this writer can furnish us with enow: As when he says [e], " Salvation " is *all* of free grace, and good works, the fruits of holiness, a part of salva-" tion, are absolutely necessary to *complete* salvation." The word *complete*, in this proposition, is so placed, as that it may be thought to be either a verb of the infinitive mood; and then the sense is, salvation is *all* of grace, and yet good works are absolutely necessary to *complete* it ; or as an adjective to the word salvation; and then the sense is, salvation is *all* of grace, and good works are absolutely necessary to salvation *complete* without them: Take it either way, the self-contradiction is manifest enough. As also, when giving the character of a deceased minister of the gospel, whose ashes he might have spared; he says [f], " he " was

---

[d] Ego autem illa ipsa, quæ vix in gymnasiis & in otio Stoici probant, ludens conjeci in communeis locos; quæ quia sunt admirabilia, contraque opinionem omnium, ab ipsis etiam παράδοξα appellantur. Tentare volui possentne proferri in lucem, id est, in forum ; & ita dici, ut probarentur, an alia quædam esset erudita, alia popularis oratio; eoque scripsi libentius, quod mihi ista παράδοξα, quæ appellantur, maxime videntur esse Socratica, longeque verissima. Ciceron. Paradox. p. 2140.

[e] In an Advertisement at the end of Mr Wallin's Funeral Sermon.  [f] Address, &c. p. 14.

"was a person of *real piety*, but discovered *so much pride and wrath* in his writ-
"ings and conduct, (By the way, how could a man so wretchedly guilty of
"these things, write this without shame and blushing?) that it is hard to ac-
"count for it; except we allow, that he had *a tincture of enthusiasm*." The
first of these instances is a *real* self-contradiction, and the other, at least, a *seeming* one; and both paradoxes. Again; why should this proposition, *good works
are not necessary to salvation*, be represented as leading to doctrinal Antinomianism? This man ought to have informed his students what doctrinal Antinomianism is. Since he has not, I will. Doctrinal Antinomianism, properly
speaking, is a denying, or setting aside the law of God, as a rule of life, action,
or conversation. Now what tendency has the above proposition to such a notion?
Or how does it appear, that the very quintessence of doctrinal Antinomianism is
couched in it, as is suggested [g]? Though we say, that good works are not necessary to salvation; do we say, that they are not necessary to any thing else? Do
we say, that they are not necessary to be done? Do we say, that they are not
necessary to be done in obedience to the law of God? Do we say, that the commands of the law are not to be regarded by men? That they are things indifferent, that may be done, or not done? No; we say none of these things, but all
the reverse. *Do we then make void the law*, through this doctrine? *God forbid:
Yea, we establish the law* [h], as it is in the hands of Christ our Lawgiver; to which
we desire to yield a chearful obedience; to shew our subjection to him as King
of saints, and to testify our gratitude for the many blessings of every kind we
receive from him. It is not worth my while to take notice of the flirt [i] at the
everlasting love of the divine persons being on all accounts *the same, yesterday,
to day, and for ever*; which he knows, in his own conscience, only regards that
love as in the breast of the divine persons, and not the manifestations of it; which
are more or less to different persons, and so, to the same persons at different
times.

[g] Address, &c. p. 5.   [h] Rom. iii. 31.   [i] Address, &c. p. 35.

# THE ANCIENT MODE OF BAPTIZING,

BY

IMMERSION, PLUNGING, OR DIPPING INTO WATER;

MAINTAINED and VINDICATED;

Against the Cavils and Exceptions of the Author of a late Pamphlet, intitled, *The manner of Baptizing with Water cleared up from the Word of God and right Reason, &c.*

TOGETHER WITH SOME

REMARKS upon the Author's REASONS for the Practice of a FREE or mixt Communion in Churches.

## CHAP. I.

*Some Remarks upon the Title of the Book, and the Author's method of writing.*

THE controversy about Baptism, both with respect to its mode of administration, and proper subjects, has been of late so diligently searched into, and thoroughly discussed, that it may well seem needless to trouble the world with any further writings upon that subject, it being in a great measure only *actum agere*, to do the same thing over again, which has been well done already; but those of a different persuasion from us, being continually thrusting their *crambe millies cocta* upon us, and repeating the same things over and over again, though they have been sufficiently answered already, makes it necessary for us, in the

defence

defence of truth, and for the honour of Christ in his ordinance, to reply. A late anonymous author has thought fit to let the world know what a talent he has in that part of the controversy, which concerns the mode of administering this ordinance, by publishing a tract, whose title page runs thus, *The Manner of baptizing with Water, cleared up from the Word of God, and right Reason, in a plain free Debate upon that subject, between Mr* J.P. *and Mr* B.W. June 6th. 1726. *Published for instruction in righteousness.* How he has acquitted himself in the management thereof, and what improvements and discoveries he has made beyond others, is our present business to consider. It seems our author has not thought fit to say any thing concerning the subjects of baptism, but has confined himself to the mode of administration of it; whether it was because he did not care to engage in that part of the controversy, or whether he thought that it has been sufficiently handled already, and this not so, is what I do not pretend to determine; therefore seeing he has not thought proper to take notice of it, I shall not think myself concerned to say any thing about it. From the title page we are given to expect, that *the manner of baptizing with water* shall be *cleared up* to us; for it seems we were all in the dark before about it, or at least, there were such mists and fogs beclouding our apprehensions concerning this ordinance, that there was no seeing *clearly* into it, until the publication of this treatise, by which the author fancies these are dissipated, and the affair set in a *clear* light; but I hope to make it appear, before I have done, that instead of giving more light, he has *darkened counsel by words without knowledge.* The title also promises that this shall be cleared up *from the word of God, and right reason.* By the *word of God,* I suppose he means the written word of God, the scriptures of truth, which indeed are the only rule of our faith and practice; and from whence, under the conduct of the blessed Spirit, all our light in faith and worship springs; but what he means by *right reason,* needs explaining, and is not so easy to determine. If he means a just and strong way of reasoning, one might justly expect to find somewhat of it in this his performance; but the case being otherwise, I shall not, at present, farther inquire what else he designed by it; but only observe to him, that we ought to believe and act in matters of faith and worship, upon the sole credit and authority of the great God, as he has revealed his mind and will in the sacred writings.

The method which our author has taken, in order to set this matter in a clear light, is dialogue-wise, or in the form of a conference between two persons, or to use his own words, *in a plain free debate.* What moved him to take this method does not indeed much concern me to know, but yet I cannot forbear thinking, one reason might be, that he might have the opportunity of making his antagonist speak what he himself pleased; for it would have betrayed his weakness

ness yet more, to have produced such arguments and objections which he was not, in his own way, able to solve: though at the same time it is an instance of his disingenuity, not fairly to propose those arguments which are made use of, nor give them their full weight and force, which he ought to have done in handling a controversy honestly and faithfully; as well as making his friend speak such weak and ridiculous things as never were, at least publicly, made use of in this controversy. Had he had a mind to have made a trial of his skill and his talents and abilities this way, why did not he take out the arguments of some such writers as *Tombs, Danvers, Keach, Stennet,* or *Gale,* and fairly propose them in their own words, and give an answer to them? But this would not have answered his design, which seems to be, exposing to ridicule and contempt the ordinance of Baptism, by plunging or dipping; and would, moreover, have been a task too difficult and laborious for him. Perhaps he also thought, this method best to conceal himself from being known to be the author of it; but if it is truth he is in search of, and bearing a testimony to, why should he be ashamed of it? why did not he put his name to his book? This is such a poor, mean, and cowardly way of writing, as manifestly betrays either shame or fear to appear publicly in the cause he has espoused; if he thinks he is fighting *the Lord's battles,* why does not he appear like a man, in the open field, and not lie scouting behind the hedges? But perhaps this is to keep off a full blow that he is afraid might be given to him. But to go on, this debate or conference is represented, as managed by two persons, under the fictitious names of Mr *J. P.* a plunger in water, and Mr *B. W.* a baptizer with water; for it seems, according to our author, that plunging *in* water, and baptizing *with* water, are directly opposite to each other; but unless he can tell us, how a person can be baptized or dipped *into* water, without being baptized *with* it, they will not appear so opposite as he imagines; but of this more hereafter.

It is scarce worth my while to take any notice of the time when this conference was held, unless it be just to remark, that it would have been as well for the credit of the author, the good and peace of the churches of Christ, and the glory of his name, or better, if it had never been, or at least, if it had never been published; but it seems it is *published for instruction in righteousness;* but if any are instructed by it in that way, in which our blessed Lord thought it became him and his followers *to fulfil all righteousness,* it will be contrary to the design and intention of the author; though I am credibly informed, that two persons have been already convinced by reading his book, that plunging or dipping the whole body in water, is the right way and mode of administering Baptism; such is the force of truth, that it will break out and appear, in spite of all opposition made against it.

I have

I have nothing more to observe here, but only, that seeing the author has not thought fit to discover his name, the reader is desired to observe, that I shall call him by the name of Mr B. W, which is what he has been pleased to assume to himself; and so proceed to the consideration of this wild, jumbling, and confused debate, in the best order and method into which I am capable of ranging it: Though I should have observed to the reader, the terms or articles agreed upon in this conference. As, 1. "That whatever was spoke, should " be tried by the written word of God, and that only." But I thought from the title page, that right reason was to be joined to the word of God, in the management of this debate; but perhaps the mode of baptizing, the thing debated, is to be tried by the one, and *cleared* up by the other. 2. "That in all they should use plainness of speech, without any cunning craftiness; granting unto him that spoke, the liberty of explaining his own words, and meaning;" but if *cunning craftiness* is not made use of, and *a handling the word of God deceitfully*, in this debate, by Mr B. W. I am much mistaken. 3. "That all be done with the spirit of meekness, and true christianity; without passion, prejudice, bitter reflection, or railing accusation." How Mr B. W. has conformed and acted agreeably to this article, may be very easily observed, when he calls baptism, as administered by plunging, a *superstitious invention*; and a pleading for it, *fathering foolish lies upon God*, p. 23. *and will-worship*, p. 24. The last article is, " That they both should keep within the bounds of brevity and civility; the one must not be tedious in speaking, nor the other trouble-" som in interrupting." Which terms being agreed upon, to work they go, and what they made of it, is now our business to inquire.

## CHAP. II.

*The first argument for dipping or plunging in water, as the right mode of baptizing, taken from* John's *practice, and our Lord's example, in* Matt. iii. 16. *with the objections of Mr* B. W. *thereunto, considered.*

MR B. W. introduces his antagonist in p. 6. producing the instance of Christ's being baptized by *John* in *Jordan*, in favour of plunging or dipping in water, as the right and only mode of baptizing: the text cited is, *Matt.* iii. 16. *And Jesus, when he was baptized, went up straightway out of the water;* from whence he argues, that he had been in it, seeing he could never be said to go out of that wherein he had not been. To which Mr B. W. replies

1. That

1. That the words signify no more than that he *went up* from *the water*; as, says he, persons of your judgment have been often told. It is true, it is kind in such learned Gentlemen as Mr B. W. that they will condescend to instruct such poor ignorant creatures as we plungers are commonly represented, and as I suppose this author takes us to be; but when they have done their part, we are left without excuse, and cannot say, that we have not been *told* to the contrary; though it is prodigiously affronting, that after all the pains they have taken to instruct us, yet that we should strenuously insist on the justness of our translation, as we think, to be a little more serious, we have just reason to do. The reason of this low criticism is, because the preposition ἀπὸ, and not ἐκ, is here made use of, but ἀπὸ signifies *out of*, as well as *from*, and answers to the Hebrew מן, which also is of the same signification; and the rather it should be rendered so here, not only because it suits best with the scope of the place, but agrees with that parallel text in *Acts* viii. 39. where ἐκ is made use of: So that there can be no foundation there for this trifling criticism. But if Mr B. W. should question whether the word ἀπὸ is ever used in this sense, let him turn to the Septuagint in *Psalm* xl. 2. which he seems to have some regard for, and there he will find it, where *David* says, the Lord *brought* him *up out of an horrible pit*, ἐξ ἀπὸ πηλοῦ ἰλυώδους, *and out of the miry clay*. But,

2. He adds, "Supposing the translation very right, I wonder, says he, where "dipping, overwhelming, or plunging, can be seen therein!" What a prodigious deal of strong reasoning is here? And I as much wonder too, where washing with water, either by pouring or sprinkling, can be seen therein. He goes on, "you say, he went out of the water, therefore he had been in it; but if "you had said, he had been dipped, overwhelmed, or plunged, I should have "denied the consequence." It seems, however, that he is willing to grant, that Christ's going into the water, and being there, is a necessary inference and consequence, justly deduced from his coming up out of the water; though he is unwilling to allow plunging to be so, for otherwise I doubt not, but that he would have denied the one as well as the other; and I hope he will be willing to grant, that Christ went down into the water, in order to be baptized, and that he came up out of it as a baptized person; therefore he is desired to observe, that we do not infer plunging merely from Christ's going down into the water, nor from his coming up out of it, but from his going down into it in order to be baptized, and from his coming up out of it as a baptized person; for that a person may go into water, and come again out of it, and not be plunged into it, we know as well as he; but that a person should go into water, and be baptized in it, as Christ was, without being dipped or plunged into it, is what we deny; and if those circumstances of *John*'s administering this ordinance

in

in the river *Jordan*, and Chriſt, when baptized, coming up out of the water, are not demonſtrative proofs of plunging, yet they are at leaſt ſtrong preſumptive ones, and ſuch as I challenge him to produce the like, in favour of this ordinance being adminiſtered to Chriſt, by waſhing with water, either by pouring or ſprinkling. If plunging is not a *neceſſary inference* from what is revealed concerning Chriſt's baptiſm, I am ſure ſprinkling or pouring of water can never be; and I will leave it to any *impartial man of judgment*, to uſe his own phraſe, whether there is not a greater probability, to put it upon no other foot, of Chriſt's being baptized by immerſion, when he went into the river *Jordan* to be baptized, and accordingly was baptized there by *John*, than there is of his being baptized in that river only by an affuſion or ſprinkling of water upon him: So that he has but little reaſon, with that air of aſſurance, and in that dogmatical way, to ſay, " *that John baptized in Jordan is true, but he never dipped nor plunged any in his life*;" as he does in p. 10. And here I cannot forbear mentioning a paſſage of thoſe excellent divines, *John Polyander, Andrew Rivet, Antbony Walæus,* and *Antbony Thyſius*, who at the ſame time that they are endeavouring to have the mode of baptiſm, either by plunging or ſprinkling, accounted an indifferent thing, acknowledge this inſtance of Chriſt's baptiſm to be an example of plunging. Their words are theſe *, " Whether baptiſm is to be adminiſtered
" by a ſingle or a trine immerſion, was always judged a thing indifferent in the
" chriſtian church; as alſo whether plunging or ſprinkling is to be uſed, ſeeing
" no expreſs command is extant concerning it; and examples of ſprinkling as
well as of plunging may be found in ſcripture; for as in *Matt.* i. i. Chriſt went into the water, and came out of it, as alſo the *Ethiopian*, Acts viii. So, many thouſands are ſaid to be baptized in one day, in the city of *Jeruſalem*, Acts ii.
" Likewiſe many in private houſes, *Acts* xvi. and xviii. 1 *Cor.* i. 16. where ſuch
" a going into water was ſcarcely poſſible:" Which, by the way, is a miſtake in thoſe great men, for none of the texts alledged, though they prove a baptiſm of whole houſholds, yet they do not prove that it was adminiſtered in their houſes; for moſt of them plainly ſhew, that this was performed before the apoſtles entrance into them; and if it had been done there, it would be no proof or evidence that it was done by ſprinkling, ſeeing proper accommodations to baptize by immerſion might be had, even in a houſe: Though there is no reaſon, as I have

Vol. II.     D d     hinted,

* An vero una, an trina merſione fit baptizandum, indifferens ſemper judicatum fuit in eccleſia chriſtiana; quemadmodum etiam an immerſione an vero adſperſione utendum, cum illius expreſſum mandatum nullum extet; & exempla adſperſionis non minus quam immerſionis in ſcripturis poſſint deprehendi, ſicuti enim *Matt.* 3. Chriſtus in aquam ingreſſus, & ex ea egreſſus eſt, & Ethiops. *Act.* 8. Sic multa millia uno die in ipſa urbe Jeruſalem dicuntur fuiſſe baptizata, *Act.* 2. item multi in domibus privatis, *Act.* 16, & 18. 1 *Cor.* i. 16. ubi egreſſus ejuſmodi in aquas vix eſſe potuit. Synop. Pur. Theolog. Diſp. 44. Theſ. 19.

hinted, to suppose it was done there; all that I produced this passage for, is to show, that though those valuable writers were fond of these instances, as evidences of sprinkling; yet they could not but acknowledge, that the baptism of Christ, and of the Eunuch, were examples of plunging. But to return: I desire, when our author insinuates, that Christ's being plunged by *John* in the river *Jordan*, when he was baptized by him, is a *human conjecture*, which he is not willing to build his faith upon; I desire, I say, that he would consider whether his suppositions that Christ went *ankle* or *knee* deep into the water, and was baptized by pouring or sprinkling water upon him, and that the multitudes baptized by *John* in *Jordan*, went down *some little way* into the water, from whence, being baptized, without any such thing as *stripping*, and *shifting*, and *plunging*, as his words are, "they straightway came up, and went about their business," are not *human conjectures*; and whether, seeing things are so, he may not be justly numbered among those who build their faith upon human conjectures, which he seems to be resolved against. And if nothing but conjectures can be formed from Christ's baptism, concerning the mode of it, I persuade myself, that to every thinking and unprejudiced person, the conjecture, if it must be called so, of Christ's being plunged, when baptized, will appear more probable, and much preferable to that of his having water poured or sprinkled on him. As for his rejecting the observation which some have made on *Mark* i. 9. and saying, that it might as well be let alone, I do not much wonder at it, it no ways agreeing with his notion of baptism. The observation is this, that whereas it is said in *Mark* i. 9. that *Jesus was baptized of John in Jordan*, it might have been rendered εις τον Ιορδανην, into *Jordan*, as the preposition εις is frequently translated. Now to say, that he was *poured* or *sprinkled* of *John* into *Jordan*, would want sense, but to say, that he was plunged or dipped into *Jordan*, runs very smooth, and is very good sense; for a person cannot be said to be baptized, or dipped *in* a river, without being baptized or dipped *into* it; and indeed this is the meaning of all those scriptures which speak of *John*'s baptizing in *Jordan*, as *Matt.* iii. 6. *Mark* i. 5. And whereas he says, that the Holy Ghost intends by it *a baptizing in Jordan*; he ought to observe, that this cannot be without a baptizing into it; to which, I suppose, he will readily reply, that this is taking for granted that the word properly signifies *to dip* or *plunge*; and he may take it for granted that we will do so, until he, or somebody else, can give us an instance where the word is otherways used; which I believe he, and greater masters of the Greek tongue than himself, will never be able to do. But,

3. Mr *B. W.* not only represents plunging, as urged from Christ's baptism, to be a mere *non sequitur*, and an human conjecture, but also attended with nonsense, and very gross absurdities; as when he says, p. 9. " By the same way
" of

"of reasoning, you may as well persuade an impartial man of judgment, that
"Christ is under water still, because it is said, that he went into the place where
"*John* at first baptized, and there he abode, *John* x. 40." As if Christ's
going to *Bethabara*, a place where *John* had formerly baptized, and Christ had
dwelt in, was a parallel case to his going down into the river *Jordan*, to be baptized by *John* there. But I am persuaded, that the very mention of this, without
making any further remarks upon it, will much more expose our author to the
scorn and contempt of every *impartial man of judgment*, than our way of reasoning,
for plunging, from Christ's baptism, ever will do us. He goes on in a trifling
manner, to shew how weak and ridiculous our method of arguing from *John*'s baptism is, "they were baptized in *Jordan*, says he; therefore they were plunged
"over head and ears;" which he fancies is as absurd, and as inconsequential,
"as if one should say, the staff stands in the corner, therefore it rains; or be-
"cause, says he, it is said that *John* baptized in the wilderness, therefore in
"baptizing he thrust the people into thorns and briars." What he means by
all this ludicrous stuff I cannot tell, unless it be to banter the ordinance of
water-baptism in general, and so join forces with the Quakers, utterly to explode it; for what he seems here to direct against the mode of baptizing by
immersion, may be retorted upon any other, and particularly his own; thus,
they were baptized in *Jordan*, therefore they went *ankle or knee deep* into it, and
had water poured or sprinkled on them; which is equally as silly and ridiculous,
as if one should say, "the staff stands in the corner, therefore it rains;" or
because it is said, that *John* baptized in the wilderness, therefore in baptizing,
he put the people *knee deep into thorns and briars*, and scratched their faces with
them. But away with such ridiculous impertinencies as these. Could not the
man distinguish between the place where *John* was preaching the doctrine of
baptism unto repentance, and the place where he was administering the ordinance of it, the one being in the wilderness, and the other in the river *Jordan*, as
he might have been informed, if he had more diligently consulted the text he has
reference to, in *Mark* i. 4, 5. But what he fancies will most affect us, is, that
*John* is said to baptize *with* water: now says our author, if "baptizing and
"plunging signify the same thing, then *John* might have said, I plunge you
"indeed with water;" all persons, adds our author, but those of your judgment,
"would readily conclude, that such an expression wanted sense;" that is, because he looks upon us plungers, as he is pleased to call us, no doubt, as persons exceeding illiterate, and who are altogether unacquainted with language;
whilst he, and those of his persuasion, must be considered as the only men of
sense and learning; but if this penetrating man, this man of sense, can tell us,
how a person can be plunged *in* water, without being plunged *with* it, what a

prodigious

prodigious difcovery would he make to the world! and if it would want fenfe to read the words, " I plunge you indeed *with* water ; ". then pray let them be read, *I plunge you indeed* in *water*, and I hope they will not want fenfe then; aye, " but, fays Mr *B. W. John* tells us himfelf, that he baptized them *with* " water; and, fays he, left plungers fhould not obferve this, all the four evan- " gelifts take notice of it," *Matt.* iii. 11. *Mark* i. 8. *Luke* iii. 16. *John* i. 26. I confefs I have confulted all thofe texts, and find the words to be read thus, *I indeed baptize you*, ἐν ὑδατι, *in water*, only in *Luke* iii. 16. the prepofition ἐν is omitted, which fome, as *Pafor* and *Schmidius* think, in the other texts, is an Hebraifm, or an Attic pleonafm, and then the fenfe and reading will be, either way, the fame as what I have given; but then here is another prodigious abfur- dity behind, which thofe of a different perfuafion from us think we are inevitably thrown into by this reading, and that is, that then we muft be obliged to read the other part of the text thus, *he fhall baptize you* in *the holy Ghoft and in fire*; and this our author feems to have regard unto, when he fays, " It is impoffible " that any impartial man of judgment can fo much as imagine, that by being " baptized with the holy Ghoft, a being plunged in the holy Ghoft fhould be " underftood; for the Lord himfelf tells us, that by baptizing he means " pouring;" for the proof of which, he mentions *Ifai.* xliv. 3. and *Acts* x. 44. That the donation of the Spirit is fometimes expreffed by pouring, fometimes by fprinkling, I frankly own; but this which *John* has reference to, is the ex- traordinary donation of the Spirit on the day of *pentecoft*, as is manifeft from *Acts* i. 5. and therefore another word is made ufe of, as being more expreffive of the glory and greatnefs of that difpenfation; and when we confider the ac- count that is given of it, by the infpired writer, as that *there came a found from heaven, as of a rufhing mighty wind, which* filled *the houfe where they were fitting*; and that *cloven tongues, like as of fire*, fat *upon each of them*; and that *they were all* filled *with the holy Ghoft* ; it will not feem fo very ftrange, incongruous, and difagreeable to fay, that they were as if they had been dipped or plunged all over therein. I am perfuaded our author will acknowledge the learned *Cafaubon* to be an *impartial man of judgment*, and yet he fpeaks of, and explains this affair much in the fame language. His words are thefe, with which I fhall conclude this chapter: " Although, fays he [b], I do not difapprove of the word " *baptizare* being retained here, that the antithefis may be full, yet I am of opi-
" nion,.

---

[b] Etfi nos improbo ut hic quoque retineatur verbum baptizare quo plena fit ἡ ἀντιθεσις, tamen habendam hoc loco propriæ fignificationis rationem cenfeo, βαπτιζειν enim tanquam ad tingendum mergere eft. Atque hoc fenfu vere dicuntur apoftoli βαπτισθηναι. Domus enim in qua hoc peractum eft, Spiritu fancto fuit repleta, ita ut in eam tanquam in κολυμϐηθρα quandam apoftoli demerfi fuiffe videantur. Cafaub. in Act. i. 5.

"mion, that a regard is had in this place to its proper signification, for βαπτιζην is to immerse, so as to tinge or dip, and in this sense the apostles are truly said to be baptized, for the house in which this was done, was filled with the holy Ghost, so that the apostles seemed to be plunged into it as into a fish-pool." And in the same way, their being baptized or dipped in fire, may be accounted for, that being expressive of the same thing, unless our author should think, that this is still a much more improper way of speaking, but among the best Greek authors, we have this phrase of dipping in fire made use of, and particularly in *Moschus* ᶜ

## CHAP. III.

*The second argument in favour of baptism by immersion, taken from the place* John *chose to baptize in, and the reason of that choice,* John iii. 23. *with the weak replies, and foolish shifts and evasions which Mr* B. W. *makes thereunto, considered.*

MR *B. W.* next introduces his friend Mr *P.* in p. 11, 12. arguing for immersion, from those words in *John* iii. 26. *And John also was baptizing in Enon, near to Salim, because there was much water there,* after this manner; namely, " *John* was baptizing in *Enon,* because there was much water there; therefore " all that were baptized were overwhelmed with water. They were dipped, " they were plunged, because there was much water there." But this argument is not very fairly represented; for we do not argue merely from there being much water there, that they were dipped or plunged, but from their being *baptized* in a place of much water, and which was chose for that very reason. We know that there may be much water where no person is dipped or plunged into it; but that any person should be *baptized* in a place of much water, without being dipped or plunged into it, is what we deny. Moreover the reasonableness of concluding that baptism, in those times, was performed by immersion, we think may be fairly argued from *John's* choosing of, and baptizing in a place where there was much water, and we believe it will appear so to every thinking and unprejudiced person; but let us consider what Mr *B. W.* has to reply. And,

*1st,* To shew his learning and skill in chorography, he inquires what *Enon* was, whether it was a river or no, and seems to call in question its being so, and therefore tells us, p. 13. *That such a river cannot be found in the best accounts we have of the*
*land*

---

ᶜ Idyll. 1. Μητι θιγης πλανα δωρα, ταγαρ πυρι παντα βιβαπται.

*land of* Ifrael: and adds, *and it is very probable, that* Enon *was either a village, or a tract of land, where there were abundance of springs and little rivulets of water.* Whether *Enon* is the name of a river, or of a city, town or village, or of a tract of land abounding with water, does not *much* affect our controversy, if it is but granted that there was much water there, for which reason *John* made choice of it to baptize in; and I hope it will be granted, that there was a sufficiency of water to baptize by immersion, especially seeing Mr *B.W.* tells us in p. 17. that *for plunging of people there need not be much water.* The *Arabic* version divides the word into two, and calls it *Ain-Nun*, which may be rendered, the *fountain of Nun*; as does also the *Syriac*, *Ain-Yon*, which *Junius* renders *the fountain of the Dove*: And as for *Salim*, near to which was *Enon*, and which is the best direction for the finding where it was; this was either *Shalem*, a city of *Shechem*, mentioned in *Gen.* xxxiii. 18. as some think, though this is not very likely, seeing that was in *Samaria*, with the inhabitants of which *John* had nothing to do; or else it is the same with *Shalim*, in 1 *Sam.* ix 4. as *Junius* and others think, though it seems rather to be that place which *Arias Montanus*[d] calls *Salim juxta torrentem*, Salim *by the brook*, which he places in the tribe of *Issachar*, not far from the lake of *Genesaret*; and may be called so, perhaps, either because it was near this *Enon*, where there was much water, or else because it was not far from the place where the two rivers *Jaboc* and *Jordan* met; as *Calvin*, from the geographers, observes upon this place. But supposing that our present best accounts of the land of *Israel*, make no mention of any such river as *Enon*; nor can it be determined by them what it was, or where it was; yet I hope it will be acknowledged, that the account of it in the sacred text is just, and that whether it be a river, village, or tract of land, yet there was *much water* there; for which reason *John* made choice of it as a proper place to baptize in, which is sufficient for our purpose. But,

2*dly*, From inquiring into the place itself, he proceeds to give us *the notation of the word*, or the reason of its name; for he says, the *learned tell us, that the word does signify a place of springs*: And the learned[e] also tell us, that it signifies an *eye*, as well as a spring or fountain; and also *soothsaying*, and *clouds*, or a *beclouding*; so that there is not much to be learned from that. And here I cannot forbear mentioning the observation of *Aretius*, upon this place; though I suppose that Mr *B.W.* will think that he might as well have let it alone, who, after he had said that it was a town near *Jordan*, observes[f], that *it signifies affliction, humility, and weeping*: I suppose he derives it from the Hebrew word עֲנָה *Anab*, which sometimes signifies to humble and afflict; " thereby, says he, teaching us,
" that

---

[d] Antiqu. Jud. l. 2. c 3.   [e] Vid. Stephan. Dictionar. Geograph.

[f] Significat afflictionem, humilitatem & fletum, admonens nos tales requiri in baptismo & vera pœnitentia, Aretius in Joh. iii. 23.

" that such we are required to be in baptism and true repentance." But to go on: In order to strengthen this sense of the word, which Mr *B. W.* says is given by the learned, he informs us, that " it is observable, that the town called *Mid-* " *din*, in *Joshua* xv. 61. is called *Enon*, by the seventy Greek interpreters of " the Old Testament;" whether this is an observation of his own, or of the learned with whom he converses, he does not tell us; if of the latter, he might have been so kind as to have told us who they were, that we might have consulted them, and have considered their proofs of it. By what goes before and after, it seems as if he meant that it was one of their's; which when one comes to examine, it looks, according to the order of the text, as if it was *Secacah*, and not *Middin*, that is rendered *Enon*; the words in *Joshua* xv. 61. *in the wilderness, Beth-arabah, Middin & Secacah*, are by the Septuagint thus rendered, *& Baddargeis, & Tharabaam, & Ænon*; so that if a regard is to be had to the order of the words, then as *Baddargeis* answers to *Beth-arabah*, so *Tharabaam* to *Middin*, and *Ænon* to *Secacah*; and if so, here is a fine piece of critical learning spoiled: But supposing that *Baddargeis* answers to *Bamidbar*, which we render, *in the wilderness*; and *Tharabaam* to *Beth-arabah*, and so *Ænon* to *Middin*, because the Septuagint make seven cities here, and in the following verse, when there are but six, to what purpose is this produced? or what is gained by it? or how does this prove that the word signifies a place of springs? Yes, in Mr *B. W*'s. imagination, it serves a very good purpose, and sufficiently proves this signification of the word; but how? why *they* (the learned) *also observe*, says he, " that in *Judges* v. 10. there " is mention made of those that sit in, upon, or near *Middin*, we read *in judg-* " *ment*, where immediately the holy Ghost takes notice of *the places of drawing* " *water*; so that, if any body would know wherefore *Middin* is rendered *Enon* " by the Septuagint, the reason is ready, because of the *places of drawing water*." A fine way of arguing indeed! what, because *Middin*, in *Joshua* xv. 61. is rendered *Ænon* by the Septuagint, and because a word of the same form and sound, is rendered in *Judges* v. 10. by the same εν Κειτηειν, " upon the judgment-seat;" and we read *in judgment*, where the holy Ghost immediately takes notice of the places of drawing water; therefore the reason is ready for any body to know why *Middin* is rendered by *Enon*, in the former text, and that is, because of *the places of drawing water*." Can any man in the world see any connection here? and how does this appear to be the ready, plain and easy reason of this version: Had either *Middin* or *Enon* been in the Septuagint text of *Judges* v. 10. there had been some tolerable colour and pretence for all this, though that would have fell short of proving it to be the reason of such a version in *Joshua* xv. 61. but here is not the least appearance of either; though it is true, there are some interpreters

terpreters who think that the word rendered *judgment*, is the proper name of a place either of that city mentioned in *Joshua* xv. 61. or of a *path* or road-way which bore this name; so the *Masora*, R. *David Kimchi*, and R. *Levi Ben Gersom*; though the Targum, Septuagint, R. *Solomon Jarchi*, R. *Isaiah*, understand it of *judgment*, as we do, as well as many other interpreters and expositors; but granting that the word does signify a place of fountains and springs, and was so called, because of the places of drawing water, then I hope there was a plenty of water there, and what was sufficient for the baptizing of persons by immersion of the whole body, for which reason *John* made choice of it. But,

3. He goes on and says, " You and your friends must grant, that the words " of the holy Ghost do not denote much water in one great channel, but many " waters, streams or rivulets, in a certain tract or neighbourhood." By *the words of the holy Ghost*, I suppose he means πολλα υδατα, which our translators have very well rendered *much water*; and he seems in this passage to have reference to that poor low criticism, which those of his persuasion are often obliged to have recourse to, which is, that these words are not expressive of a large quantity of water, but signify only, many little streams and rivulets, which are not sufficient for an immersion of the whole body, and therefore should have been rendered, not *much water*, but *many waters*. We grant that υδατα πολλα may be literally rendered *many waters*; but that they signify some little small streams and rivulets of water, and not a large quantity thereof, is what we deny. That *John* intends a large and not a small quantity of water, is manifest from his use of the phrase in other of his writings, as for instance, in *Rev.* i. 15. it is said of Christ, that *his voice* was *as the sound*, υδατων πολλων, *of many waters*; but what sound does little purling streams, and small rivulets of water make? And who can imagine the allusion should be made to them; or that these should be expressive of the voice of Christ in the gospel, especially in the ministry of it by the apostles, whose *sound went into all the earth, and their words unto the end of the world?* Again, in *Rev.* xvii. 1. the great whore is represented as sitting επι των υδατων των πολλων, " upon many waters," by which are metaphorically set forth unto us, those many people, kingdoms, and nations over whom she exercised a lawless and tyrannical power, as appears from ver. 15. where the angel tells *John*, that the waters which he saw, where the *whore sitteth, are peoples, and multitudes, and nations, and tongues:* from whence it is manifest, that by this phrase is intended, not a small quantity of people, or some little petty nations and kingdoms, which were subject to the see of *Rome*; but a large quantity of people, even *multitudes*, and of nations and kingdoms, the chief and greatest; besides, our author, as well as others, would do well to consider,

that

that ὕδατα πολλα is an Hebraism, and answers to מים רבים *Rabbim Mayim*, and by which the Septuagint frequently render these words; and that where small streams and rivulets cannot be intended, but large and great waters are spoken of, nay where indeed, the waters of the sea are plainly meant: As for instance, in *Psalm* lxxvii. 19. it is said concerning God's leading his people through the *Red sea*, *Thy way is in the sea, and thy path, ἐν ὕδασι πολλοις, in many waters*, or as we justly read it, *in the great waters*; for surely the waters of the sea may be called so, and I hope that ὕδατα πολλα, here, does not signify many little streams and rivulets. Again, in *Psalm* cvii. 23. sea-faring persons are thus described, *they that go down to the sea in ships, that do business, ἐν ὕδασι πολλοις, in many waters*, that is, *in great waters*, as the waters of the sea are; and I persuade myself, that none can be so weak as to imagine, that ships can sail in small streams and rivulets, or the business that the *Psalmist* speaks of, to be done in such places where there is not a sufficiency of water to dip or plunge into. Moreover, if this phrase may not be allowed to be an Hebraism, it will be hard to prove that many waters signify a small quantity, and only some little streams or rivulets: Sure I am, some persons, of far superior learning to what Mr *B. W.* discovers, have thought the contrary, as *Gratius, Piscator, Lightfoot*, and others; but if these may not be allowed to be good judges of the Greek tongue, I hope *Nonnus Panopolitanus* may, who flourished about the year 420. was a famous Greek and Christian poet, and turned this gospel, according to *John*, into Greek verse, who not only says, that the place where *John* was baptizing, was βαθυκυμων⸳, " a place of deep waters," but also expresses ὕδατα πολλα by ἀφθονον ὕδωρ, *copiosa aqua*, " a large water, or abundance of water:" But because his version of the whole text makes much for the elucidation of it, I will transcribe it from him "

Ἠν δε ϰ αυτος.
Θε⸳ Ιωαννης θιοπηθια λαον αλητην.
Ὑδατι βαπτιζων, βαθυκυμον⸳ εγγυθι Σαλημ,
Κειθι γαρ ευρυποργιο κυλινδομων ποταμοιο,
Χευμασιν αιπαοις κυμαινεται αφθονον ὕδωρ,
Αρκιον ειμι σι πασιν.

Which may be rendered in English thus: " And the divine *John* himself also was baptizing in water, the straying people, who were obedient to God, at or in a place of deep waters, near to *Salem*, because there abundance of water, sufficient for them altogether, flowed in the ever-running streams of the winding river, whose passage over is very broad." But supposing that much water in one great channel is not intended, though I must confess I can see no reason why it should not, and that many waters, streams, or rivulets are here meant;

meant; yet, who does not know that many of these together, can not only fill large and capacious pools, sufficient enough for immersion, but also frequently form and feed very great rivers? so that I do not see that this will much help his cause, or affect our argument.

But Mr *B. W.* says, p. 14. "But what and if the holy Ghost intends to give "us the reason why the place was called *Enon,* because there were many waters, "springs or rivulets there? what will become of your argument then, and how "will you help yourself?" Where he insinuates, as if the design of the holy Ghost in these words, *because there was much water there,* is not to inform us of the conveniency of this place for baptizing, or that it was the reason why *John* made choice of it, but to explain the meaning of the word *Enon,* and to let us know, that the place was so called, because there was much water, or many springs or rivulets there: How trifling and ridiculous is this? Does the holy Ghost take such a method as this in other parts of the Bible, where the proper names of places are mentioned? and what necessity can there be for explaining of this any more than there is of others? and why is not the meaning of *Salim* as well as *Enon* given? Surely we need not be afraid of losing our argument from such interpretations and senses of scriptures as these, which will appear vain and trifling at the first view, to every impartial man of judgment; nor need we be much solicitous about helping ourselves, when pressed with such silly nonsense as this. But,

4. Mr *B. W.* proceeds to charge the argument for plunging in baptism, taken from hence, not only with want of consequence, but as a vain conjecture: his words are these; "Granting, says he, that *Enon* was a great river, or a great "water, yet it can never be proved that *John* plunged persons all over in it; "that is nothing at all but your vain conjecture;" and then in his usual, positive, and dogmatical way, adds, "he baptized them, but he never plunged "them." Here I need only reason as I did before, with regard to the baptism of Christ, and others, in *Jordan,* that if *John's* pitching upon *Enon,* as a convenient place to baptize in, *because there was much water there,* and his baptizing in that place is not a demonstrative proof of his baptizing by plunging, yet at least must be a strong presumptive one, and such an one as he can never produce in favour of his baptizing there by an affusion or sprinkling of water: And again, if to suppose that *John* baptized there by immersion, is a vain and trifling conjecture, I am sure, and I believe it will appear to every unprejudiced person, that to suppose that he did it by sprinkling or pouring, is much more so. And if we poor ignorant creatures may not be allowed to infer and conclude immersion from hence, without being charged with making vain and trifling conjectures; yet I hope he will be a little more sparing of the great *Calvin,* for whom, I do

not

not doubt, from some few hints I have observed in this conference, he has a value and respect, and whom I persuade myself he will allow to be an *impartial man of judgment*, and to whose judgment he will always pay a deference: His note, upon this text, is this; "Geographers write, says he, that these two towns, *Enon* and *Salim*, were not far from the confluence of *Jaboc* and *Jordan*, nigh to which they place *Scythopolis*. Moreover, from those words we may gather that baptism was performed by *John* and Christ, by a plunging of the whole body under water ᶠ;" and I think we may conclude this very fairly too, whatever Mr *B. W.* may think of it. But,

5*thly*, Our ingenious author, by a new turn and mighty stretch of thought, has found out another reason, besides that of conveniency, for baptizing, which made *John* fix upon, and determined him in the choice of this place, there being much water there, and that is, that *the vast multitudes* which flocked to, and attended upon his ministry, might be *refreshed*, as also their horses, or their camels, or whatsoever we may suppose many of them did ride upon; by which, I suppose, he means *asses*, I cannot but observe, that he seems to speak this with some caution or guard upon himself, as he does also in p. 17. where he says, speaking of the people which flocked to *John's* ministry, "a great number of them, doubtless, must travel many miles; and we must suppose, many on foot, and many otherwise:" and this I cannot but attribute to a self-consciousness in him, that he deserved to be numbered among those animals, or at least, to his being aware that this would be turned upon him, for his foolish and ridiculous glosses on the sacred writings. What seems the most to strengthen him in his folly, and upon which he lays much stress, is the vast multitudes of people which followed *John*, and attended upon his ministry; and the unwise part *John* would have acted, if he had not chose places where refreshment might be had for themselves and their cattle: But surely the man forgets himself, or at least, does not give himself time to consider, that *John* was now upon the declining hand, and had not those vast numbers and multitudes following him as formerly he had; the crowd was now after Christ, and not *John*; and though he had some which came to him, and were baptized, yet they were but few in comparison of what he had formerly, or what now followed Christ; as he might easily have observed, by reading this third chapter of *John*; and therefore there was no need for him to be so solicitous for accommodations for the people and their cattle, as is here by our author intimated; and to make his sense appear the more plausible, he tells us, that "by *John's* baptizing, we are to understand *John's* preaching, administering in his office, and fulfilling his course;" for which he cites,

E E 2 *Matt.*

ᶠ Fuisse autem duo hæc oppida Ænon & Salim, non procul à confluente Jordanis & Jaboc tradunt geographi, quibus viciniam faciunt Scythopolim. Cæterum ex his verbis colligere licet, baptismum fuisse celebratum à Joanne & Christo totius corporis submersione. Calvin in Joh. iii. 23.

*Matt.* xxi. 25. *Acts* x. 47. It is readily granted, that sometimes by *John's* baptism, we are to understand his whole ministry, and particularly the doctrine of baptism, preached by him, as distinct from the administration of the ordinance; but that by his baptizing here is meant his preaching, must be denied; for that it intends his administration of the ordinance of water-baptism, not only his act of *baptizing*, but the people's submission to it; for the text says, *they came and were baptized*, manifestly prove it; to say nothing of the place where it was performed, being a place of much water, the thing now in debate. He also insinuates, that great part of the land of *Judea* was sandy and barren; but not so barren as his arguments are. " You may understand, says he, what sort of a " country, for water, a great part of that land was, from the great contentions " between *Isaac's* servants, and others, about digging, finding, and enjoying " wells of water;" but these contentions did not arise so much from the scarcity of water, as from the envy of the *Philistines* on the one hand, and from *Isaac's* servants, stiffly insisting upon their right and property, on the other: For though persons may have never such plenty of things, yet they are not willing to be defrauded of what is their just right.

He goes on: " Glad at heart they were when they found plenty of water, for " their own refreshment, and the refreshment of their cattle." One would be almost tempted to think that the man was describing the sandy deserts of *Arabia*, rather than the fertile land of *Canaan*, and representing *the travelling companies of Dedanim* who being almost scorched with heat, are thrown into a transport of joy, at the sight of a spring of water ; but who will it be most proper to give credit to, *Moses*, an inspired writer, who told the people of *Israel*, that God was bringing them into a *good land, a land of brooks of water, of fountains and depths, that spring out of valleys and hills*; or our blundering geographer, who represents it as a desert and wilderness. Moreover, it seems, that there need not be much water for the plunging of persons, and therefore *John* need not have chose this place upon that account; but I hope, so much is needful, as will cover the persons all over. And there is one thing therefore that we need not be afraid of being pressed with by our author, as we are by some, and that is, the scarcity of water in some parts. But what he says of the practice of our friends in *London*, is entirely false, which is, that they *plunge in little holes or tubs* ; for I cannot see, but he must mean them, and not those in other places; because he adds, rather than the Thames, that is just by. Now there are but two places, in and about *London*, that I know of, which are made use of for the administration of this ordinance, the one is in the midst of a public meeting-house, and the other in an open place, where there are conveniencies for a large number of spectators; and it is very rare that this ordinance is administered by us

in

in a private manner, as some other performances commonly are, in a lying-in chamber; and that only in the presence of a midwife, a nurse, and two or three gossipping women.

As for the instance of a certain plunger in the country, performing the ordinance in an horse-pond, in the middle of a town, I shall suspend my thoughts about it, and neither condemn nor commend his practice, unless I had a better account of it, with its circumstances, than Mr B. W. has given; though I can see no great damage in it, as he has related it, provided the water was not dirty and filthy: But I suppose he designs it as a banter upon us, and a diversion for his reader; much good may do him with it, and let him make the best of it he can.

## CHAP. IV.

*The third argument insisted on, in favour of plunging or dipping, as the right mode of baptizing, taken from the practice of the apostles, and particularly from the instance of the Eunuch's baptism in* Acts viii. 38, 39. *with the cavils and exceptions of Mr B. W. against it, considered.*

THE next argument which our author, p. 18. produces, as insisted on by us, for the proof of baptism by immersion, and which he excepts against, is taken from the practice of the apostles, and particularly the instance of *Philip*'s baptizing the Eunuch, recorded in *Acts* viii. 38, 39. thus; *And he commanded the chariot to stand still; and they went down both into the water, both Philip and the Eunuch, and he baptized him. And when they were come up out of the water,* &c. Here I must again observe, as I have already, in a parallel case, that we do not from this instance infer plunging, merely from *Philip* and the *Eunuch*'s going down into, and coming up out of the water; for we know, as well as he, that persons may go hundreds of times into water, as he says, without any design of plunging, or of being plunged; but we argue from both of them going down into the water; the one in order to administer the ordinance of water-baptism, and the other to submit unto it; and from their coming up out of it, as having performed it; from whence we think we have sufficient reason to conclude, that this was performed by immersion, or a plunging of the whole body under water; for to what purpose should they both go down into the water, if the ordinance was to be performed any other way? or what need would there have been of it? But if plunging cannot be inferred from hence, I am sure it is impossible that pouring or sprinkling should. But let us see what Mr B. W. will infer from this instance, and has to except against our argument from hence. And,

*1st,* From *Philip* and the *Eunuch's* both going down into the water, and coming up out of it, in a profane and irreligious manner, he infers, that neither of them were *drowned there*. Does this become a minister of the gospel, to treat the sacred writings, and the accounts they give of a solemn ordinance of Christ, after this manner? Whatever profane loose he may give himself in his attempts to be witty on the mode of baptizing by immersion, which he supposes to be unscriptural, yet, at least, he ought to set bounds to himself, and not be so free in playing with, and bantering the very words of the holy Ghost. But,

*2dly,* If that is rejected, why then he infers from hence, that they were *both plunged* over head and ears in the water. This, I suppose, is designed to shew the absurdity of our way of reasoning, as he imagines: But does not the man consider, that the one went down as an *administrator*, the other as a *subject* of baptism; the one *to baptize,* the other *to be baptized?* But suppose the ordinance was administered by pouring or sprinkling water, might it not be as justly inferred, that because they both went down into the water, one to perform, and the other to have it performed, and came up again out of it, when it was done, therefore they both had water poured upon them, or were sprinkled with it? And then,

*3dly,* When he is asked why he could not have concluded, that *one* was plunged and the *other* not: he replies, "Why truly, says he, because I thought it out "of the way of all sense, reason and revelation so to infer." I hope he will not say that it is out of the way of *all sense, reason,* and *revelation* to infer, that the one went down in order to administer the ordinance of baptism, and the other to have it administered to him; but I suppose he means that it is out of the way of all sense, reason and revelation, to infer plunging from hence: But how then came the judicious *Calvin* to be so much out of the way, to conclude from hence that plunging was the antient mode of baptizing, as he does, when he says, "here "we see what was the rite of baptizing with the ancients; for they plunged the "whole body into water [b]?" How came this great man to be guilty of making such a *vain conjecture* as our author says it is? especially when he affirms there is not in sacred history, the least *shadow of a foundation* for it. But to proceed,

*4thly,* In order to elude the force of our argument, from their going down into the water, he observes, that whosoever goes to any water, especially out of a chariot, must go down to it. But he is desired to observe, that it is not said, that they both went down *to* the water, but they both went *into* it. As for the text in *Psalm* cvii. 23. which speaks of persons going *down to the sea in ships*, I hope our author does not think that they went by land in ships to the sea-side: If he would know what is meant by this, let him read ver. 26. where the distress

---

[b] Hic perspicimus quisnam apud veteres baptizandi ritus fuerit: totum enim corpus in aquam mergebant. Calvin in Act. viii. 38.

tress that seafaring men are often in, is thus elegantly and beautifully described, *they mount up to the heaven, they go down again to the depths, their soul is melted because of trouble*; and what this means, those who have used the seas know full well, when their ships have been tossed up as it were to the heavens, and then again plunged into the depths of the sea, where they have been immersed in, and covered over with the waves thereof for a while, and on a sudden, have sprang out from thence. It is then they see the wondrous works of the Lord, in his remarkable appearance for them, and providential preservation of them.

5thly, He tells us, that "had he been in the Eunuch's place, he should not "have chosen to have water poured upon him in the chariot, but for several "reasons should have been entirely for going down to the water.". He does not tell us what these *reasons* are, that we might have considered them; but with his usual air of confidence affirms, that "there was no stripping, nor "plunging, nor putting on change of raiment in the case;" and all the reason he has to assign for it, is, because "*Philip* was directly caught away by the "Spirit of the Lord, and the Eunuch immediately went on his way rejoicing:" But I hope he will allow that *Philip* was come up out of the water first, before he was caught away, and that the Eunuch was got into his chariot, before he went on his way; and to suppose so much time as was necessary to change their raiment, is no way contrary to the account in the sacred text; and he would also do well to consider, that those words *directly*, and *immediately*, are not to be found there. But,

6thly, He argues, that if those who were baptized by the apostles were plunged or overwhelmed, "then what prodigious labour must the apostles go "through, when three thousand were baptized in one day, yea perhaps in less than half of it!" To which I answer; There does not seem to be any necessity of concluding from *Acts* ii. 41. that they were all baptized in one day; but if they were, when we consider that there were twelve apostles, and seventy disciples, who were employed in the ministry of the word, *Luke* x. 1. and so no doubt in baptizing, it will not appear so prodigiously fatiguing as our author intimates; for a single person, without having the strength either of *Hercules*, or *Samson*, and without much fatiguing himself, may baptize, in this way, a considerable number in a very little time. But then here is another difficulty behind, and that is, "What great trouble must they be at in stripping, and shift-"ing, and changing apparel! and what abundance of plunging garments they "must have ready!" To which I reply, no more trouble than a single person has for himself, and no more plunging garments to be provided than every one to provide for themselves, which is no more trouble than when five or ten persons only are baptized: and when we consider how much *bathing* was in use

among

among the Jws, it will not seem so strange, where, and how they should be so easily provided with plunging garments. Our objector goes on, and adds, "In what a poor condition was *Paul*, when he was plunged, having been so ill, and so long without eating or drinking! and after that, how unfit must *Paul* himself be under his wounds and bruises, and in the dead of the night, to go into some deep water, and take up the jailor and plunge him!". Here I cannot but remark the wretched blunder that our author makes, or at least the inadvertency, to say no worse of it, that he is guilty of, in talking as if the baptism of *Paul* and the jailor was in one and the same night. But if he objects this is not his meaning, why did he write in such a blundering manner, and many times with want of sense, as when he talks of *Paul's taking up the jailor*, and many such like passages which are to be found in this his performance. But to proceed, that *Paul* was three days before his baptism without eating or drinking, is true, but that he was so very *ill* as our author represents, does not appear so manifest; however, it is plain, that he was not so ill, but he was able to *arise and be baptized*, which he need not have done, had it been performed by pouring or sprinkling water upon him. As to *Paul's* unfitness, under his wounds and bruises, to plunge the jailor, I need only ask, how he and *Silas* were capable of praying and singing the praises of God, and that so loud as the other prisoners heard them? and after that preached the gospel to the jailor and his family, which must be a much more laborious work, and more spending and fatiguing to them, than baptizing of them was; but that same God who enabled them to perform the one, carried them through the other.

Again, he says, "how improperly did *Peter* speak in *Cornelius*'s house, when he talked of *forbidding water*! whereas he should have said, can any man forbid these men from going to the river to be plunged?" to which I answer, if there is any impropriety in this text, it is not to be charged upon the words or sense of the holy Ghost, but upon our translation; for ὕδωρ, "water," ought not to be put in construction with κωλύσαι, "forbid," but with βαπτίσθναι, "to be baptized;" and so the whole be rendered thus, "Can any man forbid, that these should be baptized with water, which have received the holy Ghost as well as we?" and then the sense is this; has any man any thing to object why these who have received the holy Ghost, even as we, should not be admitted to the ordinance of water-baptism? for seeing they have received the greater privilege, why should they be deprived of the lesser? And this reading and sense of the words are confirmed by the learned *Erasmus*, in his notes upon the text, which are these, "the Greeks, says he [1], read after this manner, μητι ὕδωρ, &c. and the "sense

---

[1] Græci legunt in hunc modum μητι ὕδωρ, &c. et apparet hunc esse sensum: num quis vetare potest, quo minus aqua baptizentur ii, qui spiritum sanctum acceperunt, sicut & nos? veluti plus sit spiritus quam

### BAPTIZING BY IMMERSION, &c.

"fenfe appears to be this: Can any man forbid that thefe fhould be baptized in water, who have received the holy Ghoft as well as we? for as the fpirit is preferable to water, and feeing they have him, it will be no great matter if this be added alfo: Moreover the accufative το ὕδωρ, "water;" either depends upon the prepofition κατα, which may be underftood, or elfe adheres to the verb βαπτισθηναι, "to be baptized;" juft in the fame form in which we fay, βαπτιζομαι βαπτισμα, "to be baptized with a baptifm."

As to what Mr *B. W.* fays, concerning the ufe of plunging garments in baptifm, that therefore the water comes to the body only *a filtering*, or as it can work its way through, which, fays he, at beft is only equivalent to fprinkling. I need only reply, it is fufficient in baptifm that the whole body be plunged into and covered under water; nor does it much concern us, to obferve and know, how it works its way through to the body. I hope he will acknowledge, that a corps may be faid to be truly buried, when covered with earth, though it is wrapt up in a fhroud, or in its funeral clothes, and put up clofe in a coffin, fo that the earth with which it is covered, does not as yet touch it; even fo a perfon may be truly faid to be baptized, when in the name of the three Divine Perfons, he is plunged into, and covered over with water, even though the water may not be fuppofed to have had time enough to have worked its way through to his body; and when it has done fo, how that is equivalent to fprinkling, no man can devife. But enough of this, I proceed to the next argument.

### CHAP. V.

*The fourth argument taken from* Romans vi. 4. Coloffians ii. 12. *with the fenfe given of thofe fcriptures, by Mr* B. W. *confidered.*

OUR next argument for baptifm by immerfion, which Mr *B. W.* has thought fit to produce in p. 24. and except againft, is taken from *Rom.* vi. 4. *Col.* ii. 12. where this ordinance is took notice of by the apoftle, as a burial, and as reprefenting the burial and refurrection of Chrift; which argument may be formed thus, and not in the loofe rambling way, in which he has reprefented it, and which, no doubt, he thought would beft anfwer his purpofe; namely, "If the end and defign of baptifm are to reprefent the burial and refurrection of Chrift, then it ought to be performed by plunging into, and overwhelming with water; but the end and defign of baptifm, are to reprefent the burial and re- "furrection

---

quam aqua, cumque ille contingerit, nihil effe magni fi hoc accefferit: Cæterum το ὕδωρ accufativus aut pendet a præpofitione fubaudita κατα, aut adhæret verbo βαπτισθηναι, ea forma qua dicimus, βαπτιζομαι βαπτισμα. Erafmus in Act. x. 47.

"surrection of Christ, therefore it ought to be performed by plunging into, and
"overwhelming with water; the reason is, because no other mode of baptizing
"either by pouring or sprinkling a little water on the face, can answer this end."
But let us attend to what Mr *B. W.* has to except. And,

1. He seems to deny this to be the end and design of the institution of this ordinance, when he asks, "But did Christ ever institute baptism for any such "end? As for the Lord's Supper, he hath said, *Do this in remembrance of me*; "and it is plain from the word, that in the Lord's Supper we *shew forth his* "*death till he come*: but where has he said, be plunged or baptized, to repre- "sent my burial or resurrection?" To which I answer, that though we have not the end of this institution declared, in so many express words, yet we think it may be fairly concluded from those texts now mentioned, and must continue to be of the same mind, for ought Mr *B. W.* has advanced against it: Nor are we alone in our sentiments: For that Christ's burial and resurrection are represented by baptism, has been acknowledged by many, both ancient and modern divines, whose words I forbear to transcribe, partly because they have been many of them produced by others already, and partly because I would not fill my book with citations, and therefore shall only direct the reader to the reference in the margent [k]. Though Mr *B. W.* is of opinion, that to infer this from those words, *buried with him in baptism*, is very absurd and inconclusive; and that "we may as well be hanged up against a tree, to represent "Christ crucified, because it is said, that we *are* crucified with Christ." But can any mortal see this to be a parallel case? to say nothing how shocking this expression must be to every serious mind, and not to be borne with; no more than the wretched jargon which follows it, when he says, "and to make a fair "end of you, be sure to see *you* dead under the earth or under the water;" which, I doubt not, to every impartial intelligent reader, will appear to have as little of argument as it has of sense in it. Besides, who does not see that all this, whatever he can mean by it, may be levelled as much against the ordinance of the Lord's-Supper, as that of Baptism. Moreover, there are other texts, besides these mentioned, which demonstrate the representation of Christ's resurrection, which supposes his burial to be the end of baptism; as for instance, 1 *Peter* iii. 21. where *baptism* is said to *save us, by the resurrection of Jesus Christ*. But how does it do that, but by representing the resurrection of Christ unto us, and thereby leading our faith to it, to behold our justification and discharge, by a risen Saviour? To which I might also add, 1 *Cor.* xv. 29. where the apostle

---

[k] Gregory Nazianzen, Basil, Chrysostome, Ambrose, Daille, Fowler, Cave, Towerson, cited by Mr Stennett, in his answer to Russen, p. 144, 145, 147, 156, 157. See also Dr Goodwin's Christ set forth. Sect. 3. Ch. 7.

apostle evincing the truth of the resurrection of the dead, thus argues, *else what shall they do, which are baptized for the dead, if the dead rise not?* that is, "Who are baptized into the faith of the resurrection of Christ, which is re-"presented thereby, and which is the confirmation of our resurrection;" the thing that is there debated; and which, if not true, the apostle argues that their baptism, as well as their faith, and his preaching, was in vain. Besides, if our author removes this end of baptism, he ought to have substituted another, and have told us what was the end and design of it, which he has not done; for all the ordinances of the gospel are, no doubt, designed for the comfort and edification of believers, and the confirmation of their faith in the person of Christ; and seeing there appears nothing more manifestly to be the end of it, than what has been mentioned, we shall think fit to abide by it. But,

2*dly,* Our author asks, "What there is in your plunging that represents "Christ's burial and resurrection;" and to shew that there is no agreement, he runs the parallel between them, and observes, that Christ was *carried* to his grave, where, being *dead,* he was buried, and lay there *three days, and three nights,* and that in the *earth,* where a great *stone* was *rolled* at the mouth of the sepulchre, and when he arose, it was *by his own power,* and thereby declared to be *the Son of God:* But as for us, we *go* ourselves into the water, are plunged *alive,* and that not *three minutes,* in *water*; and that our *plunger dares not leave* us, nor *roll a stone upon* us; *and it is he that puts* us *in that pulls* us *out, and* we *are declared to be what* we *are:* What would the man have us be declared to be, what we are not? and then in a taunting manner says, "and this is the repre-"sentation and the mighty resemblance." These are some of our author's masterly strokes, and when the candor of the reader has supplied the want of sense in his expression, and charitably conjectured at his meaning, I need only reply, that the things instanced in are only circumstantial, and not essential to a burial, and therefore unnecessary to be represented in baptism; nay, it would have been absurd to have had them: It is enough that the things themselves are, namely, the burial and resurrection of Christ, which are sufficiently represented by an immersion into water, and an emersion out of it.

But who does not see that a Quaker, or any other person that denies the ordinance of the Lord's-Supper, may argue after the same manner, and say, you say that this ordinance represents a crucified Christ, and shews forth his death and sufferings, but pray how does it appear? you take a loaf of bread, and break it in pieces, and a bottle of wine, and pour it out; but Christ, when he was crucified, was hanged on a tree, his head was crowned with thorns, his hands and feet were pierced with nails, and his side with a spear; but here are no thorns, nails, or spear made use of by you, his *real body* was treated after this manner, but yours is only a *loaf of bread*; he poured out his *blood*, you only *wine*; " and this is the reprefentation, and the mighty refemblance." And I think all this may be faid with as much juftnefs as the other. But,

3. Mr *B. W.* has got another way of getting off the argument taken from thefe texts, in *Rom.* vi. 3, 4. *Col.* ii. 12. and that is, by afferting that the baptifm of Chrift's fufferings, and not water-baptifm, is intended in them. It would be endlefs, and perhaps our author will fay needlefs, to oppofe to him the feveral expofitors and interpreters, who underftand, bv baptifm, the ordinance of water-baptifm, in thofe texts; as well as a large number of them who think the allufion is made to the ancient practice of baptizing by immerfion; as *Grotius, Vorftius, Paræus, Pifcator, Diodate*, and the *Affembly of Divines* on *Romans* vi. 4. and *Zanchy* and *Davenant* on *Col.* ii. 12. I fuppofe that Mr *B. W.* will reply, that thefe are but men, and their judgment fallible; I hope he does not think that he is more than a man, or that his judgment is infallible; and it will fcarcely be accounted modefty in him, to fet himfelf upon a level with them: Though I confefs that his fenfe of the words is not difagreeble to the analogy of faith, yet I wonder that he fhould be fo pofitive as to fay that this is *the only meaning* of them, as he does in p. 31. As to what he fays with refpect to thofe texts, one of them being produced as an argument to promote holinefs in believers, and the other to ftrengthen their faith in the doctrine of juftification; I cannot fee, but to underftand them of water-baptifm, fuits very well with the fcope thereof, however it is ridiculed by our author: For why may not our baptifm, wherein we profefs our faith in a buried Chrift, and that we are dead by him to the law, the world, and particularly to fin, be urged and made ufe of by the fpirit of God, as an argument why we fhould not live any longer therein. And are there no force, power and cogency in this argument? Again, in baptifm we profefs our faith in the refurrection of Chrift, which is reprefented hereby, and that we are rifen with him, and therefore are under the higheft obligations to walk in newnefs of life, as the apoftle himfelf argues. Moreover, what can have a greater tendency to ftrengthen our faith in the doctrine of juftification, than this ordinance has? by which it is led to fee where our Lord lay, and how our fins were left in the grave by him; and he, as our glorious reprefentative, rifing again *for our juftification,* by whom we are acquitted and difcharged from all fin and *condemnation*; and is fuch a way of arguing from hence, to promote holinefs, and ftrengthen us in the doctrine of juftification, to be wondered at, what is meant by it? But to proceed,

*4tbly,* Suppofing that the baptifm of Chrift's fufferings is intended here, and that we are buried with him therein, as our head and reprefentative, it muft be allowed, that Chrift's fufferings are called fo, in allufion to water-baptifm; and if we are said to be *buried* with him in them, it must be in allusion to a person's being buried in water in that ordinance, which cannot be by pouring or sprinkling of water upon him, but by an immersion into it. So that our argument for plunging, from hence, is like to lose nothing by this sense of the words. That Christ's sufferings are called a *baptism*, in *Matt.* xx. 22. *Luke* xii. 50. as also that by a *Synechdoche*, they are called *the blood of his cross*, is granted; but then the shedding of his blood was not the whole of Christ's sufferings, but a part only, and this is called the *blood of sprinkling*, not with regard to its being called a baptism; but because it is sprinkled upon a believer's conscience, and being so, speaks peace and pardon there; but when the greatness and multitude of Christ's sufferings are set forth, they are represented, not by a sprinkling of water, but by mighty floods of water, which overflowed him, so that he seemed, as it were, to be plunged into them, and overwhelmed with them; as he says, in *Psalm* lxix 2. *I am come into deep waters, where the floods* overflow *me*; where the Septuagint use the word κατποντίζω, as they do also in verse 15. which Mr *B. W.* in page 45. grants is very proper to express plunging by; and therefore no wonder then that his sufferings are compared to a baptism, and such an one as is administered by immersion: So that the argument from hence, notwithstanding all those cavils and exceptions, stands firm and unshaken. As to the argument taken from the universality of Christ's sufferings in every part of his body, which he makes his antagonist plead in page 32. he acknowledges it was never made use of by the greatest men of our persuasion, why then does he produce it? If every thing that has been dropt by weak christians, in private conversation on the subject of infant-baptism, was published to the world, how silly and ridiculous would it appear?

## CHAP. VI.

*The fifth and last argument taken from the signification of the word* βαπτίζω, *which always signifies to dip or plunge, with Mr* B. W*'s. exceptions to it, considered.*

THE fifth and last argument used by us, for immersion in baptism, taken from the constant signification of the word βαπτίζω, *baptizo*, to *dip* or *plunge*, Mr *B.W.* has thought fit to produce in p. 33. and except against, which we hope, notwithstanding, to make good, however we may be represented by our author, as uncapable of reading our mother tongue. And,

1. Mr *B. W.* denies that βάπτω, *bapto*, and βαπτίζω, *baptizo*, signify one and the same thing; but the reason he gives, is not a sufficient one, and that is, because

because the holy Ghost never makes use of the former, when this ordinance is expressed, but the latter; for the holy Ghost may make use of what words he pleases, without destroying the sense of others; and by the way, then it may be observed, that ῥαντίζω, *rantizo*, and βαπτίζω, *baptizo*, do not signify one and the same thing; because the holy Ghost never makes use of the former, when the ordinance is expressed, but the latter. Besides, all the Lexicographers that I have been able to consult, tell me, that βάπτω and βαπτίζω do signify one and the same thing; for they render both by the very same words, and they are both promiscuously used by Greek authors: And indeed, why should not βαπτίζω, *baptizo*, the derivative, signify the same as its primitive? what, is its signification lessened by the addition of a syllable to it? Dr Gale[1] has given instances enough of derivatives in ζω, which signify the same with their primitives. And indeed, some have taken the word, under consideration, to be what grammarians call a frequentative, which signifies more than the derivative does. But,

2. It seems our author will scarcely allow βάπτω, *bapto*, to signify *dip* or *plunge*, and therefore puts it upon us to prove, that *Judas*, when he put his hand in the dish, thrust it all over in the sauce, *Matt.* xxvi. 23. where the word ἐμβάψας, *embapsas*, is used; but he should have observed, that it was not his hand, but the sop in his hand, by a metonymy of the subject, as *Piscator* observes, which he dipt into the sauce, as he might have learned, by comparing the text with *John* xiii. 26. And in p. 45. he says, " yea, with respect unto βάπτω itself, it
" is very evident that the Greeks did not directly mean plunging thereby; for
" when the Septuagint tell us in *Dan.* iv. 33. that *Nebuchadnezzar*'s body was
" wet with the dew of heaven, they make use of the very word;" and I would also add, very justly, it exactly answered to the Chaldee word יצטבע here used, which word always signifies to tinge or dip, as dyers dip their clothes in their vatts, and so is expressive of what a condition *Nebuchadnezzar*'s body was in, he being as wet with the dew of heaven, as if he had been dipt or plunged all over in water. But enough of this; let us consider,

3. How we are like to come off with the word βαπτίζω, *baptizo*; and here our author in p. 41. tells us, *ore rotundo*, and with confidence enough, in so many words, that " it never does signify plunging; washing with water by pouring
" or sprinkling, is the only meaning of it." The man has got a good assurance, but yet by his writing, he does not seem to have such a stock of learning; however what he wants in one, he makes up in the other. It is strange that all our Lexicographers, so many learned critics, and good divines, should be so much mistaken, as to render the word to *dip* or *plunge*, and allow this to be the proper signification of it. I have myself consulted several Lexicons, as those of *Suidas*, *Scapula*,

---

[1] Reflections on Mr Wall's History of Infant-baptism, p. 217.

Scapula, Hadrian, Junius, Pasor, as also another made by *Budæus, Tusanus, Gesner, Junius, Constantine, Hartung, Hopper,* and *Xylander,* who all unanimously render the word by *mergo, immergo,* to *plunge* or *dip into:* And though they afterwards add also, *abluo, lavo, to wash,* yet it is plain they mean such a washing, as is by dipping; and we are very willing to grant it, for we know that there can be no dipping without washing: But had they meant a washing by pouring or sprinkling, they would have rendered it by *perfundo,* or *aspergo,* to *pour upon,* or *sprinkle;* but this they never do. And, to these I might add a large number of learned critics, and good divines, who grant, that the word in its first and primary sense, signifies to *dip* or *plunge* only; and to *wash* only in a secondary, remote, and consequential one; as *Casaubon, Camerarius, Grotius*[m], *Calvin*[n], *Alting*[o], *Alsted*[p], *Wendelin*[q], and others. But what need I heap up authors, to prove that which no man of any tolerable learning will deny: But what will not ignorance, attended with a considerable share of confidence, carry a man through? I might oppose to him, the use of the word in many Greek authors, but this has been done better already than I am capable of doing it, to which I refer him[r], and shall content myself, with just mentioning that passage of *Plutarch*[s], βαπτίζων σαυτὸν εἰς θάλασσαν, which I think the author I have reference to, has took no notice of; and let him try how his sense of pouring or sprinkling will agree with it. I am sure it will sound very harsh, to render the words *pour* or *sprinkle thyself into the sea,* but will read very well to be rendered thus, *plunge thyself into the sea:* But I suppose he will take this to be a breach of the first article agreed upon in this conference; but why the Greek authors should not be allowed as evidences, in the sense of a Greek word, I cannot see: I am sure this is not very consistent with *right reason,* which the thing in debate was to be *cleared up from,* as well as from the word of God. But let us consider the use of the word with the Septuagint, which I suppose he will not except against, because he has himself brought it into the controversy. And there are but two places, which I have as yet met with, where the word is used by them, and the first is in 2 *Kings* v. 14. where it is said of *Naaman* the Syrian, that *he went down,* ἐβαπτίσατο, *and baptized* or *dipped himself seven times in Jordan:* I presume our author will not say, that this is to be understood of a washing, by pouring or sprinkling; especially, seeing it answers to the Hebrew word טבל, which always signifies to dip or plunge, and is the word, which is so often rendered by βαπτω, *bapto,* and which, by the way, proves these two to be of the same

---

[m] All three on Matthew iii. 6.    [n] Institut. l. 4. c. 15. f. 19.
[o] Loc commun. p. 198. & Explic. Catech. p. 311.    [p] Lexic. Theolog. p. 221, 222.
[q] Christ. Theolog. l. 1. c. 22.    [r] Dr Ga'e's Reflections on Mr Wall's History of Infant-baptism, letter 3.    [s] De Superstitione.

same signification, seeing they are promiscuously used by them, to express one and the same word.

The other place is in *Isai*. xxi. 4. where what we read, *fearfulness affrighted me*, they render η ανομια με βαπτιζει, *iniquity hath plunged me*; for to translate the words, *iniquity hath washed*, or *poured*, or *sprinkled me*, would be intolerable; but both the language and the sense are smooth and easy, by rendering them, *iniquity hath plunged me*; that is, into the depths of misery and distress; so that I am overwhelmed with horror and terror: And hereby also the sense of the Hebrew word בעת, here used, is very beautifully expressed. But let us now consider,

4*thly*, What exceptions Mr *B. W.* makes against this universal sense of the word, and there are three places in the New Testament which he opposes to it.

The first is in *Mark* vii. 4. *And when they come from the market, except they wash, they eat not, and many other things there be, which they have received to hold, as the washing of cups and pots, brazen vessels, and of tables.* Whereupon Mr *B. W.* observes, that the words of the holy Ghost are, except they first *baptize* themselves; and many other such things they have, as the *baptizing* of tables. Excellent observations indeed! But how does this prove that the word signifies only a washing, by pouring or sprinkling? I believe it will appear, that this is meant of the washing of the whole body by dipping, which might be done, without their going *into a pond or a river* before they came home; for they had, no doubt, proper conveniencies for immersion, when they came home, seeing bathing was in many cases required of the people, as well as of the priests; and to understand it of such a washing, seems better to express their superstitious solicitude to cleanse themselves from all impurity they might contract by conversing with others in the market; it seems to be distinct from washing of hands in the former verse, where a different word is used. But supposing that washing of hands was intended here, does not every body know, that the usual manner of doing that, is not by pouring or sprinkling water upon them, but by putting them into it. And here I cannot but take notice of the observation of *Beza* ⸸ upon this text; "βαπτιζεσθαι, says he, in this "place, is more than χερνιπτειν; for the former seems to respect the whole "body, the latter only the hands, nor does βαπτιζειν signify to wash, but only "by consequence, for it properly denotes to immerse for the sake of dipping." As for the washing or baptizing of cups, pots, &c. it is well known that the cleansing of vessels, which were polluted by the falling of any dead creature

that

---

⸸ Plus autem est βαπτιζεσθαι, hoc in loco, quam χερνιπτειν, quod illud videatur de corpore universo, istud de manibus duntaxat intelligendum. Neque το βαπτιζειν significat lavare, nisi à consequenti, nam proprie declarat tingendi causa immergere. Beza in Marc. 7. 4.

that was unclean into them, was by putting into the water, and not by pouring or sprinkling water upon them. The express command in *Levit.* xi. 32, is, that *it must be put into the water,* or as the Septuagint render it βαφησιται, *it must be dipt into water.* Moreover, their superstitious washing of vessels, which our Lord seems here to mean, and justly reprehends, of which we read many things in their Mishnah [u], or oral law, their book of traditions, was performed this way, where they make use of the word טבל to express it by, which always signifies to dip or plunge. But what need I use many words to prove this, when every old woman could have informed him of the usual manner of washing their vessels, which is not by pouring or sprinkling water upon them, but by putting them into it: And if he asks, did the Jewish women wash their tables so? There appears no reason to conclude the contrary; and if he should say, how and where could they do it? I answer, in or near their own houses, where they had conveniencies for bathing themselves, and washing their garments, at proper times, without carrying them to a river

The next place instanced in by him, is *Heb.* ix. 10. where the ceremonial law is said to stand *only in meats and drinks, and divers washings*; it is in the Greek text, *in divers baptisms*; and, says our author, "it is evident from the "word of God, that those washings generally stood in pouring or sprinkling of "water;" but that is a mistake of his, for they neither stood in them generally, nor particularly; for those ceremonial ablutions were always performed by bathing or dipping in water, and are called διαφοροις, *divers,* or *different,* not because they were performed different ways, as some by sprinkling, others by pouring, and others by plunging, but because of the different persons and things, the subjects thereof; as the priests, Levites, Israelites, vessels, garments, &c. And here it may not be amiss to observe what *Maimonides* [w], who was one of the most learned of the Jewish writers, says concerning this matter, "Wherever, says he, the washing of the flesh or garments is mentioned in the "law, it means nothing else than the washing of the whole body; for if a man "washes himself all over, excepting the very tip of his little finger, he is still "in his uncleanness." Nay, he says it is necessary that every hair of his head should be washed; and therefore the apostle might well call these washings, *baptisms.*

The third and last instance produced by him, is 1 *Cor.* x. 1, 2. where the apostle says, that *all our fathers were under the cloud, and all passed through the sea;*

[u] Tract. Mikvaoth. c. 10. f. 1, 5, 6.

[w] Ubicunque in lege memoratur ablutio carnis aut vestium, nihil aliud vult, quam ablutionem totius corporis, nam siquis se totum abluat, excepto ipsissimo apice minimi digiti ille adhuc in immunditie sua, Maimon. in Mikvaoth. c. 1, 4. in Lightfoot Hor. Hebr. in Matt. p. 47.

*sea;* and *were all baptized unto Moses in the cloud, and in the sea;* which when our author has mentioned, he very briskly asks, "Pray how were our fathers bap- "tized there?" to which, I hope, we shall be capable of returning an answer, without appearing to be so *bitterly gravelled* with this place, as he is pleased to make his friend say we are. As for the manner in which he represents some of our friends accounting for it; namely, that when the people of *Israel* passed through the Red sea, they had the waters stood up, both on their right hand, and on their left, and a cloud over them; so that there was a very great resemblance of a person's being baptized, or plunged under water. This, I say, is not so much to be despised, nor does it deserve so much ridicule and contempt, as he has pleased to cast upon it; and I believe will appear to any unprejudiced person, a much better way of accounting for it, than he is capable of giving, consistent with his way of administering the ordinance: Though I cannot but think that the Israelites were *first baptized in the cloud, and then in the sea,* according to the order of the apostle's words; and agreeable to the story in *Exodus* xiv. where we read, that *the cloud went from before their face, and stood behind them,* and was between the two camps, to keep off the Egyptians from the Israelites. I am therefore of opinion, with the learned *Gataker* [x], that the cloud when it passed over them, let down a plentiful rain upon them, whereby they were in such a condition, as if they had been all over dipt in water; so that they were not only covered by it, but baptized in it: Therefore our author very improperly directs us to *Psalm* lxxvii. 17. *the clouds poured out water,* as the better way of resolving the case; for the apostle does not say, that they were baptized *in the clouds,* but *in the cloud* which went before them, but now passing over them, in order to stand behind them, they were, as it were, immersed in it. But supposing that the text in *Psalm* lxxvii. may be a direction in this case, and serve to explain what the apostle means by baptizing, it will no ways agree either with our author's sense of the word, nor his way of administering the ordinance: For were the Israelites baptized under the clouds, by their pouring or sprinkling a small quantity of water upon their faces? the Hebrew word זרם here used, signifies an overflow, or an inundation of water: And *Ainsworth* reads it *streamed down* or *gushed with a tempest;* so that they were as persons overwhelmed, and plunged over head and ears in water; and therefore the apostle might well call it a being *baptized.*

But now let us consider also, how they might be said to be *baptized in the sea;* and there are several things, in which the Israelites passage through the Red sea, resembled our baptism. As for instance, their following of *Moses* into it, which may be meant by their being *baptized into* him, was an acknowledgment of their

regard

---

[x] In Adversar. Miscellan. p 30.

## BAPTIZING BY IMMERSION, &c.

regard unto him, as their Guide and Governor; as our baptism is a following of Christ as our Prophet, who has taught and led us the way; as well as a profession of our faith in him, as our Surety and Saviour, and a subjection to him, as our King and Governor: Theirs was at their first entrance upon their journey to *Canaan*, as ours is, when, in a way of profession, we publicly begin our christian race: They, when they came out of it, could sing and rejoice, in the view of all their enemies being destroyed; as the believer also can in this ordinance, in the view of all his sins being drowned in the sea of Christ's blood, witness the instances of the Eunuch and Jailor. But in nothing is there a greater resemblance between them, than in their descending into it, and coming up out of it; which is very much expressive of the mode of baptism by immersion. And this I choose to deliver in the words of the judicious *Gataker*[y].

" The descent, (that is, of the Israelites) says he, into the inmost and lowest
" parts of the sea, and their ascent out of it again upon dry land, hath a very
" great agreement with the rite of christian baptism, as it was administered in
" the primitive times; seeing in baptizing they went down into the water, and
" came up again out of the same; of which descent and ascent express mention
" is made in the dipping of the Ethiopian Eunuch, *Acts* viii. 38, 39. Moreover,
" as in the christian rite, when they were immersed, they were overwhelmed
" in water, and as it were buried; and in some measure, seemed to be buried
" together with Christ. And again, when they emersed, they seemed to rise,
" even as out of a grave, and to be risen with Christ, *Rom.* vi. 4, 5. and *Col.* ii. 12.
" So likewise, the waters of the sea standing up higher than the heads of those
" that passed through it, they might seem to be overwhelmed; and in some
" respects, to be buried therein, and to emerse and rise out again, when they
" came out safe on the other side of the shore."

And having now considered all those exceptions, which our author has made against this sense of the word, which is contended for, I hope it will appear, that he has little reason to make that vain triumph he does, in p 38. where, he asks, " Where now is your *baptizo*, that signifies nothing else but plunging and " overwhelming?" As for his comparing the passage of the Israelites through

---

[y] Magnam habet convenientiam ille in maris intima infimaque descensus, ex eodem ascensus denuo in aridam, cum baptismi christiani ritu, prout is primis temporibus administrabatur. Siquidem inter baptizandum in aquas descendebant, & ex eisdem denuo ascendebant: Cujus καταβασεως ἡ αναβασεως in Eunuchi Æthiopis tinctione mentio expressa reperitur, Act. viii. 38, 39. Quin &, sicuti in ritu christiano, quum immergerentur aquis obruti, & quasi sepulti & Christo ipsi consepulti quodammodo videbantur; rursusque cum emergerent, a sepulchro quodammodo resurgere, ac cum Christo resuscitare præ se ferebant. Rom. vi. 4, 5. Col. ii. 12. Ita maris illius aquis capitibus ipsis transeuntium altius extantibus obruti ac sepulti quodammodo poterunt videri & emergere ac resurgere denuo, cum ad littus objectum exeuntes evasissent. Gatak. ibid.

the Red sea, to his travelling to *Scotland* with the Irish sea on his left hand, and the German on his right, and to his journeying to *Cornwal*, with the British channel at some distance from him, on his left hand, and the channel of *Bristol* on his right, I cannot see it can be of any service, unless it be to lay aside the Israelites passage through the sea as a miracle, and so furnish the atheist and deist with an argument, such an one as it is, for their purpose. As for his sneer upon plunging in it, I can easily forgive him, and pass it by, as well as that of the plunging of the Egyptians, with the same contempt in which he delivers them. Having thus considered his exceptions to those arguments produced for plunging, I shall in the next chapter take notice of his reasons against it.

## CHAP. VII.

*Mr B. W's. reasons against plunging in baptism, considered.*

MR *B.W.* in the next place, proceeds to give us some reasons in p. 43. why he is against the administration of the ordinance of baptism by plunging. And his

*First* reason is, "Because there is not any foundation for it in the word of "God; no precept, no example, says he, no necessary consequence, no words "nor sound of words to favour it;" and a little lower, "There is not a word, "he means of plunging, nor the shadow of a word; and therefore I think I "have good reason against it." Words are the shadows, representations, and expressions of our minds; but what the *shadow of a word* is, I cannot devise, unless he means the least appearance of a word, as perhaps he may; and that I suppose is an initial letter of a word, or an abbreviation, *&c.* But the holy Ghost does not write in such a manner, and therefore we expect to find whole words, or none at all. But to proceed, does he want a *precept?* let him read *Matt.* xxviii. 19. or an *example?* let him take Christ for one, *Matt.* iii. 16. and the Eunuch, *Acts* viii. 38, 39. And is no necessary consequence to be deduced from the places *John* and the apostles baptized in? nor from the circumstances which attended it, of going down and coming up out of the water? I hope it will appear to every thinking, and unprejudiced person, that it has been proved that not only the sound of words, but the true sense of words favour it.

His *other* reason is, "Because it is not only without foundation in the word "of God, but it is directly against it;" but how does that appear? Why, "sup- "pose some poor creatures, says he, upon a bed of languishing, under consump- "tions, catarrhs, pains, sores, and bruises, be converted, and that perhaps "in the depth of winter, it is their duty to be baptized, that is true? but is it
"their

" their duty to be plunged? no, to be sure; for the whole word of God com-
" mands self-preservation; and therefore it is evident, that plunging is against
" the commands of God." I suppose he takes it to be contrary to the sixth
command; but if it is the duty of persons to be baptized, it is their duty to
be plunged; for there is no true baptism without it? But what, in the depth of
winter? why not? what damage is like to come by it? Our climate is not near
so cold as *Muscovy*, where they always dip their infants in baptism, to this very
day; as does also the Greek church in all parts of the world. But what, plunge
persons when under consumptions, catarrhs, &c.? why not? perhaps it may be
of use to them for the restoration of health; and its being performed on a sacred account, can never be any hindrance to it. Whoever reads Sir *John Floyer*'s
*History of Cold-bathing*, and the many cures that have been performed thereby,
which he there relates, will never think that this is a sufficient objection against
plunging in baptism; which learned physician has also of late published *An
Essay to restore the dipping of Infants in their Baptism*; which he argues for, not
only from the signification of baptism, and its theological end, but likewise
from the medicinal use of dipping, for preventing and curing many distempers.
If it may be useful for the health of tender infants, and is in many cases now
made use of, it can never be prejudicial to grown persons: He argues from the
liturgy and rubric of the church of *England*, which requires *dipping* in baptism,
and only allows *pouring of water* in case of weakness, and never so much as granted
a permission for *sprinkling*. He proves in this book, and more largely in his
former, that the constant practice of the church of *England*, ever since the plan-
tation of christianity, was to dip or plunge in baptism; which he says continued
after the reformation until King *Edward* the sixth's time and after: Nay, that
its disuse has been within this hundred years: And here I cannot forbear mentioning a passage of his, to this purpose [a], " Our fonts are built, says he, with
" a sufficient capacity for dipping of infants, and they have been so used for
" five hundred years in *England*, both Kings and Common people have been
" dipped; but now our fonts stand in our churches as monuments, to upbraid
" us with our change or neglect of our baptismal immersion." And I wish he
had not reason to say as he does [a], that sprinkling was first introduced by the
Assembly of Divines, in 1643, by a vote of 25 against 24, and established by an
ordinance of parliament in 1644. Which complaint Mr *Wall* [b] has taken up,
who wrote the last in this controversy, having studied it for many years; and
has fairly acknowledged, that immersion is the right mode of baptism; for which
reason he calls upon his brethren, the clergy, to a reformation in it: As for those
who

---

[a] Essay to restore the Dipping of Infants in their Baptism, p. 60.   [a] Ibid. p. 4, 12, 31.
[b] Defence of the History of Infant-Baptism, p. 129, 130, 131, 146, 147.

who would willingly conform to the liturgy, he lays before them the difficulties they muſt expect to meet with; which, beſides the general One of breaking an old cuſtom, he mentions two more: The one is from thoſe *who are preſbyterianly inclined*, who as they were the firſt introducers of it, will be tenacious enough to keep it. And the other is, from midwives and nurſes, &c. whoſe pride in the fine dreſſing of the child will be entirely loſt. But to return from whence I have digreſſed. Mr *B. W.* it ſeems, is of opinion, that baptiſm by plunging, is not only againſt the ſixth, but alſo againſt the ſeventh command, for which reaſon he muſt be againſt it. To baptize by plunging, he inſinuates is " a practice contrary to the whole current of Chriſt's pure precepts, of an un-
" comely aſpect, and ſeemingly ſcandalous and ignominious to the honour of
" chriſtianity; and that one would think a man would as ſoon deny all right
" reaſon, and religion, as believe Chriſt would ever command ſuch a practice."
But I appeal to any, even our worſt adverſaries, that make any conſcience of what they ſay or do, who have ſeen the ordinance adminiſtered, whether it is of ſuch an uncomely aſpect, and ſo ſeemingly ſcandalous, as this defamer has repreſented it. " And, ſays he, to uſe the words of a ſervant of Chriſt, can we
" therefore imagine, that Chriſt's baptiſm ſhould intrench ſo much upon the
" laws of civility, chaſtity, and modeſty, as to require women and maids to
" appear openly in the light of the ſun, out of their wonted habit, in tranſpa-
" rent and thin garments, next to nakedneſs, and in that poſture be took by
" a man in his arms, and plunged in the face of the whole congregation, be-
" fore men and boys!" Who this ſervant of Chriſt is, whoſe words he uſes, and has made his own, he does not tell us. I ſhall therefore inform the reader, they are the words of one *Ruſſen*, an author he might well be aſhamed to mention in the manner he does: However I ſhall not be aſhamed to give Mr *Stennett*'s reply to this paragraph, in his excellent anſwer to that ſcurrilous writer, which I have put in the margent ᵉ; and would alſo recommend that book to

the

---

ᵉ It does not ſhock me ſo much, to find Mr R. uſe ſuch terms as are ſcarce reconcileable to good ſenſe, as it does to find him uſing ſuch expreſſions, and making ſuch deſcriptions, as are hardly conſiſtent with that civility and modeſty, for which he would appear to be an advocate. I can bear with him, when, on this occaſion, he calls thin garments a *poſture* inſtead of a *habit*, and tells us of things that are ignominious to the honour of chriſtianity, being now pretty well acquainted with his ſtile. But I muſt confeſs myſelf offended with that air of levity, and thoſe indecent terms, in which he condemns the pretended immodeſty of others. For the words by which he ſometimes deſcribes the vicious acts and inclinations which he cenſures, ſeem not ſo much adapted to excite horror and averſion in the reader, as to defile his imagination, and to diſpoſe him to that imprudent temper of making a mock of ſin. And the true reaſon why I do not quote Mr R's words at large in this place, as I do in many others, is not to evade the force of his argument, but to avoid the mode of his expreſſion, by which he has given too much occaſion of offence to virtuous minds, and perhaps too much gratified thoſe that are viciouſly inclined. Stennett's Anſw. to Ruſſen, p. 137.

the readers of our author, but especially to himself; for had he read it before he published his, perhaps it might have prevented it, or at least, have made him ashamed to quote those expressions, with such a complement upon the author of them. How does this become one, who calls himself a minister of the gospel, to be guilty of such a scandal and defamation as this is? What, did the man never see the ordinance administered? If he has, his wickedness in publishing this is the greater; if not, he ought to have took an opportunity to have informed himself, before he had made so free with the practice, as to asperse it after this manner. It is well known, that the clothes we use in baptism, are either the person's wearing apparel, or else those which are on purpose provided, which are made of as thick, or thicker stuff, than what are usually worn in the performance of the most servile work. Those who have seen the ordinance administered, know with what decency it is performed, and with such, I am persuaded what our author says will find but little credit. I have nothing else, I think, to observe now, unless it be, his arguing for the preferableness of applying water to the person, to any other mode of baptism, from the application of grace to us, and not us to that, in p. 46. which I suppose was forgot in the conference, or else he had not an opportunity to croud it in. To which I need only reply, that there does not appear to be any necessity of using a mode in baptism, that must be conformable to that; besides, if there was, does not every body know, that in plunging a person, there is an application of the water to him, as well as an application of him to the water? For as soon as ever a person is plunged, the water will apply itself to him. As to the vanity which he thinks we are guilty of, in monopolizing the name of *baptists* to ourselves, he may take the name himself if he pleases, seeing he thinks we have nothing to do with it, for we will not quarrel with him about it: But since it is necessary to make use of some names of distinction in civil conversation, he does well to tell us, what name we should be called by, and that is *plungers*; but then he will be hard put to it to shew the difference between a *baptist* and a *plunger*: Besides, the old objection against the name *baptist* being peculiar to *John*, or to an administrator, may as well be objected against this name as the other, because we are not all *plungers*, but by far the greatest part, are only persons *plunged*. However I could wish, as well as he, that all names were laid aside, especially as terms of reproach, and the great name of Christ alone exalted.

CHAP.

## CHAP. VIII.

*Concerning the free or mixt communion of churches.*

MR B. W. here and there drops a sentence, signifying his love and affection to persons of our persuasion, as in p. 42. "Christians of your persuasion, "I hope, I dearly love;" this and such like expressions, I can understand no otherwise than as a wheedling and cajoling of those of his members, who are of a different persuasion from him in this point, whom he knows he must have grieved and offended, by this shameful and scandalous way of writing. And at the same time, when he expresses so much love to them, he lets them know, that he " does not admire their plunging principle, though he does not love " to make a great noise about it." I think he has made a great noise about it, and such an one as, perhaps by this time, he would be glad to have laid. He signifies his readiness " to carry on evangelical fellowship, in all the acts thereof, " with chearfulness," with those who are differently minded from him. That those of a different persuasion from us, should willingly receive into their communion such whom they judge believers in Christ, who have been baptized by immersion; I do not wonder at, seeing they generally judge baptism performed so, to be valid; but how Mr B. W. can receive such, I cannot see, when he looks upon it to be no *ordinance of God*, p. 41. and a *superstitious invention*, p. 23. nay, *will-worship*, p. 24. There are *two* churches in *London*, which, I have been informed, will not receive persons of our persuasion into their communion; but whether it is, because they judge our baptism invalid, and so we not proper persons for communion, or whether it is a prudential step, that their churches may not be over-run by us, I cannot tell; I think those of our persuasion act a very weak part in proposing to belong to any such churches, who, when they are in them, are too much regarded only for the sake of their subscriptions, are but *noun substantives* therein, and too many like *Issachar*'s ass, *bow down between two burdens*. But to return, Mr *B. W.* has thought fit, in the close of this conference, to produce " some few reasons for the equity and necessity of com- " munion with saints as saints, without making difference in judgment about " water-baptism, a bar unto evangelical church fellowship;" which I shall now consider.

1st, "God has received them, and we should *be followers of God as dear chil- " dren.* We are commanded to *receive one another, as Christ hath received us " to the glory of God.*" That we should be followers of God in all things, which

he

he has made our duty, is certain, but his, and his Son's reception of perſons, is no rule for the reception of church-members. A ſovereign lord may do what he pleaſes himſelf, but his ſervants muſt act according to his orders: God and Chriſt have received unconverted ſinners, but that is no rule for churches; God the Father has ſo received them into his love and affections, as to ſet them apart for himſelf, provide all bleſſings of grace for them, nay, give himſelf in covenant to them, ſend his Son to die for them, his Spirit to convert them, and all previous to it. Chriſt alſo hath received them, ſo as to become a ſurety for them, take the charge both of their perſons and grace, give himſelf a ranſom for them, and beſtow his grace upon them; for we are firſt apprehended by Chriſt, before we are capable of apprehending and receiving him: Muſt we therefore receive unconverted perſons into church-fellowſhip, becauſe God and Chriſt have received them? It is what God has commanded us to do, and not all that he himſelf does, that we are to be followers of him in, or indeed can be; beſides, the churches of Chriſt are oftentimes obliged, according to Chriſt's own rules, to reject thoſe whom Chriſt has received, and cut them off from church-communion; witneſs the inceſtuous perſon; ſo that they are not perſons merely received by Chriſt, but perſons received by Chriſt, ſubjecting themſelves to his ordinances, and to the laws of his houſe, that we are to receive, and retain in churches. The text in *Romans* xv. 7. which ſpeaks of receiving one another, as Chriſt hath received us to the glory of God, can never be underſtood of the receiving of perſons into church-fellowſhip. For the perſons who are exhorted both to receive and be received, were members of churches already; therefore that text only regards the mutual love and affection which they ſhould have to one another, as brethren and church-members; which is enforced by the ſtrong love and affection Chriſt had to them.

2. "All ſaints are alike partakers of the great and fundamental privileges of "the goſpel." If by the great and fundamental privileges of the goſpel, he means union to Chriſt, juſtification by him, faith in him, and communion with him, who denies that ſaints are partakers of theſe things? Though in ſome of them, not all *alike*; for ſome have more faith in Chriſt, and more communion with him, than others have: But what is this argument produced for? or indeed, is there any argument in it? does he mean that therefore they ought to partake of goſpel ordinances? who denies it? And we would have them partake of them *alike* too, both of Baptiſm and the Lord's ſupper; it is the thing we are pleading for.

3. "All believers, though in leſſer things differently minded, are in a capa- "city to promote mutual edification in a church-ſtate." But then their admittance into it, and walk with it, muſt be according to goſpel order, or elſe they are like to be of little ſervice to promote mutual edification in it.

4. "It is observable that the churches for the free communion of saints, are "the most orderly and prosperous." This observation is wrong, witness the churches in *Northamptonshire*, where there is scarcely an orderly or prosperous one of that way; they having been made a prey of, and pillaged by others, to whose capricious humours they have been too much subject.

5. "Many waters should not in the least quench love, nor should the floods "drown it." This is foolishly and impertinently applied to water-baptism: But what is it that some men cannot see in some texts of Scripture?

6. "Behold how good and how pleasant it is!" I think I must also make a note of admiration too, as wondering what the man means by giving us half a sentence! But perhaps this is to give us a specimen of what *shadows of words* are, though I suppose he means *for brethren to dwell together in unity*; it would have been no great trouble to have expressed it; but he is willing to let us know that he has got a concise way of speaking and writing. For brethren to dwell together in unity, is indeed very pleasant and delightful: But *how can two walk*, or dwell together thus, *except they are agreed!*

7. "All the saints shall for ever dwell in glory together." Who denies it? But does it from thence follow, that they must all dwell together on earth? And if he means that it may be inferred from hence, that they ought to be admitted, whilst here, to church-fellowship, who denies it? But I hope it must be in a way agreeable to gospel order; and he ought to have first proved, that admission to church-fellowship without water baptism, is according to gospel order. Jesus Christ, no doubt, receives many unbaptized persons into heaven; and so he does no doubt, such who never partook of the Lord's supper; nay, who never were in church-fellowship: But are these things to be laid aside by us upon that account? We are not to take our measures of acting in Christ's church here below, from what he himself does in heaven, but from those rules which he has left us on earth to go by.

Having thus considered our author's reasons, for the free and mixt communion of saints, without making water baptism a bar to it; I shall take the liberty to subjoin some reasons against it, which I desire chiefly might be regarded and considered by those who are of the same persuasion with us, with respect to the ordinance of water-baptism. They are as follow:

1. Because such a practice is contrary to Christ's commission, in *Matt.* xxviii. 19. where Christ's orders are to baptize those that are taught. It is not only without a precept of Christ, which in matters of worship we should be careful that we do not act without, (for he has no where commanded to receive unbaptized persons into churches) but it is also contrary to one which requires all believers to be baptized; and this must be either before they are church members

or after they are so, or never. The two latter, I dare say, will not be asserted, and therefore the former is true.

2. It is contrary to the order and practice of the primitive churches; it is not only without a precept, but without a precedent: The admission of the first converts after Christ's death, resurrection, and ascension, into church fellowship, was after this manner. First, *they gladly received the word*, then *were baptized*, and after that, *added to the church*, Acts ii. 41. So the apostle *Paul* first believed, then was baptized, and after that assayed to join himself to the disciples, *Acts* ix. 18, 26. Who therefore that has any regard to a command of Christ, and an apostolical practice, would break in upon such a beautiful order as this? I challenge any person, to give one single instance of any one that was ever received into those primitive churches without being first baptized.

3. It has a tendency to lay aside the ordinance entirely. For upon the same foot that persons, who plead their baptism in their infancy, which to us is none at all, may be received, those who never make pretensions to any, yea, utterly deny water-baptism, may also. Moreover, if once it is accounted an indifferent thing, that may, or may not be done; that it is unnecessary and unessential to church-communion, to which persons may be admitted without it, they will lie under a temptation wholly to omit it, rather than incur the trouble, shame, and reproach that attend it.

4. It has a tendency to lay aside the ordinance of the Lord's-Supper, and indeed all others. For, suppose a person should come and propose for communion, to any of those churches who are upon this foundation, and give a satisfactory account of his faith and experience to them, so that they are willing to receive him; but after all, he tells them he is differently minded from them, with respect to the ordinance of the Lord's-Supper: I am willing to walk with you, says he, in all other ordinances but that; and, as to that, I am very willing to meet when you do, and with you; to remember Christ's dying love: I hope I shall be enabled to feed by faith, upon his flesh and blood as well as you; but I think to eat the bread, and drink the wine, are but outward ceremonies, and altogether needless. I should be glad to know, whether any of these churches would reject this man? I am sure, according to their own principles, they cannot. Therefore has not this a tendency to lay aside the ordinance of the Lord's Supper? For if it is warrantable for one man, it is for ten or twenty, and so on *ad infinitum*. All that I can meet with, as yet, that is objected to this, is, that the Lord's-Supper is a church-ordinance, and cannot be dispensed with in such a case; but baptism is not, and therefore may. But baptism is an ordinance of Christ, and therefore cannot be dispensed

with no more than the other: By a church-ordinance, they either mean an ordinance of the church's appointing; or else one that is performed by persons when in a church state. The former, I presume, they do not mean, because the Lord's-Supper is not in that sense a church-ordinance: And if they mean in the latter sense, that baptism is not a church-ordinance, then certainly it ought to be performed before they are in a church state; which is the thing pleaded for. When they talk of baptism's not being essential to salvation, who says it is? but will this tolerate the abuse, neglect, or omission of it? Is any thing relating to divine worship essential to salvation? but what, must it all be laid aside because it is not? is not this an idle way of talking?

5. It is a rejecting the *pattern* which Christ has given us, and a trampling upon his legislative power; is this doing all things according to his direction, when we step over the first thing, after believing, that is enjoined us? Is not this making too free with his legislative power, to alter his rules at pleasure? and what else is it, but an attempt to jostle Christ out of his throne? It is no other than an imputation of weakness to him, as if he did not know what was best for his churches to observe; and of carelesness, as if he was unconcerned whether they regarded his will or no. Let such remember the case of *Nadab* and *Abihu*. In matters of worship, God takes notice of those things that seem but *small*, and will contend with his people upon that account. A power to dispense with Christ's ordinances, was never given to any men, or set of men or churches upon earth. An ordinance of Christ does not depend upon so precarious a foundation, as persons having, or not having light into it: If they have not, they must make use of proper means, and wait till God gives them it.

6. We are commanded to withdraw from *every brother that walks disorderly*; not only from persons of an immoral conversation, but also from those who are corrupt in doctrine, or in the administration of ordinances; if this is not a disorderly walking, to live in the abuse, or neglect and omission of a gospel ordinance, I know not what is: We are not to suffer sin upon a brother, but reprove him for it; bear our testimony against it, lest we be partakers of his guilt; and if we are to *withdraw* from such disorderly persons, then we ought not to *receive* them.

7. This practice makes our separation from the Established church, look more like a piece of obstinacy, than a case of conscience: What, shall we boggle at reading the Common-prayer-book, wearing the surplice, kneeling at the Lord's supper, &c. and can at once drop an ordinance of Christ? if this is not straining at gnats, and swallowing of camels, I must confess myself mistaken.

To all this I might have added also, that it is contrary to the constant and universal practice of the churches of Christ, in all ages of the world. To receive
an

an unbaptized perſon into communion, was never once attempted among all the corruptions of the church of *Rome:* This principle of receiving only baptized perſons into communion, was maintained by the authors of the glorious Reformation from Popery, and thoſe who ſucceeded them. As for the preſent practice of our *Presbyterians* and *Independents,* they proceed not upon the ſame foot as our *Semi-Quakers* do. They judge our baptiſm to be valid, and their own too; and therefore promiſcuouſly receive perſons; but, according to their own principles, will not receive one that is unbaptized. And could we look upon their baptiſm valid too, what we call mixed communion would wholly ceaſe, and conſequently the controverſy about it be entirely at an end; therefore the *Presbyterians* and *Independents* do not maintain a free and mixt communion in the ſame ſenſe, and upon the ſame foundation, as ſome of our perſuaſion do, which thoſe perſons would do well to conſider.

It may be thought neceſſary by ſome, that before I conclude, I ſhould make an apology for taking notice of ſuch a trifling pamphlet as this is, which I have been conſidering. Had it not been for the importunity of ſome of my friends, as well as the vain ovations, and ſilly triumphs, which thoſe of a different perſuaſion from us are ready to make upon every thing that comes out this way, however weak it be, I ſhould never have given myſelf the trouble of writing, nor others of reading hereof. If it ſhould be aſked, why I have been ſo large in conſidering ſeveral things herein, to which a ſhorter reply would have been ſufficient? I anſwer, It is not becauſe I thought the author deſerved it, but having obſerved that the arguments and exceptions which he has licked up from others, have been, and ſtill are, received by perſons of far ſuperior judgment and learning to himſelf, and who are better verſed in this controverſy than he appears to be; it is upon that account, as well as to do juſtice to the truth I have been defending, I have taken this method. But if any ſhould think me blame-worthy, in taking notice of ſome things herein, which do not carry in them the appearance of an argument, I perſuade myſelf they will eaſily forgive me, when they conſider how ready ſome captious perſons would have been to ſay, I had paſſed over ſome of his material objections. However, without much concerning myſelf what any one ſhall ſay of this performance, I commit it to the bleſſing of God, and the conſideration of every impartial reader.

A DEFENCE

# A

# DEFENCE

Of a BOOK, intitled,

## THE ANCIENT MODE OF BAPTIZING

BY

IMMERSION, PLUNGING, or DIPPING in WATER, &c.

AGAINST

Mr MATTHIAS MAURICE's Reply, called,
*Plunging into Water no Scriptural Mode of Baptizing, &c.*

---

## CHAP. I.

*Some Remarks on Mr M's entrance to his Work*

HAVING lately attempted to vindicate the ancient mode of baptizing, by immersion, plunging, or dipping into water, against the exceptions of an anonymous pamphlet, intitled, *The manner of baptizing with water, cleared up from the word of God and right reason, &c.* The author, who appears to be Mr *Matthias Maurice* of *Rowell* in *Northamptonshire*, has thought fit to reply. He seems angry at the treatment he has met with; but if he thought that his name would have commanded greater respect, why did not he put it to his book?

## ANCIENT MODE OF BAPTIZING.

book? and why did he refuse to give satisfaction to his friends when inquired of about the author of it? Would he be treated as a gentleman, a scholar, or a christian? he ought to have wrote as such. Who is the aggressor? who gave the first provocation? If I have any where exceeded the bounds of christianity, or humanity, I would readily acknowledge it upon the first conviction; but who indeed " can touch pitch, without being defiled with it?" Three or four pages are filled up with a whining, insinuating harangue, upon the nature of controversies, and the disagreeable temper and spirit with which they are frequently managed; designing hereby to wipe himself clean, whilst he is casting reproach upon others. I would not be an advocate for burlesk and banter in religious controversies; but if he would have them banished from thence, why does he make use of them, even in this his performance, which begins with such loud exclamations against them. As for instance, how does he pun upon presumptive proofs, p. 13. and in p. 27. speaking of our baptizing in *holes* or *cisterns*, as he is pleased to call them, " Thus, says he, you have forsook the " scriptural way of baptizing *with* water, and have hewn out unto yourselves " cisterns," referring to *Jer.* ii. 13. besides the frequent sneers with which his book abounds. Now if burlesk and banter, in general, ought to be laid aside, much more punning and bantering with the words of scripture, which are sacred and awful. Is this the man that directs others to "write in the fear of God, " having the awful Judge, and the approaching judgment in view;" and yet takes such a liberty as this? He says, p. 7. " I shall not entertain the reader " with any remarks upon his performance, as it is ludicrous, virulent and de-" faming:" Which, itself is a manifest defamation, as the reader cannot but observe; it being asserted without attempting to give one single instance wherein it appears to be so. With what face can he call it ludicrous; when he himself, in the debate, has been so wretchedly guilty that way? when he talks, p. 9. of " Christ's being under water still: and in p. 10. of *John's* thrusting the people " into thorns and briars, when he baptized in the wilderness;" as also his concluding from *Philip* and the Eunuch's coming up out of the water, p. 19. " that neither of them was drowned there;" with other such like rambling stuff, which he might have been ashamed to publish to the world. Moreover, what defamation has he been guilty of, in representing it, as the judgment of " some of us " to baptize naked?" p. 22. And in the words of a *servant of Christ*, as he calls him, p. 44. tells the world that we " baptize persons in thin " and transparent garments;" which, in other cases, would be accounted down right lying. Nay even in this his last performance, p. 44. he has the assurance to insinuate, as if we ourselves thought plunging to be immodest, because we put lead at the bottom of our plunging garments; why could not he as well

have

have argued from our making use of clothes themselves? it is strange that a carefulness to prevent every thing that looks like immodesty, should be improved as an evidence of it: None but a man that is ill-natured and virulent, would ever be guilty of such an insinuation.

What his friends, at *Rowell*, may think of his performances, I cannot tell; but I can assure him, that those of his persuasion at *London* think very meanly of them; and, as the most effectual way to secure the honour of their cause, which is endangered by such kind of writing as his, say, "he is a weak man that has "engaged in the controversy;" though, perhaps, some of his admirers may think that he is one of the mighty men of *Israel*, who, like another *Samson*, has *smote* us *hip and thigh*; but if I should say, that it is with much such an instrument as he once used, I know that I should be very gravely and severely reprimanded for it, my grace and good manners called in question, and perhaps be pelted into the bargain, with an old musty proverb or sentence, either in Greek or Latin; but I will forbear, and proceed to the consideration of his *work*, as he calls it.

His first attack, p. 8. is upon a small sentence of Latin, made use of to express the nauseous and fulsom repetition, of threadbare arguments in this controversy, to which he has thought fit, to give no less than three several answers.

1. He says the Latin is false, because of an erratum of *coctum* for *cocta*; which had I observed before the last half sheet had been worked off, should have been inserted among the *errata*; whereby he would have been prevented making this learned remark; though had it not fallen under my notice, before he pointed it to me, he should have had the honour of this great discovery. He does well indeed to excuse his making such low observations, as being beneath the vast designs he has in view. I might as well take notice of his Greek proverb, p. 25. where οσμε, is put for οσμη, and charge it with being false Greek, though I should rather chuse to ascribe it to the fault of the printer, than the inadvertancy of the writer. However, he does well to let his readers know that he can write Greek; which they could not have come at the knowledge of, by his former performance. But why does not he give a version of his Latin and Greek scraps, especially seeing he writes for the benefit of the *Lord's people*, *the Godly*, and *poor men and women*, that cannot look into *Dictionaries*, and consult *Lexicons*; besides, all the wit therein will be lost to them, as well as others be left unacquainted with his happy genius for, and skill in translating.

2. He says, "the application of this *sentence* is false:" But how does it appear? why, because at *Rowell* he and his people are very moderate in the affair of baptism, they *seldom* discourse of it; when every body knows, that has read my book, that the paragraph referred to, regards not the private conversation of

persons on that subject, but the repeated writings which have been published to the world on his side the question. If the different sentiments of his people, about Baptism, "make no manner of difference in affection, church-relation," &c. as he says p. 9. why does he give them any disturbance? what could provoke him to write after the manner he has done? He knows very well, however mistaken they may be about this ordinance, in his apprehensions, yet that they are conscientious in what they do; why should he then sneer at them, as he does for their practice of plunging, and fix upon them the heavy charges of superstition and will-worship? Is not this man a wise shepherd, that will give disturbance to his flock, when the sheep are still and quiet?

3. He would have his reader believe, that in using this sentence, I would insinuate, that the notions wherein they differ from us about Baptism are poisonous, when I intend no such thing; nor does the proverb, as expressed by me, lead to any such thought, but is used for a nauseous repetition of things, with which his performance, we are considering, very plentifully abounds. We do not look upon mistakes about the grace of God, the person of Christ, and the person and operations of the Spirit, to be of a lesser nature than those about Baptism, as he reproachfully insinuates; for we do with a becoming zeal and courage, oppose such erroneous doctrines in those who are of the same mind with us, respecting baptism, as much as we do in those who differ from us therein.

Page 10. He seems to be angry with me for calling him an *anonymous* author; what should I have called him, since he did not put his name to his book? he asks, "Who was the penman of the epistle to the *Hebrews*?" Very much to the purpose indeed! and then brings in a scrap of Greek out of *Synesius*, with whom, however he may agree in the choice of an obscure life, yet will not in the affair of Baptism; for *Synesius* was baptized upon profession of his faith, and after that made bishop of *Ptolemais*. " Hundreds of precious tracts, he says, have " been published without the names of their authors;" among which, I hope, he does not think his must have a place, it having no authority from the scripture, whatever else it may pretend to; as I hope hereafter to make appear.

### CHAP. II.

*The proofs for immersion, taken from the circumstances which attended the Baptism of* John, Christ, *and his Apostles, maintained: and Mr* M's *demonstrative proofs, for pouring or sprinkling, considered.*

THE ordinance of water-baptism, is not only frequently inculcated in the New Testament, as an ordinance that ought to be regarded; but also many instances of persons who have submitted to it, are therein recorded, and those attended with such circumstances, as manifestly show, to unprejudiced minds, in what manner it was performed.

1. The baptism of Christ administered by *John* deserves to be mentioned, and considered first: This was performed in the river *Jordan*, Matt. iii. 6, 13. and the circumstance of his *coming up out of the water*, as soon as it was done, recorded *ver.* 16. is a full demonstration that he was *in* it; now that he should go into the river *Jordan*, to have water poured, or sprinkled on him, is intolerable, and ridiculous to suppose. Mr *M*. in his debate, p. 6. tells us, that " the words " only signify, that he went up from the water ;" to which I replied, that the preposition *αm* signifies *out of*, and is justly rendered so here. I gave him an instance of it, which he has not thought fit to except against; yet still he says, " the criticism delivers us from a necessity of concluding, that Christ was in the " water :" though it has been entirely baffled; neither has he attempted to defend it. And, because I say, that " we do not infer plunging, merely from " Christ's going down into, and coming up out of the water ;" therefore he would have the argument from hence, as well as from the same circumstances attending the baptism of the Eunuch, wholly laid aside; which I do not wonder at, because it presses him hard. He seems to triumph, because I have not, in his positive and dogmatical way, asserted those circumstances, to be demonstrative proofs of immersion; as though they were entirely given up as such; but he is more ready to receive, than I am to give. This is a manifest indication, I will not say, of a wounded cause only, but of a dying one, which makes him catch at every thing to support himself under, or, free himself from those pressures, which lie hard upon him. We insist upon it, that those proofs are demonstrative, so far as proofs from circumstances can be so; and challenge him to give the like in favour of pouring or sprinkling. Is it not a wretched thing, to use our author's words; that not one text of scripture can be produced, which will vindicate the practice of sprinkling in baptism; and that among all the instances of the performance of the ordinance, which are recorded in scripture, not one single circumstance can render it so much as probable ?

2. We not only read of many others baptized by *John*, but also the places which he chose to administer it in, which will lead any thinking, and considering mind to conclude, that it was performed by immersion: Now, one of those places, where *John* baptized a considerable number, and among the rest Christ Jesus, was the river *Jordan*, Matt. iii. 6. Mark i. 5, 9. the latter of which texts Mr *M*. says, p. 12. " leads us to *no* other thought, than that Jesus was bap-
" tized of *John* at *Jordan* ; as the preposition *αt*, he says, is sometimes tran-
" slated ;" though he gives us no one instance of it. Now in his debate, p. 7. he says, " that the holy Ghost himself tells us, that nothing else is intended by

"it than baptizing *in* Jordan;" and yet this man takes a liberty to differ from him. What will he be at next? to such straits are men driven, who oppose the plain words of the holy Ghost, as he is pleased to say in another case.

*Enon* was another of those places, which *John* chose to baptize in; and the reason of his making choice of it was, *because there was much water there*, John iii. 23. which was proper and necessary, for the baptizing of persons by immersion. Mr *M.* says, p. 19. " that the holy Ghost does not say that they were " baptized there, because there was much water; but that *John* was also bap- " tizing in *Enon* because there was much water there;" but what difference is there? Why only between *John*'s administering the ordinance, and the persons to whom it was administered. He says, p. 21. " that I have granted that the " words, he means ύδατα πολλα, literally denote, " many rivulets or streams; " which is notoriously false; for I do in express words utterly deny it; and have proved from the use of the phrase in the New Testament, and in the Septuagint version of the Old, as well as from *Nonnus*'s paraphrase of the text, that it signifies " large waters, or abundance of them : " I do assure him, that neither of the editions of *Nonnus*, which he has the vanity to mention, was made use of by me; but if there had been any material difference in them, from what I have made use of, I suppose he would have observed it to me, if he has consulted them; and I would also inform him, that *Nonnus* has not always a Latin version printed along with it, as he wrongly asserts.

I have consulted *Calvin* upon the place directed to by him: the text says, that *Jesus and his disciples came into the land of Judea*; and *Calvin* upon it says, that " he came into that part of the country which was nigh to *Enon*;" but neither the text, nor *Calvin* upon it, say that they were both at *Enon*, as our author insinuates; so that from hence there appears no necessity of concluding that choice was made of this place for the accommodation of the large number of people which attended, either upon the ministry of Christ or *John*; that so both they and their cattle might be refreshed, as he ridiculously enough suggests. As to the account he has given of the land of *Canaan*, it is manifest, notwithstanding all his shifts and cavils, that he did represent it in general as a land that wanted water, especially a great part of it; now whatever little spots (for the land itself was not very large) might not be so well watered, yet it is certain, that in general it was; and is therefore called *a land of brooks of water*, *&c.* But since he acknowledges there was plenty of water at *Enon*, where *John* was baptizing, which is sufficient for our purpose, we need not further inquire about the land.

3. Another remarkable instance of baptism is that of the Eunuch's, in *Acts* viii. 38. which is attended with such circumstances, as would leave any person,

that is seriously inquiring after truth, without any scruple or hesitation, in what manner it was performed. In verse 36 we are told, that *they came* unto *a certain water*, where the Eunuch desiring baptism, and *Philip* agreeing to it, after he had made a confession of his faith, it is said, verse 38. that *they went down both* into *the water*; they first came *to* it, and then went *into* it; which leaves that observation without any real foundation, which *supposes* that their going down into the water signifies no more than the descent which led to the river, for they were come thither before, as appears from verse 36. where a phrase is made use of different from this in verse 38. Now though I had observed to our author, that it was not *to*, but *into* the water they went, to which he has not thought fit to reply; yet he still produces his impertinent instance of *going down to the sea in ships*; which is all that can be obtained from him, to set aside the force of this evidence; which, how weak and ridiculous it is, will easily appear to every judicious reader.

Now if persons will but diligently consider those plain instances of baptism, in an humble and hearty search after truth, they will find that they amount to little less than a full demonstration that it was performed in those early times of *John*, Christ, and his apostles, by an immersion or plunging of the whole body under water, as has been fully acknowledged by many great and excellent divines. But now let us consider Mr *M*'s demonstrative proofs for pouring or sprinkling water in baptism, produced by him, p. 14.

He says, "pouring water in baptism, is a true representation of the donation of the Spirit; being, according to God's word, instituted for that end \*." But the word of God no where expresses, or gives the least intimation, that baptism was instituted for any such end; it is true, the donation of the Spirit is sometimes called *a baptism*, and so are the sufferings of Christ; but do we make use of such mediums as these to prove the representation of them to be the end of this ordinance? though it would with equal strength conclude the one as the other: Besides, he might as well argue, that the end of baptism is to represent the passage of the Israelites through the Red sea, because that is called *a Baptism* also. But how does pouring of water in baptism, according to the practice of our modern Pædobaptists, represent the donation of the Spirit, when they only let fall a few drops of water upon the face? But the Spirit's grace is expressed by pouring *floods of water* upon his people in *Isaiah* xliv. 3. one of the texts referred to by our author. Though I have acknowledged, and still do, that the ordinary donation of the Spirit is sometimes expressed by pouring, and sometimes by sprinkling, yet that it was the extraordinary one which the disciples received on the day of Pentecost, that is particularly called *the baptism of the Spirit and of fire*,

by

---

\* Isai. xliv. 3. Ezek. xxxvi. 25. Matt. iii. 11. 1 Cor. xii. 13.

by *John* and Chriſt. Now ſays Mr *M*. p. 17. if this was by pouring, then you are undone: perhaps not. But what does he think will undo us? why the prophecy of *Joel*, cited in *Acts* ii. 16, 17. *I will* pour *out of my ſpirit upon all fleſh*. To which I reply, that though this extraordinary inſtance of the Spirit's grace is expreſſed, as well as the more ordinary ones are, by pouring, under the Old-Teſtament-diſpenſation, in alluſion to thoſe frequent libations, or drink offerings, which were then uſed; yet it need not ſeem ſtrange, that when this prophecy was nearer accompliſhing, and there was a greater diſplay of divine grace, that another word ſhould be uſed which more largely expreſſed the abundance of it: It is no wonder that it ſhould be more abundant in the exhibition than in the prophecy; beſides this text, and all others in the Old Teſtament, which expreſs the Spirit's grace in this, or any other form of language whatever, can never be looked upon as ſufficient proofs of the manner in which a New-Teſtament-ordinance is to be adminiſtered, which was never inſtituted with a view to repreſent it.

2. He ſays, *it*, that is, "pouring water in baptiſm, exactly anſwers to *John*'s "baptiſm: he ſaid that *he baptized with water* [b]." But it ſeems, according to him in p. 15. that the phraſe of baptizing *with* water, regards the ſtrength of the adminiſtrator's arms, *wherewith* he performs, and not the mode of baptizing; ſo that he can pretty eaſily tell us *wherein* and *wherewith* a perſon may be plunged, though he ſtill ſays plunging *with* water is an expreſſion without ſenſe; but he cannot yet inform us how a man can be plunged *in* it, without being plunged *with* it. I urged that in all the evangeliſts the words are ἐν ὕδατι, "in "water," excepting *Luke* iii. 16. where the prepoſition is omitted, which has occaſioned ſome to think it redundant in the other Evangeliſts, which I obſerve no ways hurts our ſenſe and reading of the words; now he wonders that this ſhould make for our reading, or be of any uſe to us; when all that I obſerve is, that it does not make againſt us; if it does, let him make it appear. *John* baptized *in* water, perſons were baptized by him *in* the river *Jordan*, and not *with* it.

3. Another demonſtrative proof of "pouring water in baptiſm, is, that it is "exactly agreeable to the ſignification of the word, as the Lord gives it to us "in the New Teſtament [c]." Which place I ſhall more fully conſider hereafter, and make it appear, that it is there to be underſtood in the ſenſe of dipping or plunging.

4. His laſt proof is, "that it directly anſwers the promiſe of what Chriſt "ſhould do, *Iſaiah* liii. 15. *ſo ſhall he* ſprinkle *many nations*;" to this text he ſays, p. 43. the commiſſion in *Matthew* xxviii. 19. refers, which if it does,

though

[b] Luke iii. 15.   [c] 1 Cor. x. 2.

though I cannot see it can without a very large stretch, it must be only in that part of it which concerns the *teaching* of the Gentiles by the ministry of the apostles, and not that which respects the *baptizing* of them; for the word here rendered *sprinkle*, is עניו דבור expressive of *speaking*, as *Kimchi* on the place observes; and the meaning is, that Christ shall speak to the Gentiles in the ministry of the gospel by the apostles, with so much power, majesty, and authority, that *Kings* themselves *shall shut their mouths at him*; that is, shall silently submit to the scepter of his grace, and to the doctrines of his gospel; *for that which had not been told them, shall they see; and that which they had not heard, shall they consider.* Moreover, who, in the world, could ever imagine, that the ordinance of water baptism, with the mode of its administration, should be intended here? a man must have his imagination prodigiously heated indeed, and his mind captivated with a mere jingle of words, that can look upon such proofs as these, fetch'd out of the Old Testament, as demonstrative ones of the true mode of baptizing under the New. Thus we have had a *taste*, as he calls it, of his *demonstrations* of pouring or sprinkling water in baptism.

## CHAP. III.

*A vindication of* Erasmus, *and of his version of* Acts x. 47.

THE author of the debate in p. 22. urges the impropriety of *Peter*'s speech in *Cornelius*'s house, when he talked of *forbidding water* in *baptism*, if plunging was the right mode of its administration; to which I replied, that if there was any impropriety in the text, it was not to be charged, either upon the words or sense of the holy Ghost, but upon our translation; and urged, that the word *water* should be put in construction with the word *to be baptized*, and not with the word *forbid*, and the whole text be rendered thus, *Can any man forbid that these should be baptized in water, which have received the holy Ghost as well as we?* and produced the testimony of *Erasmus* to confirm it. Now let us attend to Mr *M*'s animadversions upon it. And,

1. Within the compass of four or five lines, he tells two palpable and notorious untruths; for first, he affirms that I say that the words in *Acts* x. 47. are not good sense, when it is he that insinuates an impropriety in *Peter*'s manner of speaking, supposing plunging to be the mode of baptism; what I say, is, that "*if* there is any impropriety in it, it is not to be charged upon the words or "sense of the holy Ghost, but upon our translation;" and yet he would have it, that I assert that the words are not good sense; where do I say so? It is true, I think the words are better rendered according to *Erasmus*'s version; and, for

what

what I can yet see to the contrary, I shall abide by it. Again, he says, that I think there is something wanting in the original. With what face can he say so? Or have I attempted a supplement to any part of it? How unfair is this? Yet this is the man that complains of rank injustice, wresting of words and wracking of sentences in polemical writings. He says, he fears God; I hope he does; but he has given but very little evidence of it, in his management of this controversy.

2. He next falls foul upon *Erasmus*, calling him *old Erasmus*; and represents him as disapproved of by the learned; when almost every body knows how much the learned world owes to that great man, and what deference is always paid to him; but why *old Erasmus*, and *great Beza*? Not that I would go about to diminish the praise of *Beza*, yet I cannot but be of opinion, that to set *Erasmus* upon a level with him, in respect of learning, can be no lessening of him; but it seems to me, that the reason of those different epithets which Mr *M.* has given to those excellent men, is only because the version of the one removes the foundation of his impertinent cavil, and the note of the other, as he imagines, secures it to him.

3. He proceeds, in the next place, to find fault with my translation of *Erasmus*'s version; but if he had had that candour which he would have the world believe he shews in the management of this controversy, he would have easily overlooked this, which he thinks is so much blame-worthy; especially when he could not but observe, that in the very same page, this text is rendered according to the transposition of *Erasmus*, without the negative particle, which hurts the sense: so that he might easily have perceived that this did not arise from a want of knowledge in translating, but from an inadvertency in writing.

4. As to what *Beza* says of this trajection, that it is *dura ac plane insolens*; I shall only say *cum pace tanti viri*, that the trajections in scripture, which he himself approves of, for which see his notes on *John* viii. 25. and *Acts* i. 2. are not more easy or more usual.

5. The sense of the text requires such a transposition of the words; for the meaning is not, as if *Peter* thought that any person would go about to hinder them of water convenient for the administration of the ordinance of baptism; for such a sense of the words would be trifling and jejune, and yet this our version seems to incline to; but that there might be some who would be displeased with, and to their utmost oppose, the baptizing of those Gentiles. Hence *Peter* says, *Who can forbid that these should be baptized in water?* Therefore, and what will further confirm this sense and reading of the words, he commands them in the next verse to be baptized: he does not order water to be brought unto them, but that they *be baptized in the name of the Lord.* To all which,

6. Might

6. Might be added, that this transposition of the words has not its confirmation only from the authority, judgment and learning of *Erasmus*, which is not inconsiderable, but also from others; for, as *Cornelius à Lapide* has observed, both the *Tigurine* version, and that of *Pagnine*'s, read the words the same way: so that however *Erasmus* may be disapproved of by the learned, as our author asserts, yet it seems this version is regarded by them.

## CHAP. IV.

*The end of the institution of the ordinance of Baptism, considered.*

AS the ordinance of water-baptism derives its authority from Christ, so it was instituted by him for some end or other, which may make for his own glory, as well as for the comfort, edification, and increase of faith in his people; and what that end is, we shall now inquire.

Mr *M.* p. 33. says, "the manifest end of it is a representation of the dona-"tion of the Spirit to us in the new covenant [c]." As for the former of these proofs, I need only say, that an Old-Testament-text can never be a proof or evidence of what is the end of the institution of a New-Testament-ordinance: Besides, if it could be thought to have any reference to the affair of Baptism, it would only regard the mode, and not the end of this ordinance, for which he has cited it already, and to what purpose has been also shown. As for the two latter texts here produced by him, they only inform us, that the Spirit's grace is called *a Baptism*, and so are the sufferings of Christ, *Luke* xii. 50. the representation of which he will not own to be the end of baptism, though every body will see that this may be as strongly concluded from hence, as what he contends for; besides, the martyrdom of the saints is called *a Baptism*, Matt. xx. 23. as also the passage of the Israelites through the Red sea, 1 *Cor.* x. 2. yet no body ever thought that the design of baptism was to represent either of these. Now these are what he calls the plain proofs of the manifest end of baptism, without any force upon scripture. What sort of readers does Mr *M.* expect to have, that will be imposed upon by such proofs as these? But there are manifest proofs which fully discover to us, that the end of this ordinance is to represent the sufferings, death, burial, and resurrection of Christ Jesus.

Christ has particularly instituted two ordinances, *Baptism* and the *Lord's-Supper*, to be observed by his people; and the end of the one is no less evident than that of the other. It is said of the Lord's-Supper, *As often as ye eat this bread, and drink this cup, ye do shew the Lord's death till he come* [d]. It is also said

---

[c] Isai xliv. 3. Matt. iii. 11. 1 Cor. xii. 13.  [d] 1 Cor. xi. 25.

## ANCIENT MODE OF BAPTIZING. 249

said of Baptism, *That so many of us, as were baptized into Christ, were baptized into his death* [e]. Did Christ say in the celebration of the Ordinance of the Supper? *This is my blood of the New Testament, which is shed for many for the remission of sins* [f]. His disciples in his name have also said, *Repent and be baptized every one of you, in the name of Jesus Christ, for the remission of sins* [g]: that is, that their faith in that ordinance might be led to the blood of Christ, by which remission of sins was procured; to the grave of Christ, where they were left; and to a risen Saviour, where they have a full discharge from them; all which, in a very lively manner, is represented in this ordinance of baptism. There are many other texts, besides these, which would lead any truly serious and inquiring mind to observe this to be the true end of baptism, as *Rom.* vi. 4. *Col.* ii. 12. 1 *Peter* iii. 21. 1 *Cor.* xv. 29. but because those texts are excepted against by Mr *M.* it will be proper more particularly to consider them, and what he is pleased to advance against the commonly received sense of them.

1st, " *Rom.* vi. 4. *Col.* ii. 12. he says, are not to be understood of water-bap-
" tism, but of the baptism of Christ's sufferings, in which his people were con-
" sidered in him, and with him, as their head and representative " I firmly believe the doctrine of Christ's being a common head, representative, and surety of all the elect of God; for which reason, in my reply, I acknowledged his sense of those texts to be agreeable to the analogy of faith; on the account of which he triumphs, as if it shone *with an unconquerable evidence*, as his expression is, p. 34. when I never owned it to be the true sense of the words; for a sense may be given of a text that is agreeable to the analogy of faith, which is foreign enough to the mind of the holy Ghost therein; as for instance, if of *Gen.* i 1. *In the beginning God created the heaven and the earth*; a man should give such a sense as this, that God chose a certain number of men in Christ unto salvation, before he created the heaven and the earth: This is a sense that is agreeable enough to the analogy of faith, but none will say that it is the sense of the text. But let us a little consider the exposition of those texts, so much boasted of, and see how well it will bear. As for *Rom.* vi. 4. it does not say, that *we are buried with him in baptism*, but *by baptism into death:* So that according to Mr *M*'s exposition, it runs thus, " *We are buried with* Christ representatively in
" the grave, by his sufferings on the cross, *into* that *death* he there submit-
" ted to;" in which, how oddly things hang together, every judicious reader will observee. As to *Col.* ii. 12. though we are said to be *buried with him* in baptism, yet it is added, *Wherein also you are risen with him*; but how we can be said to be risen with him in the baptism of his sufferings, will, I believe, not be very easy to account for. It is better therefore to understand those texts, in the more generally received sense both of ancient and modern divines, who unani-

VOL. II. K k mously

[e] Rom. vi. 3. [f] Matt. xxvi. 28. [g] Acts ii. 38.

mously interpret them of water-baptism; in which the death, burial, and resurrection of Christ are very evidently represented, when performed by immersion.

2*dly*, He says, 1 *Pet.* iii. 21. is not meant of water-baptism, but of the blood of Christ sprinkled upon the conscience. That the blood of Christ, as sprinkled upon a believer's conscience, is ever called a *Baptism*, I never yet met with; and, I will venture to say, can never be proved. Besides, the baptism that *Peter* speaks of was a *figure*, αντιτυπον, "an antitype" of *Noah*'s ark, and of the deliverance of him and his family by water; which was a kind of resurrection from the dead, and did well prefigure our salvation by the resurrection of Christ, represented to us in the ordinance of water-baptism.

3*dly*, The sense of 1 *Cor.* xv. 29. given by me, is also objected against by Mr *M.* p. 32. and another substituted in its room. Let the readers of the controversy between us judge which is most agreeable. The text is difficult, and has employed the thoughts and pens of the most able and learned men in all ages: Both the senses have their defenders. I shall only refer the reader to the learned notes of Sir *Norton Knatchbull*, on 1 *Peter* iii. 21. where both those texts are considered by him; and where he has sufficiently proved, from scripture, fathers, schoolmen, and modern interpreters, that the ordinance of baptism is a true figure, and just representation of the resurrection of Christ, and of ours by him.

## CHAP. V

*A consideration of the signification of the Greek word* βαπτιζω, *and particularly the use of it in* Mark vii. 4. Luke xi. 38. Heb. ix. 10.

THAT the proper, primary, common, and natural sense of the Greek word βαπτιζω, is to *dip* or *plunge*, has been acknowledged by the greatest masters of that language; and it is a rule which should be carefully attended to, that the first, natural, and common sense of a word ought to be used in the interpretation of scripture, unless some very good reason can be given why it should be used in a remote, improper, and consequential one. Now though the nature, end, and circumstances of the ordinance of Baptism, manifestly shew that immersion is the right mode of administering it, and do abundantly confirm the sense of the Greek word, directing us to the proper and primary use thereof; yet some have endeavoured to confine it to a more low and remote sense, but none have attempted to do it with more positiveness and confidence than our author. But what method does he take to effect it, and how does he succeed therein?

Why, 1*ft*, he will exclude all the teftimonies of the ufe of the word among Greek authors uninfpired, efpecially Heathens; which is unreafonable: If our tranflators had confined themfelves to this rule, they would have made but poor work in their verfion of fome part of the Bible, where a word is but once ufed, or at leaft but very rarely in that fenfe in which it is to be taken. Now if a controverfy concerning the ufe of a Greek word in fcripture atifes, which cannot be determined by it, though I do not fay this is the cafe in hand, what methods muft be taken? Will it not be very proper to confult Greek authors, either Chriftian or Heathen, and produce their teftimonies, efpecially the latter? who cannot be fufpected of perverting the ufe of a word, having never been concerned in our religious controverfies. But it feems, if we will make ufe of them, we muft be laid under an obligation to prove that " they were delivered under the immediate infpiration of the holy Ghoft:" was ever fuch an unreafonable demand made in this world before? Or was the infpiration of the holy Spirit ever thought neceffary to fix and determine the fenfe of a word? But I am willing to lay afide thofe teftimonies in this controverfy. And,

2*dly*, Be confined, as he would have me, to the ufe of the word in the New Teftament; but then I muft, it feems, be confined to the ufe of it, as applied to the ordinance of baptifm, which is alfo unreafonable: He fays the word, whenever applied to the ordinance, fignifies *pouring* or *fprinkling* only; which is a fhameful begging of the queftion; and if I fhould fay it only fignifies *dipping* or *plunging*, whenever applied to it, how muft the controverfy be decided? Muft we not refer the decifion of it to other texts of fcripture? It is true, the circumftances, which attend the adminiftration of the ordinance are fufficient to determine the true fenfe of the word, and I am willing to put it upon that iffue; but I know he will not ftand to it: Befides, why has he himfelf brought other texts of fcripture into the controverfy, where the ordinance of baptifm is not concerned? as *Mark* vii. 4. *Heb.* ix. 10. 1 *Cor.* x. 2 as alfo the Septuagint verfion in *Daniel* iv. 33. why may not others take the fame liberty? And what miferable replies has he made to my inftances out of the latter? that in 2 *Kings* v. 14. he fays, difcovers that they, that is, the Septuagint, underftood no more by it than, λυω. *No more* than λυω! Is not that enough? Is not λυω a word that includes in it all kinds of wafhing, efpecially bathing of the whole body; and is always ufed by the Septuagint to exprefs the Jewifh bathings, which were always performed by immerfion; and that *Naaman* underftood the prophet of fuch a kind of wafhing, is manifeft from his ufe of it; he *dipped* himfelf in *Jordan*, κατα το ρημα Ελισαιε, *according to the word of Elifha*.

As for the other in *Isai.* xxi. 4. he says, " it is no wonder they made use of " the word, for they knew very well that sin procures showers of divine dis- " pleasure to be poured upon a person, people, and nation." I desire the next time he pretends to baptize an infant, that he would *pour showers* of water upon it, if he thinks proper, according to this sense of the word βαπτιζω, which he allows of. But however, though those testimonies must be laid aside, yet,

3*dly*, I hope Lexicons may be made use of to direct us in the sense of the word, if it is only as it is used in the New Testament. Yes, that will be allowed of; for Mr *M.* himself consults Lexicons, though he does well to let us know so; for one would have thought, by his positiveness, that he had never looked into one in all his life. Well, but what do the Lexicons say? How do they render the word βαπτιζω? Why by *mergo, immergo,* to *dip* or *plunge into*; and this they give, as the first, and primary sense of the word; but do they make use of no other words to express it by? Yes, they also use *abluo, lavo,* to *wash*; and they mean such a washing as is by dipping, but Mr *M.* p. 38. asks, where do they tell us so? I answer in their Lexicons. Let *Scapula* be consulted, who thus renders the word βαπτιζω, *mergo seu immergo: Ut quæ tingendi aut abluendi gratia aquæ immergimus.* But,

4*thly*, Let us now consider those texts where the word is used in the New Testament; I am willing to be confined to those which Mr *M.* himself has fixed upon, and we will begin,

*First*, With *Mark* vii. 4. *and when they come from the market, except they wash* or baptize (*themselves*) *they eat not*; which may be understood either,

1. Of the things they bought in the market, which they did not eat until they were washed: Thus the *Syriac* version reads the words; *and what they buy in the market, unless it be washed, they eat not:* The same way read all the oriental versions, the *Arabic, Ethiopic,* and *Persic.* Now this must be understood of those things that may be, and are proper to be washed, as herbs, *&c.*. And nobody will question, but that the manner of the washing these was by putting them into water. But,

2. If the words design the washing of persons, they must be understood, either of the washing of their whole bodies, or else of some part only; as their hands or feet: It seems most likely, that the washing of the whole body is intended, as *Grotius*[h], *Vatablus, Drusius*[i], and others think; because washing of hands is mentioned in the preceding verse. Besides, to understand it thus, better expresses the outward, affected sanctity of the more superstitious part of the people. All the Jews washed their hands and feet before eating; but those who pretended to a greater degree of holiness, washed their whole bodies, especially

[h] In loc.      [i] De tribus Sect. Jud. lib. 2. c. 15.

## ANCIENT MODE OF BAPTIZING. 253

pecially when they came from a market; and of this total ablution of the body is *Luke* xi. 38. to be underſtood. And here I cannot forbear mentioning a paſſage of the great *Scaliger*[k] to this purpoſe. "The more ſuperſtitious part of the Jews, ſays he, not only waſhed their feet, but their whole body. Hence they were called *Hemerobaptiſts*, who every day waſhed their bodies before they ſat down to food; wherefore, the Phariſee, which had invited Jeſus to dine with him, wondered that he ſat down to meat before he had waſhed his whole body, *Luke* xi. But thoſe that were more free from ſuperſtition, were contented with waſhing of their feet, inſtead of that univerſal immerſion. Witneſs the Lord himſelf, who being entertained at dinner by another Phariſee, objected to him, when he was ſat down to meat, that he had given him no water for his feet, *Luke* vii."

3. If, by this waſhing, we underſtand only the waſhing of their hands when they came from market; then it will be proper to inquire in what manner this was performed: And it muſt be obſerved, that whatever was the manner which they uſed, it was not uſed as a national cuſtom, or as it was according to the word of God; but what was moſt agreeable to the traditions of the elders, as is manifeſt from the text itſelf. Now this tradition is delivered in their *Miſna* in theſe words; "They waſhed their hands before they eat common food, by an elevation of them; but before they eat the tithes, the offering, and the holy fleſh, they waſhed by immerſion[l]." It is reported in the ſame tract, that *Johanan Ben Gud-Gada*, who, they ſay, was one of the moſt religious in the prieſthood, "always eat his common food after the manner of purification for eating of the holy fleſh;" that is, he always uſed immerſion before eating; and it is highly reaſonable to ſuppoſe, that the Phariſees, eſpecially the more ſuperſtitious part, who pretended to a greater ſtrictneſs in religion than others, uſed the ſame method. It deſerves alſo to be remarked, that this tradition, which ſome of the Jews have been ſo tenacious of, that they would rather die than break it, is by them ſaid to be founded on *Lev.* xv. 11. *and hath not rinſed his hands in water*; where the Hebrew word שטף is uſed, which ſignifies a waſhing by immerſion: and ſo *Buxtorf* renders it. Moreover, in the aboveſaid *Miſna*[m]

we

---

[k] Judæi vero ſuperſtitioſiores non pedes tantum, ſed & corpus totum intingebant. Hinc ἡμεροβαπτισται dicti, qui quotidie, ante diſcubitum, corpus intingebant. Quare Phariſæus ille, qui Jeſum ad cœnam invitaverat, mirabatur eum, antequam totum corpus abluiſſet, diſcubuiſſe: οτι ȣ πρωτον εβαπτισθη προ τȣ αριϛȣ, Luc. xi. Puriores vero a ſuperſtitione, pro univerſali illa βαπτιζειν contenti erant ποδονιπτρῳ, hoc eſt, pedilavio. Teſtis dominus ipſe, qui alii Phariſæo, a quo cœna exceptus fuerat, objicit, ſibi diſcubituro aquam ad pedes datam non fuiſſe. Luc. vii. υδωρ επι τȣς ποδας μȣ ȣκ ιδωκας. Scaliger de Emend. Temp. lib. vi. p. 571.

[l] Trad. Chagigah. c. 2. §. 5.

[m] Tract. Yadaim. c. i. §. 1—3. &c. ii. §. 3.

we are told many things concerning this tradition, as the quantity and quality of the water they used, the vessels they washed in, as well as how far this washing reached, which was עד פרק, by which they meant, either the *back of the hand* or the *wrist*, or else the *elbow*, as *Theophylact* observes on *Mark* vii. 3. who in this is followed by *Capellus* [n]. Now some one of these, the word πυγμη, intends, which we translate *oft*. As to their manner of washing, it was either by taking water in one hand and pouring it upon the other, and then lifting it up [o], that the water might run down to the aforesaid parts, that so it might not return and defile them; or else it was performed by an immersion of them into water; which latter was accounted the most effectual way, and used by the more superstitious part of the Jews. Now those who contend the most for a washing of hands, and not the whole body, as *Pocock* [p] and *Lightfoot*, yet frankly acknowledge that it must be understood of washing of them by immersion. *Lightfoot*'s words are these, "The Jews used, says he, נטילת ידים " a washing of hands [q];" that is, by "lifting them up in the manner before described; and טבילת ידים an immersion "of the hands; and the word νίψωνται, used by our Evangelist, seems to answer "to the former, and βαπτίζωνται, to the latter." So that from the whole, suppose washing of hands is here intended; yet the sense of the Greek word, βαπτίζω contended for, is nevertheless effectually secured: Nor need we be much concerned at 2 *Kings* iii. 11. being thrown in our way by Mr *M.* p. 41. For,

1. The text does not say that *Elisha* poured water upon the hands of *Elijah*, to wash his hands withal: and if he asks what did he then do it for; suppose I should answer, I cannot tell, how will he help himself? it lies upon him to prove that he did it for that end, which he will not find very easy to do.

2. Some of the Jewish writers [r] think, that washing of hands, is not intended, but some very great miracle, which followed upon *Elisha*'s pouring water on *Elijah*'s hands, and is therefore mentioned as a thing known, and what would serve to recommend him to the kings of *Judah*, *Israel*, and *Edom*. But taken in the other sense, the recommendation would be but very inconsiderable; besides, they were now in a very great strait for water, ver. 9. and they might expect, from his former performance, some miracle would be now wrought by him for their relief, as was ver. 17, 20. But,

3. Suppose

[n] Spicileg. in Mar. vii. 3.

[o] Buxtorf. Synag. Jud. c. 8. & Lex. Talm. p. 1335. Pocock not. misc. p. 375, 376, 393. Scaliger. Elenchus Tritæres. Serrar. c. 7. [p] Pocock. not. misc. p. 397, 398.

[q] Adhibuerunt Judæi נטילת ידים lotionem manuum, & טבילת ידים immersionem manoum & videtur vocabulum νίψωνται, apud Evangelistam nostram, priori respondere, & βαπτίζωνται posteriori. Lightfoot. Hor. Heb. in Mar. vii. 4.

[r] Vid. R. David Kimchi & R. Sol. Jarchi in loc.

3. Suppose washing of hands is intended, and that this phrase is expressive of *Elisha*'s being *Elijah*'s ministering servant, and that it was his usual method to wash his master's hands by pouring water upon them; it makes nothing aginst the sense of the word in *Mark* vii. 4. since that regards the superstitious washing of hands, as has been observed, which was performed by an immersion of them, and is there justly reprehended by our Lord.

*Secondly,* The other text produced by Mr *M.* in p. 41. is *Heb.* ix. 10. where the apostle speaks of *divers washings* or *baptisms*, which I have asserted to be performed always by bathing or dipping, and never by pouring or sprinkling. And I still abide by my assertion, the instances produced by him being insufficient to disprove it

1. He mentions *Heb.* ix. 19. where the apostle speaks of *Moses*'s sprinkling the book and people with blood; but does he say that they were washed therewith? or was ever this instance of sprinkling reckoned among the ceremonial ablutions? When only a few drops of blood or water are sprinkled upon persons or things, can they be said, in any just propriety of speech, to be washed therewith?

2. He instances in *Exodus* xxix. 4. which speaks of the washing of *Aaron* and his sons, but not a word either of sprinkling or pouring, so that it makes nothing for his purpose: Besides, the Septuagint here use the word λυω, by which they always express the Jewish bathings, which were performed by a total immersion of the body in water.

3. His next instance is *Numbers* viii. 6, 7. *Take the Levites from among the children of Israel, and cleanse them; and thus shalt thou do unto them to cleanse them; sprinkle water of purifying upon them.* But why did not he read on? *and let them shave all their flesh, and wash their clothes, and so make themselves clean;* that is, by bathing their whole bodies, which was done, as the *Targum* of *Jonathan* upon the place says, *in forty measures of water.* Now, it was thus the Levites were washed. Sprinkling the water of purification, was indeed a ceremony used preparatory to this bathing, but was itself no part of it, as will more fully appear from,

4. His other instance in *Numbers* xix. 18. where it is said, that *tents, vessels,* or *persons,* that *touched a bone, or one slain, or one dead, or a grave,* were to be *sprinkled;* but why did not he transcribe the 19th verse? where his readers would have been informed, that as this sprinkling was to be done on the *third* and *seventh days,* so after that, on the seventh day, the unclean person was to *purify himself, and wash his clothes, and bathe himself in water:* So that all those aspersions before, were but so many preparations to the general washing or bathing himself all over in water, on the seventh day. I shall therefore still abide by it,

it, that none of the ceremonial washings were performed by sprinkling; and indeed, to talk of washing by sprinkling, deserves rather to be laughed at, than to have a serious answer; it being no more reconcilable to good sense, than it is to the just propriety of language, or universal customs of nations. From the whole it appears, that *Maimonides* was not mistaken in his observation; and that the word in *Hebrews* ix. 10. properly signifies *bathings* or *dippings*. And now,

*Thirdly*, We are come, as he says, to that great text, 1 *Cor.* x. 2. which he directs to, as the poor man and woman's Lexicon; and it is pity but that they should know how to make use of it. Here the children of *Israel* are said to be *baptized in the cloud, and in the sea*. But since the word is here used in a figurative sense, it is not very fair in our antagonists to urge us with it, nor, indeed, any other place where it is so used; yet we are not afraid of engaging with them in the consideration of those places, and particularly this; wherein there is enough to justify the apostle in the use of the word, and at the same time secure its sense on our side. When we consider, that the cloud in which they are said to be baptized, passed over them, so that they were covered therewith; and if it let down, at the same time, a shower of rain upon them, it makes it still look more like a baptism; which also is aptly resembled by their passage through the sea, the waters standing up on both sides, so that they seemed to be buried in them. Which things being considered, justifies the apostle, I say, in the use of the word, which strictly and properly signifies dipping or plunging. Words, when used in a figurative sense, though what is expressed by them is not literally true; yet the literal sense is not lost thereby: For instance, in the word *dip*. When a person has been in a large shower of rain, so that his clothes and body are exceeding wet, we often say of such an one, *he is finely dipt*; the meaning of which is, that he is as wet as if he had been dipt all over in a brook or river. So likewise of a person that has just looked into a book, controversy, art, or science; we say, that he has just *dipt into it*; whereby we mean, that he has arrived but to a small acquaintance with, or knowledge in those things. Now would it not be a vain thing for a man, from hence, to attempt to prove, that the word *dip* is not to be understood in its native, common, and literal sense, in which we mostly use it. This observation will serve to vindicate my way of accounting for the use of the word in the present text, as well as for βαπτω, in *Dan.* iv. 33. In fine, from the whole, we may well conclude that Baptism ought to be performed by immersion, plunging, or dipping in water, according to the practice of *John*, Christ, and his apostles, the nature and end of the ordinance, and the true and native signification of the word; which mode of baptizing has been used in all ages of the world, and I doubt not but will be, notwithstanding all opposition made against it.

As

## ANCIENT MODE OF BAPTIZING.

As to the endangering of health by immersion, I referred the reader to Sir *John Floyer*'s *History of Cold-bathing*. Mr *M*. insinuates that I have misrepresented him. I only intimate to the reader, that Sir *John* gives a relation of several cures performed by cold-bathing: And I could easily fill up several pages with a catalogue of diseases for which he says it is useful, together with instances of cures performed by it. He asks, "Why I do not inform *my* reader in how "many cases Sir *J. F.* and Dr *B.* thought cold-bathing inconvenient and dan- "gerous?" I could, indeed, soon acquaint the reader, that Sir *John Floyer* thought it not proper to be used when persons were hot and sweating, nor after excessive eating or drinking; as also, that they should not stay in it too long, until they were chilled; and that if any danger came by it, it was usually in such cases: But this will do his cause no service, nor affect ours. I could also have told my reader, that he thinks cold-bathing to be useful in Consumptions, Catarrhs, *&c.* the cases which Mr *M.* instances in; who cites Dr *Cheyne*'s *Essay on Health*, p. 108. where the Doctor says, "that Cold-bathing should never be "used under a fit of a chronical distemper, with a quick pulse, or with a head- "ach, or by those that have weak lungs." But why does he not acquaint his reader that the Doctor in the very same paragraph, says, "that cold-bathing "is of great advantage to health—It promotes perspiration, enlarges the circu- "lation, and prevents the danger of catching cold." So that every body will easily see, as all experience testifies, that there is no force in the argument, taken from the endangering of health by immersion. By this time the reader will be capable of judging whether Mr *Gill* is *fairly answered* or no, as Mr *M.* has ex- pressed in his title-page; though it would have been as well to have left it for another to have made the remark, and so took the advice of the wise man, *Let another praise thee, and not thine own mouth; a stranger, and not thine own lips* [*]: But before I conclude, I shall take liberty to ask Mr *M.* four or five questions.

1. Why does he not tell the world who that servant of Christ is, whose words he uses; he says, I am mistaken in saying that they are the words of *Russen*; but I still aver, that they are used by him; but whether *Russen* took them from his servant of Christ, or his servant of Christ from *Russen*, I cannot tell; for that two men, without the knowledge of one another's words, should fall into the same odd, and aukward way of speaking, and commit the very same blun- ders, is not reasonable to suppose; but however, let him be who he will, Mr *Stennett*'s reply to *Russen*, which I have transcribed, fully detects the sin and folly of those indecent expressions. As to what Mr *M.* says, p. 44. "that "he is very willing that both *Stennett* and *Russen* should lie dormant;" I be- lieve

[*] Proverbs xxvii. 2.

lieve it, for as the latter will never be of any service to his cause, so the former would give a considerable blow to it, was his book more diligently perused.

2. What does he mean by the *word of the Lord*, he so often mentions, when speaking of the sense of the Greek word? Does he mean the original text of the New Testament? That uses a word in the account it gives of this ordinance, which, as has been made appear, always signifies to *dip* or *plunge*. Or, by *the word of the Lord*, does he mean our translation; which uses the word *baptize*, thereby leaving the sense of the Greek word undetermined, had not the circumstances, attending the accounts we have of the administration of this ordinance, sufficiently explained it; as will clearly appear to every one who considers them: Had this rendered it *dip*, as some other versions have done, none, one would think, would have been at a loss about the right mode of administering this ordinance; though in *Holland*, where they use no other word but *dipping* to express baptism by, yet they nevertheless use sprinkling; nay, as I am informed, the minister when he only sprinkles or pours water upon the face of the infant, says, " I dip thee in the name of the Father, of the Son, and of the " holy Ghost." Such a force have prejudice and custom on the minds of men, that it puts them on doing what is contrary to the plain and manifest sense of words.

3. Why has he dropt his new-found name of *Plungers*, which he seemed to be so fond of in his former performance, and thought so exceeding proper for us, and revived the old name of *Anabaptists?* which we cannot be, neither according to his principles, nor our own; not according to ours, because we deny pouring or sprinkling to be baptism; not according to his, because he denies dipping or plunging to be baptism.

4. Why are Dr *Owen*'s arguments for Infants-baptism published at the end of his book? How impertinent is this? When the controversy between us, is not about the subjects, but the mode of baptism: Perhaps his bookseller did this, seeing Mr *M.* says nothing of them himself, nor recommends them to others; but if he thinks fit to shew his talent in this part of the controversy, he may expect attendance thereto, if what he shall offer deserves it.

5. Why has he not defended his wise reasons for mixt communion, and made some learned strictures upon those arguments of mine, which he has been pleased to call *frivolous*, without making any further reply to them? He has very much disappointed many of his friends, who promised both me and themselves an answer, to that part of my book especially; but perhaps a more elaborate performance may be expected from him, upon that subject, or some other learned hand. However, at present, I shall take my leave of him; but not with *Prov.* xxvi. 4. which he has been ashamed to transcribe at length, lest

his

his readers should compare the beginning and end of his book together; whereby they would discover, how much he deserves the character of a Gentleman, a Scholar, or a Christian; as also, how well this suits the whining insinuations, with which he begins his performance. I shall add no more, but conclude with the words of *Job, Teach me, and I will hold my tongue; and cause me to understand wherein I have erred. How forcible are right words? But what doth your arguing reprove?*

---

## THE DIVINE RIGHT OF INFANT-BAPTISM, EXAMINED AND DISPROVED;

Being an ANSWER to a Pamphlet, intitled,

*A brief Illustration and Confirmation of the Divine Right of Infant-Baptism.*

Printed at BOSTON in NEW-ENGLAND, 1746.

---

## CHAP. I.

*The Introduction, observing the Author, Title, method and occasion of writing the Pamphlet under consideration.*

MANY being converted under the ministry of the word in *New-England*, and enlightened into the ordinance of believers baptism, whereby the churches of the Baptist persuasion at *Boston* and in that country have been much increased, has alarmed the pædobaptist ministers of that colony; who have applied to one Mr *Dickenson*, a country minister, who, as my correspondent informs me, has wrote with some success against the Arminians, to write in favour of infant sprinkling; which application he thought fit to attend unto, and accordingly wrote a pamphlet on that subject; which has been printed in several places, and several thousands have been published, and great pains have been taken to spread them about, in order to hinder the growth of the Baptist interest. This performance has been transmitted to me, with a request to take some notice of it by way of reply, which I have undertook to do.

The running-title of the pamphlet, is *The Divine Right of Infant-Baptism*; but if it is of divine right, it is of God; and if it is of God, if it is according to his mind, and is instituted and appointed by him, it must be notified somewhere or other in his word; wherefore the scriptures must be searched into, to see whether it is so, or no: and upon the most diligent search that can be made, it will be found that there is not the least mention of it in them; that there is no precept enjoining it, or directing to the observation of it; nor any instance, example, or precedent encouraging such a practice; nor any thing there said or done, that gives any reason to believe it is the will of God that such a rite should be observed; wherefore it will appear to be entirely an human invention, and as such to be rejected. The title-page of this work promises an *Illustration and Confirmation* of the said divine right; but if there is no such thing, as it is certain there is not, the author must have a very difficult task to illustrate and confirm it; how far he has succeeded in this undertaking, will be the subject of our following inquiry.

The writer of the pamphlet under consideration has chose to put his thoughts together on this subject, in the form of a *dialogue* between a *minister* and one of his *parishioners*, or *neighbours*. Every man, that engages in a controversy, may write in what form and method he will; but a by-stander will be ready to conclude, that such a way of writing is chose, that he may have the opportunity of making his antagonist speak what he pleases; and indeed he would have acted a very unwise part, had he put arguments and objections into his mouth, which he thought he could not give any tolerable answer to; but, inasmuch as he allows the person the conference is held with, to be not only *a man of piety and ingenuity, but of considerable reading*, he ought to have represented him throughout as answering to such a character; whereas, whatever *piety* is shewn in this debate, there is very little *ingenuity* discovered; since, for the most part, he is introduced as admitting the weak reasonings of the minister, at once, without any further controversy; or if he is allowed to attempt a defence of the cause and principles he was going over to, he is made to do it in a very mean and trifling manner; and, generally speaking, what he offers is only to lead on to the next thing that presents itself in this dispute: Had he been a man of considerable reading, or had he read Mr *Stennett*, and some others of the Antipædobaptist authors, as is said he had, which had occasioned his doubt about his baptism, he would have known what answers and objections to have made to the minister's reasonings,

sonings, and what arguments to have used in favour of adult-baptism, and against infant-sprinkling. What I complain of is, that he has not made his friend to act in character, or to answer the account he is pleased to give of him: However he has a double end in all this management; on the one hand, by representing his antagonist as a man of ingenuity and considerable reading, he would be thought to have done a very great exploit in convincing and silencing such a man, and reducing him to the acknowledgment of the truth; and, on the other hand, by making him talk so weakly, and so easily yielding to his arguments, he has acted a wise part, and taken care not to suffer him to say such things, as he was not able to answer; and which, as before observed, seems to be the view of writing in this dialogue-way.

## CHAP. II.

*Of the Consequences of renouncing Infant-Baptism.*

THE minister, in order to frighten his parishioner out of his principle of adult-baptism, he was inclined to, suggests terrible consequences that would follow upon it; as his renouncing his baptism in his infancy; vacating the covenant between God and him, he was brought into thereby; renouncing all other ordinances of the gospel, as the ministry of the Word, and the sacrament of the Lord's-Supper; that upon this principle, Christ, for many ages, must have forsaken his church, and not made good his promise of his presence in this ordinance; and that there could be no such thing as baptism in the world now, neither among Pædobaptists, nor Antipædobaptists.

1*st*, The first dreadful consequence following upon a man's espousing the principle of believers baptism, is a renunciation of his baptism; not of the ordinance of baptism, that he cannot be said to reject and renounce; for when he embraces the principle of adult-baptism, and acts up to it, he receives the true baptism, which the word of God warrants and directs unto, as will be seen hereafter: But it seems it is a renunciation of his baptism in his infancy; and what of that? it should be proved first, that that is baptism, and that it is good and valid, before it can be charged as an evil to renounce it; it is right to renounce that which has no warrant or foundation in the word of God: But what aggravates this supposed evil is, that in it a person in his early infancy is dedicated to God the Father, Son, and holy Ghost; it may be asked, by whom is the person in his infancy dedicated to God, when baptism is said to be administered to him? Not by himself, for he is ignorant of the whole transaction; it must be either by the minister, or his parents: The parents indeed desire

the

the child may be baptized, and the minister uses such a form of words, *I baptize thee in the name of the Father, of the Son, and of the holy Ghost*; but what dedication is here made by the one, or by the other? However, seeing there is no warrant from the word of God, either for such baptism, or dedication; a renunciation of it need not give any uneasiness to any person so baptized and dedicated.

2*dly*, To embrace adult-baptism, and to renounce infant-baptism, is to vacate the covenant into which a person is brought by his baptism, page 4. by which covenant the writer of the dialogue means the covenant of grace, as appears from all his after-reasonings from thence to the right of infants to baptism.

1. He supposes that unbaptized persons are, as to their external and visible relation, strangers to the covenants of promise; are not in covenant with God; not so much as visible christians; but in a state of heathenism; without hope of salvation, but from the uncovenanted mercies of God, p. 4, 5, 6. The covenant of grace was made from everlasting; and all interested in it were in covenant with God, as early, and so previous to their baptism, as to their secret relation God-wards; but this may be thought to be sufficiently guarded against by the restriction and limitation, " as to external and visible relation : " But I ask, are not all truly penitent persons, all true believers in Christ, though not as yet baptized, in covenant with God, even as to their external and visible relation to him, which faith makes manifest? Were not the three thousand in covenant with God visibly, when they were pricked to the heart, and repented of their sins, and gladly received the word of the gospel, promising the remission of them, though not as yet baptized? Was not the Eunuch in covenant with God? or was he in a state of heathenism, when he made that confession of his faith, *I believe that Jesus Christ is the Son of God*, previous to his going down into the water, and being baptized? Were the believers in *Samaria*, or those at *Corinth*, in an uncovenanted state, before the one were baptized by *Philip*, or the other by the apostle *Paul*? Was *Lydia*, whose heart the Lord opened, and who attended to the things that were spoken; and the Jailor, that believed and rejoiced in God, with all his house, in an uncovenanted state, before they submitted to the ordinance of baptism? Are there not some persons, that have never been baptized, of whom there is reason to believe they have an interest in the covenant of grace? Were not the Old Testament saints in the covenant of grace, before this rite of baptism took place? Should it be said, that circumcision did that then, which baptism does now, enter persons into covenant, which equally wants proof, as this; it may be replied, that only commenced at a certain period of time; was not always in use, and belonged to a certain

people

people only; whereas there were many before that, who were in the covenant of grace, and many after, and even at the same time it was enjoined, who yet were not circumcised; of which more hereafter: From all which it appears, how false that assertion is.

2. That a man is brought into covenant by baptism, as this writer affirms; seeing the covenant of grace is from everlasting; and those that are put into it, were put into it so soon; and that by God himself, whose sole prerogative it is. Parents cannot enter their children into covenant, nor children themselves, nor ministers by sprinkling water upon them; it is an act of the sovereign grace of God, who says, *I will be their God, and they shall be my people:* The phrase of *bringing into the bond of the covenant*, is but once used in scripture; and then it is ascribed to God, and not to the creature; not to any act done by him, or done to him, *Ezekiel* xx. 37. and much less,

3. Can this covenant be vacated, or made null and void, by renouncing infant-baptism: The covenant of grace is ordered in all things, and sure; its promises are Yea and Amen in Christ; its blessings are the sure mercies of *David*; God will not break it, and men cannot make it void; it is to everlasting, as well as from everlasting; those that are once in it can never be put out of it; nor can it be vacated by any thing done by them. This man must have a strange notion of the covenant of grace, to write after this rate; he is said to have wrote against the Arminians with some success; if he has, it must be in a different manner from this; for upon this principle, that the covenant of grace may be made null and void by an act of the creature, how will the election of God stand sure? or the promise of the covenant be sure to all the seed? What will become of the doctrine of the saints perseverance? or of the certainty of salvation to those that are chosen, redeemed, and called?

3*dly*, Another consequence said to follow, on espousing the principle of adult-baptism, and renouncing that of infants, is a renouncing all other ordinances of the gospel, as the ministry of the word, and the sacrament of the Lord's supper, practically denying the influences of the Spirit in them, and all usefulness, comfort and communion by them. All which this author endeavours to make out, by observing, that if infant-baptism is a nullity, then those, who have received no other, if ministers, have no right to administer sacred ordinances, being unbaptized; and, if private persons, they have no right to partake of the Lord's supper, for the same reason; and so all public ordinances are just such a nullity as infant-baptism; and all the influences of the Spirit, in conversion, comfort, and communion, by them, must be practically denied, p. 5, 6. To which may be replied, that though upon the principle of adult-baptism, as necessary to the communion of churches, it follows, that no unbaptized person is regularly called to the preaching of the word, and administration ordinances, or can be a regular communicant; yet it does not follow, that a man that renounces infant baptism, and embraces believers baptism, must renounce all other ordinances, and look upon them just such nullities as infant-baptism is, and deny all the comfort and communion he has had in them; because the word may be truly preached, and the ordinance of the Lord's supper be duly administered, by an irregular man, and even by a wicked man; yea, may be made useful for conversion and comfort; for the use and efficacy of the word and ordinances, do not depend upon the minister or administrator; but upon God himself, who can, and does sometimes, make use of his own word for conversion, though preached by an irregular, and even an immoral man; and of his own ordinances, for comfort, by such an one, to his people, though they may be irregular and deficient in some things, through ignorance and inadvertency.

4*thly*, Another consequence following upon this principle, as supposed, is, that if infant-baptism is no institution of Christ, and to be rejected, then the promise of Christ, to be with his ministers in the administration of the ordinance of baptism, to the end of the world, *Matt.* xxviii. 19, 20. is not made good; since for several ages, even from the fourth to the sixteenth century, infant-baptism universally obtained, p. 6—8. To which the following answer may be returned; That the period of time pitched upon for the prevalence of infant-baptism is very unhappy for the credit of it, both as to the beginning and end; as to the beginning of it, in the fourth century, a period in which corruption in doctrine and discipline flowed into the church, and the man of sin was ripening apace, for his appearance; and likewise as to the end, the time of the reformation, in which such abuses began to be corrected: The whole is a period of time, in which the true church of Christ began gradually to disappear, or to be hidden, and at last *fled into the wilderness*; where she has not been forsaken of Christ, but is, and *will be, nourished, for a time, and times, and half a time*; this period includes the gross darkness of popery, and all the depths of Satan; and which to suffer was no ways contrary to the veracity of Christ, in his promise to be with his true church and faithful ministers to the end of the world. Christ has no where promised, that his doctrines and ordinances should not be perverted; but, on the contrary, has given clear and strong intimations, that there should be a general falling-away and departure from the truth and ordinances of the gospel, to make way for the revelation of antichrist; and though it will be allowed, that during this period infant-baptism prevailed, yet it did not universally obtain. There were witnesses for adult-baptism in every age; and Christ had a church in the wilderness, in obscurity, at this time; namely, in the valleys of *Piedmont*; who were, from the beginning of the apostacy, and witnessed against it, and bore

their

their testimony against infant-baptism, as will be seen hereafter, and with these his presence was; nor did he promise it to any, but in the faithful ministration of his word and ordinances, which he has always made good; and it will lie upon this writer and his friends, to prove the gracious presence of Christ in the administration of infant-baptism

*5thly*, It is said, that, upon these principles, rejecting infant-baptism, and espousing believers-baptism, it is not possible there should be any baptism at all in the world, either among Pædobaptists or Antipædobaptists; the reason of this consequence is, because the madmen of *Munster*, from whom this writer dates the first opposition to infant-baptism; and the first Antipædobaptists in *England*, had no other baptism than what they received in their infancy; that adult-baptism must first be administered by unbaptized persons, if infant-baptism is no ordinance of Christ, but a mere nullity; and so by such as had no claim to the gospel ministry, nor right to administer ordinances; and consequently the whole succession of the Antipædobaptist churches must remain unbaptized to this day; and so no more baptism among them, than among the Pædobaptists, until there is a new commission from heaven, to renew and restore this ordinance, which is, at present, lost out of the world, p. 6, 8, 9. As for the madmen of *Munster*, as this writer calls them, and the rise of the Antipædobaptists from them, and what is said of them, I shall consider in the next chapter. The English Antipædobaptists, when they were first convinced of adult-baptism, and of the mode of administering it by immersion, and of the necessity of setting a reformation on foot in this matter, met together, and consulted about it: when they had some difficulties thrown in their way, about a proper administrator to begin this work; some were for sending messengers to foreign churches, who were the successors of the ancient *Waldenses* in *France* and *Bohemia*; and accordingly did send over some, who being baptized, returned and baptized others. And this is a sufficient answer to all that this writer has advanced. But others thought that this was a needless scruple, and looked too much like the popish notion of an uninterrupted succession, and a right conveyed through that to administer ordinances; and therefore judged, in such a case as theirs, there being a general corruption as to this ordinance, that an unbaptized person, who appeared to be otherwise qualified to preach the word, and administer ordinances, should begin it; and justified themselves upon the same principles that other reformers did, who, without any regard to n uninterrupted succession, set up new churches, ordained pastors, and administered ordinances: It must be owned, that in ordinary cases, he ought to be baptized himself, that baptizes another, or preaches the word, or administers other ordinances; but in an extraordinary case, as this of beginning a reformation

tion from a general corruption, where such an administrator cannot be had, it may be done; nor is it essential to the ordinance that there should be such an administrator, or otherwise it could never have been introduced into the world at all at first; the first administrator must be an unbaptized person, as *John* the Baptist was. According to this man's train of reasoning, there never was, nor could be any valid baptism in the world; for *John*, the first administrator, being an unbaptized person, the whole succession of churches from that time to this day must remain unbaptized. It will be said, that he had a commission from heaven to begin this new ordinance; and a like one should be shewn for the restoration of it. To which I answer, that there being a plain direction for the administration of this ordinance, in the Word, there was no need of a new commission to restore it from a general corruption; it was enough for any person, sensible of the corruption, to attempt a reformation, and to administer it in the right way, who was satisfied of his call from God to preach the gospel, and administer ordinances, according to the word. I shall close this chapter with the words of *Zanchy*\*, a Protestant Divine, and a Pædobaptist, and a man of as great learning and judgment, as any among the first reformers: " It is a " fifth question, he says, proposed by *Augustin. contra Parmen.* l. 2. c. 13. col. " 42. but not solved, whether he that never was baptized may baptize an- " other; and of this question he says, that is, *Austin*, nothing is to be affirmed " without the authority of a council. Nevertheless, *Thomas (Aquinas)* takes " upon him to determine it, from an answer of Pope *Nicholas*, to the inquiries " of the Dutch, as it is had in *Decr. de Confec.* dist. 4. can. 22." where we thus read; " You say, by a certain Jew, whether a christian or a heathen, you know " not, (that is, whether baptized or unbaptized) many were baptized in your " country, and you desire to know what is to be done in this case; truly if " they are baptized in the name of the holy Trinity, or only in the name of " Christ, they ought not to be baptized again." And *Thomas* confirms the same, by a saying of *Isidore*, which likewise is produced in the same distinction, can. 21. where he says, " that the Spirit of Christ ministers the grace of bap- " tism, though he be a heathen that baptizes. Wherefore, says *Thomas*, if " there should be two persons not yet baptized, who believe in Christ, and " they have no lawful administrator by whom they may be baptized, one may, " without sin, be baptized by the other; the necessity of death obliging to it. " All this, adds *Zanchy*, proceeds from hence, that they thought water-baptism " absolutely necessary; but what cannot be determined by the word of God, " we should not dare to determine. But, says he, I will propose a question, " which, I think, may be easily answered; supposing a Turk in a country " where

---

\* Quinta quæstio proponitur ab Augustino, &c. Explicat. Epist. ad Ephes. c. 5. p. 125.

" where he could not eafily come at chriftian churches; he, by reading the
" New Teftament, is favoured with the knowledge of Chrift, and with faith;
" he teaches his family, and converts that to Chrift, and fo others likewife;
" the queftion is, whether he may baptize them whom he has converted to
" Chrift, though he himfelf never was baptized with water-baptifm? I do not
" doubt but he may; and, on the other hand, take care that he himfelf be
" baptized, by another of them that were converted by him; the reafon is,
" becaufe he is a minifter of the Word, extraordinarily raifed up by Chrift; fo
" that fuch a minifter may, with them, by the confent of the church, appoint
" a collegue, and take care that he be baptized by him." The reafon which
*Zanchy* gives, will, I think, hold good in the cafe of the firft Antipædobaptifts
in *England*.

## CHAP. III.

*Of the Antiquity of Infant-Baptifm; when firft debated; and concerning the* Waldenfes.

THE minifter, in this dialogue, in order to ftagger his neighbour about the principle of adult-baptifm, he had efpoufed, fuggefts to him, that infant-baptifm did univerfally obtain in the church, even from the apoftles times; that undoubted evidence may be had from the antient fathers, that it conftantly obtained in the truly primitive church; and that it cannot be pretended that this practice was called in queftion, or made matter of debate in the church, till the madmen of *Munfter* fet themfelves againft it; and affirms, that the antient *Waldenfes* being in the conftant practice of adult-baptifm, is a mere imagination, a chimerical one, and to be rejected as a groundlefs figment, p. 7, 9.

I. This writer intimates, that the practice of infant-baptifm univerfally and conftantly obtained in the truly primitive church. The truly primitive church is the church in the times of Chrift and his apoftles: The firft chriftian church was that at *Jerufalem*, which confifted of fuch as were made the difciples of Chrift, and baptized; firft made difciples by Chrift, and then baptized by his apoftles; for *Jefus himfelf baptized none*, only they baptized by his order ª. This church afterwards greatly increafed; three thoufand perfons, who were pricked to the heart under *Peter*'s miniftry, repented of their fins, and joyfully received the good news of pardon and falvation by Chrift, were baptized, and added to it; thefe were adult perfons; nor do we read of any one infant being baptized, while this truly primitive church fubfifted. The next chriftian church was that

ª John iv. 1, 2. Acts i. 15.

at *Samaria*; for that there was a church there, is evident from *Acts* ix. 31. This seems to have been founded by the ministry of *Philip*; the original members of it were men and women baptized by *Philip*, upon a profession of their faith in the things preached by him, concerning the kingdom of God, and the name of Jesus Christ [b]; nor is there the least intimation given that infant-baptism at all obtained in this church. Another truly primitive christian church, was the church at *Philippi*; the foundation of which was laid in the two families of *Lydia* and the Gaoler, and which furnish out no proof of infant-baptism obtaining here, as we shall see hereafter; for *Lydia*'s houshold are called brethren, whom the apostles visited and comforted; and the Gaoler's houshold were such as were capable of hearing the word, and who believed in Christ, and rejoiced in God as well as he [c]. So that it does not appear that infant-baptism obtained in this church. The next christian church we read of, and which was a truly primitive one, is the church at *Corinth*, and consisted of persons who, hearing the apostle *Paul* preach the gospel, believed in Christ, whom he preached, and were baptized [d]: but there is no mention made of any infant being baptized, either now or hereafter, in this truly primitive church state. These are all the truly primitive churches of whose baptism we have any account in the *Acts of the apostles*, excepting *Cornelius*, and his family and friends, who very probably founded a church at *Cæsarea*; and the twelve disciples at *Ephesus*, who very likely joined to the church there, and who are both instances of adult-baptism [e]. Let it be made appear, if it can, that any one infant was ever baptized in any of the above truly primitive churches, or in any other, during the apostolic age, either at *Antioch* or *Thessalonica*, at *Rome*, or at *Colosse*, or any other primitive church of those times. But though this cannot be made out from the writings of the New Testament, we are told,

II. That undoubted evidence may be had from the antient fathers, that infant-baptism constantly obtained in the truly primitive church. Let us a little inquire into this matter:

1. The christian writers of the first century, besides the evangelists and apostles, are *Barnabas, Hermas, Clemens Romanus, Ignatius* and *Polycarp*. As to the two first of these, *Barnabas* and *Hermas*, the learned Mr *Stennett* [f] has cited some passages out of them; and after him Mr *David Rees* [g]; for which reason, I forbear transcribing them; which are manifest proofs of adult-baptism, and that as performed by immersion; they represent the persons baptized, the one [h] as hoping in the cross of Christ, the other [i] as having heard the word, and being

willing

---

[b] Acts viii. 12.  [c] Acts xvi. 14, 15, 32—34, 40.  [d] Acts xviii. 8
[e] Acts x. 48. and xix. 1—7.  [f] Answer to Russen, p. 142, 143.
[g] Answer to Walker, p. 157, &c.  [h] Barnabæ Epist. c. 9. p. 235, 236. Ed. Voss.
[i] Hermæ Pastor. l. 1. vis. 3. s. 7. & l. 3. s. 16.

willing to be baptized in the name of the Lord; and both as going down into the water, and coming up out of it. *Clemens Romanus* wrote an epistle to the *Corinthians*, still extant; but there is not a syllable in it about infant-baptism. *Ignatius* wrote epistles to several churches, as well as to particular persons; but makes no mention of the practice of infant-baptism in any of them: what he says of baptism, favours adult-baptism; since he speaks of it as attended with faith, love and patience: "Let your baptism, says he [k], remain as armour; faith as an "helmet, love as a spear, and patience as whole armour." *Polycarp* wrote an epistle to the *Philippians*, which is yet in being; but there is not one word in it about infant-baptism. So that it is so far from being true, that there is undoubted evidence from the antient fathers, that this practice universally and constantly obtained in the truly primitive church, that there is no evidence at all that it did obtain, in any respect, in the first century, or apostolic age; and which is the only period in which the truly primitive church of Christ can be said to subsist. There is indeed a work called *The constitutions of the apostles*, and sometimes the *constitutions of Clemens*, because he is said to be the compiler of them; and another book of *Ecclesiastical Hierarchy*, ascribed to *Dionysius* the *Areopagite*, out of which, passages have been cited in favour of infant-baptism; but these are manifestly of later date than they pretend to, and were never written by the persons whose names they bear, and are condemned as spurious by learned men, and are given up as such by Dr *Wall*, in his *History of Infant-Baptism* [l].

2. The christian writers of the second century, which are extant, are *Justin Martyr*, *Athenagoras*, *Theophilus* of *Antioch*, *Tatian*, *Minutius Felix*, *Irenæus*, and *Clemens* of *Alexandria*; and of all these writers, there is not one that says any thing of infant-baptism; there is but one pretended to, and that is *Irenæus*, and but a single passage out of him; and that depends upon a single word, the signification of which is doubtful at best; and besides the passage is only a translation of *Irenæus*, and not expressed in his own original words; and the chapter, from whence it is taken, is by some learned men judged to be spurious; since it advances a notion inconsistent with that ancient writer, and notoriously contrary to the books of the evangelists, making Christ to live to be fifty years old, yea, to live to a senior age: The passage, produced in favour of infant-baptism, is this; speaking of Christ, he says [m], "Sanctifying every age, by "that likeness it had to him; for he came to save all by himself; all, I say, "*qui per eum renascuntur in Deum*, "who by him are born again unto God;" in- "fants, and little ones, and children, and young men, and old men; therefore "he

[k] Ignatii Epist. ad Polycarp. p. 14. Ed. Voss.  [l] Part I. c. 23.
[m] Irenæus adv. Hæres. l. 2. c. 39. p. 191.

"he went through every age, and became an infant, to infants sanctifying in-
"fants; and to little ones a little one, sanctifying those of that age; and like-
"wise became an example of piety, righteousness, and subjection:" Now, the
question is about the word *renascuntur*, whether it is to be rendered *born again*,
which is the literal sense of the word, or *baptized*; the true sense of *Irenæus* seems
to be this, that Christ came to save all that are regenerated by his grace and
spirit; and none but they, according to his own words, *John* iii. 3, 5. and that
by assuming human nature, and passing through the several stages of life, he
has sanctified it, and set an example to men of every age. And this now is all
the evidence, the undoubted evidence of infant-baptism, from the fathers of
the first two centuries; it would be easy to produce passages out of the above
writers, in favour of believers-baptism; I shall only cite one out of the first of
them; the account, that *Justin Martyr* gave to the emperor *Antoninus Pius* of
the christians of his day; though it has been cited by Mr *Stennett* and Mr *Rees*,
I shall choose to transcribe it; because, as Dr *Wall* says [n], it is the most antient
account of the way of baptizing next the scripture. " And now, says *Justin* [o],
"we will declare after what manner, when we were renewed by Christ, we de-
"voted ourselves unto God; lest, omitting this, we should seem to act a bad
"part in this declaration. As many, as are persuaded, and believe the things,
"taught and said by us, to be true, and promise to live according to them,
"are instructed to pray, and to ask, fasting, the forgiveness of their past sins
"of God, we praying and fasting together with them. After that, they are
"brought by us where water is, and they are regenerated in the same way
"of regeneration, as we have been regenerated; for they are then washed in
"water, in the name of the Father and Lord God of all, and of our Saviour
"Jesus Christ, and of the holy Spirit." There is a work, which bears the
name of *Justin*, called *Answers to the orthodox, concerning some necessary questions*;
to which we are sometimes referred for a proof of infant-baptism; but the book
is spurious, and none of *Justin's*, as many learned men have observed; and as
Dr *Wall* allows; and is thought not to have been written before the fifth century. So stands the evidence for infant-baptism, from the ancient fathers of
the first two centuries.

3. As to the third century, it will be allowed, that it was spoken of in it;
though as soon as it was mentioned, it was opposed; and the very first man that
mentions it, speaks against it; namely, *Tertullian*. The truth of the matter is,
that infant-baptism was moved for in the third century; got footing and establishment in the fourth and fifth; and so prevailed until the time of the reformation: Though, throughout these several centuries, there were testimonies bore

to

---

[n] History of Infant-Baptism, part I. c. 2.
[o] Οι τϱοπον δε ανεθηκαμεν εαυτυς, &c. Justin. Apolog. II. p. 93, 94. Ed. Paris.

to adult-baptism; and at several times, certain persons rose up, and opposed infant-baptism; which brings me,

III. To consider what our author affirms, that it cannot be pretended that this practice was called in question, or made matter of debate in the church, until the madmen of *Munster* set themselves against it, p. 7. Let us examine this matter, and,

1. It should be observed, that the disturbances in *Germany*, which our Pædobaptist writers so often refer to in this controversy about baptism, and so frequently reproach us with, were first begun in the wars of the boors, by such as were Pædobaptists, and them only; first by the Papists, some few years before the reformation; and after that, both by Lutherans and Papists, on account of civil liberties; among whom, in process of time, some few of the people called Anabaptists mingled themselves; a people that scarce in any thing agree with us, neither in their civil, nor religious principles; nor even in baptism itself; for if we can depend on those that wrote the history of them, and against them; they were for repeating adult-baptism, not performed among them; yea, that which was administered among themselves, when they removed their communion to another society; nay, even in the same community, when an excommunicated person was received again [p]; besides, if what is reported of them is true, as it may be, their baptism was performed by sprinkling, which we cannot allow to be true baptism; it is said, that when a community of them was satisfied with the person's faith and conversation, who proposed for baptism, the pastor took water into his hand, and sprinkled it on the head of him that was to be baptized, using these words, *I baptize thee in the name of the Father, of the Son, and of the holy Ghost* [q]: And even the disturbances in *Munster*, a famous city in *Westphalia*, were first begun by *Bernard Rotman*, a Pædobaptist minister of the Lutheran persuasion, assisted by other ministers of the reformation, in opposition to the Papists in the year 1532; and it was not till the year 1533, that *John Matthias* of *Harlem*, and *John Bocoldus* of *Leyden* came to this place [r]; who, with *Knipperdolling* and others, are, I suppose, the madmen of *Munster* this writer means; and he may call them madmen, if he pleases; I shall not contend with him about it; they were mad notions which they held, and mad actions they performed; and both disavowed by the people who are now called Anabaptists; though it is not reasonable to suppose, that these were the only men concerned in that affair, or that the number of their followers should increase to such a degree in so small a time,

[p] Cloppenburg. Gangræna, p. 366. Spanhem. Diatribe Hist. Sect. 27.
[q] Budneus apud Meshov. Hist. Anabapt. l. 4. p. 96.
[r] Sleidan. Comment. l. 10. p. 257, 269. Spanhem. Diatribe Histor. de Origine Anabaptist. Sect. 18.

time, as to make such a revolution in so large a city: However, certain it is, that it was not their principle about baptism, that led them into such extravagant notions and actions: But what I take notice of all this for, is chiefly to observe the date of the confusions and distractions, in which these madmen were concerned; which were from the year 1533 to 1536: And our next inquiry therefore is, whether there was any debate about the practice of infant-baptism before this time. And,

2. It will appear, that it was frequently debated, before these men set themselves against it, or acted the mad part they did: In the years 1532 and 1528, there were public disputations at *Berne* in *Switzerland*, between the ministers of the church there and some Anabaptist teachers'; in the years 1529, 1527 and 1525, *Oecolampadius* had various disputes with people of this name at *Basil* in the same country'; in the year 1525, there was a dispute at *Zurich* in the same country about Pædobaptism, between *Zwinglius*, one of the first reformers, and Dr *Balthasar Hubmeierus*ᵘ, who afterwards was burnt, and his wife drowned at *Vienna*, in the year 1528; of whom *Meshovius*ᵛ, though a Papist, gives this character; that he was from his childhood brought up in learning; and for his singular erudition was honoured with a degree in divinity; was a very eloquent man, and read in the scriptures, and fathers of the church. *Hoornbeck* ˣ calls him a famous and eloquent preacher, and says he was the first of the reformed preachers at *Waldshut*: There were several disputations with others in the same year at this place; upon which an edict was made by the senate at *Zurich*, forbidding rebaptization, under the penalty of being fined a silver mark, and of being imprisoned, and even drowned, according to the nature of the offence. And in the year 1526, or 1527, according to *Hoornbeck*, *Felix Mans*, or *Mentz*, was drowned at *Zurich*; this man, *Meshovius* saysʸ, whom he calls *Felix Mantscher*, was of a noble family; and both he, and *Conrad Grebel*, whom he calls *Cunrad Grebbe*, who are said to give the first rise to Anabaptism at *Zurich*, were very learned men, and well skilled in the Latin, Greek, and Hebrew languages. And the same writer affirms, that Anabaptism was set on foot at *Wittenberg*, in the year 1522, by *Nicholas Pelargus*, or *Stork*, who had companions with him of very great learning, as *Carolostadius*, *Philip Melanchthon*, and others; this, he says, was done, whilst *Luther* was lurking as an exile in the castle of *Wartpurg* in *Thuringia*; and that when he returned from thence to *Wittenberg*, he banished *Carolostadius*, *Pelargus*, *More*, *Didymus*, and others ᶻ, and only received

---

* Spanhem. ibid Sect. 14. Meshov. Anabaptist. Histor. l. 3. c. 16, 18.
t Spanhem. Sect. 13. Meshovius, ibid. c. 2.    ᵘ Spanhem. Sect. 11. Meshov. l. 2. c. 4.
ᵛ Ibid c. 15.    ˣ Summa Controvers. l. 5. p. 356.    ʸ Meshov. l. 2. c. 1.
ᶻ Meshovius, l. 1. c. 2, 3.

ceived *Melancthon* again. This carries the opposition to Pædobaptism within five years of the reformation, begun by *Luther*; and certain it is, there were many and great debates about infant-baptism at the first of the reformation, years before the affair of *Munster*: And evident it is, that some of the first reformers were inclined to have attempted a reformation in this ordinance, though they, for reasons best known to themselves, dropped it; and even *Zuinglius* himself, who was a bitter persecutor of the people called Anabaptists afterwards, was once of the same mind himself, and against Pædobaptism. But,

3. It will appear, that this was a matter of debate, and was opposed before the time of the reformation. There was a set of people in *Bohemia*, near a hundred years before that, who appear to be of the same persuasion with the people, called Anabaptists; for in a letter, written by *Costelecius* out of *Bohemia* to *Erasmus*, dated *October* 10, 1519 [a], among other things said of them, which agree with the said people, this is one; " such as come over to their sect, must " every one be baptized anew in meer water;" the writer of the letter calls them *Pygbards*; so named, he says, from a certain refugee, that came thither ninety-seven years before the date of the letter. Pope *Innocent* the third, under whom was the Lateran council, A. D. 1215, has, in the decretals, a letter, in answer to a letter from the bishop of *Arles* in *Provence*, which had represented to him [b], that " some Heretics there had taught, that it was to no purpose to " baptize children, since they could have no forgiveness of sins thereby, as " having no faith, charity, &c." So that it is a clear point, that there were some that set themselves against infant-baptism in the thirteenth century, three hundred years before the reformation; yea, in the twelfth century there were some that opposed Pædobaptism. Mr *Fox*, the martyrologist, relates from the history of *Robert Guisburne* [c], that two men, *Gerbardus* and *Dulcinus*, in the reign of *Henry* the second, about the year of our Lord 1158; who, he supposes, had received some light of knowledge of the *Waldenses*, brought thirty with them into *England*; who, by the king and the prelates, were all burnt in the forehead, and so driven out of the realm; and after were slain by the Pope. *Rapin* [d] calls them German Heretics, and places their coming into *England* at the year 1166: But *William* of *Newbury* [e] calls them *Publicans*, and only mentions *Gerbardus*, as at the head of them; and whom he allows to be somewhat learned, but all the rest very illiterate, and says they came from *Gascoigne*; and being convened before a council, held at *Oxford* for that purpose, and interrogated concerning

[a] Inter Colomes. Collect. apud Wall's History of Infant-Baptism, part II. p. 200.
[b] Opera Innocent. tertii, tom. II. p. 776. apud Wall, ibid. p. 178.
[c] Acts and Monuments, vol. I. p. 262.   [d] History of England, vol. I. p. 233.
[e] Neubrigensis de Rebus Anglicanis, l. 2. c. 13. p. 155.

cerning articles of faith, said perverse things concerning the divine sacraments, detesting holy baptism, the eucharist and marriage: And his annotator, out of a manuscript of *Radulph Picardus*, the monk, shews, that the Heretics, called *Publicans*, affirm, that we must not pray for the dead; that the suffrages of the saints were not to be asked; that they believe not purgatory; with many other things; and particularly, *afferunt isti parvulos non baptisandos donec ad intelligibilem perveniant ætatem*; " they assert that infants are not to be baptized, till " they come to the age of understanding[e]." In the year 1147, St *Bernard* wrote a letter to the earl of St *Gyles*, complaining of his harbouring *Henry*, an Heretic; and among other things he is charged with by him, are these; " the " infants of christians are hindered from the life of Christ, the grace of bap- " tism being denied them; nor are they suffered to come to their salvation, " though our Saviour compassionately cries out in their behalf, *Suffer little* " *children to come unto me, &c.*" and, about the same time, writing upon the *Canticles*, in his 65th and 66th sermons, he takes notice of a sort of people, he calls *Apostolici*; and who, perhaps, were the followers of *Henry*; who, says he, laugh at us for baptizing infants[f]; and among the tenets which he ascribes to them, and attempts to confute, this is the first, " Infants are not to be bap- " tized:" In opposition to which, he affirms, that infants are to be baptized in the faith of the church; and endeavours, by instances, to show, that the faith of one is profitable to others[g]; which he attempts from *Matt*. ix. 2. and xv. 28. 1 *Tim*. ii. 15.

In the year 1146, *Peter Bruis*, and *Henry* his follower, set themselves against infant-baptism. *Petrus Cluniacensis*, or *Peter* the Abbot of *Clugny*, wrote against them; and among other errors he imputes to them, are these: " That infants " are not baptized, or saved by the faith of another, but ought to be baptized " and saved by their own faith; or, that baptism without their own faith does " not save; and that those, that are baptized in infancy, when grown up, " should be baptized again; nor are they then rebaptized, but rather rightly " baptized[h]:" And that these men did deny infant-baptism, and pleaded for adult-baptism, Mr *Stennett*[i] has proved from *Caffander* and *Prateolus*, both Pædobaptists: And Dr *Wall*[k] allows these two men to be Antipædobaptists; and says, they were " the first Antipædobaptist preachers that ever set up a church, " or society of men, holding that opinion against infant-baptism, and rebap- " tizing such as had been baptized in infancy;" and who also observes[l], that

the

---

[e] Not. in ibid. p. 720—723.  [f] Wall, ibid. p. 175, 176.
[g] Hist. Eccl. Magdeburg. Cent. XII. c. 5. p. 338, 339.  [h] Ibid. p. 332.
[i] Answer to Russen, p. 83, 84.  [k] History of Infant-Baptism, part II. p. 184.
[l] Ibid. p. 179.

the *Lateran* council, under *Innocent* the II<sup>d</sup>, 1139, did condemn *Peter Bruis*, and *Arnold* of *Brescia*, who seems to have been a follower of *Bruis*, for rejecting infant-baptism: Moreover, in the year 1140, or a little before it, *Evervinus*, of the diocese of *Cologn*, wrote a letter to St *Bernard*; in which he gives him an account of some heretics, lately discovered in that country; of whom he says, "they condemn the sacraments, except baptism only; and this only in "those who are come to age; who, they say, are baptized by Christ himself, "whoever be the minister of the sacraments; they do not believe infant-bap- "tism; alledging that place of the gospel, *he that believeth, and is baptized,* "*shall be saved* ¹." These seem also to be the disciples of *Peter Bruis*, who began to preach about the year 1126; so that it is out of all doubt, that this was a matter of debate, four hundred years before the madmen of *Munster* set themselves against it: And a hundred years before these, there were two men, *Bruno*, bishop of *Angiers*, and *Berengarius*, archdeacon of the same church, who began to spread their particular notions about the year 1035; which chiefly respected the sacraments of Baptism and the Lord's-Supper. What they said about the former, may be learned from the letter sent by *Deodwinus*, bishop of *Liege*, to *Henry* I. King of *France*; in which are the following words ᵐ: "There is a re- "port come out of *France*, and which goes through all *Germany*, that these "two (*Bruno* and *Berengarius*) do maintain, that the Lord's body (the Host) is "not the body, but a shadow and figure of the Lord's body; and that they do "disannul lawful marriages; and, as far as in them lies, overthrow the bap- "tism of infants:" And from *Guimundus*, bishop of *Aversa*, who wrote against *Berengarius*, who says, "that he did not teach rightly concerning the baptism "of infants, and concerning marriage ⁿ." Mr *Stennett* ° relates from Dr *Allix*, a passage concerning one *Gundulphus* and his followers, in *Italy*; divers of whom, *Gerard*, bishop of *Cambray* and *Arras*, interrogated upon several heads in the year 1025. And, among other things, that bishop mentions the following reason, which they gave against infant-baptism; "because to an infant, that "neither wills, nor runs, that knows nothing of faith, is ignorant of its own "salvation and welfare; in whom there can be no desire of regeneration, or "confession; the will, faith and confession of another seem not in the least to "appertain." Dr *Wall*, indeed, represents these men, the disciples of *Gundulphus*, as Quakers and Manichees in the point of baptism; holding that water-baptism is of no use to any: But it must be affirmed, whatever their principles were, that their argument against infant-baptism was very strong. So then we have testimonies, that Pædobaptism was opposed five hundred years before the

affair

---

¹ Wall, ibid. p. 172.  ᵐ Apud Wall, ibid. p. 159.
ⁿ Hist. Eccl. Magdeburg. Cent. XI. c. 5. p. 116.  ° Answer to Russen, p. 84, 85.

affair of *Munster*. And if the Pelagians, Donatists, and Luciferians, so called from *Lucifer Calaritanus*, a very orthodox man, and a great opposer of the Arians, were against infant-baptism, as several Pædobaptist writers affirm; this carries the opposition to it still higher; and indeed it may seem strange, that since it had not its establishment till the times of *Austin*, that there should be none to set themselves against it: And if there were none, how comes it to pass that such a canon should be made in the Milevitan council, under pope *Innocent* the first, according to *Carranza*°; and in the year 402, as say the Magdeburgensian centuriators ᴾ; or be it in the council at *Carthage*, in the year 418, as says Dr *Wall* ᑫ, which runs thus, "Also, it is our pleasure, that whoever "denies that new-born infants are to be baptized; or says, they are indeed to "be baptized for the remission of sins; and yet they derive no original sin "from *Adam* to be expiated by the washing of regeneration; (from whence it "follows, that the form of baptism for the forgiveness of sins in them, cannot "be understood to be true, but false) let him be anathema:" But if there were none, that opposed the baptism of new-born infants, why should the first part of this canon be made, and an anathema annexed to it? To say, that it respected a notion of a single person in *Cyprian's* time, 150 years before this, that infants were not to be baptized, until eight days old; and that it seems there were some people still of this opinion, wants proof. But however certain it is, that *Tertullian* ʳ, in the beginning of the third century, opposed the baptism of infants, and dissuaded from it, who is the first writer that makes mention of it: So it appears, that as soon as ever it was set on foot, it became matter of debate; and sooner than this, it could not be: And this was thirteen hundred years before the madmen of *Munster* appeared in the world. But,

IV. Let us next consider the practice of the ancient Waldenses, with respect to adult-baptism, which this author affirms to be a chimerical imagination, and groundless figment. It should be observed, that the people called Waldenses, or the Vaudois, inhabiting the valleys of *Piedmont*, have gone under different names, taken from their principal leaders and teachers; and so this of the Waldenses, from *Peter Waldo*, one of their barbs, or pastors; though some think, this name is only a corruption of Vallenses, the inhabitants of the valleys: And certain it is, there was a people there before the times of *Waldo*, and even from the apostles time, that held the pure evangelic truths, and bore a testimony to them in all ages, and throughout the dark times of popery, as many ˢ learned

men

---

° Summa Concil. p. 122, 123.　　ᴾ Cent. V. c. 9. p. 468.
ᑫ History, &c. Part II. p. 275, 276.　　ʳ De Baptismo, c. 18.
ˢ Dr Allix's Remarks on the ancient churches of Piedmont, p. 188, 207, 210, 286. Morland's History of the evangelical Churches of the valleys of Piedmont, book I. c. 3. p. 8, &c. Et Bezæ Icones apud ibid. In reduction to the history, p. 7.

men have observed; and the sense of these people concerning baptism may be best understood,

1. By what their ancient barbs or pastors taught concerning it. *Peter Bruis*, and *Henry* his successor, were both, as *Morland* affirms [t], their ancient barbs and pastors; and from them these people were called Petrobrussians and Henricians; and we have seen already, that these two men were Antipædobaptists, denied infant-baptism, and pleaded for adult-baptism. *Arnoldus* of *Brixia*, or *Brescia*, was another of their barbs, and is the first mentioned by *Morland*, from whom these people were called Arnoldists. Of this man Dr *Allix* says [u], that besides being charged with some ill opinions, it was said of him, that he was not found in his sentiments concerning the sacraments of the altar and the baptism of infants; and Dr *Wall* allows [v], that the Lateran council, under *Innocent* the second, in 1139, did condemn *Peter Bruis*, and *Arnold* of *Brescia*, who seems to have been a follower of *Bruis*, for rejecting infant-baptism. *Lollardo* was another of their barbs, who, as *Morland* says, was in great reputation with them, for having conveyed the knowledge of their doctrine into *England*, where his disciples were known by the name of Lollards; who were charged with holding, that the sacrament of baptism used in the church by water, is but a light matter, and of small effect; that christian people be sufficiently baptized in the blood of Christ, and need no water; and that infants be sufficiently baptized, if their parents be baptized before them [x]: All which seem to arise from their denying of infant-baptism, and the efficacy of it to take away sin.

2. By their ancient confessions of faith, and other writings which have been published. In one of these, bearing date A. D. 1120, the 12th and 13th articles run thus [y]: "We do believe that the sacraments are signs of the holy
" thing, or visible forms of the invisible grace; accounting it good that the
" faithful sometimes use the said signs, or visible forms, if it may be done.
" However we believe and hold, that the abovesaid faithful may be saved with-
" out receiving the signs aforesaid, in case they have no place, nor any means
" to use them. We acknowledge no other sacrament but baptism and the
" Lord's-Supper." And in another ancient confession, without a date, the 7th article is [z]: " We believe that in the sacrament of baptism, water is the visible
" and external sign, which represents unto us that which (by the invisible vir-
" tue of God operating) is within us; namely, the renovation of the Spirit,
" and the mortification of our members in Jesus Christ; *by which also we are*
" *received into the holy congregation of the people of God, there protesting and de-*
" claring

[t] History, book I. ch. 8. p. 184.    [u] Remarks, &c. p. 171, 172.
[v] Hist. of Infant-Baptism, part II. p. 179.    [x] Fox's Acts and Monuments, vol. I p. 868.
[y] Morland's History, &c. book I. ch. 4. p. 34.    [z] Ibid. p. 38.

278    THE DIVINE RIGHT OF INFANT-BAPTISM,

"claring openly our faith and amendment of life." In a tract [a], written in the language of the ancient inhabitants of the valleys, in the year 1100, called *The Noble Lesson*, are these words; speaking of the apostles, it is observed of them, "they spoke without fear of the doctrine of Christ; they preached to Jews and "Greeks, working many miracles, and *those that believed* they baptized in the "name of Jesus Christ." And in a treatise concerning Antichrist, which contains many sermons of the barbs, collected in the year 1120, and so speaks the sense of their ancient pastors before this time, stands the following passage [b]: "The third work of antichrist consists in this, that he attributes the regenera- "tion of the holy Spirit, unto the dead outward work (or faith) *baptizing chil-* "*dren in that faith*, and teaching, that thereby baptism and regeneration must "be had, and therein he confers and bestows orders and other sacraments, and "groundeth therein all his christianity, which is against the holy Spirit." There are indeed two confessions of theirs, which are said to speak of infant-baptism; but these are of a late date, both of them in the sixteenth century; and the earliest is not a confession of the *Waldenses* or *Vaudois* in the valleys of *Piedmont*, but of the *Bohemians*, said to be presented to *Ladislaus* king of *Bohemia*, A. D. 1508, and afterwards amplified and explained, and presented to *Ferdinand* king of *Bohemia*, A. D. 1535; and it should be observed, that those people say, that they were falsly called *Waldenses* [c]; whereas it is certain there were a people in *Bohemia* that came out of the valleys, and sprung from the old *Waldenses*, and were truly so, who denied infant-baptism, as that sort of them called *Pygbards*, or *Picards*; who, near a hundred years before the reformation, as we have seen by the letter sent to *Erasmus* out of *Bohemia*, rebaptized persons that joined in communion with them; and *Scultetus* [d], in his annals on the year 1528, says, that the united brethren in *Bohemia*, and other godly persons of that time, were rebaptized; not that they patronized the errors of the Anabaptists, (meaning such that they were charged with which had no relation to baptism) but because they could not see how they could otherwise separate themselves from an unclean world. The other confession is indeed made by the ministers and heads of the churches in the valleys, assembled in *Angrogne*, September 12, 1532 [e]. Now it should be known, that this was made after that "Peter Masson "and George Morell were sent into *Germany* in the year 1530, as *Morland* [f] says, "to treat with the chief ministers of *Germany*, namely, *Oecolampadius*, *Bucer*, "and others, touching the reformation of their churches; but *Peter Masson* "was taken prisoner at *Dijon*." However, as *Fox* says [g], "*Morell* escaped,
"and

[a] Morland's History, &c. ch. 6. p. 99, 112.   [b] Ibid. ch. 7. p. 142, 148.
[c] Morland's History, ch.4. p. 43.   [d] Apud Hoornbeck. Summa Controvers. l. 5. p. 387.
[e] Morland, ibid.ch.4. p.39.   [f] Ibid. ch.8. p.185.   [g] Acts & Monuments, vol.II. p.186.

# EXAMINED AND DISPROVED.

"and returned alone to *Merindol*, with the books and letters he brought with "him from the churches of *Germany*; and declared to his brethren all the "points of his commission; and opened unto them how many and great errors "they were in; into the which their old ministers, whom they called *Barbs*, "that is to say *Uncles*, had brought them, leading them from the right way of "true religion." After which, this confession was drawn up, signed, and sworn to: From hence we learn, where they might get this notion, which was now become matter of great debate in *Switzerland* and *Germany*; and yet, after all this, I am inclined to think, that the words of the article in the said confession, are to be so understood, as not to relate to infant-baptism: They are these[h]; "We have but two sacramental signs left us by Jesus Christ; the one "is *Baptism*; the other is the *Eucharist*, which we receive, to shew that our "perseverance in the faith, is such, as we promised, when we were baptized, "being little children." This phrase, *being little children*, as I think, means, their being little children in knowledge and experience, when they were baptized; since they speak of their receiving the Eucharist, to shew their perseverance in the faith, they then had promised to persevere in: Besides, if this is to be understood of them, as infants in a literal sense; what promise were they capable of making, when such? Should it be said, that "they promised by "their sureties;" it should be observed, that the *Waldenses* did not admit of godfathers and godmothers in baptism; this is one of the abuses their ancient *Barbs* complained of in baptism, as administered by the Papists[i]. Besides, in a brief confession of faith, published by the reformed churches of *Piedmont*, so late as A. D. 1655, they have these words in favour of adult-baptism[k]; "that "God does not only instruct and teach us by his word, but has also ordained "certain sacraments to be joined with it, *as a means to unite us unto Christ, and* *to make us partakers of his benefits*. And there are only two of them belonging "in common *to all the members of the church* under the New Testament; to wit, "*Baptism* and the *Lord's-Suppper*; that God has ordained the sacrament of "baptism to be a testimony of our adoption, and of our being cleansed from "our sins by the blood of Jesus Christ, and renewed in holiness of life:" Nor is there one word in it of infant-baptism.

Upon the whole, it will be easily seen, what little reason the writer of the dialogue under consideration had to say, that the ancient *Wa'denses*, being in the constant practice of adult-baptism, is a chimerical imagination, and a groundless fiction; since there is nothing appears to the contrary, but that they were in the practice of it until the sixteenth century; for what is urged against it,

[h] Morland, ibid. c. 4, p. 41.  [i] Morland, ibid. c. 7. p. 173.
[k] Ibid. c. 4. p. 61, 67.

it, is since that time: And even at that time, there were some, that continued in the practice of it; for *Ludovicus Vives*, who wrote in the said century, having observed, that "formerly no person was brought to the holy baptistery, " till he was of adult age, and when he both understood what that mystical " water meant, and desired to be washed in it, yea, desired it more than once," adds the following words; " I hear, in some cities of *Italy*, the old custom is " still in a great measure preserved [1]." Now, what people should he mean by some cities of *Italy*, unless the remainders of the Petrobrussians, or Waldenses, " as Dr *Wall* observes [m],- who continued that practice in the valleys of *Piedmont*: And it should be observed, that there were different sects, that went by the name of Waldenses, and some of them of very bad principles; some of them were Manichees, and held other errors: And indeed, it was usual for the Papists in former times, to call all by this name, that dissented from them; so that it need not be wondered at, if some, bearing this name, were for infant-baptism, and others not. The Vaudois in the valleys, are the people chiefly to be regarded; and it will not be denied, that of late years infant-baptism has obtained among them: But that the ancient Waldenses practised it, wants proof.

C H A P.   IV.

*The Argument for Infant-Baptism, taken from the Covenant made with Abraham, and from Circumcision, the Sign of it, considered.*

THE minister in this debate, in answer to his neighbour's requiring a plain scripture institution of infant-baptism, tells him; if he would " consider " the covenant of grace, which was made with *Abraham*, and with *all* his seed, " both after the flesh, and after the Spirit, and by God's express command to " be sealed to infants, he would there find a sufficient scripture instance for " infant-baptism:" And for this covenant he directs him to *Gen.* xvii. 2, 4, 7, 10, 12. He argues, that this covenant was a covenant of grace; that it was made with all *Abraham*'s seed, natural and spiritual, Jews and Gentiles; that circumcision was the seal of it; and that the same institution, which requires circumcision to be administered to infants, requires baptism to be also administered to them, that succeeding circumcision, p. 10—18. Wherefore,

*First*, The leading inquiry is, whether the covenant made with *Abraham*, Genesis xvii. was the covenant of grace; that is, the pure covenant of grace, in

---

[1] Audio in quibusdam Italiæ Urbibus morem veterem magna ex parte adhuc conservari, Comment. in Aug. de Civ. Dei, Lib. I. c. 27.   [m] History of Infant-Baptism, part II. c. 2. p. 12.

in distinction from the covenant of works; which is the sense in which it is commonly understood, and in which this writer seems to understand this covenant with *Abraham*; for of it, he says, p. 13. "it was the covenant of grace, "that covenant by which alone we can have any grounded hope of salvation:" But that it was *the* covenant of grace, or a pure covenant of grace, must be denied: For,

1. It is never called the covenant of grace, nor by any name which shews it to be so; it is called *the covenant of circumcision*, which God is said to give to *Abraham* ª, but not a covenant of grace; circumcision and grace are opposed to one another; circumcision is a work of the law, which they that sought to be justified by, fell from grace ᵇ.

2. It seems rather to be a covenant of works, than of grace; for this was a covenant to be kept by men. *Abraham* was to keep it, and his seed after him were to keep it; something was to be done by them; they were to circumcise their flesh; and not only he and his seed were to be circumcised, but all that were born in his house, or bought with his money; and a severe penalty was annexed to it: In case of neglect, or disobedience, such a soul was to "be cut "off from his people ᶜ." All which favour nothing of a covenant of grace, a covenant by which we can have a grounded hope of salvation, but the contrary.

3. This was a covenant that might be broken, and in some instances was ᵈ; but the covenant of grace cannot be broken; God will not break it ᵉ, nor man cannot: It is *a covenant ordered in all things, and sure*; it cannot be moved; it stands firmer than hills, or mountains.

4. It must be owned, that there were temporal things promised in this covenant, such as a multiplication of *Abraham's* natural seed; a race of kings from him, with many nations, and a possession of the land of *Canaan* ᶠ. Things which can have nothing to do with the pure covenant of grace, any more than the change of his name from *Abram* to *Abraham*, ver. 5.

5. There were some persons, included in this covenant made with *Abraham*, of whom it cannot be thought they were in the covenant of grace, as *Ishmael*, *Esau*, and others; and on the other hand, there were some, and even living at the time when this covenant was made, and yet were not in it; who, nevertheless, were in the covenant of grace, as *Arphaxad*, *Melchizedek*, *Lot*, and others; wherefore this can never be reckoned the pure covenant of grace.

6. The covenant of grace was only made with Christ, as the federal head of it; and who is the only head of the covenant, and of the covenant-ones; wherefore,

Vol. II.                    O o                         

ª Acts vii. 8.     ᵇ Gal. v. 2—4.     ᶜ Gen. xvii. 9—14.     ᵈ Gen. xvii. 14.
ᵉ Psalm lxxxix. 34.     ᶠ Gen. xvii. 6, 8.

fore, if the covenant of grace was made with *Abraham*, as the federal head of his natural and spiritual seed, of Jews and Gentiles; then there muſt be two heads of the covenant of grace, contrary to the nature of ſuch a covenant, and the whole current of ſcripture: Yea, this covenant of *Abraham*'s, ſo far as it reſpected his ſpiritual ſeed, or ſpiritual bleſſings for them, it and the promiſes were made to Chriſt [g]. No mere man is capable of covenanting with God, of ſtipulation and reſtipulation; for what has man to reſtipulate with God? The covenant of grace is not made with any ſingle man; and much leſs with him on the behalf of others: When, therefore, at any time we read of the covenant of grace, being made with a particular perſon, or with particular perſons, it muſt always be underſtood of making it manifeſt to them; of a revelation of the covenant, and of an application of covenant-bleſſings to them; and not of any original contract with them; for that is only made with them in Chriſt. To which may be added,

7. That the covenant of grace was made with Chriſt, and with his people, as conſidered in him, from everlaſting; for ſo early was Chriſt ſet up as the mediator of it; the promiſe of eternal life in it was before the world was; and thoſe intereſted in it, were bleſſed with all ſpiritual bleſſings and grace before the foundation of it; now could there be a mediator ſo early, a promiſe of eternal life ſo ſoon, and bleſſings of grace provided, and no covenant ſubſiſting? wherefore the covenant made with *Abraham* in time, could not, ſtrictly and properly ſpeaking, be the covenant of grace. But,

8. To ſhorten this debate, it will be allowed, that the covenant made with *Abraham* was a peculiar covenant, ſuch as was never made with any before, or ſince; that it was of a mixed kind; that it had in it promiſes and mercies of a temporal nature, which belonged to his natural ſeed; and others of a ſpiritual ſort, which belonged to his ſpiritual ſeed: The former are more numerous, clear, and diſtinct; the latter are compriſed chiefly in *Abraham*'s being *the father of many nations*, or of all that believe, and in God being a God to him and them [h]. Which obſervation makes way for the next inquiry,

*Secondly*, With whom this covenant was made, ſo far as it reſpected ſpiritual things, or was a revelation of the covenant of grace; as for the temporal things of this covenant, it does not concern the argument. It is allowed on all hands, that they belonged to *Abraham*, and his natural ſeed: But the queſtion is, whether this covenant, ſo far as it may be reckoned a covenant of grace, or a revelation of it, or reſpected ſpiritual things, was made with all *Abraham*'s ſeed after the fleſh, and with all the natural ſeed of believing Gentiles? This queſtion conſiſts of two parts,

*1ſt*, Whether

[g] Gal iii. 16.  [h] See Rom. iv. 11, 12, 16, 17.

*1st*, Whether the covenant made with *Abraham*, so far as it was a covenant of grace, was made with all *Abraham*'s seed, according to the flesh? Which must be answered in the negative. For,

1. If it was made with all the natural seed of *Abraham*, as such, it must be with his more immediate offspring; and so must be equally made with a mocking and persecuting *Ishmael*, *born after the flesh, the son of the bond-woman*, as with *Isaac*, *born after the Spirit, and the son of the free-woman*; and yet we find, that *Ishmael* was excluded from having a share in spiritual blessings, only temporal ones were promised him; and, in distinction and opposition to him, the covenant was established with *Isaac*[i]. Again, if this was the case, it must be equally made with a profane *Esau*, as with plain-hearted *Jacob*; and yet it is said, *Jacob have I loved, and Esau have I hated*[k].

2. If it was made with all *Abraham*'s seed according to the flesh, it must be made with all his remote posterity, and stand good to them in their most corrupt estate; it must be made with them who believed not, and whose carcases fell in the wilderness, and entered not into rest; it must be made with the ten tribes, that revolted from the pure service of God, and who worshipped the calves at *Dan* and *Bethel*; it must be made with the people of the Jews in *Isaiah*'s time, when they were *a sinful nation, a people laden with iniquity, a seed of evil-doers, children that were corrupters*; whose rulers are called the *rulers of Sodom*, and the people *the people of Gomorrah*[l], it must be made with the Scribes and Pharisees, and that wicked, adulterous, and hypocritical generation of men in the time of our Lord, who were his implacable enemies, and were concerned in his death; who killed him, persecuted his apostles, *pleased not God, and were contrary to all men*. What man, that seriously considers these things, can think that the covenant of grace belonged to these men, at least to all; and especially when he observes, what the apostle says, *they are not all Israel, which are of Israel; neither because they are the seed of Abraham, are they all children*[m]? Yea,

3. If it was made with all that are the seed of *Abraham* according to the flesh, then it must be made with Ishmaelites and Edomites, as well as with Israelites; with his posterity by *Keturah*, as well as by *Sarah*; with the Midianites and Arabians; with the Turks, as well as with the Jews, since they descended and claim their descent from *Abraham*, as well as these. But,

4. To shut up this argument; this covenant made with *Abraham*, be it a covenant of grace, seeing it could be no more, at most, than a revelation, manifestation, copy, or transcript of it, call it which you will; it can never be thought to comprehend more in it than the original contract, than the eternal

covenant

[i] Gen. xvii. 19, 20, 21.    [k] Mal. i. 1, 2.    [l] Isai. i. 4, 6, 10.    [m] Rom. ix. 6, 7.

covenant between the Father and the Son. Now the only persons interested in the everlasting covenant of grace, are the *chosen of God and precious*; whom he has loved with an everlasting love; gave to his Son to be redeemed by his blood; for whom provision is made in the same covenant for the sanctification of their nature, for the justification of their persons, for the pardon of their sins, for their perseverance in grace, and for their eternal glory and happiness: So that all that are in that covenant are chosen to grace here, and glory hereafter, and shall certainly enjoy both: they are all secured in the hands of Christ, and are redeemed from sin, law, hell, and death, by his precious blood; and shall be saved in him with an everlasting salvation; they have all of them the laws of God put into their minds, and written on their hearts; they have new hearts and new spirits given them, and the stony heart taken away from them; they have the righteousness of Christ imputed to them; they have their sins forgiven them for his sake, and which will be remembered no more; they have the fear of God put into their hearts, and shall never finally and totally depart from him; but, being called and justified, shall be glorified [n].

Now if this covenant was made with all *Abraham*'s natural seed, and comprehends all of them, then they must be all *chosen of God*; whereas there was only *a remnant* among them, *according to the election of grace* [o]: they must be all given to Christ, and secured in his hands; whereas there were some of them, that were not of his sheep, given him by his Father, and so did not believe in him [p]; they must be all redeemed by his blood; whereas he laid down his life for his sheep, his friends, his church, which all of *Abraham*'s seed could never be said to be: In a word, they must be all regenerated and sanctified, justified and pardoned; must all have the grace of God, and persevere in it to the end, and be all eternally saved; and the same must be said of all the natural seed of believing Gentiles, if they also are all of them in the covenant of grace. But what man, in his senses, will affirm these things? And, upon such a principle, how will the doctrines of personal election, particular redemption, regeneration by efficacious grace, not by blood or the will of man, and the saints final perseverance, be established?

This Gentleman, whose pamphlet is before me, is said to have written with some success against the Arminians; but sure I am, that no man can write with success against them, and without contradiction to himself, that has imbibed such a notion of the covenant of grace, as this I am militating against.

2*dly*, The other part of the question is, whether the covenant made with *Abraham*, so far as it was a covenant of grace, was made with all the natural seed

---

[n] Jer. xxxi. 33, 34. and xxxii. 40.   Ezek. xxxvi. 25—27.   Rom. viii. 30.
[o] Rom. xi. 5.              [p] John x. 26.

seed of believing Gentiles? which also must be answered in the negative: For,

1. It will be allowed, that this covenant respects *Abraham*'s spiritual seed among the Gentiles; even all true believers, all such that walk in the steps of his faith; for he is the Father of all them that believe, whether circumcised or uncircumcised, Jews or Gentiles ⁋; but not the natural seed of believing Gentiles. They, indeed, that are of the faith of *Abraham*, are his children in a spiritual sense, and they are blessed with him with spiritual blessings, and are such, as Christ has redeemed by his blood; and they believe in him, and the blessing of *Abraham* comes upon them: But then this spiritual seed of *Abraham* is the same with the spiritual seed of Christ, with whom the covenant was made from everlasting, and to them only does it belong; and to none can spiritual blessings belong, but to a spiritual seed, not a natural one. Let it be proved, if it can, that all the natural seed of believing Gentiles, are the spiritual seed of *Abraham*, and then they will be admitted to have a claim to this covenant. But, though it appears, that believing Gentiles are in this covenant, what clause is there in it, that respects their natural seed, as such? Let it be shown, if it can; by what right and authority, can any believing Gentile pretend to put his natural seed into *Abraham*'s covenant? The covenant made with him, as to the temporal part of it, belonged to him, and his natural seed; and with respect to its spiritual part, only to his spiritual seed, whether Jews or Gentiles; and not to the natural seed of either of them, as such.

2. The covenant made with *Abraham*, and his spiritual seed, takes in many of the seed of unbelieving Gentiles; who being called by grace, and openly believing Christ, are *Abraham*'s spiritual seed, with whom the covenant was made: That there are many among the Gentiles born of unbelieving parents, who become true believers in Christ, and so appear to be in the covenant of grace, must be allowed; since many are received as such into the communion of the Fædobaptists, as well as others; and, on the other hand, there are many born of believing Gentiles, who do not believe in Christ, are not partakers of his grace, on whom the spiritual blessings of *Abraham* do not come; and so not in his covenant. Wherefore, by what authority do men put in the infant seed of believing Gentiles, as such, into the covenant, and restrain it to them, and leave out the seed of unbelieving Gentiles; when, on the contrary, God oftentimes takes the one, and leaves the other?

3. That all the natural seed of believing Gentiles cannot be included in the covenant of grace, is manifest, from the reason above given, against all the natural seed of *Abraham* being in it; shewing, that all that are in it are the elect

⁋ Rom. iv. 11, 12, 16.

of God, the redeemed of Chrift, are effectually called by grace, perfevere to the end, and are eternally faved; all which cannot be faid of all the natural feed of believing Gentiles: And if all the natural feed of *Abraham* are not in this covenant made with him, as it was a covenant of grace, it can hardly be thought that all the natural feed of believing Gentiles fhould.

4. Seeing it is fo clear a cafe, that fome of the feed of unbelieving Gentiles are in this covenant, and fome of the feed of believing Gentiles are not in it, and that it cannot be known who are, until they believe in Chrift, and fo appear to be *Abraham*'s fpiritual feed; it muft be right to put off their claim to any privilege fuppofed to arife from covenant intereft, until it appear that they have one.

5. After all, covenant intereft gives no right to any ordinance, without a pofitive order and direction from God. So, for inftance, with refpect to circumcifion; on the one hand, there were fome perfons living at the time that ordinance was inftituted, who undoubtedly had an intereft in the covenant of grace, as *Shem, Arphaxad, Lot,* and others, on whom that was not injoined, and who had no right to ufe it; and, on the other hand, there have been many that were not in the covenant of grace, who were obliged to it: And fo with refpect to baptifm, it is not covenant intereft that gives a right to it; if it could be proved, as it cannot, that all the infant feed of believers, as fuch, are in the covenant of grace, it would give them no right to baptifm, without a pofitive command for it; the reafon is, becaufe a perfon may be in covenant, and as yet not have the prerequifite to an ordinance, even faith in Chrift, and a profeffion of it; which are neceffary to baptifm and the Lord's Supper. This leads me on,

*Thirdly,* To another inquiry, whether circumcifion was a feal of the covenant of grace to *Abraham*'s natural feed; the writer, whofe performance I am confidering, affirms, that it was by God's exprefs command to be fealed to infants; and that circumcifion is the feal of it, p. 10, 16. But this muft be denied: circumcifion was no feal of the covenant of grace; for,

1. If it was, the covenant of grace, before that took place, muft be without a feal; the covenant fubfifted from everlafting, and the revelation of it was quickly made after the fall of *Adam*; and there were manifeftations of it to particular perfons, as *Noah,* and others, before this to *Abraham,* and no circumcifion injoined: Wherefore, from *Adam* to *Abraham,* according to this notion, the covenant muft be without a feal; nay, there were fome perfons living at the time it was inftituted, who were in the covenant, yet this was not injoined them; as it would, if this had been defigned as a feal of it.

2. Circumcifion

*2.* Circumcifion, in the inftitution of it, is called a fign, but not a feal; it is faid to be אות *Oth*, a *Token*, or *Sign*[f]; but not חותם *Chothem*, a *Seal*; it was a fign or mark in the flefh, which *Abraham*'s natural feed were to bear, until the promifes made in this covenant were accomplifhed; it was a typical fign of the pollution of human nature, propagated by natural generation, and of cleanfing from it by the blood of Chrift, and of the inward circumcifion of the heart; but did not feal or confirm any fpiritual blefling of the covenant, to thofe on whom this mark or fign was fet; it is never called *a feal* throughout the whole Old Teftament; and fo far is there from being any exprefs command, that the covenant of grace fhould be fealed to infants by it, that there is not the leaft hint of it given.

3. It is indeed in the New Teftament called *a feal of the righteoufnefs of faith*[g]; but it is not faid to be a feal of the covenant of grace, nor a feal to infants: it was not a feal to *Abraham*'s natural feed; it was only fo to himfelf. The plain meaning of the apoftle is, that circumcifion was a feal to *Abraham*, and affured him of, or confirmed his faith in this, that he fhould be the father of many nations, in a fpiritual fenfe; and that the righteoufnefs of faith which he had, when he was an uncircumcifed perfon, fhould alfo come upon, and be imputed unto the uncircumcifed Gentiles: and accordingly, this mark and fign continued until the gofpel, declaring juftification by the righteoufnefs of Chrift, was preached, or ordered to be preached to the Gentiles; and could it be thought that circumcifion was a feal to others befides him, it could at moft be only a feal to them that had both faith and righteoufnefs, and not to them that had neither.

4. If it was a feal of the covenant of grace to *Abraham*'s natural feed, it muft be either to fome or all; if only to fome, it fhould be pointed out who they are; and if to all, then it muft be fealed, that is, confirmed, and an intereft in it affured of, to a mocking *Ifhmael*; to a profane *Efau*; to *Korah, Dathan,* and *Abiram,* and their accomplices, whom the earth fwallowed up alive; to *Achitophel,* that hanged himfelf; to *Judas,* that betrayed our Lord; and to all the Jews concerned in his crucifixion and death; fince there is reafon to believe they were all circumcifed. But,

5. The covenant made with *Abraham,* fo far as it was a covenant of grace, was not made, as we have feen, with all *Abraham*'s natural feed; and therefore circumcifion could not be a feal of it to them. I pafs on,

*Fourthly,* To another inquiry, whether baptifm fucceeded circumcifion, and fo became a feal of the covenant of grace to believers, and their natural feed? This muft be anfwered in the negative; for,

1. There

---

[f] Gen. xvii. 11.  [g] Rom. iv. 11.

1. There is no agreement between them, in the subjects to whom they are administered; circumcision was administered to Jews only, or such as became proselytes; baptism both to Jews and Gentiles, without any distinction, that believe in Christ; circumcision was administered to infants, baptism only to adult persons; circumcision belonged only to the males, baptism to male and female: Seeing then the subjects of the one and the other are so different, the one cannot be thought to succeed the other.

2. The use of the one and the other is not the same; the use of circumcision was to distinguish the natural seed of *Abraham* from others, until Christ was come in the flesh; the use of baptism is to be a distinguishing badge of the spiritual seed of Christ, such as have believed in him, and put him on; the use of circumcision was to signify the corruption of human nature, the necessity of regeneration, of the circumcision without hands, and of cleansing by the blood of Christ; the use of baptism is to answer a good conscience towards God, to represent the sufferings, burial, and resurrection of Christ, and prerequires repentance and faith.

3. The manner of administering the one and the other is very different; the one is by blood, the other by water; the one by an incision made in one part of the body, the other by an immersion of the whole body in water; the one was done in a private house, and by a private hand; the other, for the most part, publicly, in open places, in rivers, and before multitudes of people, and by a person in public office, a public minister of the word. Now, ordinances so much differing in their subjects, use, and manner of administration, the one can never be thought to come in the room and place of the other. But,

4. What puts it out of all doubt, that baptism can never be said to succeed circumcision is, that baptism was in force and use before circumcision was abolished, and its practice discontinued, or ought to be discontinued. Circumcision was not abolished till the death of Christ, when, with other ceremonies of the law, it was made null and void; but, unto that time, it was the duty of Jewish parents to circumcise their infants; whereas some years before this, *John* came preaching the doctrine of baptism, and administered it to multitudes; our Lord himself was baptized, three or four years, according to the common computation, before his death; now that which is in force before another is out of date, can never, with any propriety, be said to succeed or come in the room of that other.

5. It has been proved already, that circumcision was no seal of the covenant of grace to *Abraham*'s natural seed; and therefore, could it be proved, as it cannot, that baptism succeeds it, it would not follow that baptism is a seal of the covenant of grace; there are many persons who have been baptized, and
yet

yet not in the covenant of grace, and to whom it was never sealed, as *Simon Magus*, and others; and, on the other hand, a person may be in the covenant of grace, and it may be sealed to him, and he may be comfortably assured of his interest in it, though, as yet, not baptized in water. The author of the dialogue before me says, p. 16. that it is allowed on all hands, that baptism is a token or seal of the covenant of grace; but it is a popular clamour, a vulgar mistake, that either that or the Lord's-Supper are seals of the covenant of grace. The blood of Christ is the seal, and the only seal of it, by which its promises and blessings are ratified and confirmed; and the holy Spirit is the only earnest pledge, seal, and sealer of the saints, until the day of redemption †. And so all that fine piece of wit of our author, about the red and white seal, is spoiled and lost, p. 17.

Upon the whole, we may see what sufficient scripture institution for infant-baptism is to be found in the covenant made with *Abraham*; since the spiritual part of that covenant did not concern his natural seed, as such, but his spiritual seed, and so not infants, but adult persons, whether among Jews or Gentiles, that walked in the steps of his faith; and seeing there is not one word of baptism in it, and much less of infant-baptism; nor was circumcision a seal of it, nor does baptism succeed that, or is a seal of the covenant of grace:

Hence also, it will appear, what little reason there is for that clamorous outcry, so often made, and is by our author, of lessening and abridging the privileges of infants under the gospel dispensation, and of depriving them of what they formerly had; or for an harangue upon the valuable blessing, and great and glorious privilege they had, of having the covenant of grace sealed unto them by circumcision; or for that demand, how, why, and when, children were cut off from this privilege? or for such a representation, this being the case, that the gospel is a less glorious dispensation, with respect to infants, than the former was, p. 19, 20, 22, 30. Seeing the covenant of grace was never sealed to infants by circumcision; nor was that bloody and painful rite accounted a rich and glorious privilege; far from it; especially as it bound them over to keep the whole law, it was a yoke of bondage, an insupportable one: and it is a rich mercy, and glorious privilege of the gospel, that the Jews and their children are delivered from it; and that Gentiles and their children are not obliged to it: And as for the demand, how, why, and when, children were cut off from it, it is easily answered, that this was done by the death of Christ, and at the time of it, when all ceremonies were abolished; and that for this reason, because of the weakness, unprofitableness, and burdensomeness of that, and them: And as for the gospel-dispensation, that is the more glorious, for infants being left out of its church-state; that is to say, for its being not national

† Heb. xiii. 20. compared with Dan. ix. 27. Ephes. i. 13. 14. and iv. 30.

and carnal, as before, but congregational and spiritual; for its consisting, not of infants without understanding, but of rational and spiritual men, of believers in Christ, and professors of his name; and these not in a single and small country, as *Judea*, but in all parts of the world, as it has been, at one time or another, and it will be in the latter day: And as for infants themselves, their case is as good, and their privileges as many and better, than under the legal dispensation; their salvation is not at all affected by the abrogation of circumcision, or through want of baptism to succeed it. As the former did not seal the covenant to them, and could not save them, so neither could the latter, were it administered to them: To which may be added, that being born of christian parents, and having a christian education, and the advantage of hearing the gospel, as they grow up, and this not in one country, but many, must exceed all the privileges the Jewish children had under the former dispensation.

## CHAP. V.

*A consideration of the several texts of scripture produced in favour of Infant-Baptism.*

THE minister in the dialogue before me, being pressed by his neighbour to declare what were the numerous texts of scripture he referred to, as proving the continuance of childrens privileges under the gospel-dispensation, meaning particularly baptism, mentions the following.

1st, The passage in *Acts* ii. 39. *For the promise is unto you, and to your children, and to all that are afar off, even as many as the Lord our God shall call.* This scripture is often made use of by our author, and seems to be his dernier resort on all occasions, and the sheet-anchor of the cause he is pleading for. The promise spoken of, he says, undoubtedly, was the covenant made with *Abraham*; and was urged as a reason with the Jews, why they and their children ought to be baptized; and as a reason with the Gentiles, why they and their children, when called into a church-state, should be also baptized, p. 11, 12. He makes use of it, to prove that this promise gives a claim to baptism, and that an interest in it gives a right unto it, p. 15, 16, 18, 29, 30.

1. It is easy to observe the contradictions, that such are guilty of, that plead for infant-baptism, from the covenant or promise made with *Abraham*, as this writer is. One while, he tells us, that persons are by baptism brought into the covenant of grace; and what a dreadful thing it is to renounce baptism in infancy; whereby the covenant is vacated, and the relation to the glorious God disowned,

owned, they were brought into by baptism, p. 4. And yet here we are told, that interest in this promise gives a right and claim to baptism; but how can it give a previous right and claim to baptism, when it is by baptism, according to this writer, that persons are brought into this covenant?

2. The promise here observed, be it what it will, is not taken notice of, as what gives a claim and right to baptism, but as an encouraging motive to persons pricked in the heart, and in distress, both to repent, and be baptized for the remission of sins, and as giving them hope of receiving the holy Ghost, since such a promise was made; wherefore repentance and baptism were urged, in order to the enjoyment of the promise; and, consequently, can be understood of no other than adult persons, who were capable of repentance, and of a voluntary subjection to the ordinance of baptism.

3. The *children*, here spoken of, do not design infants, but the posterity of the Jews, and such, who might be called children, though grown up: And nothing is more common in scripture ª, than the use of the phrase in this sense; and, unless it be so understood in many places, strange interpretations must be given of them: wherefore the argument, from hence, for Pædobaptism, is given up by some learned men, as Dr *Hammond*, and others, as inconclusive; but some men, wherever they meet with the word *children*, it immediately runs in their heads, that infants must be meant.

4. The promise, be it what it will, is restrained *to as many as the Lord our God shall call*, whether they be Jews or Gentiles, as well as to repenting and baptizing persons; and therefore can furnish out no argument for infant-baptism, but must be understood of adult persons, capable of being called with an holy calling, of professing repentance, and of desiring baptism upon it; and of doing this, that their faith might be led to the blood of Christ, for the remission of sin.

5. It seems clear from the context, that not the covenant made with *Abraham*, but either the promise of the Messiah, and salvation by him, the great promise made in the Old Testament to the Jews, and their posterity; or the particular promise of remission of sins, a branch of the new covenant made with the house of *Israel*, and mentioned in the preceding verse, and which was calculated for comfort, and pertinently taken notice of; or of the pouring out of the holy Ghost, which is last mentioned: And indeed all may be included in this promise, and used as a means to comfort them under their distress, and as an argument to encourage them to do the things they are pressed to in the foregoing verse.

2*dly*,

ª See Exod. i. 8, 12. and iii. 23. and xii. 26, 27, 28, 35, 40, 50. and xiv. 8, 10, 22, 29. Jer. l. 4; and a multitude of other places.

*2dly*, To the former is added another scripture in *Matthew* xix. 14. *Suffer little children, and forbid them not to come unto me, for of such is the kingdom of heaven.* Upon which, it is asked, how, and which way, should we bring our little children to Christ, but in the way of his ordinances? If they belong to the kingdom of heaven, they must have a right to the privileges of that kingdom, p. 20. To which I answer,

1. These little children do not appear to be new-born babes; the words used by the evangelists do not always signify such, but are sometimes used of such as are capable of going alone, yea, of receiving instructions, of understanding the scriptures, and of one of twelve years of age [v]. Nor is it probable that children just born, or within the month, should be had abroad. Moreover, these were such as Christ called unto him [x], and were capable of coming to him of themselves, as these words suppose; nor does their being brought unto him, or his taking them in his arms, contradict this; since the same things are said of such as could walk of themselves [y].

2. It is not known whose children these were, whether the children of those that brought them, or of others; and whether their parents were believers in Christ, or not, or whether their parents were baptized or unbaptized; and if they were unbelievers and unbaptized persons, the Pædobaptists themselves will not allow that their children ought to be baptized.

3. Certain it is, that they were not brought to Christ, to be baptized by him; for the ends for which they were brought are mentioned; *Matthew* says, they brought them unto him, *that he should put his hands on them, and pray*; that is, for them, and bless them; as was usual with the Jews to do [z]: and it was common with them to bring their children to venerable persons, men of note for religion and piety, to have their blessing and their prayers; and such an one the persons that brought these children might take Christ to be, though they might not know him to be the Messiah. *Mark* and *Luke* say, they were brought to him, *that he would touch them* [a]; as he sometimes used to do, when he healed persons of diseases; and probably some of these children, if not all of them, were diseased, and were brought to be cured; otherwise it is not easy to conceive what they should *be touched* by him for; however, they were not brought to be baptized: If the persons that brought them had their baptism in view, they would not have brought them to Christ, but to his disciples; seeing not he but they baptized the persons fit for it; they might have seen the disciples administer that ordinance, but not Christ; and from hence it is certain, that they were not baptized by Christ, since he never baptized any.

4. This

---
[v] Matt. xviii. 2.   2 Tim. iii. 15.   Mark v. 39, 42.   [x] Luke xviii. 16.
[y] Matt. xii. 22. and xvii. 16.   Mark ix. 36.   [z] See Gen. xlix. 14—16.
[a] Mark x. 13.   Luke xviii. 15.

4. This passage concludes against Pædobaptism, and not for it; for it seems, by this, that it had never been the practice of the Jews, nor of *John* the Baptist, nor of Christ and his disciples, to baptize infants; for had this been then in use, the apostles would scarcely have rebuked and forbid those that brought these children, since they might have concluded they brought them to be baptized; but knowing of no such usage, that ever obtained in that nation, neither among those that did or did not believe in Christ, they forbad them; and Christ's entire silence about the baptism of infants at this time, when he had such an opportunity of speaking of it to his disciples, had it been his will, has no favourable aspect on such a practice.

5. This writer's reasoning upon the passage, is beside the purpose for which he produces it; if he brings it to prove any thing respecting baptism, it must be to prove that infants were brought to Christ, in order to be baptized by him, and not to him in the way of his ordinance, or in the way of baptism: the reason our Lord gives why they should be suffered to come to him, *for of such is the kingdom of heaven*, is to be understood of such as were comparable to little children, for modesty, meekness, and humility, and for freedom from rancour malice, ambition, and pride [b]. And so the *Syriac* version is, *who are as these*; and the *Persic* version, which is rather a paraphrase, shewing the sense, *who have been humble as these little children*; and such are the proper subjects of a gospel church-state, sometimes called *the kingdom of heaven*, and shall inherit eternal happiness. If the words are to be literally understood of infants, and of their belonging to the kingdom of heaven, interpreted of the kingdom of grace, or of the gospel church-state, according to this author's reasoning, they will prove too much, and more than he cares for; namely, that belonging to that kingdom, they have a right to the privileges of it, even to all of them, to the Lord's supper, as well as to baptism; but the kingdom of glory seems to be designed And we are not unwilling to admit the literal sense, for the eternal salvation and happiness of infants dying in infancy, is not denied by us; and, according to this sense, our Lord's reasoning is strong, that seeing he thought fit to save the souls of infants, and introduce them into the kingdom of heaven, why should they be forbid being brought to him, to be touched by him, and healed of their bodily diseases? The argument is from the greater to the lesser; but furnishes out nothing in favour of Pædobaptism.

3dly, The next text mentioned is *Matt.* xviii. 6. *But whoso shall offend one of these little ones which believe in me, it were better for him, that a millstone were hanged about his neck, and that he were drowned in the depth of the sea.* Upon which it is observed, that the little one referred to was in an infant state, as appears

[b] See Matt. xviii. 2.

pears from verse 2ᵈ, and *Mark* ix. 36. and that little children are reputed, by Christ, believers in him: And so here is a full anticipation of the common objection against the baptism of infants, and a justification of their claim to the seal of the righteousness of faith; as well as a strong declaration of the awful danger of offending these little ones, by denying them the covenant privileges, to which they have a righteous claim, p. 20, 21, 23, 27. But,

1. Though the little child, in verse 2ᵈ, which our Lord set in the midst of his disciples, and took an occasion from thence to rebuke and instruct them, was in an infant-state, yet those our Lord here speaks of, were not little ones in age; for how capable soever they may be of having the principle or habit of faith implanted in them, they cannot be capable of exercising it, or of acting faith, which the phrase used expresses; for if they are not capable of exercising reason, though they have the principle of it in them, they cannot be capable of exercising faith; nor indeed of being offended in the sense the word is here used, and to such a degree, that the offenders of them had better have died a violent death, than to be guilty of such offence. But,

2. The disciples of Christ are meant, his apostles, who were contending among themselves who should be greatest in the kingdom of heaven; which ambition our Lord rebukes, by placing a little child in the midst of them, ver. 1, 2. saying to them, *Except ye be converted, and become as little children, ye shall not enter into the kingdom of heaven*; adding, that whoever humbled himself as the child before him, should be the greatest in it; and that such who received such humble disciples of his, received him; but those that offended them, would incur his resentment, and the greatest danger expressed in the words under consideration, ver. 3—6. And these were such, not only who by faith looked to Christ, and received him as their Saviour, and made a profession of him; but preached the doctrine of faith; who, *having believed, therefore spoke*; and who may be said to be offended, when their persons were despised, their ministry rejected, and they reproached and persecuted; and, when it would go ill with them that should treat them in this manner. These were such, who were *little ones*, in their own esteem, and in the esteem of others.

3. Admitting that infants in age could be meant, and these to have the principle and habit of faith in them, yet this would not justify their claim to baptism, which this writer means, by the seal of the righteousness of faith; though not baptism, but circumcision is designed by that phrase; since actual faith, yea, a profession of it, is a necessary pre-requisite to baptism; *If thou believest with all thine heart, thou mayest* ᵉ.

4. This

---

ᵉ Acts viii. 37.

4. This writer seems conscious to himself, that faith in Christ is necessary to baptism, and is that which justifies a claim unto it; since he seems glad to lay hold on this text, and the sense he puts upon it, in order to anticipate the objection to infant-baptism taken from faith in Christ, being a pre-requisite to it; which he knows not how otherwise to get rid of, than to suppose that infants have faith, and that this is a proof of it. But,

5. Supposing this, either all infants have faith, or only some: If all; how comes it to pass, that there are so many, when grown up, that are manifestly destitute of it: Can the grace be lost? Is it not an abiding one? Is not He, who is the Author, the Finisher of it? If only some have it, how can it be known, who have it, and who not? Wherefore, to baptize upon this supposed faith, is to proceed on a very precarious foundation: It seems, therefore, much more eligible, to defer their baptism, till it appears, that they do truly and actually believe in Christ.

*4thly*, The next passage of scripture, produced in favour of infant-baptism, is. 1 *Cor.* vii. 14. *For the unbelieving husband is sanctified by the wife, and the unbelieving wife is sanctified by the husband, else were your children unclean; but now are they holy.* Upon which, our author thus reasons; " If either of the parents " be a believer, the children are reputed holy ; that is, they have a covenant " holiness, and have, therefore, a claim to covenant-privileges;—they are holy, " by virtue of their covenant-relation to God, and must, therefore, have a " right to have that covenant sealed to them in baptism, p. 21." But,

1. It ought to be told, what these covenant-privileges are, that children have a claim unto, by virtue of their covenant-relation, this writer so often speaks of. If baptism is one of them, as it seems to be his intention, that must be denied to be a covenant-privilege, or a privilege of the covenant of grace ; for then all the covenant ones in all ages, ought to have enjoyed it; whereas they have not: And we have seen already, that covenant interest gives no right to any positive institution, or ordinance, without a divine direction; and that baptism is no seal of the covenant:

2. It should be told, what this covenant is, whether it is a real or imaginary thing; it seems to be the latter, by our author's way of expressing himself. He says, children are *reputed* holy ; that is, have a covenant-holiness: So that covenant-holiness is a reputed holiness ; but such a holiness can never qualify persons for a New Testament ordinance ; nor has the covenant of grace any such holiness belonging to it; that provides, by way of promise, for real holiness, signified, by putting and writing the laws of God in the heart, by giving new hearts and new spirits, and taking away the stony heart, and by cleansing from all impurity ; this is real, inward holiness, and shews itself in an outward holy conversation

conversation: Where this appears, such have an undoubted right to the ordinance of baptism, since they must have received the holy spirit, as a spirit of sanctification [d].

3. A holiness, appertaining to the covenant of grace, can never be meant, since it is such a holiness, as unbelievers, yea, as heathens are said to have; it is such a holiness, as unbelieving husbands, and unbelieving wives are said to have, by virtue and in consequence of their relation to believing wives and believing husbands; and which they have prior to the holiness of their children; and on which their childrens holiness depends. Now, surely, unbelievers and heathens, will not be allowed to be in covenant, or to be possessed of a covenant holiness, by virtue of their yoke-fellows; and yet, theirs, and their childrens holiness, must be of the same kind and nature. Wherefore,

4. If children, by virtue of this holiness, have a claim to covenant-privileges, and to have the covenant sealed to them by baptism; then, much more, their unbelieving parents, because they are sanctified before them, by their believing yoke-fellows, and they are as near to them, as their children; and if the holiness of the one gives a right to baptism, why not the holiness of the other? And yet, our Pædobaptists do not pretend to baptize the unbelieving husband or wife, though sanctified, whose holiness is the more near; but the children, that become holy through the sanctification of both, whose holiness is the more remote. For, it should be observed, that the holiness, spoken of in the text, be it what it will, is derived, or denominated, from both parents, believing and unbelieving; yea, the holiness of the children depends upon the sanctification of the unbelieving parent; for if the unbeliever is not sanctified, the children are unclean, and not holy. Besides, the words are not necessarily to be understood of infants, or young children, but of the posterity of such persons, whether of 40, or 50 years of age, or of what age soever; and must be unclean in the sense of the word, here used, if their unbelieving parent is not sanctified by, or to the believing one. But,

5. These words are to be understood of a matrimonial holiness; not merely of the holiness of marriage, as it is an institution of God, but of the very act of marriage, which, in the language of the Jews, is frequently expressed, by being *sanctified*. Innumerable instances might be given of this; I have produced one in my exposition of this place, in which the word, קדש *Kadash*, "to sanctify," is used no less than ten times, *to espouse*. And, for the sake of those who have it not, I shall transcribe the passage: And it is, as follows [e]; "a man מקדש *Me-kaddesh*, "sanctifies," or espouses a wife by himself, or by his messenger; a woman, מתקדש *Mithkaddesh*, "is sanctified," or espoused by herself, or by "her

[d] Acts x 47.   [e] Misn. Kiddushin, c. 2. §. 1.

"her messenger; a man, מקדש *Mekaddesh*, "sanctifies," or espouses his daugh-
"ter, when she is a young woman, by himself, or by his messenger: If any one
"says to a woman, התקדשי *Hitbkaddeshi*, "be thou sanctified," or espoused to
"me by this date (the fruit of the palm tree) התקדשי *Hitbkaddeshi*, "be thou
"sanctified," or espoused by this (or any other thing:) If there is in any one
"of these things the value of a farthing, מקודשת *Mekuddesheth*, "she is sancti-
"fied," or espoused; and if not, she is not מקודשת *Mekuddesheth*, "sanctified,"
"or espoused: If he says, by this, and by this, and by this; if there is the va-
"lue of a farthing in them all, מקודשת *Mekuddesheth*, "she is sanctified," or
"espoused; but if not, she is not, מקודשת *Mekuddesheth*, "sanctified," or
"espoused: If she eats one (date) after another, she is not, מקודשת *Mekudde-
"sheth*, "sanctified," or espoused, unless one of them is the value of a farthing."
In the *Mishnah*, the oral law of the Jews, there is a whole treatise of קידושי *Kiddushin*, "sanctifications," or espousals; out of which the above passage is taken:
And in the *Gemara* is another, full of the disputes of the doctors on this subject:
And *Maimonides* has also written a treatise of women and wives; out of which
might be produced almost innumerable instances, in proof of the observation;
and such, as can read, and have leisure to read the said tracts, may fully satisfy
themselves in this matter. And in the same sense, the apostle uses the word
αγιαζω here: And the passage should be rendered thus; *the unbelieving hufband is espoused*, or married *to the wife*, or rather *has been espoused*; for it relates
to the act of marriage past, as valid; *and the unbelieving wife has been espoused
to the husband*. The preposition εν, translated *by*, should be rendered *to*, as it
is in the very next verse, *God hath called us*, εν ειρηνη, "to peace." The passage
is introduced, to support the advice the apostle had given to believers married to unbelievers, not to depart from them, but live with them, who had had
some scruple upon their minds, whether they ought to cohabit with them, being
unbelievers; he advises them, by all means, to dwell with them, unless the
unbeliever departed, seeing they were duly, rightly, and legally espoused to
each other; and, therefore, ought not, notwithstanding their different sentiments of religion, to separate from one another; otherwise, if they were not
truly married to one another, as such a departure and separation would suggest,
this consequence must necessarily follow, that children, born in such a state of
cohabitation, where the marriage is not valid, must be spurious, and not legitimate: which is the sense of the next clause, *else were your children unclean, but
now are they holy*; that is, they would have been accounted illegitimate, but
now legitimate. And,

6. This sense of the words is not novel, nor singular: It is agreeable to the
minds of several interpreters, ancient and modern; as *Jerom, Ambrose, Erasmus,
Camerarius,*

*Camerarius, Musculus,* and others: which last writer, and who was a zealous Pædobaptist, makes this ingenuous confession; "formerly, says he, I have abused this place against the Anabaptists, thinking the meaning was, that the children were holy for the parents faith; which, though true, the present place makes nothing for the purpose."

5*thly,* To all which, this writer adds the commission in *Matthew* xxviii. 19. *Go, teach all nations, baptizing them, &c.* Concerning which, he says, that as the commission to the sacred ministry enjoined the baptizing of *all nations,* whereof infants are a very great part; it also enjoined the baptizing infants, as a part of the nations they were to *disciple* and *baptize,* p. 21. And, elsewhere, he says, the words ought to be read, *Go, disciple all nations, baptizing them;* and should be understood, as requiring the ministers of the gospel to make all nations disciples by baptizing them,—whereby every one is constituted *a learner* of Christ: And to prove, that infants are called disciples, he refers to *Acts* xv. 10. *Why tempt ye God to put a yoke on the neck of the disciples, &c.* and to all such scriptures, that respect the education of children, p. 24, 25. But,

1. The commission does not enjoin the baptizing of all nations, but the baptizing of such as are taught; for the antecedent to the relative *them* cannot be *all nations,* since παντα τα εθνη, the words for "all nations," are of the neuter gender; whereas αυτυς "them," is of the masculine; but μαθητας, "disciples;" is supposed and contained in the word μαθητευσατε, "teach, or make disciples;" such as are first taught, or made disciples by teaching under the ministry of the word, by the Spirit of God, Christ's orders are to baptize them.

2. If infants, as a part of all nations, were to be baptized, and because they are such; then the infants of Heathens, Turks and Jews, ought to be baptized, for they are a part of all nations, as well as the children of christians, or believers.

3. We are very willing, the words should be rendered *disciple all nations,* or *make all nations disciples;* that is, disciples of Christ, which is the same, as believers in him; for they are the true disciples of Christ, that have learned the way of life, and salvation by him; that deny themselves, sinful, righteous, and civil self, for his sake; who forsake all, take up the cross, and follow him; who bear, and bring forth much fruit, love one another, and continue in the doctrine of Christ [f]. And such, and such only, are the proper subjects of baptism: so, agreeable to this commission and the sense of it, Christ first made disciples, and then baptized them, or ordered them to be baptized [g].

4. These two acts, *discipling* and *baptizing,* are not to be confounded together; they are two distinct acts, and the one is previous to the other, and absolutely

necessary

---

[f] Luke xiv. 27, 33. John xv. 8. and xiii. 35. and viii. 31.  [g] John iv. 1, 2.

neceſſary thereunto. Men are not made diſciples by baptizing them, as this writer ſuggeſts, but they muſt be firſt diſciples, and then baptized. So *Jerom* [h] long ago underſtood the commiſſion, who has theſe words upon it; "fitſt, they "teach all nations, then dip thoſe that are taught in water: For, it cannot "be, that the body ſhould receive the ſacrament of baptiſm, unleſs the ſoul has "before received the truth of faith." To the ſame purpoſe, *Athanaſius* ſays [i], "wherefore the Saviour does not ſimply command to *baptize*, but firſt ſays, "*teach*; and then baptize thus, *in the name of the Father, and of the Son, and* "*of the holy Ghoſt*; that faith might come of teaching, and baptiſm be perfected."

5. Such a diſciple, as this writer ſuppoſes to be conſtituted by baptiſm, namely, a *learner* of Chriſt, cannot agree with an infant. What can a new-born babe learn of Chriſt? What can it be taught of him, or receive by way of teaching, at the time of its baptiſm, or by being baptized? If learners and diſciples are ſynonymous terms, as this author ſays, they cannot be diſciples before they are learners; and they cannot be learners of Chriſt, unleſs they have learned ſomething of him: And, according to this notion, they ought to learn ſomething of him, before they are baptized in his name. But what can an infant learn of Chriſt?

6. The text in *Acts* xv. 10. is not to be underſtood of infants, but of adult perſons; even converted Gentiles, who believed in Chriſt, and were his diſciples; and upon whom, the falſe teachers would have impoſed the yoke of the ceremonial law; and, particularly, circumciſion: Which, becauſe it bound over to the whole law, the apoſtle repreſents as an inſupportable one; and calls this impoſition of it on the believing Gentiles, a tempting of God: And as for any other paſſages that enjoin the education of children, or ſpeak of it, they are never from thence called the diſciples of Chriſt, nor any where elſe.

6*thly*, This writer aſſerts, that "it is plain that the apoſtles thus underſtood "our Saviour's meaning, and accordingly baptized *Lydia* and her houſhold, and "the Gaoler and all his [k]; and the houſhold of *Stephanas* [l]." P. 21. But,

1. Seeing the underſtanding of our Saviour's meaning in the commiſſion, depends upon thoſe inſtances of baptiſm, and ſo the warrant for the baptizing of infants, the Pædobaptiſts ought to be ſure that there were infants in theſe families, and that they were baptized, or otherwiſe they muſt baptize them, at moſt, upon a very precarious foundation; for if the commiſſion of itſelf is not clear for it, and thoſe inſtances in which the apoſtles acted according to the commiſſion, are not ſufficient to vouch it, it muſt ſtand upon a very bad bottom,

[h] Primum docent omnes Gentes, deinde doctas intingunt Aqua, &c. Hieron. in Matt. xxviii. 19.
[i] Διατυτο γυν κỳ ο σωΐης ουχ απλως ιντηλαῖο το βαπτιζειν, αλλα πρωτον φησι μαθητιυσατι, &c. Athanaſ. contr. Arianos. Orat. III. p. 209.
[k] Acts xvi. 15, 33.    [l] 1 Cor. i. 16.

tom, having neither precept nor precedent for it; and they must know, that there are families that have no infants in them, and how can they be sure there were any in these? And,

2. It lies upon them to prove there were infants in these families, and that these infants were baptized, or the allegation of those instances is to no purpose; how they can satisfy themselves without it, they best know; they ought not to put it upon us to prove a negative, to prove that there were none, this is unfair; and one would think, should not sit very easy upon their minds, to rest their practice on so poor a shift, and so unreasonable a demand. But,

3. We are able to make it appear, that there are many things in the account of the baptism of these families, which are inconsistent with infants, and which make it at least probable, that there were none in them; and certain, that those that were baptized were adult persons, and believers in Christ. As for *Lydia*, it is not certain in what state of life she was, whether single or married, whether maid, widow, or wife; whether she had any children, or ever had any; or if she had, and them living, whether they were infants or adult; and if infants, it does not seem probable that she should bring them along with her from her native place *Thyatira* to *Philippi*, where she seems to have been upon business, and so had hired a house during her stay there; wherefore, her houshold seems to have consisted of menial servants she brought along with her, to assist her in her business; and certain it is, that those that the apostles found there, when they entered into it, after they came out of prison, were such as are called *brethren*, and were capable of being *comforted* by them [m]. And as for the Jailer's houshold, they were such as were capable of having the word of God spoken to them, and of rejoicing at it, and in the conversation of the apostles, at what was said and done by them; and are even expresly said to believe in God, as the Jailer did, and together with him; and as for the houshold of *Stephanas*, that is, by some, thought to be the same with the Jailer's; but, if not, it is certain it consisted of adult persons, believers in Christ, and very useful in the public service of religion; for they were the first-fruits of *Achaia*, and addicted themselves to the ministry of the saints [n]. All which, in each of the instances, can never be said of infants. But,

7thly, This writer adds one text more, which, he says, must be allowed to be decisive in the present case, and that is *Romans* xi. 17—25. from whence he thinks it is most evident, that since the believing Gentiles are grafted into all the privileges and spiritual blessings of the Jewish church, they cannot be cut off from that great blessing and privilege of having the covenant sealed to their infant seed, p. 21. To which I reply,

1. It

[m] Acts xvi. 15, 40.      [n] 1 Cor. xvi. 15.

1. It will readily be allowed, that believing Gentiles shared in all the spiritual blessings and privileges of the Jewish church, or of believers under the former dispensation; the same blessings of imputed righteousness and pardon of sin came upon the uncircumcision, as well as upon the circumcision, who walk in the steps of the faith of *Abraham*°, for such that *are Christ*'s, true believers in him, they *are Abraham's seed*, his spiritual seed, and *heirs, according to the promise*, of all spiritual blessings and privileges ᵖ. But,

2. The covenant of grace was never sealed to *Abraham*'s natural seed; the covenant of grace itself did not belong to them, as such; nor was circumcision a seal of it to them; nor is baptism a seal of the covenant of grace to any; and therefore it is a great impropriety and impertinence to talk of cutting off from, that which was never had, and never was.

3. Though believing Gentiles share in the spiritual blessings and privileges which the Jewish church, or Jewish believers enjoyed, they never were grafted into that church; that church-state, with all the peculiar ordinances of it, was utterly abolished by Christ, signified by the *shaking of the heavens and the earth*, and *removing of those things that are shaken, that those which cannot be shaken may remain* ᵠ. The Jewish church is not the olive-tree, of whose root and fatness the Gentiles partake; they are not grafted into the old Jewish stock; the ax has been laid to the root of that tree; and it is entirely cut down, and no engraftment is made upon it. But,

4. The olive-tree, of whose root and fatness believing Gentiles partake, is the gospel church-state, out of which the Jews that rejected Christ were left, and are the broken branches; and those that believed in Christ were taken in, and laid the first foundation of it; these are the first-fruits, and the root, which being holy, are a pledge of the future conversion and holiness of that people; they of them that received the first-fruits of the Spirit, were first incorporated into a gospel church-state; and then the Gentiles which believed were received among them, and were engrafted into them; and this engrafture or coalition was first at *Antioch*, where and when, and hereafter, the Gentiles partook of the root and fatness of the olive-tree; enjoyed the same privileges, communicated in the same ordinances, and were satisfied with the goodness and fatness of the house of God; and of this engrafture, and of this only, does this text speak; so that it is so far from being decisive in the present case, that there is not one word, one syllable about baptism in it, and still less can any thing, in favour of infant-baptism, be inferred from it.

I shall conclude this chapter, and with it the affair of the divine right of infant-baptism, which, whether illustrated and confirmed in the *Dialogue*, must be left

to

° Rom. iv. 6—12.   ᵖ Gal. iii. 29.   ᵠ Heb. xii. 26, 27.

to the judicious reader, by observing, that the minister in it being required to give express New Testament proof for infant-baptism, which he was conscious to himself he could not do, in answer to it, requires express New Testament proof, 'that *women* should partake of the *Lord's Supper*, and offers to prove infant-baptism by the same arguments that this should be proved. But,

1. We do not go about to prove womens right to partake of the Lord's Supper, by such arguments as this writer forms for us; as, by their covenant-interest, by their claim to have the covenant sealed to them, and by their being a part of all nations; and though we look upon their being believers and disciples of Christ, proper qualifications for their admission to the Lord's supper, when these can be made to appear to belong to infants, we shall readily admit them to baptism. But,

2. We prove their right to the ordinance of the Lord's Supper, by their right to the ordinance of baptism; for they that have a right to one ordinance, have to the other; that women believing in Christ have a right to baptism, is clear, from *Acts* viii. 12. *They were baptized, both men and women*, and therefore should partake of the Lord's Supper. Let it be proved, that infants ought to be baptized, and it will be allowed and insisted upon, that they partake of the Lord's Supper.

3. We prove it by their being church members; *Mary* the mother of *Jesus*, with other women, were of the number of the disciples that formed the first gospel church at *Jerusalem*; *Sapphira*, the wife of *Ananias*, was, with her husband, of the multitude that *believed, and were together, and had all things common*; after whose awful death, *believers were the more added to the Lord*, that is, to the church, *both men and women*[r]. There were women in the church at *Corinth*; concerning whom the apostle gives rules respecting their conduct[s]. Now all those that are members of gospel churches, ought to eat the bread and drink the cup, in remembrance of Christ[t]. Women are members of gospel churches; and therefore ought to eat and drink in like manner.

4. We prove this by example: *Mary*, the mother of our Lord, and other women, being of the number of the disciples, which constituted the gospel church state at *Jerusalem*, as they continued with one accord in prayer and supplication, so likewise in breaking of bread[u].

5. We prove this by a divine direction, exhortation, and command, *Let a man examine himself, and so let him eat*[w]. The word used is ανθρωπ⊙, a word of the common gender, and signifies both men and women; in which sense it must be often understood, as in 1 *Timothy* ii. 5. for is Christ a mediator only between

---

[r] Acts i. 14, 15. and iv. 32. and v. 9, 14.   [s] 1 Cor. xi. 5, 6, 13. and xiv. 34, 35.
[t] 1 Cor. xi. 26.   [u] Acts i. 14, 15. and ii. 1, 44, 46.   [w] 1 Cor. xi. 29.

between God and men, and not women? Under the gospel dispensation, in a gospel church state, *there is neither male nor female*; they are *all one in Christ*, and enjoy the same privileges and ordinances [a]. Let the same proof, or as good, be given for infant-baptism, and we have done; let it be proved that infants have a right to any other gospel ordinance as such; that they are or ought to be members of gospel churches; that there is either precept or precedent for the baptizing of them, and we shall readily admit them.

## CHAP. VI.

*Concerning the Mode of administering the Ordinance of Baptism, whether by immersion or by sprinkling.*

THE author of the *dialogue* under consideration affirms, that there is not one single Lexicographer, or critic upon the Greek language, he has ever seen, but what agrees, that though the word *baptizo* sometimes signifies to *dip*, yet it also naturally signifies to *wash*; and that washing, in any mode whatsoever, is the native signification of the word *baptismos*, p. 31. that the words *baptize* and *baptism*, as used in the New Testament, do not, from their signification, make *dipping* or *plunging* the necessary mode of administering the ordinance, p. 33. and that one single instance of that mode of administering the ordinance, is not to be found in all the New Testament, p. 34. nor is it probable it should be the mode, p. 38. and that the mode of administering it by sprinkling is a more lively emblem of what is signified and represented by it, than dipping or plunging can be supposed, and therefore the most proper one, p. 39.

*First,* As to the lexicographers, and critics on the Greek language, they agree that the word βαπτιζω, signifies, in its first and primary sense, "to *dip or plunge*," and only in a secondary and consequential sense, to *wash*, but never to *pour* or *sprinkle*; there being no proper washing, but what is by dipping; and for this we appeal to all the writers of this kind, and even to those this author mentions.

Scapula, the first of them, renders βαπτιζω, by *mergo, seu immergo, ut quæ tingendi, aut, abluendi gratia aquæ immergimus*, "to dip or plunge into, as what for the sake of dying or washing we dip into water;" item *mergo, submergo, obruo aqua*, "also to plunge, plunge under, overwhelm in water;" item *abluo, lavo*, "also to wash off, wash;" and βαπτιζομαι, he renders, by *mergor, submergor*, "to be plunged, plunged under;" and observes, that it is used metaphorically for *obruor*, to be overwhelmed; and βαπτισμος, and βαπτισμα, he says, is, *mersio, lotio,*

[a] Gal. iii. 28.

*lotio, ablutio, ipfe immergendi, item lavandi, feu abluendi actus,* "plunging, wafh-"ing, ablution, the act itfelf of plunging, alfo of wafhing or ablution." In all which he makes dipping, or plunging, to be the firft and preferable fenfe of the words.

*Stephens* gives the fame fenfe of the words, and fo *Schrevelius,* who renders βαπτίζω, by *baptizo, mergo, lavo,* " baptize, plunge, wafh." *Pafor* only renders it *baptize,* baptize, without determining its fenfe. And *Leigh,* in his *Critica Sacra,* obferves, that " the nature and proper lignification of it, is *to dip* " *into water,* or *to plunge under water;*" and refers to *John* iii. 22, 23. *Matt.* iii. 16. *Acts* viii 38. And cites *Cafaubon, Bucanus, Bullinger,* and *Zanchy,* as agreeing and teftifying to this fenfe of it; and *baptifma,* he fays, is " dipping " into water, or wafhing with water." And thefe are the Lexicographers and Critics our author refers us to : To which I may add the Lexicon compiled by *Budæus, Conftantine,* and others, who render the word βαπτίζω, by *immergo, mergo, intingo, lavacro tingo, abluo, madefacio, lavo, mundo ;* " plunge, plunge " into, dip into, dip in a laver, wafh off, make wet, wafh, cleanfe :." And βαπτισμός, they fay, is *tingendi, hoc eft mergendi actio, in quo fignificatu tinctura dicitur ;* " the action of tinging, that is, of plunging ; in which fignification it " is called a *tincture,* or dying ;" and another by *Hadrian Junius,* who renders βαπτίζω, by *immergo,* " to plunge into ;" and βαπτισμός, by *immerfio, lotio, baptifmus,* " immerfion, wafhing, baptifm."

As for other critics on the Greek language, who affert, that the proper fignification of the word *baptizo,* is to *dip,* or *plunge;* they are fo numerous, that it would be tedious to reckon them up : I fhall only mention a few of them, and their words. *Calvin* [a] fays, " *Ipfum baptizandi verbum mergere fignificat, & " mergendi ritum veteri ecclefiæ obfervatum fuiffe conftat;*" the word *baptize,* fig- " nifies *to plunge*; and, it is plain, that the rite of plunging was obferved in " the ancient church." *Beza,* who muft be allowed to be a learned critic in the Greek language, fays, on *Mark* vii. 4. " *Neque vero* το βαπτίζειν, *fignificat " lavare nifi a confequenti, nam proprie declarat tingendi caufa immergere ;* " nei- " ther does the word *baptizo,* fignify *to wafh,* unlefs confequentially ; for it " properly fignifies, *to plunge into,* for the fake of tinging, or dying ;" and on *Matt.* iii. 11. he fays, " *fignificat autem* τὸ βαπτίζειν, *tingere quum* παρὰ τὸ βάπτειν, " *dicatur, & quum tingenda mergantur ;*" the word *baptizo,* fignifies *to dip* " (as Dyers in the vatt) feeing it comes from *bapto,* to dip, and feeing things, " that are to be dyed, are dipped." *Cafaubon,* another great critic on the Greek language, has thefe words on *Matt.* iii. 6. " *Hic enim fuit baptizandi ritus* " *ut in aquas immergerentur, quod vel ipfo vox* βαπτίζειν, *declarat fatis—unde intelligimus*

[a] Inftitut. L. IV. c. 15 §. 19.

"*ligimus non esse ab re, quod jam pridem non nulli disputarant de toto corpore immer-*
"*gendo in ceremonia baptismi; vocem enim βαπλιζειν, urgebant;*" for this was the
" rite of baptizing, that persons should be plunged into water, which the word
" *baptizo,* sufficiently declares.—Hence, we understand, that it was not fo-
" reign from the matter, which some some time ago disputed, concerning
" plunging the whole body in the ceremony of baptism; for they urged the
" signification of the word *baptizo.*" And, that this is the proper signification
of the word, he observes, in his notes on *Acts* i. 5. and ii. 4. To which, I shall
only add one more critic, and that is *Grotius*; who, on *Matthew* iii. 6. thus
writes; "*Mersatione autem non perfusione agi solitum hunc ritum indicat & vocis*
"*proprietas, & loca ad eum ritum delecta,* John iii. 23. Acts viii. 38. *& allusiones*
"*multæ apostolorum quæ ad aspersionem referri non possunt,* Rom. vi. 3. Col. ii. 12.
" that this rite used to be performed by *plunging,* and not by *pouring,* both the
" propriety of the word, and the places chosen for this rite, shew, *John* iii. 23.
" *Acts* viii. 38. and the many allusions of the apostles, which cannot be referred
" to *sprinkling,* Rom. vi. 3, 4. Col. ii. 12." I might have here subjoined, some
instances of the use of the word in Greek authors, by which it appears to have
the sense of dipping and plunging, and not of pouring, or sprinkling; but this
has been largely done by Dr *Gale,* and others. I shall, therefore, proceed,

*Secondly,* To consider the use of the words, *baptize* and *baptism,* in the New
Testament; which our author says, do not, from their signification, make dipping or plunging, the necessary mode of administering the ordinance of baptism: And the places enumerated by him, in which they are used, are as follow.

1. The descent of the holy Ghost on the apostles, and on *Cornelius,* and his
company, is called *baptizing,* Acts i. 5. and xi. 16. where he observes, it cannot
be pretended that there was the least allusion to, or resemblance of dipping, or
plunging, in this use of the word. But the learned *Casaubon,* a very great critic in the Greek tongue, before-mentioned and referred to, does pretend, that
there is such an allusion and resemblance, his words on *Acts* i. 5. are these, "*etsi*
" *non improbo,* &c. although I do not disapprove of the word *baptized,* being
" retained here, that the antithesis may be full; yet, I am of opinion, that
" regard is had, in this place, to its proper signification; for βαπτιζειν, is to
" *immerse,* so as to *tinge* or *dip :* And, in this sense, the apostles are truly said
" to be baptized; for the house, in which this was done, was filled with the
" holy Ghost : So that the apostles seemed to be plunged into it, as into some
" pool." And the extraordinary descent of the spirit in those instances, is much
more strongly expressed by a word, which signifies *plunging,* than if it had been
expressed by a word, that signifies bare perfusion, and still less by sprinkling.

2. "Christ's crucifixion is called a baptism, *Mark* x. 38. but, being buffeted, spit upon, and lifted up upon the cross, says our author, bear no resemblance, nor can have any allusion to dipping, or plunging. But, it is easy to observe, that the sufferings of our Lord, which are compared to a baptism, in the place referred to, and in *Luke* xii. 50. because of the greatness and abundance of them, are, sometimes, expressed by deep waters, and floods of waters; and he is represented as plunged into them, and covered and overwhelmed with them;" For so he says himself; *The waters are come into my soul; I sink in deep mire, where is no standing; I am come into deep waters, where the floods overflow me*, Psalm lxix. 1, 2. And, therefore, a word signifying *immersion*, and a covering of the whole body in water, is a very apt one to express the multitude of Christ's sufferings, and the overwhelming nature of them; and must, more fitly, express the same, than a word, which only signifies *pouring*, or sprinkling a few drops of water.

3. The text in *Mark* vii. 4. is next mentioned; which speaks of the Jews, when come from the market, not eating, *except they wash* (*baptizoontai*); and of *the washing* (*baptismous*) *of cups and pots, brazen vessels, and of tables*, or *beds*, as the word signifies. And this, our author thinks, is an unexceptionable instance of these words signifying *washing*, without dipping, or plunging; since it can hardly be supposed, that they dipped themselves under water, every time they came from market, or, that they dipped their beds, every time they sat, or lay upon them. But, in answer to this, it should be observed, that our Lord is here speaking of the superstition of the Pharisees, who, when they came from market, or any court of judicature, if they touched any common persons, or their clothes, reckoned themselves unclean; and, according to the traditions of the elders, were to immerse themselves in water, and did: So that a most proper word is here made use of, to express their superstition. And, as for cups, pots and brazen vessels, what other way of washing them is there, than by dipping, or putting them into water? And, in this way, unclean vessels were to be washed, according to the law, *Lev.* xi. 32. as well as all that were reckoned so by the traditions of the elders; and even beds, pillows and bolsters, when they were unclean in a ceremonial sense, and not, as this author puts it, every time they lay, or sat upon them, were to be washed by immersion, or dipping them in water; as I have proved from the Jews oral law, which our Lord has respect to, in my Exposition of this place; to which, I refer the reader. Wherefore, the words are here used in their primary sense, as signifying dipping; and, if they did not so signify, they would not truly represent the superstition, they are designed to do.

4. The

# EXAMINED AND DISPROVED.

4. The next passage produced, is 1 *Cor.* x. 1, 2. which speaks of the Jewish fathers, being *baptized unto Moses in the cloud, and in the sea*. Upon which, this writer observes, that he thinks, he need not seriously undertake to convince his friend, he is debating with; "that the fathers were not dipped in the cloud, "but that the rain from the cloud bore a much greater resemblance to sprink- "ling, or affusion, than to dipping." But let us a little examine this matter, and see wherein the agreement lay, between baptism and the Israelites passage under the cloud, and through the sea. Which may be considered, either together, or separately: If together, the agreement between it and baptism, lay in this; the Israelites, when they passed through the Red sea, had the waters on each side of them, which stood up, as a wall, higher than they, and the cloud over them; so that they were, as persons immersed in, and covered with water; and, in this view, it is easy to see, that the resemblance is much greater to immersion, than to sprinkling, or affusion: or this may be considered separately, as baptized in the cloud, and as baptized in the sea; in the cloud, when, as *Gataker*\*, a Pædobaptist writer, thinks, it passed from before the face of the Israelites, and stood behind them, and was between the two camps, to keep off the Egyptians; and which, when it passed over them, let down a plentiful rain upon them, whereby they were in such a condition, as if they had been dipped all over in water; or, when under the cloud they were all over covered with it, as a person, when baptized by immersion, is all over covered with water; and they might be said to be *baptized* in the sea, when, as they passed through it, the waters standing up above their heads, they seemed, as if they were immersed. The resemblance to plunging, therefore, considered in either way, must be nearer, than to pouring, or sprinkling a small quantity of water. To which may be added, that the descent of the Israelites into the sea, when they seemed as though they were buried in the waters of it; and their ascent out of it again on the shore, have a very great agreement with baptism, as administered by immersion; in which, the person baptized, goes down into the water, is buried with Christ therein; and comes up out of it, as out of a grave, or as the children of *Israel* out of the Red sea.

5. The last text mentioned, where the word *baptism* is used, is *Heb.* ix. 10. where our author observes, "the apostle, speaking of the ceremonial dispensa- "tion, tells us, that it *stood only in meats, and drinks, and divers washings* (bap- "tismous) *and carnal ordinances*; and the principal of these washings, he ex- "emplifies to us, ver. 13. to be *the blood of bulls and goats, and the ashes of an* "*heifer, sprinkling the unclean:* Here, therefore, the word cannot, with any "appearance of modesty, be explained in favour of immersion." To which, I reply,

\* Adversar. Miscellan. p. 30.

reply, that the afhes of an heifer, fprinkling the unclean, were fo far from being the principal part of the Jewifh wafhings or baptifms, that it was no part at all; nor is this mentioned by the apoftle, as any exemplification of them, who underftood thefe things better. Sprinkling the afhes of the heifer, and the wafhing, or bathing of the perfon in water, which was by immerfion, are fpoken of, as diftinct and feparate things, in the ceremony referred to, *Numb.* xix. 19. and indeed, wafhing by fprinkling, is not reconcileable to good fenfe, to the propriety of language, and to the univerfal cuftom of nations. However, certain it is, that the priefts, Levites, Ifraelites, veffels, garments, &c. which were enjoined wafhing by the ceremonial law, and which wafhings, or baptifms, are here referred to, were done, by putting them into water, and not by pouring, or fprinkling water upon them. It is a rule with the Jews [t], that, "where"foever, in the law, wafhing of the flefh, or of the clothes is mentioned, it "means nothing elfe, than טבילת כל הגוף *Tebileth Col hagoph, the dipping of* "*the whole body* in a laver—for if any man dips himfelf all over, except the tip "of his little finger, he is ftill in his uncleannefs." From the whole, it appears, that the words, *baptize* and *baptifm*, in all the places mentioned, do, from their fignification, make dipping, or plunging, the neceffary mode of adminiftering the ordinance of baptifm. I now go on,

*Thirdly*, To vindicate thofe texts of fcripture, which afford inftances of the mode of adminiftering baptifm by immerfion, from the exceptions of this writer, who confidently affirms, "that none of thofe texts will neceffarily prove "that any one perfon was baptized by dipping, by *John* Baptift, our bleffed "Saviour, or his apoftles." P. 34. And,

1. The firft text brought into the debate, and excepted to, is *Matthew* iii. 6. *And were baptized by him in Jordan, confeffing their fins.* But we do not argue on this place, from thofe perfons being *baptized*, to their being *dipped*, as this writer makes his neighbour to do, but from their being *baptized in the river Jordan*; for why fhould *John* chufe the river *Jordan* to baptize in, and baptize in that river, if he did not adminifter the ordinance by immerfion? Dr *Hammond*, a Pædobaptift, thought that thefe words afford an argument for dipping in baptifm, though our author will not allow it: His paraphrafe of them is; "And he received them by baptifm, or *immerfion* in the water of *Jordan*, pro"mifing them pardon upon the fincerity of their converfion and amendment, "or reformation of their lives." And in his note on *Matthew* iii. 1. having refpect to this place, fays, "*John* preaching repentance to the Jews in the de"fert, received all that came unto him as new profelytes, forfaking their old "relations, that is, their fins, and in token of their refolved change, *put them*
"*into*

[t] Maimon. Hilchot. Mikvaot. c. 1. §. 2.

"*into the water, dipped them all over, and so took them out again*; and upon the
"sincerity of their change, promised them the remission of their sins, and told
"them of the Messiah which was suddenly to appear among them, and warned
"them to believe on him." The instances of washing in the pool of *Siloam*,
in *Solomon*'s ten lavers, or the hands in a bason, mentioned by our author, are
very impertinent; and besides, such washing is not performed without dipping.
Who ever washes his hands without dipping them in the water he washes in?

2. Another text mentioned, is *John* iii. 23. *John was baptizing in Enon near
to Salim, because there was much water there.* Upon which this writer observes,
that "the words in the original are *many waters*; which implies many springs
"or brooks of water; waters suited to the necessity and conveniency of the
"vast multitudes that resorted to *John*, as a supply of drink for themselves,
"and for the horses and camels which they rode upon, as well as for their
"baptism. Here is no appearance of dipping in the case.—Had *John* baptized
"all these multitudes by dipping, he must have stood almost continually in
"water, up to his waste, and could not have survived the employment but
"by miracle." To which I reply,

(1.) Admitting that the words in the original, *many waters*, imply many
springs or brooks, this shews there was a confluence of water there; and every
body knows, that many springs and brooks being together, could easily fill large
pools, sufficient for immersion; and even form and feed great rivers, which is
often the case; and besides, the use this author finds for these springs and
brooks, requires a considerable quantity of water, namely, for the vast multitudes of men, and for their horses and camels; and surely, therefore, there
must be a sufficient quantity to cover a man's body in.

(2.) The words πολλα υδατα, *many waters*, signify a large quantity, great
abundance, both in the literal and metaphorical sense of the phrase, as it is used
by the evangelist *John* elsewhere, see *Rev.* i. 15. and xvii. 1, 15. and by the
*Septuagint* interpreters, it is used even for the waters of the sea, *Psalm* lxxvii. 19.
and cvii. 23. and answers to מים רבים, *Mayim Rabbim*, in *Cant.* viii. 7: *many
waters cannot quench love*; which surely must refer not to a small, but a large
quantity of water; and which phrase there, the Septuagint render by *much water*, as we do the phrase here.

(3.) These words are given as a reason, not for the conveniency of drink
for men and their cattle, but for the baptizing of men, and the conveniency of
that; that the men that came to *John*'s baptism came on horses and camels, we
know not; however, the text assigns no reason for the choice of the place upon
the account of conveniency for them, but for baptism only; and therefore, we
should

should not overlook the reason in the text, that is certain, and receive one, which, at most, is very precarious and uncertain; besides, *John* had not, at this time, such vast multitudes that followed him; those followed Christ, and not him: he was decreasing: Christ made and baptized more disciples than he. See ver. 26, 30. and chap. iv. 1.

(4.) Supposing that vast multitudes still followed him, and were baptized by him, this affords no argument against dipping in baptism; and especially since this was performed in a place where there was much water. Nor was the baptizing of such great multitudes by immersion so great an undertaking, as that he could not survive it without a miracle; admit the work to be hard and laborious, yet *as his day was, his strength was*; according to the divine promise. We have had instances in our own nation, in our climate, of persons that have baptized great multitudes in rivers, and even in the winter time, and that for many days successively, if credit is to be given to our own writers. Mr *Fox* the martyrologist, relates [x], from *Fabian*, that *Austin*, archbishop of *Canterbury*, baptized ten thousand in one day, in the river *Swale*; and observes upon it, that whereas he then baptized in rivers, it followeth, there were then no use of fonts. And the same, *Ranulph*, the monk of *Chester* affirms, in his history [z], and says, it was on a day in the middle of winter; and, according to *Fox*, it was on a *Christmas-day*. And our historian *Bede* says [y], that *Paulinus*, for six and thirty days successively, did nothing else, than instruct the people, which from all parts flocked unto him, and baptized them that were instructed in the river *Glen*; and who also baptized in one day vast numbers in the river *Trent*, King *Edwin* being present.

(5.) Though, this writer says, here is no appearance of dipping, in the case referred to in the text, yet there are several Pædobaptists, who are of another opinion, and think there was. *Calvin*, on the text, thus writes; "from these "words, we may gather, that baptism was performed by *John* and Christ, by "a plunging of the whole body under water." *Piscator*, on the place, has these words; "this is mentioned, to signify the rite of baptism which *John* used; "namely, plunging the whole body of the man, standing in the river; hence, "Christ, being baptized of *John* in *Jordan*, is said to come up out of the water, "*Matt*. iii. 16. The same mode *Philip* observed, *Acts* viii. 38." *Aretius*, on the passage, writes in the following manner; " but, why did *John* stay here? " He gives a reason, *because there was much water here*; wherefore penitent per- " sons might be commodiously baptized; and, it seems to intimate, that a
"large

---

[x] Acts and Monuments, vol. I. p. 154.  [z] Polychronicon, lib. V. c. 10.
[y] Eccles. Hist. l. II. c. 14. p. 77. & c. 16. p. 79.

"large quantity of water was neceſſary in baptizing, that they might, perhaps, immerſe the whole body." To which, I ſhall only add the words of *Grotius*, on the clauſe, *much water:* "Underſtand, ſays he, not many rivulets, but, ſimply, a plenty of water; ſuch, namely, in which a man's body could eaſily be immerſed: In which manner baptiſm was then performed."

3. Another text, produced in favour of dipping in baptiſm, is *Matt.* iii. 16. *And Jeſus, when he was baptized, went up ſtraightway out of the water.* To which is objected, that "there is no more in the original, than that our Saviour *went up ſtraightway* ἀπὸ, "from the water;" which Greek prepoſition "always naturally ſignifies *from*, but never *out of*, and therefore, this inſtance "can ſtand in no ſtead." But if the prepoſition never ſignifies *out of*, it is ſtrange that our learned tranſlators ſhould ſo render it here, as alſo the *Vulgate Latin, Syriac, Perſic,* and *Ethiopic* verſions; and ſo it is rendered in the New Teſtament in ſeveral places, as in *Mark* xvi. 9. *Luke* iv. 35, 41. *Acts* ii. 9. and xvii. 2. and xxviii. 23. and in others. And, moreover, it ſhould be obſerved, that this prepoſition anſwers to the Hebrew מן *Min*, which ſignifies *out of*, as well as *from*; and which the *Syriac* verſion uſes here: And, as a proof of both, let *Pſalm* xl. 2. be conſulted, and the Septuagint verſion of it, where *David* ſays, the Lord *brought* him *up out of an horrible pit,* ϰ̓ ἀπὸ πηλε ιλυϑ-, *and out of the miry clay.* And, if our Lord came up *out of the water*, it is a clear caſe, that he muſt have been in it; that he went down into it, in order to be baptized; and that he was baptized in it: And, is it reaſonable to think, he ſhould be baptized in the river *Jordan*, in any other way, than by immerſion? See the note of *Piſcator*, upon the preceding text.

4. *Acts* viii. 38, 39. goes in company with the former; *and they went down both into the water—and when they were come up out of the water.* And the following remark is made; "there can be no more proved from this text, than "that *Philip* and the Eunuch went down *to* the water, and came up *from* it. "The prepoſition ἐις, rendered *into*, naturally ſignifies *unto*, and is commonly "ſo uſed in the New Teſtament—and the prepoſition ἐκ, rendered *out of*, properly ſignifies *from*—ſo that there is no evidence from this text, that the "Eunuch was baptized by dipping." Here our author ſeems to have in view, a very falſe piece of criticiſm, frequently uſed upon this text; as if the going down into the water ſignified no more, than going down to the bank of the water, to the water-ſide: And, to ſupport which, his ſenſe of the prepoſition ἐις, which he would have rendered *unto*, is calculated. But, it ſhould be obſerved, that the hiſtorian relates in *ver*. 36. that, before this, *they were come to a certain water*, to the water-ſide; and, therefore, this, their going down, muſt be into it. Wherefore, as it cannot be denied, but that this prepoſition frequently ſignifies

*into,*

*into*, it muſt have this ſignification here; and this determines, and ſettles the ſenſe of the other prepoſition, and ſhews, that that muſt be rendered, as it is, *out of*; ſeeing, whereas they went down into the water, when they came up, it muſt be out of it: All which gives evidence, that the Eunuch was baptized by dipping. *Calvin* thought ſo, who, on the text, has theſe words; " *hic perſpi-* " *cimus*, &c. Here we ſee, what was the manner of baptizing with the antients, " for they plunged the whole body into water."

5. The laſt text, mentioned in the debate, is *Romans* vi. 4. *We are buried with him by baptiſm into death.* Where baptiſm is called a burial; a burial with Chriſt, a repreſentation and reſemblance of his; which it cannot be, unleſs it is adminiſtered by dipping. But this writer obſerves, it is alſo ſaid, *we are baptized into Chriſt's death*; and aſks, " What reſemblance is there in baptiſm to " Chriſt's dying upon the croſs, if we are baptized by dipping? Was there " any thing like dipping in our Saviour's crucifixion?—would you have ſuch " a manner of death reſembled in baptiſm, by drowning men when you baptize " them? And affirms, that this text has no reference at all to the imitation ei- " ther of Chriſt's death or burial, or to any particular mode of adminiſtering " that ordinance; but the ſcope is to ſhew us our obligation, by baptiſm, unto " a conformity to the death and reſurrection of Chriſt, by dying unto ſin, and " riſing again unto newneſs of life." But, we have ſeen already, that there is a reſemblance between the crucifixion and death of Chriſt and baptiſm, as adminiſtered by dipping. The overwhelming ſufferings of Chriſt are fitly ſignified, by a perſon's being plunged into water; and a great likeneſs there is between the burial of Chriſt and baptiſm, as performed by immerſion: And, indeed, there is no other mode of adminiſtering that ordinance, that can repreſent a burial, but immerſion. And be it ſo, that the ſcope of the place is to ſhew us our obligation, by baptiſm, unto a conformity to the death and reſurrection of Chriſt, by dying unto ſin, and riſing again to newneſs of life; then that ordinance ought to be ſo adminiſtered, that it may repreſent unto us, the death and reſurrection of Chriſt, and our dying unto ſin, and riſing unto newneſs of life; which are done, in a moſt lively manner, by an immerſion into water, and an emerſion out of it. And, that there is an alluſion, in this paſſage, to the primitive mode of baptizing by dipping, is acknowledged by many divines and annotators; too many to recite: I will juſt mention two or three. The *Aſſembly of divines*, on this place, ſay, " in this phraſe, the apoſtle ſeemeth " to allude to the ancient manner of baptiſm; which was to *dip* the parties bap- " tized, and, as it were, to *bury* them under the water, for a while; and then " to *draw* them out of it, and *lift* them up, to repreſent the burial of our old " man,

"man, and our refurrection to newnefs of life." Dr *Hammond*'s paraphrafe of the words, is this; "it is a thing, that every chriftian knows, that the immerfion in baptifm, refers to the death of Chrift; the putting the perfon baptized into the water, denotes and proclaims the death and burial of Chrift; and fignifies our undertaking in baptifm, that we will give over all the fins of our former lives (which is our being *buried* together with Chrift, or baptized into his death) that fo we may *live* that regenerate new life (anfwerable to Chrift's refurrection) which confifts in a courfe of all fanctity, a conftant chriftian walk all our days." So *Pifcator*, on the text, "*videtur refpicere ad veterem ritum*, &c. It feems to refpect the antient rite, when, in the whole body, they were plunged into water, and fo were, as if they had been *buried*; and immediately were drawn out again, as out of a grave." But,

*Fourthly*, This writer thinks, it is not probable, from the inftances of adminiftering this ordinance in fcripture, that it was performed by dipping. And,

1. He obferves, "that in *Acts* ii. 41. there were three thoufand baptized in *Jerufalem*, in one day; moft certainly, adds he, towards the clofe of the day; and afks, was there any probability (I had almoft faid poffibility) that they fhould all be baptized by dipping, in fo fhort a time? Or, is it probable that they could fo fuddenly find water fufficient in that city, for the dipping of fuch a multitude; efpecially while they were fo firmly attached to the ceremonial inftitution, which made it unlawful for two perfons to be dipped in the fame veffel of water." To which I reply,

(1.) That though three thoufand were added to the church on one and the fame day, it does not neceffarily follow from the text, that they were all baptized in one day, the words do not oblige to fuch a fenfe; I am indeed willing to allow it, and am of opinion they were baptized in one day; though it does not appear that it was moft certainly at the clofe of the day, as this writer affirms; for it was but the third hour, or nine o'clock in the morning, when *Peter* began his fermon, which does not feem to be a long one; and when that was ended, after fome difcourfe with the converted perfons, and exhortations to them, this ordinance was adminiftered. And if *Auftin*, as we have feen from our hiftorians, could baptize ten thoufand in a fhort winter's day, it need not feem improbable, and much lefs impoffible, that three thoufand fhould be baptized, even at the clofe of a day; when it is confidered that there were twelve apoftles to adminifter baptifm to them, and it was but two hundred and fifty perfons apiece; and befides, there were the feventy difciples, who were adminiftrators of this ordinance; and fuppofing them all employed, they would have no more than fix or feven and thirty perfons apiece to baptize; and as for the difference between administering the ordinance by dipping, and by sprinkling, it is very inconsiderable; for the same form of words must be pronounced in administering it one way as another; and a person being ready, is very near as soon dipped into water, as water can be taken and sprinkled or poured on his face. And,

(2.) Whereas a difficulty is made of finding suddenly water sufficient in the city of *Jerusalem*, for the dipping of such a multitude; it should be observed, that besides baths in private houses, for purification by immersion, in case of menstrua's, gonorrhæa's, &c. there was in the temple an apartment called the dipping-room, for the high-priest to dip himself in, on the day of atonement; and there were ten lavers of brass, each of which held forty baths of water, sufficient for the immersion of the whole body of a man; and there was the molten sea, for the priests to wash in, which was done by immersion; and there were also several pools in the city, as the pools of *Bethesda, Siloam, &c.* where persons bathed or dipped themselves, on certain occasions: So that there were conveniencies enough for baptism by immersion in this place. And,

(3.) As for what this author says, that according to the ceremonial institution, it was unlawful for two persons to be dipped in the same vessel of water: I must own my ignorance of it, till some proof is given; the laver in the temple was in common for the priests.

2. The narrative of *Paul*'s baptism, he says, makes it appear to be administered in his bed-room, *Acts* ix. 9, 18. but that he was in his bed-room when *Ananias* came to him, is not so clear; however, certain it is, that *he arose, and was baptized*. Whether he arose off of his bed, or off of his chair, cannot be said; but be that as it will, had the ordinance been to have been performed by sprinkling or pouring a little water on him, he need not have rose up from either; but he arose, and went either to a bath that might be in *Judas*'s house, fit for such a purpose, or to some certain place without doors, convenient for the administration of the ordinance.

3. The words of the text, *Acts* x. 47. *Can any man forbid water, that these should not be baptized?* he says, seem plainly to contradict the dipping of *Cornelius* and his houshold. But why so? there is nothing in the text contradicts it; for the sense is, " Can any man forbid the use of his river or bath, or what conve- " niency he might have, for the baptizing of those persons?" Which shews, that it required a place of some quantity of water, sufficient for baptizing by immersion; otherwise it would not have been in the power of any man to hinder them having a little water, to be sprinkled or poured on the face. And what follows confirms it; *And he commanded them to be baptized in the name*

*of*

*of the Lord*; besides, the words of the text may be rendered, *Can any man forbid that these should be baptized with water?* See *Erasmus* on the place. Wherefore, what this writer says, that the apostle did not speak of forbidding the water to run in the river, or to remain in any other receptacle or reservoir of water, and therefore must speak of bringing water for their baptism, is very impertinent and ridiculous.

4. He observes, that "the Gaoler and his houshold were baptized in the "dead of the night, in the same hour of his conversion by the earthquake; "and therefore, there was no probability (nor indeed possibility) of their going "to any depth of water for that purpose, *Acts* xvi. 33." But where is the impossibility, or improbability of it? *Grotius* thinks it probable, that there was a pool in the prison, where he washed the stripes of the apostles, and here the ordinance might be administered; but, if not, it is not unreasonable to suppose, that they went out of the prison, to the river near the city, where the oratory, or place of prayer was, *ver.* 13. and there administered the ordinance, and then returned to the prison again, before morning, unobserved by any: compare ver. 30. and 34. together.

And now let it be considered, whether these instances, as our author says, are sufficient to convince an unprejudiced person, that the ordinance was not administered by dipping, in the apostolic times.

5. He concludes, that seeing sprinkling was the greatest purification among the Jews, and the blood of Christ, and the influences of the holy Spirit, are frequently represented by sprinkling, but never by dipping; therefore, it must be the most proper mode of administration. But,

1. It must be denied, that sprinkling was the greatest purification among the Jews; their principal purifications, and which were most frequently used in cases of ceremonial uncleanness, were performed by immersion, and therefore they are called *washings*, or *baptisms*, in *Heb.* ix. 10. and even the purification by the ashes of the red heifer, which this writer instances in, was not performed without bathing the person all over in water, *Numb.* xix. 19. and which was the closing and finishing part of it.

2. It is not fact, that the blood of Christ, and the influences of the Spirit, are never represented by dipping. The bloody sufferings of Christ, and the large abundance of his blood-shed, are called a *baptism*, or dipping, *Luke* xii. 50. And his blood is represented, as a fountain opened to wash in, for sin, and for uncleanness, *Zech.* xiii. 1. And the donation of the Spirit, on the day of *Pentecost*, is also called a *baptism*, or dipping, *Acts* i. 5. But, it is not on those allusive expressions, that we lay the stress of the mode of the administering this

ordinance, though they are only such, this author attempts to mention, in favour of sprinkling.

Wherefore, upon the whole, let the reader judge, which is the most proper and significative rite, used in the administration of the ordinance of baptism; whether immersion, which is the proper and primary sense of the word *baptism*, and is confirmed to be the rite used, by the places in which baptism was administered; and by several scriptural instances and examples of it, as well as by allusive expressions; and which fitly represents the death, burial and resurrection of Christ; or, sprinkling, which the word *baptism* never signifies; and is not confirmed by any of the said ways; nor does it represent any thing for which baptism is administered. Let it be, therefore, seriously considered, what a daring thing it is to introduce into this ordinance subjects which Christ never appointed, and a mode of administering it never used by him or his apostles. In matters of worship, God is a jealous God. The case of *Nadab* and *Abibu* ought to be remembered by us, who offered strange fire, the Lord commanded not. In things relating to religious worship, as this ordinance of baptism is a part of divine worship, we ought to have a direction from God, either a precept, or a precedent: And we ought to keep to the rule, both as to matter and manner, and not dare to innovate in either, lest it should be said to us, *who hath required this at your hands?* and become chargeable with will-worship, and with *teaching for doctrines, the commandments of men.*

THE

# ARGUMENT FROM APOSTOLIC TRADITION,

## IN FAVOUR OF INFANT-BAPTISM,

With OTHERS, advanced in a late Pamphlet, called,

*The Baptism of Infants a reasonable Service*, &c. considered;

AND ALSO

An ANSWER to a *Welch* Clergyman's Twenty Arguments for Infant-Baptism.

To which are added,

The DISSENTERS REASONS for separating from the Church of *England*.

Occasioned by the said WRITER

---

IT is with reluctance I enter again into the controversy about baptism; not from any consciousness either of the badness or weakness of the cause I am engaged in; but partly on account of other work upon my hands, which I chose not to be interrupted in; and partly because I think there has been enough written already, to bring this controversy to an issue; and it is not our fault that it has not been closed long ago; for there has been scarce any thing wrote by us these *fifty* years past, but in our own defence; our Pædobaptist brethren being continually the aggressors, and first movers of the controversy; they seem as if they were not satisfied with what has been done on their side, and therefore are always attempting either to put the controversy upon a new foot, or to throw the old arguments into a new form; and even say the same things over and over again, to make their minds, and the minds of their people easy, if possible. If persons are content to search the scriptures, and form their judgment of this matter by them, there has been enough published on both sides.

the

the question to determine themselves by; and we are willing things should rest here: but this is our case; if we reply to what is written against us, then we are litigious persons, and lovers of controversy; though we only rise up in our own vindication, for which surely we are not to be blamed; and if we make no reply, then what is written is unanswerable by us, and we are triumphed over.

No less than half a dozen pamphlets have been published upon this subject, within a very little time; without any provocation from us, that I know of. Some of them indeed are like mushrooms, that rise up and die almost as soon as they live; it has been the luck of the pamphlet before me, to live a little longer, and which is cried up as an unanswerable one, for no other reason, that I can see, but because it has not yet been answered in form; otherwise the arguments advanced in it, have been answered before it was in being; for there is nothing new throughout the whole of it. Is there any one argument in it, but what has been brought into the controversy before? not one. Is the date of infant-baptism, as it appears from the writings of the ancients, from antiquity, for which this performance is mostly boasted of, carried one year, one month, one day, one hour, or moment higher, than it was before? not one. Is there any one passage of the ancients cited, which has not been produced and been under consideration before? not one. What then has this Gentleman been doing? just nothing at all. However an answer would have been made to him before this time, had not some things in providence prevented. My late worthy friend, the Reverend Mr *Samuel Wilson*, intended to have drawn up one, as he signified to me; for which reason, I did not give myself the trouble to read this pamphlet: His view was first to publish his *Manual*, and then to take this under consideration; but he dying before the publication of the former, prevented his design; nor did he, as I could ever find, leave any materials behind him relating to this affair. Some time after Mr *Killingworth* published an answer to Dr *Foster* on the subject of communion, and added some remarks upon this pamphlet; when I ordered my Bookseller to get me that, and the strictures on it; upon reading of which, I found that Mr *Killingworth* expected a formal answer to it was preparing, and would be published by a Gentleman he represents as the occasion of its being written; which for some time I have been waiting for: but hearing nothing of it, and the boasts of the party increasing, because of no answer, determined me to take it under examination in the manner I have done; but whether after all I am not too *forward*, I cannot tell; but if any thing is preparing or prepared by another hand, I hope what I have written will not hinder the publication of it.

Infant-baptism is sometimes put upon one footing, and sometimes on another; as on the covenant of grace; on circumcision; on the baptism of Jewish proselytes;

lytes; on scripture consequences; and by our author it is rested on *apostolic tradition*. This he says is *an argument of great weight*[a]; and that it is principally for the sake of this, that his performance appears in the world[b]; for which reason, I shall chiefly attend unto it. Whatever weight this argument may be thought to have in the present controversy, it has none in others; not in the controversy with the Papists, nor with the church of *England* about rites and ceremonies, this Gentleman himself being judge; who I understand is the author of *The dissenting Gentleman's answer to Mr White's Three Letters*. In his controversy with him, Christ is the *only* lawgiver and head of the church, and no man upon earth, or body of men, have authority to make laws, or prescribe things in religion, or to set aside, alter or new-make any terms fixed by him; and apostolical authority, or what is directed to by the apostles, as fallible and unassisted men, is no authority at all, nor obligatory as a law on men, they having no dominion over their faith and practice; and the scriptures are the *only*, *common*, *sufficient* and *perfect* rule: but in the controversy about infant-baptism, apostolic tradition is of great weight; if the dispute is about sponsors and the cross in baptism, then fathers and councils stand for nothing; and the testimonies of the antients for these things, though *clear* and *indubitable*, and about the sense of which there is no contest, and are of as *early* antiquity as any thing can be produced for infant-baptism, are not allowed sufficient; but if it is about infant-baptism itself, then fathers and councils are called in, and their testimonies produced, insisted upon, and retained, though they have not one syllable of baptism in them; and have senses affixed to them, strained and forced, contrived to serve an hypothesis, and what the good old fathers never dreamed of; is this fair dealing? can this be said to be *sincerity*, *integrity* and *honesty*? no surely. This Gentleman should know that we, who are called Anabaptists, are Protestants, and the Bible is our religion; and that we reject all pretended apostolic tradition, and every thing that goes under that name, not found in the Bible, as the rule of our faith and practice.

The title of the pamphlet before me is, *The baptism of Infants a reasonable service, founded upon Scripture, and undoubted Apostolic Tradition*; but if it is founded upon scripture, then not upon tradition; and if upon tradition, then not on scripture; if it is a scriptural business, then not a traditional one; and if a traditional one, then not a scriptural one: if it can be proved by scripture, that is enough, it has then no need of tradition; but if it cannot be proved by that, a cart-load of traditions will not support it.—This put me in mind of what I have heard, of a countryman offering to give the Judge a *dozen* reasons why his neighbour could not appear in court; in the *first* place, my Lord, says he,

[a] Reasonable Service, p. 30.     [b] Preface, p 5.

*be is dead*; that is enough, quoth the Judge, I shall spare you the trouble of giving me the rest: so prove but infant-baptism by scripture, and there will be no need of the weighty arguments from tradition. However, by putting the case as it is, we learn that this author by *apostolic tradition*, means *unwritten* apostolic tradition, since he distinguishes it from the scripture; and not apostolic tradition delivered in the scriptures, which is the sense in which sometimes *tradition* is used, both in the word of God [c], and in ancient writers [d]. So we are not at a loss about the sense of it; it is *unwritten*, uninspired apostolic tradition; tradition not *in*, but *out* of the scriptures; not delivered by the apostles in the sacred writings, but by word of mouth to their successors, or to the churches.

It is pretty much that infant-baptism should be called an *undoubted* apostolic tradition, since it has been *doubted* of by some learned Pædobaptists themselves; nay, some have affirmed that it is not observed by them as an apostolic tradition, particularly *Curcellæus* [e], and who gives a very good reason for it: his words are these; "Pædobaptism was unknown in the two first ages after Christ; in the third and fourth it was approved by a few; at length, in the fifth and following ages it began to obtain in divers places; and therefore this rite is indeed observed by us as an *ancient custom*, but not as an *apostolic tradition*." Bishop *Taylor* [f] calls it a *pretended* apostolical tradition; and says, that the tradition cannot be proved to be apostolical, we have very good evidence from antiquity. Since then the Pædobaptists disagree about this point among themselves, as well as it is called in question and contested by others; one would think, this writer should not be so confident as to call it an *undoubted* apostolic tradition.

Besides, apostolic tradition, at most and best, is a very precarious and uncertain thing, and not to be depended on; we have a famous instance of this, in the controversy that arose in the second century, about the time of keeping *Easter*; whether it should be observed on the 14th day of the first moon, let it fall on what day of the week it would, or on the Sunday following; the former was observed by the churches of *Asia*, and the latter by the church of *Rome*; both pleaded the custom and usage of their predecessors, and even ancient apostolic tradition [g]; the Asiatic churches said, they had it by tradition from *Philip* and *John*; the Roman church from *Peter* and *Paul*; but not being able to settle this point, which was in the right, *Victor*, the then bishop of *Rome*, excommunicated

---

[c] 1 Cor. xv. 3. 2 Thes. ii. 15. [d] Irenæus adv. Hæres. l. 3. c. 4. Cyprian. Ep. 63. ad Cæcilium, p. 146. Athanas. ad Adelph. p. 333. [e] Institut. Rel. Christ. l. 1. c. 12. § 4. p. 25. [f] Of the liberty of Prophesying, p. 320, 321. Ed. 3d.
[g] Euseb. Eccl. Hist. l. 5. c. 23—25. Socrat. Eccl. Hist. l. 5. c. 22. p 285.

nicated the other churches that would not fall in with the practice of him and his church; this was in the year 196; and even before this, in the year 157, this same controversy was on foot; and *Polycarp* bishop of *Smyrna*, who had been a hearer and disciple of the apostle *John*, made a journey to *Rome*, and conversed with *Anicetus* bishop of that place, about this matter; they talked it over candidly, parted friendly, but without convincing each other, both retaining their former customs and tradition [h]; if now it was so difficult a thing to fix a tradition, or settle what was an apostolic tradition, about the middle of the second century, fifty or sixty years after the death of the apostle *John*, and when some of the immediate successors of the apostles were living; what judgment can we form of apostolic traditions in the eighteenth century?

Moreover, it is *doubtful* whether there ever was any such thing as apostolic tradition; or that ever any thing was delivered by the apostles to their successors, or to the churches, to be observed by them, which was not delivered in the sacred writings; and I defy this Gentleman, and demand of him to give me one single instance of any apostolic tradition of this nature; and if no such instance can be given, it is in vain to talk of *undoubted apostolic tradition*; and upon what a miserable foundation must infant-baptism stand, that rests upon this? unwritten apostolic tradition is a *non-entity*, as the learned *Alting* [i] calls it; it is a mere chimæra; a refuge of heretics formerly, and of papists now; a favourite argument of theirs, to prove by it what they please.

But be it so, that there is such a thing as *apostolic tradition*; let it be proved that infant-baptism is such; let the apostles be pointed out that delivered it. Were they all the apostles or only some of them that delivered it? let them be named who they were, and to whom they delivered it, and when, and where. The apostles *Peter* and *Paul*, who were, the one the apostle of the circumcision, and the other the apostle of the uncircumcision, one would think, should be the most likely to hand down this tradition; the one to the christian Jews, and the other to the christian Gentiles; or however, to their successors or companions: but is there any proof or evidence that they did so? none at all; though there are writings of persons extant that lived in their times. If *Clemens Romanus* was a successor of *Peter*, as the papists say, it might have been expected, that it would have been delivered to him, and he would have published it; but there is not a word of it in his epistles still in being. *Barnabas* was a companion of the apostle *Paul*; and had it been a tradition of his, it might be justly thought, it would be met with in an epistle of his now extant; but there is not the least hint of it in it, but on the contrary, several passages in favour of be-
lievers-

[h] Euseb. Ib. l. 4. c. 14. See Bower's Lives of the Popes, vol. I. p 27, 37.
[i] Loc. Commun. p. 287.

## THE ARGUMENT FROM APOSTOLIC TRADITION,

lievers-baptism. Perhaps, as *John* was the last of the apostles, and outlived them all, it was left with him to transmit it to others; and had this been the case, it might have been hoped it would have been found in the writings of *Polycarp*, a hearer and disciple of the apostle *John*; but not a syllable of it is to be found in him. Nay *Papias*, bishop of *Hierapolis*, one that was a hearer of *John* the elder of *Ephesus*, and a companion of *Polycarp*, and who had conversed with those who were familiar with the apostles, and made it his business to pick up sayings and facts, said or done by the apostles, not recorded in scripture, has not a word of this; which *childish* business would have been a very pretty thing for that weak-headed man, as *Eusebius*[k] represents him, to have gone prattling about with; here is an apostolic tradition then, which no body knows by whom it was delivered, nor to whom, nor when and where: the companions and successors of the apostles say nothing of it. The [l] Jews talk of a Mosaic tradition and oral law, delivered from one to another for several thousand years running; they tell you by whom it was first given and received; and can name the persons to whom it was transmitted in succeeding ages; this is something to the purpose; this is doing business roundly; but here is a tradition no body can tell from whence it comes, nor who received it, and handed it down; for there is not the least mention of it, nor any pretended to in the first century or apostolic age. But let us attend to what evidence is given of it, in the next or second century.

Two passages are produced out of the writers of this age, to prove this *un-doubted* apostolic tradition; the one out of *Justin Martyr*; the other out of *Irenæus*. That from *Justin* is as follows [m]; " several persons among us, men " and women, of sixty and seventy years of age, οι εκ παιδων εμαθητευθησαν τω Χειςω, " who from their childhood were *instructed in Christ*, remain incorrupt:" for so the phrase on which the whole depends should be rendered, and not *discipled* or *proselyted to Christ*; which rendering of the words, as it is unjustifiable, so it would never have been thought of, had it not been to serve a turn; and is not agreeable to *Justin*'s use of the word, who frequently makes use of it in the sense of instruction and teaching; as when he speaks of persons being μαθητευθηναι, *instructed* into divine doctrines [n]; and of others being μαθητευομενους, *instructed* in the name (person or doctrine) of Christ, and leaving the way of error [o]; and of Christ's sending his disciples to the Gentiles, who by them εμαθητευσαν, *instructed* them [p]: nor should εκ παιδων, be rendered *in infancy*, but *from childhood*; and is a phrase of the same signification with that in 2 *Tim*. iii. 15. where *Timothy* is said απο βρεφους, *from a child* to know the holy scriptures; and *Justin*'s sense is, that

---

[k] Euseb. ib. l. 3. c. 39.
[n] Apolog. 1. p. 43.
[l] Pirke Abot. c. 1. §. 1.
[o] Dialog. cum Tryph. p. 258.
[m] Apolog. 2. p. 62.
[p] Ib. p. 272.

that notwithstanding the strict and severe commands of Christ in *Matthew* v. 28, 29, 30, 44. as they might seem to be, and which he cites; yet there were several persons of the age he mentions, then living, who had been instructed in the person, offices, and doctrines of Christ, or had been trained up in the christian religion from their childhood, who had persevered hitherto, and were incorrupt in their practices, and in their principles; and which is no other than a verification of what the wise man observes, *Prov.* xxii. 6. *Train up a child in the way he should go, and when he is old, he will not depart from it:* and we are able in our day, to point out persons of an age that *Justin* mentions, who have been trained up in the christian religion from their childhood; and who in riper years have made a public profession of it, and have held fast their profession without wavering, and lived unblemished lives and conversations; and yet never were baptized in their infancy. Behold, here the first proof and evidence of infant-baptism being an *undoubted apostolic tradition*; when there is not a word of baptism in it, much less of infant-baptism; nor any hint of it, or reference unto it. Can the most sanguine Pædobaptist sit down, and in cool reflection conclude, upon reading and considering this passage, that it proves infant-baptism to be an *undoubted apostolic tradition?* surely he cannot.

The other passage is out of *Irenæus,* and stands thus[q]; " He (Christ) came " to save all; all I say, qui per eum renascuntur in Deum, *who by him are born* " *again unto God,* infants, and little ones, and children, and young men, and " old men." For so the words are to be rendered, and not *baptized unto God*; for the word *renascor* is never used by *Irenæus,* or rather by his translator, in such a sense; nor had it as yet obtained among the ancients to use the words *regenerated* and *regeneration,* for *baptized* and *baptism.* Likewise, it is certain that *Irenæus* speaks elsewhere of regeneration as distinct from baptism, as an inward spiritual work, agreeable to the scriptures; which never speak of it but as such, no not in *John* iii. 5. *Tit.* iii. 5. And what reason can there be to depart from the literal and scriptural sense of the word, and even the sense which *Irenæus* uses it in; and especially, since infants are capable of regeneration in such a sense of it? besides, to understand *Irenæus* as speaking of baptism, is to make him at least to suggest a doctrine which is absolutely false; as if Christ came to save all and only such, who are baptized unto God; when it is certain, he came to save the Old-Testament-saints, who never were baptized, as well as New-Testament-saints; and no doubt many now are saved by him, who never were baptized with water at all: and on the other hand, nothing is more true than that he came to save all and only those, who are regenerated by the Spirit and grace of God, of whatsoever age they be. And after all, when it is observed

[q] Adv. Hæref. l. 3. c. 39.

served that the chapter out of which this paſſage is taken, is thought by ſome learned men to be none of *Irenæus*'s, but a ſpurious piece; and if it is his, it is only a tranſlation, as almoſt all his works be, and a very fooliſh, uncouth and barbarous one, as learned men obſerve; ſo that it is not certain that theſe are his words, or are a true tranſlation of them; what wiſe and conſiderate man will ſay, that this is a proof of infant-baptiſm being an *undoubted apoſtolic tradition*? ſeeing the paſſage is ſo much conteſted, and ſo much is to be ſaid againſt it; ſeeing, at moſt and beſt, the ſenſe of it is doubtful; and ſeeing it is certain that *Irenæus* uſes the word *regeneration* in a different ſenſe from baptiſm [r]; who can be ſure he uſes it of baptiſm here? Upon the whole, what thoughtful man will aaffirm from hence, that infant-baptiſm is an *undoubted* apoſtolic tradition? And ſeeing theſe two teſtimonies are the only ones produced in favour of infant-baptiſm in the ſecond century; and the latter Dr *Wall* [s] confeſſes, "is the firſt "expreſs mention that we have met with of infants baptized;" though there is no mention at all made of it in it, any more than in the former; he muſt have a ſtrong faith to believe, and a good aſſurance upon ſuch evidence to aſſert [t], " that the baptiſm of infants was the *undoubted* practice of the chriſtian " church in its pureſt and firſt ages; the ages immediately ſucceeding the " apoſtles." Let us now proceed to the third century.

*Tertullian* is the firſt man that ever made mention of infant-baptiſm, that we know of; and as he was the firſt that ſpoke of it, he at the ſame time ſpoke againſt it, diſſuaded from it, and adviſed to defer it; and though he was quite *ſingular*, as our author ſays, in this his advice; it ſhould be obſerved, that he is alſo quite *ſingular* in his mention of the thing itſelf; there being no writings of any cotemporary of his extant, from which we might learn their ſenſe of this affair. We allow that infant-baptiſm was moved in the third century; that it then began to be talked of, and became matter of debate, and might be prac-tiſed in the African churches, where it was firſt moved. We do not deny the *probability* of the practice of it then, though the *certainty* of it does not appear; it is probable it might be practiſed, but it is not certain it was; as yet it has not been proved. Now here we ſtick, by this we abide, that there is no mention made of it in any authentic writer before *Tertullian*'s time. And this writer himſelf elſewhere [u] obſerves, that " by *his* time, it is well known, a great va-" riety of ſuperſtitious, and ridiculous, and fooliſh rites were brought into the " church." The date of infant-baptiſm cannot, we apprehend, be carried higher than his time; and we require of any of our learned Pædobaptiſt brethren,

---

[r] Ib. l. 1. c 18. & l. 4. c. 59. & l. 5. c. 15.
[s] Hiſtory of Infant baptiſm. p. 1. ch. 3. §. 6.     [t] Reaſonable Service, p. 30.
[u] The Diſſenting Gentleman's Third Letter, &c. p. 32.

thren, to produce a single passage out of any authentic writer before *Tertullian*, in which infant-baptism is expresly mentioned, or clearly hinted at, or plainly supposed, or manifestly referred unto. This being the case, as we own it began in this century, and might be practised by some, it might be needless in a good measure to consider after-testimonies; however, I shall not think fit wholly to neglect them.

*Origen* is next quoted, and *three* passages out of him; shewing that the baptism of infants is a tradition of the apostles, and an usage of the church for the remission of sins; but it should be observed, that these quotations are not from the Greek of *Origen*; he wrote much in that language, and there is much still extant in it; and yet nothing is produced from thence, that can fairly be construed in favour of infant-baptism; though many things may be observed from thence, in favour of adult-baptism. The three passages are quoted out of some Latin translations, greatly interpolated, and not to be depended on. His Homilies on *Leviticus*, and exposition of the epistle to the *Romans*, out of which *two* of them are taken, are translated by *Ruffinus*; who with the former, he himself owns, he used much freedom, and added much, and took such a liberty in both of adding, taking away, and changing, that, as *Erasmus* says [w], whoever reads these pieces, it is uncertain whether he reads *Origen* or *Ruffinus*; and *Vossius* observes [x], that the former of these was interpolated by *Ruffinus*, and thinks therefore, that the passage cited was of the greater authority against the *Pelagians*, because *Ruffinus* was inclined to them. The Homilies on *Luke*, out of which is the other passage, were translated by *Jerom*, of whom *Du Pin* says [y], that "his "versions are not more exact than *Ruffinus*'s." Now both these lived at the latter end of the fourth century, and it looks very probable, that these very passages, are additions, or interpolations of these men, since the language agrees with those times, and no other; for no cotemporary of *Origen*'s, nor any writer before him or after him, until the times of *Ruffinus*, *Jerom* and *Austin*, speak of infant-baptism as an usage of the church, or an apostolical tradition; in short, as bishop *Taylor* observes [z], "a tradition apostolical, if it be not consigned with a fuller "testimony than of one person (*Origen*,) whom all after-ages have condemned "of many errors, will obtain so little reputation amongst those, who know that "things have upon greater authority pretended to derive from the apostles, and "yet falsly; that it will be a great argument, that he is credulous, and weak, "that shall be determined by so weak a probation, in a matter of so great con- "cernment."

*Cyprian.*

---

[w] In Rivet. critici sacri, l. 2. c. 12. p. 202.  [x] Hist. Pelag. par. 1. l. 2. p. 147.
[y] Hist. Eccles. vol. I. p. 132.  [z] Liberty of Prophesying, p. 320.

*Cyprian*, with his council of sixty-six bishops, are brought as witnesses of infant-baptism, a little after the middle of the third century. We allow that as infant-baptism was moved for in *Tertullian*'s time, so it obtained in the *African* churches in *Cyprian*'s time; but then by *Fidus* the country bishop, applying to the council to have a doubt resolved, whether it was lawful to baptize infants until they were eight days old; it appears to be a novel practice; and that as yet it was undetermined, by council or custom, when they were to be baptized, whether as soon as born, or on the eighth day, or whether it was to be left to every one's liberty: and it should also be observed, that in this age, infant communion was practised as well as infant-baptism; and very likely both began together, as it is but reasonable, that if the one be admitted, the other should. But of this more hereafter.

The *Clementine Constitutions*, as they are called, are next produced, as enjoining infant-baptism; but why does this Gentleman call them the *Clementine Constitutions*, unless he is of opinion, and which he suggests by this title of them, that *Clemens Romanus* was the compiler of them from the mouths of the apostles? and if so, he might have placed the passage out of them with greater advantage, at the head of his testimonies; but he must know, that these writings are condemned as spurious, by almost all learned men, excepting Mr *Whiston*; and were not heard of till the times of *Epiphanius*, in the latter end of the fourth century, if so soon: and it should be observed, that these same *Constitutions*, which direct to the baptizing of infants, injoin the use of godfathers in baptism; the form of renouncing the devil and all his works; the consecration of the water; trine immersion; the use of oil, and baptizing fasting; crossing with the sign of the cross in the forehead; keeping the day of Christ's nativity, *Epiphany*, the *Quadragesima* or *Lent*; the feast of the passover, and the festivals of the apostles; fasting on the fourth and sixth days of the week; praying for saints departed; singing for the dead, and honouring their relicks; with many other things foreign enough from the simplicity of the apostolic doctrine and practice. A testimony from such a work, can be of very little credit to the cause of infant-baptism.

And now we are come to a very remarkable and decisive testimony, as it is called, from the writings of *Austin* and *Pelagius*; the sum of which is, that there being a controversy between these two persons about original sin, the latter, who denied it, was pressed by the former, with an argument taken from the baptism of infants for the remission of sins; with which *Pelagius* seemed exceedingly embarassed, when it greatly concerned him to deny it if he could; and had it been an innovation, so acute, learned, and sagacious a man as he was, would have discovered it; but on the contrary, when he was charged with a denial of it as the consequence of his opinion, he warmly disclaims it, and complains of a slander; and adds, that he never heard that even any impious heretic denied
it,

it, or refused it to infants; and the same says *Austin*, that it never was denied by any man, catholic or heretic, and was the constant usage of the church; for all which vouchers are produced. To which may be replied,

1. However embarassed *Pelagius* might be with the argument, it did not lead to a controversy about the subject, but the end of baptism, and about the latter, and not the former was the dispute; nor was he under so great a temptation, and much less necessity, nor did it so greatly concern him to deny the baptism of infants, on account of his tenet; since he was able upon his principles to point out other ends of their baptism, than that of remission of sin; and particularly, their receiving and enjoying the kingdom of heaven; and as a late writer [*] observes, this proposition " *baptism ought to be administered to* " *children, as well as to the adult*; was not inconsistent with, nor repugnant to " his doctrine; for though he denied original sin, he allowed baptism to be " administered even to children, but only for their sanctification."

2. It should be known and observed, that we have no writings of *Pelagius* extant, at least under his name, only some passages quoted by his adversaries, by which we can judge what were his sentiments about infant baptism; and it is well known that a man's words often are misquoted, or misunderstood, or misrepresented by an adversary; I will not say that this is the case of *Pelagius*; I would hope better things of his adversaries, particularly *Austin*, and that he has been used fairly; I am willing to allow his authorities, though it would have been a greater satisfaction to have had these things from himself, and not at second hand. Nor,

3. Would I detract from the character of *Pelagius*, or call in question his acuteness, sagacity, and learning; yet two doctors of the age in which he lived, are divided about him in this respect, *Austin* and *Jerom*; the former speaks of him as a very considerable man, and of great penetration; but the latter, as if he had no genius, and but very little knowledge [b]; it must be owned, that *Austin* was the most candid man, and *Jerom* a sour one, who seldom spoke well of those he opposed, though he was a man of the greatest learning, and so the best judge of it: but however acute, learned, and sagacious *Pelagius* was, yet falling in with the stream of the times, and not seeing himself concerned about the subject, but the end of baptism, might give himself no trouble to inquire into the rise of it; but take it for granted, as *Austin* did; who perhaps was as acute, learned and sagacious as he, that it had been the constant usage of the church, and an apostolic tradition; as he had many other things, in which he was mistaken, as will soon appear.

4. Though

---

[*] Bower's History of Popes, vol. I. p. 339.
[b] Bower ibid. p. 329, c. 330.

## THE ARGUMENT FROM APOSTOLIC TRADITION,

4. Though *Pelagius* complained that he was defamed, and slandered by some who charged him with denying infant-baptism; yet this, *Austin* observes, was only a shift of his, in order to invert the state of the question, that he might more easily answer to what was objected to him, and preserve his own opinion. And certain it is, according to *Austin*[c], that the Pelagians did deny baptism to some infants, even to the infants of believers, and that for this reason, because they were *holy*; what others made a reason for it, they make a reason against it.

5. *Pelagius* says no such thing, that he never heard, no not even any impious heretic, who denied baptism to infants. His words indeed are[d], *nunquam se vel impium aliquem hæreticum audisse, qui hoc,* quod proposuit, *de parvulis diceret*; " that he never heard, no not any impious heretic, that would say concerning infants, what he had proposed or mentioned:" the sense depends upon the meaning of the phrase, *quod proposuit*, " what he had proposed or mentioned," of whom, and what that is to be understood; whether of *Austin*, and the state of the case as proposed and set down by him; so our author seems to understand it, since by way of explanation, he adds, *viz.* "that unbaptized infants are not liable to the condemnation of the first man; and that they are not to be cleansed by the regeneration of baptism:" but this gentleman has not put it as *Austin* has stated it, which is thus; "it is objected to them (the Pelagians) that they will not own that unbaptized infants are liable to the condemnation of the first man; *& in eos transisse originale peccatum regeneratione purgandum,* and that original sin has passed upon them to be cleansed by regeneration:" and according to this sense the meaning cannot be, that he never heard that any heretic denied baptism to infants; but either that he never heard that any one should say, that unbaptized infants are not liable to the condemnation of the first man, and that original sin had not passed upon them to be cleansed by regeneration; but then this is to bring the wicked heretics as witnesses against himself, and to make himself worse than they: or the meaning is, that he never heard that any of them should say, that unbaptized infants are liable to the condemnation of the first man, and that original sin has passed upon them to be cleansed by regeneration, which is most likely: but then this makes rather against, than for the thing for which it is brought; since it makes the heretic as never saying that infants stood in need of being cleansed by baptism: or else, *quod proposuit*, " what he had proposed or mentioned," refers to *Pelagius*, and to the state of the question as he had put it; representing that he was charged with promising the kingdom of heaven to some, without the redemption of Christ; and of this he might say, he never heard the most impious heretic to say; and this seems to be the sense by what he subjoins; "for who is so ignorant of what is read

in

---
[c] De peccator. merit. & remiss. l. 2. c. 25.  [d] In Aug. de peccator. originali, l. 2. c. 18.

" in the gospel, not only as to attempt to affirm it, but even lightly mention
" it, or even imagine it? Moreover, who so impious that would exclude in-
" fants from the kingdom of heaven, *dum eos baptizari & in Christo renasci pu-*
" *tat?* whilst he thinks, or is of opinion that they are baptized and regene-
" rated in Christ?" for so it is in my edition [e] of *Austin*; *putat*, and not *vetat*,
as Dr *Wall* quotes it; and after him this Gentleman: and *Pelagius* further adds,
" who so impious as to forbid to an infant, of whatsoever age, the common re-
" demption of mankind?" but this, *Austin* says, like the rest is ambiguous;
what redemption he means, whether from bad to good, or from good to better:
now take the words which way you will, they cannot be made to say, that he
had never heard that any heretic denied baptism to infants, but that they denied
the kingdom of heaven to them; and indeed every one must allow, whoever is
of that opinion, that infants are by baptism really regenerated in Christ; which
was the prevailing notion of those times, and the light in which it is put; that
they must belong to the kingdom of heaven, and share in the common redemption by Christ.

6. *Austin* himself does not say, that he had never heard or read of any catholic, heretic, or schismatic, that denied infant-baptism; he could never say any
such thing; he must know, that *Tertullian* had opposed it; and he himself was
at the council of *Carthage*, and there presided, and was at the making of that
canon which runs thus; "also it is our pleasure, that whoever denies that
" new-born infants are to be baptized — let him be anathema:" but to what
purpose was this canon made, if he and his brethren knew of none that denied
infant-baptism? To say that this respects some people, who were still of the
same opinion with *Fidus*, an African bishop, that lived 150 years before this
time, that infants were not to be baptized until they were eight days old, is an
idle notion of Dr *Wall* [f]: can any man in his senses think, that a council, consisting of all the bishops in *Africa*, should agree to *anathematize* their own brethren, who were in the same opinion and practice of infant-baptism with themselves; only they thought it should not be administered to them as soon as born,
but at eight days old? *Credat Judæus Apella*, believe it who will; he is capable
of believing any thing, that can believe this. *Austin* himself makes mention of
some that argued against it, after this manner [g]; "men are used to ask this ques-
" tion, says he, of what profit is the sacrament of christian baptism to infants,
" seeing when they have received it, for the most part they die before they know
" any thing of it?" and as before observed, he brings in the Pelagians [h] saying,

[e] Ed. Antwerp. by Plantine, 1576.  
[g] De libero Arbitrio, l. 3. c. 23.  
[f] Hist. of Infant-baptism. part I. ch. 19 §. 37.  
[h] De Peccator. n erit. l. 2. c. 25.

that the infants of believers ought not to be baptized: and so *Jerom*[1], who was a cotemporary of his, speaks of some christians, *qui dare noluerint baptisma*, " who " refused to give baptism to their children;" so that though infant-baptism greatly obtained in those times, yet it was not so general as this author represents it. *Austin* therefore could not say what he is made to say: but what then does he say, that he never remembered to have read in any catholic, heretic, or schismatic writer? why, " that infants were not to be baptized, that they might " receive the remission of sins, but that they might be sanctified in Christ:" it is of this the words are spoken, which our author has quoted, but are not to be found in the place he refers to; having through inadvertence mistaken Dr *Wall*, from whom I perceive he has taken this, and other things. This, and not infant-baptism itself, was what was transiently talked of at *Carthage*, and cursorily heard by *Austin* some little time ago, when he was there: this was the novelty he was startled at, but did not think it seasonable to enter into a debate about it then, and so forgot it: for surely it will not be said, that it was the denial of infant-baptism that was defended with so much warmth against the church, as he says this was; and was committed to memory in writing; and the brethren were obliged to ask their advice about it; and they were obliged to dispute and write against; for this would prove the very reverse of what this gentleman produces it for. Now, though *Austin* could not say that he never remembered to have heard or read of any catholic, schismatic, or heretic, that denied infant-baptism; yet he might say he never remembered to have heard or read of any that owned and practised infant-baptism, but who allowed it to be for the remission of sin; which is widely different from the former: it is one thing what *Austin* says, and another, what may be thought to be the consequence of his so saying; and in the same sense are we to understand him, when he says [k], " and this the church has *always* had, has *always* held." What? why, that infants are diseased through *Adam*; and stand in need of a physician; and are brought to the church to be healed. It was the doctrine of original sin, and the baptism of infants for the remission of it, he speaks of in these passages; it is true indeed, he took infant-baptism to be an ancient and constant usage of the church and an apostolic tradition [l]; which perhaps he had taken up from the Latin translations of *Origen* by *Jerom* and *Ruffinus* before-mentioned; since no other ecclesiastical writer speaks of it as such, before those times: but in this he was deceived and mistaken, as he was in other things which he took for apostolic traditions; which ought to be equally received as this, by those who are influenced by his authority; and indeed every *honest* man that receives infant-baptism upon

the

---

[1] Ep. ad Lætam, t. I. fol. 19. M.     [k] De verbis Apostoli, serm 10. c. 2.
[l] De Genesi, l. 10. c. 22. De baptismo. contr. Donat. l. 4. c. 23, 24.

the foot of tradition, ought to receive every thing else upon the same foot, of which there is equally as *full*, and as *early* evidence of apostolic tradition, as of this: let it then be observed,

1. That the same *Austin* that asserts infant-baptism to be an apostolic tradition, affirms infant-communion to be so likewise, as Bishop *Taylor* [m] observes; and thus *Austin* says [n], "if they pay any regard to the apostolic authority, or rather to the Lord and Master of the apostles, who says, that they have no "life in themselves, *unless they eat the flesh of the son of man, and drink his blood*, "which they cannot do unless baptized; will sometimes own that unbaptized "infants have not life;"—and a little after, "no man that remembers that he "is a christian, and of the catholic faith, denies or doubts that infants, not hav- "ing the grace of regeneration in Christ, and without eating his flesh, and drink- "ing his blood, have no life in them; but are hereby liable to everlasting pu- "nishment;" by which he means the two sacraments of baptism, and the Lord's supper; the necessity of both which to eternal life he founded upon a mistaken sense of *John* iii. 5. and vi. 53. as appears from what he elsewhere says [o]; where having mentioned the first of those passages, he cites the latter, and adds; "let "us hear the Lord, I say, not indeed speaking this of the sacrament of the holy "laver, but of the sacrament of the holy table; whither none rightly come, "unless baptized. *Except ye eat my flesh, and drink my blood, ye shall have no* "*life in you*; what do we seek for further? what can be said in answer to this, "unless one would set himself obstinately against clear and invincible truth? "will any one dare to say this, that this passage does not belong to infants; and "that they can have life in themselves, without partaking of his body and blood?" And of the necessity of this, as well as of baptism to eternal life, he says [p] the *African* christians took to be an ancient and apostolic tradition.

*Innocent* the first, his cotemporary, was also of the same mind; and the giving of the eucharist to infants generally obtained; and it continued six hundred years after, until transubstantiation took place; and is continued to this day in the Greek church: and if we look back to the times before *Austin*, we shall find that it was not only the opinion of *Cyprian*, but was practised in his time; he tells [q] a story which he himself was a witness of; how that " a little child being "left in a fright by its parents with a nurse, she carried the child to the magis- "trates, who had it to an idol's sacrifice; where because the child could not "eat flesh, they gave it bread soaked in wine: some time after, the mother "had her child again; which not being able to relate to her what had passed,

[m] Liberty of Prophesying, p. 119.
[o] De Peccator. merit. & remiss. l. 1. c. 20.
[q] Cyprian de lapsis, p. 244.
[n] Ep. 106. Bonifacio, contr. Pelag.
[p] Ibid. c. 24.

"it was brought by its parent to the place where *Cyprian* and the church were celebrating the Lord's-fupper; and where it fhrieked, and was dreadfully diftreffed; and when the cup was offered it in its turn by the deacon, it fhut its lips againft it; who forced the wine down its throat; upon which it fobbed, and threw it up again." Now here is a plain inftance of infant-communion in the third century; and we defy any one to give a more early inftance, or an inftance fo early, of infant-baptifm: it is highly probable that infant-baptifm was now practifed; and that this very child was baptized, or otherwife it would not have been admitted to the Lord's-fupper; and it is reafonable to fuppofe, they both began together; yet no inftance can be given of infant-baptifm, fo early as of infant-communion; wherefore whoever thinks himfelf obliged to receive the one upon fuch evidence and authority, ought to receive the other; the one has as good a claim to apoftolic authority and tradition, as the other has.

2. The fign of the crofs in baptifm was ufed by the ancients, and pleaded for as an apoftolic tradition. *Bafil*, who lived in the fourth century obferves [r], that fome things they had from fcripture; and others from apoftolic tradition, of which he gives inftances; and, fays he, "becaufe this is the firft and moft common, I will mention it in the firft place; as that we *fign with the fign of the crofs* thofe who place their hope in Chrift; and then afks who taught this in fcripture?" *Chryfoftom*, who lived in the fame age, manifeftly refers to it, when he fays [s], "how can you think it fitting for the minifter to make *the fign on its* (the child's) *forehead*, where you have befmeared it with the dirt?" which *Cyril* [t] calls the *royal feal* upon the forehead.

*Cyprian* in the middle of the third century relates the cuftom of his times [v]; "what is now alfo in ufe among us is, that thofe who are baptized, are offered to the governors of the church; and through our prayers and impofition of hands, they obtain the holy Spirit, and are made compleat *fignaculo Dominico*, with the feal of the Lord:" and in another place [w] he fays, "they only can efcape, who are regenerated and *figned* with the *fign of Chrift*." And *Tertullian*, in the beginning of the fame century, fpeaking of baptifm fays [x], "the flefh is wafhed, that the foul may be unfpotted; the flefh is anointed, that the foul may be confecrated; *caro fignatur*, "the flefh is figned," that the foul alfo may be fortified." Now this ufe of the crofs in baptifm, was as early as any inftance of infant-baptifm that can be produced; higher than *Tertullian's*

---

[r] Bafil. de Spiritu Sanct. c. 27.     [s] Homil. 12. in 1 Ep. ad Corinth.
[t] Catechef 12. §. 4.     [v] Ep. 73. ad Jubajanum. p. 184.     [w] Ad. Demetrian. prope finem.
[x] De refurrectione carnis. c. 8.

*tullian*'s time it cannot be carried: what *partiality* then is it, I know to whom I speak, to admit the one upon the foot of tradition, and reject the other? The same *Tertullian*[y] also speaks of *sponsores*, sponsors, or godfathers, in baptism; which this writer himself has mentioned, and thus renders; "what occasion is "there—except in cases of necessity, that the sponsors or *godfathers* be brought "into danger;" not to take notice of the *Clementine Constitutions*, as our author calls them, which enjoin the use of them; and which appear to be as early as infant-baptism itself; and indeed it is but reasonable that if infants are baptized, there should be sponsors or sureties for them.

3. The form of "renouncing the devil and all his works," used in baptism, is also by *Basil*[z] represented as an apostolic tradition; for having mentioned several rites in baptism, received upon the same foot, he adds; "and the rest "of what is done in baptism, as to renounce the devil and his angels, from what "scripture have we it? is it not from this private and secret tradition?" *Origen* before the middle of the third century relates the usage of his times[a], "let every "one of the faithful remember when he first came to the waters of baptism; when "he received the first seals of faith, and came to the fountain of salvation; what "words there he then used; and what he denounced to the devil, *non se usurum* "*pompis ejus*, "that he would not use his *pomps*, nor his *works*, nor any of his "service, nor obey his pleasures:" and *Tertullian*[b] before him; "when we "enter into the water, we profess the faith of Christ, in the words of his law; "we protest with our mouth that *we renounce the devil, and his pomp, and his* "*angels*;" and in another place[c], in proof of unwritten tradition, and that it ought to be allowed of in some cases, he says; "to begin with baptism; when "we come to the water, we do there, and sometimes in the congregation under "the hand of the pastor, protest that we *renounce* the devil, and his pomp, and "angels; and then we are thrice immersed; answering something more than "the Lord has enjoined in the gospel:" now this is as early as any thing can be produced in favour of infant-baptism.

4. Exorcisms and exsufflations are represented by *Austin*[d], as rites in baptism, *priscæ traditionis*, "of ancient tradition," as used by the church every where, throughout the whole world. He frequently presses the Pelagians with the argument taken from thence, and suggests, that they were pinched with it, and knew not how to answer it; he observes, that things the most impious and absurd, were the consequences of their principles, and among the rest these[e]: "that "they (infants) are baptized into a Saviour, but not saved; redeemed by a deli-
"verer

---

[y] De Baptismo. c. 18.   [z] Ut supra.   [a] Homil. 12. in Numeros, fol. 114. D.
[b] De spectaculis, c. 4.   [c] De corona, c. 3.
[d] De peccato originali, l. 2. c. 40. de nupt. & concup. l. 1. c. 20. & l. 2. c. 18.
[e] Contr. Julian. l. 3. c. 5.

verer, but not delivered; washed in the laver of regeneration, but not washed from any thing; exorcised and exsufflated, but not freed from the power of darkness:" and elsewhere he says [f], that "notwithstanding their craftiness, they know not what answer to make to this, *that infants are exorcised and exsufflated*; for this, without doubt, is done in mere show, if the devil has no power over them; but if he has power over them, and therefore are not exorcised and exsufflated in mere show, by what has the prince of sinners power over them, but by sin?" And *Gregory Nazianzen* before him, as he exhorts to confession of sin in baptism, so to exorcism; "do not refuse, says he [g], the medicine of exorcism—for that is the trial of sincerity, with respect to that grace (baptism)." And says *Optatus* of *Milevis* [h], "every man that is born, though born of christian parents, cannot be without the spirit of the world, which must be excluded and separated from him, before the salutary laver; this exorcism effects, by which the unclean spirit is driven away, and is caused to flee to desert places." *Cyprian*, in the third century, speaking of the efficacy of baptism to destroy the power of Satan, relates what was done in his days [i]; "that by the exorcist the devil was buffeted, distressed, and tortured, with an human voice, and by a divine power." And *Cornelius* bishop of *Rome*, a cotemporary of his, makes mention [k] of the same officers in the church; and this is also as early as the practice of infant-baptism.

5. Trine immersion is affirmed to be an apostolic tradition, nothing is more frequently asserted by the ancients than this. *Basil* [l], among his instances of apostolic tradition, mentions this; "now a man is thrice immersed, from whence is it derived?" his meaning is, is it from scripture or apostolic tradition? not the former, but the latter. And *Jerom* [m], in a dialogue of his, makes one of the parties say after this manner, which clearly appears to be his own sense; "and many other things which by tradition are observed in the churches, have obtained the authority of a written law; as to dip the head thrice in the laver," &c. And so *Tertullian* in the third century as above, in support of tradition, mentions [n] this as a common practice; "we are thrice immersed;" and elsewhere speaking [o] of the commission of Christ, he says, "he commanded them to dip into the Father, and the Son, and the holy Ghost; not into one, for not once, but thrice are we dipped, at each name, into each person;" and he is the first man that makes mention of infant-baptism, who relates this as the then usage of the church: and *Sozomen* [p] the historian observes, that it was said, that "*Eunomius* was the first that dared to assert, that the divine baptism should be "performed

---

[f] Ep. 105. Bonifacio, prope finem.    [g] Orat. 40. p. 657.    [h] Adv. Parmenian. l. 4. p. 92.
[i] Ep 76. ad Magnum.    [k] Apud Euseb. Eccl. Hist. l. 6. c. 43.    [l] Ut supra.
[m] Adv. Luciferianos, fol. 47. H. tom. 2.    [n] De corona, c. 3.    [o] Adv. Praxeam c. 26.
[p] Hist. Eccles. l. 6. c. 26.

"performed by one immersion; and so corrupted the apostolic tradition, which till now had been every where observed."

6. The consecration of the water of baptism is an ancient rite, and which ° *Basil* derives from apostolic tradition; "we consecrate, says he, the water of baptism, and the anointing oil, as well as the person that receives baptism, from what scripture? is it not from private and secret tradition?" by which he means apostolic tradition, as he in the same place calls it; which was done, not only by the prayer of the administrator over the water, but by signing it with the sign of the cross; which rite was in use in the times of *Austin* ᵖ, who says, "baptism is signed with the sign of Christ, that is, the water where we are dipped;" and *Ambrose*, who lived in the same age, relates, that exorcism was also used in consecration: he describes the manner of it thus ᑫ; "why did Christ descend first, and afterwards the Spirit, seeing the form and use of baptism require, that first the font be consecrated, and then the person that is to be baptized, goes down? for where the priest first enters, he makes an exorcism, next an invocation on the creature of the water, and afterwards prays that the font may be sanctified, and the eternal Trinity be present." *Cyprian*, in the middle of the third century, makes mention of this ceremony of consecrating the baptismal water; he says ʳ, "the water must first be cleansed and *sanctified* by the priest, that it may, by his baptizing in it, wash away the sins of the man that is baptized." And *Tertullian* before him, though he makes no difference between the water of a pool, river or fountain, *Tyber* or *Jordan*, yet supposes there is a sanctification of it through prayer; "all waters, he says ˢ, from their ancient original prerogative, (referring to *Genesis* i. 2.) obtain the sacrament of sanctification, *Deo invocato*, God being called upon;" for immediately the Spirit comes down from heaven, and rests upon the waters, sanctifying them of himself; and so being sanctified, they drink in together the sanctifying virtue." This also is as high as the date of infant-baptism can be carried.

7. Anointing with oil at baptism, is a rite that claims apostolic tradition. *Basil* ᵗ mentions it as an instance of it, and asks; "the anointing oil, what passage in scripture teaches this?" *Austin* ᵘ speaks of it as the common custom of the church in his time; having quoted that passage in *Acts* x. 38; "*how God anointed him* (Jesus) *with the holy Ghost*; adds, not truly with visible oil, but with the gift of grace, which is signified by the visible ointment, *quo baptizatos ungit ecclesia*, "with which the church anoints those that are baptized:" several parts of the body were wont to be anointed. *Ambrose* ʷ makes mention of

---

° Ut supra.   ᵖ De tempore sermo, 119. c. 8.   ᑫ De sacramentis, l. 1. c. 5.
ʳ Ep. 70. ad Januarium.   ˢ De baptismo, c. 4.   ᵗ Ut supra.
ᵘ De trinitate, l. 15. c. 26.   ʷ De sacramentis, l. 3. c. 1.

of the ointment on the head in baptism, and gives a reason for it. *Cyril*[x] says, the oil was exorcised, and the forehead, ear, nose and breast, were anointed with it, and observes the mystical signification of each of these; the necessity of this anointing is urged by *Cyprian*[y] in the third century; "he that is baptiz-
"ed must needs be anointed, that by receiving the chrysm, that is, the *anointing*,
"he may be the anointed of God, and have the grace of Christ. And *Tertullian*, in the beginning of the same century, says[z], as before observed, "the flesh
"is anointed, that the soul may be consecrated;" and in another place[a], "when
"we come out of the laver, we are anointed with the blessed ointment, accord-
"ing to the ancient discipline, in which they used to be anointed with oil out
"of the horn, for the priesthood;" this was the custom used in the times of the man that first spoke of infant-baptism.

8. The giving a mixture of milk and honey to a person just baptized, is a rite that was used in the churches anciently through tradition; *Jerom*[b] makes mention of it, as observed upon this footing, and as an instance, among other things which obtained authority in that way: "as to dip the head thrice in the laver,
"and when they *came out* from thence, *to taste of a mixture of milk and honey*, to
"signify the new birth;" and elsewhere he says[c], it was a custom observed in the western churches to that day, to give *wine and milk* to them that were regenerated in Christ. This was in use in *Tertullian*'s time; for, speaking of the administration of baptism, he says[d], "we come to the water—then we are thrice dipped—then being taken out from thence. we taste a mixture of *milk and honey*; and this, as well as anointing with oil, he observes, was used by heretics themselves, for so he says of *Marcion*[e]; "he does not reject the water of the creator,
"with which he washes his disciples; nor the oil with which he anoints his
"own; *nor the mixture of milk and honey*, by which he points them out as new-
"born babes;" yea, even *Barnabas*, a companion of the apostle *Paul*, is thought to refer to this practice, in an epistle of his still extant[f]; not to take notice of the white garment, and the use of the ring and kiss in baptism, in *Cyprian* and *Tertullian*'s time[g].

Now these several rites and usages in baptism, claim their rise from *apostolic tradition*, and have equal evidence of it as infant-baptism has; they are of as early date, have the same vouchers, and more; the testimonies of them are clear and full; they universally obtained, and were practised by the churches throughout the whole world; and even by heretics and schismatics; and this is

---

[x] Catechef. myftagog 2. §. 3. & 3. §. 3.   [y] Ep. 70. ad Januariam, p 175.
[z] De refurrectione carnis, c. 8.   [a] De baptifmo, c 7.   [b] Adv. Luciferianos, fol. 47.
[c] Comment. in Efaiam. c. 55. 1. fol. 94. E.   [d] De corona, c. 3.
[e] Adv Marcion, l. 3 c. 14.   [f] C. 5. prope finem.   [g] Tertullian de pudicitia,
c. 9. Cyprian. Ep. 59. ad Fidum, vid. Aug. contr. 2. Epift. Pelag. l. 4. c. 8.

is to be said of them, that they never were *opposed* by any within the time referred to, which cannot be said of infant-baptism; for the very first man that mentions it, dissuades from it: and are these facts which could not but be *publicly* and perfectly known, and for which the ancient writers and fathers may be appealed to, not as reasoners and interpreters, but as historians and witnesses to public standing facts; and all the reasoning this gentleman makes use of, concerning the apostles forming the churches on one uniform *plan* of baptism, the *nearness* of infant-baptism to their times, from the testimony of the antients, the difficulty of an innovation, and the easiness of its detection, may be applied to all and each of these rites.

Wherefore whoever receives infant-baptism upon the foot of apostolic tradition, and upon such proof and evidence as is given of it, as above, if he is an honest man; I say again, if he is an honest man, he ought to give into the practice of all those rites and usages. We do not think ourselves indeed obliged to regard these things; we know that a variety of superstitious, ridiculous, and foolish rites, were brought into the church in these times; we are not of opinion, as is suggested, that even the authority of the apostles a hundred years after their death, was sufficient to keep an innovation from entering the church, nor even whilst they were living; we are well assured, there never was such a sett of impure wretches under the christian name, so unsound in principle, and so bad in practice, as were in the apostles days, and in the ages succeeding, called the *purest* ages of christianity. We take the Bible to be the only authentic, perfect and sufficient rule of faith and practice: we allow of no other head and lawgiver but one, that is, Christ; we deny that any men, or set of men, have any power to make laws in his house, or to decree rites and ceremonies to be observed by his people, no not apostles themselves, uninspired: and this gentleman, *out of this controversy*, is of the same mind with us, who asserts the above things we do; and affirms, without the least hesitation, that what is "ordained
" by the apostles, without any precept from the Lord, or any particular direc-
" tion of the holy Spirit, is not at all obligatory as *a law* upon the consciences
" of christians;—even *the apostles* had no *dominion* over the *faith* and *practice* of
" christians, but what was given them by the special presence, and Spirit of
" Christ, the only Lawgiver, Lord, and Sovereign of the church: they were
" to teach *only* the things which he should command them; and whatever they
" enjoined under the influence of that Spirit, was to be considered and obeyed
" as the injunctions of Christ; but if they enjoined any thing in the church,
" without the peculiar influence and direction of this Spirit, that is, as merely
" fallible and unassisted men, in that case, their injunctions had no authority
" over conscience; and every man's own reason had authority to examine and

"discuss their injunctions, as they approved themselves to his private judg-
"ment, to observe them or not: should we grant thee what you ask—says he
"to his antagonist—that the church in the present age, has the same authority
"and power, as the church in the apostolic age, considered, as not being under
"any immediate and extraordinary guidance of the holy Ghost — what will you
"gain by it? This same authority and power is you see, Sir, really no power
"nor authority at all [b]."

The controversy between us and our brethren on this head, is the same as between Papists and Protestants about tradition, and between the church of *England* and Dissenters, about the church's power to decree rites and ceremonies; namely, whether Christ is the sole head and lawgiver in his church; or whether any set of men have a power to set aside, alter, and change any laws of his, or prescribe new ones? if the latter, then we own it is all over with us, and we ought to submit, and not carry on the dispute any further: but since we both profess to make the Bible our religion, and that only the rule of our faith and practice; let us unite upon this common principle, and reject every tradition of men, and all rites and ceremonies which Christ hath not enjoined us; let us join in pulling down this *prop* of *Popery*, and remove this *scandal* of the Protestant churches, I mean infant-baptism; for sure I am, so long as it is attempted to support it upon the foot of apostolic tradition, no man can write with success against the Papists, or such, who hold that the church has a power to decree rites and ceremonies.

However, if infant baptism is a tradition of the apostles, then this point must be gained, that it is not a scriptural business; for if it is of tradition, then not of scripture; whoever appeals to tradition, when a doctrine or practice can be proved by scripture? appealing to tradition, and putting it upon that foot, is giving it up as a point of scripture: I might therefore be excused from considering what this writer has advanced from scripture in favour of infant-baptism, and the rather, since there is nothing produced but what has been brought into the controversy again and again, and has been answered over and over: but perhaps this gentleman and his friends will be displeased, if I take no notice of his arguments from thence; I shall therefore just make some few remarks on them. But before I proceed, I must congratulate my readers upon the blessed times we are fallen into! what an enlightened age! what an age of good sense do we live in! what prodigious improvement in knowledge is made! behold! *tradition* proved by *scripture!* *apostolic tradition* proved by *Abraham's* *covenant!* undoubted *apostolic tradition* proved from writings in being *hundreds* of years *before* any of the *apostles*
were

[b] The dissenting Gentleman's Second Letter, &c. p. 29, 30.

were born! all extraordinary and of the marvellous kind! but let us attend to the proof of thefe things.

The *firſt* argument is taken from its being an *inconteſtable faƈt*, that *the infants of believers* were received with their parents into covenant with God, in the former difpenfations or ages of the church; which is a great privilege, a privilege ſtill fubſiſting, and never revoked; wherefore the infants of believers, having ſtill a right to the fame privilege, in confequence have a right to baptifm, which is now the only appointed token of God's covenant, and the only rite of admiffion into it[1]. To which I reply, that it is not an inconteſtable faƈt, but a *faƈt conteſted*, that the *infants of believers* were with their parents taken into covenant with God, in the former difpenfations and ages of the church; by which muſt be meant, the ages preceding the *Abrahamic* covenant; fince that is made, to furnifh out a *fecond* and diſtinƈt argument from this; and fo the fcriptures produced are quite impertinent, *Gen.* xvii. 7, 10—12. *Deut.* xxix. 10—12. *Ezek.* xvi. 20, 21. feeing they refer to the *Abrahamic* and *Mofaic* difpenfations, of which hereafter. The firſt covenant made with man, was the covenant of works, with *Adam* before the fall, which indeed included all his poſterity, but had no *peculiar* regard to the infants of believers; he ſtanding as a federal head to all his feed, which no man fince has ever done: and in him they all finned, were condemned, and died. This covenant, I prefume, this Gentleman can have no view unto: after the fall of *Adam*, the covenant of grace was revealed, and the way of life and falvation by the Meffiah; but then this revelation was only made to *Adam* and *Eve* perfonally, as interefted in thefe things, and not to their natural feed and poſterity as fuch, as being interefted in the fame covenant of grace with them; for then all mankind muſt be taken into the covenant of grace; and if that gives a right to baptifm, they have all an equal right to unto it; and fo there is nothing *peculiar* to the infants of believers; and of whom, there is not the leaſt fyllable mentioned throughout the whole age or difpenfation of the church, reaching from *Adam* to *Noah*; a length of time almoſt equal to what has run out from the birth of Chriſt, to the prefent age. The next covenant we read of, is the covenant made with *Noah* after the flood, which was not made with him, and his immediate offspring *only*; nor were they taken into covenant with him as the *infants of a believer*; nor had they any facrament or rite given them as a token of *Jehovah* being their God, and they his children, and as ſtanding in a peculiar relation to him; will any one dare to fay this of *Ham*, one of the immediate fons of *Noah*? The covenant was made with *Noah* and all mankind, to the end of the world, and even with every living creature, and all the beaſts of the earth, promifing them fecurity from an uni-

verfal

---

[1] Baptifm of Infants a reafonable Service, &c. p. 14, 15.

versal deluge, as long as the world stands; and had nothing in it *peculiar* to the infants of believers: and these are all the covenants the scripture makes mention of, till that made with *Abraham*, of which in the next argument.

This being the case, there is no room nor reason to talk of the greatness of this privilege, and of the continuance of it, and of asking when it was repealed, since it does not appear to have been a fact; nor during these ages and dispensations of the church, was there ever any *sacrament, rite,* or *ceremony,* appointed for the admission of *persons adult,* or *infants,* into covenant with God; nor was there ever any such rite in any age of the world, nor is there now: the covenant with *Adam,* either of works or grace, had no ceremony of this kind; there was a token, and still is, of *Noah*'s covenant, the rainbow, but not a token or rite of admission of persons into it, but a token of the continuance and perpetuity of it in all generations: nor was circumcision a rite of admission of *Abraham*'s seed into his covenant, as will quickly appear; nor is baptism now an *initiatory rite,* by which persons are admitted into the covenant. Let this Gentleman, if he can, point out to us where it is so described; persons ought to appear to be in the covenant of grace, and partakers of the blessings of it, the Spirit of God, faith in Christ, and repentance towards God, before they are admitted to baptism. This Gentleman will find more work to support his first argument, than perhaps he was aware of; the premises being bad, the conclusion must be wrong. I proceed to,

The *second* argument, taken from the *Abrahamic* covenant, which stands thus: The covenant God made with *Abraham* and his seed, *Genesis* xvii. into which *his infants* were taken together with himself, *by the rite of circumcision,* is the *very same we are now* under, the same with that in *Gal.* iii. 16, 17. still in force, and not to be disannulled, in which we believing Gentiles are included, *Romans* iv. 9—16, 17. and so being *Abraham*'s seed, have a right to all the grants and privileges of it, and so to the admission of our infants to it, by the sign and token of it, which is changed from circumcision to baptism [k]. But, 1. though *Abraham*'s seed were taken into covenant with him, which designs his adult posterity in all generations, on whom it was enjoined to circumcise their infants, it does not follow that his infants were; but so it is, that wherever the words *seed, children,* &c. are used, it immediately runs in the heads of some men, that infants must be meant, though they are not necessarily included; but be it so, that *Abraham*'s infants were admitted with him, (though at the time of making this covenant, he had no infant with him, *Ishmael* was then *thirteen* years of age) yet not as *the infants of a believer*; there were believers and their infants then living, who were left out of the covenant; and those that were taken in in successive

[k] Baptism of Infants a reasonable Service, &c. p. 16—19

cessive generations, were not the infants of believers only, but of unbelievers also; even all the natural seed of the Jews, whether believers or unbelievers.—2. Those that were admitted into this covenant, were not admitted *by the rite of circumcision*; *Abraham*'s female seed were taken into covenant with him, as well as his male seed, but not by any *visible rite* or ceremony; nor were his male seed admitted by any such rite, no not by circumcision; for they were not to be circumcised until the eighth day; to have circumcised them sooner would have been criminal; and that they were in covenant from their birth, this gentleman, I presume, will not deny.—3. The covenant of circumcision, as it is called *Acts* vii. 8. cannot be the same covenant we are now under, since that is abolished, *Gal.* v. 1—3. and it is a *new* covenant, or a new administration of the covenant of grace, that we are now under; the old covenant under the *Mosaic* dispensation is waxen old, and vanished away, *Heb.* viii. 8, 13. nor is the covenant with *Abraham, Gen.* xvii. the same with that mentioned in *Gal.* iii. 17. which is still in force, and not to be disannulled; the distance of time between them does not agree, but falls short of the apostle's date, four and twenty years; for from the making of this covenant to the birth of *Isaac*, was one year, *Gen.* xvii. 1. and xxi. 5. from thence to the birth of *Jacob*, sixty years, *Gen.* xxv. 26. from thence to his going down to *Egypt*, one hundred and thirty years, *Gen.* xlvii. 9. where the Israelites continued two hundred and fifteen [1]; and quickly after they came out of *Egypt*, was the law given, which was but four hundred and six years after this covenant. The reason this gentleman gives, why they must be the same, will not hold good, namely, "this is the only covenant in which "God ever *made* and *confirmed* promises to *Abraham*, and to *his seed*;" since God made a covenant with *Abraham* before this, and confirmed it to his seed, and that by various rites, and usages, and wonderful appearances, *Gen.* xv. 8—18. which covenant, and the confirmation of it, the apostle manifestly refers to in *Gal.* iii. 17. and with which his date exactly agrees, as the years are computed by *Paræus*[m] thus; from the confirmation of the covenant, and taking *Hagar* to wife, to the birth of *Isaac*, fifteen years; from thence to the birth of *Jacob*, sixty, *Gen.* xxv. 26. from thence to his going down to *Egypt*, one hundred and thirty, *Gen.* xlvii. 9. from thence to his death, seventeen, *Gen.* xlvii. 28. from thence to the death of *Joseph*, fifty three, *Gen.* l. 26. from thence to the birth of *Moses*, seventy-five; from thence to the going out of *Israel* from *Egypt*, and the giving of the law, eighty years; in all four hundred and thirty years.—4. It is allowed, that the covenant made with *Abraham, Gen.* xvii. is of a mixed kind, consisting partly of temporal, and partly of spiritual blessings; and that there is a twofold seed of *Abraham*, to which they severally belong; the temporal blessings, to his natural seed the Jews, and the spiritual blessings,

to

[1] See Pool's Annotation on Gal. iii. 17.  [m] In ibid.

to his spiritual seed, even all true believers that walk in the steps of his faith, *Jews or Gentiles*, Rom iv. 11, 12, 16. believing Gentiles are *Abraham*'s spiritual seed, but then they have a right only to the spiritual blessings of the covenant, not to *all* the grants and privileges of it; for instance, not to the land of *Canaan*; and as for their natural seed, these have no right, as such, to any of the blessings of this covenant, temporal or spiritual: for either they are the natural, or the spiritual seed of *Abraham*; not his natural seed, no one will say that; not his spiritual seed, for only believers are such; *they which are of faith* (believers) *the same are the children of Abraham*; *and if ye be Christ's*, (that is, believers) *then are ye Abraham's seed, and heirs according to the promise*; and it is time enough to claim the promise, and the grants and privileges of it, be they what they will, when they appear to be believers; and as for the natural seed of believing Gentiles, there is not the least mention made of them in *Abraham*'s covenant.
—5. Since *Abraham*'s seed were not admitted into covenant with him, by any visible rite or token, no not by circumcision, which was not a rite of admission into the covenant, but a token of the continuance of it to his natural seed, and of their distinction from other nations, until the Messiah came; and since therefore baptism cannot succeed it as such, nor are the one or the other seals of the covenant of grace, as I have elsewhere ° proved, and shall not now repeat it; upon the whole, this second argument can be of no force in favour of infant-baptism: and here, if any where, is the proper time and place for this gentleman to ask for the *repeal* of this *ancient privilege*, as he calls it ᵖ, of infants being taken into covenant with their parents, or to shew when it was repealed; to which I answer, that the covenant made with *Abraham*, into which his natural seed were taken with him, so far as it concerned them as such, or was a national covenant, it was abolished and disannulled when the people of the Jews were cut off as a nation, and as a church; when the *Mosaic* dispensation was put an end unto, by the coming, sufferings, and death of Christ, and by the destruction of that people on their rejection of him; when God wrote a *Loammi* upon them, and said, *Ye are not my people, and I will not be your God*, Hosea i. 9. when he *took his staff, beauty, and cut it asunder, that he might break* his *covenant he had made with this people*, Zech. xi. 10. when the old covenant and old ordinances were removed, and the old church-state utterly destroyed, and a new church-state was set up, and new ordinances appointed; and for which new rules were given; and to which none are to be admitted, without the observance of them; which leads me to

The *third* argument, taken from the commission of Christ for baptism, *Matt.* xxviii. 19. and from the *natural* and *necessary* sense in which the apostles would
understand

---
° The divine right of Infant-baptism disproved, p. 56—61.   ᵖ Reasonable service, &c. p. 16.

understand it *; though this gentleman owns that it is delivered in such general terms, as not certainly to determine whether adult believers only, or the infants also of such are to be baptized; and if so, then surely no argument can be drawn from it for admitting infants to baptism. And,

1. The rendering of the words, *disciple* or *proselyte all nations, baptizing them*, will not help the cause of infant-baptism; for one cannot be a proselyte to any religion, unless he is taught it, and embraces and professes it; though had our Lord used a word which conveyed such an idea, the evangelist *Matthew* was not at a loss for a proper word or phrase to express it by; and doubtless would have made use of another clear and express, as he does in chap. xxiii. 15.— 2. The suppositions this writer makes, that if, instead of *baptizing them*, it had been said *circumcising them*, the apostles without any farther warrant would have naturally and justly thought, that upon proselyting the Gentile parent, and circumcising him, his infants also were to be circumcised: or if the twelve patriarchs of old had had a divine command given them, to go into *Egypt, Arabia*, &c. *and teach them the God of Abraham, circumcising them*, they would have understood it as authorizing them to perform this ceremony, not upon the parent only, but also upon the infants of such as believed on the God of *Abraham*. As these suppositions are without foundation, so I greatly question whether they would have been so understood, without some instructions and explanations; and besides the cases put are not parallel to this before us, since the circumcision of infants was enjoined and practised before such a supposed commission and command; whereas the baptism of infants was neither commanded nor practised before this commission of Christ; and therefore could not lead them to any such thought as this, whatever the other might do.—3. The characters and circumstances of the apostles, to whom the commission was given, will not at all conclude that they apprehended infants to be actually included; some in which they are represented being entirely false, and others nothing to the purpose: Jews they were indeed, but men that knew that the covenant of circumcision was not still in force, but abolished: men, who could never have observed that the infants of believers with their parents had always been admitted into covenant, and passed under the same initiating rite: men, who could not know, that the Gentiles were to be taken into a joint participation of all the privileges of the Jewish church; but must know that both believing Jews and Gentiles were to constitute a new church, state, and to partake of new privileges and ordinances, which the Jewish church knew nothing of:—men, who were utter strangers to the baptism of Gentile proselytes, to the Jewish religion, and of their infants; and to any baptism, but the ceremonial ablutions, before the times of *John* the Baptist:—men, who were not

* Reasonable service, &c. p. 19—22.

not tenacious of their antient rites after the Spirit was poured down upon them at Pentecoſt, but knew they were now aboliſhed, and at an end:—men, though they had ſeen little children brought to Chriſt to have his hands laid on them, yet had never ſeen an infant baptized in their days:—men, who though they knew that infants were ſinners, and under a ſentence of condemnation, and needed remiſſion of ſin and juſtification, and that baptiſm was a means of leading the faith of adult perſons to Chriſt for them; yet knew that it was not by baptiſm, but by the blood of Chriſt, that theſe things are obtained:—men, that knew that Chriſt came to ſet up a new church-ſtate; not national as before, but congregational; not conſiſting of carnal men, and of infants without underſtanding; but of ſpiritual and rational men, believers in Chriſt; and therefore could not be led to conclude that infants were comprehended in the commiſſion: nor is Chriſt's ſilence with reſpect to infants to be conſtrued into a ſtrong and moſt manifeſt preſumption in their favour, which would be preſumption indeed; or his not excepting them, a permiſſion or order to admit them: perſons capable of making ſuch conſtructions, are capable of doing and ſaying any thing. I haſten to

The *fourth* argument, drawn from the evident and clear conſequences of other paſſages of ſcripture[r]; as,

1. From *Romans* xi. 17. and *if ſome of the branches be broken off*, &c. here let it be noted, that the *olive-tree* is not the *Abrahamic* covenant or church, into which the Gentiles were grafted; for they never were grafted into the Jewiſh church, that, with all its peculiar ordinances, being aboliſhed by Chriſt; ſignified by the ſhaking of the heaven and the earth, and the removing of things ſhaken[s], but the goſpel church-ſtate, out of which the unbelieving Jews were left, and into which the believing Gentiles were engrafted, but not in the ſtead of the unbelieving Jews: and by the *root* and *fatneſs* of the olive-tree, are meant, not the religious privileges and grants belonging to the Jewiſh covenant or church, which the Gentiles had nothing to do with, and are aboliſhed; but the privileges and ordinances of the goſpel-church, which they with the believing Jews jointly partook of, being incorporated together in the ſame church-ſtate; and which, as it is the meaning of *Romans* xi. 17. ſo of *Epheſians* iii. 6. in all which there is not the leaſt ſyllable of baptiſm; and much leſs of infant baptiſm; or of the faith of a parent grafting his children with himſelf, into the church or covenant-relation to God, which is a mere chimera, that has no foundation either in reaſon or ſcripture.

2. From *Mark* x. 14. *Suffer little children to come unto me*, &c. and *John* iii. 5. *Except any one is born of water*, &c. from theſe two paſſages put together, it is ſaid, the

right

---

[r] Reaſonable ſervice, &c. p. 23—28.    [s] Heb. xii. 26, 27.

## IN FAVOUR OF INFANT-BAPTISM.

right of infants to baptism may be clearly inferred; for in one they are declared actually to have a place in God's kingdom or church, and yet into it, the other as expresly says, none can be admitted without being baptized. But supposing the former of these texts is to be understood of infants, not in a metaphorical sense, or of such as are compared to infants for humility, &c. which sense some versions lead unto, and in which way some Pædobaptists interpret the words, particularly *Calvin*, but literally; then by *the kingdom of God*, is not meant the visible church on earth, or a gospel church-state, which is not national, but congregational; consisting of persons gathered out of the world by the grace of God, and that make a public profession of the name of Christ, which infants are incapable of, and so are not taken into it: besides, this sense would prove too much, and what this writer would not chuse to give into, viz. that infants, having a place in this kingdom or church, must have a right to all the privileges of it; to the Lord's supper, as well as to baptism; and ought to be treated in all respects as other members of it. Wherefore it should be interpreted of the kingdom of glory, into which we doubt not that such as these in the text are admitted; and then the strength of our Lord's argument lies here; that since he came to save such infants as these, as well as adult persons, and bring them to heaven, they should not be hindered from being brought to him to be touched by him, and healed of their bodily diseases: and so the other text is to be understood of *the kingdom of God*, or heaven, in the same sense; but not of water-baptism as necessary to it, or that without which there is no entrance into it; which mistaken, shocking and stupid sense of them, led *Austin*, and the *African* churches, into a confirmed belief and practice of infant-baptism; and this sense being imbibed, will justify him in all his monstrous, absurd and impious tenets, as this writer calls them, about the ceremony of baptismal water, and the absolute necessity of it unto salvation: whereas the plain meaning of the words is, that *except a man be born again* of the grace of the Spirit of God, comparable to water, *he cannot enter into the kingdom of God*, or be a partaker of the heavenly glory; or without the regenerating grace of the Spirit of God, which in *Titus* iii. 5. is called *the washing of regeneration, and renewing of the holy Ghost*, there can be no meetness for, no reception into, the kingdom of heaven; and therefore makes nothing for the baptizing of infants.

3. A distinction between the children of believers and of unbelievers, is attempted from 1 *Cor.* vii. 14. as if the one were in a visible covenant-relation to God, and the other not; whereas the text speaks not of two sorts of children, but of one and the same, under supposed different circumstances; and is to be understood not of any federal, but matrimonial holiness, as I have shewn elsewhere,

elsewhere¹, to which I refer the reader. As for the *Queries* with which the argument is concluded, they are nothing to the purpose, unless it could be made out, that it is the will of God that infants should be baptized, and that the baptism of them would give them the remission of sins, and justify their persons; neither of which are true: and of the same kind is the *harangue* in the *introduction* to this treatise: and after all a poor, slender provision is made for the salvation of infants, according to this author's own scheme, which only concerns *the infants of believers*, and leaves all others to the uncovenanted mercies of God, as he calls them; seeing the former are but a very small part of the thousands of infants, that every day languish under grievous distempers, are tortured, convulsed, and in piteous agonies give up the ghost. Nor have I any thing to do with what this writer says, concerning the moral purposes and use of infant-baptism in religion; since the thing itself is without any foundation in the word of God: upon the whole, the baptism of infants is so far from being a *reasonable service*, that it is a *most unreasonable one*; since there is neither precept nor precedent for it in the sacred writings; and it is neither to be proved by *scripture* nor *tradition*.

---

¹ The divine right of Infant-baptism disproved, &c. p. 73—78.

# AN ANSWER

TO

WELCH CLERGYMAN's TWENTY ARGUMENTS IN FAVOUR OF INFANT-BAPTISM,

WITH

Some STRICTURES on what the said AUTHOR has advanced concerning the Mode of BAPTISM.

A Book some time ago being published in the *Welch* language, intitled, "A Guide to a saving Knowledge of the Principles and Duties of Religion, *viz.* Questions and Scriptural Answers, relating to the Doctrine contained in the Church Catechism," &c. Some extracts out of it respecting the ordinance of baptism, its subject, and mode, being communicated to me, with a request from our friends in *Wales* to make some *Reply* unto, and also to draw up some *Reasons* for dissenting from the church of *England*, both which I have undertook, and shall attempt in the following manner.

I shall take but little notice of what this author says, part 5. p. 40. concerning sponsors in baptism, but refer the reader to what is said of them in the *Reasons* for dissenting, hereunto annexed. This writer himself owns, that the practice of having sureties is not particularly mentioned in scripture; only he would have it, that it has in general obtained in the churches from the primitive times, and was enacted by the *powers which God has appointed*, and whose *ordinances are to be submitted to*, when they are not contrary to those of God [*]; and must be allowed to be of great service, *if* the sureties fulfilled their engagements. The answer to all which is, that since it is not mentioned in scripture, it deserves no regard; at least, this can never recommend it to such, who make the Bible the rule

---

[*] 1 Pet. ii. 13. Rom. xiii. 1, 2. Tit. iii. 1, 2.

rule of their faith and practice; and as to its obtaining in primitive times, it is indeed generally ascribed to Pope *Hyginus*, as an invention of his; but the genuineness of the epistles attributed to him and others, is called in question by learned men, and are condemned by them as spurious; but were they genuine, neither his office nor his age would have much weight and authority with us, who are not to be determined by the decrees of popes and councils: the *powers* spoken of in the scriptures referred to, were Heathen magistrates, who surely had no authority to enact any thing relating to gospel-worship and ordinances; nor can it be reasonably thought they should; and submission and obedience to them, are required in things of a civil nature, not ecclesiastical, as the scope of the passages, and their context manifestly shew; nor has God given power and authority to any set of men whatever, to enact laws and ordinances of religious worship; nor are we bound to submit to all ordinances of men in religious matters, that are not contrary to the appointments of God, that is, that are not expresly forbidden in his word; for by this means, all manner of superstition and will-worship may be introduced. *Oil* and *spittle* in baptism are no where forbidden, nor is the baptizing of *bells*; yet these ordinances of men are not to be submitted to, and a multitude of others of the like kind: we are not only to take care to do what God has commanded, but to reject what he has not commanded; remembering the case of *Nadab* and *Abihu*, who offered *strange fire* to the Lord, which he commanded not. And whereas it is suggested, that this practice would be very serviceable were the engagements of sureties *fulfilled*, it is not practicable they should; it is impossible to do what they engage to do, even for themselves, and much less for others, as is observed in the *Reasons*, before referred to.

But passing these things, I shall chiefly attend to the *twenty* arguments, which this writer has advanced in favour of infant-baptism, page 41—45.

The *first* argument runs thus: "Baptism, which is a seal of the covenant of "grace, should not be forbid to the children of believers, seeing they are under "condemnation through the covenant of works; and if they are left without "an interest in the covenant of grace, they then would be, to their parents great "distress, under a dreadful sentence of eternal condemnation, without any sign "or promise of the mercy of God, or of an interest in Christ; being *by nature* "*children of wrath as others*, and consequently *without any hope* of salvation, if "they die in their infancy." In which there are some things true, and others false, and nothing that can be improved into an argument in favour of infant-baptism. 1. It is true that the infants of believers, as well as others, are by nature the children of wrath, and under condemnation through the covenant of works; so all mankind are as considered in *Adam*, and in consequence of his sin

and

and fall [b]. But, 2. It is not baptifm that can fave them from wrath and condemnation; a perfon may be baptized in water, and yet not faved from wrath to come, and ftill lie under the fentence of condemnation, *being* notwithftanding that, *in the gall of bitternefs, and bond of iniquity*, as the cafe of *Simon Magus* fhews. Though this writer feems to be of opinion, that baptifm is a faving ordinance, and that a perfon cannot be faved without it; and indeed he exprefsly fays, p. 27. that "in general it is neceffary to falvation;" as if falvation was by it, (which is a popifh notion) and there was none without it; but the inftance of the penitent thief, is a proof to the contrary: the text does not fay, *he that is baptized fhall be faved*, but *he that* BELIEVETH *and is baptized*; nor is it any where fuggefted, that a perfon dying without baptifm fhall be damned. It is CHRIST only, and not *baptifm*, that faves from *wrath and condemnation*. 3. Being unbaptized, does not leave without an intereft in the covenant of grace, or exclude from the hope of falvation, or the mercy of God, or an intereft in Chrift; perfons may have an intereft in all thefe, and yet not be baptized. See the ftrange contradictions men run into when deftitute of truth; one while the covenant of grace is faid to be made with believers, and their feed, as in the next argument, and fo their infants being in it, have a right to *baptifm*; at another time it is *baptifm* that puts them into the covenant; and if they are not baptized they are left without intereft in it, and, to the great grief of their parents, under a dreadful fentence of eternal condemnation. But, 4. as the falvation of an infant dying in its infancy is one of *the fecret things which belong unto the Lord*, a judicious chriftian parent will leave it with him; and find more relief from his diftrefs, by hoping in the grace and mercy of God through Chrift, and in the virtue and efficacy of his blood and righteoufnefs, which may be applied unto it without baptifm, than he can in baptifm; which he may obferve, may be adminiftered to a perfon, and yet be damned. For, 5. baptifm is no feal of the covenant of grace, nor does it give any perfon an intereft in it, or feal it to them; a perfon may be baptized, and yet have no intereft in the covenant, as *Simon Magus* and others, and to whom it was never fealed; and on the other hand, a perfon may be in the covenant of grace, and it may be fealed to him, and he affured of his intereft in it, and not yet be baptized: the blood of Chrift is the feal of the covenant, and the Spirit of Chrift is the fealer of the faint's intereft in it. And, after all, 6 if baptifm has fuch virtue in it, as to give an intereft in the covenant of grace, to be a fign and promife of mercy, and of our intereft in Chrift, and furnifh out hope of falvation, and fecure from wrath and condemnation, why fhould not compaffion be fhewn to the children of unbelievers, who are in the fame ftate and condition by nature? for, I obferve all along, that in this and the following

arguments,

[b] See Rom. v. 12, 18.

arguments, baptism is wholly restrained to the children of believers; upon the whole, the argument from the state of infants to their baptism is impertinent and fruitless; since there is no such efficacy in baptism, to deliver them from it[f].

The *second* argument is: "The children of believers should be admitted to baptism, since as the covenant of works, and the seal of it belonged to *Adam* and his children, so the covenant of grace, and the seal thereof belongs, through Christ, to believers and their children:" to which it may be replied, 1. That it is indeed true, that the covenant of works belonged to *Adam* and his posterity, he being a federal head unto them; but then it does not appear, that that covenant had any seal belonging to it, since it needed none, nor was it proper it should have any, seeing it was not to continue. And if the tree of life is intended, as I suppose it is, whatever that might be, a sign of, it was no seal of any thing, nor did it belong to *Adam*'s children, who were never suffered to partake of it. 2. There is a great disparity between *Adam* and believers, and the relation they stand in to their respective offspring: *Adam* stood as a common head and representative to all his posterity; not so believers to theirs: they are no common heads unto them, or representatives of them; wherefore though the covenant of works belonged to *Adam* and his posterity, it does not follow, that the covenant of grace belongs to believers and their children, they not standing in the same relation he did. There never were but two covenant-heads, *Adam* and CHRIST, and between them, and them only, the parallel will run, and in this form; that as the covenant of works belonged to *Adam* and his seed, so the covenant of grace belongs to Christ and his seed. 3. As it does not appear there was any seal belonging to the covenant of works, so we have seen already, that baptism is not the seal of the covenant of grace; wherefore this argument in favour of infant-baptism is weak and frivolous; the reason this author adds to strengthen the above argument, is very lamely and improperly expressed, and impertinently urged; "for we are not to imagine, that there is more efficacy in the covenant of works, to bring condemnation on the children of the unbelieving, through the fall of *Adam*; than there is virtue in the covenant of grace, through the mediation of the son of God, the second *Adam*, to bring salvation to the seed of those that believe[d]." For the covenant of works being broken by the fall of *Adam*, brought condemnation, not on the children of the unbelieving only, but of believers also, even on all his posterity, to whom he stood a federal head; and so the covenant of grace, of which Christ the second *Adam* is the mediator, brings salvation, not to the seed of those that believe, many of whom never believe, and to whom salvation is never brought, nor they

to

---
[c] See the *Introduction* to the *Baptism of Infants a reasonable Service*, &c. to which this is an answer.
[d] Rom. v. 15, 18.

to that; but to all Christ's spiritual seed and offspring, to whom he stands a federal head; which is the sense of the passages of scripture referred to, and serves no ways to strengthen the cause of infant-baptism.

The *third* argument runs thus. " The seed of believers are to be baptized
" into the same covenant with themselves; seeing infants, while infants, as na-
" tural parts of their parents, are included in the same threatenings, which are
" denounced against wicked parents, and in the same promises as are made to
" godly parents, being branches of one root*." Here let it be observed, 1. that it is pleaded that infants should be baptized into the same covenant with their parents, meaning no doubt the covenant of grace; that is, should by baptism be brought into the covenant as it is expressed in Argument 7th, or else I know not what is meant by being baptized into the same covenant; and yet in the preceding argument it is urged, that the covenant of grace belongs to the infants of believers, that is, they are in it, and therefore are to be baptized: an instance this of the glaring contradiction before observed. 2. Threatenings indeed are made to wicked parents and their children, partly to shew the heinousness of their sins, and to deter them from them; and partly to express God's hatred of sin, and his punitive justice; and also to point out original sin and the corruption of nature in infants, and what they must expect when grown up if they follow the examples of their parents, and commit the same or like sins; but what is all this to infant-baptism; Why, 3. In like manner promises are made to godly parents and their children, and several passages are referred to in proof of it; some of these are of a temporal nature, and are designed to stir up and encourage good men to the discharge of their duty, and have no manner of regard to any spiritual or religious privilege; and such as are of a spiritual nature, which respect conversion, sanctification, &c. when these take place on the seed of believers, then, and not till then, do they appear to have any right to Gospel-ordinances, such as baptism and the Lord's supper; wherefore the argument from promises to such privileges, before the things promised are bestowed, is of no force.

The *fourth* argument is much of the same kind with the foregoing, namely,
" There are many examples recorded in scripture wherein the infants of ungod-
" ly men are involved with their parents in heavy judgments; therefore as the
" judgment and curse which belong to the wicked, belong also to their seed,
" so the privileges of the saints belong also to their offspring, unless they reject
" the God of their fathers. The justice and wrath of God, is not more extensive
" to

* Rom. xi. 16. Deut. iv. 37, 40. and xxviii. 1—4. and xxx. 6, 19. Psal. cii. 28. Prov. xi. 21. and xx. 7. Jer. xxxii. 38, 39. Exod. xx. 5. and xxxiv. 7. Deut. xxviii. 15, 18, 45, 46. Psal. xxi. 10. and cxix. 9, 10. Isai. xiv. 20, 21. Jer. xxii. 28. and xxxvi. 31.

" to deftroy the offspring of the wicked, than his grace and mercy is to fave
" thofe of the faithful; therefore baptifm, the fign of the promifes of God's
" mercy, is not to be denied to fuch infants f." The anfwer given to the former may fuffice for this: to which may be added, 1. That the inflicting judgments on the children of fome wicked men, is an inftance of the fovereign juftice of God; and his beftowing privileges on the children of fome good men, is an inftance of his fovereign grace, who punifhes whom he will, and has mercy on whom he will: for, 2. God does not always proceed in this method; he fometimes beftows the bleffings of his grace on the children of the wicked, and inflicts deferved punifhment on the children of good men; the feed of the wicked do not always inherit their curfes, nor the feed of the godly their bleffings; wherefore fuch difpenfations of God can be no rule of conduct to us; and particularly with refpect to baptifm. And, 3. Whatfoever privileges belong to the feed of believers, we are very defirous they fhould enjoy; nor would we deprive them of any; let it be fhewn that baptifm belongs to them as fuch, and we will by no means deny it to them. But, 4. Whereas it is faid that the privileges of faints belong to their offspring, adding this exceptive claufe, " unlefs they reject
" the God of their fathers;" it feems moft proper, prudent and advifeable, particularly in the cafe before us, to wait and fee whether they will receive or reject, follow or depart from the God of their fathers.

The *fifth* argument is formed thus: " The children of believers are to be bap-
" tized now, as thofe of the Jews were circumcifed formerly; for circumcifion
" was then the feal of the covenant, as baptifm is now, which Chrift has appoint-
" ed in lieu thereof. *Abraham* and his fon *Ifhmael*, and all that were born in
" his houfe, were circumcifed the fame day; and God commanded all *Ifrael* to
" bring their children into the covenant with them, to give them the feal of it,
" and circumcife them ᵍ." To all which I reply, 1. that circumcifion was no feal of the covenant of grace; if it was, the covenant of grace from *Adam* to *Abraham* was without a feal. It is called a *fign* in *Genefis* xvii. the paffage referred to, but not a feal: it is indeed in *Romans* iv. 11. faid to be *a feal of the righteoufnefs of the faith*, not to infants, not to *Abraham*'s natural feed, only to himfelf; affuring him, that he fhould be the father of many nations, in a fpiritual fenfe, and that the righteoufnefs of faith he had, fhould come upon the Gentiles: wherefore this mark or fign continued until the gofpel, in which *the righteoufnefs of God is revealed from faith to faith*, was preached unto the Gentiles, and received by them; to which may be added, that there were many living who were interefted in the covenant of grace, when circumcifion was appointed, and yet it was not ordered to them; as it would have been, had it been a feal

of

---

f Numb. xiv. 33.  2 Kings v. 27.  Jofhua vii. 24, 25.  Jer. xxii. 28.
g Gen. xvii.  Deut. xxix. 10—12.  Col. ii. 11, 12.

of that covenant; and on the other hand, it was enjoined such who had no interest in the covenant of grace, and to whom it could not be a seal of it, as *Ishmael*, *Esau*, and others. And, 2. it has been shewn already, that baptism is no seal of the said covenant. Nor, 3. is it appointed by Christ in lieu of circumcision, nor does it succeed it; there is no agreement between them in their subjects, use, and manner of administration; and what most clearly shews that baptism did not come in the room of circumcision, is, that it was in force and use before circumcision was abolished; which was not till the death of Christ; whereas, years before that, multitudes were baptized, and our Lord himself; and therefore it being in force before the other was out of date, cannot with any propriety be said to succeed it.

This writer, p. 28. has advanced several things to prove that baptism came in the room of circumcision.

*1st*, He argues from the Lord's supper being instead of the paschal lamb, that therefore baptism must be in the room of circumcision, which is ceased; or else there must be a deficiency. But it does not appear that the Lord's supper is in the room of the passover; it followed that indeed, in the institution and celebration of it by Christ, but it was not instituted by him to answer the like purposes as the passover; nor are the same persons admitted to the one as the other; and besides, was the Lord's supper in the room of the passover, it does not follow from thence that baptism *must* be in the room of circumcision: but then it is said there will be a deficiency; a deficiency of what? all those ceremonial rites, the passover and circumcision, with many others, pointed at Christ, and have had their fulfilment in him; he is come, and is the body and substance of them; and therefore there can be no deficiency, since he is in the room of them, and is the fulfilling end of them: nor can any other but he, with any propriety, be said to come in the room of them. And there can be no deficiency of grace, since he is full of it, nor of ordinances, for he has appointed as many as he thought fit.

*2dly*, This author urges, that it is proper there should be *two* sacraments under the gospel, as there were *two* under the law, one for adult persons, the other for their children, as were the paschal lamb and circumcision. But if every thing that was typical of Christ, as those two were, were sacraments, it might as well be said there were two and twenty sacraments under the law, as two; and, according to this way of reasoning, there should be as many under the gospel. Moreover, of these two, one was not for adult persons only, and the other for their children; for they were, each of them, both for adult persons and children too; they that partook of the one had a right to the other; all that were circumcised might eat of the passover, and none but they; and if this is a rule and direction to us now, if infants have a right to baptism, they ought to be admitted to the Lord's supper.

*3dly*, Baptism, he says, is appointed for a like end as circumcision; namely, for the admission of persons into the church, which is not true; circumcision was appointed for another end, and not for that: the Jewish church was national, and as soon as an infant was born, it was a member of it, even before circumcision; and therefore it could not be admitted by it; nor is baptism for any such end, nor are persons admitted into a visible church of Christ by it; they may be baptized, and yet not members of a church: what church was the eunuch admitted into, or did he become a member of, by his baptism?

*4thly*, This writer affirms, that "the holy Spirit calls baptism circumcision, "that is, *the circumcision made without hands*, having the same spiritual design; "and is termed the *christian* circumcision, or that of Christ; it answering to "circumcision, and being ordained by Christ in the room of it." To say that baptism is ordained by Christ in the room of circumcision, is begging the question, nor is there any thing in it that answers to circumcision, nor is it called the circumcision of Christ, in *Col.* ii. 11. which I suppose is the place referred to; for not that, but internal circumcision, *the circumcision of the heart* is meant, which Christ by his Spirit is the author of, and therefore called his; and the same is the circumcision *made without hands*, in opposition to circumcision *in the flesh*; it being by the powerful and efficacious grace of God, without the assistance of men; nor can baptism with any shew of reason, or appearance of truth, be so called, since that is made with the hands of men; and therefore can never be the circumcision there meant.

*5thly*, He infers that baptism is appointed in the room of circumcision, from their signifying like things, as original corruption, regeneration, or the circumcision of the heart [h]; being seals of the covenant of grace [i]; initiating ordinances, and alike laying men under an obligation to put off the body of sin, and walk in newness of life [k]; and also being marks of distinction between church-members and others [l]. But baptism and circumcision do not signify the like things; baptism signifies the sufferings, death, burial, and resurrection of Christ, which circumcision did not; nor does baptism signify original corruption, which it takes not away; nor regeneration, which it does not give, but pre-requires it; nor is baptism meant in the passage referred to, *Titus* iii. 5. nor are either of them seals of the covenant of grace, as has been shewn already; nor initiating ordinances, or what enter persons into a church-state: Jewish infants were church-members, before they were circumcised; and persons may be baptized, and yet

not

---

[h] Deut. xxx. 6. Tit. iii. 5.    [i] Rom. iv. 11.    [k] Rom. vi. 4, 6.
[l] Ezek. xvi. 21. Matt. xvi. 26.

not be members of churches; and whatever obligations the one and the other may lay men under to live in newness of life, this can be no proof of the one coming in the room of the other. Circumcision was indeed a mark of distinction between the natural seed of *Abraham* and others; and baptism is a distinguishing badge, to be wore by those that believe in Christ, and put him on, and are his spiritual seed; but neither of them distinguish church-members from others; the passages referred to are impertinent. But I proceed to consider

The *sixth* argument in favour of infant-baptism, taken from " the sameness of the covenant of grace made with Jews and Gentiles, of which circumcision was the seal; from the seal and dispensation of which, the Jews and their children are cut off, and the Gentiles and their seed are engrafted in ᵐ." In answer to which, let it be observed, 1. That the covenant of grace is indeed the same in one age, and under one dispensation, as another; or as made with one sort of people as another, whether Jews or Gentiles; the same blessings of it that came upon Abraham, come upon all believers, Jews or Gentiles; and the one are saved by the grace of our Lord Jesus Christ, as the other; but then, 2. The covenant of grace was not made with *Abraham* and his natural seed, or with all the Jews as such; nor is it made with Gentiles and their natural seed as such; but with Christ and his spiritual seed, and with them only, be they of what nation, or live they in what age they will. 3. Circumcision was no seal of the covenant of grace, nor does *Romans* iv. 11. prove it, as has been shewn already; and therefore nothing can be inferred from hence with respect to baptism. 4. The root or stock from whence the unbelieving Jews were cut off, and into which the believing Gentiles are engrafted, is not the covenant of grace, from which those who are interested in it can never be cut off; but the gospel church-state, from which the unbelieving Jews were rejected and left out, and the believing Gentiles took in, who partook of all the privileges of it ⁿ: though no mention is made throughout the whole of the passage of the children of either; only of some being broken off through unbelief, and others standing by faith; and therefore can be of no service in the cause of infant-baptism.

The *seventh* argument is taken from " the extent of the covenant of grace being the same under the New Testament, as before the coming of Christ, who came not to curtail the covenant, and render worse the condition of infants; if they were in the covenant before, they are so now; no spiritual privilege given to children or others can be made void °." To which may be replied, 1. That the extent of the covenant, as to the constitution of it, and persons interested in it, is always the same, having neither more nor fewer; but with

respect

Gal. iii. 14. Acts xv. 11. Rom. iv. 11. and xi. 15, 17.  ⁿ Rom. xi. 17—25.
° Rom. xi. 29. Jer. xxx. 29.

respect to the application of it, it extends to more persons at one time than at another; and is more extensive under the gospel-dispensation than before; it being applied to Gentiles as well as Jews: and with respect to the blessings and privileges of it, they are always the same, are never curtailed or made void, or taken away from those to whom they belong; which are all Christ's spiritual seed, and none else, be they Jews or Gentiles. But, 2. It should be proved that the infant-seed of believers, or their natural seed as such, were ever in the covenant of grace; or that any spiritual privileges were given to them as such; or it is impertinent to talk of curtailing the covenant, or taking away the privileges of the seed of believers. 3. If even their covenant-interest could be proved, which it cannot, that gives no right to any ordinance, or to a positive institution, without a divine direction; there were many who were interested in the covenant of grace, when circumcision was appointed, who yet had nothing to do with that ordinance. 4. Baptism not being allowed to infants, does not make their condition worse than it was under the former dispensation; for as then circumcision could not save them, so neither would baptism, were it administered to them; nor was circumcision really a privilege, but the reverse; and therefore the abrogation of it, without substituting any thing in its room, does not make the condition of infants the worse; and certain it is, that the condition of the infants of believing Gentiles, even though baptism is denied them, is much better than that of the infants of Gentiles before the coming of Christ; yea, even of the infants of Jews themselves; since they are born of christian parents, and so have a christian education, and the opportunity and advantage of hearing the gospel preached, as they grow up, with greater clearness, and in every place *p* where they are. The text in *Romans* xi. 29. regards not external privileges, but internal grace; that in *Jeremiah* xxx. 20. respects not infants, but the posterity of the Jews; adult persons in the latter day.

The *eighth* argument is taken from the everlastingness of the covenant of grace, and runs thus; " The example of *Abraham* and the Israelites in circum-
" cising their children according to the command of God, should oblige us
" to baptize our children; because circumcision was then a seal of the ever-
" lasting covenant, a covenant that was to last for ever, and not cease as the
" legal ceremonies; which God hath confirmed with an oath; and therefore
" can have suffered no alteration for the worse in any thing with respect to
" infants *q* " The answer to which is, 1. That the covenant of grace is everlasting, will never cease, nor admit of any alteration, is certain; but the covenant of circumcision, which is called an everlasting covenant, *Genesis* xvii. 7.

was

---

*p* This also is an answer to what the author of *The baptism of Infants a reasonable Service* suggests in p. 7, 12, 16.   *q* Gen. vii. 17. Heb. vi. 13, 18. Mic. vii. 18, 20. Gal. iii. 8.

was only to continue during the Mosaic dispensation, or unto the times of the Messiah; and is so called for the same reason, and just in the same sense as the covenant of the priesthood with *Phinehas* is called, *the covenant of an everlasting priesthood* [r]. Though the covenant of grace is everlasting, and whatever is in that covenant, or ever was, will never be altered; yet it should be proved there is any thing in it with respect to infants, and particularly which lays any foundation for, or gives them any claim and right to baptism. 3. Though circumcision was a sign and token of the covenant made with *Abraham*, and his natural seed, it never was any seal of the covenant of grace. And, 4. The example of *Abraham* and others, in circumcising their children according to the command of God, lays no obligation upon us to baptize ours, unless we had a command for their baptism, as they had for their circumcision.

The *ninth* argument is formed thus; "Baptism is to be administered to the "seed of believers, because it is certainly very dangerous and blameworthy, "to neglect and despise a valuable privilege appointed by God from the begin- "ning, to the offspring of his people." But it must be denied, and should be proved, that baptism is a privilege appointed by God from the beginning, to the offspring of his people; let it be shewn, if it can, when and where it was appointed by him. This argument is illustrated and enforced by various observations; as that "that soul was to be cut off that neglected circumcision; and "no just excuse can be given for neglecting infant-baptism, which is ordained "to be the seal of the covenant instead of circumcision:" but we have seen already, that baptism does not come in the room of circumcision, nor is it a seal of the covenant of grace; and there is good reason to be given for the neglect of infant-baptism, because it never was ordained and appointed of God. Moreover it is said, "that the seed of believers were formerly, under the Old Testa- "ment, in the covenant together with their parents; and no one is able to shew "that they have been cast out under the New, or that their condition is worse, "and their spiritual privileges less, under the gospel, than under the law:" but that believers with their natural seed as such, were together in the covenant of grace under the Old Testament, should not be barely affirmed, but proved, before we are put upon to shew that they are cast out under the New; though this writer himself, before in the *sixth* argument, talks of the Jews and their children being cut off from the seal and dispensation of the covenant; which can never be true of the covenant of grace; nor do we think that the condition of infants is worse, or their privileges less now, than they were before, though baptism is denied them, as has been observed already. It is further urged, that "it is not to be imagined, without presumption, that Christ ever intended to
"cut

[r] Numb. xxv. 13.

"cut them off from an ordinance, which God had given them a right unto; nor do we imagine any such thing; nor can it be proved that God ever gave the ordinance of baptism to them. As for what this writer further observes, that had Christ took away circumcision, without ordaining baptism in the room of it, for the children of believers; the Jews would have cried out against it as an excommunication of their children; and would have been a greater objection against him than any other; and would now be a hindrance of their conversion; and who, if they were converted, would have baptism or circumcision to be a seal of the covenant with them and their children, it deserves no answer; since the clamours, outcries, and objections of the Jews, and their practice on their legal principles, would be no rule of direction to us, were they made and gave into, since they would be without reason and truth; for though Christ came not to destroy the moral law, but to fulfil it ᶠ; yet he came to put an end to the ceremonial law, of which circumcision is a part, and did put an end to it \*: the text in *Jeremiah* xxx. 20. respects the restoration of the Jews in the latter day, but not their old ecclesiastical polity, which shall not be established again, but their civil liberties and privileges.

The *tenth* argument stands thus; "Children are to be baptized under the "covenant of grace, because all the covenants which God ever made with men "were made not only with them, but also with their children;" and instances are given in *Adam, Noah, Abraham, Isaac* and *Jacob, Levi, Phinehas,* and *David*. The covenant of works was indeed made with *Adam* and his seed, in which covenant he was a federal head to his offspring; but the covenant of grace was not made with him and his seed, he was no federal head in that; nor is that made with all mankind, as it must, if it had been made with *Adam* and his seed: this is an instance against the argument, and shews that *all* the covenants that ever God made with men, were not made with them and their seed; for certainly the covenant of grace was made with *Adam*, and made known to him ᵗ; and yet not with his seed with him; nor can any instance be given of the covenant of grace being made with any man, and his natural seed. There was a covenant made with *Noah* and his posterity, securing them from a future deluge, but not a covenant of grace securing them from everlasting destruction; for then it must have been made with all mankind, since all are the posterity of *Noah*; and where then is the distinction of the seed of believers and of unbelievers? Besides *Ham*, one of *Noah*'s immediate offspring, was not interested in the covenant of grace. As for the covenant made with *Abraham*, his son *Ishmael* was excluded from it ᵘ; and of *Isaac*'s two sons one of them was rejected ᵛ;
and

---

ᶠ Matt. v. 17.  \* Which may likewise be an answer to the same thing hinted by the author of *The baptism of Infants a reasonable Service*, p. 28.  Gen. iii.15.
ᵘ Gen. xvii. 19—21.  ᵛ Rom. ix. 10—13.

and all were not *Israel* that were of *Israel*, or of *Jacob*, ver. 6. The covenant of the priesthood was indeed made with *Levi* and *Phinehas*, and their posterity; and though it is called an *everlasting* one, it is now made void; nor is there any other in its room with the ministers of the word and their posterity; and yet no outcry is made of the children of gospel-ministers being in a worse condition, and their privileges less than those of the priests and Levites: and as for *David*, the sad estate of his family, and the wicked behaviour of most of his children, shew, that the covenant of grace was not made with him and his natural offspring; and whatever covenants those were that were made with these persons, they furnish out no argument proving the covenant of grace to be made with believers and their carnal seed, and still less any argument in favour of infant-baptism [x].

The *eleventh* argument is; " The seed of believers ought to be baptized
" under the covenant of grace, otherwise they would be reckoned pagans,
" and the offspring of infidels and idolaters, to whom there is neither a promise
" nor any sign of hope; whereas the scripture makes a difference, calling them
" *holy* on account of their relation to the holy covenant, when either their
" father or mother believe [y], *disciples* [z]; reckoning them among them that *be-*
" *lieve*, because of their relation to the houshold of faith [a]; styling them *the*
" *seed of the blessed*, and their offspring with them [b]; accounting them *for a*
" *generation to the Lord* [c], as *David* says; who, ver. 10. observes, that God
" was his God from his mother's belly; and also calling them the *children of*
" *God* [d]; therefore they ought to be dedicated to him by that ordinance which
" he has appointed for that purpose." To all which may be replied, 1. That the children of believers are by nature *children of wrath even as others*; and are no better than others; and were they baptized, they would not be at all the better christians for it. Though, 2. It will be allowed that there is a difference between the offspring of believers, and those of infidels, pagans and idolaters; and the former have abundantly the advantage of the latter, as they have a christian education; and consequently as they are brought up under the means of grace, there is hope of them; and it may be expected that the promise of God to such who use the means will be accomplished. But, 3. the characters mentioned either do not belong to children, or not for the reason given; and those that do, do not furnish out an argument for their baptism. Children are said to be *holy*, born in lawful wedlock [e]; not on account of their relation to the holy covenant, but on account of the holiness of a believing parent, which
surely

---

[x] Let this also be observed, together with the answer to the first argument of the author of *The bap-tism of Infants a reasonable Service*, &c. p. 14.   [y] 1 Cor. vii. 14.   [z] Acts xv. 10.
[a] Matt. xviii. 6.   [b] Isai. lxv. 23.   [c] Psal. xxii. 30.   [d] Ezek. xvi. 20, 21.
[e] 1 Cor. vii. 14.

surely cannot be a federal holiness, but a matrimonial one; the marriage of a believer with an unbeliever being valid, or otherwise their children must be *unclean* or illegitimate, and not *holy* or legitimate. The disciples in *Acts* xv. 10. are not young children, but adult persons, the converted Gentiles, on whom the false teachers would have put the yoke of the ceremonial law, and particularly circumcision. The little ones reckoned among those that believe in Christ, *Matt.* xviii. 6. were not infants in age, but the apostles of our Lord, who were little in their own account, and in the account of others, whom to offend was criminal, highly provoking to Christ, and of dangerous consequence. The text, *Isai.* lxv. 23. speaks of the spiritual seed of the church, and not the carnal seed of believers [f]; and these are the same who are *accounted to the Lord for a generation*; even a spiritual seed that shall serve him, *Psal.* xxii. 30. and the words in ver. 10. are the words, not of *David*, but of Christ. And the sons and daughters born to God, and whom he calls his children, *Ezekiel* xvi. 20, 21. were so, not by grace or by covenant, but by creation. And from the whole there is not the least reason why the children of believers should be dedicated to God by baptism, which is an ordinance that never was appointed by him for any such purpose.

The *twelfth* argument is; "The seed of believers are to be baptized, because church-relation belongs to them, as citizenship belongs to the children of freemen; and it is by baptism that they are first admitted into the visible church; and there is neither covenant nor promise of salvation out of the church; for the church of Christ is his kingdom on earth, and Christ says this belongs to children [g]." In answer to which, 1. There is a manifest contradiction in the argument. Church-relation belongs to infants, that is, they are related to the church, and members of it, and therefore should be baptized; and yet they are first admitted into the church by baptism; what a contradiction this! in it, and out of it, related, and not related to it, at one and the same time. 2. Church-membership does not pass from father to son, nor is it by birth, as citizenship, or the freedom of cities; the one is a civil, the other an ecclesiastical affair; the one is of nature, the other of grace; natural birth gives a right to the one, but the spiritual birth or regeneration only intitles to the other. 3. Church-membership gives no right to baptism, but rather baptism to church-membership, or however is a qualification requisite to it; persons ought to be baptized before they are church-members; and if they are church-members, and not regenerate persons and believers in Christ, for such may be in a church, they have no right to baptism. 4. To talk of there being no covenant or promise of salvation out of the church, smells rank of popery. The

covenant

---

[f] Vide ibid, p. 24.      [g] Mark x 13, 14.

covenant and promife of falvation are not made with and to perfons as members of churches, or as in a vifible church-ftate, but with and to the elect of God in Chrift, and with perfons only confidered in him; who have an intereft in the covenant and promife of falvation, though they may not be in a vifible church-ftate; and doubtlefs many are faved who never were members of a vifible church. 5. The kingdom of God, in *Mark* x. 13, 14. be it the church of Chrift on earth, or eternal glory in heaven, only belongs to fuch perfons who are like to little children for their meeknefs and humility, and freedom from malice and rancor, as ver. 15. fhows. 6. Could infants in age, or the feed of believers as fuch be here meant, and the kingdom of God be underftood of Chrift's vifible church, and they as belonging to it, it would prove more than this writer chufes; namely, that they have a right to all church-privileges, and particularly and efpecially to the Lord's fupper.

The *thirteenth* argument is; "Children are the lambs of Chrift's flock and "fheep; and the lambs ought not to be kept out of Chrift's fold, nor hindered "from the wafhing that is in his blood; he particularly promifes to be their "fhepherd; and his Spirit has declared, that little children fhould be brought "to him under the gofpel, in the arms, and on the fhoulders of their parents [h]." On which may be obferved, 1. That there is indeed mention made of the lambs of Chrift in *Ifai.* xl. 11. *John* xxi. 15. which he gathers in his arms, and ordered *Peter* to feed; yet not infants in age are intended in either place, but adult perfons, weak believers, who, in comparifon of others, becaufe of their fmall degree of knowledge and ftrength, are called *lambs*; and are to be gently and tenderly dealt with; and fuch as thefe are not kept out of Chrift's fold, but are received into it, though weak in the faith, but *not to doubtful difputations*; and are fed with knowledge and underftanding, which infants in age are not capable of. 2. The infant-feed of believers are no where called the fheep of Chrift, nor has he promifed to be the fhepherd of them; let the paffages be directed to, if it can be, where this is faid. 3. Thofe who are truly the lambs and fheep of Chrift, are not hindered from the wafhing of his blood; though that is not to be done, nor is it done by baptifm; perfons may be wafhed with water, as *Simon Magus*, and yet not wafhed in the blood of Chrift: *Canticles* vi. 6. does not intend wafhing in either fenfe; but either the regenerating grace of the fpirit, or the purity of converfation, and refpects not infants at all. 4. Nor is it declared by the Spirit of God, that parents fhould bring their children to Chrift in their arms, and on their fhoulders; the paffage in *Ifai.* xlix. 22. brought in fupport of it, fpeaks of the fpiritual feed of the church, and not of the carnal feed of believers; and of their being brought, not in the arms and on the fhoulders

[h] Ifai. xl. 11. and xlix. 22. Cant. vi. 6. John xxi. 15.

ders of their natural parents, but of the Gentiles; and not to Chrift, but to the church, through the miniftry of the word in the latter day, in which the Gentiles would be very affifting.

The *fourteenth* argument runs thus: "The feed of the faithful ought to be "baptized, becaufe they were partakers of all the former baptifms mentioned "in fcripture, as the children of *Noah* in the ark[¹]; the Ifraelites at the Red fea, "and in the cloud[ᵏ]. Several children were baptized with the baptifm of the "Spirit, for feveral were filled with the holy Ghoft from their mother's womb; "all the children of *Bethlehem* under two years old, with the baptifm of mar- "tyrdom[¹]; and many children with *John*'s baptifm, fince he baptized the "whole country." But, 1. It unhappily falls out, for the caufe of infant-baptifm, that *Noah*'s children in the ark were all adult and married perfons[ᵐ]. 2. That there were children among the Ifraelites when they were *baptized in the cloud, and in the fea*, is not denied; but then it fhould be obferved, that *they did all eat the fame fpiritual meat, and did all drink the fame fpiritual drink*; and therefore, if this does not give a fufficient claim to infants to partake of the Lord's fupper, neither will the other prove their right to baptifm: moreover, if any arguments can be formed from this and the former inftance, for the adminiftration of baptifm under the New Teftament, they will clearly fhew, that it ought to be adminiftered by immerfion; for, as in the former, when the fountains of the great deep were broke up under them, and the windows of heaven were opened over them, they were as perfons immerfed in water; fo when the waters of the Red fea ftood up on each fide, and the cloud was over the Ifraelites, they were, as it were overwhelmed in water. 3. Though this writer fays, that feveral children were filled with the holy Ghoft from their mother's womb, yet we read but of one that was fo, *John* the Baptift, a very extraordinary perfon, and extraordinarily qualified for extraordinary work, an inftance not to be mentioned in ordinary cafes; befides, it is a rule in logic, *a particulari ad univerfalem non valet confequentia*, "from a particular to an univerfal, the confequence "is not conclufive." Moreover, in what fenfe *John* was filled with the holy Ghoft fo early, is not eafy to fay; and be it what it will, the fame cannot be proved of the feed of believers in general; and could it, it would give no right to baptifm, without a pofitive inftitution; it gave no right to *John* himfelf. 4. That the infants at *Bethlehem* were murdered, will be granted, but that they fuffered martyrdom for Chrift, will not eafily be proved; fince they knew nothing of the matter, and were not confcious on what account their lives were taken away. 5. That many or any children were baptized with *John*'s baptifm

we

[¹] 1 Pet. iii 20.     [ᵏ] 1 Cor. x. 1, 2. Exod. xii. 37.     [¹] Matt. ii.
[ᵐ] Gen. vii. 7.

we deny, and call upon this writer to prove it, and even to give us one single instance of it; what he suggests is no evidence of it, as that the whole country in general were baptized by him, who could not be all childless; but I hope he does not think, that every individual person in the country of *Judea* was baptized by *John*; it is certain, that there were many even adult persons that were refused by him, and such as were baptized by him, were such as *confessed their sins*, which infants could not do[a]: and as to the probability of the displeasure of Jewish parents, suggested if their children had not been baptized by *John*, since they were used, and under a command of God, to bring their children to the covenant and ordinances of God[b], it deserves no regard, since whatever probability there was of their displeasure, though I see none, there could be no just ground for it; since in the instances given, they had the command of God for what they did, for this they had none.

The *fifteenth* argument is: "It is contrary to the apostle's practice, to leave "any unbaptized in christian families; for they baptized whole families when "the heads of them believed; as the families of *Lydia*, the Jailor, and *Ste-* "*phanas*; and it is evident, that the words, family and houshold, in scripture, "mean chiefly children, sons, daughters, and little ones[c]." To which I reply, that whatever these words signify in some places of scripture, though in the passages mentioned they do not chiefly intend new-born infants, but grown persons; it should be proved, that there were infants in families and housholds that were baptized, and that these were baptized together with the head of the family; for it is certain, there are many families and housholds that have no little children in them; and as for those that are instanced in, it is not probable that there were any in them; and it is manifest, that such as were baptized, were adult persons and believers in Christ. It is not evident in what station of life *Lydia* was, whether married or unmarried, and whether she had young children or not; and if she had, it is not likely they should be with her, when at a distance from her native place, and upon business; it is most probable, that those that were with her, called her houshold, were her servants, that assisted her in her business; and it is certain, that when the apostles entered her house, those that were there, and who doubtless are the same that were baptized, were called *brethren*, and such as were capable of being *comforted*[d]; and the Jailor's houshold were such as had the word of God spoken to them, and received it with joy, took pleasure in the company and conversation of the apostles, and believed in God together with him, and so were adult persons,

believers.

[a] Matt. iii. 5—7.  [b] Gen. xvii. Deut. xxix. 10, 13. Joel ii. 16.
[c] Compare Exod. i. 1, 7. w'th Gen. xlvi. 5. and xlv. 18, 19. compare 1 Sam. xxvii. 3. with chap. xxx. 5. 1 Tim. iii. 8. Gen. xxx. 30. Numb. iii. 15.   [d] Acts xvi. 15, 40.

believers, and very proper subjects of baptism¹. *Stephanas* is by some thought to be the same with the Jailor; but if he was another person, it is plain his houshold consisted of adult persons, men called by grace, and who were made use of in public work; they were *the first-fruits of Achaia*, and addicted themselves to the ministry of the saints¹.

The *sixteenth* argument is: " None that truly fear God, can seriously and with certainty say, that there were not many infants among the three thousand baptized by the apostles at once; for the Jews were not content with any ordinances without having their children with them. The apostle directs those who were at age to repent, but he commands every one of them to be baptized, and objects nothing against their children; because, as he says, the promise was unto them and their children also; and this is a plain command for infant-baptism to all that will judge impartially." But, 1. A man that carefully reads the account of the baptism of the three thousand, having the fear of God before his eyes, may with the greatest seriousness and strongest assurance affirm, not only that there were not many infants, but that there were not one infant among the three thousand baptized by the apostles; for they were all of them such as *were pricked to the heart, and cried out, Men and brethren what shall we do? they gladly received the word* of the gospel, joined to the church, and *continued stedfastly in the apostles doctrine, in fellowship, and in breaking of bread and prayer*; all which cannot be said of infants. 2. What this author suggests, agreeable to what he elsewhere says, that the Jews were not pleased with any ordinance unless they had their children with them, is without foundation; what discontent did they ever shew at a part of their children being left out of the ordinance of circumcision, and no other appointed for them in lieu of it? And had they been discontented, what argument can be formed from it? 3. The distinction between those that were of age, whom the apostle directed to repent, and the *every one of them* whom he commanded to be baptized, has no ground nor reason for it, yea is quite stupid and senseless; and even, according to this writer himself, is a distinction without any difference, since the *every one* to be baptized are supposed by him to have children, and so to be at age; since he adds, " and objects nothing against their children." And a clear case it is, that the self-same persons that were exhorted to be *baptized*, were exhorted to *repent*, and that as previous to their baptism; and therefore must be adult persons, for infants are not capable of repentance, and of giving evidence of it. 4. Those words, *the promise is unto you and to your children*, are so far from being a plain command for infant-baptism, that there is not a word of baptism in them, and much less of infant-baptism; nor do they regard infants, but the posterity of the Jews, who are often called *children*, though grown

---

¹ Acts xvi. 31—34.   ¹ 1 Cor. xvi. 15. Let this be observed, in answer to what the author of The baptism of Infants a reasonable Service, &c. has advanced in p. 43.

grown up, to whom the promise of the Messiah, and remission of sins by him, and the pouring out of the holy Ghost, was made; and are spoken for the encouragement of adult persons only, to repent and be baptized; and belong only to such as are called by grace, and to all such, whether Jews or Gentiles.

The *seventeenth* argument is; "The seed of believers should be baptized, be-
"cause the privileges and blessings which are signified and sealed in baptism are
"necessary to their salvation, and there is no salvation without them; namely,
"an interest in the covenant of grace, the remission of original sin, union with
"Christ, sanctification of the holy Spirit, and regeneration, without which
"none can be saved [1]." The answer to which is, 1. That the things indeed mentioned are necessary to salvation, and there can be none without them; but then baptism is not necessary to the enjoyment of these things, nor to salvation; a person may have an interest in these blessings, and be saved, though not baptized; these are things necessary to baptism, but baptism is not necessary to them; and indeed a person ought to have an interest in these, and appear to have one, before he is baptized. Wherefore, 2. These things are not signified in baptism, and much less sealed by it; other things, such as the sufferings, death, and the resurrection of Christ, are signified in it; these, as regeneration, &c. are prerequisites unto baptism, and are not communicated by it, or sealed up to persons in it, who may be baptized, and yet have no share and lot in this matter, witness the case of *Simon Magus*.

The *eighteenth* argument is: "The children of the faithful ought to be bap-
"tized, because this lays them under strong obligation to shun the works of Sa-
"tan; and many have received much benefit from hence in their youth. Com-
"fortable symptoms, or signs of a work of grace, have appeared very early in
"several, though perhaps bad company has afterwards corrupted them. Besides
"infant-baptism keeps up a general profession of faith and religion, and makes
"the word and means of grace of more virtue and efficacy, than if men had
"utterly renounced christianity, and declared themselves infidels; and further,
"it lays a powerful obligation on their parents and others, to teach them their
"duty, which is a main end of all the ordinances God has instituted [2]." But, 1. Is there nothing besides baptism, that can lay persons under strong obligation to shun the works of the Devil? certainly there are many things: if so, then it is not absolutely necessary on this account; besides, though the baptism of adult persons does lay them under obligation to walk in newness of life [3], yet the baptism of infants can lay them under no such obligation as infants, and while they are such, because they are not conscious of it, nor can it take any such effect upon them. 2. What that much benefit or advantage is, that many
have

[1] John iii. 5.    [2] Psalm lxxviii. 5, 6.    [3] Rom. vi. 4.

have received from infant-baptism, I am at a loss to know, and even what is intended by this writer, unless it be what follows, that signs of a work of grace have appeared very early in several, which may be, and yet not to be ascribed to baptism; baptism has no such virtue and influence, as to produce a work of grace in the soul, or any signs of it; besides, a work of grace has appeared very early in several, and has been carried on in them, who have never been baptized at all. 3. Infant-baptism keeps up no public or general profession of faith or religion, since there is no profession of faith and religion made in it by the person baptized; nor is it of any avail to make the word and means of grace powerful and efficacious, which only become so by the Spirit and grace of God; and a wide difference there is between the disuse of infant-baptism, and renouncing christianity, and professing infidelity; these things are not necessarily connected together, nor do they go together; persons may deny and disuse infant-baptism, as it is well known many do, and yet not renounce the christian faith, and declare themselves infidels. 4. Parents and others, without infant-baptism, are under strong obligations to teach children their duty to God and men, and therefore it is not necessary on that account.

The *nineteenth* argument is; " The seed of believers are to be baptized, " though they have not actual faith, since Christ speaks not of these but of " adult persons, *Mark* xvi. 16. And certain it is they have as much fitness " for baptism as for justification and eternal life, without which they must all " perish; the Spirit of God knows how to work this fitness in them, as well " as in grown persons: *Jeremiah*, *John* the Baptist, and several others, were " sanctified from their mother's womb ˣ." To which may be returned for answer, 1. That if the text in *Mark* xvi. 16. speaks not of infants, but of adult persons only, as it certainly does, I hope it will be allowed to be an instruction and direction for the baptism of adult believers, and to be a sufficient warrant for our practice. 2. If the infants of believers have no more fitness for baptism than they have for justification and eternal life, they have none at all, since they are *by nature children of wrath, even as others*; and therefore can have none, but what is given them by the Spirit and grace of God. 3. We dispute not the power of the Spirit of God, or what he is able to do by the operations of his grace upon the souls of infants; we deny not but that he can and may work a work of grace upon their hearts, and clothe them with the righteousness of Christ, and so give them both a right and meetness for eternal life; but then this should appear previous to baptism; actual faith itself is not sufficient for baptism, without a profession of it; the man that has it ought to declare it to the satisfaction of the administrator, ere he admits him to the ordinance ʸ. 4. Of the several

children

---

ˣ John iii. 8, 9. Eccles. xi. 5. Luke i. 15, 44. Jer. i. 5. Isai. xliv. 3. Psal. viii. 2.
ʸ ?? viii. 36, 37.

children said to be sanctified from their mother's womb, no proof is given but of one, *John* the Baptist, who was filled with the holy Ghost from thence, which has been considered in the answer to the *fourteenth* argument; as for *Jeremiah*, it is only said of him that he was *sanctified*, that is, set apart, designed and ordained, in the purpose and counsel of God to be a prophet, before he was born; and is no proof of internal sanctification so early. *Isaiah* xliv. 3. speaks of the Spirit of God being poured down, not upon the carnal seed of believers, but upon the spiritual seed of the church; and *Psalm* viii. 2. is a prophecy, not of new-born infants, but of children grown up, crying *Hosanna* in the temple ˣ: no argument from a particular instance or two, were there more than there are, is of avail for the sanctification of infants in general; it should be proved, that all the infant-seed of believers are sanctified by the Spirit of God; for if some only, and not all, how shall it be known who they are? let it first appear that they are sanctified, and then it will be time enough to baptize them.

The *twentieth* argument is; "The children of believers are to be baptized, "because their right to the covenant and church of God is established from "the first, much clearer than several other necessary ordinances; there is no "express command nor example of womens receiving the Lord's supper; no "particular command in the New Testament for family-worship, and for the "observation of the first day of the week as a sabbath; and yet none dare call "them in question; and there is no objection against infant-baptism, but the "like might formerly have been made against circumcision; and may now "be objected against many other ordinances and commands of God." To hich I reply, 1. That with respect to womens receiving the Lord's supper, it is certain, that not only they were admitted to baptism ᵃ, and became members of churches ᵇ, but there is an express command for their receiving the Lord's supper in 1 *Cor.* xi. 29. where a word is used of the common gender, and includes both men and women; who are both one in Christ, and in a gospel church-state, and have a right to the same ordinances ᶜ. 2. As to family-worship, that is not peculiar to the New Testament-dispensation, as baptism is; it was common to the saints in all ages, and therefore needed no express command for it under the New; though what else but an express command for it is *Ephesians* vi. 4.? for can children be brought up in the nurture and admonition of the Lord, without family-worship? 3. As to the observation of the first day, though there is no express command for it, there are precedents of it; there are instances of keeping it ᵈ: now, let like instances and examples of

infant-

---

ˣ See Matt. xxi. 15, 16.    ᵃ Acts viii. 12.    ᵇ Acts i. 14, 15. and iv. 37. and v. 9, 14. 1 Cor. xi. 5, 6, 13. and xiv. 34, 35.    ᶜ Gal. iii. 28.    ᵈ John xx. 19, 26. Acts xx. 7. 1 Cor. xvi. 1, 2.

infant-baptifm be produced if they can: though no exprefs command can be pointed at, yet if any precedent or example of any one infant being baptized by *John*, or Chrift, or his apoftles, can be given, we fhould think ourfelves obliged to follow it. 4. That the fame objections might be made againft circumcifion formerly, as now againft infant-baptifm, is moft notorioufly falfe; it is objected, and that upon a good foundation, that there is neither precept nor precedent for infant-baptifm in all the word of God; the fame could never be objected againft circumcifion, fince there was fuch an exprefs command of it to *Abraham*, Genefis xvii. and fo many inftances of it are in the facred writings; let the fame be fhewn for infant-baptifm, and we have done. 5. What the other ordinances and commands of God are, to which the fame objections may be made as to infant-baptifm, is not faid, and therefore no reply can be made.

I have nothing more to do, than to take fome little notice of what this writer fays, concerning the mode of adminiftering the ordinance of baptifm, p. 33. We are no more fond of contentions and ftrifes about words, than this author, and thofe of the fame way of thinking with himfelf can be; but furely, modeftly to inquire into, and attempt to fix the true manner of adminiftering an ordinance of Chrift, according to the fcriptures, and the inftances of it; according to the fignification of the words ufed to exprefs it, and agreeable to the end and defign of it; can never be looked upon as a piece of impertinence, or be traduced as cavil and wrangling. And,

1*ft*, Since this writer obferves, that he does not find that either the facred fcripture or the church of *England*, have exprefsly determined, whether baptifm is to be performed by plunging or fprinkling, but have left the one and the other indifferently to our choice; I hope he will not be difpleafed, that we choofe the former, as moft agreeable to the facred writings, and the examples of baptifm in them; as thofe of our Lord and others in *Jordan*[e]; and in *Ænon*, where *John* was baptizing, becaufe there was much water [f]; and of the Eunuch [g]; and as beft reprefenting the death, burial, and refurrection of Chrift [h]: as well as beft fuits with the primary fenfe of the Greek word, βαπτιζω, which fignifies to plunge or dip. And,

2*dly*, Since, according to this writer, one mode is not more effential to the ordinance than another, but a *reverential* receiving of the fign; it may be afked, what of this nature, namely, a reverential receiving of the fign, the application of the water to the body, fignifying the fpiritual application of Chrift and his gifts

---

[e] Matt. iii. 6, 16.  [f] John iii. 23.  [g] Acts viii. 36—38.
[h] Rom. vi. 4. Col. ii. 12.

gifts to the soul, can be observed in an infant when sprinkled, which is not conscious of what is done to it?

3*dly*, Whereas, he says, " it is not improbable but the apostles baptized by sprinkling, since several were baptized in their houses, *Acts* ix. 17, 18. and xvi. 33. and others, in former times, sick in their beds:" it may be replied, that it is not probable that the apostle *Paul* was baptized by sprinkling¹; since had he, he would have had no occasion to have *arose* in order to be baptized, as he is said to do, *Acts* ix. 18. It is most probable, that when he arose off of his bed or chair, he went to a bath in *Judas*'s house; or out of the house, to a certain place fit for the administration of the ordinance by immersion; and since there was a pool in the prison, as *Grotius* thinks, where the Jailor washed the apostles stripes, it is most probable, that here he and his houshold were baptized; or since they were brought out of the prison, and after baptism brought into the Jailor's house, ver. 33, 34. it is most likely they went out to the river near the city *where prayer was wont to be made*, and there had the ordinance administered to them, ver. 13. As for the baptism of sick persons in their beds, this was not in the times of the apostles, but in after-times, when corruptions had got into the church; and so deserves no regard.

4*thly*, In favour of sprinkling, or pouring water in baptism, he urges that " it is a sign of the pouring or sprinkling of the holy Ghost, and of the blood of Christ ᵏ:" but it should be observed, that baptism is not a sign or significative of the sprinkling of clean water, or the grace of the Spirit in regeneration, or of the blood of Christ on the conscience of a sinner, all which ought to precede baptism; but of the death, and burial, and resurrection of Christ; which cannot be represented in any other way than by covering a person in water, or an immersion of him.

5*thly*, " Water in baptism, he says, is but a sign and seal; a little of it is " sufficient to signify the gifts which Christ has purchased, as a small quantity of " bread and wine does in the other sacrament, and as a small seal is as much " security as a larger one." But as baptism is no sign of the things before-mentioned, so it is no seal, as we have seen, of the covenant of grace; wherefore these similitudes are impertinent to illustrate this matter: and though a small quantity of bread and wine is sufficient in the other sacrament, to signify our partaking of the benefits of the death of Christ by faith; yet a small quantity of water is not sufficient to signify his sufferings and death, with his burial and resurrection, themselves. And though we do not expect benefit from the quantity of the water, yet that best expresses the end and design of the ordinance.

6*thly*,

¹ Acts ix. 17, 18.     ᵏ Ezek. xxxvi. 25. Heb. xii. 24.

*6tbly* and *laftly*, He obferves, that " fprinkling of water on the face, a part of the body, is a fign fufficient for the whole; fince the nature of the foul appears more in it, and often in fcripture fignifies the whole man." But be it fo that it does; fprinkling water on the face is not a fufficient fign for the whole; for this ordinance reprefents a burial, and fprinkling a little water is not fufficient for that; the ordinance fo performed cannot be called a burial, or a perfon faid to be buried in it; cafting a little earth upon the face of a corps, can never be fufficient for its burial, or be accounted one.

I have now gone through the confideration of the feveral arguments of this author, with refpect both to the fubjects and mode of baptifm; fhould he upon reading this anfwer, and after he has confidered the advice of the wife man, *Prov.* xxvi. 4, 5. which he propofes to do, think fit to reply, perhaps, upon the like confideration, a rejoinder may be made to what he fhall hereafter offer.

THE

# DISSENTERS REASONS

For separating from the

## CHURCH OF ENGLAND,

OCCASIONED BY

A LETTER wrote by a *Welch* Clergyman on the *Duty of Catechising Children.*

Intended chiefly for the use of Dissenters of the *Baptist* Denomination in *Wales.*

WHEREAS Dissenters from the church of *England* are frequently charged with schism, and their separation is represented as unreasonable, and they are accounted an obstinate and contentious people; it may be proper to give some reasons why they depart from the Established church; by which it will appear that their separation does not arise from a spirit of singularity and contention, but is really a matter of conscience with them; and that they have that to say for themselves, which will sufficiently justify them, and remove the calumnies that are cast upon them; and our reasons are as follow.

I. We dislike the church of *England* because of its *Constitution*, which is human; and not divine: it is called *The church of England as by law Established*; not by the law of God, but by the law of man: it is said to be the best constituted church in the world, but we like it never the better for its being constituted by men: a church of Christ ought to be constituted as those we read of in the *Acts of the Apostles*, and not established by *Acts of Parliament*; as the articles, worship, and discipline of the church of *England* be; a *parliamentary* church we do not understand; Christ's *kingdom* or church is *not of this world*; it is not established on worldly maxims, nor supported by worldly power and policy.

II. We

II. We are not satisfied that the church of *England* is a true church of Chrift becaufe of the *form* and order of it; which is national, whereas it ought to be congregational, as the firft chriftian churches were; we read of the church at *Jerufalem*, and of the churches in *Judea* befides, fo that there were feveral churches in one nation; and alfo of the churches of *Macedonia*, and likewife of *Galatia*, and of the feven churches of *Afia*, which were in the particular cities mentioned; yea of a church in an houfe, which could not be national; there were alfo the church at *Corinth*, and another at *Cenchrea*, a few miles diftant from it, and a fea-port of the Corinthians. A church of Chrift is a congregation of men who are gathered out of the world by the grace of God, and who feparate from it and meet together in fome one place to worfhip God; and to this agrees the definition of a church in the XIX$^{th}$ Article of the church of *England*, and is this; " The vifible church of Chrift is a congregation of faith-" ful men:" which is againft herfelf; for if a congregation, then not a nation; if a congregation then it muft be gathered out from others; and if a congregation, then it muft meet in one place, or it cannot with any propriety be fo called; as the church at *Corinth* is faid to do, 1 *Cor.* xi. 18, 20. and xiv. 23. but when and where did the church of *England* meet together in one place? and how is it the vifible church of Chrift? where and when was it ever feen in a body together? is it to be feen in the King, the head of it? or in the Parliament, by whom it was eftablifhed? or in the upper and lower houfes of Convocation, its reprefentatives? To fay, that it is to be feen in every parifh, is either to make a building of ftone the church, which is the ftupid notion of the vulgar people; or to make the parifhioners a church, and then there muft be as many churches of *England* as there are parifhes, and fo fome thoufands, and not one only.

III. We object to the *matter* or materials of the church of *England*, which are the whole nation, good and bad; yea, inafmuch as all the natives of *England* are members of this church, and are fo by birth, they muft in their original admiffion, or becoming members, be all bad; fince they are all conceived and born in fin, and great part of them as they grow up are men of vicious lives and converfations; whereas a vifible church of Chrift ought to confift of *faithful men*, as the above mentioned Article declares, that is, of true believers in Chrift; and fuch were the materials of the firft chriftian churches; they were made up of fuch as were *called to be faints, fanctified in Chrift Jefus*, and *faithful brethren in him*; as were the churches at *Rome, Corinth, Ephefus* and *Coloffe*: thefe were *churches of faints*; but the church of *England* is a church of the world, or confifts for the moft part of worldly men; and therefore we cannot hold communion with it.

IV. We

IV. We are dissatisfied with the *doctrine* preached in the church of *England*, which generally is very corrupt, and not agreeable to the word of God; and therefore cannot be a true church of Christ, which ought to be *the pillar and ground of truth*; for the visible church of Christ, as the XIXth article runs, is " a congregation of faithful men, in the which the pure word of God is preach- " ed;" of which pure word, the doctrines of grace are a considerable part; such as eternal election in Christ, particular redemption by him, justification by his imputed righteousness, pardon through his blood, atonement and satisfaction by his sacrifice, and salvation alone by him, and not by the works of men; the efficacy of divine grace in conversion, the perseverance of the saints, and the like; but these doctrines are scarce ever, or but seldom, and by a very few, preached in the church of *England:* since two thousand godly and faithful minis- ters were turned out at once, Arminianism has generally prevailed; and scarce any thing else than Arminian tenets and mere morality are preached, and not Christ and him crucified, and the necessity of faith in him, and salvation by him; wherefore we are obliged to depart from such a communion, and seek out elsewhere for food for our souls. And though the XXXIX Articles of the church of *England* are agreeable to the word of God, a few only excepted; yet of what avail are they, since they are seldom or ever preached, though sworn and subscribed to by all in public office; and even these are very defective in many things: There are no articles relating to the *two covenants* of grace and *works*; to creation and providence; to the fall of man; the nature of sin and punishment for it; to adoption, effectual vocation; sanctification, faith, repen- tance, and the final perseverance of the saints; nor to the law of God; christian liberty; church-government and discipline; the communion of the saints; the resurrection of the dead, and the last judgment.

V. We dissent from the church of *England*, because the ordinances of Baptism and the Lord's supper are not duly administered in it, according to the word of God, and so is not a regular church of Christ; for, as the above Article says, " The visible church of Christ is a congregation of faithful men, in the which " —the sacraments be duly ministered, according to Christ's own ordinance, " in all those things that of necessity are requisite to the same:" but the said ordinances are not duly administered in the church of *England*, according to the appointment of Christ; there are some things which are of necessity requisite to the same, which are not done; and others which are not of necessity requisite, which are enjoined, and with which we cannot comply.

*First*, The ordinance of Baptism is not administered in the said church, ac- cording to the rule of God's word: there are some things used in the adminis- tration of it, which are of human invention, and not of Christ's ordination;

and

and other things absolutely necessary to it, which are omitted; and indeed the whole administration of it, has nothing in it agreeable to the Institution of Christ, unless it be the bare form of words made use of, *I baptize thee in the name of the Father*, &c.

1. The sign of the cross used in baptism is entirely unscriptural, an human invention, a rite and ceremony which the Papists are very fond of, and ascribe much unto; and indeed the church of *England* makes a kind of a sacrament of it, since the minister when he does it says, that it is done " in token, that hereafter he " (the person baptized) shall not be ashamed to confess the faith of Christ cru" cified, and manfully to fight under his banner against sin, the world, and " the devil, and to continue Christ's faithful soldier unto his life's end:" this is such an human addition to a divine ordinance, as by no means to be admitted.

2. The introduction of sponsors and sureties, or godfathers and godmothers, is without any foundation from the word of God; it is a device of men, and no ways requisite to the administration of the ordinance: besides, they are obliged to promise that for the child, which they cannot do for themselves, nor any creature under heaven; as " to renounce the devil and all his works, " the vain pomp and glory of the world, with all covetous desires of the same, " and the carnal desires of the flesh, so as not to follow or be led by them; and " constantly believe God's holy word, and obediently keep God's holy will and " commandments, and walk in the same all the days of his life."

3. The prayers before and after baptism may well be objected to, suggesting that remission of sins and regeneration are obtained this way; and that such as are baptized are regenerated and undoubtedly saved: in the prayer before baptism are these words; " We call upon thee for this infant, that he coming to " thy holy baptism, may receive remission of his sins by spiritual regenera" tion;" and when the ceremony is performed, the minister declares, " that " this child is regenerate, and grafted in the body of Christ's church;" and in the prayer after it, he says, " We yield thee hearty thanks, most merciful Fa" ther, that it hath pleased thee to regenerate this infant with thy holy Spirit:" and in the rubric are these words; " It is certain by God's word, that children " which are baptized, dying before they commit actual sin, are undoubtedly " saved;" yea in the Catechism, the person catechized is instructed to say, that in his baptism he " was made a member of Christ, the child of God, and an " inheritor of the kingdom of heaven:" which seems greatly to favour the popish notion, that the sacraments confer grace *ex opere operato*, upon the deed done. These are things which give disgust to many Dissenters, that are for in-

fant-baptism; but some of us have greater reasons than these against the administration of baptism in the church of *England*; for,

4. The subjects to which it is administered are not the proper ones, namely infants; we do not find in all the word of God, that infants were commanded to be baptized, or that ever any were baptized by *John*, the first administrator of that ordinance, nor by Christ, nor by his apostles, nor in any of the primitive churches: the persons we read of, that were baptized in those early times, were such as were sensible of sin, had repentance for it, and had faith in Christ, or professed to have it; all which cannot be said of infants: nor can we see, that any argument in favour of infant-baptism can be drawn from *Abraham*'s covenant, from circumcision, from the baptism of housholds, or from any passage either in the Old or New Testament. Moreover,

5. We cannot look upon baptism as administered in the church of *England*, to be valid, or true christian baptism; because not administered in a right way, that is, by immersion, but either by sprinkling or pouring water, which the rubric allows of in case of weakness; nor do we understand, that it is ever performed in any other way, at least, very rarely; whereas we have abundant reason to believe, that the mode of immersion was always used by *John* the baptist, and by the apostles of Christ, and by the churches of Christ for many ages.

*Secondly*, There are many things in the administration of the Lord's supper, which we think we have reason to object unto, and which shew it to be an undue one: and not to take notice of the bread being ready cut with a knife, and not broken by the minister, whereas it is expresly said, that Christ *brake* the bread, and did it in token of his *broken* body; nor of the time of administering it, at noon, which makes it look more like a dinner, or rather like a breakfast, being taken fasting, than a supper; whereas to administer it in the evening best agrees with its name, and the time of its first institution and celebration; but not to insist on these things.

1. *Kneeling* at the receiving of it is made a necessary requisite to it, which looks like an adoration of the elements, and seems to favour the doctrine of the *real presence*; and certain it is, that it was brought in by pope *Honorius*, and that for the sake of transubstantiation and the real presence, which his predecessor *Innocent* the III<sup>d</sup>. had introduced; and though the church of *England* disavows any such adoration of the elements, and of Christ's corporal presence in them; yet inasmuch as it is notorious that this has been abused, and still is, to idolatry, it ought to be laid aside; and the rather *sitting* should be used, since it is a table-gesture, and more suitable to a feast; and was what was used by Christ and his apostles, and by the primitive churches, until transubstantiation obtained; or however, since kneeling at most is but an indifferent rite, it

ought

ought not to be imposed as necessary, but should be left to the liberty of persons to use it or not.

2. The ordinance is administered to all that desire it, whether qualified for it or not; and to many of vicious lives and conversations; yea the minister, when he intends to celebrate it, in the exhortation, which in the book of Common Prayer he is directed to use, says; " unto which, in God's behalf, " *I bid you, all that are here present*, and beseech you for the Lord Jesus Christ's " sake, that ye will not refuse to come thereto." Whereas it cannot be thought, that all present, every one in a public congregation, or in a parish, are fit and proper communicants; and there are many persons described in the word of God, we are not to eat with, 1 *Cor.* v. 11. Yet the rubric enjoins, " that every " parishioner shall communicate, at the least, three times in the year; " and directs, " that new-married persons should receive the holy communion at the " time of their marriage, or at the first opportunity after it; " though none surely will say, that all married persons are qualified for it.

3. This sacred ordinance is most horridly prostituted, and most dreadfully profaned, by allowing and even obliging persons, and these oftentimes some of the worst of characters, to come and partake of it as a civil Test, to qualify them for places of profit and trust; whereas the design of this ordinance is to commemorate the sufferings and death of Christ, and his love therein; to strengthen the faith of christians, and increase their love to Christ and one another, and to maintain communion and fellowship with him and among themselves.

4. This ordinance is sometimes administered in a private house, which took its rise from saying of private mass; and to sick persons, to whom it seems to be given as a *viaticum*, or a provision for the soul in its way to heaven; and to two or three persons only, and even in some cases to a single person; whereas it is a church-ordinance, and ought to be administered only in the church, and to the members of it.

VI. As the church of *England* has neither the form nor matter of a true church, nor is the word of God purely preached, and the ordinances of the gospel duly administered in it; so neither is it a truly *organized* church, it having such ecclesiastical officers and offices in it, which are not to be found in the word of God; and which is another reason why we separate from it. The scripture knows nothing of Archbishops and Diocesan Bishops, of Archdeacons and Deans, of Prebends, Chantors, Parsons, Vicars, Curates, &c. The only two officers in a christian church are Bishops and Deacons; the one has the care of the spiritual, the other of the temporal affairs of the church; the former is the same with Pastors, Elders, and Overseers; and such men ought to be of
sound

found principles, and exemplary lives and conversations; and moreover ought to be chosen by the people; nor should any be imposed upon them contrary to their will: this is an hardship, and what we cannot submit to: and it is a reason of our separation, because we are not allowed to choose our own pastors.

VII. The church of *England* has for its *head* a temporal one, whereas the church of Christ has no other head but Christ himself. That our lawful and rightful sovereign King GEORGE is head of the Church of *England*, we deny not; he is so by *Act of Parliament*, and as such to be acknowledged; but then that church can never be the true church of Christ, that has any other head but Christ; we therefore are obliged to distinguish between the church of *England* and the church of Christ. A woman may be, and has been head of the church of *England*, but a woman may not be head of a church of Christ; since she is not allowed to speak or teach there, or do any thing that shews authority over the man [a].

VIII. The want of *discipline* in the church of *England*, is another reason of our dissent from it. In a regular and well-ordered church of Christ, care is taken that none be admitted into it but such as are judged truly gracious persons, and of whom testimony is given of their becoming conversations; and when they are in it, they are watched over, that their walk is according to the laws and rules of Christ's house; such as sin, are rebuked either privately or publicly, as the nature of the offence is; disorderly persons are censured and withdrawn from; profane men are put out of communion, and heretics, after the first and second admonition, are rejected: but no such discipline as this is maintained in the church of *England*. She herself acknowledges a want of godly discipline, and wishes for a restoration of it; which is done every *Lent* season, and yet no step taken for the bringing of it in: what discipline there is, is not exercised by a minister of a parish, and his own congregation, though the offender is of them, but in the Bishop's Court indeed, yet by laymen; the admonition is by a set of men called Apparitors, and the sentence of excommunication and the whole process leading to it by Lawyers, and not Ministers of the word.

IX. The *Rites* and *Ceremonies* used in the church of *England*, are another reason of our separation from it. Some of them are manifestly of pagan original; some favour of Judaism, and are no other than abolished Jewish rites revived; and most, if not all of them, are retained by the papists; and have been, and still are, abused to idolatry and superstition. Bowing to the east, was an idolatrous practice of the heathens, and is condemned in scripture as an abominable thing [b]. Bowing to the altar, is a relic of popery, used by way of adoration of the elements, and in favour and for the support of transubstantiation, and the real

[a] 1 Cor. xiv. 34, 35. 1 Tim. ii. 11, 12.   [b] Ezek. viii. 15, 16.

real presence; and therefore by no means to be used by those that disbelieve that doctrine, and must be an hardening of such that have faith in it. Bowing, when the name of Jesus is mentioned, is a piece of superstition and will-worship, and has no countenance from *Phil.* ii. 10. The words should be rendered *in*, and not *at* the name of Jesus; nor is it *in the name Jesus*, but *in the name of Jesus*, and so designs some other name, and not Jesus; and a name given him after his resurrection, and not before, as the name of Jesus was at his birth; and besides some are obliged to bow in it, who have no knees in a literal sense to bow with, and therefore bowing of the knee cannot be meant in any such sense. And as for such ceremonies which in their own nature are neither good nor bad, but indifferent, they ought to be left as such, and not imposed as necessary; the imposition of things indifferent in divine service as necessary, as if without which it could not be rightly performed, is a sufficient reason why they ought not to be submitted to: such and such particular garments worn by persons in sacred office, considered as indifferent things, may be used or not used; but if the use of these is insisted on, as being holy and necessary, and without which divine worship cannot rightly be performed, then they ought to be rejected as abominable. Nor can we like the surplice ever the better for being brought in by pope *Adrian*, A. D. 796. The cross in baptism, and kneeling at the Lord's-supper, have been taken notice of before.

X. The book of *Common Prayer*, set forth as a rule and directory of divine worship and service, we have many things to object to.

1. Inasmuch as it prescribes certain stinted set forms of prayer, and ties men up to the use of them: we do not find that the apostles of Christ and the first churches used any such forms, nor christians for many ages; and of whatever use it can be thought to be unto persons of weak capacities, surely such that have spiritual gifts, or the gift of preaching the gospel, can stand in no need of it, and who must have the gift of prayer; and to be bound to such precomposed forms, as it agrees not with the promise of the Spirit of grace and supplication, so not with the different cases, circumstances, and frames that christians are sometimes in; wherefore not to take notice of the defectiveness of these prayers, and of the incoherence and obscurity of some of the petitions in them; the frequent tautologies and repetitions, especially in the Litany, so contrary to Christ's precept in *Matt.* vi. 7. are sufficient to give us a distaste of them.

2. Though we are not against reading the scriptures in private and in public, yet we cannot approve of the manner the Liturgy directs unto; namely, the reading it by piece-meals, by bits and scraps, so mangled and curtailed as the Gospels and Epistles are: we see not why any part of scripture should be omitted;

ted; and the order of these being an invention of a Pope of *Rome*, and the fixing them to mattins and even-songs smelling so rank of popery, no ways serve to recommend them to us: not to take notice of the great impropriety of calling passages out of *Isaiah*, *Jeremiah*, *Joel*, *Malachi*, and the *Acts* of the apostles, by the name of Epistles: but especially it gives us much uneasiness to see lessons taken out of the *Apocrypha*, and appointed to be read as if of equal authority with the sacred scriptures; nay not only out of the books of *Baruch*, *Wisdom*, and *Ecclesiasticus*, but out of the histories of *Tobit*, *Judith*, *Susanna*, *Bel and the dragon*, and such lessons out of them as contain the most idle and fabulous stories.

3. The book of Common Prayer, enjoins the reading of the book of *Psalms* in the corrupt translation of the *Vulgate Latin*, used by the papists; in which there are great omissions and subtractions in some places; as every where, the titles of the *Psalms* are left out, and in all places these words *Higgaion* and *Selah*, and the last verse of *Psalm* lxxii. and in others, there are manifest additions, as in *Psalm* ii. 12. and iv. 8. and xiii. 6. and xxii. 1, 31 and xxxix. 12. and cxxxii. 4. and cxxxvi. 27. and cxlvii. 8. and three whole verses in *Psalm* xiv. whereas nothing should be taken from, nor added to the word of God; some sentences are absurd and void of sense, as *Psalm* lviii. 8. and lxviii. 30, 31. and in others the sense is perverted, or a contrary one given, as in *Psalm* xvii. 4. and xviii. 26. and xxx. 13. and cv. 28. and cvi. 30. and cvii. 40 and cxxv. 3. This translation of the *Psalms* stands in the *English* Liturgy, and is used and read in the churches in *England*.

4. It directs to the observation of several fasts and festivals, which are no where enjoined in the word of God, and for which it provides collects, gospels and epistles to be read: the fasts are, *Quadragesima* or *Lent*, in imitation of Christ's forty days fast in the wilderness, *Ember* weeks, *Rogation* days, and all the *Fridays* in the year; in which men are commanded to abstain from meats, which God has created to be received with thanksgiving. The festivals, besides, the principal ones, *Christmas*, *Easter* and *Whitsuntide*, are the several saints days throughout the year; which are all of popish invention, and are either moveable or fixed, as the popish festivals be; and being the relics of popery makes us still more uneasy and dissatisfied with them.

5. Besides the corruptions before observed in the ordinances of Baptism and the Lord's supper, in the order for the Visitation of the Sick stands a form of Absolution, which runs thus; "And by his (Christ's) authority committed to "me, I absolve thee from all thy sins, in the name of the Father, and of the "Son,

"Son, and of the holy Ghost;" which is a mere popish device; Christ having left no such power to his church, nor committed any such authority to any set of men in it; all that the ministers of Christ have power or authority to do, is only ministerially to declare and pronounce, that such who believe in Christ shall receive the remission of sins, and that their sins are forgiven them; and that such who believe not shall be damned.

6. It appoints some things merely civil, as ecclesiastical and appertaining to the ministry, and to be performed by ecclesiastical persons and ministers, and provides offices for them: as,

1. Matrimony; which seems to favour the popish notion of making a sacrament of it; whereas it is a mere civil contract between a man and a woman, and in which a minister has nothing to do; nor do we ever read of any priest or Levite, that was ever concerned in the solemnization of it between other persons, under the Old Testament, or of any apostle or minister of the word, under the New; not to say any thing of the form of it, or of the ceremonies attending it.

2. The Burial of the Dead; which is a mere civil action, and belongs not to a gospel-minister, but to the relations of the deceased or other neighbours, friends or acquaintance [c]: nor is there any necessity for a place to be consecrated for such a purpose. *Abraham* and *Sarah* were buried in a cave, *Deborah* under an oak, *Joshua* in a field, *Samuel* in his house, and Christ in a garden [d]. Nor do the scriptures ever make mention of any service being read, or of any divine worship being performed at the interment of the dead; and was any thing of this kind necessary, yet we must be obliged to object unto, nor could we comply with, the service used by the church of *England* on this occasion; we cannot in conscience call every man and woman, our *dear brother*, or our *dear sister*, as some who have lived vicious lives, and have not appeared to have had true repentance towards God or faith in Christ, have been called; or " com-
" mit their bodies to the ground in sure and certain hope of the resurrection to
" eternal life;" since we know there will be a resurrection to damnation as well as to eternal life; nor can we give thanks to God on account of many, " that
" it has pleased him to deliver them out of the miseries of this sinful world;"
nor join in the following petition, which seems to favour the popish notion of praying for the dead; " beseeching—that we, with all those that are departed in the true faith of thy holy name, may have our perfect consummation and bliss, both in body and soul," &c.

XI. We

[c] Matt. viii. 21, 22. Act. viii. 2.
[d] Gen. xxiii. 9. and xxxv. 8. Josh. xxiv. 30. 1 Sam. xxv. 1. John xix. 41.

XI. We cannot commune with the church of *England*, because it is of a persecuting spirit; and we cannot think such a church is a true church of Christ: that the *Puritans* were persecuted by it in Queen *Elizabeth*'s time, and the Dissenters in the reign of King *Charles* the second, is not to be denied; and though this spirit does not now prevail, this is owing to the mild and gentle government of our gracious sovereign King GEORGE, the head of this Church, for which we have reason to be thankful; and yet it is not even now quite clear of persecution, witness the Test and Corporation-acts, by which many free-born *Englishmen* are deprived of their native rights, because they cannot conform to the church of *England*; besides, the reproaches and revilings which are daily cast upon us, from the pulpit and the press, as well as in conversation, shew the same: and to remove all such calumnies and reproaches, has been the inducement to draw up the above Reasons for our dissent; and which have been chiefly occasioned by a late *Letter* on the duty *of Catechizing Children*, in which the author, is not content highly to commend the church of *England*, as the purest church under heaven, but reflects greatly on Dissenters, and particularly on such whom he calls *rebaptizers*; and repeats the old stale story of the *German Anabaptists*, and their errors, madnesses and distractions; and most maliciously insinuates, that the people who now go by this name are tinctured with erroneous principles; for he says, they spread their errors in adjacent countries, which are not fully extinguished to this day: whereas they are a people that scarce agree with us in any thing; neither in their civil nor in their religious principles, nor even in baptism itself; for they were for the repetition of adult-baptism in some cases, which we are not: and used sprinkling in baptism, which we do not: the difference between them and us is much greater than between the papists and the church of *England*; and yet this letter-writer would think it very hard and unkind in us, should we rake up all the murders and massacres committed by Pædobaptists, and that upon principle, believing that in so doing they did God good service; I mean the Papists, who are all Pædobaptists; and yet this might be done with as much truth and ingenuity, as the former story is told: and besides, the disturbances in *Germany* were begun by Pædobaptists; first by the Papists before the reformation, and then by Lutherans after it, whom *Luther* endeavoured to dissuade from such practices; and even the disturbances in *Munster* were begun by Pædobaptist ministers, with whom some called Anabaptists joined, and on whom the whole scandal is laid. But what is all this to us, who as much disavow their principles and practices, as any people under the heavens? nor does our different way of thinking about baptism any ways tend to the same.

*ANTI-*

# ANTIPÆDOBAPTISM;
## OR,
## INFANT-BAPTISM AN INNOVATION.
### BEING A
Reply to a late Pamphlet, intitled, PÆDOBAPTISM; or, *A Defence of* Infant-Baptism, *in point of Antiquity,* &c.

A Pamphlet being published some time ago by a nameless author, intitled, *The baptism of Infants a reasonable Service,* &c. I wrote an answer to it, chiefly relating to the antiquity of infant-baptism, called, *The argument from Apostolic tradition, in favour of Infant-baptism,* &c. *considered*; and of late another anonymous writer has started up in defence of the antiquity of it, from the exceptions made by me to it; for it seems it is not the same author, but another who has engaged in this controversy; but be he who he will, it does not greatly concern me to know; though methinks, if they judge they are embarked in a good cause, they should not be ashamed of it, or of their names, and of letting the world know who they are, and what share they have in the defence of it: but just as they please, it gives me no uneasiness; they are welcome to take what method they judge most agreeable, provided truth and righteousness are attended to.

In my answer, I observe that apostolic tradition at most and best is a very uncertain and precarious thing, not to be depended upon; of which I give an instance so early as the second century, which yet even then could not be settled; and that it is doubtful whether there is any such thing as apostolic tradition, not delivered in the sacred writings; and demand of the Gentleman, whose performance was before me, to give me one single instance of it; and if infant-baptism is of this kind, to name the apostle or apostles by whom it was delivered, and to whom, when, and where; to all which no answer is returned;
only

only I observe a deep silence as to *undoubted apostolic tradition*, so much boasted of before.

The state of the controversy between us and the Pædobaptists, with respect to the antiquity of infant-baptism, lies here; and the question is, whether there is any evidence of its being practised before the third century; or before the times of *Tertullian*. We allow it began in the third century, and was then practised in the African churches, where we apprehend it was first moved; but deny there was any mention or practice of it before that age; and affirm that *Tertullian* is the first person known that spoke of it, and who speaks against it: I have therefore required of any of our learned Pædobaptists to produce a single passage out of any authentic writer before *Tertullian*, in which infant-baptism is expresly mentioned, or clearly hinted at, or plainly supposed, or manifestly referred to: if this is not done, the controversy must remain just in the same state where it was, and infant-baptism carried not a moment higher that it was before; and whatever else is done below this date, is all to no purpose. How far this Gentleman, who has engaged in this controversy, has succeeded, is our next business to inquire.

The only christian writers of the first century, any of whose writings are extant, are *Barnabas, Clemens Romanus, Hermas, Polycarp*, and *Ignatius*; nothing out of *Barnabas, Polycarp*, and *Ignatius*, in favour of infant-baptism, is pretended to. " The most ancient writer that we have (says this Gentleman, " in the words of Mr *Bingham*) is *Clemens Romanus*, who lived in the time of " the apostles; and he, though he doth not directly mention infant-baptism, " yet says a thing that by consequence proves it; for he makes infants liable to original sin, which is in effect to say that they have need of baptism to purge it away, *&c*." The passage or passages in *Clemens*, in which he says this thing, are not produced; I suppose they are the same that are quoted by Dr *Wall*, in neither of which does he say any such thing; it is true, in the first of them he makes mention of a passage in *Job* xiv. 4. according to the Greek version, *no man is free from pollution, no not though his life is but of one day*; which might be brought indeed to prove original sin, but is not brought by *Clemens* for any such purpose, but as a self-accusation of *Job*; shewing, that though he had the character of a good man, yet he was not free from sin: and the other only speaks of men coming into the world as out of a grave and darkness, meaning out of their mother's womb; and seems not to refer to any moral death and darkness men are under, or to the sinful state of men as they come into the world: but be it so, that in these passages *Clemens* does speak of original sin, what is this to infant-baptism, or the necessity of it? is there no other way to purge away original sin, but baptism? nay, is there any such virtue in baptism as to

purge

purge it away? there is not; it is the blood of Chrift, and that only, that purges away fin, whether original or actual. Should it be faid that this was the fenfe of the ancients in fome after-ages, who did afcribe fuch a virtue to baptifm, and did affirm it was neceffary to be adminiftered, and did adminifter it to infants for that purpofe, what is this to *Clemens*? what, becaufe fome perfons in fome after-ages gave into this ftupid notion, that baptifm took away original fin, and was neceffary to infants, and ought to be given them for that reafon, does it follow that *Clemens* was of that mind? or is there the leaft hint of it in his letter? What though he held the doctrine of original fin, does it follow therefore that he was for infant-baptifm? how many Antipædobaptifts are there who profefs the fame doctrine? will any man from hence conclude that they are for and in the practice of infant-baptifm? It follows in the words of the fame writer; " *Hermes paftor* (*Hermas* I fuppofe it fhould be) lived about the fame time with " *Clemens*; and hath feveral paffages to fhew the general neceffity of *water*, " that is, baptifm, to fave men:" the paffages referred to are thofe Dr *Wall* has produced. *Hermas* had a vifion of a tower built on *water*; inquiring the reafon of it, he is told, it was " becaufe your life is, and will be faved by water:" and in another place, " before any one receives the name of the Son of God, " he is liable to death; but when he receives that feal, he is delivered from " death, and is affigned to life; and that feal is water." Now by *water Hermas* is fuppofed to mean baptifm; but furely he could not mean real material water, or the proper ordinance of water-baptifm, fince he fpeaks of the patriarchs coming up through this water, and being fealed with this feal *after they were dead*, and fo entering into the kingdom of God: but how difembodied fpirits could be baptized in real water, is not eafy to conceive; it muft furely defign fomething myftical; and what it is, I muft leave to thofe who better underftand thefe vifionary things: but be it fo, that baptifm in water is meant, falvation by it may be underftood in the fame fenfe as the apoftle *Peter* afcribes falvation to it, when he fays, that *baptifm faves by the refurrection of Chrift from the dead*; that is, by directing the baptized perfon to Chrift for falvation, who was delivered for his offences, and rofe again for his juftification; of which refurrection baptifm by immerfion is a lively emblem; and *Hermas* is only fpeaking of adult perfons, and not of infants, or of their baptifm, or of the neceffity of it to their falvation: in another place indeed he fpeaks of fome that were as infants without malice, and fo more honourable than others; and, adds he, all infants, are honoured with the Lord, and accounted of firft of all; that is, all fuch infants as before defcribed: but be it that infants in age are meant, they may be valued and loved by the Lord; he may fhew mercy to them, chufe, redeem, regenerate, and fave them, and yet not order them to be baptized; nor has he ordered

it:

it: however *Hermas* has not a word about the baptism of them, and therefore these passages are impertinently referred to.

Now these are all the passages of the writers of the first century brought into this controversy; in which there is so far from being any express mention of infant-baptism, that it is not in the least hinted at, nor referred unto; nor is any thing of this kind pretended to, till we come to the middle of the next age; and yet our author upon the above passages concludes after this manner: " thus—we have traced up the *practice* of infant baptism to the time of the " apostles;" when those writers give not the least hint of infant-baptism, or have any reference to it, or the practice of it. It is amazing what a *face* some men have! proceed we now to

The second century. The book of *Recognitions*, this writer seems to be at a loss where to place it, whether after or before *Justin*; however, Mr *Bingham* tells him, " it is an antient writing of the same age with *Justin Martyr*, men-" tioned by *Origen* in his *Philocalia*, and by some ascribed to *Bardesanes Syrus*, " who lived about the middle of the second century." It is indeed mentioned by *Origen*, though not under that name, and is by him ascribed to *Clemens*, as it has been commonly done; and if so, might have been placed among the testimonies of the *first* century; but this Gentleman's author says it is ascribed by some to *Bardesanes Syrus:* it is true, there is inserted in it a fragment out of a dialogue of his concerning fate, against *Abydas* an astrologer; but then it should rather be concluded from hence, as *Fabricius* observes [a], that the author of the *Recognitions*, is a later writer than *Bardesanes* : but be it so that it is him, who is this *Bardesanes?* an arch-heretic, one that first fell into the Valentinian heresy; and though he seemed afterwards to change his mind, he was not wholly free, as *Eusebius* says [b], from his old heresy; and he became the author of a new sect, called after his name Bardesanists; who held that the devil was not a creature of God; that Christ did not assume human flesh; and that the body rises not [c]. The book of *Recognitions*, ascribed to him, is urged by the Papists, as Mr *James* observes [d], to prove the power of exorcists, free-will, faith alone insufficient, the chrysm in baptism, and *Peter*'s succession; though the better sort of writers among them are ashamed of it. Sixtus Senensis says [e], that " most things in " it are uncertain, many fabulous, and some contrary to doctrines generally " received." And *Baronius* [f] has these words concerning it: " Away with such " monstrous lies and mad dotages, which are brought out of the said filthy

" ditch

[a] Bibliothec. Græc. l. 5. c. 1. f. 12. p. 36.   [b] Eccl. Hist. l. 4. c. 30.
[c] Ittigius de Heresiarchis, sect. 2. c. 6. p. 133. Vid. Epiphan. Hæres. 56. August. de Hæres. c. 35. Corruption of the Fathers, part 1. p. 6.
[d] Apud Rivet. Critic. Sacr. l. 1. c. 7. p. 130.   [f] Ibid.

"ditch of the *Recognitions,* which go under the name of *Clemens:*" but all this is no matter, if infant-baptism can be proved out it; but how? "This author speaks of the necessity of baptism in the same stile as *Justin Martyr* did—was undeniably an assertor of the general necessity of baptism to salvation:" wherever this wretched tenet, this false notion of the absolute necessity of baptism to salvation is met with, the Pædobaptists presently smell out infant-baptism, one falshood following upon another; and true it is, that one error leads on to another; and this false doctrine paved the way for infant-baptism; but then the mystery of iniquity worked by degrees; as soon as it was broached infant-baptism did not immediately commence: it does not follow, because that heretic asserted this notion, that therefore he was for or in the practice of infant-baptism; besides this book, be the author of it who will, is not made mention of before the third century, if so soon; for the work referred to by *Origen* has another title, and was in another form; he calls it *the circuits of Peter,* an apocryphal, fabulous and romantic writing; and though the passage he quotes is in the *Recognitions,* which makes some learned men conclude it to be the same with that; yet so it might be, and not be the same with it. But I pass on to a more authentic and approved writer of the second century:

*Justin Martyr,* who lived about the year 150; and the first passage produced from him is this [s] : "We bring them (namely, the new converts) to some "place where there is water, and they are regenerated by the same way of "regeneration by which we were regenerated; for they are washed with water "in the name of God the Father and Lord of all things, and of our Saviour "Jesus Christ, and of the holy Spirit." In this passage, it is owned, "*Justin* "is describing the manner of adult baptism only; having no occasion to de- "scend to any farther particulars; nor is it alledged, it is said, as a proof of "infant-baptism directly; but only to shew, that this ancient writer used the "word *regeneration* so as to connote *baptism*—yet his words cannot be thought "to exclude the baptism of infants in these days:" but if infant-baptism had been practised in those days, it is not consistent with that sincerity and impartiality which *Justin* sets out with, when he proposed to give the Roman Emperor an account of christian baptism, not to make any mention of that; for he introduces it thus: "We will declare after what manner, when we were "renewed by Christ, we devoted ourselves unto God, left omitting this we "should seem to act a bad part (prevaricate or deal unfairly) in this declara- "tion;" whereas it was not dealing fairly with the Emperor, and not giving him a full and fair account of the administration of the ordinance of baptism to all its proper subjects, if infants had used to be baptized; which he could

easily

[s] Apolog. 2. p. 93, 94.

easily have introduced the mention of, and one would think could not have omitted it: besides, as Dr *Gale*[b] observes, he had an occasion to speak of it, and to descend to this particular, had it been used; since the christians were charged with using their infants barbarously; which he might have removed, had this been the case, by observing the great regard they had to them in devoting them to God in baptism, and thereby initiating them into their religion, and providing for the salvation of their souls: but *Justin* is so far from saying any thing of this kind, that he leaves the Emperor and every body else to conclude that infants were not the subjects of baptism in this early age; for as the above writer observes, immediately follow such words as directly oppose infant-baptism; they are these: " And we have been taught by the apostles " this reason for this thing; because we being ignorant of our first birth, were " generated by necessity, *&c.* that we should not continue children of that " necessity and ignorance, but of will (or choice) and knowledge; and should " obtain forgivenfs of the sins in which we have lived, by water:" so that in order to obtain these things by water or baptism, which *Justin* speaks of, there must be free choice and knowledge, which infants are not capable of: but it seems the main thing this passage is brought to prove, is, that the words *regenerated* and *regeneration* are used for *baptized* and *baptism*; and this agreeing with the words of Christ in *John* iii. 5. shews that this construction of them then obtained, that baptism is necessary to salvation. Now, it should be observed, that the persons *Justin* speaks of are not represented by him as regenerated by baptism, because they are spoken of before as converted persons and believers; and it is as clear and plain that their baptism is distinguished from their regeneration, and is not the same thing; for *Justin* uses the former as an argument of the latter; which if the same, his sense must be, they were baptized because they were baptized; whereas his sense, consistent with himself, and the practice of the primitive churches, is; that these persons, when brought to the water, having made a profession of their regeneration, were owned and declared regenerated persons; as was manifest from their being admitted to the ordinance of water-baptism; and from hence it appears, that, then no such construction of *John* iii. 5. obtained, that baptism is necessary to salvation: and this now seems to be the passage referred to, in which *Justin* is said to speak of the necessity of baptism, in a stile the author of the *Recognitions* agreed with him in; but without any reason.

The next passage out of *Justin* is in his dialogue with *Trypho* the Jew; where he says that " concerning the influence and effect of *Adam*'s sin upon mankind, " which the ancient writers represent as the ground and reason of infant- " baptism—"

[b] Reflections, &c. p. 455.

" baptism—" The words, as cited by Dr *Wall*, to whom our author refers us, are these: *Justin*, speaking of the birth, baptism, and crucifixion of Christ, says [h], " he did this for mankind, which by *Adam* was fallen under death, and " under the guile of the serpent; beside the particular cause which each man " had of sinning." Now, allowing that this is spoken of original sin, as it seems to be, what is this to infant-baptism? I have already exposed the folly of arguing from persons holding the one, to the practice of the other. It is added by our author, " in the same book, he (*Justin*) speaks of baptism being " to christians in the room of circumcision, and so points out the analogy be-
" tween those two initiatory rites." The passage referred to is this [i]: " We " also who by him have had access to God, have not received this carnal cir-
" cumcision, but the spiritual circumcision, which *Enoch*, and those like him, " have observed; and we have received it by baptism by the mercy of God, " because we were sinners; and it is enjoined to all persons to receive it the same " way." Now let be observed, that this spiritual circumcision, whatever *Justin* means by it, can never design baptism; since the patriarch *Enoch*, and others like him, observed it: and since christians are said to receive it *by baptism*, and therefore must be different from baptism itself: nor does *Justin* say any thing of the analogy between baptism and circumcision, or of the one being in the room of the other; but opposes the spiritual circumcision to carnal circumcision; and speaks not one word of infants, only of the duty of adult persons, as he supposes it to be. The last passage, and on which this Gentleman intends to dwell awhile, is this [k]: " Several persons (says *Justin*) among us of both sexes, of " sixty and seventy years of age, οι εκ παιδων εμαθητευθησαν τω Χριςω, " who were " discipled to Christ in their childhood, *&c.*" which I have observed should be rendered, " who from their childhood were instructed in Christ;" and which I have confirmed by several passages in *Justin*, in which he uses the word in the sense of instruction; and from whom can we better learn his meaning than from himself? all which this author takes no notice of; but puts me off with a passage out of *Plutarch*, where *Antiphon* the son of *Sophilus*, according to his version, is said to be *discipled* or *proselyted* to his father: I leave him to enjoy his own sense; for I do not understand it; and should have thought that μαθητευσας Δ τω πατρι, might have been rendered more intelligibly, as well as more truly, " instructed by his father;" since, as it follows, his father was an orator. He thinks he has catched me off of my guard, and that I suppose the word *disciple* includes baptism; because in my commentary on *Acts* xix. 3. I say, " the apostle takes it for granted that they were *baptized*, since they were not " only believers, but *disciples*;" but had he read on, or transcribed what follows,

---

[h] Dialog. cum Trypho p. 316. Ed. Paris.   [i] Ib. p. 261.   [k] Ib. Apolog. p. 62.

lows, my sense would clearly appear; "such as not only believed with the "heart, but had made a profession of their faith, and were followers of Christ:" nor is the sense of the word *disciple*, as including the idea of baptism, confirmed by *Acts* xiv. 21. where it is said, *when they had preached the gospel to that city,* χ μαθητυσαντες, "*and taught many*, or made them disciples;" which may be interpreted without tautology, and yet not include the idea of baptism; since the first word, *preached*, expresses the bare external ministry of the word; and the latter, *taught*, or made disciples, the influence and effect of it upon the minds of men; the former may be where the latter is not; and both, where baptism is not as yet administered. The reason why ικ παιδος, must be rendered *in*, and not *from their childhood*, because the baptism of any persons being not a continued, but one single transient act, to speak of their being baptized *from* their childhood would be improper, is merry indeed; when *Justin* is not speaking of the baptism of any person at all; but of their being trained up in the knowledge of Christ, and the christian religion from their childhood, in which they had persevered to the years mentioned. Upon the whole, in all these passages of *Justin* quoted, there is no express mention of infant-baptism, nor any hint given of it, nor any reference unto it. Proceed we now to the next writer in this century, brought into this controversy:

*Irenæus*; who lived towards the close of it, and wrote about the year 180; the only passage in him, and which has been the subject of debate a hundred years past, is this; speaking of Christ, he says[1], "he came to save all, all I "say, *qui per eum renascuntur in Deum*, "who by him are *born again* unto God;" "infants, and little ones, and children, and young men, and old men." Now not to insist upon the works of *Irenæus* we have being mostly a translation, and a very poor one, complained of by learned men; nor upon this chapter wherein this passage is, being reckoned spurious by others; which weaken the force of this testimony, and will have their weight with considering persons; I shall only take notice of the sense of the phrase, *born again unto God*; and the injury done to the character of *Irenæus*, to make it signify baptism, or any thing else but the grace of regeneration. Our author begins his defence of this passage in favour of infant-baptism, with a remark of the learned *Feuardentius*, as he calls him; "that by the name of regeneration, according to the phrase of Christ and "his apostles, he (*Irenæus*) understands *baptism*, clearly confirming the apos- "tolical tradition concerning the baptism of infants." As for the learning of this monk, I cannot discern it, unless his lies and impudence against the reformers, which run through his notes, are to be so called. Whether our author is a junior or senior man, I know not; by his writing he seems to be the former, but

[1] Adv. Hæref. l. 2. c. 39.

but the advice of *Rivet*, who was without doubt a man of learning, is good; " only, says he [m], I would have the younger, that shall light on the works of " *Irenæus* advised, to beware of those editions, which that most impudent monk " *Feuardentius*, a man of large assurance, and uncommon boldness, and of no " faith nor faithfulness, has in many things foully corrupted and defiled with " impious and lying annotations:" and a false gloss this of his is, which is quoted; for Christ and his apostles no where call baptism by the name of the *new birth*. I have observed, that as yet, that is, in *Irenæus's* time, it had not obtained among the ancients, to use the words *regenerated* or *regeneration* for *baptized* or *baptism*; nor is this author able to prove it. The passage in *Justin* before-mentioned falls short of it, as has been shewn; and the passages in *Tertullian* and *Clemens* of *Alexandria*, concerning being *born in water*, and *begotten of the womb of water*, are too late; and beside, the one is to be interpreted of the grace of God compared to water; this is clearly *Tertullian's* sense; for he adds [n], " nor " are we otherwise safe or saved, than by remaining in water;" which surely can never be understood literally of the water of baptism: and as for *Clemens* [o], he is speaking not of regeneration, but of the natural generation of man, as he comes out of his mother's womb, naked, and free from sin, as he supposes; and as such, converted persons ought to be.

To have recourse to heathens to ascertain the name of christian baptism, is monstrous; though this, it is said, there is no need of, " since *several* christian " writers, who lived *with* or *before Irenæus*, speak the same language, as will " be seen hereafter:" and yet none are produced but *Barnabas* and *Justin*; the latter of which has been considered already, and found not to the purpose; and his reasoning upon the former is beyond my comprehension; for whatever may be said for the giving of milk and honey to persons just baptized, being a symbol of their being born again, it can be no proof of the words *regeneration* and *regenerated* being used for *baptism* and *baptized*; when these words neither the one nor the other are mentioned by *Barnabas*; so that I have no reason to retract what I have said on that point. And now we are returned to *Irenæus* himself; and two passages from him are produced in proof of the sense of the word contended for; and one is where he thus speaks [p], " and again giving the power " of regeneration unto God to his disciples, he said unto them, *Go and teach all nations, baptizing them*, &c." By which power or commission is meant, not

the

---

[m] Juniores qui in opera Irenæi incident monitos volo, ut caveant ab illis editionibus quas impudentissimus ille monachus Feuardentius, homo projectæ audaciæ, & nullius fidei, fœde in multis corrupit & annotationibus impiis & mendacibus conspurcavit, Rivet. Critic. Sacr. l.2.c.6. p. 188, 189.

[n] Nos pisciculi in aqua nascimur. Nec aliter quam in aqua permanendo salvi sumus, Tertullian. de baptismo, c 1.

[o] Stromat l. 4. p. 538. Ed. Paris.     [p] Adv. Hæref. l. 3. c. 19.

the commiſſion of baptizing, but more plainly the commiſſion of teaching the doctrine of regeneration by the Spirit of God, and the neceſſity of that to ſalvation, and in order to baptiſm; and which was the firſt and principal part of the apoſtles commiſſion, as the order of the words ſhew; and it is moſt reaſonable to think, that he ſhould ſo call the commiſſion, not from its more remote and leſs principal part, but from the firſt and more principal one. The other paſſage is where *Irenæus* mentions ⁹ by name "the *baptiſm* of *regeneration* to God:" but this rather proves the contrary, that baptiſm and regeneration are two different things, and not the ſame; juſt as the ſcriptural phraſe, the *baptiſm of repentance*, and which ſeems to have led the ancients to ſuch a way of ſpeaking, means ſomething different from repentance, and not the ſame : baptiſm is ſo called, becauſe repentance is a prerequiſite to it, in the ſubjects of it; and for the ſame reaſon it is called the *baptiſm of regeneration*, becauſe regeneration is abſolutely neceſſary in order to it: to all which I only add, that *Irenæus* not only uſes the word *regeneration* in a different ſenſe from baptiſm elſewhere ʳ, but moſt clearly uſes it in another ſenſe in this very paſſage; ſince he ſays, Chriſt came to ſave all who *by him* are born again unto God; who are regenerated by Chriſt, and not by baptiſm; and which is explained both before and after by his *ſanctifying* all ſorts of perſons, infants, little ones, young men, and old men; which cannot be underſtood of his baptizing them, for he baptized none; and therefore they cannot be ſaid to be regenerated by him in that ſenſe: and I ſay again, to underſtand *Irenæus* as ſpeaking of baptiſm, is to make him ſpeak what is abſolutely falſe; that Chriſt came to ſave *all* and *only* ſuch who are baptized unto God. It ſeems *Le Clerc* is of the ſame ſentiment with me, an author I am a ſtranger to; whom this writer lets paſs without any reaſoning againſt him, only with this chaſtizement; "he ſhould have underſtood (being an *eccleſiaſtical hiſtorian*) the ſentiments and language of the primitive fathers better;" but what their language and ſentiments were, we have ſeen already; and let them be what they will, *Irenæus* muſt expreſs a downright falſehood, if he is to be underſtood in the ſenſe contended for: on the one hand, it cannot be true that Chriſt came to ſave *all* that are baptized; no doubt but *Judas* was baptized, as well as the other apoſtles, and yet it will not be ſaid Chriſt came to ſave him; *Simon Magus* was certainly baptized, and yet was *in the gall of bitterneſs, and bond of iniquity*, and by all the accounts of him continued ſo till death; there were many members of the church at *Corinth*, who doubtleſs were baptized, and yet were unworthy receivers of the Lord's ſupper, and eat and drank damnation to themſelves, for which reaſon there were many weak, ſickly, and aſleep ˢ; and it is to be feared, without any breach of charity, that this has been the caſe of

thouſands

⁹ Ibid. l. 1. c. 18.    ʳ Vid. l. 4. c. 59. and l. 5. c. 15.    ˢ 1 Cor. xi. 29, 30.

thousands besides: and on the other hand, it cannot be with truth suggested, that Christ came to save *only* such as are baptized; he came to die for the transgressions that were under the First Testament, or to save persons under that dispensation, who never received Christian baptism; he said to one and to another, unbaptized persons, *thy sins are forgiven thee*[1]; and no doubt there are many saved, and whom Christ came to save, who never were baptized in water; and the Pædobaptists themselves will stand a bad chance for salvation, if this was true; for they will find it a hard task to prove that any one of them, only sprinkled in infancy, was ever truly baptized; and yet as uncharitable as we are said to be, we have so much charity to believe that every good man among them, though unbaptized, shall be saved. And now since the words of *Irenæus* taken in this sense contain a manifest falshood, and they are capable of another sense, agreeable to truth, without straining them; as that Christ came to save all that are regenerated by himself, by his spirit and grace, we ought in a judgment of charity to believe that this latter sense is his, and not the former; and the rather, since his words in their proper and literal sense have this meaning; and since they are expressed with so much caution; left it should be thought it was his meaning that Christ came to save *all men*, good and bad, he describes the persons he came to save, not by their baptism, which is a precarious and uncertain evidence of salvation, but by their regeneration, which is a sure proof of it; and since this sense of his words is agreeable to his use of the phrase elsewhere, and to the context likewise, and is suited to all sorts of persons of every age here mentioned; and indeed to depart from this clear literal sense of his words, which establishes a well-known truth, and fix a figurative, improper one upon them, which makes him to say a notorious untruth, to serve an hypothesis, is *cruel* usage of the good old father, and is contrary to all the *rules* of *honour, justice, truth*, and *charity*. To put our Lord's words in *Mark* xvi. 16. upon a level with the false sense of *Irenæus*, is mean and stupid; they need no qualifying sense; the meaning is plain and easy; that every baptized believer shall be saved, and leave no room to suggest that unbaptized believers shall not; but that every unbeliever, be he who he will, baptized or unbaptized, shall be damned. And now what a wretched cause must the cause of infant-baptism be, that requires such managing as this to maintain it? what a wretched cause is it, that at its first setting out, according to the account of the advocates of it; for Dr *Wall* says[2], "this is the first express mention that we have met with of infants "baptized?" I say again, what a wretched cause must this be, that is connected with lies and falshood at its first appearance, as pleaded for; is established upon downright injustice to a good man's character, and supported by real injury to
it?

[1] Matt. ix. 5. Luke vii. 48.     [2] History of Infant-baptism, part I. c. 3. §. 6.

## INFANT-BAPTISM AN INNOVATION.

it? and yet notwithstanding all this, our author has the *front* to say, "so much then for the testimony, the *plain, unexceptionable* testimony, of *Irenæus*, for the practice of infant-baptism."

And now we are come to the close of the second century; but before we pass to the next, we must stop a little, and consider a passage our author, after Dr *Wall*, has produced out of *Clemens* of *Alexandria*, who lived at the latter end of this century, about the year 190; and it is this: speaking of rings worn on the fingers, and the seals upon them, advises against every thing idolatrous and lascivious, and to what is innocent and useful; "let our seals, says he[*], be a dove, or a fish, or a ship running with the wind, or a musical harp—or a mariner's anchor———and if any one is a fisherman, Ἀποςολν μιμνηται ϗ τον ἐξ ὑδατ@ ἀναςπωμενον παιδων, "let him remember the apostle, and the children drawn out of the water." This passage was sent by two Gentlemen from different places to Dr *Wall*, after he had published two editions of his history; and he seems to have been ashamed of himself for not having observed it, and fancies that this refers to the baptizing of a child, and the taking, drawing, and lifting it out of the water. Now, though I do not pretend to support my conjecture by any manuscript or printed copy, nor do I think it worth while to search and inquire after it, whether there is any various reading or no, but shall leave it to others who have more leisure and opportunity; yet I persuade myself my conjecture will not be condemned as a groundless one by any man of sense and learning, especially out of this controversy: my conjecture then is, that it should be read not παιδων, "children," but ιχθυων "fishes;" for who ever heard of a *draught of children*; when a *draught of fishes* is common? and why should a fisherman, more than any other, remember an apostle and a draught of children? surely a draught of fishes is more proper to him: the words I think therefore should be read, "let him remember the apostle, and the fishes drawn out of the water;" and the sense is, let him remember the apostle *Peter*, and the draught of fishes taken by him, recorded either in *Luke* v. 6, 9. or in *John* xxi. 6, 8, 11. for the words manifestly refer to some particular and remarkable fact, which should be called to mind, and not to a thing that was done every day; which must be the case, if infant-baptism now obtained: besides, the word used cannot with any decency and propriety be applied to the baptizing of a child; a wide difference there is in the expression, between taking and lifting a child out of the font, and a drawing or dragging it out of the water; the word is expressive of strength and force necessary to an action [x], and well agrees with the drawing or dragging of a net full of fishes. However, if this instance is continued to be urged, I hope

[*] Pædagog. l. 3. c. 11. p. 246, 247.  [x] Luke xiv. 15. Acts xi. 10.

it will be allowed that baptifm in thofe early times was performed by immerfion; fince thefe children are faid to be drawn out of the water, and therefore muft have been in it: moreover, let it be what it will that *Clemens* refers unto, it muft be fomething that was not common to every man, but peculiar to a fifherman; as he afterwards fays, a fword or a bow are not proper for thofe that purfue peace; nor cups for temperate perfons; and I infift upon it, that it be faid what that is which is peculiar to fuch a one, except it be that which I have fuggefted: and after all, he muft have a warm brain, a heated imagination, and a mind prepoffeffed, that can believe that infant-baptifm is here referred to. Upon the whole, it does not appear from any authentic writer of the fecond century, that there is any exprefs mention of infant-baptifm in it, nor any clear hint of it, or manifeft reference to it; and therefore it muft be an innovation in the church, whenever it afterwards took place. I proceed now to

The third century, at the beginning of which *Tertullian* lived; who is the firft perfon that ever gave any hint of infant-baptifm, or referred unto it, or made exprefs mention of it, that is known; and he argued againft it, and that very ftrongly, from the more ufual delay of the adminiftration of it, according to every one's age, condition, and difpofition; from the danger fureties might be brought into by engaging for infants; from the neceffity of firft knowing and underftanding what they were about; from their innocent age, as it comparatively is, not being yet confcious of fin, ftanding in no need of the application of pardoning grace, which the ordinance of baptifm leads adult believers to; from the propriety of their firft afking for it; and from a different method being taken in worldly affairs: his words are thefe, and as they are tranflated by Dr *Wall* himfelf; "therefore according to every one's condition and difpo-
" fition, and alfo their age, the delaying of baptifm is more profitable, efpe-
" cially in the cafe of little children; for what need is there that the godfathers
" fhould be brought into danger? becaufe they may either fail of their pro-
" mifes by death, or they may be miftaken by a child's proving of a wicked
" difpofition. Our Lord fays indeed, *Do not forbid them to come to me:* there-
" fore let them come when they are grown up: let them come when they un-
" derftand: when they are inftructed whither it is that they come: let them be
" made chriftians when they can know Chrift; what need their guiltlefs age
" make fuch hafte to the forgivenefs of fins? Men will proceed more warily
in worldly things; and he that fhould not have earthly goods committed to
" him, yet fhall have heavenly. Let them know how to defire this falvation,
" that you may appear to have given to one that afketh [x]." It is obferved by
our

[x] Tertullian. de baptifmo, c. 18.

our author, after Dr *Wall*, that in the clause about sponsors, in the older editions, these words come in, *si non tam necesse*, which are rendered, *except in case of necessity*. But these *older editions* are but *one Gagnæus*, whose reading is rejected by *Rigaltius* as a foolish repetition; censured by *Grotius*, as affording no tolerable sense [y]; received by *Pamelius* for no other reason that he gives, but because it softens the opinion of the author about the delaying of baptism to infants [z]; and it is for this reason it is catched at by the Pædobaptists; and yet they do not seem to be quite easy with it, because of the nonsense and impertinence of it; " *what need is there, except there is a need?*" wherefore our author attempts an emendation, and proposes to read *tamen* for *tam*, which does not make it a whit the better, but rather increases the nonsense; " what need is there, except not-
" withstanding there is need?" but what is of more importance is, it is said,
" these words of *Tertullian seem* fairly to imply that infant baptism was not only
" moved for, but actually practised in his time:" to which I answer, that they neither do imply, nor *seem* to imply any such thing, at least not necessarily; for supposing the baptism of infants moved for, and sureties promised to be engaged for them, which seems likely to be the case as soon as mentioned, the better to get it received; *Tertullian* might say all that he does, though as yet not one infant had ever been baptized, or any sureties made use of: and indeed it would have been very strange, if nothing of this kind had been said previous to the observance of them; the bare motion of these things was sufficient to bring out the arguments against them: and what though *Tertullian* might have some odd notions and singular opinions, about which he talked wrong and weakly, does it follow that therefore he so did about these points? Nor is there any reason to interpret his words of the infants of infidels, since he makes no distinction in the passage, nor gives the least hint of any; and what he elsewhere says of the children of believers being holy, he explains of their being *designed for holiness* [a]; and says men are not *born*, but *made* christians [b]: nor does he any where allow of the baptism of infants, in case of necessity, which is only established upon that impertinent reading before-mentioned: and with respect to his notion of the necessity of baptism to salvation, it is sufficient to observe what he says; " if any
" understand the importance of baptism, they will rather fear the having it,
" than the delaying it: true faith is secure of salvation [c]." And the reason why he does not produce infant-baptism among his unwritten customs, is very easy

3 E 2   to

---

[y] See Dr Gale's Reflections, &c. p. 511.   [z] Ex eodem Gagnæo iterum adjicio, si non tam necesse; nam illud mitigat auctoris opinionem, &c Pamelii. adnot. p. 348.

[a] Designatos sanctitati, Tertull. de anima. c. 39.

[b] Fiunt, non nascuntur christiani, Apologet. c. 18.

[c] Si qui pondus intelligant baptismi, magis timebunt consecutionem quam dilationem: fides integra secura est de salute. Ibid. de baptismo, c. 18.

to observe, because as yet no such custom had obtained, and as yet the apostolical tradition of it had never been heard of: the first that speaks of that, if he does at all, is the following person;

*Origen*, who flourished about the year 230, and comes next under consideration: and three passages are usually cited out of him in favour of infant-baptism; shewing not only that infants should be baptized, but that this was an ancient usage of the church, and a tradition of the apostles. Now these things are only to be met with in the Latin translations of this ancient writer; and though there is much of his still extant in Greek, yet in these his genuine works there is not the least hint of infant-baptism, nor any reference to it; and much less any express mention of it; and still less any thing said of it, being a custom of the church, and an apostolical tradition: This has justly raised a suspicion, that he has not been fairly used in the translations of him by *Ruffinus* and *Jerom*: and upon inquiry, this is found to be the truth of the matter; and it is not only *Erasmus*, whom Dr *Wall* is pleased to represent as angrily saying, that a reader is uncertain whether he reads *Origen* or *Ruffinus*; for *Scultetus*[d] says the same thing; and it is the observation of many others, that it was the common custom of *Ruffinus* to interpolate whatever he translated. The learned *Huetius*, who has given us a good edition of all *Origen's* commentaries of the scripture in Greek, and who was as conversant with his writings, and understood them as well as any man whatever, was very sensible of the foul play he has met with, and often complains of the perfidy and impudence of *Ruffinus*; he says of him, that whatever he undertook to translate, he interpolated; that he so distressed and corrupted the writings of *Origen* by additions and detractions, that one is at a loss to find *Origen* in *Origen*: that whereas he undertook to translate his commentary on the *Romans*, at the instance of *Heraclius*, yet he asks, with what faithfulness did he do it? namely, with his own, that is, which is the worst; and when *Huetius* produces any thing out of these translations, it is always with diffidence, as not to be depended upon; and sometimes he adds when he has done, "but let us remember again the perfidy of *Ruffinus*;" and speaking particularly of his commentaries on the *Romans*, he says; "Let the learned reader remember that *Origen* is not so much to be thought the author of them, as *Ruffinus*, by whom they are not so much interpreted, as *new coined* and *interpolated*[e]." But what need I produce

[d] Medulla Patrum, part 1. l. 6. c. 2. p. 124.

[e] Interpolare enim omnia Ruffinus quæcunque suscepit interpretanda—solenne habuit. Huetii Origeniana, l. 2. p. 116. nam ejus scripta interpretans, ita additamentis & detractionibus vexavit & corrupit ut Origenem in Origene desideres, ibid. l. 3. c. 1. p. 233. Ruffinus Heraclii impulsu viginti tomos commentariorum Origenis in epistolam ad Romanos Latinæ linguæ donandos suscepit:

produce these testimonies? *Ruffinus* himself owns, not only that he used great freedom in translating the homilies on *Leviticus*, and added much of his own to them, as I have observed; but also in his translation of the commentary on the *Romans*, he grants the charge against him, "that he added some things, "supplied what was wanting, and shortened what were too long[f];" and it is from these two pieces that the two principal passages which assert infant-baptism to be the custom of the church, and an apostolical tradition, are taken: and now of what use is this Gentleman's quotation from *Marshall?* it is good for nothing. The other passage, which stands in *Jerom's* translation of *Origen's* homilies on *Luke*, speaks indeed of the baptism of infants, and the necessity of it; but not a word of its being a custom of the church, and an apostolical tradition, as in the other; and beside, his translations being no more exact than *Ruffinus's*, and which appears by his other versions; in which he takes the same liberty as *Ruffinus* did, are no more to be depended upon than his. And now, where is his highest *probability* and *moral certainty*, that there are no additions and interpolations in *Origen?* I appeal to the whole world, whether such sort of writings as these, so manifestly corrupted, so confessedly interpolated, would be admitted an evidence in any civil affair in any court of judicature whatever; and if not, then surely these ought not to be admitted as an evidence in religious affairs, respecting an ordinance of our Lord Jesus Christ. But it is said, "supposing all this, what does it signify in the present case, unless it could be "proved that the particular passages under consideration were additions or "interpolations?" To which I answer; since the whole is so *interpolated*, and so deformed, that it can scarcely be known, as has been observed, what dependence can there be on any part of it? I have observed, that the passage in the homilies on *Leviticus*, is by *Vossius* thought to be of the greater authority against the Pelagians, because of the interpolations of *Ruffinus*. This Gentleman says, I have *unluckily* observed this; I do not see any *unluckiness* in it; it is *lucky* on my side, that *Vossius*, a Pædobaptist, should suggest that this passage is interpolated, however unlucky *Ruffinus* was in doing it; and it is no unusual thing for a writer to insert that in his works, which makes or may be improved against himself: beside, what makes these very passages suspected of interpolation, is, not only that no cotemporary of *Origen's*, nor any writer

before

---

sed qua fide? sua nempe, hoc est, pessima. Ibid. p. 253. Sed Ruffini tamen perfidiam denuo recordemur. Ibid. l. 2. p. 59. vide etiam, p. 35. meminerit eruditus lector non tam illorum auctorem existimandum esse Origenem quam Ruffinum, a quo non tam interpretati, quam recusi & interpolati sunt. Ibid. p. 144.

[f] Addere aliqua videor, & explere quæ desunt, aut breviare quæ longa sunt. Ruffini Peroratio in Ep. ad Rom. fol. 224. C.

before him, nor any after him, till the times of *Ruffinus* and *Jerom*, ever speak of infant-baptism as a custom of the church, or an apostolic tradition; but neither *Cyprian* who came after him, and pleaded for infant-baptism, ever refers to *Origen* as saying these things, or uses such language as he is said to do; nor does *Austin*, who made such a bluster about infant-baptism being an apostolical tradition, ever appeal to *Origen*'s testimony of it; which one would think he would have done, had there been any such testimony: our author, because I have said that many things may be observed from the Greek of *Origen* in favour of adult-baptism, hectors most manfully; "the assertion, he says, is either "*false*, or very *impertinent*;" but surely he must be a little too premature to pass such a censure before the things are produced. I greatly question whether he has ever read the writings of *Origen*, either the Latin translations of him, or his works in Greek; and indeed there are scarce any of his quotations of the fathers throughout his whole work, but what seem to be taken at second hand from Dr *Wall*, or others: I say more than I should have chose to have said, through his insulting language. I am quite content he should have all the credit his performance will admit of; only such a writer, who knows his own weakness, ought not to be so *pert* and *insolent*: however, to stop the mouth of this *swaggering blade*, whoever he is, I will give him an instance or two out of the Greek of *Origen*, in favour of adult-baptism, to the exclusion of infant-baptism, and as manifestly against it. Now, not to take notice of *Origen*'s [f] interpretation of *Matthew* xix. 14. as not of infants literally, but metaphorically; which, according to his sense, destroys the argument of the Pædobaptists from thence, in favour of infant-baptism: "It is to be observed, says *Origen*, that the four
" evangelists saying that *John* confessed he came to baptize in water, only
" *Matthew* adds *unto repentance*; teaching, that he has the profit of baptism
" who " is baptized of his own will and choice:" Now if the profit of baptism is tied to " a person baptized of his own will and choice," according to *Origen*, then baptism must be unprofitable and insignificant to infants, because they are not baptized of their own will and choice: and a little after he says;
" The laver by the water is a symbol of the purification of the soul washed
" from all the filth of wickedness; nevertheless also of itself it is the beginning
" and fountain of divine gifts, because of the power of the invocation of the
" adorable Trinity, "to him that gives up himself to God [g];" which last clause excludes infants, since they do not and cannot give up themselves to God in
that

[f] Orig. Comment. in Matt. p. 372, 375. Ed. Huet.

[g] Παρατηρητεον δε οτι των τεσσαρων ειρηκοτων το εν υδατι ομολογω Ιωαννης ελιλυθναι βαπτιζων, μον⊙- Ματθαι⊙- τουτω προστιθηκε το εις μετανοιαν, διδασκων το, απο του βαπτισματ⊙- ωφιλναι εχιθαι της προαιρεσεως του βαπτιζομενω, & Paulo post το δια του υδατ⊙- λουτρον —ιμπαριχοντι εαυτον τη θεοτητι—χαρισματων θειων αρχη κ̣ πηγη. Origen. Comment. in Joannem. p. 124.

that ordinance. Let this Gentleman, if he can, produce any thing out of those writings of *Origen*, in favour of infant-baptism; the passage Dr *Wall* [b] refers to has not a syllable of it, nor any reference to it; and though he supposes *Jerom* must some where or other have read it in his writings, what *Jerom* says [1] supposes no such thing; since the passage only speaks of *Origen*'s opinion of sins in a pre-existent state, being forgiven in baptism, but not a word of the baptism of infants, or of their sins being forgiven them in their baptism: and now where is the clear testimony of the great *Origen*, not only for the practice of infant-baptism in his own days, but for the continual use of it all along from the time of the apostles? and where is our author's vaunt of the superior antiquity of infant-baptism to infant-communion? which, as we shall see presently, began together.

*Cyprian* is the next, and the only remaining writer of this century, quoted in favour of infant-baptism; who lived about the middle of it, and is the first pleader for it that we know of. We allow it was practised in his time in the African churches, where it was first moved; and at the same time infant-communion was practised also, of which we have undoubted and incontestable evidence; and it is but reasonable that if infants have a right to one ordinance, they should be admitted to the other; and if antiquity is of any weight in the matter, it is as early for the one as for the other: but though infant-baptism now began to be practised, it appears to be a novel-business; not only the time of its administration being undetermined; which made *Fidus*, a country bishop, who had a doubt about administering it before the eighth day, apply to the council under *Cyprian* for the resolution of it; but the exceeding weakness of the arguments then made use of for baptizing new-born infants, of which the present Pædobaptists must be ashamed, shew that Pædobaptism was then in its *infant-state*: the arguments used by *Cyprian* and his brethren for it, were taken from the grace of God being given to all men; and from the equality of the gift to all; and this proved from the spiritual equality of the bodies of infants and adult-persons; and both from the prophet *Elisha*'s stretching himself on the Shunamite's child; they argue the admission of all to baptism from the words of *Peter*, who says he was shewn, that *nothing is to be called common or unclean*; and reason, that infants ought to be more easily admitted than grown persons, because they have less guilt; and their weeping and crying are to be interpreted praying; yea, they suggest that baptism gives grace, and that a person is lost without it: but that it may appear I do not wrong them, I will transcribe their own words; and that as they are translated by Dr *Wall*, so far as they relate to this matter: "All of us judged that the grace and mercy of God is to be denied

"to

[b] Comment. in Matt. p. 391, 392.   [1] Adv. Pelag. l. 3. fol. 102. tom. 2.

" to no person that is born; for whereas our Lord in his gospel says, *the Son*
" *of Man came not to destroy mens souls,* (or lives) *but to save them*; as far as lies
" in us, no soul, if possible, is to be lost. The scripture gives us to under-
" stand the equality of the divine gift on all, whether infants or grown persons:
" *Elisha*, in his prayer to God, stretched himself on the infant-son of the *Shuna-*
" *mite* woman, that lay dead, in such manner, that his head, and face, and
" limbs, and feet, were applied to the head, face, limbs, and feet of the child;
" which, if it be understood according to the quality of our body and nature,
" the infant would not hold measure with that grown man, nor his limbs fit
" to reach to his great ones; but in that place a spiritual equality, and such
" as is in the esteem of God, is intimated to us; by which persons that are
" once made by God are alike and equal; and our growth of body by age,
" makes a difference in the sense of the world, but not of God; unless you
" will think that the grace itself which is given to baptized persons, is greater
" or less according to the age of those that receive it; whereas the holy Spirit
" is given, not by different measures, but with a fatherly affection and kind-
" ness, equal to all; for God, as he accepts no one person, so not his age;
" but with a just equality shews himself a Father to all, for their obtaining
" the heavenly grace—so that we judge that no person is to be hindered from
" the obtaining the grace by the law that is now appointed; and that the spi-
" ritual circumcision ought not to be restrained by the circumcision that was
" according to the flesh; but that all are to be admitted to the grace of Christ;
" since *Peter*, speaking in the *Acts of the Apostles*, says, *the Lord has shewn me,*
" *that no person is to be called common or unclean.* If any thing could be an ob-
" stacle to persons against their obtaining the grace, the adult, and grown,
" and elder men, would be rather hindered by their more grievous sins. If
" then the graceless offender, and those that have grievously sinned against
" God before, have, when they afterwards come to believe, forgiveness of
" their sins; and no person is kept off from baptism and the grace; how much
" less reason is there to refuse an infant, who, being newly born, has no sin,
" save the being descended from *Adam* according to the flesh: he has from
" his very birth contracted the contagion of the death anciently threatened;
" who comes, for this reason, more easily to receive forgiveness of sins, because
" they are not his own, but others sins that are forgiven him. This therefore,
" dear brother, was our opinion in the assembly, that it is not for us to hinder
" any man from baptism and the grace of God, who is merciful and kind and
" affectionate to all; which rule, as it holds for all, so we think it more espe-
" cially to be observed in reference to infants, and persons newly born; to
whom our help, and the divine mercy, is rather to be granted; because by
" their

## INFANT-BAPTISM AN INNOVATION.

"their weeping and wailing, at their first entrance into the world, they do in-
"timate nothing so much as that they implore compassion [k]."

Every one that compares what *Cyprian* and his collegues say for infant-baptism, and what *Tertullian* says against it, as before related, will easily see a difference between them, between *Tertullian* the Antipædobaptist, and *Cyprian* the Pædobaptist; how manly and nervous the one! how mean and weak the other! no doubt, as is known, being raised about infant-baptism at this time, or any objection made to it, does not prove it then to be an ancient custom; since the same observation, which may be made, would prove infant-communion to be equally the same. Now as we allow that henceforward infant-baptism was practised in the African churches, and prevailed in

The fourth century, here the controversy might stop: and indeed all that we contend for in this century, is only that there were some persons that did call it in question and oppose it; and if this will not be allowed, we are not very anxious about it, and shall not think it worth while to contest it.— This writer would have it observed, that I have given up the *greatest lights* of the church in this century as vouchers for infant baptism, and particularly St *Jerom*, *Ruffinus*, and *Auzustin*; they are welcome to them; they have need of them to enlighten them in this dark affair: we do not envy their having them, especially that perfidious interpolater *Ruffinus*; nor that arch-heretic *Pelagius*, whom this Gentleman takes much pains to retain, as ignorant as he either was, or would be, or is thought to be; as that he never heard that any one whatever denied baptism to infants, and promised the kingdom of heaven without the redemption of Christ, or refused that unto them. This ignorance of his was either affected or pretended, in order to clear himself from the charge of those things against him; as men generally do run into high strains and extravagant expressions, when they are at such work; or it was real ignorance, and who can help that? It does not follow that therefore none had, because he had never heard of it; one would think his meaning rather was, that he had never heard of any that denied the kingdom of heaven and the common redemption to infants, who *think* they ought to be baptized, *dum putat*, while he is of opinion, that in baptism they are regenerated in Christ; but about this I shall not contend; truth does not depend upon his hearing and knowledge, judgment and observation. I think it is not insisted upon that *Austin* should say, he never heard or read of any catholic, heretic, or schismatic, that denied infant-baptism; however, it seems he *could* say it if he did not, and that notwithstanding the reasons I alledged; as,

VOL. II.     3 F     1. *Austin*

[k] Cyprian. ad Fidum. Ep. 59. p. 317.

1. *Auſtin* muſt know that *Tertullian* had oppoſed it. Here our author quibbles about the terms *oppoſing* and *denying*, and diſtinguiſhes between them; and obſerves, that whatever *Tertullian* ſaid *againſt* it, he did not properly *deny* it. He may ſay the ſame of me, or any other writer againſt infant-baptiſm, that though we ſpeak againſt it, contradict and oppoſe it, and uſe arguments againſt it, yet we do not *deny* it. Dr *Wall* indeed thinks neither *Auſtin* nor *Pelagius* had ſeen *Tertullian*'s book of baptiſm, or they could not have ſaid what he thinks they did.

2. *Auſtin* preſided at the council of *Carthage*, when a canon was made that anathematized thoſe who denied baptiſm to new-born infants; and therefore muſt know there were ſome that denied it. This Gentleman ſays, it is demonſtrably certain, that this canon was not made againſt perſons that denied infant-baptiſm, becauſe it was made againſt *Pelagius* and *Celeſtius*. It is true, the latter part of the canon was made againſt them; but the former part reſpected a notion or tenet of ſome other perſons, who denied baptiſm to new-born infants. Dr *Wall* ſaw this, and ſays, this canon mentions the baptiſm of infants, condemning two errors about it; the one reſpecting the baptiſm of new-born infants; the other the doctrine of original ſin, and the baptiſm of infants for forgiveneſs of ſins, denied by the Pelagians; but the former he ſuppoſes was the opinion of *Fidus*, embraced by ſome perſons now, which he had vented a hundred and fifty years before, that infants ſhould not be baptized till they were eight days old; whereas *Fidus* is repreſented as having been alone in his opinion; and if he retained it, which is doubtful, it does not appear he had any followers; nor is there any evidence of there being any of his ſentiment in this age[1]; and were there, it is unreaſonable to imagine, that a council of all the biſhops in *Africa* ſhould agree to anathematize them, becauſe they thought proper to defer the baptizing of infants a few days longer than they did; and beſides, infants only eight days old may be properly called newly-born infants; and therefore ſuch could not be ſaid to deny baptiſm to them; and it would have been a marvellous thing, had they been anathematized for it: though this writer ſays, "wonder who will; a council, conſiſting of all the biſhops of *Africa*, did in fact agree to anathematize their own brethren, who were in the ſame opinion and practice of infant-baptiſm with themſelves." It is true, they did anathematize the Pelagians, who were in the ſame opinion and practice of infant-baptiſm with themſelves in general; though I queſtion whether they reckoned them their *own brethren*; but then not on account of any difference about the time of baptiſm, a few days odds between them, the thing to be wondered at; but their denial of original ſin, and the baptiſm of infants to be on account of that:

[1] Hiſtory of Infant-baptiſm, p. 1. ch. 4. §. 13.

## INFANT-BAPTISM AN INNOVATION.

that: and now since the Pelagians are distinct from those in the canon that denied baptism to new-born infants; and it is unreasonable to suppose any who were of the sentiments of *Fidus* are intended; it remains, that there must be some persons different both from the one and the other, who denied baptism to babes, and are by this canon anathematized for it, which *Austin* must know.

3. It is observed by me, that *Austin* himself makes mention of some that argued against it, from the unprofitableness of it to infants; since for the most part they die before they have any knowledge of it. These men our author does not know what to make of; sometimes it is questionable whether they were christians, and suggests that they were men of atheistical principles; and then again they are supposed to be christians, and even might be Pædobaptists, notwithstanding this their manner of arguing. I am content he should reckon them what he pleases; but one would think they could not be any good friends to infant-baptism, that questioned the profitableness of baptism to infants, and brought so strong an objection to it.

4. It is further observed by me, that according to *Austin* the Pelagians denied baptism to the infants of believers, because they were holy. This is represented by this Gentleman as a mistake of mine, understanding what was spoken *hypothetically*, to be *absolutely* spoken. I have looked over the passage again, and am not convinced upon a second reading of it, nor by what this writer has advanced, of a mistake: the words are absolutely expressed and reasoned upon; " but, says the apostle, *your children would be unclean, but now they are holy*; " therefore, say they (the Pelagians) the *children of believers ought not now to* " *be baptized*." The observation our author makes, though he does not insist upon it, is very impertinent; that not infants but *children* are mentioned, and so may include the adult children of believers, and consequently make as much against adult-baptism as infant-baptism; since children in the text, on which the argument is grounded, are always by themselves understood of infants. *Austin* wonders that the Pelagians should talk after this manner, that holiness is derived from parents, and reasons upon it, when they deny that sin is originally derived from *Adam*: it is true, indeed, he presses them with an argument this Gentleman calls *ad hominem*, taken from their shutting up the kingdom of God to unbaptized infants; for though they believed that unbaptized infants would not perish, but have everlasting life, yet not enter the kingdom of God; absurdly distinguishing between *the kingdom of God*, and *eternal life*. What they were able to answer, or did answer to this, it is not easy to say; " it is a disadvantage, " as our author says, that we have none of their writings entire, only scraps " and quotations from them:" Perhaps as they had a singular notion, that the infants of believers ought not to be baptized, though the infants of others should;

they

they would, in anfwer to the above argument, fay, that the infants of believers unbaptized enter the kingdom, though the unbaptized infants of others do not. I only guefs this might be their anfwer, confiftent with their principles: however, if I am miftaken in this matter, as I think I am not, it is in company with men of learning I am not afhamed to be among. The learned *Danæus* fays ᵐ, "the "Pelagians deny that baptifm is to be adminiftered to the children of *believers*," having plainly in view this paffage of *Auftin*'s; and the very learned *Forbefius* ⁿ brings in this as an objection to his fenfe of 1 *Corinthians* vii. 14. "the Pelagians "abufed this faying of the apoftle, that they might fay, that the infants of "believers ought not to be baptized, as we read in *Auguftin* º."

5. The words quoted by me out of *Jerom*, I own, are fpoken by way of fuppofition; but then they fuppofe a cafe that had been, was, and might be again; and it fhould be obferved, that the fuppofition *Jerom* makes, is not a *neglect* of the baptifm of infants, as this Gentleman fuggefts, but a *denial* of it to them, a *refufing* to give it to them; which is expreffive of a rejection of it, and of an oppofition to it. So that from all thefe inftances put together, we cannot but conclude that there were fome perfons that did oppofe and reject infant-baptifm in thofe times, and think it may be allowed, which is all we contend for; however, as I have faid before, we are not very anxious about it. Mr *Marfhall* ᵖ, a favourite writer of our author's, fays, fome in thofe times queftioned it (infant-baptifm) as *Auguftin* grants in his fermons *de verbis Apoftol.* but does not refer us to the particular place; it feems to be his *fourteenth fermon* on that fubject, intitled, *Concerning the baptifm of infants, againft the Pelagians*; where *Auftin* tells us how he was led to the fubject; and though he had no doubt about it, yet "fome men raifed difputes, which were now become frequent, and endea-"voured to fubvert the minds of many ᵠ:" by whom he feems to mean perfons diftinct from the Pelagians, fince he reprefents them as having no doubt about it: and this is further confirmed by a paffage out of the fame difcourfe; "that infants are to be baptized, *let no one doubt* (which is an addrefs to others, "and implies, that either they did doubt of infant-baptifm, or were in danger "of it) fince they doubt not, who in fome refpect contradict it;" which our author has placed as a motto in his title-page.

*Auftin*, we allow, in this age, frequently fpeaks of infant-baptifm as an ancient ufage of the church, and as an apoftolical tradition; but what proof does he give

---

ᵐ Baptifmum parvulis fidelium negant dandam Pelagiani. Danæus de facramentis ad calcem Auguft. de Hæref. ⁿ Abutebantur hoc Apoftoli dicto, ut dicerent infantes fidelium baptizari minime deberi, ut legimus apud Aug. de peccator. merit. & remiff. l. 2. c. 25. Forbef. Inftruct. Hiftor. Theolog. l 10 c. 10. §. 5. º L. 2. de Peccator. merit. & remiff. c. 25.
ᵖ Sermon on baptizing of Infants, p. 5. ᵠ Sed difputationes quorundam, quæ modo crebiefcere, & multorum animos evertere moliuntur, Aug. de verb Apoftol. Serm. 14.

give of it? what testimonies does he produce? does he produce any higher testimony than *Cyprian?* not one; who, it is owned, speaks of infant-baptism, but not as an apostolical tradition; *Cyprian* uses no such language: those phrases, " which were understood and believed *from the beginning,* and what the *church* " *always thought,* or *anciently* held," are *Austin*'s words, and not *Cyprian*'s; and only express what *Austin* inferred and concluded from him: and besides, his testimony is appealed to, not so much for infant-baptism, the thing itself, as for the reason of it, original sin, which gave rise unto it in *Cyprian*'s time: and it is for the proof of this, and not infant-baptism, that *Austin* himself refers to the *manifest faith of an apostle*; namely, to shew that not the flesh only, but the soul would be lost, and be brought into condemnation through the offence of *Adam,* if not quickened by the grace of Christ, for which he refers to *Romans* v. 18. and yet our author insinuates, that by this he did not consider the baptism of infants for original sin as a novel thing in *Cyprian*'s time, but refers it to the authority of an apostle: and by the way, since *Cyprian,* the only witness produced by *Austin,* speaks not of infant-baptism as an ancient usage of the church, or an apostolic tradition, there is no agreement between his language and that of *Origen,* he is made to speak in his Latin translations, as this author elsewhere suggests; and it confirms the proof of his having been dealt unfairly with, since *Cyprian,* coming after him, uses no such language, nor does *Austin* himself ever refer unto him.

I have observed that there are many other things, which by *Austin,* and other ancient writers, are called apostolic traditions; such as infant-communion, the sign of the cross in baptism, the form of renouncing the devil and all his works, exorcism, trine immersion, the consecration of the water, anointing with oil in baptism, and giving a mixture of milk and honey to the baptized persons: and therefore if infant-baptism is received on this foot, these ought likewise; since there is as early and clear proof of them from antiquity, as of that: and my further view in mentioning these, was to observe, not only how *early,* but how *easily* these corruptions got into the church, as infant-baptism did.

This writer has thought fit to take notice only of one of these particulars, namely, infant-communion; and the evidence of this, he says, is not so full and so early as that of infant-baptism. Now, let it be observed, that there is no proof of infant-baptism being practised before *Cyprian*'s time; nor does *Austin* refer to any higher testimony than his for the practice of it for original sin; and in his time infant-communion was in use beyond all contradiction: there is an instance of it given by himself, which I have referred to; and that is more than is or can be given of infant-baptism, which can only be deduced by consequences from that instance, and from *Cyprian* and his collegues reason--
ing

ing about the necessity of the administration of it to new-born children. He suggests that *Austin* expresses himself-differently, when he is speaking of the one and of the other as an apostolic tradition; but if he does, it is in higher strains of infant-communion; for thus begin the passages, "if they pay any regard " to the *apostolic authority*, or rather *to the Lord and Master of the apostles*, &c. " and no man that remembers that he is *a christian, and of the catholic faith,* " *denies or doubts* that infants, without eating his flesh, and drinking his blood, " have no life in them, *&c.*" The *Punici Christiani*, which *Austin* speaks of, are not to be restrained, as they are by our author, to the christians of *Carthage*, but take in other *African* christians, particularly at *Hippo*, where *Austin* was bishop, and where they spoke the Punic language, and in many other places: and surely if *Austin* is a good witness for an apostolical tradition, who lived at the latter end of the *fourth* century; he must know what was the sense of the *African* christians in his time, among whom he lived, and upon what they grounded their practice of infant-communion; which he says was upon an ancient and apostolic tradition.

The other rites and usages, he says, I make mention of, are spoken of by *Basil* as *unwritten traditions*; and infant-baptism is not mentioned among them, and so was considered as standing upon a better evidence and testimony: now, not to observe that I produce earlier authorities than *Basil*, for these apostolical traditions so called, even as early as *Tertullian*, the first man that spoke of infant-baptism; neither are infant-communion, sponsors at baptism, exorcism in it, and giving milk and honey at that time, mentioned by *Basil* among them; does it therefore follow that they stand upon a better foot than the rest? besides, since Apostolic tradition is distinguished from Scripture, by the author of *The baptism of infants a reasonable Service*, with whom I had to do; it can be considered in the controversy between us, no other than as an *unwritten tradition*. This writer further observes, that it does not appear that these unwritten traditions were ever put to the test, and stood the trial, particularly in the Pelagian controversy, as infant-baptism: it is manifest that the exorcisms and exsufflations used in baptism, and the argument from them, as much pinched, puzzled, and confounded the Pelagians, as ever infant-baptism did: and it is notorious, that signing with the sign of the cross has stood the test in all ages, from the beginning of it, and is continued to this day; and prevails not only among the Papists, but among Protestant churches. Upon the whole then, it is clear there is no *express mention* of infant-baptism in the *two first* centuries, no nor any *plain hint* of it, nor any *manifest reference* to it; and that there is no evidence of its being practised till the *third* century; and that it is owned, it prevailed in the *fourth:* and so rests the state of the controversy.

A REPLY

A

# REPLY to a DEFENCE

OF THE

## DIVINE RIGHT OF INFANT BAPTISM,

By PETER CLARK, *A. M.* Minister at SALEM,

IN

LETTER to a FRIEND at BOSTON in *New-England*.

To which are added,

Some STRICTURES on a late TREATISE, called,
*A Fair and Rational Vindication of the Right of Infants to the Ordinance of Baptism.*

Written by DAVID BOSTWICK, *A. M.*
Late Minister of the Presbyterian Church in the City of *New-York*.

---

## The PREFACE.

IT is necessary that the reader should be acquainted with the reason of the republication of the following treatise. In the year 1746, a pamphlet was printed at *Boston* in *New England*, called, "A brief Illustration and Confir-
" mation of the Divine Right of Infant-Baptism," written by Mr *Dickinson*;
which being industriously spread about in great numbers, to hinder the growth
of the Baptist-Interest in those parts, it was sent over to me by some of our friends
there, requesting an answer to it; which I undertook, and published in the
year 1749, intitled, " The Divine Right of Infant-Baptism examined and dis-
" proved." Upon which *Peter Clark*, A.M. Minister at *Salem* in *New-England*,
was

was employed to write againſt it, and which he did; and what he wrote was printed and publiſhed at *Boſton* in 1752, called, "A Defence of the Divine Right of Infant-Baptiſm." This being ſent over to me, I wrote a Reply, in a letter to a friend at *Boſton*, in the year 1753, as the date of my letter ſhews, giving leave to make uſe of it, as might be thought fit; and which was printed and publiſhed at *Boſton* in 1754, together with a Sermon of mine on Baptiſm, preached at *Barbican*, 1750. The controverſy lying beyond the ſeas, I choſe it ſhould continue there, and therefore never reprinted and republiſhed my Reply here, though it has been ſolicited; but of late Mr *Clark*'s Defence has been ſent over here, and publiſhed, and advertiſed to be ſold; which is the only reaſon of my reprinting and republiſhing the following Reply; to which I have added ſome ſtrictures on a treatiſe of Mr *Boſtwick*'s on the ſame ſubject, imported from *America*, with the above Defence, and here reprinted. The Pædobaptiſts are ever reſtleſs and uneaſy, endeavouring to maintain and ſupport, if poſſible, their unſcriptural practice of Infant-Baptiſm; though it is no other than a pillar of Popery; that by which antichriſt has ſpread his baneful influence over many nations; is the baſis of national churches, and worldly eſtabliſhments; that which unites the church and the world, and keeps them together; nor can there be a full ſeparation of the one from the other, nor a thorough reformation in religion, until it is wholly removed: and though it has ſo long and largely obtained, and ſtill does obtain; I believe with a firm and unſhaken faith, that the time is haſtening on, when Infant-Baptiſm will be no more practiſed in the world; when churches will be formed on the ſame plan they were in the times of the apoſtles; when goſpel-doctrine and diſcipline will be reſtored to their primitive luſtre and purity; when the ordinances of baptiſm and the Lord's ſupper will be adminiſtered as they were firſt delivered, clear of all preſent corruption and ſuperſtition; all which will be accompliſhed, when *the Lord ſhall be king over all the earth, and there ſhall be one Lord, and his name one*.

A REPLY

# A REPLY, &c.

## In a LETTER to a FRIEND.

SIR,

I Acknowledge the receipt of your Letter on the 22ᵈ of laſt *March,* and with it Mr *Clark*'s *Defence of the Divine Right of Infant-Baptiſm,* &c. which I have ſince curſorily read over; for I thought it a too great waſte of time to give it a *ſecond* reading. Nor will my engagement in a work of greater importance permit me to write a ſet and laboured anſwer to it; nor am I willing to beſtow ſo much time and pains as are neceſſary to cleanſe that Augean ſtable, and remove all the dirt and rubbiſh this writer has collected together. The remarks I made in reading, I here ſend you. At firſt ſetting out, I ſoon found I muſt expect to be dealt *rudely* and *roughly* with, and accordingly prepared myſelf for it; and I aſſure you, Sir, I was not diſappointed.

The *firſt* chapter of my book, which the above Gentleman has undertook to anſwer, is ſhort, and only an *introduction,* obſerving the author's title, method, and occaſion of writing the pamphlet before me. In Mr *Clark*'s Reply to which I obſerve; 1. That he is diſpleaſed at calling the ordinance of baptiſm as truly and properly adminiſtered, Believer's-baptiſm, and the pretended adminiſtration of it, to infants, Infant-ſprinkling; whereas this is calling things by their proper names: it is with great propriety, we call baptiſm as adminiſtered to believers, the proper ſubjects of it, Believer's-baptiſm; and with the ſame propriety we call that which is adminiſtered to infants, Infant-ſprinkling; from the nature of the action performed, and the perſons on whom it is performed. Does this Gentleman think, we ſhall be ſo complaiſant to ſuit our language and way of ſpeaking to his miſtaken notion and practice? though indeed we too often do, through the common uſe of phraſes which obtain. 2. He is unwilling to allow of any increaſe of the Baptiſt intereſt in *New England,* either at *Boſton* or in the country; whereas I am credibly informed, and you, Sir, I believe, can atteſt the truth of it, that there have been confiderable additions to the Baptift intereft at *Bofton*; and that many hundreds in the country have been baptized within a few years. 3. He fays, it is an egregious miftake, that the minifters of *New-England* applied to Mr *Dickinfon* (the author of the pamphlet I wrote againft) to write in favour of Infant-fprinkling; and he is certain that not one of the minifters in *Bofton* made application to him, (which was never affirmed,) and is perfuaded it was not at the motion of any minifters in *New-England*, that he wrote his Dialogue, but of his own mere motion; and yet he is obliged to correct himfelf by a marginal note, and acknowledge that it was wrote through minifterial influence. 4. This writer very early gives a fpecimen of his talent at reafoning; from the rejection of Infant-baptifm, as an human invention, he argues to the rejection of baptifm itfelf, as fuch; that if Infant-baptifm is intirely an human invention, and a rite not to be obferved, then baptifm itfelf is an human invention, and not to be obferved: this is an argument drawn up *fecundum artem*, like a mafter of arts; and to pretend to anfwer fo ftrong an argument, and fet afide fuch a mafterly way of reafoning, would be weaknefs indeed! 5. It being obferved of the Dialogue-writer, "that he took care, not to put fuch "arguments and objections into the mouth of his antagonift as he was not able "to anfwer;" this Gentleman rifes up, and blufters at a great rate, and defies the moft zealous, learned, and fubtil of the Antipædobaptifts to produce any other arguments and objections againft Infant-baptifm, for matter or fubftance, different from, or of greater weight, than thofe produced in the Dialogue; but afterwards lowers his topfail, and fays, that the defign of the author of that pamphlet was to reprefent in a few plain words, the moft material objections againft Infant-baptifm, with the proper anfwers to them; and at laft owns, that a great deal more has been faid by the Antipædobaptifts.

The *fecond* chapter, you know, Sir, treats of "the confequences of em- "bracing Believer's-baptifm; fuch as, renouncing Infant-baptifm, vacating "the covenant, and renouncing all other ordinances of the gofpel;" that Chrift muft have forfaken his church for many ages, and not made good the promife of his prefence, and that there now can be no baptifm in the world. In Mr *Clark*'s Reply to what I have faid on thofe heads, I obferve the following things.

The *firft* confequence is the renunciation of Infant-baptifm; which confequence, to put him out of all doubt and pain, about my owning or not owning it, I readily allow, follows upon a perfon's being fprinkled in infancy, embracing adult-baptifm by immerfion; in which he is to be juftified, the one being an invention of man's, the other according to the word of God; nor is

there

## DIVINE RIGHT OF INFANT-BAPTISM.

there any thing this Gentleman has said, that proves such a renunciation to be an evil.

1. He is very wrong in supposing it must be my intention, that the age of a person, or the time of receiving baptism, are essential to the ordinance. The Antipædobaptists do not confine this ordinance to any age, but admit old or young to it, if proper subjects; let a man be as old as *Methuselah*, if he has not faith in Christ, or cannot give a satisfactory account of it, he will not be admitted to this ordinance by reason of his age; on the other hand, if a little child is called by grace, and converted, and gives a reason of the hope that is in it, of which there have been instances; such will not be refused this ordinance of baptism. The essentials to the right administration of baptism, amongst other things, are, that it be performed by immersion, without which it cannot be baptism; and that it be administered upon a profession of faith; neither of which are to be found in Infant-sprinkling.

2. It is in vain and to no purpose in this writer to urge, that infants are capable of baptism; so are bells, and have been baptized by the Papists. But it is said, infants are capable of being cleansed by the blood of Christ; of being regenerated; of being entered into covenant, and of having the seal of it administered to them. And what of all this? are they capable of understanding the nature, design, and use of the ordinance, when administered to them? are they capable of professing faith in Christ, which is a pre requisite to this ordinance? are they capable of answering a good conscience towards God in it? are they capable of submitting to it in obedience to the will of Christ, from a love to Him, and with a view to his glory? they are not. But,

3. It seems, in baptism, infants are dedicated unto God; wherefore to renounce Infant-baptism, is for a man to renounce his solemn dedication to God, and much is said to prove that parents have a Right to dedicate their children to him. It will be allowed, that parents have a right to devote or dedicate their children to the Lord; that is, to give them up to him in prayer; or to pray for them, as *Abraham* did for *Ishmael*, that they may *live in his sight*; and it is their duty to *bring them up in the nurture and admonition of the Lord*; but they have no direction to baptize them, nor warrant to dedicate them by baptism; nor is baptism an ordinance of dedication, either of a man's self, or of others; a dedication ought to be previous to baptism; and Believers first give up themselves to the Lord, and then are baptized in his name.

4. After all, a renunciation of baptism in infancy must be a matter of great impiety, because witches are solicited by the Devil to renounce it, in order to their entering into confederacy with them. I thought, Sir, your country of

*New-England* had been cured of thefe fooleries about witchcraft, and diabolical confederacies long ago, but I find the diftemper continues. This argument, I own, is unanfwerable by me; I muft confefs myfelf quite a ftranger to this dark bufinefs.

5. What the ftory of Mr *Whifton* is told for, is not eafy to fay; fince it feems, he did not renounce his Infant-baptifm: it looks, by the reference, as if it was intended to fuggeft, that an Antitrinitarian could not fo well fhelter himfelf among a people of any denomination, as the Baptifts; whereas the ordinance as adminiftered by them, as ftrongly militates againft fuch a principle, as it does by being adminiftered by Pædobaptifts: but it may be, it is to recommend a fpirit of moderation among us, to receive unbaptized perfons into our communion by this example; but then unhappy for this writer, fo it is, that the congregation Dr *Fofter* was paftor of, and Mr *Whifton* joined himfelf to, is, and always was of the Pædobaptift denomination, and have for their prefent minifter one of the Prefbyterian perfuafion.

The *fecond* confequence of receiving the principle of adult-baptifm, and acting up to it, is, vacating the covenant between God and the perfon baptized in infancy, into which he was brought by his baptifm.

Now you will obferve, Sir, 1. That Mr *Clark* has offered nothing in proof of infants being brought into covenant with God, by baptifm; and indeed I cannot fee how he can confiftently with himfelf undertake it; fince he makes covenant relation to God, the main ground of infants right to baptifm; and therefore they muft be in it before their baptifm, and confequently are not brought into it by it; wherefore fince they are not brought into covenant by it, that cannot be vacated by their renouncing of it.

2. It being obferved, that no man can be brought into the covenant of grace by baptifm, fince it is from everlafting, and all interefted in it were fo early in covenant, and confequently previous to their baptifm; this writer fets himfelf with all his might and main to oppofe this fentiment, that the covenant of grace was from everlafting; this, he fays, is unfcriptural, irrational, and contrary to fcripture. But if Chrift was fet up from everlafting as mediator; for only as fuch could he be fet up [a]; if there was a promife of eternal life made before the world began, and this promife was in Chrift, who then exifted as the federal head and reprefentative of his people, in whom they were chofen fo early, to receive all promifes and grace for them [b]; and if grace was given to them in him before the world was, and they were bleffed with all fpiritual bleffings in him fo early [c]; then, furely, there muft be a covenant tranfaction between the Father and the Son on their account fo early; for could there be all

---

[a] Prov. viii. 22.  [b] Titus i. 2. 2 Tim. i. 1.  [c] 2 Tim. i. 9. Eph. i. 3,4.

all this and no covenant fubfifting? The diftinction between a covenant of redemption and a covenant of grace, is without any foundation in the word of God. Nor is this notion irrational; two parties were fo early exifting, when the covenant was made; *Jehovah the Father* was one, *and the Son of* God the other, in the name of his people; who, though they had not then a perfonal, yet had a reprefentative being in Chrift their head; and this was fufficient for them to have grace given them in him before the world was.

His metaphyfical arguments from eternal acts being imminent, will equally militate againft eternal election, as againft an eternal covenant; and perhaps this writer has as little regard to the one, as he has to the other: nor is this notion contrary to fcripture; for though the covenant is called a *new* and *second* covenant, yet only with refpect to the former adminiftration of it, under the legal difpenfation; and both adminiftrations of it, under the law and under the gofpel, are only fo many exhibitions and manifeftations of the covenant under different forms, which was made in eternity. The fcriptures which promife the *making* of a covenant, only intend a clearer manifeftation and application of the covenant of grace to perfons to whom it belongs; things are faid in fcripture to be *made*, when they are made manifeft or declared [a]: it is a previous intereft in the covenant of grace that gives perfons a right to the bleffings of it; and the application of thefe bleffings, fuch as pardon of fin, *&c.* flows from this previous intereft: nor does this notion render the miniftry of the word and the operation of the Spirit for that end ufelefs, and fuperfluous; but on the contrary fo early an intereft in the covenant of grace is the ground and reafon of the Spirit being fent down in time to make the word effectual to falvation. Nor is the ftate of unregeneracy, the elect of God are in by nature, inconfiftent with this eternal covenant; fince that covenant fuppofes it, and provides for, promifes, and fecures the regeneration and fanctification of all interefted in it; affuring them that *the heart of ftone shall be taken away, and an heart of flesh* given them; *a new heart and a new Spirit*, yea the Spirit of God fhall be put into them, and the laws of God written in their minds.

The text in *Ephefians* ii. 12. defcribes the Gentiles only, who were ftrangers from the covenants of promife; the covenant of circumcifion, and the covenant at *Sinai*; covenants peculiar to the Jews; as well as ftrangers to the fcriptures, which contain the promife of the Meffiah; all which might be, and was, and yet be interefted in the covenant of grace. If this is to be an Antinomian, I am quite content to be called one; fuch bug-bear names do not frighten me. It is not worth while to take notice of this man's Neonomian rant; of the terms

and

[a] See Acts ii. 36.

and conditions of the covenant; of its being a rule of moral government over man in a state of unregeneracy, brought hereby into a state of probation; which turns the covenant into a law, and is what the Neonomians call a *remedial* law, (as this writer calls the covenant a *remedial* one) a law of milder terms; nor of his Arminian strokes in making the endeavours and acts of men to be the turning point of their salvation, and conversion, as being foreign to the controversy in hand.

3. This writer makes a distinction between a man's being in covenant in respect of the spiritual dispensation of the grace of it, and in respect of the external administration of it: by the spiritual dispensation of it, I apprehend, he means the application of spiritual blessings in the covenant to persons regenerated and converted, by which they must appear to be in it; and in this sense, all the persons, I have instanced in, must be manifestly in the covenant of grace, previous to baptism: and consequently not brought into it by it. By the external administration of it, I suppose, he means the administration of the ordinances of the gospel, particularly baptism; and then it is only saying a man is not baptized before he is baptized; which no body will contest with him.

4. No man, I observe, is entered into the covenant of grace by himself, or others; this is an act of the sovereign grace of God, who says, *I will be their God, and they shall be my people*; which this writer owns, though not exclusive of human endeavours; as if God could not take any into his covenant without their own endeavours; such wretched divinity deserves the utmost contempt. Since the above phrase, *I will be their God*, &c. is a proof of the sovereign grace of God in bringing men into covenant; he hopes it will be allowed that a like phrase, *I will be the God of thy seed*, will be admitted as strongly to conclude the reception of the Infant-children of believers into covenant. I answer, whenever it appears that there is such an article in the covenant of grace, that so runs, that God will be the God of the natural Seed of believers as such, it will be admitted; and whereas I have observed, that the phrase of *bringing into the bond of the covenant*, which the Pædobaptists often make use of, is but once mentioned in scripture, and then ascribed to God; this, as it no ways contradicts a being in covenant from everlasting, so it fails not of being a proof of the sovereign grace of God in that act. By the *bond of the covenant*, is not meant faith and repentance on man's part; which some stupidly call the terms and conditions of the covenant, when they are parts and blessings of it; but the everlasting love of God, which is the source and security of it, and which lays men under obligation to serve their covenant-God; and to be brought into it, is to be brought into a comfortable view of interest in it, and to an open participation
of

of the bleſſings of it; which is all according to, and conſiſtent with the eternal conſtitution of it.

5. The covenant of grace can never be vacated, ſince it is everlaſting, *ordered in all things and ſure:* this is owned by our author in reſpect of its divine conſtitution, and of the immutability of the divine promiſe, to all under the ſpiritual diſpenſation of it; but there are others who are only in it by a viſible and baptiſmal dedication; and theſe may make void the covenant between God and them; and this it ſeems is the caſe of the greateſt part of infants in covenant. Now let me retort this Gentleman's argument upon himſelf, which he makes uſe of againſt the covenant being from everlaſting. " Thoſe, whom God ad-
" mits into the covenant of grace, have an intereſt in the benefits of that cove-
" nant, pardon of ſin, the gift of the Spirit, reconciliation, adoption, &c. for
" it is a ſort of contradiction to ſay, that any man is admitted into the covenant,
" and yet debarred from an intereſt in all the privileges of it." Now, either infants are admitted into the covenant of grace, or they are not; if they are, then they have an intereſt in the benefits of it, pardon of ſin, and the other bleſſings, and ſo ſhall all certainly be ſaved with an everlaſting ſalvation, and not apoſtatize, as it ſeems the greateſt part of them do; for to ſay they are in the external, but not in the ſpiritual part of the covenant, is to make a poor buſineſs of their covenant-intereſt indeed. The inſtance of *Simon Magus,* which he thinks I have forgot, will not make for him, nor againſt me; it is a clear proof, that a man is not brought into covenant by baptiſm; ſince though baptiſm was adminiſtered to this perſon in the pure, primitive way, by an apoſtolic man, yet he was *in the gall of bitterneſs and bond of iniquity.*

3*dly,* The other *three* conſequences following upon the renouncing of Infant-baptiſm, as renouncing all other ordinances, the promiſe of Chriſt's preſence not made good, and no baptiſm now in the world, are in ſome ſort given up, and are allowed not to be clear, at leaſt not alike clear; and are only adverted to in a general way, and ſome expreſſions of mine catched at, and remarked upon, and theſe miſtaken or perverted.

1. I obſerve, this author repeats his former miſtake, that we make age eſſential to baptiſm, which is but circumſtantial; and then uſes an argument from the leſſer to the greater, as he thinks, that if a defect in ſuch a circumſtance nullifies the ordinance, then much more the want of proper adminiſtrators: but it is not age that we object to, but a want of underſtanding, and faith, and an incapacity to make a profeſſion of it, as well as the mode of adminiſtration; things of greater importance in this ordinance; at leaſt they are ſo with us. However, it is kind in this Gentleman to direct us how we may avoid this inconvenience his argument has thrown us into, by exerciſing a little more moderation.

moderation and charity for Infant-baptism; and upon this foot he seems to be willing to compound the matter with us.

2. As to the presence of Christ with his church and ministers, it is sufficient to make that good, that he grants it where his Church is, and wheresoever he has a people, be they more, or fewer, and wheresoever his ordinances are administered according to his direction; but he has no where promised, that he will have a continued succession of visible congregated churches. Certain indeed it is, that he will have a number of chosen ones in all ages; that his invisible church, built on Christ the rock, shall not fail; and he will have a seed to serve him, or some particular persons, whom he will reserve to himself from a general corruption; but that these shall be gathered always into a visible gospel church-state, is no where promised; and for many hundreds of years it will be hard to find any one such church, unless the people in the valleys of *Piedmont* are allowed to be such.

3. This writer is not willing to admit such a supposition, that any of the laws and institutions of Christ have failed, ceased, or been annulled in any one age, and much more for several ages together; but, besides the ordinance of baptism, which through the change of mode and subjects, together with the impure mixtures of salt, oil, and spittle, and other superstitious rites, which became quite another thing than what was instituted by Christ, and practised by his apostles; the ordinance of the Lord's-supper was so sadly perverted and corrupted, as to be a mere *mass* indeed of blasphemy and idolatry; in the communion of which the gracious presence of Christ cannot be thought to be enjoyed: and yet this continued some hundreds of years; only now and then some single persons rose up, and bore a testimony against it, who for a while had their followers.

4. He seems to triumph from Dr *Wall*'s account of things, that there never was, nor is, to this day, any *national* church in the world but Pædobaptists, either among the Greeks, or Roman Catholicks, or the Reformed; and that Antipædobaptism never obtained to be the established religion of any country in the world. We do not envy his boast; we know that national churches are good for nothing, as not being agreeable to the rule of the divine word; one small church or congregation, gathered out of the world by the grace of God, according to gospel-order, and whose principles and practices are agreeable to the word of God, is to be preferred before all the national churches in the world.

5. According to this Gentleman's own account of the English Antipædobaptists, there could be none to administer the ordinance to them in their way; since those that came from *Holland*, it seems, gained no proselytes, but were
soon

soon extinct, being cruelly persecuted and destroyed; so that it was necessary they should send abroad for an administrator, or make use of an unbaptized one: but which way soever they took, they are able to justify their baptism on as good a foundation as the Reformers are able to justify theirs received from the Papists, with all the fooleries, corruptions, and superstitious rites attending it.

My *third* chapter, you will remember, Sir, is concerning *The Antiquity of Infant-baptism*, and the practice of the Waldenses.

I. The enquiry is, whether Infant-baptism constantly and universally obtained in the truly primitive church, which truly pure and primitive church must be the church in the times of Christ and his apostles; since towards the close of those times, and in the two following Ages, there arose such a set of impure men, both for principle and practice, under the christian name, as never were known in the world: now by an induction of particular instances of churches in this period of time, it does not appear, that Infant-baptism at all obtained. In Mr Clark's reply to which, I observe, 1. That he says, the evidence of Infant-baptism is not pretended to lie in the history of fact, or in any express mention of it in the New Testament. That the penman of the *Acts of the Apostles* did not descend to so minute a particular, as the baptizing of infants,—and that the baptism of the *adult* was of the greatest account to be recorded. 2. Yet he thinks there are pretty plain intimations of it in most of the characters instanced in, and particularly in the church at *Jerusalem*; which he endeavours to make good by a criticism on *Acts* ii. 41. And it is pleasant to observe, how he toils and labours to find out an antecedent to a relative not expressed in the text; for the words, *to them*, are not in the original; it is only *and the same day there were added about three thousand souls*; or, the same day there was an addition of about three thousand souls; and all this pains is taken to support a whimsical notion, that this addition was made, not to the church, but to the new converts; and by a wild fancy he imagines, that infants are included among the three thousand souls that were added: his argument from ver. 39. and the other instances mentioned, as well as some other passages alledged, such as *Luke* xviii. 16. *Acts* xv. 10. 1 *Cor.* vii. 14. as they come over in the debate again, are referred to their proper places. But, 3. It must not be forgotten, what is said, that this may be a reason why Infant-baptism is so sparingly mentioned, (not mentioned at all) because the custom of the Jews to baptize the children of proselytes to their religion with their parents, was well known; and there can be little doubt, that the apostles proceeded by the same rule in admitting the infants of christian proselytes into the christian covenant by baptism. This is building Infant-baptifm on a bog indeed; fince this Jewifh cuftom is not pretended to be of divine inftitution; and fo a poor argument in *the Defence of the Divine Right of Infant-baptifm*; and at moft and beft, is only a tradition of the elders, which body of traditions was inveighed againft by Chrift and his apoftles; and befides, this particular tradition does not appear to have obtained fo early among the Jews themfelves, as the times of the apoftles, and therefore could be no rule for them to proceed by; and about which the firft reporters of it difagree, the one affirming there was fuch a cuftom, and the other denying it; and had it then obtained, it is incredible the apoftles fhould make this the rule of their procedure in adminiftering an ordinance of Chrift: and after all, was this the cafe, this would be a reafon for, and not againft the exprefs mention of Infant-baptifm by the divine hiftorian; fince it is neceffary that in agreement with this Jewifh cuftom, fome inftance or inftances of chriftian profelytes being baptized with their children fhould be recorded, as an example for chriftians in fucceeding ages to go by. But, 4. A fuppofition is made of fome Pædobaptifts fent into an heathen country to preach, and giving an account of their fuccefs, declaring that fome families were baptized, fuch a man and all his, fuch another and his houfhold; upon which a queftion is afked, who could raife a doubt whether any infants were baptized in thofe feveral families? To which I anfwer, there is no doubt to be made of it, that Pædobaptifts would baptize infants; and if the apoftles were Pædobaptifts, which is the thing to be proved, they no doubt baptized infants too; but if no other account was given of the baptizing of houfholds, than what the apoftles give of them, Infant-baptifm would ftill remain a doubt. For who can believe, that the brethren in *Lydia*'s houfe whom the apoftles comforted, and of whom her houfhold confifted, or that the Jailor's houfhold, that believed and rejoiced with him, or the houfhold of *Stephanas*, who addicted themfelves to the miniftry of the faints, were infants? however it feems, as there is no evidence of fact for Infant-baptifm in the New Teftament, it is referred to the teftimony of the ancient fathers; and to them then we muft go.

II. The teftimony of the fathers of the three firft centuries is chiefly to be attended to; and whereas none in the firft century are produced in favour of Infant-baptifm, we muft proceed to the fecond. In it, I obferve, there is but one writer, that it is pretended fpeaks of Infant-baptifm, and that is *Irenæus*, and but one paffage in him; and this is at beft of doubtful meaning, and by fome learned men judged fpurious; as when he fays, Chrift "came to fave all, "all, I fay, who are regenerated (or born again) unto God; Infants, and little "ones, and children, and young men, and old men." Now, admitting the chapter in which this paffage ftands, is genuine and not fpurious, which yet is

not

not a clear case; it is objectible to, as being a translation, as the most of this author's works are, and a very foolish, uncouth and barbarous one it is, as learned men observe; wherefore there is reason to believe that justice is not done him; and it lies not upon us, but upon our antagonists that urge this passage against us, to produce the original in support of it: but allowing it to be a just translation, yet what is there of Infant-baptism in it? Not a word. Yes, to be *regenerated*, or *born again*, is to be baptized; this is the sense of the antients, and particularly of *Irenæus*, it is said; but how does this appear? Dr *Wall* has given an instance of it out of Lib. iii. chap. 19. where this ancient writer says, "when "he gave the disciples the commission of regenerating (or rather of regenera-"tion) unto God, he said unto them, *Go, teach all nations, baptizing them in* "*the name of the Father, and of the Son, and of the Holy Ghost;*" where the commission of regenerating, adds Dr *Wall*, plainly means the commission of baptizing; whereas, it more plainly means the commission of teaching the doctrine of regeneration by the spirit, and the necessity of that unto salvation, and in order to baptism; and which was the first and principal part of the apostles commission, as the very order of the words shews; and certain it is, that *Irenæus* uses the word *Regeneration* in a different sense from baptism ᵉ, as an inward work, agreeable to the scriptures; and besides, such a sense of his words contended for, is to make him at least to suggest a doctrine which is absolutely false, as if Christ came to save all, and only such, who are baptized unto God; whereas he came to save baptized and unbaptized ones, Old and New Testament saints; and many no doubt are saved by him who never were baptized at all, and some baptized not saved; but on the other hand nothing is more true than that he came to save all, and only those, who are regenerated by the spirit and grace of God, of whatsoever age; and which is clearly this ancient writer's sense, and so no proof of Infant-baptism.

To support this notion of regeneration signifying baptism so early, our author urges a passage cited by me from *Justin*; who, speaking of converted persons, says, " they are brought by us where water is, and they are regenerated in the " same way of regeneration as we have been regenerated; for they are then " washed in water *in the name of the Father, &c.*" Now, it is evident, that those persons are not represented as regenerated by baptism; because they are spoken of before as believers and converted ones; and it is as clear, that their baptism is distinguished from their regeneration, and not the same thing; for *Justin* uses the former, as an argument of the latter; which, if the same, his sense must be, they were baptized, because they were baptized; which is making him guilty of what Logicians call proving *Idem per Idem*: whereas, *Justin*'s sense,

---

ᵉ Vid. Irenæum adv. Hæres. l. 1. c. 18. and l. 4. c. 59. and l. 5. c. 15.

sense, consistent with himself, and the practice of the primitive churches, is, that those persons when brought to the water, having made a profession of their regeneration, were owned and declared regenerated persons, as is manifest from their being admitted to the ordinance of water-baptism: and that *Justin* speaks of the baptism of the *adult*, is owned by this writer; though he thinks it is unquestionable, that he speaks only of such who were converted from Heathenism; and is sure of it, that there were none among them born of christian parents; this he will find a hard task, with all his confidence, to prove. And he has ventured to produce a passage out of *Justin*, as giving suffrage to Infant-baptism in the second century; and it is this from Dr *Wall*; "We also, who by him have had access to God, have not received this carnal circumcision, but the spiritual circumcision, which *Enoch* and those like him observed; and we have received it by baptism, by the mercy of God, because we were sinners, and it is enjoined to all persons to receive it the same way." Now let it be observed, that this spiritual circumcision, whatever *Justin* means by it, can never design baptism; since the patriarch *Enoch*, and others like him, observed it; and since with christians it is received *by* baptism, he says; and therefore must be different from it: and, after all, not a word of infants in the passage; nor is baptism called a spiritual circumcision; nor, as our author elsewhere stiles it, christian circumcision, in *Colossians* ii. 11. since the circumcision there spoken of, is called *a circumcision made without hands*, which surely cannot be said of baptism. In short, I must once more triumph, if it may be so called, and say, this is all the evidence, the undoubted evidence of Infant-baptism from the fathers of the two first centuries. Proceed we to

The third century; and the fathers of this, brought into the controversy about baptism are *Tertullian*, *Origen*, and *Cyprian* The first of these, is the first writer we know of that ever made mention of Infant-baptism; and he dissuades from it, and advises to defer baptism to riper years; and is therefore claimed on our side of the question: nor can he be made to unsay what he has said; and therefore is traduced as a man of heterodox notions, and of odd and strange opinions; and, it seems, afterwards turned Montanist; and all this is said, to weaken the credit of his testimony, when not a word is said of *Origen*'s gross errors and monstrous absurdities: the reason is, because it seems he was a Pædobaptist, and *Tertullian* an Antipædobaptist; though it is some comfort to this writer, that he was not quite so bad as the present Antipædobaptists are. As to *Origen*, there are *three* passages quoted out of him; to which we object, not only, that they are *translations*, the fidelity of which cannot be depended upon, when there is much of this writer still extant in the language in which he wrote, and yet nothing from thence produced; but that these are *interpolated*, and not a clear cafe; it is objectible to, as being a tranflation, as the moft of this author's works are, and a very foolifh, uncouth and barbarous one it is, as learned men obferve; wherefore there is reafon to believe that juftice is not done him; and it lies not upon us, but upon our antagonifts that urge this paffage againft us, to produce the original in fupport of it: but allowing it to be a juft tranflation, yet what is there of Infant-baptifm in it? Not a word. Yes, to be *regenerated*, or *born again*, is to be baptized; this is the fenfe of the antients, and particularly of *Irenæus*, it is faid; but how does this appear? Dr *Wall* has given an inftance of it out of Lib. iii. chap. 19. where this ancient writer fays, "when " he gave the difciples the commiffion of regenerating (or rather of regeneration) unto God, he faid unto them, *Go, teach all nations, baptizing them in* " *the name of the Father, and of the Son, and of the Holy Ghoft*;" where the commiffion of regenerating, adds Dr *Wall*, plainly means the commiffion of baptizing; whereas, it more plainly means the commiffion of teaching the doctrine of regeneration by the fpirit, and the neceffity of that unto falvation, and in order to baptifm; and which was the firft and principal part of the apoftles commiffion, as the very order of the words fhews; and certain it is, that *Irenæus* ufes the word *Regeneration* in a different fenfe from baptifm*, as an inward work, agreeable to the fcriptures; and befides, fuch a fenfe of his words contended for, is to make him at leaft to fuggeft a doctrine which is abfolutely falfe, as if Chrift came to fave all, and only fuch, who are baptized unto God; whereas he came to fave baptized and unbaptized ones, Old and New Teftament faints; and many no doubt are faved by him who never were baptized at all, and fome baptized not faved; but on the other hand nothing is more true than that he came to fave all, and only thofe, who are regenerated by the fpirit and grace of God, of whatfoever age; and which is clearly this ancient writer's fenfe, and fo no proof of Infant-baptifm.

To fupport this notion of regeneration fignifying baptifm fo early, our author urges a paffage cited by me from *Juftin*; who, fpeaking of converted perfons, fays, " they are brought by us where water is, and they are regenerated in the " fame way of regeneration as we have been regenerated; for they are then " wafhed in water *in the name of the Father, &c.*" Now, it is evident, that thofe perfons are not reprefented as regenerated by baptifm; becaufe they are fpoken of before as believers and converted ones; and it is as clear, that their baptifm is diftinguifhed from their regeneration, and not the fame thing; for *Juftin* ufes the former, as an argument of the latter; which, if the fame, his fenfe muft be, they were baptized, becaufe they were baptized; which is making him guilty of what Logicians call proving *Idem per Idem*: whereas, *Juftin*'s

* Vid. Irenæum adv. Hæref. l. 1. c. 18. and l. 4. c. 59. and l. 5. c. 15.

sense, consistent with himself, and the practice of the primitive churches, is, that those persons when brought to the water, having made a profession of their regeneration, were owned and declared regenerated persons, as is manifest from their being admitted to the ordinance of water-baptism: and that *Justin* speaks of the baptism of the *adult*, is owned by this writer; though he thinks it is unquestionable,—that he speaks only of such who were converted from Heathenism; and is sure of it, that there were none among them born of christian parents; this he will find a hard task, with all his confidence, to prove. And he has ventured to produce a passage out of *Justin*, as giving suffrage to Infant-baptism in the second century; and it is this from Dr *Wall*; "We also, who by him "have had access to God, have not received this carnal circumcision, but the "spiritual circumcision, which *Enoch* and those like him observed; and we "have received it by baptism, by the mercy of God, because we were sinners, "and it is enjoined to all persons to receive it the same way." Now let it be observed, that this spiritual circumcision, whatever *Justin* means by it, can never design baptism; since the patriarch *Enoch*, and others like him, observed it; and since with christians it is received *by* baptism, he says; and therefore must be different from it: and, after all, not a word of infants in the passage; nor is baptism called a spiritual circumcision; nor, as our author elsewhere stiles it, christian circumcision, in *Colossians* ii. 11. since the circumcision there spoken of, is called *a circumcision made without hands*, which surely cannot be said of baptism. In short, I must once more triumph, if it may be so called, and say, this is all the evidence, the undoubted evidence of Infant-baptism from the fathers of the two first centuries. Proceed we to

The third century; and the fathers of this, brought into the controversy about baptism are *Tertullian*, *Origen*, and *Cyprian* The first of these, is the first writer we know of that ever made mention of Infant-baptism; and he dissuades from it, and advises to defer baptism to riper years; and is therefore claimed on our side of the question: nor can he be made to unsay what he has said; and therefore is traduced as a man of heterodox notions, and of odd and strange opinions; and, it seems, afterwards turned Montanist; and all this is said, to weaken the credit of his testimony, when not a word is said of *Origen*'s gross errors and monstrous absurdities: the reason is, because it seems he was a Pædobaptist, and *Tertullian* an Antipædobaptist; though it is some comfort to this writer, that he was not quite so bad as the present Antipædobaptists are. As to *Origen*, there are *three* passages quoted out of him; to which we object, not only, that they are *translations*, the fidelity of which cannot be depended upon, when there is much of this writer still extant in the language in which he wrote, and yet nothing from thence produced; but that these are *interpolated*,

and

## DIVINE RIGHT OF INFANT-BAPTISM.

and confessedly so. His homilies on *Leviticus* and exposition of the epistle to the *Romans*, from whence two of the passages are taken, were translated by *Ruffinus*, who owns he took liberty to *add* of his own to them; so that, as *Erasmus*[f] observes, it is uncertain whether one reads *Origen* or *Ruffinus*; and *Scultetus*[g] says the same thing; and *Huetius*, who has given us a good edition of the Greek commentaries of this father, and well understood him, says[h], that " his writings are so corrupted by him, that you are at a loss to find *Origen* in " *Origen*, and so deformed and unlike the original, they can scarce be known;" and one of these particular passages *Vossius*[i] takes to be an interpolation, and so of the greater force against the Pelagians, because *Ruffinus* the translator and interpolator was inclined to them: the homilies on *Luke*, out of which is the other passage, are said to be translated by *Jerom*, of whom *Du Pin* says[k], that his versions are not more exact than the other's; so no credit is to be given to them, nor are they to be depended on. *Cyprian* is the next that is produced, and it will be allowed that Infant-baptism began to be practised in his time in some churches, though it seems to be an upstart notion; since it was not till then determined at what time it should be administered; and also at the same time, and in the same churches, Infant-communion was practised; of which *Cyprian* gives an instance; and that is more than is, or can be given of the practice of Infant-baptism so early; and if his testimony is of any weight for the one, it ought to be of the same for the other; and if infants are admitted to baptism, it is but reasonable they should partake of the Lord's-supper, and especially as there is as early antiquity for the one as for the other.

The quotations out of *Gregory Nazianzen*, *Optatus*, *Ambrose*, *Chrysostom*, and *Austin*, fathers of the fourth century, which Mr *Clark* has collected from Dr *Wall*, might have been spared; seeing this does not come into his own account of the truly primitive church; and since it is not denied, Infant-baptism obtained in it; and yet it is certain, there were persons in this age against it, as will be observed hereafter; nor was *Pelagius*, in this age, so pressed and puzzled with the argument taken from it in favour of original sin; since it was not contrary to his doctrine, who allowed baptism to be administered to them " on account of the kingdom of God, but not for forgiveness of sin;" and the controversy did not lead to dispute about the *subject*, but the *end* of baptism.

The

[f] Apud Rive'. Critic. Sacr. l. 2 c. 12. p. 202.
[g] Medulla Patrum, par. 1. l. 6. c. 2. p. 124.
[h] Origeniana. l. 2. p. 116. l. 3. c. 1. p. 233, 253.
[i] Hist. Pelag. par. 1. l. 2. p. 147.
[k] Hist. Eccl. vol. 1. p. 132.

The next thing, you will remember, Sir, brought into the controversy, is, whether the practice of Infant-baptism was called in question before the mad-men of *Munster* set themselves against it. As to the troubles in *Germany*, and in *Munster* itself, it is certain beyond all contradiction, that they were begun by Pædobaptists, and whilst they were such; and as for the German Anabaptists, as they are called, who joined with them, they were Sprinklers, and not Baptists, and so belong rather to this writer's party, than to us; but be this as it will, nothing in the controversy depends upon that; the state of the case is, whether Infant-baptism was called in question, or made matter of doubt of before these men opposed it; and here I observe, 1. That it is allowed there were debates about Infant-baptism before the affair of *Munster*, and between that and the reformation; by which it appears that it was quickly opposed after the reformation begun. 2. The letter to *Erasmus* out of *Bohemia* shews, that there were a people there near one hundred years before the reformation, who baptized anew, in mere water, such as came over to their sect: this those people did, as our author would have it, not because they judged baptism in infancy invalid, but what was received in the corrupt way of the church of *Rome*. This he says after Dr *Wall*, (though with the Doctor it is uncertain which was the case) inclining to the latter. But it should be observed, that there is no proof from any ancient history, that these people, or any Protestants and reformers that retained Infant-baptism, did, upon leaving the church of *Rome*, reject the baptism of that church, and receive a new one; and besides, *Thomas Waldensis*[l], who lived and wrote at this very time, affirms, that there were a people in *Bohemia* then, that maintained that "believers children were not to be baptized, and that baptism was to no purpose administered to them;" to which I would add the testimony of *Luther*[m], who says, "the *Waldenses* in *Bohemia*, ground the sacrament of baptism upon the person's faith; and for that reason, they annihilate the baptizing of children; for they say, children must be taught before they be baptized."

2. This Gentleman is not well pleased with Dr *Wall* in making this concession, that the Petrobrusians were Antipædobaptists; though it is some comfort to him, that he tells him, that their opinion seems to have been in a short time extinguished and forgotten. But this opinion of theirs not only continued among *Henry* and his followers, who succeeded the Petrobrusians, but among the people afterwards called Waldenses; who to this day own *Peter Bruis* for one of their Barbs or Pastors, as will be seen hereafter. However, that we may have no credit from these people, they are branded as denying the other ordinance of the Lord's Supper; and as saying, it is not to be administered since Christ's time. But what Dr *Wall*[n] afterwards cites from the abbot of *Clugny*, will

---

[l] Tom. iii. tit. 5. c. 53.  [m] Mensalla Colloqu. c.17. p. 254.  [n] Hist. par.2. c.7. 1.8.

## DIVINE RIGHT OF INFANT-BAPTISM. 423

will serve to explain this, and shew, that their meaning is only, that the real presence of Christ in the supper, was only at the time when it was administered by him to the disciples; who makes them to say, "the body of Christ was only "once made by himself at the supper, before his passion, and was only, namely "at this time, given to his disciples; since that time it was never made by any "one, nor given to any one;" or as it is expressed from the same popish writer by Dr *Allix* [o], "The fourth (article ascribed by the abbot to the Petrobrusians) "consisted not only in denying the truth of the body and blood of our Lord, "which is offered up every day, and continually by the sacrament of the church; "but also in maintaining, that it was nothing, and ought not to be offered." Upon which the Doctor makes this remark: "The fourth heresy is expressed in very "odious terms, and after the popish manner, who own nothing to be real in "the sacrament, if the flesh of Jesus Christ and his blood be not there in sub- "stance; and who do not believe he is present at the sacrament upon any other "account, but as he is offered up to God before he is eaten." It was the *real presence* in the supper, and not that itself, these people denied; so that they were brave champions for the purity of both ordinances, equally rejecting Infant-baptism and the doctrine of transubstantiation.

3. As for the other instances of persons denying Infant-baptism after *Peter Bruis*, produced by me; this writer, from Dr *Wall*, would fain fasten the charge of Manicheism upon them, and so as denying all water-baptism; I say, from Dr *Wall*, for what he here says, and indeed there is scarce any thing in this whole chapter about the antiquity of Infant-baptism, but what is borrowed from him, this Gentleman having no stock of his own; that, in fact, instead of answering Mr *Clark*, I am answering Dr *Wall*. As for those *Evervinus* writes of to *Bernard*, about the year 1140, these he observes, from Dr *Wall*, held a tenet which shews them to be Manichees; though *Evervinus* [p] distinguishes them from the Manichees, namely, "all marriage they call fornica- "tion, except that which was between two virgins;" but this was not one of the principles of the Manichees, who condemned all marriage; whereas these allowed of the marriage of persons who had never been married before; they only condemned second marriage; a notion which had prevailed with some of the christian fathers before the Manichees were in being; and this was the notion of some of the *apostolics*, and very probably of them all, the same *Bernard* makes mention of; and who, very likely, as I have observed, were the followers of *Henry*; and against these, this author has nothing of Manicheism:

Here

---

[o] Remarks on the ancient churches of the Albigenses, c. 14. p. 123.

[p] Apud Allix's Remarks on the ancient church of Piedmont, c. 16. p. 143.

Here Dr *Wall* fails him; and here it may be remarked what *Mezeray* says [1], " in the year 1163, there were two sorts of heretics; the one ignorant and " loose, who were a sort of Manichees; the other more learned, and remote " from such filthiness, who held much the same opinions as the Calvinists, and " were called Henricians;" so that the followers of *Henry* were a distinct people from the Manichees; but as for those the Bishop of *Arles* takes notice of, our author's remark upon them is, " it *may be* said, these heretics *might be* some of " the Manichean sect;" fine proof indeed! what he farther adds is more probable, " as perhaps they were some remains of the Petrobrusians;" so that it appears, that their opinion, which seems to have been in a short time extinguished and forgotten, continued however to the year 1215. As for the Gascoiners, that came over into *England* in the year 1158, and asserted, that infants ought not to be baptized till they come to the age of understanding; this, our author says, is no more than what a Manichee might say *then*, and a Quaker *now*; though they both disown all water-baptism. What! to say, that infants ought not to be baptized *till* they come to the age of understanding? is this talking like a Manichee or a Quaker? Does not this suppose that they *may* be baptized, when they come to the age of understanding, and know what they do? But this writer adds, it appears that these rejected both the sacraments of the New Testament, detesting *holy Baptism*, and the *Eucharist*: so they did, they detested Infant-baptism as an human invention, and transubstantiation as an idol of the Pope of *Rome*.

4. To what I have said concerning *Bruno* and *Berengarius*, and their opposition to Infant-baptism 100 years before the Petrobrusians, I would only add; that *Peter Bruis* was not the author of a new sect, though his followers were so called by the Papists, to suggest that they were so; whereas, they were the same with the Berengarians, and held the same principles as the Berengarians did, both with respect to Baptism and the Lord's-supper; and what were their sentiments concerning these are well known.

5. *Gundulphus* and his followers, another instance of persons denying Infant-baptism as early as the year 1025, are represented as Manichees and Quakers, in the point of baptism; and both Mr *Stennett* and myself are charged with great unfairness, partiality and disingenuity, in leaving out what Dr *Allix* has said concerning these men, namely, " that in the same examination, being further " interrogated, these men confessed, that they thought water-baptism of no " use or necessity to any one, infants or adult." This is cited from Dr *Wall*, an author not always to be depended upon, and particularly here; for Dr *Allix* gives

---

[1] Apud Allix's Remarks on the ancient churches of the Albigenses, c. 14. p. 130. c. 20. p. 189.

## DIVINE RIGHT OF INFANT-BAPTISM.

gives no account of any further interrogation of these men, by *Gerard* bishop of *Cambray*, as is suggested; nor are these words to be found in him; for though the men at their first, and only interrogation, speak of the non-necessity and unavailableness of baptism to salvation; and, as Dr *Allix* observes, said some things slightly of baptism, in opposition to the prevailing notions of those times, about the absolute necessity and efficacy of baptism to salvation; yet he is quite clear, that they were for the thing itself: "It is easy to judge, says he[*], that "they looked upon baptism only as a mystical ceremony, the end of which was "to express the engagement of him who is baptized, and the vow he makes "to live holily." *Gundulphus*, adds he, "seeing them, (the popish priests) "assert, that whosoever was baptized could never be damned, falls to an "indifference for baptism; thinking it sufficient to keep to the essentials of that "sacrament." From whence it is plain, he did not deny it, nor disuse it; and upon the whole it is evident, Dr *Wall* has abused Mr *Stennett*, and this Gentleman both him and myself.

6. It is observed, that a large stride is taken by me from the *Eleventh* to the *Fourth* century, not being able in the space of more than 600 years to find one instance of an opposer of Infant-baptism: this will not seem so strange to those who know what a time of ignorance this was; partly through the prevalence of popery, and partly through the inundation of the barbarous nations, which brought a flood of darkness upon the empire; and very few witnesses arose against the superstitions of the church of *Rome*; yet there were some in the valleys of *Piedmont*, even from the times of the apostles, and during this interval, as learned men have observed, that bore their testimony against corruptions in doctrine and practice; among which, this of Infant-baptism must be reckoned one; and whose successors, as we have seen already in the Berengarians, and the Petrobrusians, and will be seen again in the Waldenses, bore witness against this innovation.

7. Though I did not insist upon the Pelagians and others being against Infant-baptism, which some have allowed; this writer is pleased to reproach me with a good-will to admit such heretics, as our predecessors; and this is not the only instance of this sort of reflection; whereas truth is truth, let it be espoused by whom it will; and it might be retorted, that Infant-baptism has been practised by the worst of heretics, and retained by the man of sin and his followers in all the antichristian states; and this writer thinks it worth his pains to rescue the above heretics and schismatics out of our hands; and yet, after all, some of the followers of Pelagius at least argued, that the infants of believers ought

not

[*] Remarks on the ancient church of Piedmont, ch. 11. p. 95, 100.

not to be baptized; and that for this reason, because they were holy, as [*] *Austin* affirms; and who also observes [†], that some other persons argued against it, and the unprofitableness of it to infants, who for the most part died before they knew any thing of it; and *Jerom* [‖], his cotemporary, supposes it, and reasons upon it, that some christians refused to give baptism to their children. So that even in the *fourth* century, though Infant-baptism greatly prevailed, yet it was not so general, as that not one man cotemporary with *Austin* can be produced, as setting himself against it, as our author avers; nay *Stephen Marshall*, a great stickler for Infant-baptism, in his famous sermon on this subject [※], owns, that some in the times of *Austin* questioned it, and refers to a discourse of his in proof of it; and the canon of the council at *Carthage*, produced by me, notwithstanding all that this writer says, is a full proof of the same. For surely, no man in his senses can ever think, that a council consisting of all the bishops in *Africa*, should agree to anathematize their own brethren, who were in the same opinion with them about Infant-baptism; only thought it should not be administered to them as soon as born, but be deferred till they were eight days old; they that can believe this, can believe any thing; and besides, is not a child of eight days old a child newly born? Lastly, after all, *Tertullian*, in the beginning of the *third* century, as he was the first we know of that made mention of Infant-baptism, did oppose it, and dissuade from it; so that it must be once more said, it was called in question, debated and opposed twelve or thirteen hundred years before the madmen of *Munster*, as well as in some of the intervening centuries.

It remains now, Sir, to defend what I have said concerning the *Waldenses*; and it should be observed, 1. That these people had not their name from *Waldus*, as the first founder of their sect: this Dr *Allix* has undertook to make out beyond all possible contradiction, and he has done it. These people were before his time called Vaudois, Vallenses or Wallenses, from their inhabiting the vallies; which name was afterwards changed to Waldenses, when the design was laid to make men believe that *Valdo* or *Waldus* was their first founder, that they might be taken for a new and upstart people; whereas they were in being long before *Waldus*, who received his light and doctrine from them, and whose followers joined them; and this observation sets aside the exceptions of our author to the testimonies of *Peter Bruis*, their confession of faith in 1120, and their noble lesson 1100, as being before the times of the Waldenses; that is, before the times of *Waldo*, more properly speaking; and by how much the more ancient

---

[*] De peccator. merit. l. 2. c. 25.  
[†] Ep. ad Lætam. l. 1. fol. 19.  
[‖] De Libero Arbitrio, l. 2. c 23.  
[※] Sermon, page 5.

## DIVINE RIGHT OF INFANT-BAPTISM. 427

ancient thefe teftimonies are, by fo much the greater is their evidence in point of antiquity, as to thefe peoples denial of Infant-baptifm; and more ftrongly prove that the ancient Vallenfes, afterwards corruptly called Waldenfes, were againft it, and for *adult* baptifm. 2. Thefe people were not divided into various fects, but were a body of people of one and the fame faith and practice, which they retained from father to fon, as their ufual phrafe is, time out of mind.

2. It is true, they were called by different names, by their adverfaries; fome given them by way of reproach, others from their leaders and teachers, as Petrobrufians, Henricians, Arnoldifts, Waldenfians, &c. from *Peter Bruis, Henry, Arnold, Waldus*; but ftill they were the fame people; juft as the Papifts, at the Reformation, made as many heads of diftinct parties, as there were men of note in that work. Thus for inftance, the Petrobrufians were not a diftinct fect of this people, but the very people called Vallenfes, afterwards Waldenfes; and the fame may be faid of the reft: nor were there any fect among them of the Manichean principle, or any of them tinctured with that herefy, as Dr *Allix* has abundantly proved. The cafe, as he makes it appear, was this; that there were Manichees in the places where the Valdenfes and Albigenfes lived, but not that joined them; their enemies took the advantage of this, and called them by the fame name, and afcribed the fame opinions to them, efpecially if they could find any thing in them fimilar to them: thus for inftance, becaufe they denied Infant-baptifm, therefore they were againft all Water-baptifm, and fo Manichees; for as Dr *Allix* [x] obferves, "in thofe barbarous and cruel ages, a "fmall conformity of opinions with the Manichees, was a fufficient ground to "accufe them of Manicheifm, who oppofed any doctrine received by the "church of *Rome*: Thus would they have taken the Anabaptifts for downright "Manichees, fays he, becaufe they condemned the baptifm of infants:" and Mr *Clark* cannot object to this obfervation, fince he himfelf argues from the denial of Infant-baptifm, to the denial of baptifm itfelf; and has reprefented me as a Manichee, or a Quaker, for no other reafon, but for the denial of Infant-baptifm; and if his book lives to the next age, and is of any authority, and can find people foolifh enough to believe it, I muft be fet down for a Manichee or a Quaker. Indeed I muft confefs, I once thought, giving too much credit to Dr *Wall*, that there were different fects among the Waldenfes, and fome of them Manichees, and of other erroneous principles, which I now retract.

3. It is not true what this writer from Dr *Wall* affirms; "This is certain, "that no one author, that calls the people he writes of Waldenfes, does im-

[x] Remarks on the ancient church of Piedmont, c. 15. p. 138.

"pute to them the denial of Infant-baptism;" for *Claudius Couſſard*, writing against them, under this name, gives an extract of their errors out of *Raynerius*, and this is one of them; "They say, then first a man is baptized, when he is received into their sect; some of them hold that baptism is of no advantage to infants, because they cannot yet actually believe;" and concludes this extract thus, "from whence you may see, courteous reader, that this sect of the Waldenses, and the chief, yea almost all heresies now in vogue, are not of late invention, &c." and were this true, yet it is a mere evasion, and a foolish one; since the names of Henricians, Arnoldists, Cathari, Apostolici, &c. under which they are represented, as opposers of Infant-baptism, are the names of the Waldenses, as *Perrin*[y] observes, a writer whom our author says he has read.

4. It is a most clear case, that the ancient barbs or pastors of the Waldensian churches, so called, were opposers of Infant-baptism. Sir *Samuel Moreland*, as I have observed, reckons *Peter Bruis* and *Henry* among their ancient pastors; so does *Perrin* likewise, though he is mistaken in making them to follow *Waldo*; and these are allowed to be Antipædobaptists by several Pædobaptists themselves. *Arnoldus*, another of their pastors, according to the above writer, from whence they were called Arnoldists, was out of all doubt a denier of Infant-baptism, for which he was condemned by a council, as Dr *Wall* owns. *Lollardo* was another of their pastors, according to the same authors, and from whose name, *Perrin* says, the Waldenses were called Lollards; and so *Kilianus* says [z], a Lollard is also called a Waldensian heretic. These were not the followers of *Wickliff*, as our author wrongly asserts; for they were, as Dr *Allix*[a] observes, more ancient than the Wicklifites; and though this name was afterwards given to the latter, *Lollardo* was here in *England*, and had his followers before *Wickliff*'s time; and so he had in *Flanders* and *Germany*; and of the Lollards there, *Trithemius*[b] says, they derided the sacrament of baptism; which cannot be understood of their deriding baptism in general, but of their deriding Infant-baptism; which was common among the Papists to say; and the same is the sense of the Lollards in *England*, who are charged with making light of the sacrament of baptism. Now since these were the sentiments of the ancient pastors of the Waldenses, it is reasonable to believe the people themselves were of the same mind with them; nor are there any confessions of their faith, which make any mention of Infant-baptism; nor any proofs of its being practised by them until the sixteenth century, produced by our author, or any other.

5. The

---

[y] History of the Waldenses, p. 8, 9.
[z] Apud Allix's Remarks on the ancient churches of the Albigenses, c. 22. p. 202.
[a] Ibid. p. 201.  [b] Apud Allix, ibid. p. 202.

5. The Albigenses, as *Perrin*[e] says, differ nothing at all from the Waldenses, in their belief; but are only so called of the country of *Albi*; where they dwelt, and had their first beginning; and who received the belief of the Waldenses by means of *Peter Bruis*, *Henry* and *Arnold*; who, as it clearly appears, were all Antipædobaptists; and Dr *Allix*[d] observes, that the Albigenses have been called Petrobrusians; owned to be a sect of the Waldenses, that denied Infant-baptism: and that the Albigenses denied it, at least some of them, yea the greatest part of them, is acknowledged by some Pædobaptists themselves. *Chassanion* in his history of these people says[e]; "some writers have affirmed, that the " Albigeois approved not of the baptism of infants.—I cannot deny that the " Albigeois for the *greatest part* were of that opinion.—The truth is, they did " not reject this sacrament, or say it was useless, (as some, he before observes, " asserted they did) but only counted it unnecessary to infants, because they are " not of age to believe, or capable of giving evidence of their faith." Which is another proof of the ancient Waldenses being against Infant-baptism, these being the same with them. Upon the whole, if I have been too modest, in saying that the ancient Waldenses practised Infant-baptism, wants proof, I shall now use a little more boldness and confidence, and affirm, that the ancient Vallenses, or as corruptly called Waldenses, were opposers of Infant-baptism; and that no proof can be given of the practice of it among them till the sixteenth century; and that the author of the dialogue had no reason to say, that their being in the practice of adult baptism, and denying Infant-baptism, was a mere chimæra and a groundless figment.

My *fourth* chapter, you know, Sir, respects the argument for Infant-baptism; taken from the covenant made with *Abraham*, and from circumcision. Here our author runs out into a large discussion of the covenant of grace, in his way; in which he spends about fourscore pages, which I take to be the heads of some old sermons, he is fond of, and has taken this opportunity of publishing them to the world, without any propriety or pertinence. For, 1. not to dispute the point with him, whether there are two distinct covenants of redemption and grace, or whether they are one and the same, which is foreign to the argument; be it that they are two distinct ones, the spiritual seed promised to Christ, or the people given him in the one, are the same that are taken into the other; they are of equal extent; there are no more in the one, than there are concerned in the other; and this writer himself allows, " that the salvation of the *spiritual* " *seed of* Christ is promised in both covenants." Now let it be proved, if it can,

[c] History of the Albigenses, l. 1. c. 1. p. 1, 2.
[d] Ut supra, c. 14. p. 121.   [e] Apud Stennett, p. 81, 82.

can, that there are any in the covenant of grace but the *spiritual seed of Christ*; and that the natural seed of believers, and their infants as such, are the spiritual seed: and if they are, then they were given to Christ, who undertook to save them, and whose salvation was promised to him, and to whom in time the communications of grace according to the covenant are made; then they must be all of them regenerated, renewed, and sanctified, justified, pardoned, adopted, persevere in grace, and be eternally saved; all which will not, cannot be said of all the infants of believers; and consequently cannot be thought to be in the covenant of grace.

2. As to what he says concerning the conditionality of the covenant, it is all answered in one word; let him name what he will, as the condition of this covenant, which God has not absolutely promised, or Christ has not engaged to perform, or to see performed in his people, or by them. Are the conditions, faith and repentance? These are both included in the *new heart*, and *spirit*, and *heart of flesh*, God has absolutely promised in the covenant, *Ezekiel* xxxvi. 26. Is new, *spiritual*, and *evangelical* obedience, the condition? This is absolutely promised as the former, ver. 27. Or is it actual consent? *Thy people shall be willing*, Psal. cx. 3. And after all, if it is a conditional covenant, how do infants get into it? Or is it a conditional covenant to the *adult*, and unconditional to them? If faith and repentance are the conditions of it, and these must be, as this author says, "the sinner's own voluntary chosen acts, before " he can have any actual saving interest in the privileges of the covenant;" it follows, that they cannot be in it, or have interest in the privileges of it, till they repent and believe, and do these as their own voluntary chosen acts; and if "man's consent and agreement bring him into covenant with God," as this writer says; it should be considered, whether infants are capable of this consent, or no; and if they are not, according to this man, they stand a poor chance for being in the covenant.

3. Whereas the covenant of grace, as to the essence of it, has been always the same, as is allowed, under the various forms and administrations of it, both under the Old and New Testament; so the subjects of it have been, and are the same, the spiritual seed of Christ, and none else; and not the carnal seed of men as such: and if the conditions of it are the same, faith and obedience, as our author observes, then infants must stand excluded from it, since they can neither believe nor obey.

4. That the covenant of grace was made with *Abraham*, or a revelation and application of it to him; that the gospel was revealed to him, and he was justified in the same way believers are now; and that he had spiritual promises made to him, and spiritual blessings bestowed upon him; and that *gospel-believers*,

be

be they Jews or Gentiles, who are the spiritual seed of *Abraham*, are heirs of the same covenant-blessings and promises, are never denied;—this man is fighting with his own shadow.

What is denied and should be proved, is, that the covenant of grace is made with *Abraham*'s carnal seed, the Jews, and with the carnal seed of gospel-believers among the Gentiles; and that spiritual promises are made to them; and that they are heirs of spiritual blessings, as such: and let it be further observed, that the covenant in *Genesis* xvii. is not the covenant referred to in *Galatians* iii. 17. said to be *confirmed of God in Christ*, and which *could not be disannulled by the law 430 years after*; since the date does not agree, it falls short twenty-four years; and therefore must refer, not to the covenant of circumcision, but to some other covenant, and time of making it.

5. It is false, that children have been always taken with their parents into the covenant of grace, under every dispensation. The children of *Adam* were not taken into the covenant of grace with him, which was made known to him immediately after the fall; for then all the world must be in the covenant of grace. The covenant made with *Noah* and his sons, was not the covenant of grace; since it was made with the beasts of the field as well as with them; unless it will be said, that they also are in the covenant of grace. Nor were all *Abraham*'s natural seed taken into the covenant of grace with him. *Ishmael* was by name excluded, and the covenant established with *Isaac*; and yet *Ishmael* was in the covenant of circumcision; which by the way proves, that, that and the covenant of grace are two different things: nor were all *Abraham*'s natural seed in the line of *Isaac* taken into the covenant of grace, not *Esau*; nor all in the line of *Jacob* and *Israel*; for as the apostle says, *they are not all Israel which are of Israel*; *neither because they are the seed of Abraham, are they all children*; *but in Isaac shall thy seed be called*; *that is, they which are the children of the flesh, these are not the children of God, but the children of the promise are counted for the seed*[e]. The covenant at *Horeb* was indeed a national covenant, and took in all, children and grown persons; and which was no other than a civil contract, and not a covenant of grace, between God and the people of *Israel*; he as King, and they as subjects; he promising to be their protector and defender, and they to be his faithful subjects, and obey his laws; which covenant has been long ago abolished, when God wrote a *Loammi* upon them: nor is there any proof of infants under the New Testament being taken into covenant with their parents. Not *Matt.* xix. 14. 1 *Cor.* vii. 14. which make no mention of any covenant at all, as will be considered hereafter; nor *Heb.* viii. 8. since the house of *Israel*, that new covenant is said to be made with, are the *spiritual Israel*, whether

[e] Rom. ix. 6—8.

ther Jews or Gentiles, even the whole houshold of faith, and none but them; nor are their infants spoken of, nor can they be included; for have they all of them the laws of God written on their hearts? Do they all know the Lord? or have they all their sins forgiven them? which is the case with all those with whom this covenant is made, or to whom it is applied. Nor are there any predictions of this kind in the Old Testament. *Deut.* xxx. 6. *Psalm* xxii. 30. *Isaiah* ix. 21. speak only of a succession of converted persons, either in the gospel-church among the Gentiles, or in the same among the Jews, when that people shall be converted in the latter day.

6. The distinction of an *inward* and *outward* covenant, is an *Utopian* business, mere jargon and nonsense; it has no foundation in scripture, reason, nor common sense. And here I cannot but observe what Mr *Baxter*, a zealous Pædobaptist, says on this subject [f]. " Mr *Blake*'s common phrase is, that they are " in the *outward* covenant, and what that is, I cannot tell; in what sense is that " (God's covenant-act) called outward? It cannot be, as if God did as the dis- " sembling creature, *Ore tenus*, with the mouth only, covenant with them, and " not with the heart, as they deal with him. I know therefore no possible sense " but this, that it is called outward from the blessings promised, which are out- " ward; here therefore, I should have thought it reasonable for Mr *Blake* to " have told us what these outward blessings are, that this covenant promiseth; " and that he would have proved out of the scriptures that God hath such a co- " venant distinct from the covenant of grace. I desire therefore that those words " of scripture may be produced, where any such covenant is contained." And let Mr *Clark* tell us what he means by the *outward* covenant, or the outward part of it, in which infants are; if any thing can be collected from him, as his meaning, it is, that it designs the outward administration of the covenant by the word and ordinances: but if it means the outward ministry of the word, newborn infants are not capable of that to any profit; if it designs the administration of baptism and the Lord's supper, then they should be admitted to one as well as the other; and if baptism only is intended by this outward covenant, or the outward part, here is the greatest confusion imaginable; then the sense is, they are under the outward administration of the covenant, that is baptism; and this gives them a right to be baptized, that is to be baptized again, or in other words to be made Anabaptists of; and after all it is a poor covenant, or a poor part of it assigned for infants, in the bond of which, as this author says, are many real hypocrites.

7. That covenant-interest, and an evidence of it, give right to the seal of the covenant, which was circumcision formerly, and baptism now, is false; and

this

[f] Baxter's Answer to Blake, Sect 39.

this writer has not proved it, nor infants covenant-intereft, as we have feen already. He fhould have firft proved that circumcifion was a feal of the covenant of grace formerly, and baptifm the feal of it now, before he talked of covenant-intereft giving a right to either. Admitting that circumcifion was a feal of the covenant of grace formerly, (though it was not) yet intereft in that covenant and evidence of intereft in it, did not give right to all in it to the feal of it, as it is called; fince there were many who had evidently an intereft in the covenant of grace, when circumcifion was firft appointed, and yet had no right to it; as *Shem, Arphaxad, Lot,* and others; and even many who were in the covenant made with *Abraham,* as this writer himfelf will allow, who had no right to this feal, even all his female offspring: to fay, they were *virtually circumcifed in the males,* is falfe and foolifh; to have a thing virtually by another, is to have it by proxy, who reprefents another; but were the males the proxies and reprefentatives of the females? had they been fo, then indeed when they were circumcifed, the females were virtually circumcifed with them; and fo it was all one as if they had been circumcifed in their own perfons; which to have been, would have been unlawful and finful, not being by the appointment of God: as for its being unlawful for uncircumcifed perfons to eat of the pafsover, this muft be underftood of fuch who ought to be circumcifed, and does not affect the females, who ought not, and fo might eat, though they were really uncircumcifed; nor had the males themfelves any right to it till the eighth day; and fo it was not covenant-intereft, but a command from God, that gave them a a right; and fuch an order is neceffary to any perfon's right to baptifm.

Again, admitting for argument-fake, that baptifm is a feal of the covenant, does not this Gentleman alfo believe, that the Lord's-fupper is a feal of it likewife? and if covenant-intereft gives a right to the feals, why not to one feal as well as the other? and why are not infants admitted to the Lord's table, as well as to baptifm? Moreover, it is *evidence* of intereft, this writer fays, that gives a right to the feal; and what is that evidence? Surely if faith and repentance are the conditions of the covenant, as before afferted, they muft be the evidence? and therefore, according to his own argument, it fhould firft appear, that infants have faith and repentance as the evidence of their covenant-intereft, before they are admitted to the feal of it; and fuch only according to the injunction of Chrift, and the practice of his apoftles, were admitted to baptifm; as the paffages below fhew t, which our author refers us to.

And now, Sir, after a long ramble, we are come to *Abraham's* covenant itfelf, and to the queftions concerning it; as, of what kind it is; with whom made;

---

t Matt. xxviii. 19. Mark xvi. 16. Acts ii. 38, 39. and x. 47.

and whether circumcifion was the feal of the covenant of grace; and whether baptifm is come in its room, and is the feal of it. Now as to the

I. Firft of thefe, of what kind was the covenant with *Abraham*, Genefis xvii? I have afferted, that it was not the pure covenant of grace, but of a mixed kind; confifting partly of promifes of temporal things, and partly of fpiritual ones; and you will eafily obferve, Sir, that the exceptions of this writer to the arguments I make ufe of in proof of it, are for the moft part founded on his miftaken notions of the conditionality of the covenant of grace, and on that ftupid and fenfelefs diftinction of the *inward* and *outward* covenant, before exploded; wherefore fince thefe are groundlefs conceits and fandy foundations, what is built upon them muft neceffarily fall.

II. The fame may be obferved with refpect to that part of the queftion, which relates to the covenant being made with all *Abraham*'s feed according to the flefh, as a covenant of grace; by the help of which unfcriptural and irrational diftinction, he can find a place in the covenant of grace for a perfecuting *Ifhmael*, a profane *Efau*, and all the wicked Jews in all ages, in all times of defection and apoftacy; but if he can find no better covenant to put the infants of believers into, nor better company to place them with, who notwithftanding their covenant-intereft, may be loft and damned, it will be a very infignificant thing with confiderate perfons, whether they are in this *Utopian* covenant or no.

III. As to that part of the queftion which relates to the natural feed of believing Gentiles being in *Abraham*'s covenant, or to that being made with them as a covenant of grace, it is by me denied. This writer fays, I add a ftroke, as he calls it, that at once cuts off all *Abraham*'s natural feed, and all the natural feed of believing Gentiles, from having any fhare in the covenant; fince I fay, " That to none can fpiritual bleffings belong, but to a fpiritual feed, not a " natural one." But he might have obferved, that this is explained in the fame page thus, " not to the natural feed of either of them *as fuch*." He fays, " it is not requifite to a perfon's vifible title and claim to the external privileges " of the covenant, that he fhould be truly regenerate, or a fincere believer;" and yet he elfewhere fays, " that to repent and believe muft be the finner's " own voluntary chofen acts, before he can have any actual faving intereft in " the privileges of the covenant:" let him reconcile thefe together. He has not proved, nor is he able to prove, that the natural feed of believing Gentiles, as fuch, are the fpiritual feed of *Abraham*; fince only they that are Chrift's, or believers in him, or who walk in the fteps of the faith of *Abraham*, are his fpiritual feed; which cannot be faid of all the natural feed of believing Gentiles, or of any of them as fuch. That claufe in *Abraham*'s covenant, *A father of many nations have I made thee*[b], is to be understood only of the faithful, or of believers in all nations; and not of all nations that bear the christian name, as comprehending all in them, grown persons and infants, good and bad men; and only to such who are of the faith of *Abraham* does the apostle apply it[i]; the stranger, and his male seed, that submitted to circumcision, may indeed be said to be in the covenant of circumcision; but it does not follow, that these were in the covenant of grace; there were many of *Abraham*'s own natural seed that were in the covenant of circumcision, who were not in the covenant of grace; and it would be very much, that the natural seed of strangers, and even of believing Gentiles, should have a superior privilege to the natural seed of *Abraham*. Those, and those only, in a judgment of charity, are to be reckoned the spiritual seed, who openly believe in Christ, as I have expressed it; about which phrase this man makes a great pother, when the sense is plain and easy; and that it designs such who make a visible profession of their faith, and are judged to be partakers of the grace of the covenant; which certainly is the best evidence of their interest in it; and therefore it must be best to wait till this appears, before any claim of privilege can be made; and is no other than what this writer himself says in the words before referred to. Though, after all, I stand by my former assertion, that covenant-interest, even when made out clear and plain, gives not right to any ordinance without a positive order or direction from God; and he may call it a conceit of mine if he pleases; he is right in it, that according to it, no person living is capable of (that is, has a right unto) the ordinances and visible privileges of the church upon any grounds of covenant-interest, without a positive direction from God for it; as there was for circumcision, so there should be for baptism; as, with respect to the former, many who were in the covenant of grace had no concern with it, having no direction from the Lord about it; so though persons may be in the covenant of grace, yet if they are not pointed out by the Lord, as those whom he wills to be the subjects of it, they have no right unto it. To say, that *Lot* and others were under a former administration of the covenant, on whom circumcision was not enjoined, is saying nothing; unless he can tell us what that former administration of it was, and wherein it differed from the administration of it to *Abraham* and his seed; to instance in circumcision, would be begging the question, since that is the thing instanced in; by which it appears that covenant-interest gives no right to an ordinance, without a special direction; and the same holds good of baptism. His sense of *Mark* xvi. 16. is, that infants are included in the profession of their believing parents, and why not in their baptism too? and so there is no necessity of their baptism; the text countenances one as much as it does the other, and both are equally stupid and senseless.

IV. The

[b] Gen. xvii. 4, 5.  [i] Rom. iv. 16.

IV. The next inquiry is, whether circumcifion was the *feal* of the covenant of grace to *Abraham*'s natural feed. It is called a *token* or *fign*, but not a feal; this writer fays, though a token, fimply confidered, does not neceffarily imply a feal, yet the token of a covenant, or promife, can be nothing elfe: if it can be nothing elfe, it does neceffarily imply it; unlefs there is any real difference between a token fimply confidered, and the token of a covenant, which he would do well to fhew. Circumcifion was nothing elfe but a fign or mark in the flefh, appointed by the covenant; and therefore that is called *the covenant in their flefh*; and not becaufe circumcifion was any confirming token or feal of the covenant to any of *Abraham*'s natural feed: it was a fign and feal of the righteoufnefs of faith to *Abraham*; that that righteoufnefs which he had by faith before his circumcifion, fhould come upon the uncircumcifed Gentiles; but was no feal of that, nor any thing elfe, to any others: and according to our author's notion of it, it was neither a feal of *Abraham*'s faith, nor of his righteoufnefs; then furely not of any others; and yet in contradiction to this, he fays, it is "a feal of the covenant of grace, wherein this privilege of jufti-"fication by faith is confirmed and conveyed to believers;" and if to believers, then furely not to all *Abraham*'s natural feed, unlefs he can think they were all believers; though his real notion, if I underftand him right, is, that it is no confirming fign, or feal of any fpiritual bleffings to any; fince the fubjects of it, as he owns, may have neither faith nor righteoufnefs; but of the truth of the covenant itfelf, that God has made one; but this needs no fuch fign or feal; the word of God is fufficient, which declares it and affures of it.

V. The next thing that comes under confideration, is, whether baptifm fucceeds circumcifion; and is the feal of the covenant of grace to believers, and their natural feed. 1. This author endeavours to prove that baptifm fucceeds circumcifion from *Coloffians* ii. 11. but in vain; for the apoftle is fpeaking not of corporal, but of fpiritual circumcifion, of which the former was a typical refemblance; and fo fhewing, that believing Gentiles have that through Chrift which was fignified by it; and which the apoftle defcribes, by the manner of its being effected, *without hands*, without the power of man, by the efficacy of divine grace; and by the fubftance and matter of it, which lay in *the putting off the body of the fins of the flefh*; and without a tautology, as this writer fuggefts, by the author of it, Chrift, who by his Spirit effects it, and therefore is called the *circumcifion of Chrift*; and is diftinguifhed from baptifm, defcribed in the next verfe: and as weak and infignificant is his proof from the analogy between baptifm and circumcifion; fome things faid of baptifm and circumcifion are not true; as that they are facraments of admiffion into the church: Not fo

was

was circumcision; not of the Gentiles, who had it not, nor were admitted by it, and yet were in the church; nor even of the males, for they were not circumcised till eight days old, yet were of the Jewish church, which was national, as soon as born; and persons may be baptized, and yet not be entered into any visible church: Nor are they badges of relation to the God of *Israel*; since on the one hand, persons might have one or the other, yet have no spiritual relation to God; and on the other hand, be without either, and yet be related to him: nor are either of them seals and signs of the covenant of grace, as before shewn: nor is baptism absolutely requisite to a person's approach to God with confidence and acceptance in any religious duty, private or public. Baptism serves not to the same use and purpose in many things that circumcision did; it is not the middle wall of partition; nor does it bind men to keep the whole law, as circumcision; and though there may be some seeming agreement, arguments from analogy are weak and dangerous: so from the priest's offering a propitiatory sacrifice, wearing the linen ephod, and one high priest being above all other priests, the Papists argue for a minister's offering a real propitiatory sacrifice, for wearing the surplice, and for a Pope, or universal Bishop; and others from the same topic argue for tithes being due to ministers, and for the inequality of bishops and presbyters, there being an high priest and inferior ones: and to this tends our author's third argument, that either baptism succeeds circumcision, or there is nothing at all instituted in its room; nor is there any necessity that there should, any more than that there should be a Pope in the room of an high priest, or any thing to answer to Easter, Pentecost, *&c.* all which, as circumcision, had their end in Christ: nor does the Lord's-supper come in the room of the passover; what answers to that is, *Christ the passover sacrificed for us*; and did it, by this argument from analogly, infants ought to be admitted to the Lord's-supper, as they were to the passover: by this way of arguing, and at this door, may be brought in all the Jewish rites and ceremonies, under other names: and after all, what little agreement may be imagined is between them, the difference is notorious in many things; some of which this author is obliged to own; as in the subjects of them, the one being only males, the other males and females; the one being by blood, the other by water; and besides they differ as to the persons by whom, and the places where, and the uses for which, they are performed; wherefore from analogy and resemblance is no proof of succession, but the contrary.

My argument from baptism being in force before circumcision, to prove that the one did not succeed the other, is so far from being allowed by our author a proof of it, that he will not allow it to be a bare probability, unless I could prove they had been all along cotemporary: but if I cannot do it, he and his
brethren

brethren can, who give credit to the Jewish custom of baptizing their proselytes and children; and which they make to be a practice, for which the Jews fetch proof as early as the times of *Jacob*; and I hope, if he will abide by this, he will allow that baptism could not come in the room of circumcision.

2. He next attempts to prove that baptism is a seal of the covenant of grace to believers and their seed, by a wretched perversion of several passages of scripture [k], in which no mention is made of the covenant of grace, and much less of baptism as a seal of it; and which only speak of believers, and not a syllable of their infants; and all of them clear proofs, that believers, and they only, are the proper subjects of baptism; as may easily be observed by the bare reading of them.

3. My sentiment of the ordinances of baptism and the Lord's supper not being seals of the covenant of grace, he thinks, is borrowed from the Socinians. These have no better notion of the covenant of grace than himself, nor of the efficacy of the blood of Christ for the ratification of it, nor of the sealing work of the spirit of God upon the hearts of his people. My sentiment is borrowed from the scriptures, and is established by them; the blood of Christ confirms and ratifies the covenant, the blessings and promises of it, and is therefore called *the blood of the everlasting covenant*; the blessed spirit is the sealer of believers interest in it, or assures them of it [l]. So that there are not two seals of the covenant of grace, as he wrongly observes. The blood of Christ makes the covenant itself sure, and is in this sense the seal of that; the spirit of God is the seal of interest in it to particular persons; and in neither sense do or can ordinances seal.

4. Upon the whole, what has this author been doing throughout this chapter? has he proved that the natural seed of believers, as such, are in the covenant of grace? he has not. The covenant he attempts to prove they are in, according to his own account of it, is no covenant of grace. Does it secure any one spiritual blessing to the carnal seed of believers? it does not. Does it secure regenerating, renewing, sanctifying grace, or pardoning grace, or justifying grace, or adopting grace, or eternal life? it does not. And if so, I leave it to be judged of by such that have any knowledge of the covenant, if such a covenant can be called the covenant of grace; or what spiritual saving advantage is to be had from an interest in such a covenant, could it be proved.

He would have his readers believe, that the covenant, he pleads infants have an interest in, is the same under all dispensations, and in all ages: the covenant of grace is indeed the same, but the covenant he puts the infant-seed of believers into, is only an external administration; and this, he himself being judge, cannot

---
[k] See John iii. 33. Mark xvi. 16. Matt. xxviii. 19. 1 Peter iii. 21. 1 Cor. xii. 13.
[l] Heb. xiii. 20. Ephes. i. 13.

not have been always the fame. This external administration, according to himself, was first by sacrifices, and then by circumcision, and now by baptism; for what else he means by an external administration, than an administration of ordinances, cannot be conceived; and then by infants being in the covenant, is no other than having ordinances administered to them; and so their being in the covenant now, is no other than their being baptized; and yet he says, "the main foundation of the right of infants to baptism, is their interest in the covenant;" that is, the external administration they are under, or the administration of baptism to them, is the main foundation of their right to baptism. They are baptized, therefore they are and ought to be baptized; such an account of covenant-interest, and of right to baptism from it, is a mere begging the question, and proving *idem per idem*, yea is downright nonsense and contradiction: and so, when baptism is said to be the seal of the covenant, that is, of the external administration, which administration is that of baptism, the sense is, baptism is the seal of baptism. This senseless jargon is the amount of all the reasonings throughout this chapter: Such mysterious stuff, such glaring contradictions, and stupid nonsense, I leave him and his admirers to please themselves with.

5. From hence it appears, that the clamorous out-cry of cutting off infants from their covenant-right, and so abridging and lessening their privileges, is all a noise about nothing; since it is in vain to talk about cutting off from the covenant of grace, when they were never in it; as the natural seed of believers, as such, never were, under any dispensation whatever; and even what is pleaded for, is only an external administration, which neither conveys grace, nor secures any spiritual blessings; wherefore what privileges are infants deprived of by not being baptized? Let it be shewn if it can, what spiritual blessings infants said to be baptized have, which our infants unbaptized have not; to instance in baptism itself, would be begging the question; it would still be asked, what spiritual privilege or profit comes to an infant by its baptism? If our infants have as many, or the same privileges under the gospel-dispensation, without baptism, as others have with it; then their privileges are not abridged or lessened, and the clamour must be a groundless one. To say, that baptism admits into the christian church, as circumcision into the Jewish church, are both false, as has been proved already; our author, it seems, did not know, that a national church was a carnal one; whereas a national church can be no other, since all born in a nation are members of it, and become so by their birth, which is carnal; for, *whatsoever is born of the flesh is flesh*. Whereas a gospel-church, gathered out of the world, does, or should consist, only of such who are born again, and have an understanding of spiritual things. This writer seems to suggest,

gest, that if infants are not admitted to this external administration, and seal of the covenant he pleads for, their condition is deplorable, and there is no ground of hope of their eternal salvation; and does their being admitted into this external administration make their condition better with respect to everlasting salvation? not at all; since, according to our author, persons may be in this, and yet not in the covenant of grace, as hypocrites may be; and he distinguishes this visible and external administration from the spiritual dispensation and efficacy of the covenant of grace; so that persons may be in the one, and yet be everlastingly lost; and therefore what ground of hope of eternal salvation does this give? or what ground of hope does non-admission into it deprive them of? Is salvation inseparably connected with baptism? or does it ensure it to any? How unreasonable then, and without foundation, is this clamorous outcry? And now, Sir, we are come to

The *fifth* chapter of my treatise, which considers the several texts of scripture produced in favour of Infant-baptism; and the first is *Acts* ii. 38, 39. Now, not to take notice of this author's foolish impertinencies, and with which his book abounds, and would be endless to observe; for which reason I mention them not, that I might not swell this letter too large, and impose upon your patience in reading it; you will easily observe, Sir, the puzzle and confusion he is thrown into to make the exhortation to *repent*, urged in order to the enjoyment of the *promise*, to agree with infants; and which is mentioned as previous to baptism, and in order to it. That this passage can furnish out no argument in favour of Infant-baptism, will appear by the plain, clear, and easy sense of it; *Peter* had charged the Jews with the sin of crucifying Christ; their consciences were awakened, and loaded with the guilt of it; in their distress, being pricked to the heart, they inquire what they should do, as almost despairing of mercy to be shewn to such great sinners; they are told, that notwithstanding their sin was so heinous, yet if they truly repented of it, and submitted to Christ and his ordinances, particularly to baptism, the promise of life and salvation belonged to them, nor need they doubt of an interest in it: and whereas they had imprecated his blood, not only upon themselves, but upon their posterity, more immediate and more remote, for which they were under great concern; they are told this promise of salvation by Christ reached to them also, provided they repented and were baptized; and which is the reason that mention is made of their children; *yea, even to them that were afar off*, their brethren the Jews in distant countries, that should hear the gospel, repent and believe, and be baptized; or should live in ages to come in the latter day, and should *look on him whom they have pierced, and mourn*; and so has nothing to do with the covenant with
*Abraham*

*Abraham* and his natural feed, and much lefs with the Gentiles and theirs: and be it fo, that the Gentiles are meant by thofe *afar off*, which may be admitted, fince it is fometimes a defcriptive character of them; yet no mention is made of their children; and had they been mentioned, the limiting claufe, *even as many as the Lord our God ſhall call*, plainly points at, and defcribes the perfons intended; not among the Gentiles only, but the Jews alfo, as agreeable to common fenfe and the rules of grammar; and is to be underftood only of the Jews that are called by grace, and of their children, that are effectually called, and of the Gentiles called with an holy calling, as the perfons to whom the promife belongs; and which appears evident by their repentance and baptifm, which this is an encouraging motive to; and therefore can be underftood only of adult perfons, and not of infants; and of whofe baptifm not a fyllable is mentioned, nor can it be inferred from this paffage, or eftablifhed by it.

II. The next paffage of fcripture produced in favour of Infant-baptifm, and to as little purpofe, is *Matthew* xix. 14. it is owned by our author, that thefe children were not brought to Chrift to be baptized by him; and that they were not baptized by him; thefe things, he fays, they do not affirm. For what then is the paffage produced? why, to fhew, that infants become profelytes to Chrift by baptifm; and is not this to be baptized? what a contradiction is this? And afterwards another felf-contradiction follows: he imagines thefe infants had been baptized already, and yet were commanded to become profelytes by baptifm, and fo Anabaptifts; but how does it appear that it was the will of Chrift they fhould become profelytes to him this way? from the etymology of the Greek word, which fignifies *to come to*; fo, wherever the word is ufed of perfons as coming to Chrift, it is to be underftood of their becoming profelytes to him by baptifm: it is ufed in *Matthew* xvi. 1. the *Pharifees alfo with the Sadducees*—προσηλθντες, "*came tempting him*." Did they become profelytes to him by baptifm? what ftupid ftuff is this? nay the Devil himfelf is faid to come to him, *and when the Tempter*—προσελθων, *came to him, he faid*, &c. *Matthew* iv. 3. our author furely does not think he became a profelyte to him. That it was the cuftom of the Jews, before the times of Chrift, to baptize the children of profelytes, is not a fact fo well attefted, as is faid; the writings from whence the proof is taken, were written fome hundreds of years after Chrift's time; and the very firft perfons that mention it, difpute it; one affirming there was fuch a cuftom, and the other denying it; and were it fo, fince it was only a tradition of the elders at beft, and not a command of God, it is not credible that our Lord fhould follow it, or enforce fuch a practice on his followers: the coming of thefe children was merely corporal; whatever it was for, and temporary; there is no other way of coming to Chrift, or becoming profelytes to him, but by believing in him, embracing his doctrines, and obeying his commands; and when children are capable of these things, and do them, we are ready to acknowledge them the proselytes of Christ, and admit them to baptism: nor does the reason given in the text, *for of such is the kingdom of heaven*, prove their right to baptism; for not to insist on the metaphorical sense of these words, which yet *Calvin* gives into; but supposing infants litterally are meant, the *kingdom of heaven* cannot be understood of the gospel-church-state; which is not national but congregational, consisting of men gathered out of the world by the grace of God, and who make a public profession of Christ, which infants are not capable of, and so not taken into it; and were they, they must have an equal right to the Lord's supper as to baptism, and of which they are equally capable; for does the Lord's supper require in the receivers of it a competent measure of christian knowledge, the exercise of reason and understanding, and their active powers, as this writer says, so does baptism. But by the *kingdom of heaven*, is meant the heavenly glory; and we deny not, that there are infants that belong to it, though who they are, we know not; nor is this any argument for their admission to baptism; it is one thing what Christ does himself, he may admit them into heaven; it is another thing what we are to do, the rule of which is his revealed will: we cannot admit them into a church-state, or to any ordinance, unless he has given us an order so to do; and besides, it is time enough to talk of their admission to baptism, when it appears they have right unto, and a meetness for the kingdom of heaven.

III. Another passage brought into this controversy is *Matthew* xviii. 16. this is owned to be less conviclive, because interpreters are divided about the sense of it; some understanding it of children in knowledge and grace, others of children in age, to which our author inclines, for the sake of his hypothesis; though he knows not how to reject the former: my objections to the latter sense, he says, have no *great weight* in them; it seems they have some. I will add a little more to them, shewing that not little ones in a litteral, but figurative sense, are meant, even the disciples of Christ, that actually believed in him: the word here used is different from that which is used of little children, ver. 3. and is manifestly used of the disciples of Christ, *Matthew* x. 42. and the parallel text in *Mark* ix. 41, 42. most clearly shews, that the little ones that believed in Christ, which were not to be offended, were his apostles, that belonged to him; quite contrary to what this writer produces it for; who has most miserably mangled and tortured this passage: Moreover there was but one little child, Christ took and set in the midst of his disciples, whereas he has regard to several little ones then present, and whom, as it were, he points unto; one of which to offend, would be resented; and plainly designs the apostles then present, who

not

not only had the principle of faith, but exercised it, as the word used signifies; and who were capable of being scandalized, and of having stumbling-blocks thrown in their way, and taking offence at them; which infants in age are not capable of: that senseless rant of cutting off infants from their right in the covenant of salvation, and from the privileges of the gospel, (I suppose he means by denying baptism to them) being an offence and injury to them, and the whining cant upon this, are mean and despicable: his reasons, why the apostles of Christ cannot be meant, because contending for pre-eminence, they discovered a temper of mind opposite to little children, has no force in it; for Christ calls them *little ones*, partly because they ought to be as little children, ver. 3. and in some sense were so; and partly to mortify their pride and vanity, as well as to express his tender affection and regard for them, see ver. 10. and since infants are not meant, it is in vain to dispute about their faith, either as to principle or act, and what right that gives to baptism; and especially since profession of faith, and consent to be baptized, are necessary to the administration of that ordinance, and to the subjects of it.

IV. Next we have his remarks on the exceptions to the sense of 1 *Corinthians* vii. 14. contended for: the sense of internal holiness derived from parents to children is rejected by him; but there is another, which he seems to have a good will unto: he says there are some reasons to support it, and he does not object to it; yet chooses not to adhere to it, though if established, would put an end to the controversy; and that is, that the word *sanctified* signifies *baptized*, and the word *holy*, christians *baptized*; and then the sense is, " the unbelieving husband is baptized by the believing wife, and the unbelieving wife is baptized by the believing husband; else were your children unbaptized, but now they are baptized christians;" the bare mention of which is confutation sufficient. The sense our author prefers is a visible federal holiness: but what that holiness is, for any thing he has said to clear it, remains in the dark: covenant-holiness, or what the covenant of grace promises, and secures to all interested in it, is clear and plain, internal holiness of heart, and outward holiness of life and conversation flowing from that[m]: But are the infants of believers, as such, partakers of this holiness? or is such holiness as this communicated unto, or does it appear upon all the natural seed of believers? This will not be said; experience and facts are against it; they *are born in sin, and are by nature children of wrath, as others*; and many of them are never partakers of real holiness, and are as profligate as others; and on the other hand, some of the children of unbelievers are partakers of true holiness: if it be said, and which seems to be our author's meaning, that it is such a holiness the people of the

Jews

[m] Ezek. xxxvi. 25—27.

Jews had in distinction from the *Heathens*, and therefore are called an *holy seed*; this cannot be, since the holiness of the Jewish seed lay in the lawful issue of a Jewish man and a Jewish woman: if a Jewish man married an Heathen woman, their issue was not holy, as appears from *Ezra* and *Nehemiah*; whereas, according to the apostle, if a Christian man married an Heathen woman, or a Christian woman an Heathen man, their issue were holy: should it be said, as it is suggested by our author, that so indeed it was in *Ezra*'s times, according to the Jewish law; but now, since the coming of Christ, the national difference is abolished; which he makes to be the sense of the apostle, and therein betrays his ignorance of the apostle's argument and method of reasoning; for " the " particle *now*, as *Beza* observes, is not in this place an adverb of time, but a " conjunction, which is commonly used in assumptions of argument," which destroys our author's argument, and sets aside his method of reasoning, which he seems fond of, and afterwards repeats: it remains therefore, that only a matrimonial holiness is here intended; and surely marriage may be said to be *holy*, as it is by the apostle *honourable*, and for that reason [n], without favouring strong of popery, or favouring the notion of marriage being a sacrament, as this writer insinuates; who has got a strange nose, and a stranger judgment: whether he is a single or a married man, I know not; he appears to have a bad opinion of marriage. That infants born in lawful wedlock cannot be called holy, being legitimate, without favouring of popery. As he is not able to set aside the sense of the word *sanctified* given by me, as signifying *espoused*; he requires of me to prove that the word *holy* means *legitimate*; for which I refer him to *Ezra* ix. 2. where those born of parents, both Jewish, are called *an holy seed*; that is, a lawful one; in opposition to, and in distinction from a spurious and illegitimate issue, born of parents, the one Jewish and the other Heathen: and this is the same with the *godly seed*, in *Mal.* ii. 15. which *Calvin* interprets legitimate, in distinction from those that are born in polygamy: nor will any other sense suit with the case proposed to the apostle; nor with his answer and manner of reasoning about it; who says not one word of a covenant whereby an unbelieving yoke-fellow is sanctified to a believing one, or of the federal holiness of the children of both; but argues, that if their marriage, being unequal, was not valid, which was their scruple, their children *must be unclean*, as bastards were accounted [o]; whereas it being good, their children were legitimate, and so might be easy, and continue together as they ought.

· The passage out of the *Talmud*, which he has at second-hand from Dr *Lightfoot*, designs by *Holiness*, Judaism, and not Christianity, and is quite impertinent to the purpose; nor can it be thought to be alluded to, since the holiness the Jews
speak

---

[n] Heb. xiii. 4.   [o] Deut. xviii. 2.

speak of, respects the parents, as both proselytes to Judaism; whereas the apostle's case supposes one an Heathen, and the other a Christian: and he might have observed by a tradition quoted by the Doctor, in the same place, that such a marriage the apostle was considering, is condemned by the Jews as no marriage, and the issue of it as illegitimate; which asserts, that *a son begotten of a Heathen woman is not a son,* his lawful son; just the reverse of what the apostle suggested: and after all, our author himself seems to make this holiness no other than a civil holiness, and which secures a civil relation, by which " the unbelieving yoke-fellow is sanctified, so far as concerns the believing " party; that is, for lawful cohabitation, conjugal society, and the propaga- " tion of a holy covenant-seed;" for all which purposes, lawful marriages may be allowed to sanctify, if only instead of *a holy covenant-seed,* a legitimate seed is put. So that upon the whole, this passage does not furnish out the least shew of argument for Infant-baptism. Come we to

V. The next passage produced in favour of Infant-baptism, which are the words of the commission in *Matthew* xxviii. 19, 20. one would think there should be no difficulty in understanding these words; and that the plain and easy sense of them is, that such as are taught by the ministry of the word, should be baptized, and they only; and if there was any doubt about this, yet it might be removed by comparing the same commission with this, as differently expressed in *Mark* xvi. 15, 16. from whence it clearly appears, that *to teach all nations, is to preach the gospel to every creature;* and that the persons among all nations, that may be said to be taught, or made disciples by teaching, are believers, and being so, are to be baptized; *he that believeth and is baptized, shall be saved.* It is observed by this writer, that the acts of discipling and baptizing are of equal extent: it is agreed to, provided it be allowed, as it ought, that the word, *teach,* or *make disciples,* describes and limits the persons to be baptized; for such only of all nations are to be baptized, who are made disciples by teaching; not all the individuals of all nations; no, not even where the gospel comes, and is preached; for many hear it, and more might, who are not taught by it; and even when the seventh trumpet shall sound, and *all nations shall serve the Lord,* this will not be true of every individual of all nations, only of such, who are qualified for, and capable of serving the Lord; and so of adult persons only, and not of infants at all: and was this the case, that all nations in the commission are under no limitation and restriction, then not only the children of Pagans, Turks, and Jews, but even all adult persons, the most vile and profligate, should be baptized; wherefore the phrase, *all nations* to be baptized, must be restrained and limited to those who are *made disciples* out of all nations; who are the antecedent to the relative, *them* that are to be baptized, and not all nations; and though there is a frequent

change

change of gender in the Greek language, which is owned; yet as *Piscator*, a learned Pædobaptift, on the text obferves, "the fyntax (*of them*) is referred to "the fenfe, and not to the word, fince *nations* went before;" and the fame obfervation he makes on the paffage our author has produced as parallel, *Romans* ii. 14. but in order to bring infants to this reftrictive and qualifying character for baptifm, it is faid, they are made difciples with their parents, when they become fo, as parts of themfelves: and why may they not be faid to be baptized with them, when they are baptized, as parts of themfelves, and fo have no need of baptifm? No doubt, if Chrift had continued the ufe of circumcifion under the New-Teftament, and had bid his apoftles *to go and difciple the nations, circumcifing them*, they would have needed no direction as to infants, as is fuggefted; and that for this plain reafon, becaufe there had been a previous exprefs command for the circumcifion of them; but there is no fuch command to baptize infants previous to the commiffion, and therefore could not be underftood in like manner. But it feems the known cuftom of the Jews to baptize the children of profelytes with them, was a plain and fufficient direction as to the fubjects of baptifm, and is the reafon why no exprefs mention is made of them in the commiffion: But it does not appear there was any fuch cuftom among the Jews, when the commiffion was given; had it been fo early, as is pretended, even in the times of *Jacob*, it is ftrange there fhould be no hint of it in the Old Teftament: nor in the apocryphal writings; nor in the writings of the New Teftament; nor in *Jofephus*; nor in *Philo* the Jew; nor in the Jewifh *Mifnah*; only in the *Talmud*; which was not compofed till five hundred years after Chrift; and this cuftom is at firft reported by a fingle *Rabbi*, and at the fame time denied by another of equal credit and authority: and admitting that this was a cuftom that then obtained, fince it was not of divine inftitution, but of human invention, had our Lord thought fit (which is not reafonable to fuppofe) to take it into his New Teftament ordinance of baptifm; yet it would have been neceffary to have made exprefs mention of it, as his will that it fhould be obferved, in order to remove the fcruple that might arife from its being a mere Jewifh cuftom and tradition.

But to proceed: though this writer may be able to find in the fchools within his knowledge, fuch ignorant difciples and learners, that have learned nothing at all; CHRIST has none fuch in his fchool: Chrift fays, none can be a difciple of his, but who has learned *to deny himfelf, take up his crofs, and follow him*[\*], and forfake all for him; and this man fays, they may be called difciples, that have learned nothing, and be inrolled among the difciples of Chrift, who are uncapable of outward teaching: but who are we to believe, Chrift, or this man?

[\*] Luke xiv. 26, 27, 33.

man? He suggests, that it would be impracticable to put the commission in execution, if none but true disciples and believers are to be baptized, since the heart cannot be inspected, and man may be deceived; and observes, that the apostles baptized immediately upon profession, and waited not for the fruits of it, and some of which are not true disciples, but hypocrites: this is what he often harps upon; and to which I answer, the apostles had no doubt a greater spirit of discerning, and so could observe the signs of true faith and discipleship in men, without long waiting; but they never baptized any whom they did not judge to be true disciples and believers, and who professed themselves to be such: and though they were in some few instances mistaken; this might be suffered, that ministers and churches might not be discouraged, when such instances should appear in following times; and this is satisfaction enough in this point, when men keep as close as they can to the divine rule, and make the best judgment of persons they are able; and when, in a judgment of charity, they are thought to be true disciples of Christ, baptize them; in which they do their duty, though it may fall out otherwise; and in which they are to be justified by the word of God; which they could not, were they to administer the ordinance to such who have no appearance of the grace of God, and the truth of it in them. The text in *Acts* xv. 10. is far from proving infants disciples; they are not designed in that place, nor included in the character; for though no doubt the Judaizing preachers were for having the Gentiles, and their infants too, circumcised; yet it was not circumcision, the thing itself, that is meant by the intolerable yoke, attempted to be put upon the necks of the disciples; for that was what the Jewish fathers and their children were able to bear, and had borne in ages past; but it was the doctrine of the necessity of that, and other rites of *Moses*, to salvation; and which could not be imposed upon infants, but upon adult persons only. Next we proceed to

VI. The passages concerning the baptism of whole housholds, as an explanation of the commission, and of the apostles understanding it: Now since Infant-baptism, as we have seen, cannot be established by *Abraham*'s covenant, nor by circumcision, nor by any command of Christ, nor by his commission, nor by any instances of infants baptized in the times of *John* the Baptist, or of Christ; if any instances of infants baptized by the apostles are proposed, they should be clear and plain: Since there is no express precept, which might justly be demanded; if any precedent is produced, it ought to be quite unexceptionable; if it is expected, such a practice should be given into by thinking people. Three families or housholds we read of, that were baptized, and these are the precedents proposed; yet no proof is made of any one infant in these families, or of the baptism of any in them; which should be done, if the former could

be

be proved: but inftead of this, the advocates for this practice are drove to this poor and miferable fhift, to put us on proving the negative, that there were no infants in them. Our author thinks it utterly incredible, that in three fuch families there fhould be no infants, when, in fo large a country as *Egypt*, there was not a family without a child [p]; and is fo weak as to believe, or however hopes to find readers weak enough to believe, that all the firft-born of the Egyptians that were flain were infants; whereas there might be many of them twenty, thirty, or forty years of age; fo that there might be hundreds and thoufands of families in *Egypt* that had not an infant in them, and yet not an houfe in which there was not a dead perfon.

But let us attend to thefe particular families: as for *Lydia* and her houfhold, fo far as a negative in fuch a cafe as this is capable of being proved; this is certain, that no mention is made of any infants in her family; it is certain, that there were brethren in her houfe, who were capable of being comforted by the apoftles, and were; for it is exprefsly faid, that *they entered into the houfe of Lydia, and comforted the brethren*; which is a proof of what, he fays, cannot be proved, that they faw the brethren at her houfe; and nothing appears to the contrary, but that they were of her houfhold; and if there were any other befides them, that were baptized by the apoftles, it lies upon thofe that will affirm it, to prove it; without which, this inftance cannot be in favour of Infant-baptifm. As for the Jailor's family, it is owned by our author, that there were fome adult perfons in it, who believed, and were baptized at the fame time with the Jailor; but he afks, how does this argue that there were no others baptized in it, who were in the infantile ftate? It lies upon him to prove it, if there were: The word of God was fpoken to all that were in his houfe, and all his houfe believed in God, and rejoiced in the converfation of the apoftles, who muft be *all* of them adult perfons; and if he can find perfons in his houfe, befides thofe *all* that were in it, I will fet him down for a cunning man. Who thofe expofitors are, that render the words, *believing in God, he rejoiced all his houfe over*, I know not, any more than I underftand the nonfenfe of it. *Erafmus* and *Vatablus* join the phrafe *with all his houfe*, with *believing*, as we do, and *Pricæus* makes it parallel with *Acts* xviii. 8. but however, this writer has found a text to prove, that the children of believers are in their infancy accounted believers, and numbered with them, it is in *Acts* ii. 44. if he can find any wife-acres that will give credit to him. As to the houfhold of *Stephanas*, he fays, that it feems probable that it was large and numerous, which renders it more likely that there were fome infants in it: how large and numerous it was, does not appear; but be thofe of it more or fewer, it is a clear cafe they were adult perfons, that we have any

account

[p] Exod. xii. 30.

account of; since they *addicted themselves to the ministry of the saints*: and now upon what a tottering foundation does Infant-baptism stand, having no precept from God for it, nor any one single precedent for it in the word of God? Come we now,

VII. To the last text in the controversy, *Romans* xi. 17, 24. and which is the decisive one, and yet purely allegorical; when it is an axiom with divines, that symbolical or allegorical divinity is not argumentative: there is nothing, says Dr *Owen* [q], "so sottish, or foolish, or contradictious in and to itself, as may not "be countenanced from teaching parables to be instructive, and proving in "every parcel, or expression, that attends them;" of this we have an instance in our author, about ingrafting buds with the cyon, and of breaking off and grafting in branches with their buds, which he applies to parents and their children; though the apostle has not a word about it: and indeed he is speaking of an ingrafture, not according, but contrary to nature; not only of an ingrafture of an olive-tree, which is never done, but of ingrafting a wild cyon into a good stock; whereas the usual way is to ingraft a good cyon into a wild stock. The general scope and design of the allegory is to be attended to, which is to shew the rejection of the unbelieving Jews from, and the reception of the believing Gentiles into the gospel-church; for though God did not cast away the people among the Jews whom he foreknew; or the remnant according to the election of grace, of which the apostle was one; yet there was a casting-away of that people as a body politic and ecclesiastic, which now continues, and will till the fulness of the Gentiles are brought in; and then there will be a general conversion of the Jews, of which the conversion of some of them in the times of Christ and his apostles were the root, first-fruits, pledge, and earnest; and which led on the apostle to this allegorical discourse about the olive-tree; which I understand of the gospel church-state, in distinction from the Jewish church-state, now dissolved. This writer will not allow, that the Jewish church, as to its essential constitution, is abolished, only as to its outward form of administration: but God has wrote a *Lo-ammi* upon that people, both as a body politic and ecclesiastic [r]; he has unchurched them; he has broke his covenant with them, and their union with each other in their church state, signified by his breaking his two staffs, beauty and bands [s]; and if this is not the case, the people of the Jews are now the true church of God, notwithstanding their rejection of the Messiah; and if the Gentiles are incorporated into that church, the gospel-church is, and must be national, as that was, and the same with it; whereas it differs from it, both as to matter and form, consisting of persons gathered out of the world, and enjoying different ordinances, the former being utterly abolished.

[q] On Perseverance, p. 416.  [r] Hosea i. 9.  [s] Zech. xi. 10, 14.

lifhed. Our author objects to my interpretation of the good olive-tree being the gofpel church-ftate, from the unbelieving Jews being faid to be *broken-off*, and the olive-tree called their *own olive-tree*, and they *the natural branches*: to which I anfwer, that the breaking of them off, ver. 17. is the fame with the cafting away of them, ver. 15 and the allegory is not to be ftretched beyond its fcope. The Jewifh church being diffolved, the unbelieving Jews lay like broken, withered, fcattered branches, and fo continued, and were not admitted into the gofpel church-ftate, which is all the apoftle means: if I have ufed too foft a term, to fay they were *left out* of the gofpel-church, fince feverity is expreffed, I may be allowed to ufe one more harfh and fevere; as that they were caft away and rejected, they were cut off from all right, and excluded from admiffion into the gofpel church, and not fuffered to partake of the ordinances of it: and as to the gofpel-church being called *their own olive-tree*, that is, the converted Jews in the latter day, of whom the apoftle fpeaks; with great propriety may it be called their own, not only becaufe of their right of admiffion to it, being converted, but becaufe the firft gofpel-church was fet up in *Jerufalem*, was gathered out from among the Jews, and confifted of fome of their nation, which were the firft-fruits of thofe converted ones; and fo in other places, the firft gofpel-churches confifted of Jews, into which, and not into the national church of the Jews, were the Gentiles ingrafted, and became *fellow-heirs with them*, and of the fame body, partaking of gofpel-ordinances and privileges: and the *natural branches* are not the natural branches of the olive-tree, but the natural branches or natural feed of *Abraham*, or of the Jewifh people, who in the latter day will be converted, and brought into the gofpel-church, as fome of them were in the beginning of it. This fenfe being eftablifhed, it is a clear and plain cafe, that nothing from hence can be concluded in favour of Infant-baptifm; of which there is not the leaft hint, nor any manner of reference to it.

This chapter, you will remember, Sir, is concluded with proofs of womens right to the ordinance of the Lord's fupper: and which are fuch, as cannot be produced, and fupported, to prove the right of infants to baptifm. It is granted by our author, that my " arguments are in the main conclufive, and he " muft be a wrangler that will difpute them;" and yet he difputes them himfelf, and fo proves himfelf a wrangler, as indeed he is nothing elfe throughout the whole of his performance. However, he is confident, there are as good proofs of the baptifm of infants; as, from their being accounted believers and difciples [t]; from their being church-members [u]; from the probability of fome infants baptized in the whole houfholds mentioned; all which we have feen are weak, foolifh, impertinent, and inconclufive. This author does wonderful

feats

[t] Matt. viii. 6. Acts ii. 44. and xv. 10.
[u] Luke xviii. 16. 1 Cor. vii. 14. Ephes. v. 25, 26.

feats in his own conceit, in his knight-errantry way; he proves this, and confutes that, and baffles the other; and though he brings the same arguments, that have been used already; as he owns, and I may add, baffled too already, to use his own language; yet he has added some *new illustration* and *enforcement* to them, and such as have not occurred to him in any author he has seen; so that he would have his reader believe, he is some extraordinary man, and has performed wonderful well; and in this vainglorious shew, I leave him to the ridicule and contempt of men of modesty and good sense, as he justly deserves, and proceed to

The *sixth* and last chapter of my treatise, which is concerning the mode of administering the ordinance of baptism, whether by immersion, or sprinkling; and here, Sir, I observe, 1. That our author represents the controversy about this as one of the most trifling controversies that ever was managed: but if it is so trifling a matter, whether baptism is administered by immersion or sprinkling, why do he and his party write with so much heat and vehemency, as well as with so much scorn and contempt against the former, and so heavily load with calumnies those that defend it, and charge them with the breach of the *sixth* and *seventh* commands, as it has been often done? But if it is so indifferent and trifling a matter with this writer, it is not so with us, who think it to be an affair of great importance, in what manner an ordinance is to be administered; and who judge it essential to baptism, that it be performed by immersion, without which it cannot be baptism; nor the end of the ordinance answered, which is to represent the burial of Christ; and which cannot be done unless the person baptized is covered in water.

2. It is allowed that the word βαπτίζω, with the lexicons and critics, signifies *to dip*; but it is also observed, that they render it *to wash*: which is not denied, since dipping necessarily includes washing; whatever is dipped, is washed, and therefore in a consequential sense it signifies washing, when its primary sense is dipping. Our author does not attempt to prove, that the lexicons and critics ever say it signifies *to pour* or *sprinkle*; which ought to be done, if any thing is done to purpose: indeed he says, with classical writers, it has the signification of *perfusion*, or *sprinkling*; but does not produce one instance of it. He charges me with partiality in concealing part of what Mr *Leigh* says in his *Critica Sacra*; which I am not conscious of, since my edition, which indeed is one of the former, has not a syllable of what is quoted from him; and even that is more for us than against us. Hence with great impertinence are those passages of scripture produced, *Mark* vii. 3, 4. *Luke* xi. 30. *Heb.* ix. 10. which are supposed to have the signification of washing; since these do not at all militate against the sense of dipping, seeing dipping is washing; and to as vain a purpose are those

scriptures referred to, *Ephes.* v. 26. *Tit.* iii. 5. *¹ Cor.* vi. 11. 2 *Peter* i. 9. *Acts* xxii. 16. which call baptism *a washing of water,* and *the washing of regeneration,* &c. even supposing they are to be understood of baptism; which, at least in several of them, is doubtful; since nobody denies, that a person baptized, may be said to be washed, he being dipped in water.

4. It is affirmed that we do not read of one instance of any person who repaired to a river, or conflux of water, purely on the design of being baptized therein. But certain it is, that *John* repaired to such places for the convenient administration of that ordinance; and many repaired to him at those places, purely on a design of being baptized by him in them; and particularly it is said of Christ, *then cometh Jesus from Galilee to Jordan unto John, to be baptized of him* ʷ; and I hope it will be allowed, that he repaired to *Jordan,* on a pure design of being baptized in it; and though it was in a wilderness where *John* was, yet such an one in which were many villages, full of inhabitants, as our author might have learned from Dr *Lightfoot* ˣ; where *John* might have had the convenience of vessels for bringing water, had the ordinance been performed by him in any other way, than by immersion.

5. The use of the words, *baptize* and *baptism,* in scripture, comes next under consideration; and, (1.) the word is used in *Acts* i. 5. of the extraordinary Gifts of the Spirit to the apostles on the day of Pentecost, which is called a *being baptized with the holy Ghost*; and the house in which the apostles were, being *filled with it,* had in it a resemblance to baptism by immersion; and hence the use of the phrase. The main objection our author makes to this, is, that the disciples were in the house before it was filled with the holy Ghost; whereas it should have been first filled, and then they enter into it, to carry any resemblance in it to immersion: but it matters not, whether the house was filled before or after they entered, inasmuch as it was filled when they were in, whereby they were encompassed and covered with it; which is sufficient to support the allusion to baptism, performed by immersion; or covering the person in water: it is represented as dissonant from common sense, to say, *Ye shall be plunged with the holy Ghost?* and is it not as dissonant from common sense to say, *Ye shall be poured with the holy Ghost?*

(2.) The sufferings of Christ are called a baptism ʸ; and a very apt word is used to express the *abundance* of them, as ₜhaₜ signifies an immersion into water; and though the lesser sufferings of men, and God's judgments on them, may be expressed by the *pouring out* of his wrath, and the vials of it on them; yet since the holy Ghost has thought fit not to make use of such a phrase, but a very peculiar word to express the greater sufferings of Christ, this the more confirms

the

---

ʷ Matt. iii. 13.    ˣ Vol. II. p. 113, 297.    ʸ Mark x. 38. Luke xii. 50.

## DIVINE RIGHT OF INFANT-BAPTISM.

the sense of the word contended for. The phrase in *Psalm* xxii. 14. *I am poured out like water*, doth not express the sufferings of Christ, but the effect of them, the faintness of his spirits under them. The passages in *Psalm* lxix. 1, 2. which represent him as *overwhelmed* with his sufferings, as in water, do most clearly illustrate the use of the word *baptism* in reference to them, and strongly support the allusion to it, as performed by immersion, which this writer has not been able to set aside.

(3.) Mention is made in *Mark* vii. 4. of the Jews washing, or baptizing themselves, when they came from market, before they eat; and of the washing, or baptizing of their cups, pots, brazen vessels, tables or beds; all which was done by immersion. This writer says, I am contradicted by the best masters of the Jewish learning, when I say, that the Jews upon touching common people, or their clothes, at market, or in any court of judicature, were obliged by the tradition of the elders to immerse themselves in water, and did. To which I reply, that *Vatablus* and *Drusius*, who were great masters of Jewish learning, affirm, that according to the tradition of the elders, the Jews washed or immersed the whole body before they eat, when they came from market; to whom may be added the learned *Grotius*, who interprets the words the same way; and which seems most reasonable, since washing before eating, ver. 4. is distinguished from the washing of hands, ver. 3. But not to rest it here; *Maimonides*[a], that great master of Jewish learning, assures us, that " if the Pharisees touched but the " garments of the common people, they were defiled, all one as if they had " touched a profluvious person, and needed immersion," and were obliged to it: and though Dr *Lightfoot*, who was a great man in this kind of learning, yet not always to be depended upon, is of opinion, that the plunging of the whole body is not here understood; yet he thinks, that plunging or immersion of the hands in water, is meant, done by the Jews, being ignorant and uncertain what uncleanness they came near unto in the market; and observes, the Jews used the washing of the hands, and the plunging of the hands; and that the word *wash* in the Evangelist, seems to answer to the former, and *baptize* to the latter; and *Pococke*[b] himself, whom this writer refers to, confesses the same, and says, that the Hebrew word כבל to which βαπτιζειν answers in Greek, signifies a further degree of purification, than נטל or χερνιπτειν, (the words used for washing of hands) though not so as necessarily to imply an immersion of the whole body; since the greatest and most notorious uncleanness of the hands reached but to the wrist, and was cleansed by immersing or dipping up to it; and though he thinks the Greek word used in the text does not only and necessarily signify immersion, which yet he grants, specially agrees to it, as he thinks appears.

[a] In Mishnah Chagigah, c. 2. §. 7.   [b] Not. Miscell. 390, 397.

appears from *Luke* xi. 38. To this may be oppoſed what the great *Scaliger*[b] ſays; "the more ſuperſtitious part of the Jews, not only dipped the feet but the whole body, hence they were called Hemerobaptiſts, who every day before they ſat down to food, dipped the body; wherefore the Phariſee, who had invited Jeſus to dine with him, wondered he ſat down to meat before he had waſhed his whole body, *Luke* xi." and after all, be it which it will, whether the immerſion of the whole body, or only of the hands and feet, that is meant in theſe paſſages; ſince the waſhing of either was by immerſion, as owned, it is ſufficient to ſupport the primary ſenſe of the word contended for: and ſo all other things, after mentioned, according to the tradition of the elders, of which only the text ſpeaks, and not of the law of God, were waſhed by immerſion; particularly brazen veſſels; concerning which the tradition is[c], "ſuch as they uſe for hot things, as cauldrons and kettles, they heat them with hot water, and ſcour them, and *dip* them, and they are fit to be uſed."

This writer ſays, I am ſtrangely beſides my Text, when I add, that "even beds, pillows, and bolſters, when they were unclean in a ceremonial ſenſe, were to be waſhed by immerſion, or dipping them into water;" but I am able to produce chapter and verſe for what I affirm, from the traditions of the Jews, which are the only things ſpoken of in the text, and upon which the proof depends: for beds, their canons run thus; "a bed that is wholly defiled, if a man *dips* it part by part, it is pure[d]." Again, "if he *dips* the bed in it, (a pool of water) though its feet are plunged into the thick clay, (at the bottom of the pool) it is clean[e]." As for pillows and bolſters, thus they ſay; "a pillow or a bolſter of ſkin, when a man lifts up the mouth of them out of the water, the water which is in them will be drawn; what ſhall we do? he muſt *dip* them, and lift them up by their fringes[f]." Thus, according to the traditions of the elders, our Lord is ſpeaking of, theſe ſeveral things mentioned were waſhed by immerſion; which abundantly confirms the primary ſenſe of the word uſed.

(4.) The paſſage of the Iſraelites through the Red-ſea, and under a cloud, is repreſented as a baptiſm, 1 *Cor*. x. 1, 2. and very aptly, as performed by immerſion; ſince the waters ſtood up on both ſides of them, and a cloud covered them; which very fitly repreſented perſons immerſed and covered with water in baptiſm: but what our author thinks will ſpoil this fine fancy, and ſome others, as he calls them, is, that one obſervation of *Moſes* often repeated; that *the children of Iſrael went on dry ground through the midſt of the ſea*. To which I reply, that we are not under any neceſſity of owning that the cloud under
which

---

[b] De Emend. temp. l. 6. p. 271.  [c] Maimon. Maacolot Aſurot, c. 17. 1. 3.
[d] Ib. Celim, c. 26. S. 14.  [e] Miſnah Mikvaot, c. 7. S. 7.  [f] Ib. S. 6.

## DIVINE RIGHT OF INFANT-BAPTISM. 455

which the Ifraelites were, let down any rain: it is indeed the fentiment of a Pædobaptift, I have referred to, and therefore am not affected with this obfervation; befides, it fhould be confidered, that this equally, at leaft, fpoils the fine fancy of the rain from the cloud bearing a much greater refemblance to *fprinkling* or *affufion*; as is afferted by the writer of the dialogue; and our author fays, there was a true and proper ablution with water from the cloud, in which the Ifraelites were baptized, and concludes that they received baptifm by fprinkling or affufion; how then could they walk on dry ground?

(5.) The laft text mentioned is *Heb.* ix. 10. which fpeaks of *diverfe wafhings* or *baptifms* of the Jews, or *different dippings*, as it may be rendered without any impropriety, as our author afferts; though not to be underftood of different forts of dipping, as he foolifhly objects to us; nor of different forts of wafhing, fome by fprinkling, fome by affufion, others by bathing or dipping, as he would have it; but the Jewifh wafhings or baptifms are fo called, becaufe of the different perfons, or things wafhed or dipped, as *Grotius* on the place fays; there was one wafhing of the Priefts, another of the Levites, and another of the Ifraelites, when they had contracted any impurity; and which was done by immerfion; nor do any of the inftances this writer has produced difprove it. Not *Exod.* xxix. 4. *thou fhalt wafh them with water*; but whether by immerfion or affufion he knows not. The Jews interpret it of immerfion; the *Targum* of *Jonathan* is, "thou fhalt *dip* them in forty meafures of living water:" nor *Exod.* xxx. 19. which mentions the wafhing of the prieft's hands and feet at the brazen laver of the tabernacle; the manner of which our author defcribes from Dr *Lightfoot*, out of the *Rabbins*; but had he tranfcribed the whole, it would have appeared, that not only wafhing the hands and feet, but bathing of their whole body, were neceffary to the performance of their fervice; for it follows, "and none
" might enter into the court to do the fervice there, till he hath bathed; yea,
" though he were clean, he muft bathe his body in cold water before he enter."
And to this agrees a canon of theirs [f]; " no man enters into the court for fervice,
" though clean, till he has dipped himfelf; the high-prieft dips himfelf five
" times on the day of atonement." And the Priefts and Levites, before they performed any part of the daily fervice, dipped themfelves: nor 2 *Chron.* iv. 6. which fays, the molten fea in *Soloman*'s temple was *for the priefts to wafh in*; where they wafhed not only their hands and their feet, but their whole bodies, as Dr *Lightfoot* fays [h]; and for the bathing of which, they went down into the veffel itfelf; and to which agrees the *Jerufalem Talmud* [i], which fays, "the
" molten fea was a *dipping-place* for the priefts:" Nor *Numb.* viii. 6, 7. which, had the paffage been wholly tranfcribed, it would appear, that not only the water

[f] Mifnah Yoma, c. 3., S. 3.     [h] Vol. I. p. 2047.     [i] Yoma, fol. 41..1.

ter of purifying was sprinkled on the Levites, but their bodies were bathed; for it follows: "and let them shave all their flesh, and *wash* their clothes, and so make themselves clean;" that is, by bathing their whole bodies, which, as the *Targum* on the place says, was done in forty measures of water. Sprinkling *the water of purification* was a ceremony preparatory to the bathing, but was itself no part of it; and the same is to be observed of the purification by *the ashes of an heifer*, on the third and seventh days, *Numb.* xix. 19. which was only preparatory to the great purification by bathing the body, and washing the clothes on the seventh day, which was the closing and finishing part of the service; for that it was the unclean person, and not the priest, that was to wash his clothes, and bathe himself in water, ver. 19. is clear; since it is a distinct law, or statute, from that in ver. 21. which enjoins the priest to wash his clothes, but not to bathe himself in water; and indeed, the contrary sense is not only absurd, and interrupts and confounds the sense of the words; but, as Dr *Gale* also observes, it cannot be reasonably imagined that the priest, by barely purifying the unclean, should need so much greater a washing and purification than the unclean himself; this sprinkling of the ashes of the heifer, therefore, was not part of the Jewish washings, or baptisms, or any exemplification of them; so that from the whole, I see no reason to depart from my conclusion, that " the words bap-" *tize* and *baptism*, in all the places mentioned, do from their signification make " *dipping* or *plunging* the necessary mode of administering the ordinance of bap-" tism."

I proceed now, 6. To vindicate those passages of scripture, which necessarily prove the mode of baptism by immersion. And,

The first passage, is in *Matthew* iii. 6. *and were baptized of him in Jordan, confessing their sins*. We argue from hence, not merely from these persons being *baptized*, to their being *dipped*; though this is an argument that cannot be answered, seeing those that are *baptized*, are necessarily *dipped*; for the word *baptize* signifies always to *dip*, or to *wash by dipping*, and never to *pour* or *sprinkle*; but the argument is still more forcible from these persons being baptized *in* the river *Jordan*: for either the persons said to be baptized were in the river, or they were not; if they were not in the river, they could not be baptized in it; if they were in it, they went in it in order to be baptized by immersion; since no other end could be proposed, agreeable to the common sense of mankind: to say they went *into* it to have a little water sprinkled or poured on them, which could have been done without it, is ridiculous, and an imposition on common sense; wherefore this necessarily proves the mode of baptizing by immersion; since no other mode is compatible with this circumstance. The instances of the

blind

blind man's wafhing in *Siloam*, and the lavers of the temple being to wafh in, as difproving the neceffity of immerfion, I fay, are impertinent; fince the word *baptize* is ufed in neither of them; and befides, there is nothing appears to the contrary, that the blind man dipped himfelf in *Siloam*, as *Naaman* the *Syrian* did in *Jordan*; and the things that were wafhed in the lavers, were dipped there, fince they held a quantity of water fufficient for that purpofe. The author of the *dialogue* afks, "Do not we commonly wafh our face and hands in a bafon of " water without dipping in it?" But common practice proves the contrary; men commonly dip their hands into a bafon, when they wafh either hands or face; the inftance of *Elifha* pouring water on the hands of *Elijah*, doth not prove it was common to wafh hands by pouring water on them; fince this is not faid to be done to wafh his hands with; and fome interpreters have thought that wafhing of hands is not intended, but fome miracle which followed the action of pouring water, which gave *Elifha* a character, and by which he is defcribed.

The fecond paffage, is *John* iii. 23. *John was baptizing in Enon near Salim, becaufe there was much water there.* Here is not the leaft hint of *John*'s chufing of this place, and being here, for any other reafon, but for baptizing; not for drink for men and cattle, as fuggefted; befides, why did he not fix upon a place where the people could be provided with food for themfelves, and provender for their cattle? Why for drink only? This is a wild fancy, a vain conjecture. The reafon of the choice is plain, it was for the conveniency of baptizing, and that *becaufe there was much water*, fuitable to the manner of baptizing ufed by *John*; and if this reafon given agrees with no other mode of baptizing, but by immerfion, as it does not, fince fprinkling or pouring requires not much water; it follows, that this neceffarily proves the mode of baptifm by immerfion.

The third text is *Matthew* iii. 16. *And Jefus, when he was baptized, went up ftraightway* OUT *of the water*. The author of the dialogue fuggefted, that the Greek prepofition απο, always fignifies *from*, never *out of*: our author is obliged to own, that it may fometimes admit to be rendered *out of*: a great condefcenfion to the learned tranflators of our Bible! Well, if Jefus came up out of the water, he muft have been in it, where it is certain he was baptized; and the evangelift *Mark* fays, he was *baptized into Jordan*; not into the banks of *Jordan*; but into the waters of *Jordan*; now feeing fuch an expreffion as this will not fuit with any other mode of baptifm but immerfion, and it cannot be faid with any propriety, that Chrift was fprinkled into *Jordan*, or poured into *Jordan*, but with great propriety may be faid to be *dipped* or *plunged* into *Jordan*; it follows, that this neceffarily proves the mode of baptifm as adminiftered to our Lord, to be by immerfion.

The fourth passage, is concerning *Philip*'s baptizing the Eunuch in *Acts* viii. 38, 39. *they went down both into the water, and he baptized him; and when they were come up out of the water,* &c. The dialogue-writer would have it, that this proves no more than that they went down *to* the water, and came *from* it: but that this was not the case, I have observed, that previous to this, they are said to *come to a certain water*, to the water-side; and therefore after this, it cannot be understood of any thing else, but of their going *into* it; and so, consequently, the other phrase, of their coming *out of it*. Here our author has got a new fancy in his head; that coming *to a certain water* is not coming to the water-side, or to the water itself, but to the sight of it; which sense he does not pretend to confirm by any parallel place, either in sacred or profane writings, and is very absurd, improper and impertinent; since a person may come to the *sight* of a water, when he is at a great distance from it, and cannot be said with any propriety to be come *to* it: what he thinks will add strength to this fancy, and destroy the observation I made, is, that after this the chariot is still going on, and several questions and answers passed before it was bid to stand still: all which is easily accounted for, supposing them to be come to the water itself; since the road, they were now in, might be by the water-side, and so they travelled along by it, while the questions and answers passed, till they came to a proper and convenient place for baptism, at which they alighted; besides, why should the *sight* of a certain water, or confluence of water, put the Eunuch in mind of baptism, if it was not performed by immersion, of the mode of which he was doubtless acquainted? It is highly probable, that this treasurer was provided both with wine and water for his journey, which, mixed, was the usual drink of those countries; and a bottle of his own water would have done for sprinkling, or pouring, had either of them been the mode of baptism used; nor would there have been any occasion for going out of the chariot and to the water, and much less into it, which the text is express for; and seeing these circumstances of going down into the water, and coming up out of it, at the administration of baptism, agree with no other mode than that of immersion, not with sprinkling, nor pouring water, it necessarily proves immersion to be the mode of baptism.

The last text is *Romans* vi. 4. *we are buried with him by baptism into death*; where baptism is called a burial, a burial with Christ, and a resemblance of his; which only can be made by immersion: but our author says, if it is designed to represent it, there is no necessity it should be a resemblance of it; but how it can represent it without a resemblance of it, is not easy to say: he suggests, that though the Lord's supper represents the death of Christ, it is no resemblance of it. Strange! that the breaking of the bread should not be a resemblance of the

body

body of Chrift broken, and the pouring out of the wine not a refemblance of his blood fhed. Baptifm by immerfion, according to our author, is no refemblance of the burial of Chrift; fince his body was laid in a fepulchre cut out of a rock on high, and not put under ground, or covered with earth: this arifes from a miftaken notion of the Jewifh way of burial, even in their fepulchres, hewed out of rocks; for in every fepulchre of this kind, according to the nature of the rock, there were eight graves dug, fome fay thirteen, and which were dug feven cubits deep[k]: in one of thefe graves, within the fepulchre, lay the body of our Lord. So that it had a double burial, as it were, one in the fepulchre, and another in one of the graves in it: befides, how otherwife could our Lord be faid to be three days and nights in the heart of the earth[l]? Again, our author fays, "there is no more refemblance of a common burial in baptifm by " immerfion, than by fprinkling, or pouring on water; fince a corps above " ground may be properly faid to be buried by having a fufficient quantity of earth caft upon it." True; but then a corps can never be faid to be buried, that has a little duft or earth fprinkled or poured on its face; from whence it is evident, that fprinkling or pouring cannot bear any refemblance of a common burial. In fhort, feeing no other mode but immerfion, not fprinkling, nor pouring, has any refemblance of a burial, this paffage neceffarily proves the mode of baptifm by immerfion: and yet, after all, this writer inclines to that opinion, that both modes were ufed in fcripture-times; though it appears by all accounts that the manner was uniform, one and the fame word being always ufed in the relation of it; and yet he wrangles at every inftance of immerfion, and will not allow of one; what muft be faid of fuch a man! that he muft be fet down for a mere wrangler; a wrangler againft light and confcience; a wrangler againft his own opinion and fentiment; and what a worthlefs writer muft this be!

I go on, 7. To confider the inftances, which, it is faid, fhew it improbable that the ordinance of baptifm was performed by dipping. The *firft* is the baptifm of the three thoufand, *Acts* ii. 41. which, to be done by immerfion, is reprefented as improbable; from the fhortnefs of the time, and the want of convenience on a fudden, for the baptizing of fuch a multitude. As to the time, I fhall not difpute it with our author, whether *Peter's* fermon was at the beginning of the third hour, or nine o'clock, or at the clofe of it, and about noon: I am willing to allow it might be noon before the baptifm of thefe perfons came on; nay, I will grant him an hour longer if he pleafes, and yet there was time enough between that and night for the twelve apoftles, and feventy difciples, in all fourfcore and two, to baptize by immerfion three times three thoufand perfons. I pafs over his foolifh remarks on a perfon's being ready for baptifm, as I have done many others of the fame ftupid kind, as deferving no notice, nor anfwer:

[k] Mifnah Bava Bathra, c. 6. S. 8.     [l] Matt. xii. 40.

As to the want of convenience for the baptizing such a number, I have observed the great number of baths in private houses in *Jerusalem*, the several pools in it, and the many conveniencies in the temple: this writer thinks, the mention of the last is a piece of weakness in me, to imagine that the Jewish priests, in whose hands they were, the mortal enemies of Christ, should be on a sudden so good-natured as to grant the use of their baths for such a purpose: but how came they to allow the christians the use of their temple, where they met daily? And besides, it is expressly said, they *had favour with all the people* ᵐ.

The *second* instance, is the baptism of *Paul* ⁿ; here only the narrative is directed to, as representing his baptism to be in the house of *Judas:* but there is nothing in the account that necessarily concludes it was done in the house, but rather the contrary; since he *arose* from the place where he was, in order to be baptized: and supposing it was done in the house, it is not at all improbable that there was a bath in this house, where it might be performed; since it was the house of a Jew, with whom it was usual to have baths to wash their whole bodies in, on certain occasions: So that there is no improbability of *Paul*'s baptism being by immersion; besides, he was not only bid to *arise and be baptized*, which would sound very oddly, be *sprinkled* or *poured* ᵒ; but says himself, that he was *buried by baptism* ᵖ.

The *third* instance, is the baptism of *Cornelius* and his houshold ᵠ. The sense of the words given, "can any man forbid the use of his river, or *bath*, or what conveniency he might have, for baptizing;" is objected to, as not being the apostle's words, but a strained sense of them: the same objection may be made to this writer's sense, that the phrase imports the forbidding water to be brought; since no such thing is expressed, or hinted at: the principal thing, no doubt, designed by the apostle, is, that no one could, or at least ought, to object to the baptism of those who had so manifestly received the holy Ghost: but what is there in all this account, that renders their baptism by immersion improbable, for which it is produced?

The *fourth* instance is the baptism of the Jailor and his houshold ʳ; in the relation of which, there is nothing that makes it probable, much less certain, that it was performed by sprinkling or pouring water on them; nor any thing that makes it improbable that it was done by immersion: according to the account given, it seems to be a clear case, that the Jailor, upon his conversion, took the apostles out of prison into his own house, where they preached to him and his family ˢ, and that after this, they went out of his house, and were baptized; very probably in the river without the city, where the oratory was ᵗ, for it

---

ᵐ Acts ii. 46, 47.  ⁿ Acts ix. 18.  ᵒ Acts xxii. 16.  ᵖ Rom. vi. 4.
ᵠ Acts x. 47.  ʳ Acts xvi. 33.  ˢ Ver. 32.  ᵗ Ver. 13.

it is certain, that after the baptism of him and his houshold, he brought the apostles into his house, and set meat before them [u], nor is it any unreasonable and incredible thing, that he with his whole family should leave the prison and prisoners, who no doubt had servants that he could trust, or otherwise he must have been always little better than a prisoner himself: and whether the earthquake reached any farther than the prison, to alarm others, is not certain, nor any great matter of moment in this controversy to be determined; and the circumstances of the whole relation shew it more likely, that the Jailor and his family were baptized without the prison, than in it, and rather in the river without the city, than with the water out of the vessel, with which the Jailor had washed the apostle's stripes: upon the whole, these instances produced fail of shewing the improbability of the mode of baptism by immersion; which must appear clear and manifest to every attentive reader, notwithstanding all that has been opposed unto it.

There remains nothing but what has been already attended to, or worthy of regard; but the untruth he charges me with, in saying that " the dialogue-writer only attempts to mention allusive expressions in favour of sprinkling:" our author will be ashamed of himself, and his abusive language, when he looks into the dialogue again; since the writer of that never mentions the words of the institution, for any such purpose, and much less argues from them; nor does he ever shew that the word *baptize* is in the sacred pages applied to sprinkling, or that it so signifies; nor does he any where argue from the good appearance there is of evidence, that in the apostles times, the *mode of sprinkling* was used; he never attempts to prove that the word βαπτίζω, signifies to sprinkle, or is so used; nor mentions any one instance of sprinkling in baptism; what he contends for is, that the signification of the word, and the scripture instances of baptism, do not make *dipping* the necessary mode of administering that ordinance; and what he mentions in favour of *sprinkling*, are only resemblances, and allusive expressions.

These, Sir, are the remarks I made in reading Mr *Clark*'s book; which I have caused to be transcribed, and here send you for the use of yourself and friends, either in a private or in a public way, as you may judge necessary and proper.

[u] Acts xvi. 33, 34.

*I am with all due respects,*
*Yours, &c.*

LONDON,
July 26, 1753.

JOHN GILL.

# SOME
# STRICTURES
### ON

Mr BOSTWICK's Fair and Rational Vindication of the Right of Infants to the Ordinance of Baptism.

ALONG with Mr *Clark's Defence of the divine Right of Infant-baptism*, to which what is written above is a Reply, there has been imported from *America* a treatise, called, *A fair and rational Vindication of the Right of Infants to the Ordinance of Baptism*; being the substance of several discourses from *Acts* ii. 39. by *David Bostwick*, A. M. late minister of the Presbyterian church in the city of *New York*, which has been reprinted and published here; and as it comes in company with the former, it is but a piece of civility to take some notice of it, and make some few strictures upon it, though there is nothing in it but what is answered in the above Reply; to which I shall greatly refer the reader. There is scarce a single thought through the whole of it, that I can discern, is *new*; nothing but *crambe repetita*, old stale reasonings and arguments, which have been answered over and over; and yet this, I understand, has been cried up as an *unanswerable* performance; which I do not wonder at, that any thidg that has but an *appearance* of reasoning, candour, and ingenuity, as this will be allowed to have, should be so reckoned by those of that party; when the *most miserable* pamphlet that comes out on that side of the question, has the same epithet bestowed upon it. And,

*First,* This Gentleman has mistook the sense of his text, on which he grounds his discourse concerning the Right of infants to baptism, *Acts* ii. 39. *for the promise is unto you, and to your children; and to all that are afar off; even as many as the Lord our God shall call;* by which promise, he says, p. 14, 15. must be understood, "the covenant-promise made to *Abraham*, which gave his "infant-children a right to the ordinance of circumcision;" when there is not the least mention made of *Abraham*, nor of any covenant-promise made to him in it; nor was ever any covenant-promise made to him, giving his infant-children a right to the ordinance of circumcision, but the covenant of circumcision; and that can never be meant here by the promise; since this is said to be *to all that are afar off*; by whom, according to this Gentleman, Gentiles are meant; to whom the covenant of circumcision belonged not; nor did it give to them any right to the ordinance of circumcision, except they became proselytes to the Jewish religion: besides, be the promise here what it may, it is observed, not as giving any right or claim to any ordinance whatever; but as an encouraging motive to persons in distress under a sense of sin, to repent of their sin, and declare their repentance, and yield a voluntary subjection to the ordinance of baptism; when they might hope that remission of sin would be applied to them, and they should receive a larger measure of the grace of the Spirit; and therefore can only be understood of adult persons; and the promise is no other than the promise of life and salvation by Christ, and of remission of sins by his blood, and of an increase of grace from his Spirit: and whereas the persons addressed had imprecated the blood of Christ, they had shed, upon their posterity, as well as on themselves, which greatly distressed them; they are told, for their relief, that the same promise would be made good to their posterity also, provided they did as they were directed to do; and to all their brethren the Jews, in distant parts; and even to the Gentiles, sometimes described as *afar off*, of the same character with themselves, repenting and submitting to baptism; yea, to all, in all ages and places, whom God should now, or hereafter call by his grace; see my Reply to Mr *Clark*, p. 50, 51 [*]. This text is so far from being an *unanswerable argument* for the right of infants to baptism, as it is said to be, that there is not the least mention of Infant-baptism in it; nor any hint of it; nor any thing from whence it can be concluded. The baptism encouraged to by it is only of adult persons convinced of sin, and who repented of it. The passage in *Acts* iii. 25. brought for the support of the author's sense of his text, is foreign to his purpose; since it refers not to the covenant of circumcision made with *Abraham*, Gen. xvii. but to the promise of the Messiah of *Abraham*'s seed, and of the blessing of all nations in him, *Gen.* xxii. 18. and which was fulfilled in the mission and incarnation of Christ, and in the ministration of his gospel to Jews and Gentiles; which same promise of Christ, of life and salvation by him, is meant in *Acts* xiii. 26, 32, 33. and which is also a proof, that the children to whom it belongs, are to be

understood

[*] The Octavo Edit. is referred to all along.

understood, not of infant-children, but of the adult posterity of the Jews; since the apostle says, *God hath fulfilled the same to* us *their children*; for surely the apostle *Paul* must not be reckoned an infant-child.

*Secondly,* The ground on which the right of infants to baptism is founded by this author is a false one; which is the covenant made with *Abraham,* that which gave his infant-children a right to circumcision, and is said to be the covenant of grace, the same under which believers now are. This he looks upon to be the grand turning point, on which the issue of the controversy very much depends; that it is the main ground on which the right of infants to baptism is asserted; and he freely confesses, that if this covenant is not the covenant of grace, the main ground of infants right to baptism is taken away, and consequently, that the principal arguments in support of the doctrine are overturned, p. 18, 19. Now that this ground and foundation is a false and sandy one, and will not bear the weight of this superstructure laid upon it, will appear by observing,

1. That the covenant of grace gives no right to any positive institution, either circumcision or baptism: not to circumcision; the covenant of grace was in being, was made, manifested, and applied to many, from *Adam* to *Abraham,* both before and after the flood, who had no right to circumcision, nor knowledge of it; the covenant of grace did not give to *Abraham* himself a right to circumcision; he was openly interested in it, it was made, manifested, and applied unto him, many years before circumcision was enjoined him; and when it was, it was not the covenant of grace, but the express command of God, that gave him and his male seed a right to circumcision; I say his male seed, for his female seed, though no doubt many of them were interested in the covenant of grace, yet their covenant-interest gave them no right unto it: as there were also many, at the same time that circumcision was enjoined *Abraham* and his natural seed, who were interested in the covenant of grace, and yet had no right to circumcision; as *Shem, Arphaxad, Lot,* and others: and on the other hand, it may easily be observed, that there were many who had a right to circumcision, and on whom it was practised, who, without any breach of charity, it may be concluded, had no interest in the covenant of grace; not to mention particular persons, as *Ishmael, Esau,* &c. many of the idolaters and rebels among the Israelites in the wilderness, of those that bowed the knee to *Baal* in the times of *Ahab,* and of the worshippers of *Jeroboam*'s calves; those that are called the rulers of *Sodom* and *Gomorrah* in the times of *Isaiah,* and that worshipped the queen and host of heaven in the times of *Jeremiah*; and those whose characters are given in the prophecy of *Malachi,* as then living; with

with the Scribes and Pharisees, who committed the unpardonable sin in the times of Christ; these cannot be thought to be in the covenant of grace.

In short, all were not *Israel* that were of *Israel*, and circumcised: it is therefore clear to a demonstration, that interest in the covenant of grace did not give right to circumcision, but the special, particular, and express command of God: nor does it give right to baptism; it gave the Old Testament-saints no right unto it, who were four thousand years without it, and yet in the covenant of grace; and since baptism is enjoined as an ordinance of the New Testament, a person may be in the covenant of grace, and yet not known to be so by himself or others; and while he is in such a state, and in such circumstances, he cannot be thought to have any right to baptism. It is a command of God, that those that repent and believe, be baptized; the covenant of grace provides faith and repentance for those interested in it, and bestows them on them; whereby they are qualified for baptism according to the divine command. But it is not the covenant of grace, nor these qualifications, that give the right to baptism; but the command of God to persons so qualified, to profess the same, and be baptized: for men may have faith and repentance, yet if they do not make a profession of them, they have no right to baptism, nor a minister any authority to administer it to them. No doubt but the apostle *Peter* was satisfied that the three thousand pricked in their hearts were truly penitents; yet insisted on the profession of their repentance, as antecedent to baptism; and *Philip*, I make no question, was satisfied of the Eunuch's being a believer in Christ by the conversation he had with him; yet required a confession of his faith in him, in order to his baptism; for *with the mouth confession is* to be *made unto salvation*. Nor even according to our author's sentiment does the covenant of grace give a right to baptism; since, according to him, persons are not in covenant before they are baptized; for he expressly says, p. 12, 30. that *by baptism* they *enter* into the covenant, and are *taken into the covenant* by baptism; and therefore baptism rather gives them a right to the covenant, than the covenant a right to baptism, according to this Gentleman: so far is it from being true what he elsewere says, p. 32. that the covenant of grace gave *Abraham* and his children a right to circumcision under the law; and that this it is that gives parents and children a right to baptism under the gospel.

2. The covenant of circumcision, or the covenant which gave *Abraham*'s infant-children a right to circumcision, is not the covenant of grace; for the covenant of circumcision must be most certainly, in the nature of it, a covenant of works, and not of grace. It will be freely allowed, that the covenant of grace was at certain times made, and made manifest, and applied to *Abraham*, and he interested in it; and that God was the God of him, and of his spiritual seed;

seed; and that the spiritual seed of *Abraham*, both among Jews and Gentiles, are interested in the same covenant; but not his carnal seed, nor theirs as such: and that *Abraham* was justified by faith, as believers now are; and that the same gospel was preached to him as now; and that at the same time the covenant of circumcision was given unto him, there was an exhibition of the covenant of grace unto him: the account of both is mixed together; but then the covenant of circumcision, which was a covenant of peculiarity, and belonged only to him and his natural male seed, was quite a distinct thing from the covenant of grace, since it included some that were not in the covenant of grace, and excluded others that were in it: nor is that the covenant that was confirmed of God in Christ 430 years before the law was; since the covenant of circumcision falls 24 years short of that date, and therefore it refers not to that, but to an exhibition of the covenant of grace to *Abraham*, about the time of his call out of *Chaldea*; besides the covenant of circumcision is abolished, but the covenant of grace continues, and ever will; see my reply, p. 35, 36. Now as this covenant, which gave *Abraham*'s infant-children a right to circumcision, is not the covenant of grace, the main ground on which the right of infants to baptism is asserted, is taken away, and so no foundation left for it; and consequently the principal argument in support of the doctrine are overturned, as this Gentleman freely confesses; and as every one should, who is in the same way of thinking and reasoning. If the covenant of circumcision is not the covenant of grace, here of right the controversy should be closed, since this is the turning point on which the issue of it very much depends; for if this be false, all that follows as argued from it, must be so too; for,

*Thirdly*, If the covenant of circumcision is not the covenant of grace, then circumcision is not the seal of the covenant of grace it is said to be, p. 22. If it was, the covenant of grace must be without such a seal near two thousand years, before the covenant of circumcision was given; and why not then always without one? besides, it must be with a seal and without a seal at one and same time, which is absurd; for there were some interested in the covenant of grace as before observed, on whom circumcision was not enjoined, and so without this seal, when it was enjoined on *Abraham* and his natural seed, and there were such afterwards; and circumcision also must have been the seal of itself, which is another absurdity. Circumcision was a token and sign, or mark in the flesh, which *Abraham*'s natural posterity were to bear until the coming of the Messiah; but is never called a seal throughout the whole Old Testament; and much less is it any where said to be a seal of the covenant of grace: and indeed what blessing of grace could it seal, assure of, and confirm, to any of *Abraham*'s natural seed

[k] Romans iv. 11.

seed as such, or any other man's natural seed? It is indeed in the New Testament called *a seal of the righteousness of the faith which Abraham had, being yet uncircumcised* [b], but then it was no seal of that, nor of any thing else to others, but to *Abraham* only; namely, that that righteousness which he had by faith before he was circumcised, would come upon, or be imputed to the uncircumcised Gentiles; and accordingly this mark continued in the flesh of his posterity, until the gospel, publishing justification by the righteousness of faith, was ordered to be preached to the Gentiles [c]. Wherefore,

Fourthly, Seeing circumcision was no seal of the covenant of grace, baptism, which it is pretended was instituted in the room of it, can be no seal of it neither, and so not to be administered as such to the children of professed believers, as is said, p. 25. The text in *Colossians* ii. 11. falls short of proving that baptism is instituted in the room of circumcision; since the apostle is speaking, not of circumcision in the flesh, but in the Spirit; and by which he means not the outward ordinance of baptism, that is distinguished from it [d], but an inward work of grace upon the heart; spiritual circumcision, called *the circumcision of Christ*; which to understand as the same, is not to make an unreasonable *tautology*; it makes none at all, and much less *nonsense*, as this writer suggests; but beautifully completes the description the apostle gives of spiritual circumcision; first, by the manner of its performance, *without hands*; then by the matter and substance of it, *the putting off the body of the sins of the flesh*; and lastly, by the author of it, Christ, who by his spirit produces it.

The argument from *analogy* is weak and insufficient; though some little agreement between circumcision and baptism may be imagined, and seem to be in the signification of them, yet the difference between them is notorious; they differ in their subjects, uses, manner of administration, and the administrators of them; nor is it true, what is suggested, that they are both sacraments of admission into the church; nor are they badges of relation to God or Christ, nor signs and seals of the covenant of grace. Nor need we be under any concern about any ordinance coming in the room of circumcision, and answering to that Jewish rite. Nor is there any necessity of any, no more than of a pope in the room of an high priest, or of any festivals to answer to those of the passover, pentecost, and feast of tabernacles; nor does the Lord's supper answer to the passover, and come in the room of it; it is Christ that answers to it, and is the passover sacrificed for us: but what makes it quite clear and plain, that baptism does not succeed circumcision, or come in the room of it, is, that it was in force and use before circumcision was abolished, which was not until the death of

Christ;

---

[b] Rom. iv. 11. and the Reply, p. 43.  
[c] See the divine Right of Infant-baptism examined, &c. p 56, &c.  
[d] Ver 12.

Chrift, whereas *John* adminiftered baptifm, and Chrift himfelf was baptized, and many others, fome years before that time; and therefore baptifm cannot be faid, with any propriety, to fucceed circumcifion, when it was in force before the other was out of date: befides, if it did, it is no feal of the covenant of grace, nor to be adminiftered to infants for fuch an ufe; for what fpiritual blefling, what blefling of grace in the covenant, does baptifm feal, or can feal, affure of, and fecure unto the carnal feed of believers? Let it be named if it can [e].

*Fifthly*, It is not indifputably evident, as this Gentleman fays, p. 29. but indifputably falfe, that the apoftles acknowledged and allowed the covenant-relation and intereft of children, under the gofpel, as well as under the law; by which I take it for granted he means, their relation and intereft in the covenant of grace: that relation and intereft, the natural feed of *Abraham*, as fuch, had not under the law; nor have the natural feed of believers, as fuch, the fame under the gofpel. This is not to be proved from his text, as has been fhewn already: nor from *Romans* xi. 16, 17. where by the root and branches, are not meant *Abraham* and his pofterity, or natural feed; nor by the olive-tree the Jewifh church; but the gofpel church-ftate in its firft foundation, out of which were left the Jews that believed not in Chrift, meant by the *branches broken off*; and which church was conftituted of thofe that believed in him; and thefe were the *root* and *firft-fruits*, which being *holy*, are the pledge and earneft of the future converfion and holinefs of that people the apoftle is fpeaking of in the context; and into which church-ftate the Gentiles that believed were received, and are the branches *grafted in*, which partook of the root and fatnefs of the olive-tree; that is, of the goodnefs and fatnefs of the houfe of God, the ordinances and privileges of it: and in this paffage not a word is faid of the covenant-relation, and intereft of children under the gofpel; not a fyllable about baptifm, much lefs of Infant-baptifm; nor can any thing in favour of it be inferred from it [f]; nor can any thing of this kind be proved from 1 *Corinthians* vii. 14. real internal holinefs is rejected by our author, as the fenfe of this and the preceding paffage; but he pleads for a federal holinefs; but what that is, as diftinct from real holinefs, let it be faid if it can: the only holinefs which the covenant of grace promifes and provides for, and which only is proper federal holinefs, is real holinefs of heart and life [g]: no other than matrimonial holinefs, or lawful marriage, can be meant in the Corinthian text; it is fuch a holinefs with which the unbelieving parent is fanctified, hufband or wife; and if it is a federal holinefs, the unbeliever ought to be allowed to be in covenant; and if this gives a right to baptifm, ought to be baptized,

[e] See Reply, p. 44—47.  [f] See the Reply, p. 64, 65.
[g] See Jer. xxxi. 33. Ezek. xxxvi. 26, 27.

baptized, as well as their carnal issue; and have as good a right to it, surely, as they who have their holiness from them, and which even depends upon the sanctification of the unbelieving parent. I am able to prove, from innumerable instances in Jewish writings, that the words *sanctify* and *sanctified*, are used for *espouse* and *espoused*, and the apostle, being a Jew, adopts the same language; and let men wriggle and wrangle as long as they can, no other sense can be put upon the words, than of a legitimate marriage and offspring; nothing else will suit with the case proposed to the apostle, and with his answer and reasoning about it; and which sense has been allowed by many learned Pædobaptists; and I cannot forbear transcribing, what I have elsewhere done, the honest confession of *Musculus*: " Formerly, says he, I have abused this
" place against the Anabaptists, thinking the meaning was, that the children
" were holy for the parents faith, which, though true, the present place makes
" nothing for the purpose [b]"

*Sixthly*, From what has been observed, it is not proved, as our author asserts, p. 32. that the apostles looked on the children of believing parents as having an interest in the covenant of grace; and false is it, to the last degree of falshood, what he infers from thence, that " then we have undeniable evidence that
" they did in fact baptize the children of all professing believers; and that they
" understood their commission as authorizing them so to do, *Matthew* xxviii. 19." Let one single fact be produced, one undeniable instance of the apostles baptizing an infant of any, professor or profane, and we will give up the cause at once, and say no more. Nor did the apostles, nor could the apostles understand the commission as authorizing them to baptize infants. What this Gentleman observes, that the word *teach* is in the original to make disciples, or learn: Be it so, it is not applicable to new-born babes, who are not capable of learning any thing, and much less of divine and spiritual things, of Christ and his gospel, and the doctrines of it; of which kind of learning only can the commission be understood: nor are the children of believing parents called disciples, *Acts* xv. 10. adult persons are meant; and by the yoke attempted to be put on their necks, not circumcision, which was not intolerable, but the doctrine of the necessity of that, and other Mosaic rites, and even of keeping the whole law in order to salvation; this was intolerable.

This author further observes, that children must be included in the words *all nations*, mentioned in the commission. If they are included so as to be baptized, and if this phrase is to be understood without any limitation or restriction, then not only the children of christian parents, but the children of Pagans, Jews, and Turks; yea, all adult persons, be they who they may, ever so vile and profligate,

[b] See the divine Right of Infant-baptism examined, p. 73—78. and the Reply, p. 55—58.

gate, since these are included in all nations; but the limitation is to those that are taught, and learn to become the disciples of Christ, and believe in him, as appears from *Mark* xvi. 15, 16 [j]. Nor does it appear from the scripture-accounts, that there is any probability, and much less *the highest probability*, as this writer says, p. 33. that it was the general practice of the apostles to baptize infants, and which he concludes from *Lydia*, the Jailor, and *Stephanas*; which instances do not afford the least probability of it [k]. To make it probable that there might be infant-children in those families, he observes, we read, when God smote the first-born in *Egypt*, there was not an house in which there was not *one* dead, consequently not an house in *Egypt* in which there was not a child: but he did not consider, that all the first-born of *Egypt* slain, were not infant-children; but many of them might be men grown, of twenty, or thirty years of age, or more; and of these, with those under such an age, and in infancy, it is not strange that there should be found one in every house [l]. Our author adds, "suppose it had been said of one proselyted to the Jewish religion, that "he and his houshold, or that he and all his were circumcised, would any doubt "whether his infant-children were circumcised? I believe not:" and so do I too; but not for the reason given, which is a false one; for it never was a practice, either before or since *Abraham*'s covenant, to receive children with their parents into a covenant-relation, if by that relation is meant relation to, and interest in the covenant of grace; but for this very good reason, because the Jews and their proselytes were commanded to circumcise their Infant-children; but God has no where commanded any to baptize their Infant-children; and therefore when housholds are said to be baptized, this cannot be understood of infants, and especially when those in these housholds are represented as hearer of the word, believers in it, and persons possessed of spiritual joy and comfort.

*Seventhly*, The evidence this author gives of the practice of Infant-baptism, from those that lived in the first, second, and third centuries, p. 34—40. comes next. He produces no evidence from any writer of the first century, though there are several whose writings are extant, as *Barnabas, Clemens Romanus, Hermas, Polycarp*, and *Ignatius*. He begins with *Irenus*, as he is twice called; *Irenæus* is meant, of whom he says, that he only mentions Infant-baptism transiently; but he does not mention it at all: it is not once mentioned in all his writings, as corrupted as they be; being some spurious, and for the most part translations, and these barbarous, and but few original pieces: the passage produced for his use, of the word *regeneration* for baptism, is not to the purpose; since by the command of *regenerating*, Christ gave to his disciples, is not meant the

[j] See the Reply, p 58, 59, 62.   [k] See the Reply, p. 63, 64.   [l] Ibid.

the command of baptizing, but of teaching the doctrine of regeneration, and the necessity of it to salvation, and in order to baptism, the first and principal part of the commission of the apostles, as the order of the words shews. The other testimony which, he says, is plain for the baptism of infants, there is not syllable of it in it: *Irenæus* only says, "Christ came to save all; all I say, that "are born again unto God; infants, and little ones, and children, and young "men, and old men." Which is most true; for Christ came to save all of every age that are regenerated, and of which persons of every age are capable; but to interpret this of Christ's coming to save all that are baptized, is false; and is to make this ancient writer to speak an untruth: to prove that regeneration is used by him for baptism, a passage is produced out of *Justin Martyr*, said to be his cotemporary, though *Justin* lived before him, in the middle of the second century, and should have been first mentioned; but will not serve his purpose: for *Justin* is speaking of the manner of adult-baptism, and not a word of infants; and of adult persons, not as regenerated by or in baptism; for he speaks of them before as converted and believers, and consequently regenerated; and their baptism is plainly distinguished from regeneration. Of the sense of the passages of these two writers, see more in the *Reply*, p. 16—18. *The argument from apostolic Tradition*, p. 13, 14. *Antipædobaptism*, p. 9—20.

The next testimony produced is *Origen*, placed in the beginning of the third century, though it was rather towards the middle of it that he wrote and flourished in, and should have been mentioned after *Tertullian*. The passages quoted from him are, the first out of his eighth homily on *Leviticus*, though the last clause in it does not belong to that, but is in the fourteenth homily on *Luke*, and the other is out of his epistle to the *Romans*: Now these are all taken out of Latin translations, full of interpolations, additions, and detractions; so that, as many learned men observe, "one knows not when he "reads *Origen*, and is at a loss to find *Origen* in *Origen*." Now whereas there are genuine works of his still extant in Greek, in them there is not the least hint of Infant-baptism, nor any reference to it, much less any express mention of it, not even as an apostolical tradition, as in the last passage produced; for so it should be rendered, not *order*, but *tradition*; on which I shall just observe what Bishop *Taylor* says: "A tradition apostolical, if it be not consigned with "a fuller testimony than of one person (*Origen*) whom all after-ages have con- "demned of many errors, will obtain so little reputation among those, who "know that things have, upon greater authority, pretended to derive from "the apostles, and yet falsly; that it will be a great argument, that he is cre- "dulous,

"dubious and weak, that shall be determined by so weak a probation in a
"matter of so great concernment [a]."

*Tertullian* is the next writer quoted as giving plain proof that Infant-baptism was the constant practice of the church in his day: he is the first person known to have made any mention of it; who, as soon as he did, argued against it, and dissuaded from it; and though it will be owned, that it was moved in his day, and debated; yet that it was practised, and much less constantly practised, has not yet been proved.

The next evidence produced is *Cyprian*, who lived in the middle of the third century; and it will be allowed that it was practised in the African churches in his time, where it was first moved, and at the same time Infant-communion was practised also; of the practice of which we have as early proof as of Infant-baptism; and this furnishes with an answer to this author's questions, p. 42. When Infant-baptism was introduced, and by whom? It was introduced at the time Infant-communion was, and by the same persons. As for the testimonies of *Ambrose*, *Austin*, and *Pelagius*, they might have been spared, since they wrote in the fourth century, when it is not denied that Infant-baptism very much prevailed; of *Austin*, and particularly of what *Pelagius* says, see *Argument from apostolic tradition*, p. 19—26. *Antipædobaptism*, p. 33—37. And from hence it appears, that it is not true what this author suggests, p. 42, 52. that infant-baptism was the universal practice of the primitive churches in the three first centuries, called the purest times; when it does not appear to have been practised at all until the third century, when sad corruptions were made in doctrine and practice.

*Eighthly*, This author proposes to answer some of the most material objections against Infant-baptism, p. 43, &c. as, 1. "That there is no express "command for it in scripture, and therefore unwarrantable." To which the answer is; that if there is no express command, there are virtual and implicit ones, which are of equal force with an express one, and no less than four are observed; one command is enough, this is over-doing it, and what is over-done is not well done: but let us hear them; the first is God's command to *Abraham* to circumcise his infant-children, which is a virtual and implicit command to believers to baptize theirs! The reason is, because they are *Abraham's* spiritual seed, and *heirs according to the promise*; but the command to *Abraham* only concerned his natural, not his spiritual seed; and if there is any force in the reason given, or the command lays any obligation on the latter, their duty is not to baptize, but circumcise their children; since the sacramental rite commanded,

[a] Liberty of prophesying, p. 320. See the Reply, p. 19, 20. Argument from apostolic Tradition, p. 16, 17. Antipædobaptism, p. 24—29.

manded, it seems, has never been repealed, and still remains in full force. The next virtual and implicit command is in *Matthew* xix. 14. but Chrift's permission of children *to come,* or *to be brought* unto him, there spoken of, was not for baptism, or to be baptized by him, but for him to pray for them, and touch them, in order to cure them of difeases [o]. Another implicit, if not express command, to baptize infants, is in *Matthew* xxviii. 19. This has been confidered, and difproved already; fee p. 99. The fourth and laft implicit command, the author mentions, is the exhortation in his text, *Acts* ii. 38, 39. in which, as has been fhewn, there is not the leaft hint of Infant-baptifm, nor any thing from whence it can be concluded.

This author obferves, that fince virtual and implicit commands are looked on as fufficient to determine our conduct in other things, then why not in this? fuch as keeping the firft-day-fabbath, attendance on public worfhip, and the admiffion of women to the Lord's-fupper. To which I reply, he has not proved any virtual and implicit command to baptize infants; and as to the cafes mentioned, befides implications, there are plain inftances in fcripture of the practice of them; and let like inftances of Infant-baptifm be produced, and we fhall think ourfelves obliged to practife it. As to what this author fays of an exprefs, irrepealable command to children, to receive the feal of the covenant, and the conftant practice of the church to adminifter the feal of it to them; if by the covenant is meant the covenant of grace, it never had any fuch feal as is fuggefted, which has been proved; nor has it any but the blood of Chrift, called *the blood of the everlafting covenant.*

2. Another objection to Infant-baptifm is; there is no exprefs inftance in all the hiftory of the New-Teftament of an Infant-child being baptized, and therefore is without any fcripture-example. To which is replied, by obferving that whole houfholds were baptized; as there were, and which have been already confidered; and thefe were baptized, not upon the converfion of the parent, or head of the family, but upon their own faith; and fo were not infants, but adult perfons; though this author thinks that fuch accounts would eafily be underftood to include children, had the fame been faid of circumcifion. They might fo, when circumcifion was in force and ufe; for this very good reafon, becaufe there was a previous exprefs command extant to circumcife children, when there is none to baptize infants. He further obferves, that from there being no exprefs mention of Infant-baptifm in the New Teftament, it fhou'd not be concluded there was none, any more than that the churches of *Antioch,* Ico-

---

[o] Matt. xix. 13. Mark x. 13. of the fenfe of this text fee the Reply, p. 50—52.

*nium*, of the Romans, Galatians, Thessalonians and Colossians, were not baptized, because there is no express account of it in the history of the New-Testament: but of several of those churches there is mention made of the baptism of the members of them, of the Romans, Galatians and Colossians, *Rom.* vi. 3, 4. *Gal.* iii 27. *Col.* ii. 12. but what this author might imagine would press us hard, is to give a scripture-example of our own present practice. Our present practice, agreeable to scripture-examples, is not at all concerned with the parents of those baptized by us, whether believers or unbelievers, christians or not christians, Jews or Heathens, this comes not into consideration; it is only concerned with the persons themselves to be baptized, what they are. It seems, if we give a scripture-example of our practice, it must be of a person born and brought up of christian or baptized parents, that was baptized in adult years; but our present practice is not limited to such persons. We baptize many whose parents we have no reason to believe are christians, or are baptized persons; and be it that we baptize adult persons, who are born and brought up of christian or baptized parents, a scripture-example of such a person might indeed be required of us with some plausible pretext, if the history of the *Acts of the Apostles*, which this writer says continued above thirty years, had given an account of the yearly or of frequent additions of members to the churches mentioned in it, during that space of time; whereas that history only gives an account of the first planting of those churches, and of the baptism of those of which they first consisted; wherefore to give instances of those that were born of them, and brought up by them as baptized in adult years, cannot be reasonably required of us: But, on the other hand, if Infant-children were admitted to baptism in those times, upon the faith and baptism of their parents, and their becoming christians; it is strange! exceeding strange! that among the many thousands that were baptized in *Jerusalem, Samaria, Corinth*, and other places, that there should be no one instance of any of them bringing their children with them to be baptized, and claiming the privilege of baptism for them upon their own faith, or of their doing this in any short time after; this is a case that required no length of time; and yet not a single instance can be produced.

3. A third objection is, that " infants can receive no benefit from baptism, " because of their incapacity; and therefore are not to be baptized." To which our author answers; that they are capable of being entered into covenant with God, of the seal of the covenant, of being cleansed by the blood of Christ, and of being regenerated by his Spirit: And be it so; what of all this! as I have observed in the *Reply*, p. 4. Are they capable of understanding the nature, design, and use of the ordinance of baptism? Are they capable of

professing

professing faith in Christ, which is a prerequisite to it, and of exercising it in it? Are they capable of answering a good conscience to God in it? Are they capable of submitting to it in obedience to the will of Christ, from love to him, and with a view to his glory? They are not: what benefit then can they receive by baptism? and to what purpose is it to be administered to them? If infants receive any advantage, benefit, or blessing by baptism, which our infants have not without it, let it be named, if it can; if none, why administered? why all this zeal and contention about it? a mere noise about nothing.

4. A fourth and most common objection, it is said, is, that "faith and re- "pentance, or a profession of them at least, are mentioned in the New Testa- "ment as the necessary prerequisites of baptism, of which children are incap- "able, and therefore of the ordinance itself." To this it is answered; that children are capable of the habit and principle of faith: which is not denied, nor is it in the objection; and it is granted by our author, that a profession of faith is a prerequisite to baptism in adult persons, who embrace christianity; but when they have embraced it, and professed their faith, in the apostles times, not only themselves, but their housholds, and all that were theirs, were baptized. It is very true, those professing their faith also, as did the houshold of the Jailor, of whom it is said, that he was *believing in God with all his house*: His family believed as well as he, which could not have been known, had they not professed it. The instance of a professing stranger embracing the Jewish religion, in order to his circumcision, which, when done, it was always administered to his family and children, makes nothing to the purpose; since it is no rule of procedure to us, with respect to a gospel-ordinance.

*Ninthly*, The performance under consideration is concluded with observing many absurdities, and much confusion, with which the denial of Infant-baptism, as a divine institution, is attended. As,

1. It is saying the covenant made with *Abraham* is not an everlasting one; that believers under the gospel are not *Abraham*'s seed, and heirs of his promise; that the ingrafted Gentiles do not partake of the same privileges in the church, from which the Jews were broken off; and that the privileges of the gospel-dispensation are less than those of the law: all which are said to be flat contradictions to scripture. To all which I reply, that the covenant of grace made with, and made known to *Abraham*, is an everlasting covenant, and is sure to all the seed; that is, the spiritual seed; and is not at all affected by Infant-baptism, that having no concern in it. The covenant of circumcision, though called an *everlasting* covenant, *Gen.* xvii. 7. was only to continue unto the times of the Messiah; and is so called, just in the same sense, and for the same reason,

the covenant of priesthood with *Phineas* has the same epithet, *Numb.* xxv. 13. Believers under the gospel are *Abraham*'s spiritual seed, and heirs of the same promise of spiritual things; but these spiritual things, and the promise of them, do not belong to their natural seed as such; the believing Gentiles, ingrafted into the gospel church-state, partake of all the privileges of it, from which the unbelieving Jews are excluded, being for their unbelief left out of that state. The privileges of the gospel-dispensation are not less, yea far greater than those of the law; to believers, who are freed from the burdensome rites and ceremonies of the law, have larger measures of grace, a clearer ministration of the gospel, and more spiritual ordinances; nor are they less to their infants, who are eased from the painful rite of circumcision, have the advantage of a christian education, and of hearing the gospel as they grow up, in a clearer manner than under the law; which are greater privileges than the Jewish children had under the former dispensation; nor are all, nor any of these affected, or to be contradicted, by the denial of Infant-baptism.

2. It is observed, that to deny the validity of Infant-baptism, is saying that "there was no true baptism in the church for eleven or twelve hundred years after Christ; and that the generality of the present professors of christianity are now a company of unbaptized heathens," p. 52. so p. 10. To which I reply, that the true baptism continued in the church in the first two centuries; and though Infant-baptism was introduced in the third, and prevailed in the fourth, yet in both these centuries there were those that opposed it, and abode by the true baptism. Besides, in the vallies of *Piedmont*, as many learned men have observed, there were witnesses from the times of the apostles, who bore their testimony against corruptions in doctrine and practice, and among whom Infant-baptism did not obtain until the sixteenth century; so that the true baptism continued in the church till that time, and it has ever since; see the *Reply*, p. 31, 32. As for the generality of the present professors of christianity, it lies upon them to take care of their character, and remove from it what may be thought disagreeable; and clear themselves of it, by submitting to the true baptism according to the order of the gospel. As to the salvation of persons in or out of the visible church, which is the greater number, this author speaks of, I know nothing of; salvation is not by baptism in any way, but by Christ alone.

3. It is said, if Infant-baptism is a divine institution, warranted by the word of God, then they that are baptized in their adult age necessarily renounce a divine institution, and an ordinance of Jesus Christ, and vacate the former covenant between God and them. *If it be*; but it is not a divine institution, nor an

ordinance

ordinance of Jesus Christ, as appears from all that has been said about it in the foregoing pages; wherefore it is right to renounce and reject it, as an human invention: and as for any covenant between God and them vacated thereby, it will not, it need not give the renouncers of it any concern; being what they know nothing of, and the whole a chimerical business. Nay, it is farther observed, that renouncing Infant-baptism, and making it a nullity, is practically saying there are no baptized persons, no regular ministers, nor ordinances, in all professing churches but their own, and as elsewhere, p. 41. no gospel-church in the world; and that the administrations of the ministers of other churches are a nullity, and the promise of Christ to be with his ministers in the administration of this ordinance to the end of the world, must have failed for hundreds of years, in which Infant-baptism was practised. But be it so: to whom is all this owing? to whose account must it be put? to those who are the corrupters of the word and ordinances. Is it suggested by all this, that " God " in his providence would never suffer things to go such lengths?" Let it be observed, that he has given us in his word reason to expect great corruptions in doctrine and worship; and that though he will always have a seed to serve him, more or fewer, in all ages, yet he has no where promised that these shall be always in a regular gospel-church-state; and though he has promised his presence in his ordinances to the end of the world, it is only with those ministers and people among whom the ordinances are administered according to his word; and there was for some hundreds of years, in the darkness of popery, such a corruption in the ordinances of baptism, and the Lord's supper, in the administration of which the presence of God cannot be thought to be; nor were there any regular ministers, nor regular ordinances, nor a regular gospel-church, but what were to be found in the vallies of *Piedmont*; and with whom the presence of God may be supposed to be; who bore a testimony against all corruptions, and among the rest, against Infant-baptism [p].

This writer further urges, that "if Infant-baptism is a nullity, there can be " now no regular baptism in the world, nor ever will be to the end of it; and " so the ordinance must be lost, since adult baptism cannot be traced to the apos- " tles times, and as now administered, is derived from those that were baptized " in infancy; wherefore if Infant-baptism is invalid, that must be so too; so " in p. 42." To which it may be answered, that the first English Antipædobaptists, when determined upon a reformation in this ordinance, in a consultation of theirs about it, had this difficulty statted about a proper administrator to begin the work, when it was proposed to send some to foreign churches, the

successors.

[p] See Reply, p. 11, 12.

successors of the antient Waldenses in *France* and *Germany*; and accordingly did send some, who being baptized, returned and baptized others; though others were of opinion this too much favoured of the popish notion of an uninterrupted succession, and a right through that to administer ordinances; and therefore judged, that in an extraordinary case, as this was, to begin a reformation from a general corruption, where a baptized administrator could not be had, it might be begun by one unbaptized, otherwise qualified to preach the word and ordinances; which practice they were able to justify upon the same principles the other reformers justified theirs; who without any regard to an uninterrupted succession, set up new churches, ordained pastors, and administered ordinances. Nor is it essential to the ordinance of baptism, that it be performed by one regularly baptized, though in ordinary cases it should; or otherwise it could never have been introduced into the world; the first administrator of it must be an unbaptized person, as *John* the Baptist was. All which is a sufficient answer to what this writer has advanced on this subject [q].

[q] See the Divine Right of Infant-baptism examined, &c. p. 13—15. 8vo Edit.

*The Scriptures the only Guide in Matters of Religion.*

Being a SERMON Preached at the BAPTISM of several Persons in BARBICAN, *November* 2, 1750.

JEREMIAH VI. 16.

*Thus saith the Lord, Stand ye in the ways and see, and ask for the old paths, where is the good way, and walk therein; and ye shall find rest for your souls.——*

IN this chapter the destruction of *Jerusalem* by the Babylonians is threatened and foretold, and the causes of it assigned; in general, the great aboundings of sin and wickedness among the people; and in particular, their neglect and contempt of the word of God; the sin of covetousness, which prevailed among all sorts; the unfaithfulness of the prophets to the people, and the peoples impenitence and hardness of heart; their want of shame, their disregard to all instructions and warnings from the Lord, by the mouth of his prophets, and their obstinate refusal of them; which last is expressed in the clause following the words read; and which, though an aggravation of it, shew the tender regard of the Lord to his people, and may be considered as an instruction to such who had their doubts and difficulties in religious matters; who were halting between two opinions, and like men *in bivio*, who stand in a place where two or more ways meet, and know not which path to take; and in this light I shall consider them; and in them may be observed,

I. A direction to such persons what to do; *to stand in the ways, and see, and ask for the old paths, where is the good way, and walk therein.*
II. The encouragement to take this direction; *and ye shall find rest for your souls.*

I. The

I. The direction given to *stand in or on the ways, &c.* to do as men do when they are come to a place where two or more ways meet, make a stand, and view the roads, and see which they should take; they look about them, and consider well what course they should steer; they look up to the way-marks, or way-posts, and read the inscriptions on them, which tell them whither such a road leads, and so judge for themselves which way they should go. Now in religious matters, the way-marks or way-posts to guide and direct men in the way, are the scriptures, the oracles of God, and they only.

Not education-principles. It is right in parents to do as *Abraham* did, to teach their children to *keep the way of the Lord*[a]. The direction of the wise man is an exceeding good one; *Train up a child in the way he should go, and when he is old, he will not depart from it*[b]; that is, easily and ordinarily: and it becomes christians under the gospel-dispensation to *bring up* their children *in the nurture and admonition of the Lord*[c]; and a great mercy and blessing it is to have a religious education; but then, as wrong principles may be infused as well as right ones, into persons in their tender years, it becomes them, when come to years of maturity and discretion, to examine them, whether they are according to the word of God, and so judge for themselves, whether they are to be abode by or rejected. I know it is a grievous thing with some persons to forsake the religion they have been brought up in; but upon this foot, a man that is born and brought up a Turk or a Jew, a Pagan or a Papist, must ever continue so. Sad would have been the case of the apostle *Paul*, if he had continued in the principles of his education; and what a shocking figure did he make whilst he abode by them? thinking, according to them, he *ought to do many things contrary to the name of Jesus*[d].

Nor are the customs of men a rule of judgment, or a direction which way men should take in matters of religion; for *the customs of the people are* for the most part *vain*[e]; and such as are not *lawful* for us, being christians, to *receive or observe*[f]; and concerning which we should say, *We have no such custom, neither the churches of God*[g]. Custom is a tyrant, and ought to be rebelled against, and its yoke thrown off.

Nor are the traditions of men to be regarded; the Pharisees were very tenacious of the traditions of the elders, by which they transgressed the commandments of God, and made his word of no effect; and the apostle *Paul*, in his state of unregeneracy, was zealous of the same; but neither of them are to be imitated by us: it is right to observe the exhortation which the apostle gives,

when

---

[a] Gen. xviii. 19.    [b] Prov. xxii. 6.    [c] Ephes. vi. 4.
[d] Acts xxii. 3, 4. and xxvi. 9.    [e] Jer. x. 3.    [f] Acts xvi. 21.
[g] 1 Cor. xi. 16.

when a christian [h]; *beware lest any man spoil you through philosophy and vain deceit, after the traditions of men, after the rudiments of the world, and not after Christ.* Take care you are not imposed upon, under the notion and pretence of an *apostolical tradition*; unwritten traditions are not the rule, only the word of God is the rule of our faith and practice.

Nor do the decrees of popes and councils demand our attention and regard; it matters not what such a pope has determined, or what canons such a council under his influence has made; what have we to do with the man of sin, that *exalts himself above all that is called God*; who *sits in the temple of God, shewing himself as if he was God?* we know what will be his fate, and that of his followers [i].

Nor are the examples of men, no not of the best of men, in all things to be copied after by us; we should indeed be *followers* of all good men as such, *of those who through faith and patience inherit the promises*; and especially of such, who are or have been spiritual guides and governors in the church; who have made the scriptures their study, and have laboured in the word and doctrine; their *faith* we should *follow, considering the end of their conversation*; how that issues, and when it terminates in Christ, his person, truths and ordinances, *the same to-day, yesterday and for ever* [k] : but then we are to follow them no further than they follow Christ; the apostle *Paul* desired no more than this of his *Corinthians* with respect to himself; and no more can be demanded of us; it should be no bias on our minds, that such and such a man of so much grace and excellent gifts thought and practised so and so. We are to call no man father or master on earth; we have but one father in heaven, and one master, which is Christ, whose doctrines, rules, and ordinances we should receive and observe. We are not to be influenced by men of learning and wealth; though these should be on the other side of the question, it should be no stumbling to us; had this been a rule to be attended to, christianity had never got footing in the world: *Have any of the rulers or of the Pharisees believed on him? But this people, who knoweth not the law, are cursed* [l]. It pleased the Lord, in the first times of the gospel, to *hide the things of it from the wise and prudent*, and *reveal* them *unto babes*; and to call by his grace, *not many wise men after the flesh, not many mighty, not many noble*; but the *foolish, weak, and base things of the world, and things that are not, to confound the wise and mighty, and bring to nought things that are; that no flesh should glory in his presence* [m] : nor should it concern us that the greatest number is on the opposite side; we are *not to follow a multitude to do evil*; the whole world once wondered after the beast; Christ's flock is but a little flock.

Vol. II.   3 Q   The

[h] Col. ii. 8.   [i] 2 Thess. ii. 4, 5. Rev. xx. 10. and xiii. 8. and xiv. 11.
[k] Heb. vi. 12. and xiii. 7.   [l] John vii. 48, 49.   [m] Matt. xi. 25, 26. 1 Cor. i. 26—29.

The scriptures are the only external guide in matters of religion; they are the way-posts we should look up unto, and take our direction from, and should steer our course accordingly: *To the law and to the testimony: if men speak not according to this word, it is because there is no light in them* [a]; we should *not believe every spirit, but try them, whether they are of God* [o]; and the trial should be made according to the word of God; the scriptures should be searched, as they were by the noble Bereans, to see whether the things delivered to consideration are so or no; the inscriptions on these way-posts should be read, which are written so plain, that he that runs may read them; and they direct to a way, in which men, though fools, shall not err: if therefore the inquiry is,

1*st*, About the way of Salvation; if that is the affair the doubt is concerning, look up to the way-posts, look into the word of God, and read what that says; search the scriptures, for therein is the way of eternal life; life and immortality, or the way to an immortal life, is brought to light by the gospel. The scriptures, under a divine influence, and with a divine blessing, are able to make a man wise unto salvation, and they do point unto men the way of it: it is not the light of nature, nor the law of *Moses*, but the gospel-part of the scriptures which direct to this; these will shew you, that God saves and calls men with an holy calling, not according to their works, but according to his purpose and grace; that it is not by works of righteousness done by men, but according to the mercy of God, that men are saved; and that it is not by works, but by grace, lest men should boast [p]. That it is a vain thing for men to expect salvation this way; that it is a dangerous one: such *who encompass themselves with sparks of their own kindling, shall lie down in sorrow*: and that it is a very wicked thing; such *sacrifice to their own net, and burn incense to their own drag*. These will inform you that *Christ is the way, the truth, and the life*; that he is the only true way to eternal life; that there is salvation in him, and in no other: the language of them is, *Believe on the Lord Jesus Christ, and thou shalt be saved:* these words, *Salvation alone by Christ, salvation alone by Christ*, are written as with a sunbeam on them; just as the way-posts, set up in places where two or more ways met, to direct the manslayer when he was fleeing to one of the cities of refuge from the avenger of blood, had written on them in very legible characters, *refuge, refuge* [q].

2*dly*, If the question is about any point of Doctrine; if there is any hesitation concerning any truth of the gospel, look up to the way-posts, look into the scriptures, search them, see and read what they say; for they are *profitable for doctrine* [r]; for finding it out, explaining, confirming, and defending it: these will tell you
whether

---

[a] Isai. viii. 20.    [o] 1 John iv. 1.    [p] 2 Tim. i. 9. Tit. iii. 5. Ephes. ii. 8, 9.
[q] T. Hieros. Maccot. fol. 31. 4.    [r] 2 Tim. iii. 16.

## IN MATTERS OF RELIGION.

whether the thing in debate is so or no, and will direct you which side of the question to take; if you *seek for knowledge and understanding* in gospel-truths diligently and constantly, *as you would for silver*, and search after them *as for hid treasures, then will you understand the fear of the Lord, and find the knowledge of God*[*]. Thus, for instance,

If the inquiry is about the doctrine of the Trinity; as the light of nature and reason will tell you, that there is but *one* God, and which is confirmed by revelation; the scriptures will inform you, that *there are three that bear record in heaven, the Father, the Word, and the holy Spirit*, and that *these three are one*[†]; are the one God: look into the first page of the Bible, and you will see how just and right is that observation of the Psalmist[*]; *by the word of the Lord were the heavens made, and all the host of them by the breath* or *spirit of his mouth*; and that Jehovah, his word and spirit, were concerned in the creation of all things: you will learn from thence that *God made the heavens and the earth*; that *the spirit of God moved upon the face of the waters*, and brought the chaos into a beautiful order, as well as garnished the heavens; and that *God the word said, Let there be light, and there was light*; and that these three are the us that made man after their *image and likeness*[w]. This doctrine is frequently suggested in the Old Testament, but clearly revealed in the New; and no where more clearly than in the commission for the administration of the ordinance of baptism; *Go, teach all nations, baptizing them in the name of the Father, and of the Son, and of the holy Ghost*[x]; and in the administration of it itself to our Lord Jesus Christ, at which all the three persons appeared; the Father by a voice from heaven, declaring Christ his beloved Son; the Son in human nature, submitting to the ordinance; and the holy Ghost descending as a dove upon him[y]; this was thought to be so clear a testimony for this doctrine, that it was usual with the ancients to say, "Go to "Jordan, and there learn the doctrine of the trinity."

If the question is concerning the Deity of Christ, his eternal Sonship and distinct personality, look to your way-marks; inquire into the sacred records, and there you will find, that *he is the mighty God, God over all, blessed for ever; the great God, the true God, and eternal life*[z]; that all divine perfections are in him; that the fulness of the Godhead dwells in him; that he is *the brightness of his Father's glory, and the express image of his person*; to whom all divine works are ascribed, and all divine worship is given; that he is *the only begotten of the Father, the first-born of every creature*; or was begotten before any creature was in being[a]; of whom the Father says, *Thou art my Son, this day have*

3 Q 2 *I be-*

---

[*] Prov. ii. 4, 5.    [†] 1 John v. 7.    [*] Psal. xxxiii. 6.    [w] Gen. i. 1—3, 26.
[x] Matt. xxviii. 19.    [y] Matt. iii. 16, 17.    [z] Isai. ix. 6. Rom. ix. 5. Titus ii. 13. 1 John v 20.
[a] Heb. i. 3. Col. ii. 9. and i. 15.

*I begotten thee* [b]; that he is *the Word* which *was in the beginning with God*; and must be distinct from him with whom he was; and *in the fulness of time was made flesh*; which neither the Father nor the Spirit were [c]; and the same sacred writings will satisfy you about the deity and personality, as well as the operations of the blessed Spirit.

If the doubt is about the doctrine of Election, read over the sacred volumes, and there you will find, that this is an eternal and sovereign act of God the Father, which was made in Christ before the foundation of the world; that it is to holiness here, and happiness hereafter; that the means are *sanctification of the Spirit, and belief of the truth*; that it is irrespective of faith and good works, being before persons had done either good or evil; that faith and holiness flow from it, and that grace and glory are secured by it; *Whom he did predestinate, them he also called; and whom he called, them he also justified; and whom he justified, them he also glorified* [d].

If you have any hesitation about the doctrine of Original Sin, look into your Bible; there you will see, that the first man sinned, and all sinned in him; that *judgment*, through his offence, *came upon all men to condemnation*; and that *by his disobedience many were made sinners*; that men are *conceived in sin, and shapen in iniquity*; that they are *transgressors from the womb, go astray from thence, speaking lyes, and are by nature children of wrath* [e].

If the matter in debate is the Satisfaction of our Lord Jesus Christ, read over the epistles of his holy apostles, and they will inform you, that he was made under the law, and became the fulfilling end of it, in the room of his people; that he yielded perfect obedience to it, and bore the penalty of it, that the righteousness of the law might be fulfilled in them; that he *was made sin for them, that they might be made the righteousness of God in him*; and *a curse for them, that he might redeem them from the curse of the law*; that *he offered himself a sacrifice for them*, in their room and stead to God, *for a sweet-smelling savour*; that *he suffered, the just for the unjust, to bring them nigh to God*; and died for their sins according to the scriptures, and made reconciliation and atonement for them [f].

If you are at a loss about the Extent of Christ's Death, and know not what part to take in the controversy about general and particular Redemption, look to your way-marks, the scriptures, and take your direction from thence; and there you will observe, that those whom Christ saves from their sins are *his* own

people,

---

[b] Psal. ii. 7. [c] John i. 1, 14. [d] Ephes. i. 4. 2 Thess. ii. 13. Rom. ix. 11. and viii. 30. [e] Rom. v. 12, 18, 19. Psal. li. 5. and lviii. 3. Isai. xlviii. 8. Ephes. ii. 3.
[f] Gal. iv. 4. Rom viii. 3, 4. and x. 4. 2 Cor. v. 21. Gal. iii. 13. Ephes. v. 2. 1 Peter iii. 18. 1 Cor. xv. 3. Heb. ii. 17.

*people*, for whose transgressions he was stricken; that he gave his life a ransom for many, for all sorts of persons, for all his elect, Jews and Gentiles; that they were his sheep he laid down his life for; that *he loved the church, and gave himself for it*; and that *he tasted death for every one* of his brethren, and of *the children* the Father gave him; that those that are redeemed by him, are redeemed *out* of every kindred, tongue, people, and nation [g].

If the affair before you is the doctrine of Justification, and the query is, whether it is by works of righteousness done by you, or by the righteousness of Christ imputed to you, or about any thing relating to it, read over the sacred pages, and especially the epistles of the apostle *Paul*; and you will easily see, that a man cannot be justified in the sight of God by the works of the law, or by his own obedience to the law of works; that, *if righteousness comes by the law, Christ is dead in vain*; that *men are justified by faith, without the works of the law*; that is, by the righteousness of Christ, received by faith; that they are *justified by the blood of Christ, and made righteous by his obedience*; that this is the righteousness which God approves of, accepts, and *imputes* to his people, without works; and which being looked to, apprehended and received by faith, is productive of much spiritual peace and comfort in the soul [h].

If the dispute is about Free-will or Free-grace, the power of the one, and the efficacy of the other, in a sinner's regeneration and conversion; turn to your Bible, and from thence it will appear, that this work is not by the might, or power of man, but by the Spirit of the Lord of hosts; that *men are born again, not of the will of the flesh, nor of the will of man, but of God, his Spirit and grace*; that *it is not of him that willeth, nor of him that runneth, but of God that sheweth mercy*; that the work of faith is a work of power, of the operation of God, and is carried on by it, and is even *according to the exceeding greatness of his power, who works in man both to will and to do of his own good pleasure* [i].

If the demur is about the final Perseverance of the Saints, read over the gracious promises and declarations in the word of God, and they will serve to confirm you in it; as that the righteous shall hold on his way, and he that hath clean hands shall grow stronger and stronger; that God will put his fear into the hearts of his people, and they shall not depart from him; that they are preserved in Christ Jesus, and in his hands, out of whose hands none can pluck them; who is able to keep them from falling, and will; and that they are, and shall be kept by the power of God through faith unto salvation [k].

To

[g] Matt. i. 21. and xx. 28. John x. 15. Ephes. v. 25. Heb. ii. 9—12. Rev. v. 9.
[h] Rom. iii. 20, 28. Gal. ii. 16, 21. Rom. v. 1, 9. 19. and iv. 6.
[i] Zach. iv. 6. John i. 13. and iii. 5. Rom. ix. 15, 16. Col. ii. 12. 2 Thess. i. 11. Ephes. i. 19. Phil. ii. 13. [k] Job xvii. 9. Jer. xxxii. 40. John x. 28, 29. Jude i 24. 1 Peter i. 5.

To observe no more: if the doctrines of the Resurrection of the dead, and a future Judgment, should be called in question, read the divine oracles, and there you are told, that there will be *a resurrection both of the just and unjust*; that the one shall come forth from their graves to the resurrection of life, and the other to the resurrection of damnation; that there is a judgment to come; that there is a righteous Judge appointed, and a day set when just judgment will be executed; and that all, *small and great, good and bad, must appear before the judgment-seat of Christ, to receive for the things done in the body, whether they be good, or whether they be evil* [k].

3*dly*, If the inquiry is about Worship, the scriptures will direct you both as to the object and manner of it, and circumstances relating to it; they will inform you, that God only is to be worshipped, and not a creature; and that the Deity to be worshipped is *not like to gold, or silver, or stone graven by art and man's device*; that *God is a spirit, and must be worshipped in spirit and in truth*: you will there find the rules for the several parts of worship, for prayer to him, singing his praise, preaching his word, and administering his ordinances, and how every thing should be done decently, and in order [l].

4*thly*, If the inquiry is about the nature of a Church, its government, officers, and discipline; look into the ancient records of the scripture, and there you will meet with a just and true account of these things, the original of them, and rules concerning them; you will find that a church is a society of saints and faithful men in Christ Jesus, that are joined together in holy fellowship; that are incorporated into a visible church-state, and by agreement meet together in one place to carry on the worship of God, to glorify him, and edify one another [m]; that it is not national, provincial, or parochial, but congregational; that its offices or officers are only these two plain ones, Bishops, or Overseers or Elders, and Deacons [n]; where you will find nothing of the rabble of the Romish hierarchy; not a syllable of archbishops, archdeacons, deans, prebends, priests, chantors, rectors, vicars, curates, &c. there you will observe laws and rules of Christ, the sole head of the church, his own appointing, for the better ordering and regulating affairs; rules about the reception and rejection of members, for the laying on or taking off censures, for admonitions and excommunications; all which are to be done by the joint suffrage of the church.

5*thly*, If the inquiry is about the Ordinances of the Gospel, *stand in the ways and see, and ask for the old paths*, in which the saints formerly trod; if it is about the ordinance of the Lord's-supper, the scriptures will inform you of the

original

---

[k] Acts xxiv. 16. John v. 28, 29. Acts xvii. 31. Rev. xx. 12. 2 Cor. v. 10.
[l] Rom i. 25. Acts xvii. 29. John iv. 24. 1 Cor. xiv. 40.
[m] Ephes. i. 1. 1 Cor. xi. 20.    [n] Phil. i. 1.

original inftitution of this ordinance by Chrift, of the nature, ufe, and intent of it; that it is to fhew forth the death of Chrift till he come again; to commemorate his fufferings and facrifice, to reprefent his body broken, and his blood fhed for the fins of his people; and that if any one is defirous of partaking of it, he fhould firft examine himfelf whether he has true faith in Chrift, and is capable of difcerning the Lord's body °. If it is concerning the ordinance of baptifm, by confulting the facred oracles you will eafily perceive that this is of God, and not of man; that it is to be done in water; that the form of adminiftration is in the name of the Father, and of the Son, and of the holy Ghoft; that the fubjects of it are believers in Chrift, and the mode by immerfion; and that the whole is warranted by the commiffion and example of our Lord *. But,

1. If there is any doubt about the fubjects of this ordinance, whether they are infants or adult perfons, *ftand in the ways and fee, and afk for the old paths*; not which fathers and councils have marked out, but which the fcriptures point unto, and in which John the Baptift, Chrift and his apoftles, have trod. We do not decline looking into the three firft centuries of chriftianity, commonly reckoned the pureft ages of it; we readily allow, that Infant-baptifm was talked of in the third century; it was then moved in the *African* churches; but that it was practifed is not proved. I will not fay it is improbable that any were then baptized; but this I affirm, it is not certain that any were; as yet, it has not been proved: and as for the writers of the two firft centuries, not a word of it is mentioned by them. And had it, had any thing dropped from their pens that looked like it, and could by artifice be wire-drawn to the countenance of it, we fhould not think ourfelves obliged to embrace it on that account; what if *Hermas*, or *Barnabas*, or *Ignatius*, or *Polycarp*, or the two *Clements* of *Rome* and *Alexandria*, or *Irenæus*, or *Juftin Martyr*, or *Tatian*, or *Theophilus* of *Antioch*, or *Athenagoras*, or *Minutius Felix* declared it, any one or more of them, as their opinion, that infants ought to be baptized, (though none of them have) yet we fhould not think ourfelves bound to receive it, any more than the many abfurdities, weak reafonings, and filly notions thefe men gave into; and even could it be proved, (as it cannot) that it is an inconteftable fact that Infant-baptifm was adminiftered by one or more of them, it would only ferve to prove this fad truth, known by other inftances, how foon corruptions in faith and practice got into the chriftian churches, even prefently after the times of the apoftles; nay, the myftery of iniquity began to work in their days. Wherefore, in order to get fatisfaction in this point,

Look

° Matt. xxvi. 26—28. 1 Cor. xi. 24—29.
* Matt. xxi. 25. and iii. 6, 11, 16. and xxviii. 19.

Look over the accounts of the administration of the ordinance of baptism by *John*, the first administrator of it, and see if you can find that any infants were baptized by him. We are told, that *there went out to him Jerusalem, and all Judea, and all the region round about Jordan*; that is, the inhabitants of these places, great numbers of them; but surely these could not be infants, nor any among them, that *went out to John* to hear him preach, or be baptized by him: it is added, *and were baptized of him in Jordan, confessing their sins*: these also could not be infants, but adult persons, who being made truly sensible of sin, and having true repentance for it, frankly and ingenuously confessed it; which infants are not capable of. *John* preached the baptism of repentance, and required repentance previous to it, and even fruits meet for it, and evidential of it; and when the Pharisees and Sadducees came to his baptism, who also could not be infants, he objects to them, because not good men and penitent; and even though they were capable of pleading that they were the children of *Abraham*, and the seed of that great believer [q]. And indeed the notion that is advanced in our day is a very idle one, that infants must be baptized, because the seed of believers. Are not all mankind the seed of believers? Has not *God made of one man's blood all nations that are upon the face of the earth*? Were not *Adam* and *Eve* believers in Christ, to whom the first promise and declaration of a Messiah were made? And do not all men spring from them? Or come we lower to *Noah*, the father of the new world, who was a perfect man, and found grace in the sight of God; do not all men descend from him? Turks, Jews, Pagans and Papists, are all the seed of believers, and at this rate ought to be baptized: and as for immediate believers and unbelievers, their seed by birth are upon an equal foot, and are in no wise better one than another, or have any preference the one to the other, or have by birth any claim to a gospel privilege or blessing the other has not; the truth of the matter is, that they are equally by nature children of wrath.

Look farther into the account of baptism as administered by Christ, or rather by his orders, and see if you can find an infant there. *John*'s disciples come to him, and say, *Rabbi, he that was with thee beyond Jordan, to whom thou bearest witness, behold the same baptizeth, and all men come to him* [r]. These also could not be infants that came to him and were baptized; and besides, who they were that were baptized by him, or by his orders, we are afterwards told, and their characters are given; *Jesus made and baptized more disciples than John* [s] : first he made them disciples, and then baptized them, or ordered them to be baptized, and a disciple of Christ is one that has learnt him, and the way of salvation by him; who is taught to deny sinful, civil and righteous self for Christ; and such were the persons baptized in the times of Christ, who must be adult ones; and

with

---

[q] Matt. iii. 5—9.    [r] John iii. 26.    [s] John iv. 1.

with this his practice agrees the commission he gave in *Matthew* xxviii. 19. where he orders teaching before baptizing; and such teaching as issues in believing, with which compare *Mark* xvi. 16. True indeed, he says ', *suffer little children to come unto me, and forbid them not*; but they were admitted to come to him, not to be baptized by him, of which there is not one syllable, nor the least intimation, but to lay his hands on them and pray, or be touched by him, very probably to heal them of diseases that might attend them. However, it seems reasonable to conclude, that the apostles knew nothing of any such practice as Infant-baptism, enjoined, practised, or countenanced by Christ, or they would never have forbid the bringing of infants to him; and our Lord saying nothing of it when such a fair opportunity offered, looks very darkly upon it.

Once more; look over the accounts of the administration of Baptism by the apostles of Christ, and observe who they were that were baptized by them. We read indeed of housholds baptized by them; but inasmuch as there are many families that have no infants in them, nothing can be concluded from hence in favour of Infant-baptism; it should be first proved that there were infants in these housholds, before any such consequence can be drawn from them: and besides, it will appear upon a review of them, that not infants but adult persons in the several instances are intended. *Lydia*'s houshold consisted of *brethren*, whom the apostles *comforted*; who could not be infants, but adult persons; we have no account of any other, no other are named; if any other can, let them be named. The Jailor's houshold were such, to whom the word of God was spoken, who believed in God, and rejoiced with him. *Stephanas*'s houshold, which is the only other that is mentioned, is thought by some to be the same with the Jailor's; but, if not, it is certain that it consisted of adult persons, such who addicted themselves to the ministry of the saints ". It will be easy to observe, that the first persons that were baptized after our Lord's resurrection and ascension, were such as were pricked to the heart, repented of their sins, and gladly received the gospel; such were the three thousand who were baptized, and added to the church in one day. The Samaritans, hearing *Philip* preach the things concerning the kingdom of God, were baptized, both men and women. The instance of the Eunuch is notorious; this man was a Jewish proselyte, a serious and devout man, was reading in the prophecy of *Isaiah* when *Philip* joined his chariot; who, after conversation with him, desired baptism of him, to whom *Philip* replied, that if he believed with all his heart he might be baptized; intimating, that if he did not, notwithstanding his profession of religion, and external seriousness and devotion, he had no right to that ordinance; and upon professing his faith in Christ he was baptized.

*Cornelius*

' Matt. xix. 14.   " Acts xvi. 15, 32—34, 40.   ' Cor. i. 16. and xvi. 15.

*Cornelius* and his family, and those in his house, to whom *Peter* preached, and on whom the holy Ghost fell, were ordered by him to be baptized, having received the holy Ghost, and for that reason. And the Corinthians, hearing the apostle *Paul*, and believing in Christ he preached, were baptized [v]: from all which instances it appears, that not infants but adult persons were the only ones baptized by the apostles of Christ. Now, though we might justly demand a precept or command of Christ to be shewn, expresly enjoining the baptism of infants, before we can go into such a practice, since it is used as a part of religious worship; for which we ought to have a *thus saith the Lord*: yet if but one single precedent could be given us, one instance produced; or if it could be proved that any one infant was ever baptized by *John* the Baptist, by Christ, or by his orders, or by his apostles, we should think ourselves obliged to follow such an example; let this be shewn us, and we have done; we will shut up the controversy, and say no more. Strange! that in the space of sixty or seventy years, for such a course of time ran out from the first administration of baptism to the close of the canon of the scripture, that in all the accounts of baptism in it, not a single instance of Infant-baptism can be given! upon the whole, we must be allowed to say, and if not, we must and will take the liberty to say, that Infant-baptism is an unscriptural practice; and that there is neither precept nor precedent for it in all the word of God.

2. If the doubt is concerning the Mode of Baptism, whether it is to be performed by immersion of the whole body, or by sprinkling or pouring a little water on the face; take the same course as before, *ask for the old paths*; inquire how this ordinance was antiently administered in the times of *John*, Christ, and his apostles. I shall not appeal unto, nor send you to inquire the signification of the Greek word; though all men of learning and sense have acknowledged, that the primary meaning of the word is *to dip* or *plunge*; but this ordinance was appointed not for men of learning only, but for men and women also of the meanest capacities, and of the most plain and simple understandings: wherefore let all inquiring persons consult

The scriptural instances of Baptism; read over the accounts of baptism as administered by *John*, and you will find that he baptized in *Jordan*: ask yourselves why a *river* was chose, when a *bason* of water would have done, had it been performed by sprinkling or pouring; try if you can bring yourselves to believe that *John* was not in the river *Jordan*, only on the banks of it, from whence he took water, and poured or sprinkled it; and if you can seriously and in good earnest conclude (with a grave divine) that if he was in the river, he had in his hand a scoop, or some such instrument, and with it threw the water over the people

as

[v] Acts ii. 37, 41, 42. and viii. 12, 37, 38. and x. 47. and xviii. 8.

as they stood on the banks of the river on both sides of him, and so baptized them in shoals. Look over the baptism of Christ by *John*, and see if you can persuade yourselves that Christ went ancle deep, or a little more, into the river *Jordan*, and *John* stood upon a bank and poured a little water on his head, as messieurs painter and engraver have described them; or whether the most easy and natural sense of the whole is not this, that they both went into the river *Jordan*, and *John* baptized our Lord by immersion; which when done, he straightway came up *out* of the water, which supposes him to have been *in* it; and then the Spirit descended on him as a dove, and a voice was heard from his Father, saying, *This is my beloved Son* [x]. Carefully read over those words of the evangelist [y], *and John also was baptizing in Ænon near to Salim, because there was much water there*; and try if you can make *much* water to signify *little*; or *many waters*, as the words may be literally rendered, only a little rill, or some small rivulets of water, not sufficient to cover a man's body; though the phrase is used even of the waters of the great sea [z]; and persuade yourselves, if you can, that the reason of the choice of this place, because of *much water* in it, was not for baptism, as says the text, but for the convenience of men, their camels and asses on which they came to hear *John*; of which it says not one word. To which add the instance of the eunuch's baptism, in which we are told [a], that both *Philip and the eunuch went down into the water*; and that when baptism was administered, they *came up out of the water:* now try whether you can really believe that this great man, who left his chariot, went down with *Philip* into the water, ancle or knee deep, only to have a little water sprinkled and poured upon him, and then came out of it, when in this way the ordinance might as well have been administered in his chariot; or whether it is not most reasonable to believe, from the bare narrative, from the very letter of the text, that their going down into the water was in order that the ordinance might be administered by immersion; and that when *Philip* had baptized the Eunuch this way, they both came up out of the water: as for that poor weak criticism, that this is to be understood of going to and from the water-side; it may be asked what they should go thither for, what reason was there for it, if done by sprinkling? Besides, it is entirely destroyed by the observation the historian makes before this, that *they came unto a certain water* [b]; to the water-side; and therefore when they went down, it must be into the water itself; it could not with any propriety be said, that when they were come to the water-side, after that they went to the water-side. But to proceed,

Consider

---

[x] Matt. iii. 6, 16, 17.    [y] John iii. 23.    [z] Sept. in Psal. lxxvii. 19. and cvii. 83.
[a] Acts viii. 38, 39.    [b] Verse 36.

Consider the figurative or metaphorical Baptisms mentioned in scripture. Baptism is said 'to be a like figure to *Noah*'s ark, in which eight souls were saved by water; there is a likeness, an agreement between the one and the other; now see if you can make out any likeness between the ark upon the waters and baptism, as performed by sprinkling; whereas it soon appears as performed by immersion, in which persons are covered in water, as *Noah* and his family in the ark were, when the fountains of the great deep were broke up under them, and the windows of heaven were opened above them: think with yourselves, whether sprinkling or immersion best agrees with this, that baptism should be called the antitype to it; to which may be added, that *Noah* and his family, when shut up in the ark, were, as it were, buried there; and baptism by immersion is a representation of a burial. The passage of the Israelites through the Red sea is called a *being baptized in the cloud and in the sea*[d]; but why should it be so called? what is there in that account that looks like sprinkling? There is that resembles immersion; for when the waters of the sea stood up on both sides of them, as a wall, and a cloud covered them, they were as people immersed in water; and besides, their going down into the sea, and passing through it, and coming up out of it on the other side; if it may not be litterally called an immersion, it was very much like an immersion into water, and an emersion out of it; and both that and baptism represent a burial and resurrection. The sufferings of our Lord, are called a *baptism*; you would do well to consider whether only sprinkling a few drops of water on the face, or an immersion into it, best represents the abundance and greatness of our Lord's sorrows and sufferings, for which reason they are called a baptism; and the rather, since they are signified by the waters coming into his soul, and by his coming into deep waters, where the floods overflowed him[e]. Once more, the extraordinary donation of the holy Ghost on the day of Pentecost is called a baptism, or a being *baptized with the holy Ghost, and with fire*; which was done when the house in which the apostles were, was filled with a mighty wind, and cloven tongues, as of fire, sat upon them[f]: it deserves your consideration, whether this wonderful affair, and this large abundance of the Spirit, is not better expressed by baptism, as administered in a large quantity of water, than with a little. To add no more;

Consider the nature, use, and end of Baptism; it is a burial; and the use and end of it are, to represent the burial and resurrection of our Lord Jesus Christ; hence the phrase of *being buried with him in baptism*[g]: see if you can make any thing like a burial when this ordinance is administered by sprinkling;

can

* 1 Pet. iii. 20, 21.  d 1 Cor. x. 1, 2.  e Luke xii. 50. Psalm lxix. 1, 2.
f Matt. iii. 11. Acts i. 5. and ii. 1, 2, 3.  g Rom. vi. 4. Colos. ii. 12.

can you perfuade yourfelves, that a corps is properly buried, when only a little duft is fprinkled on its face? on the other hand, you will eafily perceive a lively reprefentation of a burial, when the ordinance is performed by immerfion; a perfon is then covered with water, and when he comes out of it, it clearly reprefents our Lord's refurrection, and the believer's rifing again to newnefs of life. Upon the whole, having afked for *the good old paths*, and found them, walk herein, abide by this ancient practice of baptifm by immerfion; a practice which continued for the fpace of thirteen hundred years at leaft, without any exception, unlefs a few bed-ridden people in the times of Cyprian[b], who received baptifm on their fick and death-beds, fancying there was no atonement for fins after baptifm, and therefore deferred it till fuch time.

But after all, let me advife you in the words of our text to inquire *where is the good way*, or *the better way*; for though the ordinance of baptifm, and every other, is a good way, there is a better way. This is a way of duty, but not of life and falvation; it is a command of Chrift, to be obeyed by all believers in him, but not to be trufted in and depended on; it is effential to church-communion, but not to falvation; it is indeed no indifferent thing whether it is performed or no; this ought not to be faid or thought of any ordinance of Chrift; or whether in this or the other manner, or adminiftered to this or the other fubject. It ought to be done as Chrift has directed it fhould; but when it is beft done, it is no faving ordinance: this I the rather mention, to remove from us a wicked and a foolifh imputation, that we make an idol of this ordinance, and place our confidence and dependence on it, and put it in the room of the Saviour. I call it wicked, becaufe falfe; and foolifh, becaufe contrary to an avowed and well-known principle on which we proceed, namely, that faith in Chrift alone for falvation is a prerequifite to baptifm: can any man in his fenfes think that we depend on this ordinance for falvation, when we require that a perfon fhould believe in Chrift, and profefs that he believes in Chrift alone for falvation, before he is baptized; or otherwife we judge he is not a fit fubject? but on the other hand, thofe that infinuate fuch a notion as this, would do well to confider, if their own conduct does not befpeak fomething of this kind; or otherwife what means the ftir and buftle that is made, when a child is ill, and not yet fprinkled? what means fuch language as this, "run, fetch the minifter to baptize the child, the child's a "dying?" Does it not look as if this was thought to be a faving bufinefs, or as if a child could not be faved unlefs it is fprinkled; and which, when done, they are quite eafy and fatisfied about its ftate? But to leave this, and as

the

[b] Clinici.

the apoſtle ſays, *yet ſhew I unto you a more excellent way*[1], which is *Jeſus Chriſt, the way, the truth, and the life.*

Chriſt is the way of ſalvation, which the goſpel, and the miniſters of it, point out to men; and he is the only way of ſalvation, there is ſalvation in him, and in no other; this is what the whole Bible centers in; this is the ſum and ſubſtance of it; this is the *faithful ſaying, and worthy of all acceptation, that Chriſt came into the world to ſave the chief of ſinners.* He is the way of acceſs to the Father, nor can any come to God but by him; he is the mediator between God and man, and through him there is acceſs with confidence by the faith of him. He is the way of acceptance with God: we have nothing to render us acceptable unto God; we are black in ourſelves with original and actual ſin, and are only comely in Chriſt; our acceptance is in the beloved. God is well pleaſed with him, and with all that are conſidered in him; their perſons and their ſacrifices are acceptable to God through him. He is the way of conveyance of all grace, and the bleſſings of it to us. All was given originally to him, and to us in him; and from him, and through him we receive it, even out of his fulneſs, grace for grace; all ſpiritual bleſſings are with him, and come to us from him; all grace paſſes through his hands; the firſt we have, and all the afterſupplies of it; yea, *the gift of God, eternal life, is through Jeſus Chriſt our Lord.* And he is the way to heaven and eternal happineſs; he has entered into it with his own blood already, and has opened a way by it for his people, into the holieſt of all; he is gone beforehand as their forerunner, and has taken poſſeſſion of heaven for them; he is now preparing a place for them there, and will come again and take them to himſelf, and introduce them into his kingdom and glory. And he is a plain, pleaſant, and ſafe way; plain to him that underſtands, and has a ſpiritual knowledge of him, even though but of a very mean capacity; for this is *a way in which men, though fools, ſhall not err*; and it is a very delightful one; what more delightful than to live by faith on Chriſt, or to walk by faith in him, as he hath been received. And a very ſafe one, it muſt needs be; none ever periſhed that believed in Chriſt; he is the living way, all in this way live, none in this way die; though it is a ſtrait gate and narrow way, yet it ſurely and ſafely leads to eternal life; and though it is ſometimes called a *new* way, yet not becauſe newly contrived, for it is as ancient in this reſpect as the counſel and covenant of peace; nor newly revealed, for it was made known to *Adam* immediately after the fall; nor newly made uſe of, for all the Old Teſtament ſaints were directed in this way, and walked in it, and were ſaved by the grace of our Lord Jeſus Chriſt, the Lamb ſlain from the foundation of the world, as well as we; but becauſe it is more clearly manifeſted now, and more largely

and

[1] 1 Cor. xii. 31.

and frequently walked in: otherwise it is the good old path to be asked for; there never was any other way of salvation, or ever will be. I go on,

II. To consider the encouragement given to take the direction, and make the inquiry as above; and in this I shall be very brief; it lies in this clause, *and ye shall find rest for your souls.*

There is a rest for souls to be enjoyed in ordinances, when men are arrived to satisfaction about them, and submit unto them in a becoming manner; when a man has carefully and conscientiously searched the scriptures, and is come to a point about an ordinance, his mind is easy, which before was distracted and confused; and he is the more easy in that he has acted the faithful part to himself and truth; and I cannot see how persons can have rest in their minds, who have not stood in the ways and looked about them, searched the scriptures, and inquired for *the good old paths*; and in consequence of an honest inquiry, walk therein; to such, *wisdom's ways are ways of pleasantness, and her paths paths of peace*; there is great peace enjoyed *in* them, though not *from* them; a believer comes to an ordinance, being upon inquiry satisfied about it, as for instance, the ordinance of baptism; he, I say, comes to it with delight, passes through it with pleasure, and goes away from it as the eunuch did, *rejoicing.*

There is rest for souls to be enjoyed in doctrines, which a man does enjoy, when upon a diligent search after truth, he finds it, and is at a point about it; a man that is tossed to and fro with every wind of doctrine, is like a wave of the sea, always restless and uneasy; *a double-minded man*, that halts between two opinions, and sometimes inclines to one, and sometimes to the other, *is unstable in all his ways*, and has no true rest in his mind; a man that is carried about with divers and strange doctrines, is like a meteor in the air, sometimes here, and sometimes there; a good thing it is to have the heart established in and with the doctrines of grace; and the way to this is to *search the scriptures, to see whether these things be so or no*; which when seriously and faithfully done, the issue is peace of conscience, rest in the mind.

But above all, true rest for the soul is to be had in Christ, and such who ask for the good and better way find it in him, nor is it to be found in any other; Christ is that to believers, as *Noah*'s ark was to the dove, which could find no rest for the sole of its feet, till it returned thither: there is rest in Christ, and no where else, and he invites weary souls to come to him for it; his words are [k], *Come unto me, all ye that labour and are heavy laden, and I will give you rest; take my yoke upon you, and learn of me, for I am meek and lowly in heart, and ye shall find rest unto your souls;* which last clause is the same with this in our text, and

our

[k] Matt. xi. 28, 29.

Lord seems to have had respect unto it, and to have took his language from it; and what peace and rest do weary souls find in Christ, when their faith is led to his person, fulness, blood, sacrifice and righteousness? and such who are made partakers of spiritual rest here, shall enjoy an eternal one hereafter, for still *there remains a rest to the people of God*[l].

To conclude; let us bless God for the scriptures, that we have such a way-mark to direct us, and point out unto us the way in which we should go; let us make use of them; let us search the scriptures daily and diligently, and the rather, since they testify of Christ, of his person, offices, of his doctrines and ordinances. These are *the more sure word of prophecy, to which we do well to take heed, as to a light shining in a dark place*; these are *a lamp unto our feet, and a light unto our paths*, both with respect to the way of salvation, and to the way of our duty. These guide us to the old paths, and shew us where is the good way in which we should walk; and when we are tempted to turn to the right hand, or the left, it is best to hearken to the voice of the word behind us, *saying, 'This is the way, walk in it*"*. The Bible has the best claim to antiquity of any book in the world; and the gospel, and the truths of it, have the greatest marks and evidences of it upon them. Error is old, but truth is more ancient than that; the gospel is the *everlasting gospel*; it was even *ordained before the world unto our glory*"; and the ordinances of it, as administered in the times of Christ and his apostles, should be received and submitted to, as there delivered; and we should walk in them as we have Christ and his apostles for an example: but above all things, our concern should be to walk in Him, the way; there is no way better, nor any so good as he; seek rest for your souls in him, and no where else; not in the law, and the works of it, there is none there; not in the world, and the things of it, *this is not your rest, it is polluted*°; but seek it in Christ, where you will find it here, and more fully enjoy it with him hereafter.

---

[l] Heb. iv. 9.   " John v. 39.   2 Pet. i. 19.   Psal. cxix. 105.   Isai. xxx. 21.
Rev. xiv. 6.   1 Cor. ii. 7.   ° Micah ii. 10.

*Baptism*

*Baptism a Divine Commandment to be Observed.*

Being a SERMON Preached at BARBICAN, *October* 9, 1765. at the BAPTISM of the Reverend Mr ROBERT CARMICHAEL, Minister of the Gospel in EDINBURGH.

## The PREFACE.

THE following discourse was not designed for the press; had it, the subject of it would have been a little more enlarged upon; and, perhaps, might have appeared in a little better dress; but as the publication of it is become necessary, I chose to let it go just as it was delivered, as nearly in the very words and expressions, as my memory could assist me; the sense, I am sure, is no where departed from; that it might not be said, that any thing that was spoken is concealed, changed, or altered. The warmest solicitations of my friends would never have prevailed upon me to have made it public, being unwilling to renew the controversy about baptism unnecessarily; and being determined only to write in self-defence, when attacked, or whenever the controversy is renewed by others; for I am very sensible, that the argument on both sides is greatly exhausted, and scarce any thing new can be expected, that is serious and pertinent: but the rude attack upon the sermon in two letters in a news-paper, determined me at once to send it out into the world, as being a sufficient confutation of itself, without any remarks at all, of the lies and falshoods, calumnies, cavils and impertinencies, with which the letters abound; whereby it will appear to every reader, how falsly that writer charges me *with railing against my brethren, and the whole christian world*; and how injuriously he represents me, as treating all that differ from me as *fools, unlearned, ignorant of the scriptures, and unclean.* It is hard we cannot practise what we believe, and speak in vindication of our practice, without being abused, vilified and insulted in a public news-paper; is this treating us as *brethren*, as the writer of the letters, in a canting way, affects to call us? And how does this answer to the false character of *Candidus*, he assumes? I shall not let myself down so low, nor do I think it fitting and decent to go into, and carry on a religious controversy in a news-paper, and especially with so worthless a writer, and without a name. This base and cowardly way of writing, is like the Indians manner of fighting; who set up an hideous yell, pop off their guns behind bushes and hedges, and then run away and hide themselves in the thickets. However, if the publication of this discourse should be of any service to relieve or strengthen the minds of any, with respect to their duty in the observance of the ordinance of baptism, I am content to bear the indignities of men, and shall reckon it an over-balance to all their reproaches and insults. *J. G.*

Being about to administer the Ordinance of Baptism, before we enter upon the administration of it, I shall drop a few words on the occasion, from a passage of scripture you will find in

1 JOHN V. 3.

*For this is the love of God, that we keep his commandments, and his commandments are not grievous.*

WHAT I shall say in the following discourse, will much depend upon the sense of the word *commandments*; by which are meant, not the ten commandments, or the commandments of the moral law delivered by *Moses* to the children of *Israel*; which, though they are the commands of God, and to be observed by christians under the present dispensation; since we are *not without law to God, but under the law to Christ* [a]; and are to be kept from a principle of love to God, for *the end of the commandment is charity*, or love, *out of a pure heart, and of a good conscience, and of faith unfeigned* [b]; yet these commands are not easy of observation, through the weakness of the flesh, or corruption of nature; nor can they be perfectly kept by any of *Adam*'s fallen race; *for there is not a just man upon earth, that doeth good and sinneth not* [c]; and he that *offends in one point is guilty of all* [d]; and is exposed to the curse and condemnation of the law, which runs in this tenor, *Cursed is every one that continueth not in all things which are written in the book of the law, to do them* [e]; hence this law in general is called a fiery law, the letter which kills, and the ministration of condemnation and death, which make it terrible to offenders; however, it may be delighted in by believers in Christ after the inward man: nor are the commandments of the ceremonial law intended, which being many and numerous, were burdensom; especially to carnal men, who were frequently ready to say concerning them,

[a] 1 Cor. ix. 21. [b] 1 Tim. i. 5. [c] Eccles. vii. 20. [d]
[e] Gal. iii. 10.

them, *What a weariness is it?* One of its precepts, circumcision, is called *a yoke*, which, says the apostle *Peter*, *neither our fathers nor we were able to bear* [f]; because it bound persons to keep the whole law, which they could not do; and the whole is said to be a *yoke of bondage* [g], and consequently its commandments grievous; besides this law was abrogated before the apostle *John* wrote this epistle, and its commandments were not to be kept; Christ had *abolished* this *law of commandments contained in ordinances*; and there is now a *disannulling* of the whole of it, because of its *weakness* and *unprofitableness* [h]: rather the commandments of faith and love the apostle speaks of in chap. iii. 23. may be designed; *And this is his commandment, that we should believe in the name of his Son Jesus Christ, and love one another, as he gave us commandment:* these were exhortations, injunctions and commands of Christ to his disciples, which were to be kept by them, and were not grievous. *Ye believe in God,* says he [i], *believe also in me*; and again, *A new commandment I give unto you, that ye love one another, as I have loved you* [k]; but inasmuch as Christ, as lawgiver in his church, has appointed some special and peculiar laws and ordinances to be observed, and which he calls *his* commandments, *he that hath my commandments and keepeth them, he it is that loveth me* [l]; very agreeably to our text; and after he had given his apostles a commission to preach and baptize, he adds, *teaching them to observe all things whatsoever I have commanded you* [m]; and whereas, among these commandments and ordinances, baptism and the Lord's supper are the chief and principal, I chuse to understand the text of them [n]; and since we are about to administer the first of these at this time, I shall confine my discourse chiefly to that, and shall attempt the following things.

I. To shew that baptism, water-baptism, is a command of God and Christ, or a divine command.
II. That being a divine command, it ought to be kept and observed.
III. The encouragement to keep it; it is the love of God, and it is a commandment not grievous.

I. The

---

[f] Acts xv. 10.   [g] Gal. v. 1.   [h] Ephes. ii. 15. Heb. vii. 18.   [i] John xiv. 1.
[k] John xiii. 34.   [l] John xiv. 21.   [m] Matt. xxviii. 20.

[n] Let the commandments be what they may, which are chiefly intended in the text; yet since water-baptism is a commandment of God, and allowed to be such, and the rest of the commandments mentioned are not denied to be, nor excluded from being the commandments of God; there can be no impropriety in treating on the commandment of baptism particularly and singly from this passage of scripture; and it might have escaped, one would have thought, a sneer, though it has not, of a scurrilous writer, in a late news-paper, referred to in the preface.

# BAPTISM A DIVINE COMMANDMENT

I. The ordinance of water-baptism is a divine command. *John*, the forerunner of our Lord, was the first administrator of it, and from thence was called *the Baptist*; and he did not administer it of his own mind and will, but had a mission and commission from God to do it; *There was a man sent from God, whose name was John*; and he was sent by him, not to preach the gospel only, but to baptize; for so he himself says, *he that sent me to baptize with water, the same said unto me*, &c°. Hence Christ put this question to the chief priests and elders of the Jews, *the baptism of John, whence was it? from heaven or of men*ᵖ? this brought them into such a dilemma, that they knew not what answer to give, and chose to give none; our Lord's design by the question was to shew that *John*'s baptism was of divine institution, and not human; wherefore he charges the Pharisees and Lawyers with *rejecting the counsel of God against themselves, being not baptized of him* ᵠ, that is, of *John*; and he elsewhereʳ speaks of his baptism as a part of righteousness to be fulfilled, and was fulfilled by him. Now *John*'s baptism and Christ's were, as to the substance of them, the same; *John*'s baptism was allowed of and approved of by Christ, as appears from his submission to it; and the ordinance was confirmed by the order he gave to his apostles to administer it: one of *John*'s disciples said to his master, *Rabbi, he that was with thee beyond Jordan, to whom thou bearest witness, behold, the same baptizeth, and all men come to him* ˢ; though, as is said afterwards, *Jesus himself baptized not, but his disciples* ᵗ; that is, they baptized by his orders; and which were renewed after his resurrection from the dead, saying, *Go ye therefore, and teach all nations, baptizing them*, &cᵘ. and which orders were obeyed by his apostles, as many instances in the *Acts of the Apostles* shew; and that it was water-baptism they administered, according to Christ's instructions and directions.

In matters of worship there ought to be a command for what is done; as this ordinance of baptism is a solemn act of worship, being performed *in the name of the Father, and of the Son, and of the holy Ghost*. God is a jealous God, and especially with respect to the worship of him; nor should any thing be introduced into it but what he has commanded; and careful should we be hereof, lest he should say unto us, *who hath required this at your hands*ʷ? it is not enough that such and such things are not forbidden; for on this footing a thousand fooleries may be brought into the worship of God, which will be resented by him. When *Nadab* and *Abihu* offered strange fire to the Lord, which he commanded not, fire came down from heaven and destroyed them: we should have

a precept

---

° John i. 6, 33.    ᵖ Matt. xxi. 25, 26.    ᵠ Luke vii. 30.
ʳ Matt. iii. 15.    ˢ John iii. 26.    ᵗ John iv. 2.
ᵘ Matt. xxviii. 19.    ʷ Isai. i. 12.

a precept for what we do, and that not from men, but from God; left we incur the charge of *worshipping* God *in vain, teaching for doctrines the commandments of men*[x], and involve ourselves in the guilt of superstition, and will-worship.

Wherefore, the baptism of infants must be wrong; since there is no command of God and Christ for it; if there was any, it might be expected in the New Testament, and in that only; it is absurd to send us to the Old Testament for a command to observe a New Testament-ordinance; it is a gross absurdity to send us so far back as to the xvii[th] chapter of *Genesis*[y] for a warrant for the ordinance of baptism; we might as well be sent to the first chapter of that book; for there is no more relating to that ordinance in the one than in the other. Was there a like precept for the baptism of infants under the New Testament, as there was for the circumcision of infants under the Old Testament, there could be no objection to it; but it is an absurdity of absurdities to affirm, that baptism comes in the room of circumcision; since baptism was in force and use long before circumcision was abolished; circumcision was not abolished until the death of Christ, when that, with other ceremonies, had an end in him; but baptism was administered many years before to multitudes, by *John*, by the order of Christ, and by his apostles; now where is the good sense of saying, and with what propriety can it be said, that one thing succeeds another, as baptism circumcision, when the one, said to succeed, was in use and force long before the other ceased, it is pretended it succeeded?

If there is any precept for Infant-baptism, it must be in the New Testament; there only it can be expected, but there it cannot be found; not in *Matthew* xix. 14. *Suffer little children, and forbid them not to come unto me, for of such is the kingdom of heaven*; which is no precept, but a permission, or grant, that little children might come, or be brought unto him; but for what? not for baptism; but for that for which they were brought, and which is mentioned by the evangelist in the preceding verse, *that he should put his hands on them,*

*and*

---

[x] Matt. xv. 9.

[y] That we are ever referred to this chapter, for a proof of Infant-baptism, is denied, and pronounced a wilful misrepresentation, by the above mentioned writer, in his second letter in the newspaper. This man must have read very little in the controversy, to be ignorant of this. The very last writer that wrote in the controversy, that I know of, calls the covenant made with *Abraham* in that chapter, "the grand turning point, on which the issue of the controversy very much depends; "and that if *Abraham*'s covenant, which included his infant-children, and gave them a right to "circumcision, was not the covenant of grace; then he freely confesses, that the *main ground*, on "which they assert *the right of infants to baptism*, is taken away; and, consequently, the principal "arguments in support of the doctrine, are overturned." Bostwick's Fair and Rational Vindication of the Right of Infants to the Ordinance of Baptism, &c. p. 19.

*and pray*, or give them his blessing; as it seems it was usual in those times, and with those people, as formerly, to bring their children to persons venerable for religion and piety, to be blessed by them in this way; and such an one they might take Jesus to be, though they might not know he was the Messiah. Two other evangelists say, they were brought unto him *that he should touch them*; as he sometimes touched diseased persons when he healed them; and these children might be diseased, and brought to him to be cured of their diseases; however, not to be baptized by Christ, for he baptized none; they would rather have brought them to the disciples, had it been for such a purpose; and had it been the practice of the apostles to baptize infants, they would not have refused them; and our Lord's intire silence about Infant-baptism at this time, when there was so fair an opportunity to speak of it, and enjoin it, had it been his will, has no favourable aspect on that practice. The reason given by Christ for the permission of infants to come to him, *for of such is the kingdom of heaven*, is figurative and metaphorical; and not to be understood of the infants themselves, but of such as they; of such who are comparable to them for their humble deportment, and harmless lives; or to use our Lord's words elsewhere, such who are *converted, and become as little children*, Matt. xviii. 2 [y].

Nor is a command for Infant-baptism contained in the commission to baptize, *Matthew* xxviii. 19. *Go ye, therefore, and teach all nations, baptizing them in the name of the Father, and of the Son, and of the holy Ghost*. It is argued, that " since all nations are to be baptized, and infants are a part of them, then, " according to the command of Christ, they are to be baptized." But it should be observed, that the commission is indeed *to teach* all nations, but not to

---

[y] The above letter-writer, in the news-paper, observes, "that the *kingdom of heaven* signifies " either the kingdom, or church of Christ here, or the kingdom of glory above. If the former, " they are declared, by Christ himself, real subjects of his among men; if the latter, if members " of the invisible church, why not of the visible?" But, in fact, they themselves are not intended, only such as they; such who are comparable to them for meekness and humility; for freedom from malice, pride, and ambition. But admitting that the words are to be understood of infants litterally, the kingdom of heaven cannot design the kingdom, or church of Christ under the gospel dispensation, which is not national, but congregational; consisting of men gathered out of the world, by the grace of God, and who make a public profession of Christ, which infants are not capable of, and so cannot be real subjects of it; and if they were, they must have an equal right to the Lord's supper, as to baptism, of which they are equally capable. The kingdom of glory then being meant, it is asked, if members of the invisible church, why not of the visible? They may be, when it appears that they are of the invisible church, which only can be manifest by the grace of God bestowed on them; and it is time enough to talk of their baptism when that is evident; and when it is clear they have both a right unto, and meetness for the kingdom of heaven.

to *baptize* all nations; the antecedent to the relative *them*, is not *all nations*; the words ωιτα τα εθνη, *all nations*, are of the neuter gender; but αυτυς, *them*, is of the masculine, and do not agree; the antecedent is μαθητας, *disciples*, which is understood, and supposed, and contained in the word μαθητευσατε, *teach*, or *make disciples*; and the sense is, teach all nations, and baptize them that are taught, or are made disciples by teaching. If the above argument proves any thing, it would prove too much; and what proves too much, proves nothing: it would prove, that not only the infants of christians, but the infants of Turks, Jews, and Pagans, should be baptized, since they are part of all nations; yea, that every individual person in the world should be baptized, heathens, as well as christians, and even the most profligate and abandoned of mankind, since they are part of all nations [z].

And as there is no precept for the baptism of infants, so no precedent for it in the word of God. Though there was no clear and express command for it, which yet we think is necessary, and is required in such a case; yet, if there was a precedent of any one infant being baptized, we should think ourselves obliged to pay a regard unto it; but among the many thousands baptized by *John*, by Christ, or, however, by his order, and by his apostles, not one single instance of an infant being baptized can be found. We read, indeed, of *housholds* being baptized; from whence it is argued, that there might be, and it is probable there were, infants in them, who might be baptized; but it lies upon those who are of a different mind, to prove there were any in those housholds. To put us upon proving a negative, that there were none there, is unfair. However, as far as a negative can be proved, we are capable of it [a]. There are but three families usually observed, if so many; *Lydia*'s, the Jailor's,

[z] But our letter-writer says, "When the apostles received their commission, they could not under-"stand it otherwise than to baptize the *parents* that embraced the faith of Christ, through their "preaching, and all their *children* with them, as was the manner of the ministers of God in pre-"ceding ages, by circumcision;" but if they so understood it, and could not otherways understand it, it is strange they should not practice according to it, and baptize children with their parents; of which we have no one instance. By the *ministers of God in preceding ages*, I suppose, he means the priests and prophets, under the Old Testament-dispensation; but these were not the operators of circumcision, which was done by parents and others: and surely it cannot be said, it was the usual manner of ministers to baptize parents, and their children with them in those ages; and it is pretty unaccountable how they should baptize them by circumcision, as is affirmed; this is something unheard of before, and monstrously ridiculous and absurd.

[a] The above writer affirms, that my mannner of "proving the negative, was *by barely afferting* "there were no children in any of the families, mentioned in the scriptures, as baptized." The falsity of which appears by the following descriptive characters given of the persons in the several families, and the reasonings upon them.

Jailor's, and that of *Stephanas*, if not the same with the Jailor's, as some think. As for *Lydia*'s houshold, or those in her house, they were *brethren*; whom, afterwards, the apostles went to see, and whom they *comforted*; and so not infants. As for the Jailor's houshold, they were such as were capable of hearing the word preached to them, and of believing it; for it is said, *he rejoiced, believing in God with all his house* [b]: and if any man can find any other in his house, besides *all* that were in it, he must be reckoned a very sagacious person. As for the houshold of *Stephanas*, (if different from the Jailor's) it is said, that *they addicted themselves to the ministry of the saints* [c]: and whether this be understood of the ministry of the word to the saints, or of the ministration of their substance to the poor, they must be adult persons, and not infants. Seeing then there is neither precept nor precedent for Infant-baptism in the word of God, of which I defy the whole world to give one single precedent, we cannot but condemn it as unscriptural, and unwarrantable [d]. I proceed,

II. To shew that the ordinance of water-baptism, being a divine command, it ought to be kept, and observed, as directed to in the word of God.

*First*, I shall shew, by whom it is to be kept and observed. 1. By sensible, repenting sinners. *John*'s baptism was called *the baptism of repentance* [e]; because repentance was previous to it; and the very first persons that were baptized by him, were such who were sensible of their sins, repented of them, and ingenuously confessed them; for it is said, they were *baptized of him in Jordan, confessing their sins*; and whereas others applied to him for baptism, of whom he had no good opinion, he required of them, that they would first *bring forth fruits meet for repentance; and not to think with* themselves, *we have Abraham to*

---

[b] Acts xvi. 40, 34.   [c] 1 Cor. i. 16.—xvi. 15.

[d] In his turn, the writer in the news-paper, "defies me to produce one scripture precept, or precedent, for delaying the *baptism of children* of christian parents; or for baptizing adult persons, born of such parents. On this the controversy hinges." It is ridiculous to talk of a precept for delaying that which was not in being; and of a precedent for delaying that which had never been practised. If a warrant is required for baptizing adult persons, believers, it is ready at hand, *Mark* xvi. 16. and precedents enough: and we know of no precept to baptize any other, let them be born of whom they may; and as for precedents of the baptism of adult persons, born of christian parents, it cannot be expected, nor reasonably required of us; since the *Acts* of the Apostles only give an account of the planting of the first churches; and of the baptism of those of which they first consisted; and not of those that in a course of years were added to them. Wherefore, to demand instances of persons, born of christian parents, and brought up by them, as baptized in adult age, which would require length of time, is unreasonable; and if the controversy hinges on this, it ought to be at an end, and given up by them.   [e] Mark i. 4.

*to our father* [f]; since such a plea would be of no avail with him; and the very first persons that were baptized after our Lord had given to his apostles the commission to baptize, were penitent ones; for under the first sermon after this, three thousand were pricked in their heart, and cried out, *Men and brethren, what shall we do?* To whom the apostle *Peter* gave this instruction and direction: *Repent, and be baptized every one of you in the name of Jesus Christ* [g]; and accordingly, on their repentance, they were baptized. 2. This command is to be kept and observed by believers in Christ; *he that believeth and is baptized, shall be saved* [h]. Faith goes before baptism, and is a pre-requisite to it; as the various instances of baptism recorded in the scriptures shew. *Philip* went down to *Samaria*, and preached Christ there to the inhabitants of it; and *when they believed Philip, preaching the things concerning the kingdom of God, and the name of Jesus Christ, they were baptized both men and women* [i]. The same minister of the word was bid to join himself to the chariot of an Eunuch, returning from *Jerusalem*, where he had been to worship, and whom he found reading a prophecy in *Isaiah*; and said unto him, *Understandest thou what thou readest?* To which he answered, *How can I, except some man should guide me?* And being taken up into the chariot with him: from that scripture, *Philip* preached Jesus to him, his word, and ordinances, as the sequel shews; for when they came to a certain water, the Eunuch said, *See, here is water; what doth hinder me to be baptized?* And Philip said, *If thou believest with all thine heart, thou mayest.* Otherwise not, it seems; for notwithstanding his religion and devotion, without faith in Christ, he had no right to that ordinance; *He answered and said, I believe that Jesus Christ is the Son of God* [k]; upon which profession of his faith, he was baptized. The apostle *Paul* preached the gospel at *Corinth* with success; and it is observed by the historian, that *many of the Corinthians hearing, believed, and were baptized* [l]. First they heard the word, then they believed in Christ, the sum and substance of the word, and upon the profession of their faith, were baptized. 3. The ordinance of water-baptism is to be attended to, and observed by such who are the disciples of Christ; it is said that *Jesus made and baptized more disciples than John* [m]. First made them disciples, and then baptized them; that is, ordered his apostles to baptize them; with which his commission to them agrees, *Teach all nations, baptizing them*; make disciples, and baptize them that are so made. Now, what is it to be disciples of Christ? Such may be said to be so, who have learned to know Christ, and believe in him; who are taught to deny sinful self, righteous self, and civil self, for his sake, and to take up the cross and follow him, in the exercise of grace and in the discharge of duty:

[f] Matt. iii. 6—9. Acts viii. 36, 37.    [g] Acts ii. 38.    [i] Acts xviii. 8.    [h] Mark xvi. 16.    [m] John iv. 1.    [l] Acts viii. 12.

and, 4. Such as have received the Spirit of God, are proper persons to observe the ordinance of baptism, and submit unto it: *Can any man forbid water, that these should not be baptized, who have received the holy Ghost as well as we*[a]*?* as a Spirit of illumination and conviction, as a Spirit of sanctification, faith and consolation, and as a Spirit of adoption.

2*dly*, Next let us consider in what manner the ordinance of baptism is to be kept and observed: and, 1. It should be kept in faith; for *without faith it is impossible to please God; and whatsoever is not of faith, is sin*, Heb. xi. 6. Rom. xiv. 23. 2. In love, and from a principle of love to Christ, and which is the end of every commandment, and of this; *If ye love me*, says Christ, *keep my commandments*, John xiv. 15 3. It should be kept as it was at first delivered and observed: the manner in which it is to be performed and submitted to, is immersion, or covering the whole body in water; and which agrees with the primary sense of the word Βαπτίζω, which signifies *to dip* or *plunge*, as all learned men know [o]; and he must be a novice in the Greek language, that will take upon him to contradict what has been ingenuously owned by so many men of learning. Had our translators thought fit to have translated the word, which they have not in those

[a] Acts x 47.

[o] The letter-writer makes me to say, "All the world acknowledge Βαπτίζω, signifies to dip or plunge, and never to sprinkle or pour water on any thing," which is a false representation of my words, and of the manner in which they were delivered; however, this I affirm, that in all the Greek Lexicons I ever saw, and I have seen a pretty many, I do not pretend to have seen all that have been published; yet in what my small library furnishes me with, the word is always rendered in the first and primary sense by mergo, immergo, to *dip* or *plunge into*; and in a secondary and consequential sense, by abluo, lavo, to *wash*, because what is dipped is washed; and never by perfundo or aspergo, to *pour* or *sprinkle*; as the Lexicon published by *Constantine, Budæus*, &c. those of *Hadian, Junius, Plantinus, Scapula, Schrevelius*, and *Stockius*, besides a great number of critics that might be mentioned; and if this writer can produce any one Lexicographer of any note, that renders the word to *pour* or *sprinkle*, let him name him. This *ignorant scribbler* puts the following questions, "Did the Jews plunge their whole bodies in water always before they did eat? Did they dip their pots, brazen vessels and beds?" He does not suffer me to answer the questions, but answers for me, "He knows the contrary." But if I may be allowed to answer for myself, I must say, by the testimonies of the Jews themselves, and of others, I know they did; that is, when they came from market, having touched the common people, or their clothes, immersed themselves in water; so says *Maimonides* in Misn. Chagigah. c. 2. sect. 7. "If the Pharisees touched but the garments of the common people they were defiled, and needed immersion, and were obliged to it." And *Scaliger* observes, de Emend. Temp. l. 6. p. 271. "That the more superstitious part of the Jews, every day before they sat down to meat, dipped the whole body; hence the Pharisee's admiration at Christ, *Luke* xi. 38." According to the law of *Moses*, Lev xi. 32. unclean vessels were washed by putting or dipping them into water; and according to the traditions of the elders, to which our Lord refers, *Mark* vii. 4. not only brazen vessels and tables, but even beds, bolsters and pillows unclean, in a ceremonial sense, were washed by immersion in water. So the Jews say in their Misnah, or book of traditions, "A bed that is wholly defiled, a man dips it part by part." Celim, c. 26. sect. 14. See also Mikvaot, c 7. sect. 7.

those places where the ordinance of baptism is made mention of, for reasons easily to be guessed at, but have adopted the Greek word *baptize* in all such places; had they truly translated it, the eyes of the people would have been opened, and the controversy at once would have been at an end, with respect to this part of it, the mode of baptism; however we have proof sufficient that it was performed, and ought to be performed by immersion, as appears, 1. By the places where it was administered, as the river *Jordan*, where *John* baptized many, and where our Lord himself was baptized; and *Ænon*, near *Salim*, which he chose for this reason, *because there was much water there* ᵖ; now if the ordinance was administered in any other way than by immersion, what need was there to make choice of rivers and places abounding with water to baptize in? 2. By the instances of persons baptized, and the circumstances attending their baptism, as that of our Lord, of whom it is said, *When he was baptized, he went up straightway out of the water* ᵠ; which manifestly implies that he had been in it, of which there would have been no need, had the ordinance been administered to him in any other way than by immersion; as by sprinkling or pouring a little water on his head, as the painter ridiculously describes it. The baptism of the Eunuch is another instance proving baptism by immersion; when he and *Philip* were come to a certain water, and it was agreed to baptize him, it is said, *they went down both into the water, both Philip and the Eunuch, and he baptized him. And when they were come up out of the water, the Spirit of the Lord caught away Philip* ʳ. The circumstances of *going down into* the water, and *coming up out of* it, manifestly shew in what manner the Eunuch was baptized, namely, by immersion; for what reason can be given why they should go *into* the water, had it been performed in any other way ˢ? 3. The end of baptism, which

---

ᵖ Matt. iii. 6, 13.     ᵠ Matt. iii. 16.     ʳ Acts viii. 38, 39.

ˢ The above letter-writer asks, "How often must I be told, that the particle εις and εκ are in "hundreds of places in the New Testament rendered *unto* and *from?*" be it so; it follows not, that they must be so rendered here. Greek particles or prepositions have different significations, according to the words and circumstances with which they are used; nor is it as proper or a more just reading of the words, "they went down *unto* the water and came up *from* it;" it is neither proper nor just; for before this, they were expressly said to *come to* a certain water, to the water-side; wherefore when they went down, they went not *unto* it, if they were there before, but *into* it; as it must be allowed the preposition sometimes, at least, signifies; and circumstances require that it should be so rendered here, let it signify what it may elsewhere; and this determines the sense of the other preposition, that it must and ought to be rendered *out of*; for as they went down *into* the water, when they came up, it must be *out of* it. What he means by the strange question that follows, "What will he make of Christ's going *into a mountain?*" I cannot devise, unless he thinks the translation of *Luke* vi. 12 is wrong, or nonsense, or both; but has this wiseacre never heard or read of a cave in a mountain, into which men may go, and properly be said to go *into* the mountain; and such an one it is highly probable our LORD went into, to pray alone; such as the cave in mount Horeb,

508    BAPTISM A DIVINE COMMANDMENT

which is to reprefent the burial and refurrection of Chrift, cannot be anfwered any other way than by immerfion; that it is an emblem of the burial and refurrection of Chrift, and of the burial and refurrection of believers in him, is clear from *Rom.* vi. 4. *Colofs.* ii. 12. *buried with him by baptifm*, and *in baptifm.* Now only an immerfion or covering of the whole body in water, and not pouring or fprinkling a little water on the face, can be a reprefentation of a burial; will any man in his fenfes fay, that a corps is buried, when only a little duft or earth is fprinkled or poured on its face? 4. The figurative baptifms, or the allufions made to baptifm in fcripture, fhew in what manner it was adminiftered; the paffage of the Ifraelites under the cloud, and through the fea, is called a being *baptized in the cloud and in the fea*[t]; and with great propriety may it be called a baptifm, as that is by immerfion; for the waters ftanding up as a wall on each fide of them, through which, and the cloud over their heads, under which they paffed, they were like perfons immerfed in water [*]: likewife the overwhelming fufferings of Chrift are fitly called a baptifm, in allufion to baptifm by immerfion. *I have a baptifm to be baptized with*, fays he; *and how am I ftraitened until it be accomplifhed*[v]? and which fufferings of Chrift, in prophetic language, agreeable to baptifm by immerfion, are thus defcribed; *I am come into deep waters, where the floods overflow me*[x]. Once more; the extraordinary donation of the Spirit on the day of Pentecoft, is called a being *baptized with the holy Ghoft*[y]; the emblem of which was *a rufhing mighty wind, which filled all the houfe where they were fitting*[z]; fo that they were as if immerfed into it, and covered with

Horeb, into which *Elijah* went. But his tip-top tranflation of all is that of *John's* baptizing in *Jordan*, which he fuppofes might be rendered, by baptizing the people *with the river Jordan*. This is the man that reproaches me with very freely finding fault with the tranflators; my complaint is only of a non-tranflation, not of a wrong one; but this man finds fault with the tranflation as wrong, or however thinks it may be corrected or mended, and that in more places than one.

[t] 1 Cor x. 1, 2.

[*] The letter-writer I have often referred to, affirms, that "the learned world univerfally maintain, "that the Ifraelites were no otherways *baptized in the fea*, than by being fprinkled with the fpray "of the toffing waves, agitated by the wind that blew as they paffed through the channel." Who the learned world be, that maintain this whimfical notion, I own, I am quite ignorant of, having never yet met with any learned man that ever afferted it. It is a mere conceit and a wild imagination, and contrary to the facred fcriptures, which reprefent the waves of the fea, through which the Ifraelites paffed, not as agitated and toffed about, but as ftanding unmoved, as a wall on each fide of them, whatever was the cafe in that part where the Egyptians were; *The floods*, fays the infpired writer, *ftood upright as an heap, and the depths were congealed in the heart of the fea*, Exod. xv. 8. And if there was a continual fpray of the toffing waves, as the Ifraelites paffed through the channel, how could they pafs through the fea *on dry ground?* as they are faid to do, *Exod.* xiv. 16, 22, 29. What this man fcoffs at, the celebrated *Grotius*, who is univerfally allowed to be a man of learning and fenfe, expreffes in a note on 1 *Cor.* x. 2. "*were baptized*, that is, as if they were baptized; for there "was fome likenefs in it; the cloud was over their heads, and fo water is over them that are bap"tized; the fea encompaffed the fides of them, and fo water thofe that are baptized."

[v] Luke xii. 50.   [x] Pfal. lxix. 1, 2.   [y] Acts i. 5.   [z] Acts ii. 2.

with it, and therefore very properly called *a baptism*, in allusion to baptism by immersion [a]. I go on,

III. To observe the incouragement, motives, and reasons given to keep this ordinance, as well as others. 1. The apostle says, *this is the love of God*; that is, this shews love to God; it is a plain case, that a man loves God, when he keeps his commandments; this is an evidence, that he loves not in word, and in tongue only, but in deed and in truth. Others may say that they love God and Christ; but this is the man that truly loves them, even he that *hath my commandments*, says Christ [b], *and keepeth them; he it is that loveth me:* and it is a clear case, that such a man has a sense of the love of God and Christ; the love of the Father is in him; and the love of Christ constrains him to observe his ordinances, and keep his commands; and such may expect greater manifestations of the love of God and Christ unto them; for of such that keep the commandments of Christ, he says, *I will love him, and manifest myself to him;—and my Father will love him, and we will come unto him, and make our abode with him* [c]; which is no small inducement and incouragement to an observation of the ordinances and commands of Christ, and among the rest this of baptism.

2. Another incouraging motive and reason is, the commandments of God and Christ are not grievous, hard and difficult to be performed. The Lord's supper is not; nor is baptism. What is baptism in water, to the baptism of sufferings Christ endured for us? And yet how desirous was he of accomplishing it?

[a] The same writer is pleased to represent this explanation of the baptism of the Spirit as ridiculous; but some of greater learning than he can pretend to, have so explained it, as particularly Dr Casaubon, famous for his great knowledge of the Greek language; though perhaps this *very illiberal man* will call the learned doctor a *dunce* for what he says; his words on *Acts* i. 5. are these, "though I do not disapprove of the word *baptize* being retained here, that the antithesis may be full; yet I am of opinion that regard is had in this place to its proper signification, for βαπτίζειν is to immerse, so as to *tinge* or *dip*; and in this sense the apostles were truly said to be baptized; for the house in which this was done was filled with the holy Ghost, so that the apostles seemed to be plunged into it as into a pool." In confirmation of which, he makes mention on chap. ii. 2. of an observation in a Greek commentary on it, "the wind filled the whole house, filling it like a pool; since it was promised to them (the apostles) that they should be *baptized with the Holy Ghost.*" It seems to be the same commentary, Erasmus on the place, says went under the name of *Chrysostom*, in which are these words, as he gives them, "the whole house was so filled with fire, though invisible, as a pool is filled with water."—Our scribbler, in order to expose the notion of dipping, as used in the baptism of the spirit, and fire, condescends, for once, to read *dip*, instead of *baptize*; "*John* said I indeed dip you *with* water, but one, mightier than I, cometh, he shall *dip* you *with* the holy Ghost, and with *fire*." But not only the word *baptize* should be read *dip*, but the preposition *in* should be rendered *in*; *in* water; and *in* the holy Ghost; and *in* fire; and the phrase of *dipping in fire*, is no unusual one, both in Jewish and Greek authors; as I have shewn in my Exposition of the place, and of *Acts* ii. 3. [b] John xiv. 21. [c] John xiv. 23.

it? *Luke* xii. 50. And therefore why should we think it an hardship, or be backward to comply with his will, in submitting to the ordinance of water-baptism? When *Naaman* was bid by *Elisha* to dip himself in *Jordan*, and be clean; which he resented as too little and trifling a thing, and thought he might as well have stayed in his own land, and dipped himself in one of the rivers of *Syria*; one of his servants took upon him to allay and repress the heat of his passion and resentment, by observing, that if the prophet had bid him do some great thing, which was hard and difficult to be performed, he would have gone about it readily; how much rather then, he argued, should he attend to the direction of the prophet, when he only bid him *wash in Jordan, and be clean*<sup>d</sup>? There are many that will go into baths, and plunge themselves in them for pleasure or profit, to refresh their bodies, or cure them of disorders; but if plunging in water is directed to, as an ordinance of God, then it is a grievous thing; and, indeed, no ordinance is grateful to a carnal mind; but to believers in Christ, *wisdom's ways are ways of pleasantness, and her paths paths of peace*. Christ's yoke, if it may be called so, is easy, and his burden light. Now to close with a few words

1. Let none despise this command of God, the ordinance of baptism; remember it is a command of his; be it at your peril if you do; it is hard kicking against the pricks; it is dangerous to treat with contempt any of the commands of God, and ordinances of Christ; *beware*, lest that should come upon you, and be fulfilled in you, *behold, ye despisers, and wonder, and perish*[e].
2. Let such who see it their duty to be baptized, not tarry, but immediately submit unto it; let them make haste, and delay not, to keep this command; remembering the motives, and encouragement to it.
3. Let those that yield obedience to it, do it in the name and strength of Christ; in the faith of him, from love to him, and with a view to his glory.

<sup>d</sup> 2 Kings v. 13.  <sup>e</sup> Acts xiii. 40, 41.

# INFANT - BAPTISM,

A

PART and PILLAR of POPERY:

BEING

A VINDICATION of a Paragraph in a PREFACE to a Reply to Mr CLARKE's Defence of INFANT - BAPTISM.

To which is added,

A POSTSCRIPT, containing a full and fufficient Anfwer to SIX LETTERS of CANDIDUS, on the Subjects and Mode of BAPTISM, &c.

BEING called upon, in a public manner, to give proof of what I have faid concerning Infant-baptifm, in a Preface to my reply to Mr *Clarke*'s *Defence*, &c. or to expunge it; I readily agree to the former, and fhall endeavour to explain myfelf, and defend what I have written; but it will be proper firft to recite the whole paragraph, which ftands thus: " The Pædobaptifts are ever
" reftlefs and uneafy, endeavouring to maintain and fupport, if poffible, their
" unfcriptural practice of Infant-baptifm; though it is no other than a pillar
" of Popery; that by which Antichrift has fpread his baneful influence over
" many nations; is the bafis of national churches and worldly eftablifhments;
" that which unites the church and world, and keeps them together; nor can
" there be a full feparation of the one from the other, nor a thorough reforma-
" tion in religion, until it is wholly removed: and though it has fo long and
" largely obtained, and ftill does obtain; I believe with a firm and unfhaken
" faith, that the time is haftening on, when Infant-baptifm will be no more
" practifed in the world; when churches will be formed on the fame plan they
" were in the times of the apoftles; when gofpel-doctrine and difcipline will
" be reftored to their primitive luftre and purity; when the ordinances of bap-
" tifm

"tifm and the Lord's fupper will be adminiftered as they were firft delivered, "clear of all prefent corruption and fuperftition; all which will be accom- "plifhed, when "the Lord fhall be king over all the earth, and there fhall "be one Lord and his name one." Now the whole of this confifts of feveral articles or propofitions, which I fhall re-confider in their order.

I. That "Infant-baptifm is a part and pillar of Popery; that by which An- "tichrift has fpread his baneful influence over many nations:" I ufe the phrafe Infant-baptifm here and throughout, becaufe of the common ufe of it; other- wife the practice which now obtains, may with greater propriety be called In- fant-fprinkling. That, unwritten traditions with the Papifts are equally the rule of faith and practice, as the holy fcriptures, will not be doubted of by any converfant with their writings. The council of *Trent* afferts [a], that "traditions "refpecting both faith and manners orally delivered and preferved fucceffively "in the catholic church, are to be received with equal affection of piety and "reverence as the books of the Old and New Teftament;" yea the Popifh wri- ters prefer traditions to fcripture. *Bellarmine* fays [b], "fcriptures without tradi- "tion, are neither fimply neceffary, nor fufficient, but unwritten traditions "are neceffary. Tradition alone is fufficient, but the fcriptures are not fuffi- "cient." Another of their writers afferts [c], that "the authority of ecclefiaftic "traditions is more fit than the fcriptures to afcertain any thing doubtful, even "that which may be made out from fcripture, fince the common opinion of "the church and ecclefiaftical tradition are clearer, and more open and truly "inflexible; when, on the contrary, the fcriptures have frequently much ob- "fcurity in them, and may be drawn here and there like a nofe of wax; and, "as a leaden rule, may be applied to every impious opinion." *Bailey* the Je- fuit [d], thus expreffes himfelf, "I will go further, and fay, we have as much "need of tradition as of fcripture, yea more; becaufe the fcripture minifters "to us only the dead and mute letter, but tradition, by means of the miniftry "of the church, gives us the true fenfe, which is not had diftinctly in the fcrip- "ture; wherein, notwithftanding, rather confifts the word of God than in the "alone written letter; it is fufficient for a good catholic, if he underftands it "is tradition, nor need he to enquire after any thing elfe." And by *tradition*, they mean not tradition delivered in the fcripture, but diftinct from it, and out of it; unwritten tradition, apoftolical tradition, as they frequently call it, not delivered by the apoftles in the facred fcriptures, but by word of mouth to their fucceffors, or to the churches: that we may not miftake them. *Andra-*
*dius*

---

[a] Seff. 4. Decret. de canon. fcript.    [b] De Verbo Dei, c. 4. fect. 1, 6.
[c] Pighius apud Rivet. Cathol. Orthodox. Tract. 1, qu. 6. p. 99.    [d] Apud. ibid. p. 142.

*dius* tells us, "that of necessity those traditions also must be believed, which "can be proved by no testimony of scripture:" and *Petrus a Soto* still more plainly and openly affirms; "It is, says he, a rule infallible and catholic, that "whatsoever things the church of *Rome* believeth, holdeth and keepeth, and "are not delivered in the scriptures, the same came by tradition from the apos- "tles; also all such observations and ceremonies, whose beginning, author, "and original are not known, or cannot be found, out of all doubt they "were delivered by the apostles [e]." This is what is meant by apostolic tradition.

Now the essentials of Popery, or the peculiarities of it, are all founded upon this, even upon apostolic and ecclesiastic tradition; this is the Pandora from whence they all spring; this is the rule to which all are brought, and by which they are confirmed; and what is it, be it ever so foolish, impious and absurd, but what may be proved hereby, if this is admitted of as a rule and test? It is upon this foot the Papists assert and maintain the observation of *Easter*, on the Lord's-day following the 14th of *March*; the fast of Quadragesima or Lent; the adoration of images and relicks; the invocation of saints; the worship of the sign of the cross; the sacrifice of the mass; transubstantiation; the abrogation of the use of the cup in the Lord's-supper; holy water; extreme unction, or the chrism; prayers for the dead; auricular confession; sale of pardons, purgatory, pilgrimages, monastic vows, &c.

Among apostolical traditions Infant-baptism is to be reckoned, and it is upon this account it is pleaded for. The first person that asserted Infant-baptism and approved it, represents it as a tradition from the apostles, whether he be *Origen*, or his translator and interpolator, *Ruffinus*; his words are, "For this (that is, for original sin) "the church has received a tradition from the apostles, "even to give baptism unto infants [f]." *Austin*, who was a warm advocate for Infant-baptism, puts it upon this footing, as a custom of the church, not to be despised, and as an apostolic tradition generally received by the church [g]; he lived in the fourth century, the same *Ruffinus* did; and probably it was from his Latin translation of *Origen*, *Austin* took the hint of Infant-baptism being an apostolic tradition, since no other ecclesiastical writer speaks of it before as such; so that, as Bishop *Taylor* [h] observes, "This apostolical tradition is but a "testimony of one person, and he condemned of many errors; so that, as he "says, to derive this from the apostles on no greater authority, is a great ar-  "gument

---

[e] See the Abstract of the History of Popery, part 2. p. 252, 253.
[f] Origen. Comment. in Epist. ad Roman. l. 5. fol. 178. 1.
[g] De Genes. l 10. c. 21. & de Baptismo contr. Donat. l. 4. c. 23, 24.
[h] Liberty of Prophesying, p. 320.

"gument that he is credulous and weak, that shall be determined by so weak a probation, in a matter of so great concernment;" and yet it is by this that many are determined in this affair: and not only Popish writers, as *Bellarmine* and others, make it to be an apostolical tradition unwritten; but some Protestant Pædobaptists shew a good-will to place Infant-baptism among the unwritten sayings and traditions of Christ or his apostles, and satisfy themselves therewith. Mr *Fuller*[i] says, "We do freely confess that there is neither express *precept* nor *precedent* in the New Testament for the baptizing of infants;" yet observes, that St *John* saith, chap. xxi. 25. *And there are also many other things, which Jesus did, which are not written*; "among which, for ought appears to the contrary, the baptizing of these infants (those whom Christ took in his arms and blessed) might be one of them." In like manner, Mr *Walker*[k] argues, "It doth not follow, our Saviour gave no precept for the baptizing of infants, because no such precept is particularly expressed in the scripture; for our Saviour spoke many things to his disciples concerning the kingdom of God, both before his passion, and also after his resurrection, which are *not written* in the *scriptures*; and who can say, but that among those many unwritten sayings of his, there might be an express precept for Infant-baptism?" And Mr *Leigh*, one of the disputants in the *Portsmouth*-disputation[l], suggests, that though Infant-baptism is not to be found in the writings of the apostle *Paul* extant in the scriptures, yet it might be in some writings of his which are lost, and not now extant; all which is plainly giving up Infant-baptism as contained in the sacred writings, and placing it upon unwritten, apostolical tradition, and that too, conjectural and uncertain.

Now Infant-baptism, with all the ceremonies attending it, for which also apostolical tradition is pleaded, makes a very considerable figure in Popish pageantry; which, according to pretended apostolical tradition, is performed in a very pompous manner; as, by consecration of the water, using sponsors, who answer to the interrogatories, and make the renunciation in the name of the infant; exorcisms, exsufflations, crossings, the use of salt, spittle, and oil. Before the party is baptized, the water is consecrated in a very solemn manner; the priest makes an exorcism first; three times, he exsufflates or breathes into the water, in the figure of a cross, saying, "I adjure thee, O creature of water;" and here he divides the water after the manner of a cross, and makes three or four crossings; he takes a horn of oil, and pours it three times upon the water in the likeness of a cross, and makes a prayer that the font may be sanctified, and the eternal Trinity be present; saying, "Descend from heaven and sanctify
"this

---

[i] Infants Advocate, p. 71, 150.      [k] Modest Plea, p. 268.
[l] Narrative of the Portsmouth-Disputation, p. 16—18.

" this water, and give grace and virtue, that he who is baptized according to
" the command of thy Chrift, may be crucified, and die, and be buried, and
" rife again with him." The fponfors or fureties, inftead of the child, and in
its name, recite the creed and the Lord's-prayer, make the renunciation of the
devil and all his works, and anfwer to queftions put in the name of the child :
the form, according to the Roman order, is this; " The name of the infant
" being called, the prefbyter muft fay, " Doft thou renounce Satan ? Anfwer,
" I do renounce; and all his works? Anfw. I do renounce; and all his pomps?
" Anfw. I do renounce: three times thefe queftions are put, and three times
" the fureties anfwer." The interrogations are fometimes faid to be made by
a prieft, fometimes by a prefbyter, and fometimes by an exorcift, who was one
or the other, and to which the following queftion alfo was added : " Doft thou
" believe in God the Father Almighty, creator of heaven and earth, &c ?
" Anfw. I believe." Children to be baptized are firft exfufflated or breathed
and blown upon, and exorcifed, that the wicked fpirit might be driven from
them, that they might be delivered from the powers of darknefs, and tranflated
into the kingdom of Chrift : the Roman order is, " Let him (the minifter,
prieft, deacon, or exorcift) " blow into the face of the perfon to be baptized,
" three times, faying, Go out, thou unclean fpirit, and give place to the holy
" Ghoft, the Comforter." The form, according to St *Gregory*, is, " I exorcife
" thee, O unclean fpirit, in the name of the Father, and of the Son, and of
" the holy Ghoft, that thou go out and depart from this fervant of God." Salt
alfo is put into the mouth of the infant, after it is bleffed and exorcifed, as a
token of its being feafoned with the falt of wifdom; and that it might be preferved from the corruption and ill favour of fin : the prieft firft bleffes the falt
after this manner : " I exorcife thee, O creature of falt; and then being bleffed,
" it is put into the mouth of the infant, faying, Receive the falt of wifdom
" unto life everlafting." The nofe and ears of infants at their baptifm are
touched with fpittle by the prieft, that they may receive the favour of the knowledge of God, and their ears be opened to hear the commands of God; and
formerly fpittle was put upon the eyes and upon the tongue, though it feems
now difufed as to thofe parts; and yet no longer than the birth of king *James*
the firft, it feems to have been in ufe; fince at his baptifm his mother fent word
to the archbifhop to forbear the ufe of the fpittle, faying, " She would not have
" a pocky prieft to fpit in her child's mouth [m];" for it feems the queen knew
that the archbifhop, who was *Hamilton*, Archbifhop of St *Andrews*, then had
the venereal difeafe [n]. And fo in the times of the martyrs in queen *Mary*'s days;

[m] Abftract of the Hiftory of Popery, part 1. p. 114.
[n] Vid. Rivet. Animadv. in Grot. Annotat. in Caffander. Confultat. p. 72.

for *Robert Smith* the martyr, being afked by *Bonner*, in what point do we diffent from the word of God? meaning as to baptifm; he anfwered [o], "First, in hallowing your water, in conjuring of the fame, in baptizing children with anointing and fpitting in their mouths, mingled with falt; and many other lewd ceremonies, of which not one point is able to be proved in God's word." All which he calls a mingle-mangle. Chryfm, or anointing both before and after baptifm, is another ceremony ufed at it; the parts anointed are the breaft and fhoulders; the breaft, that no remains of the latent enemy may refide in the party baptized; and the fhoulders, that he may be fortified and ftrengthened to do good works, to the glory of God: this anointing is made in the form of a crofs; the oil is put on the breaft and beneath the fhoulders, making a crofs with the thumb; on making the crofs on the fhoulders, the prieft fays, "Flee, thou unclean fpirit, give honour to the living and true God;" and when he makes it on the breaft, he fays, "Go out, thou unclean fpirit, give place to the holy Ghoft:" the form ufed in doing it is, "I anoint thee with the oil of falvation, that thou mayeft have life everlafting." The next ceremony is that of figning the infant with the fign of the crofs: this is made in feveral parts of the body, efpecially on the forehead, to fignify that the party baptized fhould not be afhamed of the crofs of Chrift, and not be afraid of the enemy, Satan, but manfully fight againft him. After baptifm, in ancient times, honey and milk, or wine and milk, were given to the baptized, though now difufed; and infants were admitted to the Lord's-fupper; which continued fome hundreds of years in the Latin church, and ftill does in the Greek church. Now for the proof of the ufe of thefe various ceremonies, the reader may confult *Jofeph. Vicecomes*, a learned Papift, as Dr *Wall* calls him, in his treatife *de antiquis baptifmi ritibus at ceremoniis*, where and by whom they are largely treated of, and the proofs of them given. All which are rehearfed and condemned by the ancient Waldenfes in a treatife of theirs, written in the year 1120 [p]. It may be afked, to what purpofe is this account given of the ceremonies ufed by Papifts in the adminiftration of baptifm to infants by them, fince they are not ufed by Proteftant Pædobaptifts? I anfwer, it is to fhew what I propofed, namely, what a figure Infant-baptifm, with thefe attending ceremonies, makes in Popery, and may with propriety be called a part of it; befides, though all thefe ceremonies are not ufed, yet fome of them are ufed in fome Proteftant Pædobaptift churches, as fureties, the interrogations made to them, and their anfwers in the name of the infants; the renunciation of the devil and all his works, and figning with the fign of the crofs: and fince thefe and the

others,

* For's Acts and Monuments, vol. 3. p. 400.
p See Morland's Hiftory of the chuches of Piedmont, p. 173.

others, all of them claim apostolic authority, and most, if not all of them, have as good and as early a claim to it as Infant-baptism itself; those who admit that upon this foot, ought to admit these ceremonies also. See a treatise of mine, called *The Argument from Apostolic tradition in favour of Infant-baptism considered.* Most of the above ceremonies are mentioned by *Basil*[q], who lived in the fourth century, and as then in use; and which were had from apostolic tradition, as said, and not from the scriptures; and, says he, "Because this "is first and most common, I will mention it in the first place, as that we sign "with *the sign of the cross*;—Who has taught this in scripture?—We consecrate "the water of baptism and the oil of unction, as well as him who receives bap-"tism; from what scriptures? Is it not from private and secret tradition? "Moreover the anointing with oil, what passage in scripture teaches this? Now "a man is thrice immersed, from whence is it derived or directed? Also the rest "of what is done in baptism, as to renounce Satan and his angels, from what "scripture have we it? Is not this from private and secret tradition?" And so *Austin*[r] speaks of exorcisms and exsufflations used in baptism, as of ancient tradition, and of universal use in the church. Now whoever receives Infant-baptism on the foot of apostolic tradition, ought to receive those also, since they stand upon as good a foundation as that does.

The Papists attribute the rise of several of the above ceremonies to their Popes, as sponsors, chrysms, exorcisms, &c. though perhaps they were not quite so early as they imagine, yet very early they were; and Infant-baptism itself, though two or three doctors of the church had asserted and espoused it, yet it was not determined in any council until the Milevitan council in 418, or thereabouts, a provincial of *Africa*, in which was a canon made for Pædobaptism, and never till then: So says bishop *Taylor*[s], with whom *Grotius* agrees[t], who calls it the council of *Carthage*; and who says in the councils no earlier mention is made of Infant-baptism than in that council; the canons of which were sent to pope *Innocent* the first[u], and confirmed by him: And *Austin*, who must write his book against the Donatists before this time, though he says[v], the church always held it (Infant-baptism) and that it is most rightly believed to be delivered by apostolic tradition; yet observes, that it was not instituted, or determined and settled in or by councils; that is, as yet it was not, though it afterwards was in the above council confirmed by the said pope; in which
council.

[q] De Spiritu Sancto, c. 27.
[r] De Peccat. Orig. l. 2. c. 40. & de napt. & concup. l. 1. c. 20. & l. 2. c. 18.
[s] Liberty of Prophesying, p. 320, 321.   [t] Comment on Matt xix. 14.
[u] Vid. Centuriat. Magdeburg. cent. 5. c. 9. p. 468, 473. Epist. August. Ep 92, 93.
[v] De Baptismo contra Donatist. l. 4. c. 24.

council *Austin* himself presided, and in which is this canon, "Also it is our plea-
"sure, that whoever denies that new-born infants are to be baptized,—let him
"be anathema;" and which is the first council that established Infant-baptism,
and anathematized those that denied it; so that it may justly be called a part
of popery: besides baptism by immersion, which continued 1300 years in the
Latin church, excepting in the case of the Clinicks, and still does in the Greek
church, was first changed into sprinkling by the Papists; which is not an indifferent thing, whether performed with much or a little water, as is usually
considered; but is of the very essence of baptism, is that itself, and without
which it is not baptism; it being, as Sir *John Floyer* says [x], "No circumstance,
"but the very act of baptizing;" who observes [y], "that aspersion, or sprink-
"ling, was brought into the church by the popish schoolmen; and our dis-
"senters, adds he, had it from them; the schoolmen employed their thoughts
"how to find out reasons for the alteration to sprinkling, and brought it into use
"in the twelfth century:" and it must be observed, to the honour of the church
of *England*, that they have not established *sprinkling* in baptism to this day; only
have permitted *pouring* in case it is certified the child is weakly and not able to
bear dipping; otherwise, by the Rubric, the priest is ordered to *dip* the child
*warily:* sprinkling received only a Presbyterian sanction in the times of the civil
war, by the Assembly of Divines; where it was carried for sprinkling against
dipping by one vote only, by 25 against 24, and then established by an ordinance of parliament 1644 [z]: and that this change has its rise from the authority of the Pope, Dr *Wall* [a] himself acknowledges, and that the sprinkling of
infants is from popery. " All the nations of christians, says he, that do now,
"or formerly did, submit to the authority of the bishop of *Rome*, do ordina-
"rily baptize their infants by pouring or sprinkling; and though the English
"received not this custom till after the decay of Popery, yet they have since
"received it from such neighbour-nations as had began it in the times of the
"pope's power; but all other christians in the world, who never owned the
"pope's usurped power, do, and ever did, *dip* their infants in their ordinary
"use;" so that Infant-baptism, both with respect to subject and mode, may
with great propriety be called a part and branch of popery.

But it is not only a part of popery, and so serves to strengthen it, as a part
does the whole; but it is a *pillar* of it, what serves greatly to support it; and
which furnishes the Papists with one of the strongest arguments against the Protestants in favour of their traditions; on which, as we have seen, the essentials of
popery are founded, and of the authority of the church to alter the rites of divine

---

[x] Essay to restore Dipping, &c. p. 44.   [y] Ibid. p. 58.   [z] Ibid. p. 12, 32.
[a] History of Infant-baptism, part 2. p. 477.

vine worship: they sadly embarrass Pædobaptist protestants with the affair of Infant-baptism, and urge them either to prove it by scripture, both with respect to mode and subjects, or allow of unscriptural traditions and the authority of the church, or give it up; and if they can allow of unwritten traditions, and the custom and practice of the church, as of authority in one point, why not in others? This way of arguing, as Mr *Stennett* observes [b], is used by cardinal *Du Perron*, in his reply to the answer of king *James* the first, and by Mr *John Ainsworth*, against Mr *Henry Ainsworth*, in the dispute between them, and by *Fisher* the Jesuit, against archbishop *Laud*; a late instance of this kind, he adds, we have in the controversy between Monsieur *Bossuet*, bishop of *Meaux*, and a learned anonymous writer, said to be Monsieur *de la Roque*, late pastor of the reformed church at *Roan* in *Normandy*. The bishop, in order to defend the withholding the cup in the Lord's supper from the laity, according to the authority of the church, urged that Infant-baptism, both as to mode and subject, was unscriptural, and solely by the authority of tradition and custom, with which the pretended *reformed* complied, and therefore why not in the other case? which produced this ingenuous confession from his antagonist, that to baptize by sprinkling was certainly an abuse derived from the Romish church, without due examination, as well as many other things, which he and his brethren were resolved to correct, and thanked the bishop for undeceiving them; and freely confessed, that as to the baptism of infants, there is nothing formal or express in the gospel to justify the necessity of it; and that the passages produced do at most only prove that it is permitted, or rather, that it is not forbidden to baptize them. In the times of king *Charles* the second, lived Mr *Jeremiah Ives*, a Baptist minister, famous for his talent at disputation, of whom the king having heard, sent for him to dispute with a Romish priest; the which he did before the king and many others, in the habit of a clergyman: Mr *Ives* pressed the priest closely, shewing that whatever antiquity they pretended to, their doctrine and practices could by no means be proved apostolic; since they are not to be found in any writings which remain of the apostolic age; the priest after much wrangling, in the end replied, that this argument of Mr *Ives* was of as much force against Infant-baptism, as against the doctrines and ceremonies of the church of *Rome*: to which Mr *Ives* answered, that he readily granted what he said to be true; the priest upon this broke up the dispute, saying, he had been cheated, and that he would proceed no further; for he came to dispute with a clergyman of the established church, and it was now evident, that this was an Anabaptist preacher. This behaviour of the priest afforded his majesty and all present not a little diversion [c]: and as protestant Pædobaptists-

[b] Answer to Russen, p. 173, &c.     [c] Crosby's Hist. of the Baptists, vol. 4. p. 247, 248.

tifts are urged by this argument to admit the unwritten traditions of the Papifts, fo diffenters of the Pædobaptift perfuafion are preffed upon the fame footing by thofe of the church of England to comply with the ceremonies of that church, retained from the church of Rome, particularly by Dr *Whitby*[a]; who having pleaded for fome condefcenfion to be made to diffenters, in order to reconcile them to the church, adds; "And on the other hand, fays he, if notwithftand-
"ing the evidence produced, that *baptifm* by *immerfion*, is fuitable both to the
"inftitution of our Lord and his apoftles; and was by them ordained to repre-
"fent our burial with Chrift, and fo our dying unto fin, and our conformity
"to his refurrection by newnefs of life; as the apoftle doth clearly maintain
"the meaning of that rite: I fay, if notwithftanding this, all our *diffenters*
"(that is, who are Pædobaptifts, he muft mean) do agree to *fprinkle* the bap-
"tized infant; why may they not as well fubmit to the fignificant ceremonies
"impofed by our church? for, fince it is as lawful to *add* unto Chrift's infti-
"tutions a fignificant ceremony, as to diminifh a fignificant ceremony which
"he or his apoftles inftituted, and ufe another in its ftead, which they never
"did inftitute; what reafon can they have to do the latter, and yet refufe fub-
"miffion to the former? and why fhould not the peace and union of the
"church be as prevailing with them, to perform the one, as is their mercy
"to the *infant*'s body to neglect the other?" Thus Infant-baptifm is ufed as the grand plea for compliance with the ceremonies both of the church of *Rome* and of the church of *England*.

I have added, in the preface referred to, where ftands the above claufe, that Infant-baptifm is " that by which Antichrift has fpread his baneful influence " over many nations;" which is abundantly evident, fince by the *chriftening* of children, through baptifm introduced by him, he has made whole countries and nations chriftians, and has chriftened them by the name of *Chriftendom*; and thereby has inlarged his univerfal church, over which he claims an abfolute power and authority, as being Chrift's vicar on earth; and by the fame means he retains his influence over nations, and keeps them in awe and in obedience to him; afferting, that by their baptifm they are brought into the pale of the church, in which there is falvation, and out of which there is none; if there fore they renounce their baptifm, received in infancy, or apoftatize from the church, their damnation is inevitable; and thus by his menaces and anathemas he holds the nations in fubjection to him: and when they at any time have courage to oppofe him, and act in difobedience to his fupreme authority, he immediately lays a whole nation under an interdict; by which are prohibited, the adminiftration of the facraments, all public prayers, burials, chriftenings, &c.

church

[a] Proteftant Reconciler, p. 289.

church-doors are locked up, the clergy dare not or will not administer any offices of their function to any, but such as for large sums of money obtain special privileges from *Rome* for that purpose [e]: now by means of these prohibitions, and particularly of christening or baptizing children, nations are obliged or comply and yield obedience to the bishop of *Rome*; for it appears most dreadful to parents, that their children should be deprived of baptism, by which they are made christians, as they are taught to believe, and without which there is no hope of salvation; and therefore are influenced to give into any thing for the sake of what is thought so very important. Once more, the baneful influence spread by Antichrist over the nations by Infant-baptism, is that poisonous notion infused by him, that sacraments, particularly baptism, confer grace *ex opere operato*, by the work done; that it takes away sin, regenerates men, and saves their souls; this is charged upon him, and complained of by the antient Waldenses in a tract [f] of theirs, written in the year 1120. Where, speaking of the works of antichrist, they say, "the *third* work of antichrist consists
" in this, that he attributes the regeneration of the holy Spirit unto the dead,
" outward work of baptizing children in that faith, and teaching that thereby
" baptism and regeneration must be had; and therein he confers and bestows
" orders and other sacraments, and groundeth therein all his christianity, which
" is against the holy Spirit:" and which popish notion is argued against and exposed by *Robert Smith* the martyr [g]; on *Bonner*'s saying "if they (infants) die
" before they are baptized, they be damned; he asked this question; I pray
" you, my Lord, shew me, are we saved by water or by Christ? to which
" *Bonner* replied, by both; then, said *Smith*, the water died for our sins, and
so must ye say, that the water hath life, and it being our servant, and created
" for us, is our Saviour; this my Lord is a good doctrine, is it not?" And this pernicious notion still continues, this old leaven yet remains even in some Protestant churches, who have retained it from *Rome*; hence a child when baptized is declared to be regenerate, and thanks are returned to God that it is regenerate; and it is taught, when capable of being catechized, to say, that in its baptism it was "made a child of God, a member of Christ, and an inhe-
" ritor of the kingdom of heaven;" which has a tendency to take off all concern in persons when grown up, about an inward work of grace, in regeneration and sanctification, as a meetness for heaven, and to encourage a presumption in them, notwithstanding their apparent want of grace, that they are members of Christ, and shall never perish; are children and heirs of God, and shall certainly inherit eternal life. Wherefore Dr *Owen* rightly observes [h], " that the " father

[e] Abstract of the Hist. of Popery, part 1. p. 463. See Fox's Acts and Monuments, vol. 1. p. 326.
[f] Apud Morland's History of the churches of Piedmont, p. 148.
[g] Fox's Acts and Monuments, vol. 3. p. 400.   [h] Theologoumena, l. 6. c. 3. p. 477.

" father of lies himself could not easily have devised a doctrine more pernicious,
" or what proposes a more present and effectual poison to the minds of sinners
" to be drank in by them."

II. The second article or proposition in the preface is, as asserted by me, that " Infant-baptism is the basis of national churches and worldly establishments; " that which unites the church and world, and keeps them togther;" than which nothing is more evident: if a church is national, it consists of all in the nation, men, women, and children; and children are originally members of it, either so by birth, and as soon as born, being born in the church, in a christian land and nation, which is the church; or rather by baptism, as it is generally put; so according to the order of the church of *England*, at the baptism of a child, the minister says, "We receive this child into the congregation of Christ's " flock." And by the Assembly of Divines, "Baptism is called a sacrament " of the New Testament, whereby the parties baptized are solemnly admitted " into the visible church." And to which there is a strange contradiction in the following answer, where it is said, that " Baptism is not to be administered to any " that are out of the visible church;" but if by baptism the parties baptized are solemnly admitted into the visible church, then before baptism by which they are admitted, they must be out of it: one or other must be wrong; either persons are not admitted into the visible church by baptism, or if they are, then before baptism they are out of it, and have baptism administered to them in order to their being admitted into it; and *Calvin* says, according to whose plan of church-government at *Geneva*, that of the Scotch church is planned, that baptism is a solemn introduction to the church of God [1]. And Mr *Baxter* argues, " that if there be neither precept nor example of admitting church-" members in all the New Testament but by baptism; then all that are now " admitted ought to come in by baptism; but there is neither precept nor. " example in all the New Testament of admitting church-members but by " baptism; therefore they ought to come in the same way now." So then infants becoming members of a national church by baptism, they are originally of it; are the materials of which it consists; and it is by *the baptism of infants* it is supplied with members, and is supported and maintained; so that it may be truly said, that Infant-baptism is the basis and foundation of a national church, and is indeed the sinews, strength, and support of it: and infants being admitted members by baptism, continue such when grown up, even though of the most dissolute lives and conversations, as multitudes of them are; and many, instead of being treated as church-members, deserve to be sent to the
house

[1] Epist. Calvin. Ep. ad N. S. D. p. 441.

house of correction, as some are; and others are guilty of such flagitious crimes that they die an infamous death; yet even these die in the communion of the church; and thus the church and the world are united and kept together till death doth them part.

The *Independents* would indeed separate the church and the world, according to their principles; but cannot do it, being fettered and hampered with Infant-church-membership and baptism, about which they are at a loss and disagreed on what to place it; some place it on infants interest in the covenant of grace; and here they sadly contradict themselves or one another; at one time they say it is interest in the covenant of grace gives infants a right to baptism; and at another time, that it is by baptism they are brought and entered into the covenant; and sometimes it is not in the inward part of the covenant they are interested, only in the external part of it, where hypocrites and graceless persons may be; but what that external part is, no mortal can tell: others not being satisfied that their infant-seed as such are all interested in the covenant of grace, say, it is not that, but the church-covenant that godly parents enter into, which gives their children with them a right to church-membership and baptism: children in their minority, it is said [k], covenant with their parents, and so become church-members, and this intitles them to baptism; for according to the old *Independents* of *New England*, none but members of a visible church were to be baptized [l]; though Dr *Goodwin* [m] is of a different mind: hence only such as were children of members of churches, even of set members [n], as they call them, were admitted, though of godly and approved christians; and though they may have been members, yet if excommunicated, their children born in the time of their excommunication might not be baptized [o]; but those children that are admitted members and baptized, though not confirmed members, as they stile them, till they profess faith and repentance [p]; yet during their minority, which reaches till they are more than thirteen years of age, according to the example of *Ishmael*, and till about sixteen years of age, they are real members to such intents and purposes, as, that if their parents are dismissed to other churches, their children ought to be put into the letters of dismission with them [q]; and whilst their minority continues, are under church-watch, and subject to the reprehensions, admonitions, and censures thereof, for their

---

[k] Disputation concerning church-members and their children at Boston, p. 12, 13. Hooker's Survey of church-discipline, part 3. p. 23, 25. [l] Cotton's Way of the churches in New England, p. 81. Boston-disputation, p. 4. Defence of the Nine Propositions, p. 115.
[m] Government of the churches of Christ, p. 377. [n] Defence of the Nine Propositions, p. 69.
[o] Cotton's Way, p. 85. Boston-disputation, p. 25. Hooker's Survey, part 3. p. 18.
[p] Cotton's Holiness of church-members, p. 19. Boston-disputation, p. 3. [q] Ibid. p. 15.

their healing and amendment', as need fhall require; though with refpect to public rebuke, admonition, and excommunication, children in their minority are not fubject to church-difcipline, only to fuch as is by way of fpiritual watch and private rebuke'. The original *Independents*, by the covenant-feed, who have a right to church-memberfhip and baptifm, thought only the feed of immediate parents in church-covenant are meant, and not of progenitors'. Mr *Cotton* fays ", "Infants cannot claim right unto baptifm, but in the right of one " of their parents or both; where neither of the parents can claim right to the " Lord's-fupper, there their infants cannot claim right to baptifm;" though he afterwards fays ", " it may be confidered, whether the children may not be " baptized, where either the grandfather or grandmother * have made profeffion " of their faith and repentance before the church, and are ftill living to under-" take for the chriftian education of the child; or if thefe fail, what hinders " but that if the parents will refign their infant to be educated in the houfe of " any godly member of the church, the child may be lawfully baptized in the " right of its houfhold governor." But Mr *Hooker*, as he afferts <sup>y</sup>, that children as children have no right to baptifm, fo it belongs not to any predeceffors, either nearer or farther off removed from the next parents to give right of this privilege to their children; by which predeceffors, he fays, he includes and comprehends all befides the next parent; grandfather, great grandfather, *&c.* So the minifters and meffengers of the congregational churches that met at the *Savoy* declare <sup>z</sup>; " that not only thofe that do actually profefs faith in, and " obedience unto Chrift, but alfo the infants of one or both believing parents " are to be baptized, and thofe only." And the commiffioners for the review of the Common Prayer, in the beginning of the reign of king *Charles* the fecond; thofe of the *Prefbyterian* perfuafion moved, on the behalf of others, that " there " being divers learned, pious, and peaceable minifters, who not only judge it " unlawful to baptize children whofe parents both of them are Atheifts, Infi-" dels, Heretics, or Unbaptized; but alfo fuch whofe parents are excommuni-" cate perfons, fornicators, or otherwife notorious and fcandalous finners; we " defire, fay they, they may not be inforced to baptize the children of fuch, " until they have made open profeffion of their repentance before baptifm <sup>a</sup>:" but now I do not underftand, that the prefent generation of Diffenters of this denomination, adhere to the principles and practices of their predeceffors, at

leaft

<sup>r</sup> Cambridge Platform of church government, p. 18.    <sup>s</sup> Bofton-difputation, p. 14.
<sup>t</sup> Bofton-difputation, p. 19.    <sup>u</sup> Cotton's Way of the churches, p. 81.    <sup>w</sup> Ibid. p. 115.
<sup>x</sup> Of this fee Epift. Calvin. Ep. Farella, p. 175. & Salden. Otia, Theolog. Exercitat. 7. fect. 21. p. 544.    <sup>y</sup> Survey of church-difcipline, part 3. p. 13.
<sup>z</sup> Declaration of the Faith and Order, &c. c. 29. p. 48.
<sup>a</sup> Proceedings of the Commiffioner. of both Perfuafions, &c. p. 22.

least very few of them; but admit to baptism, not only the children of members of their churches, but of those who are not members, only hearers, or that apply to them for the baptism of their infants, whether gracious or graceless persons: and were only the first sort admitted, children of members, what are they? No better than others, born in sin, born of the flesh, carnal and corrupt, are of the world, notwithstanding their birth of religious persons, until they are called out of it by the effectual grace of God; and as they grow up, appear to be of the world as others, and have their conversation according to the course of it; and many of them are dissolute in their lives, and scandalous in their conversations: and yet I do not understand, that any notice is taken of them in a church-way; as to be admonished, censured, and excommunicated; but they retain their membership, into which they were taken in their infancy, and continue in it to the day of their death: and if this is not uniting and keeping the world and church together, I know not what is.

Moreover all the arguments that are made use of to prove the church of Christ under the gospel-dispensation to be congregational, and against a national church, are all destroyed by the baptism and membership of infants. It is said in favour of the one, and against the other, that the members of a visible church are saints by calling, such as in charitable discretion may be accounted so [b]; but are infants who are admitted to membership and baptized, such? The holiness pleaded for as belonging to them, is only a federal holiness, and that is merely chimerical: are they called to be saints, or saints by effectual calling? Can they, in charitable discretion, or in rational charity, be thought to be truly and really holy, or saints, as the churches of the New Testament are said to be? And if they cannot in a judgment of charity, be accounted real saints, and yet are admitted members of churches; why not others, of whom it cannot be charitably thought that they are real saints? Besides, it is said by the Independents, "that members of gospel-churches are saints by calling, visibly manifesting and evidencing by their profession and walk their obedience to that call; who are further known to each other by their confession of faith wrought in them by the power of God; and do willingly consent to walk together, according to the appointment of Christ, giving up themselves to the Lord and to one another by the will of God, in professed subjection to the ordinances of the gospel [c]:" now are infants such? Do they manifest and evidence by a profession and walk their obedience to a divine call? And if they do not, and yet are admitted members, why not others, who give no more evidence than they do? Do they make a confession of faith wrought in them? Does it

appear

---

[b] Cotton's Way of the churches, &c. p. 56. Cambridge-Platform, c. 3. p. 3.
[c] Savoy-Declaration, &c. p. 57.

appear that they have such a faith? and in a confession made, and so made as to be known by fellow-members? and if not, and yet received and owned as members, why not others that make no more confession of faith than they do. Do infants consent to walk with the church of Christ, and give up themselves to the Lord and one another, and profess to be subject to the ordinances of the gospel? and if they do not, as most certainly they do not, and yet are members, why may not others be also members on the same footing? Is it objected to a national church, that persons of the worst of characters are members of it; and by this means the church is filled with men very disreputable and scandalous in their lives? and is not this true of infants admitted members in their infancy, who when grown up are very wicked and immoral, and yet their membership continues? and why not then national churches be admitted of, notwithstanding the above objection? So that upon the whole, I think, I have good reason to say, "that there cannot be a full separation of the one from the other, that is, of the church from the world, nor a thorough reformation in religion, until it (Infant-baptism) is wholly removed."

III. In the said Preface, I express my firm belief of the entire cessation of Infant-baptism, in time to come: my words are, " though it (Infant-baptism) has so long and largely obtained (as it has from the fourth century till now, and over the greater part who have since bore the christian name) and still does obtain; I believe with a firm and unshaken faith, that the time is hastening on, when Infant-baptism will be no more practised in the world." I mean in the spiritual reign of Christ; for in his personal reign there will be no ordinances, nor the administration of them; and this is explained by what I farther say, " when churches will be formed on the same plan they were in the times of the apostles; when gospel-doctrine and discipline will be restored to their primitive purity and lustre; when the ordinances of baptism and the Lord's supper will be administered as they were first delivered; all which will be accomplished, when " the Lord shall be king over all the earth, and there shall be one Lord and his name one;" that is, when there shall be one Lord, one faith, and one baptism, acknowledged by all christians; and they will be all of one mind with respect to the doctrines and ordinances of the gospel. And as it becomes every man to give a reason of the faith and hope he has concerning divine things, with meekness and fear; the reasons of my firm belief, that Infant-baptism will be no more practised in the latter day, and spiritual reign of Christ, are some of them suggested in the above paragraph, and others may be added, as,

*First*, Because churches in the time referred to will be formed on the plan churches were in the time of the apostles; that this will be the case, see the

prophecies

prophecies in *Isai.* i. 25, 26. *Jer.* xxx, 18, 20. *Rev.* xi. 19. Now the apostolic churches consisted only of baptized believers, or of such who were baptized upon profession of their faith; the members of the first christian church, which was at *Jerusalem*, were first baptized upon their conversion; and then added to it; the next christian church, at *Samaria*, consisted of men and women baptized on believing the gospel preached by *Philip*; and the church at *Corinth*, of such who hearing, believed and were baptized; and on the same plan were formed the churches at *Rome*, *Philippi*, *Colosse*, and others; nor is there one single instance of Infant-baptism and of Infant-church-membership in them; wherefore if churches in the latter day will be on the same plan, then Infant-baptism will be no more practised.

*Secondly*, Because then the ordinances of the gospel will be administered, as they were first delivered, clear of all present corruption and superstition; this is what is meant by *the temple of God* being *opened in heaven*, on the founding of the seventh trumpet, *Rev.* xi. 19. and xv. 5. which respects the restoration of worship, discipline, doctrines and ordinances, to the free use of them, and to their original purity; when, as the ordinance of the Lord's-supper will be administered clear of all corruptions and ceremonies introduced by Papists and retained by Protestants; so likewise the ordinance of baptism, both with respect to subject and mode; which, as it was first delivered, was only administered to persons professing faith and repentance, and that by immersion only; and if this will be universally administered in the latter day, as in the first ages of christianity, Infant-sprinkling will be practised no more.

*Thirdly*, Because Christ will then be *king over all the earth* in a spiritual sense; one Lord, whose commands will be obeyed with great precision and exactness, according to his will revealed in his word; and as baptism is one of his commands he has prescribed, as he is and will be acknowledged the one Lord and head of the church, and not the pope, who will no more be submitted to; so there will be *one baptism*, which will be administered to one sort of subjects only, as he has directed, and in one manner only, by immersion, of which his baptism is an example; and therefore I believe that Infant-sprinkling will be no more in use.

*Fourthly*, At this same time the *name* of Christ will be *one*, that is, his religion; which will be the same it was at first instituted by him. Now it is various, as it is professed and practised by different persons that bear his name; but in the latter day, it will be one and the same, in all its branches, as embraced, professed, and exercised, by all that are called christians; and as baptism is one part of it, this will be practised in an uniform manner, or by all alike, that shall name the name of Christ; for since Christ's name, or the christian religion.

in all its parts, will be the same in all the professors of it; I therefore firmly believe, that baptism will be practised alike by all, according to the primitive institution; and consequently, that Infant-baptism will be no more: for,

*Fifthly*, As at this time, the *watchmen will see eye to eye*, Isai. lii. 8. the ministers of the gospel will be of one mind, both with respect to the doctrines and duties of christianity; will alike preach the one, and practise the other; so the people under their ministrations will be all agreed, and receive the truths of the gospel in the love of them, and submit to the precepts and institutions of it, without any difference among themselves, and without any variation from the word of God; and among the rest, the ordinance of baptism, about which there will be no longer strife; but all will agree that the proper subjects of it are believers, and the right mode of it immersion; and so Infant-sprinkling will be no more contended for; saints in this, as in other things, will serve the Lord with one consent, *Zeph.* iii. 9.

*Sixthly*, Another reason why I firmly believe Infant-baptism will hereafter be no more practised, is, because antichrist will be entirely *consumed* with the spirit or *breath* of Christ's *mouth*, and with *the brightness of his coming*, 2 Thess. ii. 8. that is, with the pure and powerful preaching of his word, at his coming to take to himself—his power, and reign spiritually in the churches, in a more glorious manner; when all antichristian doctrines and practices will be entirely abolished and cease, even the whole body of antichristian worship; not a limb of antichrist shall remain, but all shall be consumed. Now as I believe, and it has been shewn, that Infant-baptism is a part and pillar of Popery, a limb of antichrist, a branch of superstition and will-worship, introduced by the man of sin, when he shall be destroyed, this shall be destroyed with him and be no more.

*Seventhly*, Though the notion of Infant-baptism has been embraced and practised by many good and godly men in several ages; yet it is part of the wood, hay, and stubble, laid by them upon the foundation; is one of those works of theirs, the bright day of the gospel shall declare to be a falshood; and which the fire of the word will try, burn up, and consume, though they themselves shall be saved; and therefore being utterly consumed, shall no more appear in the world: for,

*Eighthly*, When the angel shall descend from heaven with great power, and *the earth* be *lightened with his glory*, which will be at the fall of *Babylon* and ruin of Antichrist, *Rev.* xviii. 1, 2. such will be the blaze of light then given, that all antichristian darkness shall be removed, and all works of darkness will be made manifest and cast off, among which Infant-baptism is one; and then *the earth will be full of the knowledge of the Lord, as the waters cover the sea*, Isai. xi. 9. even of the knowledge of the word, ways, worship, truths, and ordinances of
God,

'God, and all ignorance of them vanish and disappear; and then the ordinance of baptism will appear in its former lustre and purity, and be embraced and submitted to in it; and every corruption of it be rejected, of which Infant-baptism is one.

*Ninthly,* Whereas the ordinances of the gospel, baptism and the Lord's-supper, are to continue until the second coming of Christ, or the end of the world, *Matt.* xxviii. 19, 20. 1 *Cor.* xi. 26. and whereas there have been corruptions introduced into them, as they are generally administered, unless among some few; it is not reasonable to think, that those corruptions will be continued to the second coming of Christ, but that they will be removed before, even at his spiritual coming, or in his spiritual reign: and as with respect to baptism particularly, there must be a mistake on one side or the other, both with respect to subject and mode; and as this mistake I firmly believe is on the side of the Pædobaptists; so, I as firmly believe for the reason given, that it will be removed, and Infant-sprinkling for the future no more used.

*Tenthly,* The Philadelphian church-state, which answers to and includes the spiritual reign of Christ in his churches, is what I refer unto in the preface, as the time when the practice of Infant-baptism will cease; in which I am con firmed, by the characters given of that church and the members of it; as, that it *kept* the *word* of Christ; that is, not only the doctrines of the gospel, which will be then purely preached and openly professed, but the ordinances of it, baptism and the Lord's-supper; which have been (particularly baptism) sadly corrupted in almost all the periods of the churches hitherto, excepting the apostolic one; but will in this period be restored to their pristine purity and glory; hence it is promised to this church, and that it represents, that because it *kept the word* of Christ's *patience* truly and faithfully, it should be kept from the hour of temptation that should come on all the earth; and is exhorted to *hold* fast what she had, both the doctrines and ordinances, as they were delivered by Christ and his apostles, and as she now held them in the truth and purity of them. These are the reasons why I believe with a firm and unshaken faith, that the time is coming, and I hope will not be long, when Infant-baptism will be no more practised in the world.

Since, now at this time, we are greatly and justly alarmed with the increase of Popery; in order to put a stop to it, let us begin at home, and endeavour to remove all remains of it among ourselves; so shall we with the better grace, and it may be hoped, with greater success, oppose and hinder the spread of it.

## POSTSCRIPT.

THE writer who lately appeared in a news-paper, under the name of *Candidus*, having been obliged to quit his mountebank-stage, on which he held forth to the public for a few days; has, in his great humility, condescended to deal out his packets, in a less popular way; under the title of, "*The true Scripture-Doctrine of the Mode and Subjects of Christian Baptism*, &c. in six letters." It is quite unreasonable that we should be put, by every impertinent scribbler, to the drudgery of answering, what has been answered over and over again in this controversy. However I shall make short work with this writer, and therefore I have only put him to, and shall only give him a little gentle correction at *the cart's tail*; to use the phrase of *a late learned Professor* in one of our universities, with respect to the discipline of a certain *Bishop*.

The *first* and *second* letters of *Candidus*, in the news-paper, are answered in marginal notes on my Sermon upon Baptism, and published along with it. His *third* letter is a mean piece of buffoonery and scurrility; it begins with a trite, vulgar proverb, in low language, fit only for the mouth of an *Hostler* or a *Carman*; and his friends seem to have spoiled one or other of these, by making him a *Parson*. He goes on throughout the whole of the letter, as one that is in great haste, running after his wits, to seek for them, having lost them, if ever he had any; and it concludes with a poor, pitiful, foolish burlesk, mixed with slander and falshood, on an innocent gentleman; quite a stranger to him, and could never have offended him, but by a conscientious regard to what he believed was his duty. However, by this base and inhuman treatment, it appears that his moral character is unimpeachable, or otherwise it would have been nibbled at. His *fourth* letter begins with representing the sermon published, as so mangled, changed, altered, and added to, that it has scarce any remains of its original; in which he must be condemned by all that heard it: and he has most unluckily charged one clause as an addition, which, there cannot be one in ten but will remember it; it is this, "If any man can find any others in his " (the jailor's) house, besides *all* that were in it, he must be reckoned a very " *sagacious* person;" and he himself, in his *first* letter, published before the sermon was, has an oblique glance at it; calling me, in a sneering way, "the " *sagacious* doctor." What he says in the following part of the letter, concerning the subjects of baptism, and what he intended to say concerning the mode in another letter, which was prevented, I suppose are contained in a set of letters now published; and which are addressed, not to Mr Printer, who cast him off, but to *a candid Antipædobaptist*; and indeed the epithet of *candid* better agrees

with

with that sort of people than with himself, of which he seems conscious, if he has any conscience at all; for it looks as if he had not, or he could never have set out with such a most notorious untruth, and impudent falshood; affirming that I said in my sermon, that "the ten commandments, stiled the moral law, "were not binding on Christ's disciples;" a greater untruth could not well have been told: my writings in general testify the contrary, and particularly two sermons I have published, one called, "*The Law established by the Gospel*," and the other, "*The Law in the Hand of Christ*;" which are sufficient to justify me from such a wicked calumny; and the paragraph with which my sermon begins, attacked by him, and which I declare, are the words I delivered in the pulpit, that "the ten commandments, are the commands of God, and to be observed "by christians under the present dispensation;" for which I quoted 1 *Cor.* ix. 21. this I say, must stare him in the face, and awaken his guilty conscience, if not seared as with a red-hot iron; which I fear is his case. As for his flings at eternal justification, which he has lugged into this controversy, and his grand concluding and common argument against it, that it is eternal nonsense, I despise; he has not a head for that controversy: and I would only put him in mind of what Dr Owen said to Baxter, who charged him with holding it, "What would "the man have me say? I have told him, I am not of that opinion; would he "have me swear to it, that I am not? but though I am not, I know *better* and "*wiser* men than myself that do hold it."

Some body in the news-paper, observing that this man was froward and perverse, and fearing he should do hurt to religion in general, in order to divert him from it, and guide him another way; *complimented* him with being a man of wit, and of abilities; and the vain young man fancies he *really* is one: and being a witty youth, and of abilities, he has been able to produce an instance of Infant-baptism, about 1500 years before christian baptism was instituted; though he must not have the sole credit of it, because it has been observed before him: the instance is of the passage of the Israelites through the sea, at which time, he says, their children were baptized, as well as they: *come then,* says he, in very polite language, this is one scripture-instance; but if he had had his wits about him, he might have improved this instance, and strengthened his argument a little more; by observing that there was a mixed multitude, that came with the Israelites out of *Egypt*, and with them passed through the sea, with *their children* also. And since he makes mention of *Nebuchadnezzar's* baptism, it is much he did not try to make out, that his children were baptized also, then or at some other time. This is the true scripture-doctrine, of the subjects of christian baptism, according to his title.

That the Jews received their proselytes by baptism, before the times of Christ, he says, I know; but if I do, he does not. I observe, he is very ready to ascribe great knowledge of things to me, which he himself is ignorant of; I am much obliged to him: the great names he opposes to me, do not frighten me; I have read their writings and testimonies, and know what they were capable of producing, and to how little purpose; though I must confess, it is amazing to me, that any men of learning should give into such a notion, that christian baptism is founded upon a tradition of the baptism or dipping of proselytes with the Jews; of which tradition there is not the least hint, neither in the Old nor in the New Testament; nor in the Apocryphal writings between both; nor in *Josephus*; nor in *Philo* the Jew; nor in the Jewish *Mifnah*, or book of traditions; compiled in the second century, or at the beginning of the third, whether of the Jerusalem or Babylonian editions. I am content to risk that little reputation I have for Jewish learning, on this single point; if any passage can be produced in the *Mifnah*, mentioning such a tradition of the Jews, admitting proselytes by baptism or dipping, whether adult or children. I own it is mentioned in the *Gemara*, both Jerusalem and Babylonian, a work of later times, but not in the *Mifnah*; though Dr *Gale* has allowed it without examination. The only passage in it which Dr *Wall* refers to from *Selden*, though not fully expressed, is this [a], " a female stranger, a captive, a maiden, which are " redeemed and become proselytes, and are made free; being *under* (the next " paragraph is *above*) three years and one day old, are allowed the matrimonial " dowry;" that is, at marriage: but not a tittle is here, or any where else in the *Mifnah*, of receiving either minors or adult as proselytes by baptism or dipping: and supposing such a Jewish tradition, five-hundred, or three-hundred, or two-hundred years after Christ; or even so many years before Christ, of what avail would it be? He must be strangely bigoted to an hypothesis, to believe that our Lord, who so severely inveighed against the traditions of the Jews, and particularly those concerning their baptisms or dippings; should found his New Testament-ordinance of baptism, on a tradition of theirs, without excepting it from the other traditions, and without declaring his will it should be continued, which he has not done; and yet this, as Dr *Hammond* suggests, is *the basis of Infant-baptism*: to what wretched shifts must the Pædobaptists be driven for a foundation to place Infant-baptism on, to place it on such a rotten one; a tradition of men, who at other times, are reckoned by them, themselves, the most stupid, sottish, and despicable of all men upon the face of the earth? For the farther confutation of this notion, see Sir *Norton Knatchbull*

[a] Mifnah, Cetubat, c. 1. f. 2—4.

*Knatchbull* on 1 *Pet.* iii. 20, 21. *Stennett* againſt *Ruſſen*, p. 61. *Gale's Reflections* on *Wall's Hiſtory of Infant-baptiſm*, Letters 9 and 10. *Rees* on *Infant-baptiſm*, p. 17—29.

I ſhall not purſue this writer any farther, by giving particular anſwers to his arguments, objections, and queries, ſuch as they are; but ſhall only refer the reader to the anſwers that have been already given to them: as to the threadbare argument, from *Abraham's* covenant, and from circumciſion, for Old Teſtament times and caſes, are chiefly dealt in, to ſettle a New Teſtament-ordinance; ſee *Ewer's* Anſwer to *Hitchin*, *Rees* againſt *Walker*, and my Anſwers to *Dickinſon*, *Clarke*, and *Boſtwick*. Of the unreaſonableneſs of requiring inſtances of the adult baptiſm of children of chriſtian parents, in the ſcriptures, ſee my Strictures on *Boſtwick's Fair and Rational Vindication*, &c. p. 106. Of the teſtimonies of the ancient chriſtian writers in favour of Infant-baptiſm, ſee *Gale's Reflections*, &c. Letters 11, 12, 13. *Rees* on *Infant-baptiſm*, p. 150, &c. Some treatiſes of mine; *The Divine Right of Infant-baptiſm Examined*, &c. p. 20—25. *The Argument from Apoſtolic Tradition*, &c. *Antipædobaptiſm. Reply to Clarke*, p. 18—23. *Strictures on Boſtwick*, p. 100—103. 8vo. Edit.

I called upon this writer, in the notes on my Sermon, to name any lexicographer of note, that ever rendered the word $\beta\alpha\pi\tau\iota\zeta\omega$, by *perfundo* or *aſpergo*, to *pour* or *ſprinkle*; and behold! *Leigh's Critica Sacra*, is the only book quoted! and he the only lexicographer mentioned, if he may be ſo called! a book which every one of our illiterate lay-preachers, as they are called, are capable of quoting, and of confronting this writer with it; by obſerving that *Leigh* ſays, that " the native and proper ſignification of the word, is *to dip into water*, or *to plunge under water*, John iii. 22, 23. Matt. iii. 16. Acts viii. 38." In proof of baptiſm by immerſion, and of the true ſignification of the word, ſee *Gale's Reflections*, &c. Letters 3 and 4. *Rees* on *Infant-baptiſm*, p. 121, &c. my treatiſe of *The Ancient Mode of Baptizing*, and the Defence of it, with *The Divine Right of Infant-baptiſm Examined*, &c. p. 90, &c.

I bid this writer adieu: God give him repentance for his ſins, and the pardon of them; and this I am ſure he cannot charge, neither with uncharitableneſs, nor with Antinomianiſm.

When the Pædobaptiſts write again, it may be expected they will employ a better hand; or ſhould they chooſe to fix upon one of their younger ſort again; let them take care, firſt to wring the milk well out of his noſe, before they put a pen in his hand.

A DISSER-

A

# DISSERTATION

CONCERNING

The Eternal SONSHIP of CHRIST;

SHEWING

By whom it has been denied and opposed, and by whom asserted and defended, in all ages of christianity.

THE eternal Sonship of Christ, or that he is the Son of God by eternal generation, or that he was the Son of God before he was the son of *Mary*, even from all eternity, which is denied by the Socinians, and others akin to them, was known by the saints under the Old Testament; by *David*, Psalm ii. 7, 12, by *Solomon*, Prov. viii. 22, 30. by the prophet *Micah*, chap. v. 2. His Sonship was known by *Daniel*, from whom it is probable *Nebuchadnezzar* had it, *Dan.* iii. 25. from which it appears he was, and was known to be, the Son of God before he was born of the virgin, or before his incarnation, and therefore not called so on that account. This truth is written as with a sun-beam in the New Testament; but my design in what I am about is, not to give the proof of this doctrine from the sacred scriptures, but to shew who first set themselves against it, and who have continued the opposition to it, more or less, to this time; and, on the other hand, to shew that sound and orthodox christians, from the earliest times of christianity to the present, have asserted and defended it. I shall begin with

I. The first century, in which the Evangelists and Apostles lived; what their sentiments were concerning this doctrine, is abundantly manifest from their writings. The persons in this age who opposed the divine and eternal Sonship of Christ were,

1*st*, *Simon*

ETERNAL SONSHIP OF CHRIST, &c.

*1st, Simon Magus*, the father of heresies, as he is justly called; he first vented the notion afterwards imbibed by *Sabellius*, of one person in the Godhead; to which he added this blasphemy, that he was that person that so is. Before he professed himself a christian he gave out that he was some *great one*; he afterwards said, he was the one God himself under different names, the Father in *Samaria*, the Son in *Judea*, and the holy Spirit in the rest of the nations of the world [a]; or, as *Austin* [b] expresses it, he said that he in mount *Sinai* gave the law to *Moses* for the Jews, in the person of the Father; and in the time of *Tiberius* he seemingly appeared in the person of the Son, and afterwards as the holy Ghost, came upon the apostles in tongues of fire. And according to *Jerom* [c] he not only said, but wrote it; for it seems, according to him, he wrote some volumes, in which he said, "I am the Word of God, that is, the Son of God." *Menander* his disciple took the same characters and titles to himself his master did [d].

*2dly, Cerinthus* is the next, who was cotemporary with the apostle *John*, of whom that well known story is told [e], that the apostle being about to go into a bath at *Ephesus*, and seeing *Cerinthus* in it, said to those with him, "Let us flee from hence, lest the bath fall upon us in which *Cerinthus* the enemy of truth is:" he asserted that Christ was only a man, denying his deity [f], and in course his divine and eternal Sonship; he denied that Jesus was born of a virgin, which seemed to him impossible; and that he was the son of *Joseph* and *Mary*, as other men are [g] of their parents. *Jerom* says [h], at the request of the bishops of *Asia*, *John* the apostle wrote his gospel against *Cerinthus* and other hereticks, and especially the tenets of the Ebionites, then rising up, who asserted that Christ was not before *Mary*; hence he was obliged plainly to declare his divine generation; and it may be observed, that he is the only sacred writer who in his gospel and epistles speaks of Christ as the begotten and only begotten Son of God, at least speaks mostly of him as such.

*3dly, Ebion.* What his sentiment was concerning Christ, may be learned from what has been just observed, about the apostle *John*'s writing his gospel to refute it; and may be confirmed by what *Eusebius* [i] says of him, that he held that Christ was a mere man, and born as other men are: and though he makes mention of another sort of them, who did not deny that Christ was born of a virgin, and of the holy Ghost, nevertheless did not own that he existed before, being God the Word and Wisdom. Hence *Hilary* calls [k] *Photinus*, *Ebion*, because of the sameness.

[a] Irenæus adv. hæref. L. 1. c. 20.   [b] De Hæres. c. 1.
[c] Comment. in Matt. xxix. 5. tom. 9. fol. 33. A.   [d] Tertullian de præscript. hæret. c 46.
[e] Irenæus adv. hæref. l. 3. c. 3.   [f] Tertullian ut supra, c. 48.   [g] Irenæus ib. l. 1. c. 25.
[h] Catalog. scrip. eccles. c. 19. sic Irenæus l. 3. c. 11.   [i] Eccles. Hist. l. 3. c. 27. vid. Tertullian de carne Christ. c. 18.   [k] De Trinitate L 7. p. 81, 82.

ness of their principles, and *Jerom* says¹, *Photinus* endeavoured to restore the heresy of *Ebion*; now it is notorious that the notion of the Photinians was the same with the Socinians now, who say, that Christ was not before *Mary*; and so *Alexander* bishop of *Alexandria* ᵐ observes of *Arius* and his followers, who denied the natural sonship and eternal generation of Christ, that what they propagated were the heresy of *Ebion* and *Artemas*.

Besides the inspired writers, particularly the apostle *John*, who wrote his gospel, as now observed, to confute the heresies of *Ebion* and *Cerinthus*, and in vindication of the deity of Christ, and his divine and eternal generation, there are very few writings if any in this century extant. There is an epistle ascribed to *Barnabas*, cotemporary with the apostle *Paul*, in which are these words ⁿ, having made mention of the brazen serpent as a figure of Jesus, he adds, " what " said *Moses* again to Jesus the son of *Nave*, putting this name upon him, being " a prophet, that only all the people might hear that the Father hath made ma- " nifest all things concerning his Son Jesus in the son of *Nave*, and he put this " name upon him, when he sent him to spy the land—because the Son of God " in the last days will cut up by the roots the house of *Amalek*: behold again " Jesus, not the son of man, but the *Son of God*, manifested in the flesh by a " type.—Likewise *David* said, the *Lord said to my Lord*.—See how *David* calls " him "Lord, and the Son of God:" by which it appears that he believed that Christ was the Son of God before he was manifested in the flesh, or became incarnate; and that he was the Son of God according to the divine nature, as well as the Son of *David* according to the human nature, which he also expresses in the same paragraph. And elsewhere he says º, " *For this end the Son of God* " *came in the flesh*, that the full sum might be made of the sins of those who per- " secuted the prophets," so that according to him Christ was the Son of God before he came in the flesh or was incarnate.

*Clemens Romanus* was bishop of *Rome* in this century, and though the book of *Recognitions*, ascribed to him, are judged spurious, yet there is an epistle of his to the Corinthians ᵖ thought to be genuine: in which, after speaking of Christ our Saviour, and the high priest of our oblations, and the brightness of the magnificence of God, and of his having a more excellent name than the angels, observes, that the Lord thus says of his own Son, *Thou art my Son, this day have I begotten thee*; thereby declaring his belief, that Christ is the proper Son of God, and begotten by him. *Ignatius* was bishop of *Antioch* in this century, after the first bishop of that place *Evodius*, and was early in it, if any truth in these

---

¹ Catalog scrip. eccl. c 117.  ᵐ Apud Theodoret. hist. eccles. l. 1. c 4.
ⁿ Barnabæ epist. c. 9.   º Ibid. c 4.
ᵖ Clemens. epist. ad Corinth. p. 84. ed. Oxon. 16'9.

these reports that he was the child Christ took in his arms, when he rebuked his disciples; and that he saw Christ after his resurrection; but though these are things not to be depended on, yet it is certain that he lived in the latter end of the first century, and suffered martyrdom in the beginning of the second. Several epistles of his are extant, in which, as well as by words, he exhorted the saints to beware of heresies then springing up among them, and abounding, as *Eusebius* observes [q]; meaning the heresies of *Ebion* and *Cerinthus* about the person of Christ: and says many things which shew his belief, and what was their error. In one of his epistles [r] he exhorts to decline from some persons, as beasts, as ravenous dogs, biting secretly, and difficult of cure; and adds, "there is one physician, "carnal and spiritual, begotten and unbegotten, God made flesh, in a true and "immortal life, who is both of *Mary* and of God." In a larger epistle to the same [s], thought by some to be interpolated, though it expresses the same sentiment; "our physician is alone the true God, the unbegotten and invisible Lord "of all, the Father and *begetter of the only begotten one*; we have also a physi- "cian, our Lord Jesus Christ, the *only begotten Son before the world*, and the "word, and at last man of the virgin *Mary*;" and afterwards in the same [t] epistle still more expresly, "the Son of God, who was *begotten before the world was*, "and constitutes all things according to the will of the Father, he was bore in "the womb by *Mary*, according to the dispensation of God, of the seed of *David* "by the holy Ghost." And a little farther [u], "be ye all in grace by name, ga- "thered together in one common faith of God the Father, and of Jesus Christ "his only begotten Son, and the first-born of every creature; according to the "flesh indeed of the family of *David*: ye being guided by the Comforter." A plain account, as of the divine Sonship and Humanity of Christ, so of the doctrine of the Trinity. In another epistle of his [v], he speaks of Jesus Christ, "who "was with the Father before the world was, and in the end appeared," that is, in human nature in the end of the world; and exhorts all to "run to one tem- "ple of God, as to one altar, as to one Jesus Christ, who came forth from "one Father, and being in him and returning to him." And a little lower he adds, "there is one God, who hath manifested himself by Jesus Christ his Son, "who is his eternal word." And farther on he says, "study to be established "in the doctrines of the Lord, and of the apostles, that whatsoever ye do may "prosper, in flesh and spirit, in faith and love, in the Son, and in the Father, "and in the Spirit." A full confession of the Trinity, one of the principal doctrines he would have them be established in. All which is more fully ex-

VOL. II.   3 Z   pressed

[q] Eccles. hist. l. 3. c. 36.   [r] Epist. ad Ephes. p. 21. Ed. Voss.   [s] Ibid. p. 125.
[t] Ibid. p. 136.   [u] Ibid. p. 138.   [v] Epist. ad Magnes. p. 33, 34, 37.

pressed in the larger epistle[a] to the same persons: speaking of Christ, he says, "who was *begotten by the Father before the world was*; God the Word, the only begotten Son, and who remains to the end of the world, *for of his kingdom there is no end*." Again, "there is one God omnipotent, who hath manifested himself by Jesus Christ his Son, who is his Word; not spoken, but essential, not the voice of an articulate speech, but of a divine operation, begotten substance, who in all things pleased him that sent him." And farther on, "but ye have a plerophory in Christ, who was *begotten by the Father before all worlds*, afterwards made of the virgin *Mary* without the conversation of men." And in the larger epistle[y] of his to other persons, he thus speaks of some hereticks of his time; "they profess an unknown God, they think Christ is unbegotten, nor will they own that there is an holy Spirit: some of them say the Son is a mere man, and that the Father, the Son and the holy Spirit, are the same:—beware of such, lest your souls be ensnared." And in an epistle to another people[z] he says, "there is one unbegotten God the Father, and one only begotten Son, God the Word and man, and one comforter the Spirit of truth." And in an epistle[a] ascribed unto him he has these words, "there is one God and Father—there is also one Son, God the Word—and there is one comforter, the Spirit;—not three Fathers, nor three Sons, nor three Comforters, but one Father, and one Son, and one Comforter; therefore the Lord, when he sent his apostles to teach all nations, commanded them to *baptize in the name of the Father, and of the Son, and of the holy Ghost*; not in one of three names, nor into three that are incarnate, but into three of equal honour and glory." *Lucian*, that scoffing, blasphemous heathen, lived in the times of *Trajan*, and before, as *Suidas* says, wrote a dialogue[b] in derision of the christian religion, particularly of the doctrine of the Trinity: which dialogue, though it is a scoff at that doctrine, is a testimony of it, as held by the christians of that age; and among other things, he represents them as saying, that Christ is *the eternal Son of the Father*. I go on,

II. To the second century, in which the same heresies of *Ebion* and *Cerinthus* were held and propagated by *Carpocrates*, the father of the *Gnosticks*[c], by *Valentinus* and *Theodotus* the currier, whose disciples were another *Theodotus* a silversmith, and *Asclepiodotus* and *Artemon* also, according to *Eusebius*[d].

*1st. Carpocrates* was of *Alexandria* in *Egypt*, and lived in the beginning of the second century: he and his followers held that Christ was only a man, born of

*Joseph*

---

[a] Page 145, 147, 151.  [y] Ad Trallianos, p. 160.  [z] Ad Philadelph. p. 176.
[a] Ad Phillipans, p. 100.  [b] Entitled, *Philopatris*.  [c] Euseb. hist. eccles. l. 4. c. 7.
[d] Ibid. l. 5. c. 28.

## ETERNAL SONSHIP OF CHRIST, &c.   539

*Joseph* and *Mary*, of two parents, as other men[e], only he had a foul superior to others; which, having a strong memory, could remember, and so could relate, what he had seen and had knowledge of, when in the circumference (as they express it) and in conversation with his unknown and unbegotten Father; and which was endowed with such powers, that he escaped the angels, the makers of the world; and was so pure and holy, that he despised the Jews, among whom he was brought up; and afterwards returned to his unknown Father; his soul only, not his body [f]. There seems to be something similar in this notion of the human soul of Christ, to what is imbibed by some in our day.

2dly, *Valentinus*. He came to *Rome* when *Hyginus* was bishop of that place, flourished under *Pius*, and lived to the time of *Anicetus* [g]. He and his followers held, that God the creator sent forth his own Son, but that he was animal, and that his body descended from heaven, and passed through the virgin *Mary*, as water through a pipe; and therefore, as *Tertullian* observes [h], *Valentinus* used to say, that Christ was born *by* a virgin, but not *of* a virgin. This is what divines call the heretical illapse; which yet those disavow, who in our day are for the antiquity of the human nature of Christ before the world was; though how he could be really and actually man from eternity, and yet take flesh of the virgin in time, is not easy to reconcile.

3dly, *Artemon*, or *Artemas*, who lived in the time of *Victor* bishop of *Rome*. He held that Christ was a mere man [i]; and pretended that the apostles and all christians from their times to the times of *Victor*, held the same [k]; than which nothing could be more notoriously false, as the writings of *Justin*, *Irenæus*, &c. shew: and it is said that by him, or by his followers, the celebrated text in 1 *John* v. 7. was erased and left out in some copies [l].

4thly, *Theodotus* the currier held the same notion he did, that Christ was a mere man; for which he was excommunicated by *Victor* bishop of *Rome*: which shews the falsity of what *Artemon* said; for if *Victor* had been of the same opinion, he would never have excommunicated *Theodotus*. *Eusebius* says, this man was the father and broacher of this notion [m], before *Artemon*, that Christ was a a mere man, and denied him to be God. Yea, that he was not only a mere man, but born of the seed of man [n]. Though *Tertullian* says, that he held

that

---

[e] Irenæus adv. hæres, l. 1. c. 24. Tertull. de præscript. hæret. c. 48.
[f] Irenæus ib. Epiphan. contra hæret. hær. 27. Theodoret. hæret. fol. l. 1. c 7. Aug. de hæret. c. 7.
[g] Irenæus l. 3 c. 4.   [h] Ibid. l. c. 1. Tertull. de præscript. c. 49. Epiphan. hæres. 31.
[i] Adv. Valentin. c. 27. & de carne Christ. c. 20.
[k] Euseb. Eccles. Hist. l. 5. c. 25. Theodoret. hæret. fol. l. 2. c. 5.
[l] Wittichii Theolog. pacific. c. 17. f. 25.   [m] Euseb. eccles. hist. l. 5. c. 28.
[n] Epiphan. Hæres. 54.

540 A DISSERTATION CONCERNING THE

that Chrift was only a man, but equally conceived and born of the holy Ghoſt
and the virgin *Mary*, yet inferior to *Melchizedeck* °.

The contrary to theſe notions was aſſerted and maintained by thoſe apoſto-
lical men, not only *Ignatius*, who lived in the latter end of the preceding century, and the beginning of this, as has been obſerved, but by *Polycarp*, *Juſtin
Martyr*, *Irenæus*, and others.

1. *Polycarp*, biſhop of *Smyrna*, a diſciple and hearer of the apoſtle *John*, uſed
to ſtop his ears when he heard the impious ſpeeches of the hereticks of his time.
This venerable martyr, who had ſerved his maſter Chriſt eighty ſix years, when
at the ſtake, and the fire juſt about to be kindled upon him, witneſſed a good
confeſſion of the bleſſed Trinity in his laſt moments, putting up the following
prayer; "O Father of thy beloved and bleſſed Son Jeſus Chriſt, by whom we
" have received the knowledge of thee; God of angels and of powers, and every
" creature—I praiſe thee for all things; I bleſs thee, I glorify thee, by the
" eternal high prieſt Jeſus Chriſt thy beloved Son, through whom, to thee with
" him in the holy ſpirit, be glory, now and for ever, *Amen* ᵖ "

2. *Juſtin*, the philoſopher and martyr, in his firſt apology ᵠ for the chriſtians,
has theſe words; "The Father of all, being unbegotten, has no name—the Son
" of him, who only is properly called a Son, the Word, begotten and exiſting
" before the creatures (for at the beginning by him he created and beautified
" all things) is called Chriſt." And in his ſecond apology he ſays ʳ, "We pro-
" feſs to be atheiſts with reſpect to ſuch who are thought to be Gods, but not
" to the true God and Father of righteouſneſs, &c. him, and his Son who comes
" from him, and has taught us theſe things, and the prophetic Spirit, we adore
" and worſhip." Afterwards ˢ he ſpeaks of the *logos*, or word, as the *firſt birth*
of God: "which, ſays he, we ſay is begotten without mixture." And again ᵗ,
" We ſpeak that which is true, Jeſus Chriſt alone is properly the Son begotten
" by God, being his Word, and firſt-born, and power, and by his will became
" man; theſe things he hath taught us." And in his dialogue with *Trypho* the
Jew ᵘ, who is repreſented as objecting to him, "What thou ſayeſt, that this
" Chriſt exiſted God before the world, and then was born, and became man,
" does not only ſeem to be a paradox to me, but quite fooliſh." To which
*Juſtin* replies, "I know this ſeems a paradox, eſpecially to thoſe of your nation,
" —but if I cannot demonſtrate, that this is the Chriſt of God, and that he
" pre-exiſted God, the Son of the maker of all things, and became man by
" a virgin, in this only it would be juſt to ſay, that I am miſtaken, but not to
" deny

° De præſcript. Hær. c. 53.   ᵖ Euſeb. l. 4. c. 15.   ᵠ Page 44.
ʳ Page 56.   ˢ Ibid. p. 66.   ᵗ Ibid. p. 68.   ᵘ Page 267.

"deny that this is the Chrift of God, though he may feem to be begotten a man
"of men, and by choice made Chrift, as afferted by fome; for there are fome
"of our religion who profefs him to be Chrift, but affirm that he is begotten a
"man of men; to whom I do not affent, nor many who are in the fame mind
"with me." In which he plainly refers to the hereticks before mentioned, who thought that Chrift was born of *Jofeph* and *Mary*. And in another place, in the fame dialogue, he fays [w], "I will prove from fcripture that God firft
"*begat of himfelf, before all creatures*, a certain rational power, which is called
"by the holy Spirit, the Glory of the Lord, fometimes the Son, fometimes Wif-
"dom, fometimes the Angel, fometimes God, fometimes the Lord and the
"Word." And then, after obferving there is fomething fimilar in the Word begetting a Word without any rejection or diminution, and fire kindling fire without leffening it, and abiding the fame; he proceeds to give his proof from the words of *Solomon*, Prov. viii. where "the word of wifdom teftifies, that he
"is the God who is *begotten* by the Father of all, who is the word and wifdom
"and the power and the glory of him that *generates*." And then obferves, that "this is the *birth* produced by the *Father*, which *co-exifted* with the Father
"*before all creatures*, and with whom the Father familiarly converfed, as the
"word by *Solomon* makes it manifeft, that he the beginning before all creatures
"is the *birth begotten by God*, which by *Solomon* is called Wifdom." And in another place [x], in the fame dialogue, on mention of the fame words in *Proverbs* he fays, "Ye muft underftand, ye hearers, if ye do but attend, the Word declares
"that this birth was *begotten by the Father before all creatures*, and that which is
"*begotten* is *numerically* another from him that *begets*." What can be more ex-prefs for the eternal generation of the Son of God, and that as a diftinct perfon from his Father!

3. *Irenæus*, a martyr, and bifhop of *Lyons* in *France*, and a difciple of *Poly-carp*. He wrote five books againft the herefies of *Valentinus* and the Gnoftics, which are ftill extant; out of which many teftimonies might be produced con-firming the doctrine of the Trinity, and the deity of Chrift. I fhall only tran-fcribe two or three paffages relating to the divine Sonfhip and generation of Chrift. In one place he fays [y], "Thou art not increated and man, nor didft
"thou always *co-exift with God, as his own word* did, but through his eminent
"goodnefs, haft now had a beginning of beings; thou fenfibly learneft from
"the word the difpofitions of God who made thee; therefore obferve the order
"of thy knowledge, and left, as ignorant of good things, thou fhouldeft tran-
"fcend

[w] Ibid. p. 284, 285.  [x] Ibid p. 359.
[y] Adv. Hæres. l. 2. c. 43.

"fcend God himfelf." And again [y], "fhould any one fay to us, how is the Son *brought forth by the Father?* we reply to him, This bringing forth or *generation*, &c. or by whatfoever name it is called; no man knows his exifting *unfpeakable* generation; not *Valentinus*, not *Marcion*, nor *Saturninus*, nor *Bafilides*, nor angels, nor archangels, nor principalities, nor powers, only the Father, who hath *generated*, and the Son that is *generated*; therefore feeing his generation is ineffable, whoever attempts to declare fuch productions and generations (as the above hereticks did) are not in their right minds, promifing to declare thofe things which cannot be declared." And elfewhere, he fays [z], "The Son, the Word and Wifdom, was always prefent with him (God), and alfo the Spirit, by whom, and in whom, he made all things freely and willingly; to whom he fpake, faying, *Let us make man*, &c." And a little after, "that the Word, that is, the Son, was always with the Father, we have abundant proof;" and then mentions *Prov.* iii. 19. and viii. 22, &c.

4. *Athenagoras*, who flourifhed at *Athens*, in the times of *Antoninus* and *Commodus*, to which emperors he wrote an apology for the chriftians, in which he has thefe words [a], "Let not any think it ridiculous in me that I fpeak of God as having a Son, for not as the poets fable, who make their Gods nothing better than men, do we think either of God the Father, or of the Son; but the Son of God is the Word of the Father, in idea and efficacy, *for of him and by him are all things made*, feeing the Father and the Son are one; fo that the Son is in the Father, and the Father is in the Son, by the union and power of the Spirit; the mind and word of the Father is the Son of God; now if any through the fublimity of your underftanding would look further and enquire what the Son means, I will tell him in a few words, that he is the *firft birth of the Father*; not as made, for from the beginning, God being the eternal mind, he had the word in himfelf (the λογ⊙, or reafon) being *eternally rational*, (that is, never without his word and wifdom) but as coming forth, is the idea and energy of all things." For which he produces as proof *Prov.* viii. 22. and then proceeds, "Who therefore cannot wonder, to hear us called atheifts, who fpeak of God the Father, and of God the Son and the holy Spirit, fhewing their power in unity and their diftinction in order?" A little farther [b], he ftrongly expreffes the doctrine of the Trinity in Unity; "We affert God, and the Son his Word, and the holy Ghoft, united indeed according to power, the Father, the Son, the Spirit, for the Mind, Word and Wifdom, is the Son of the Father, and the Spirit an emanation, or influence, as light from fire."

5. *Theophilus,*

[y] Ibid. c. 48.   [z] L. 4. c. 37.
[a] Legatio pro Chriftian. p. 10, 11.   [b] Ibid. p. 27.

# ETERNAL SONSHIP OF CHRIST, &c.

5. *Theophilus*, bishop of *Antioch*, flourished under the emperor *Antoninus Verus*: in a treatise of his[c] he has these words concerning the Word and Son of God, "God having his λογον ενδιαθετον, internal word within himself, *begat him*, when he brought him forth with his wisdom *before all things*; this word he used in working those things that were made by him, and he made all things by him. —The prophets were not when the world was made; but the wisdom of God, which is in him, and the holy word of God, was always present with him;" in proof of which he produces *Prov.* viii. 27. And in another place[d], speaking of the voice *Adam* heard, says, "What else is the voice, but the word of God, who is his Son? not as the poets and writers of fables, who say, the sons of the gods are born of copulation; but as the truth declares, the internal Word being always in the heart of God, before any thing was made, him he had as his counsellor, being his mind and prudence, when God would do what he counselled, he begat the Word, and having begotten the Word, the first-born of every creature, he always conversed with his Word," for which he quotes *John* i. 1—3.

6. *Clemens* of *Alexandria*, flourished under the emperors *Severus* and *Caracalla*, towards the latter end of the second century, he bears a plain testimony to the doctrine of the Trinity, concluding one of his treatises thus[e], "Let us give thanks, praising the only Father and the Son, both teachers, with the holy Spirit, in which are all things, in whom are all things, and by whom all are one,—to whom be glory now and for ever, *Amen.*" He speaks[f] of Christ the perfect word, as born of the perfect Father; and says[g] of the Son of God, "that he never goes out of his watch-tower, who is not divided nor dissecated, nor passes from place to place, but is always every where, is contained no where, all mind, all paternal light, all eye; who sees all things, hears all things, knows all things by his power, searches powers, and to whom the whole militia of angels and gods (magistrates) is subject.—This is the Son of God, the Saviour and Lord whom we speak of, and the divine prophecies shew." A little after he speaks of him as, "*begotten without beginning*, that is, eternally begotten, and who, before the foundation of the world, was the Father's counsellor, that wisdom in whom the almighty God delighted; for Son is the power of God; who before all things were made, was the most antient word of the Father.—Every operation of the Lord has a reference to the almighty; and the Son is, as I may say, a certain energy of the Father." This antient writer frequently attacks and refutes the Carpocratians, Valentinians, and Gnostics, and other heretics of this and the preceding age. I proceed,

III. To

[c] Ad. Autolog. c. l. 2. p. 88.    [d] Ibid. p. 100.    [e] Pædagog. L 3. p. 266.
[f] Ibid. l. 1. c. 6. p. 92.    [g] Stromat. l. 7. p. 702, 703.

III. To the third century. The herefies which fprung up in this age refpecting the Perfon, Sonfhip, and Deity of Chrift, were thofe of *Beryllus*, who revived
that of *Artemon*, and of the Noetians or Sabellians, fometimes called Patripaffians, and of the Samofatenians.

1ft, *Beryllus*, bifhop of *Boftra* in *Aretia*, who for fome time behaved well in
his office, as *Jerom* fays[l], but at length fell into this notion, that Chrift was
not before his incarnation; or as *Eufebius*[k] expreffes it, that our Lord and
Saviour did not fubfift in his own fubftance before he fojourned among men,
and had no deity of his own refiding in him, but his Father's; but through difputations he had with feveral bifhops, and particularly with *Origen*, he was
recovered from his error and reftored to the truth.

2. The Noetians, fo called from *Noetus*, and afterwards Sabellians, from
*Sabellius*, a difciple of the former; thofe held that Father, Son and Spirit, are
one perfon under thefe different names. The foundation of their herefy was
laid by *Simon Magus*, as before obferved. They were fometimes called Praxeans
and Hermogenians, from *Praxeus* and *Hermogenes*, the firft authors of it, who
embraced the fame notions in this period, and fometimes Patripaffians, becaufe,
in confequence of this principle, they held that the Father might be faid to
fuffer as the Son[l].

3. The Samofatenians, fo called from *Paul* of *Samofate*, bifhop of *Antioch*,
who revived the herefy of *Artemon*, that Chrift was a mere man. He held that
Chrift was no other than a common man; he refufed to own that he was the
Son of God, come from heaven; he denied that the only begotten Son and
Word was God of God: he agreed with the Noetians and Sabellians, that there
was but one perfon in the Godhead[m]; of thefe notions he was convicted, and
for them condemned by the fynod at *Antioch*[n].

The writers of this age are but few, whofe writings have been continued
and tranfmitted to us; but thofe we have, ftrongly oppofed the errors now
mentioned; the chief are *Tertullian*, *Origen*, and *Cyprian*, befides in fome fragments of others.

1. *Tertullian*. He wrote againft *Praxeus*, who held the fame notion that
*Noetus* and *Sabellius* did, in which work he not only expreffes his firm belief of
the Trinity in Unity, faying[o]; " neverthelefs the oeconomy is preferved, which
" difpofes Unity into Trinity, three, not in ftate (or nature, effence) but in de-
" gree (or perfon) not in fubftance but in form, not in power but in fpecies, of
" one fubftance, of one ftate, and of one power, becaufe but one God, from whom
" thefe

---

[l] Catalog. Script. Eccles c. 70.  [k] Hift. Eccles. l. 6. c. 33.
[l] Epiphan. Hæres. 42 Aug de hæres. c 36, 41.
[m] Eufeb. Eccles Hift. l 7. c. 27, 30 Epiphan Hæret. 65. Aug de Hæres. c. 44.
[n] Eufeb. ib. c. 29.  [o] Adv. Praxeam. c. 2.

"these degrees, forms and species are deputed, under the name of the Father, "and of the Son, and of the holy Spirit." And that he means three distinct persons, is clear from what he afterwards *says*: "whatsoever therefore was the "substance of the Word, that I call a person, and to him I give the name of "Son; and whilst I acknowledge a Son, I defend a second from the Father." The distinction of the Father and Son from each other, and the eternal generation of the one from the other, are fully expressed by him: "this rule as *pro- "fessed by me, is every where held; by which I testify, the Father, Son, and "Spirit are inseparable from each other; - for lo I say, another is the Father, "and another is the Son, and another is the holy Spirit;—not that the Son is "another from the Father, by diversity, but by distribution; not another by "division, but by distinction:—another is he that *generates*, and another he that "is *generated*:—a Father must needs have a Son that he may be a Father, and "the Son a Father that he may be a Son." And again *, he explains the words in *Prov.* viii. 22. (*The Lord possessed me*) of the generation of the Son; and on the clause, *when he prepared the heavens, I was with him,* he remarks, " thereby "making himself equal to him, by proceeding from whom he became the Son "and first born, as being *begotten before all things*; and the only begotten, as "being alone begotten of God." On these words, *Thou art my Son, this day "have I begotten thee,* he observes * to *Praxeas,* "if you would have me believe "that he is both Father and Son, shew me such a passage elsewhere, *The Lord "said* unto himself, *I am* my Son, *this day have I begotten* my Self." And in another work * of his, he has these words, speaking of the Word, "this we "learn is brought forth from God, and by being brought forth, *generated,* and "*and therefore called the Son of God,* and God, from the unity of substance;— "so that what comes from God, is God, and the Son of God, and both one:" that is, one God.

2. *Origen.* Notwithstanding his many errors, he is very express for the doctrine of the Trinity, and the distinction of the Father and Son in it, and of the eternal generation of the Son: he observes * of the Seraphim, in *Isai.* vi. 3. that by saying, "*Holy, holy, holy,* they preserve the mystery of the Trinity; that it "was not enough for them to cry *holy* once nor twice, but they take up the "perfect number of the Trinity, that they might manifest the multitude of "the holiness of God, which is the repeated community of the trine holiness, "the holiness of the Father, the holiness of the only begotten Son, and of the "holy Spirit." And elsewhere *, allegorizing the shew-bread, and the two tenth deals in one cake, he asks, how two tenths become one lump? because, says

says he, " we do not feparate the Son from the Father, nor the Father from the Son, *John* xiv. 9. therefore each loaf is of two tenths, and fet in two pofitions, that is, in two rows, for if there was one pofition, it would be confufed, and the Word would be mixed of the Father and the Son, but now indeed it is but one bread; for there is one will and one fubftance; but there are two pofitions; that is, two proprieties of perfons (or proper perfons) for we call him the Father who is not the Son; and him the Son who is not the Father." Of the generation of the Son of God he thus fpeaks [x], " Jefus Chrift himfelf who is come, was *begotten of the Father before every creature was.*" And again [y], " it is abominable and unlawful to equal God the Father in the *generation of his only begotten Son*, and in his fubftance, to any one, men or other kind of animals; but there muft needs be fome exception, and fomething worthy of God, to which there can be no comparifon, not in things only, but indeed not in thought: nor can it be found by fenfe, nor can the human thought apprehend, how the unbegotten God is the Father of the only begotten Son: for *generation is eternal*, as brightnefs is generated from light, for he is not a Son by adoption of the Spirit extrinfically, but he is a *Son by nature.*"

3. *Cyprian.* Little is to be met with in his writings on this fubject. The following is the moft remarkable and particular [z]; " the voice of the Father was heard from heaven, *This is my beloved Son, in whom I am well pleafed, hear ye him*;— that this voice came from thy paternity, there is none that doubts; there is none who dares to arrogate this word to himfelf; there is none among the heavenly troops who dare call the Lord Jefus his Son. Certainly to thee only the Trinity is known, the Father only knows the Son, and the Son knows the Father, neither is he known by any unlefs he reveals him; in the fchool of divine teaching, the Father is he that teaches and inftructs, the Son who reveals and opens the fecrets of God unto us, and the holy Spirit who fits and furnifhes us; from the Father we receive power, from the Son wifdom, and from the holy Spirit innocence. The Father choofes, the Son loves, the holy Spirit joins and unites; from the Father is given us eternity, from the Son conformity to him his image, and from the holy Spirit integrity and liberty; in the Father we are, in the Son we live, in the holy Spirit we are moved, and become proficients; eternal deity and temporal humanity meet together, and by the tenour of both natures is made an unity, that it is impoffible that what is joined fhould be feparated from one another." As for the Expofition of the Creed, which ftands among

*Cyprian's*

[x] περι Αρχων proem fol. 111. 4. [y] Ibid. l. 1. c. 2. fol. 114. 4. vid. Pamphil. Apolog. pro Origen. inter opere Hieronom. tom. 4. fol. 74. M. & fol. 77. A.
[z] Cyprian. de baptifmo inter opera ejus, p. 455.

## ETERNAL SONSHIP OF CHRIST, &c.

*Cyprian*'s works, and is sometimes attributed to him, it was done by *Ruffinus*, and the testimonies from thence will be produced in the proper place.

4. *Gregory* of *Neocæsarea*, sometimes called *Thaumaturgus*, the wonder-worker, lived in this century, to whom is ascribed ª the following confession of faith; "One God, the Father of the living Word, of subsisting wisdom and power, and of the eternal character, perfect begetter of the perfect One, Father of the only begotten Son: and God the Son, who is through all. The perfect Trinity, which in glory eternity and kingdom, cannot be divided nor alienated. Not therefore any thing created or servile is in the Trinity, nor any thing superinduced, nor first and last; nor did the Son ever want a Father, nor the Son a Spirit: but the Trinity is always the same, immutable and invariable." And among his twelve articles of faith, with an anathema annexed to them, this is one ᵇ; "If any one says, another is the Son who was before the world, and another who was in the last times, and does not confess, that he who was before the world, and he who was in the last times, is the same, as it is written, let him be anathema." The interpolation follows; "how can it be said, another is the Son of God before the world was, and another in the last days, when the Lord says, *before Abraham was, I am*; and because *I came forth from the Father, and am come*; and again, *I go to my Father?*"

5. *Dionysius*, bishop of *Alexandria*, was a disciple of *Origen*: he wrote against the Sabellians ᶜ, but none of his writings are extant, only some fragments preserved in other authors. And whereas *Arius* made use of some passages of his, and improved them in favour of his own notions, *Athanasius* from him shews the contrary, as where in one of his volumes he expressly says ᵈ, that "there never was a time in which God was not a Father; and in the following acknowledges, that Christ the Word, Wisdom and Power, always was; that he is the eternal Son of the eternal Father; for if there is a Father, there must be a Son; and if there was no Son, how could he be the Father of any? but there are both, and always were.—The Son alone always co-existed with the Father.—God the Father always was: and the Father being eternal, the Son also is eternal, and co-existed with him as brightness with light." And in answer to another objection, made against him, that when he mentioned the Father, he said nothing of the Son, and when he named the Son, said nothing of the Father; it is observed, that in another volume of his, he says ᵉ, that "each of these names spoken of by me, are inseparable and indivisible from one another; when I speak of the Father, and before I introduce the Son, I

4 A 2 "signify

---

ª Expof Fidei inter opera ejus. p. 1. ed. Paris. ᵇ Ibid. p 4.
ᶜ Epist. ad Xystum apud Euseb. l. 7. c. 6. & ad Ammonium & Euphranor. apud Athanasium de Sent Dionyf. p. 433, 435. ᵈ Elench. & Apolog. vol. 1. apud Athanaf. ib. p 436, 437.
ᵉ Ibid. vol. 2. apud Athanaf. ibid. p. 437.

"signify him in the Father; when I introduce the Son, though I have not before spoken of the Father, he is always to be understood in the Son."

6. The errors of *Paulus Samosate* were condemned by the synod at *Antioch*, towards the latter end of this century, by whom a formula or confession of faith was agreed to, in which are these words [f]. " We profess that our Lord Jesus Christ was *begotten of the Father before ages*, according to the Spirit, and in the last days, born of a virgin, according to the flesh." The word ὁμοούσιος, *consubstantial*, is used in their creed. Towards the close of this century, and at the beginning of the next, lived *Lactantius*, (for he lived under *Dioclesian*, and to the times of *Constantine*) who asserts [g], that God, the maker of all things, begat " a Spirit holy, incorruptible, and irreprehensible, whom he called the Son." He asks [h], " how hath he procreated? The divine works can neither be known nor declared by any; nevertheless the scriptures teach, that the Son of God is the Word of God." Nothing more is to be observed in this century. I pass on,

IV. To the fourth century, in which rose up the Arians and Photinians, and others. 1st, The Arians, so called from *Arius*, a presbyter of the church of *Alexandria*, in the beginning of this century, who took occasion from some words dropped in disputation by *Alexander* his bishop, to oppose him, and start the heresy that goes under his name; and though the eternal Sonship of Christ was virtually denied by preceding hereticks, who affirmed that Christ did not exist before *Mary*; in opposition to whom the orthodox affirmed, that he was *begotten of the Father before all worlds*; yet *Arius* was the first, who pretended to acknowledge the Trinity, that actually and in express words set himself to oppose the eternal Sonship of Christ by generation; and argued much in the same manner as those do, who oppose it now: for being a man who had a good share of knowledge of the art of logic, as the historian observes [i], he reasoned thus, " If the Father begat the Son, he that is begotten, must have a beginning of his existence, from whence it is manifest, that there was a time when the Son was not; and therefore it necessarily follows, that he had his subsistence from things that are not;" or was brought out of a state of non-existence into a state of existence. He understood *generated* in no other sense than of being *created* or *made*; and asserted, that he was created by God before time, and was the first creature, and by which he made all others; in proof of which he urged *Prov.* viii. 22. taking the advantage of the Greek version, which, instead of *possessed me*, reads *created me the beginning of his ways*. His sentiments will more fully appear from his own words in his epistles to *Eusebius* of *Nicomedia*, and to his

[f] Apud Forbes. Instruct. Hist. Theolog. l. 1. c. 4. p. 10.    [g] De verb. Sap. l. 4. c. 6.
[h] Ibid. c. 8.    [i] Socrat. Hist. Eccl. l. 1. c. 5.

his own bishop, *Alexander* of *Alexandria*; in his letter to the former, he says [e], "Our sentiments and doctrines are, that the Son is not unbegotten, nor a part of the unbegotten in any manner, nor out of any subject matter, but that by will and counsel he subsisted before times and ages, perfect God, the only begotten, immutable; and that before he was begotten or created, or decreed or established, *he was not*, for he was not unbegotten; we are persecuted because we say, *the Son had a beginning*, but God is without beginning; for this we are persecuted, and because we say, that he is of things that did not exist (that is, out of nothing;) so we say, that he is not a part of God, nor out of any subject-matter; and for this we are persecuted." And in his letter to his bishop, he thus expresses himself [h], "We acknowledge one God, the only unbegotten; —that this God begat the only begotten Son before time, by whom he made the world, and the rest of things; that he begot him not in appearance, but in reality; and that by his will he subsisted, immutable and unalterable, a perfect creature, but as one of the creatures, a birth, but as one of the births —We say, that he was created before times and ages, by the will of God, and received his life and being from the Father; so that the Father together appointed glories for him;—The Son without time was begotten by the Father, and was created and established before the world was; he was not before he was begotten, but without time was begotten before all things, and subsisted alone from the alone Father; neither is eternal nor co-eternal, nor co-unbegotten with the Father, nor had he a being together with the Father." What he held is also manifest from his creed [i], which he delivered in the following words, "I believe in one eternal God, and in his Son whom he created before the world, and as God he made the Son, and all the Son has, he has not (of himself,) he receives from God, and therefore the Son is not equal to, and of the same dignity with the Father, but comes short of the glory of God, as a workmanship; and is less than the power of God. I believe in the holy Ghost, who is made by the Son."

The Arians were sometimes called Aetians, from *Aetius*, a warm defender of the doctrine of *Arius*, and who stumbled at the same thing that *Arius* did; for he could not understand, the historian says [k], how that which is begotten could be co-eternal with him that begets; but when *Arius* dissembled and signed that form of doctrine in the Nicene Synod, *Aetius* took the opportunity of breaking off from the Arians, and of setting up a distinct sect, and himself at the head of them. These were after called Eunomians, from *Eunomius*, a disciple of *Aetius*; he is said [l] to add to and to exceed the blasphemy of *Arius*; he with great boldness

[e] Apud Theodoret. Eccl. Hist. l. 1. c. 5.   [h] Apud Epiphan. Hæres. 69.
[i] Apud Athanas. in Nic. concil. contr. Arium disput. p. 81, 82.   [k] Socrat. Eccl. Hist. l. 2. c. 35.
[l] Theodoret. Eccl. Hist. l. 2. c. 29.

nels renewed the herefy of *Aetius*, who not only after *Arius* afferted that the Son was created out of nothing, but that he was unlike to the Father ⁿ. Hence the followers of thefe men were called Anomœans. There was another fect called Nativitarians, who were a fucker or branch that fprung from the Eunomians, and refined upon them; thefe held that the Son had his nativity of the Father, the beginning of it from time; yet being willing to own that he was co-eternal with the Father, thought that he was with him before he was begotten of him, that is, that he always was, but not always a Son, but that he began to be a Son from the time he was begotten. There is a near approach to the fentiments of thefe in fome of our days.

The Arians were alfo called Macedonians, from *Macedonius* a violent perfecutor of the orthodox, called Homooufians ⁿ, who believed that the Son is of the fame fubftance with the Father; but this man afterwards becoming bifhop of *Conftantinople*, refufed to call him a creature, whom the holy fcripture calls the Son; and therefore the Arians rejected him, and he became the author and patron of his own fect; he denied the Son was confubftantial with the Father, but taught, that in all things he was like to him that begat him, and in exprefs words called the Spirit a creature º, and the denial of the deity of the holy Spirit is the diftinguifhing tenet of his followers.

2*dly*, The Photinians rofe up much about the fame time the Arians did, for they are made mention of in the council of *Nice*, but their opinions differ from the Arians. Thefe were fometimes called Marcellians, from *Marcellius* of *Ancyra*, whofe difciple *Photinus* was, and from him named Photinians. He was bifhop of *Syrmium*; his notions were the fame with *Ebion* and *Paul* of *Samofate*, that Chrift was a mere man, and was only of *Mary*; he would not admit of the generation and exiftence of Chrift before the world was ᵖ. His followers were much the fame with our modern Socinians, and who are fometimes called by the fame name. According to *Thomas Aquinas* ᵠ, the Photinians, and fo the Cerinthians, Ebionites, and Samofatenians before them, as they held that Chrift was a mere man, and took his beginning from *Mary*, fo that he only obtained the honour of deity above others by the merit of his bleffed life; that he was, like other men, the Son of God by the Spirit of adoption, and by grace born of him, and by fome likenefs to God is in fcripture called God, not by nature, but by fome participation of divine goodnefs.

Thefe herefies were condemned by the feveral councils and fynods held on account of them, and were refuted by various found and valuable writers who
lived

Sozomen. Eccl. Hift. l 6. c. 25.     ⁿ Socrat. Eccl. Hift. l. 2. c. 38.
º Theodoret. Eccl. Hift. l 2 c. 6.     ᵖ Theodoret. ibid. l. 5. c. 11. Socrat. l. 7. c. 32.
Sozomen. l. 4. c. 6.     ᵠ Contr. Gentiles, l. 4. c. 4. p. 610.

lived in this century: to produce all their testimonies would be endless; I shall only take notice of a few, and particularly such as respect the Sonship of Christ.

1. The tenets of *Arius* were condemned by the council held at *Nice* in *Bythinia*, consisting of three hundred and eighteen bishops, by whom was composed the following creed or agreement of faith, as the historian calls it [r]: "We be-" lieve in one God the Father Almighty, the maker of all things, visible and "invisible; and in one Lord Jesus Christ, the Son of God, the only begotten, "begotten of the Father, that is, out of the substance of the Father, God of "God, light of light, true God of true God; begotten not made, consubstan-"tial (or of the same essence) with the Father, by whom all things are made "which are in heaven and in earth; who for us men, and for our salvation, de-"scended and became incarnate, and was made man and suffered, and rose again "the third day; ascended up into heaven, and will come to judge the quick "and the dead. And we believe in the holy Spirit. As for those that say, "there was a time when the Son of God was not, and before he was begotten "was not, and that he was made of what does not exist (out of nothing), and "say, he was from another substance, or essence, or created, or turned, or "changed; the holy catholic and apostolic church anathematizes."

2. *Athanasius* was a famous champion for the doctrines of the Trinity, the proper Sonship of Christ, and his eternal generation; to produce all the testimonies from him that might be produced in proof of those doctrines, would be to transcribe a great part of his writings; it may be sufficient to give his creed; not that which is commonly called the Athanasian creed, which, whether penned by him is a doubt, but that which stands in his works, and was delivered by him in a personal disputation with *Arius*, and is as follows; which he calls an epitome of his faith [t]. "I believe in one God the Father, the al-"mighty, being always God the Father; and I believe in God the Word, the "only begotten Son of God, that he co-existed with his own Father; that "he is the equal Son of the Father; and that he is the Son of God; of the same "dignity; that he is always with his Father by his deity, and that he contains all "things in his essence; but the Son of God is not contained by any, even as "God his Father: and I believe in the holy Ghost, that he is of the essence of "the Father, and that the holy Spirit is co-eternal with the Father and with the "Son. The Word, I say, was made flesh." After this I would only just observe, that *Athanasius* having said that the Son was without beginning and eternally begotten of the Father, farther says [t], that he was begotten ineffably and inconceivably; and elsewhere he says [u], "it is superfluous or rather full madness to
"call

---

[r] Socrat. Hist. l. 1. c. 8.    [s] Contr Arian. disput. inter opera ejus, vol. I. p. 83.
[t] Exposit. fidei, vol. I. p. 394.    [u] Contr. Arian. Orat. 3. p. 211, 214.

"call in queſtion, and in an heretical manner to aſk, how can the Son be eter-
"nal? or, how can he be of the ſubſtance (or eſſence) of the Father, and not
"be a part of him?" And a little farther, "it is unbecoming to enquire how
"the Word is of God, or how he is the brightneſs of God, or how God begets,
"and what is the mode of the generation of God: he muſt be a madman that
"will attempt ſuch things, ſince the thing is ineffable, and proper to the na-
"ture of God only, this is only known to himſelf and his Son."

3. *Alexander*, biſhop of *Alexandria*, whom *Arius* oppoſed, and ſhould have been mentioned firſt, in an epiſtle of his to *Alexander*, biſhop of *Conſtantinople* ▼, acquaints him with the opinion of *Arius*, that there was a time when the Son of God was not, and he that was not before, afterwards exiſted, and ſuch was he made, when he was made as every man is; and that the Son of God is out of things that are not, or out of nothing; he obſerves to him, that what was his faith and the faith of others, was the faith of the apoſtolic church: "We be-
"lieve in one unbegotten Father,—and in one Lord Jeſus Chriſt, the only
"begotten Son of God; not begotten out of that which is not, but from
"the Father; that exiſts, not in a corporal manner by inciſion, or defluctions
"of diviſions, as ſeemed to *Sabellius* and *Valentinus*, but in a manner ineffable
"and inexplicable."

4. *Epiphanius* wrote a volume againſt all hereſies, and attempts a confutation of them: and with reſpect to the Arian hereſy, he thus writes ˣ; "God exiſting,
"incomprehenſible, has begat him that is incomprehenſible, *before all ages and
"times*, and there is no ſpace between the Son and the Father, but as ſoon as
"you underſtand a Father, you underſtand a Son, and as ſoon as you name
"a Father you ſhew a Son; the Son is underſtood by the Father, and the Fa-
"ther is known by the Son; whence a Son, if he has not a Father? and whence
"a Father, if he has not begat an only begotten Son? for when is it the Father
"cannot be called a Father, or the Son, a Son? Though ſome think of a Father
"without a Son, who afterwards comes to a proficiency and begets a Son, and
"ſo after the birth is called the Father of that Son: the Father who is perfect,
"and never wants perfection, making a progreſs or proficiency in the deity."

5. *Hilary*, biſhop of *Poictiers* in *France*, wrote againſt the Arians, and ſays many things in oppoſition to their tenets, concerning the Sonſhip of Chriſt, and his eternal generation; among others, he ſays ʸ, "the unbegotten *begot* a Son
"of himſelf *before all time*, not from any ſubjacent matter, for all things are by
"the Son, nor out of nothing, for the Son is from him himſelf.—He begot the
"only begotten in an incomprehenſible and unſpeakable manner, before all
"time

▼ Apud Theodoret. Hiſt. l. 1. c. 4. ˣ Contr. Hæreſ. l. 2. tom. 2. hæreſ. 69.
ʸ De Trinitate, l. 3. p. 23, 24. vid. ibid. de Unitate filii & patris, p. 650.

"time and ages, of that which is unbegotten, and so of the unbegotten, per-
"fect and eternal Father, is the only begotten, perfect and eternal Son."

6. *Faustinus* the presbyter, wrote a treatise against the Arians; who observes, that they sometimes use the same words and phrases the orthodox do; but not in the same sense; they speak of God the Father and of God the Son, but when they speak of the Father, it is not of one who truly begets, and when they speak of the Son, it is of him as a Son by adoption, not by nature; and when they speak of him as a Son begotten before the world was, they attribute a beginning to him, and that there was a time when he was not; and so they assert him to be of things not existent; that is, of nothing[y]. He asks[z], "How is he truly a
"Father, who, according to them, does not beget (truly); and how is Christ
"truly a Son, whom they deny to be generated of him?" And again[a], "How
"is he the only begotten of the Father, since he cannot be the only begotten,
"other Sons existing by adoption? but if he is truly the only begotten by the
"Father, therefore because he only is truly generated of the Father." And elsewhere[b], "They say God made himself a Son: if he made him out of nothing,
"then is he a creature, and not a Son. What is he that you call a Son, whom
"you confirm to be a creature, since you say he is made out of nothing? there-
"fore you cannot call him both a Son and a creature; for a Son is from birth,
"a creature from being made." And again[c], "In this alone the Father differs
"from the Son, that the one is a Father, the other a Son; that is, that the one
"begets and the other is begotten; yet not because he is begotten has he any
"thing less than what is in God the Father, *Heb.* i. 3." Once more[d], "God
"alone is properly a true Father, who is a Father without beginning and end,
"for he did not sometime begin: he is a Father, but he was always a Father,
"having always a Son begotten of him, as he is always the true God, conti-
"nuing without beginning and end."

7. *Gregory*, bishop of *Nazianzum*, gives many testimonies to the doctrines of the Trinity and of the Sonship and generation of Christ, against the Arians and Eunomians; among which are the following; "We ought, says he[e], to
"acknowledge one God the Father, without beginning and unbegotten; and
"one Son, begotten of the Father; and one Spirit, having subsistence from God,
"yielding to the Father, because he is unbegotten, and to the Son, because he
"is begotten; otherwise of the same nature, dignity, honour and glory." And elsewhere he says[f], "If you ask me, I will answer you again, When was the
"Son begotten? When the Father was not begotten. When did the Spirit pro-
"ceed?

[y] De Trinitate contr. Arian c. 1. p. 36.  Ibid p. 45.  [a] Ibid. p. 77.
[b] Ibid. c. 2. p. 92.  [c] Ibid. c. 3. p. 124.  [d] Ibid. c. 7. p. 157. Ed. Oxon.
[e] Orat. 26. p. 445.  [f] Orat. 35. p. 563.

"ceed? When the Son did not proceed, but was begotten before time, and be-
"yond expreſſion.—How can it be proved, that they (the Son and Spirit) are
"co-eternal with the Father? From hence, becauſe they are of him, and not
"after him, for what is without beginning is eternal." And then he goes on
to anſwer the ſeveral objections made to the generation of the Son by the Eunomians. Again he ſays [g], "Believe the Son of God, the word that was *before*
"*all ages begotten* of the Father before time, and in an incorporeal manner;
"the ſame in the laſt days made the Son of man for thy ſake, coming forth
"from the virgin *Mary* in an unſpeakable manner." And elſewhere he ſays [h],
"Do you hear of generation? do not curiouſly enquire how it is. Do you
"hear that the holy Spirit proceeds from the Father? do not be anxiouſly ſoli-
"citous how it is: for if you curiouſly ſearch into the generation of the Son,
"and the proceſſion of the Spirit, I ſhall curiouſly enquire into the tempera-
"ment of the ſoul and body, how thou art duſt, and yet the image of God?
"How the mind remains in thee, and begets a word in another mind?"

8. *Baſil*, called the great, archbiſhop of *Cæſarea Cappadocia*, wrote a treatiſe
againſt *Eunomius*, in which he ſays [i], "As there is one God the Father, always
"remaining the Father, and who is for ever what he is; ſo there is one Son, born
"by an eternal generation, who is the true Son of God, who always is what
"he is, God the Word and Lord; and one holy Spirit, truly the holy Spirit."
Again [k], "Why therefore, O incredulous man, who doſt not believe that God
"has an own Son, doſt thou enquire how God begets? if truly thou aſkeſt
"of God how and where alſo, as in a place and when as in time; which, if ab-
"ſurd to aſk ſuch things concerning God, it will be more abominable not to
"believe." And a little after he ſays [k], "If God made all out of nothing by
"his will, without labour, and that is not incredible to us; it will certainly be
"more credible to all, that it became God to beget an own Son of himſelf, in
"the divine nature, without paſſion, of equal honour, and of equal glory, a
"counſellor of the ſame ſeat, a co-operator conſubſtantial with God the Father;
"not of a divers ſubſtance, nor alien from his ſole deity; for if he is not ſo,
"neither is he adorable, for it is written *thou ſhalt not worſhip a ſtrange God*."

9. *Gregory*, biſhop of *Nyſſa*, the brother of *Baſil*, wrote againſt *Eunomius*, in
which we have this paſſage [l]. "He (*Eunomius*) does ſay, that he (the Son) was
"truly begotten before the world. Let him ſay of whom he was begotten: he
"muſt ſay of the Father entirely, if he is not aſhamed of the truth; but from
"the eternal Father there is no ſeparating the eternity of the Son; the word
"Father contains a Son."

10. *Ambroſe*

[g] Orat. 40. p. 671.   [h] Orat. 29. p. 493.   [i] Adv. Eunom. l. 5. c. 11.
[k] Ibid. c. 14.   [l] Baſil ibid.   [m] Contr. Eunom. Orat. 1. p. 30.

10. *Ambrose*, bishop of *Milan*, after having said many things in opposition to *Arius*, *Sabellius*, *Photinus* and *Eunomius*, observes, that "when you speak of
"a Father, you also design his Son, for no man is a father to himself; and
"when you name a son, you confess his father, for no man is a son to himself;
"therefore neither the son can be without the father, nor the father without the
"son; therefore always a father and always a son." He has also these words¹
"You ask me, how he can be a son if he has not a prior father? I ask of you
"also, when or how you think the Son is generated? for to me it is impossible
"to know the secret of generation; the mind fails, the voice is silent; and not
"mine only, but that of the angels; it is above angels, above powers, above
"cherubim, above seraphim, and above all understanding; if the peace of
"Christ is above all understanding, *Phil.* iv. 7. must not such a generation be
"above all understanding?" And in another place ᵐ, "God the Father begat
"the Word *co-eternal* with himself and co-omnipotent, with whom he produced
"the holy Spirit; hence we believe that the substance of the Son and of the
"holy Spirit existed before any creature, out of all time; that the Father is the
"begetter, the Son is begotten, and the holy Spirit the holiness and the Spi-
"rit of the begetter and the begotten."

11. *Jerom* the presbyter, and a noted writer in this century, speaking of the Arians says ⁿ, "Let them understand, that they glory in vain of the testimony
"in which Wisdom speaks of being created in the beginning of the ways of
"God, and begotten and established; for if, according to them, he was created,
"he could not be begotten or born; if begotten or born, how could he be
"established and created?" And a little after he says, "God, the Father of
"our Lord Jesus Christ, is a Father according to substance (or essence), and
"the only begotten is not a Son by adoption, but by nature; whatsoever we
"say of the Father and the Son, this we know is said of the holy Spirit."
Here the creed of *Damasus* might be taken notice of, in which he says, "God
"has begot a Son, not by will nor by necessity, but by nature;" and in the explanation of it, it is said, "Not because we say the Son is begotten of the Father
"by a divine and ineffable generation, do we ascribe any time to him, for
"neither the Father nor the Son began to be at any time; nor do we any other-
"wise confess an eternal Father, but we also confess a co-eternal Son." Also
*Ruffinus*'s exposition of the apostles creed, which stands among *Jerom*'s works,
"when you hear of a Father, understand the Father of a Son, the image of
"his substance; but how God begat a Son do not discuss, nor curiously in-
"trude into the depth of this secret ᵒ."

4 B 2  The

---

ᴶ De Fide ad Gratian. c. 5. p. 119, 120.  ᵐ In symbolum apostol. c. 1. p. 87. tom. 4.
ⁿ In Epist. ad Ephes. fol. 96. A. tom. 9.  Vid. opera Hierom tom. 4. fol. 42. 1. 44; 1.

12. The errors of the Photinians were not only confuted by the several above writers, but *Photinus* himself was condemned by the synod at *Syrmium*, of which place he had been bishop; and in the formula of faith agreed on therein, among others, are the following articles °, "We believe in one God the Father " almighty, the creator and maker of all things; — and in his only begotten " Son our Lord Jesus Christ, who was *begotten of the Father before all ages*;— " and in the holy Spirit:—and as to those that say, that the Son is of things " that are not, (or of nothing) or of another substance, and not of God; and " that there was a time or age when he was not, the holy and catholic church " reckons them as aliens. — If any one dare to say, that the unbegotten or a " part of him was born of *Mary*, let him be anathema: and if any one say that " he is the Son of *Mary* by prescience, and not begotten of the Father before " the world, and was with God by whom all things are made, let him be " anathema.—If any one says, that Christ Jesus was not the Son of God before " the world was, and ministered to the Father at the creation of all things, but " only from the time he was born of *Mary* was called Son and Christ, and then " received the beginning of deity, let him be anathema, as a Samosatenian."

13. The formulas, creeds, and confessions of faith, made by different persons, and at different places, besides the Nicene creed, and even some that differed in other things from that and from one another, yet all agreed in inserting the clause respecting their faith in Christ, the only begotten Son, as *begotten of the Father before all ages*, or *the world was*; as at *Antioch, Syrmium, Ariminum, Seleucia*, and *Constantinople* ᵖ.

14. Before the Nicene creed was made, or any of the above creeds, this was an article of faith with the orthodox christians, that Christ was the eternal begotten Son of God. From the writings of *Cyril*, bishop of *Jerusalem*, who lived in the fourth century, may be collected a symbol or creed containing the faith of the church, and in which this article is fully expressed ᑫ; that Christ " is the only begotten Son of God, begotten of the Father before all worlds, the " true God by whom all things are made;" and which article he strongly asserts and defends; and the creed which he explains, is thought to be the ʳ same which the first and ancient church always professed, and from the beginning; and perhaps is what *Eusebius* ˢ refers unto, who was bishop of *Cæsarea* in *Palestine*, when he declared his faith in the council at *Nice*; our formula, says he, which was read in the presence of our emperor (*Constantine*) most dear to God, is as we received it *from the bishops that were before us*; and as when catechized and

° Socrat. eccl. Hist. l 2. c. 29, 30.   ᵖ Ib. l. 2. c. 10, 18, 19, 30, 37, 40, 41. vid. epist. hæres. 73.   ᑫ Cateches. 4. f. 5. v. xi. f. 1.   ʳ Vid. Bulli judicium eccl. cathol. p. 128.
ˢ Apud Socrat. eccl. hist. l. 1. c. 8, and Theodoret hist. l. 1. c. 12.

and received the laver (that is, were baptized,) and as we learnt from the divine writings, and is in this manner, "We believe in one God the Father Almighty, "—and in one Lord Jesus Christ, the Word of God, the only begotten Son, "the first-born of every creature, *begotten of God the Father before all worlds*, "by whom all things are made, &c." Nor indeed was the word ομοουσιος, *consubstantial*, which expresses the Son's being of the same substance, nature and essence with the Father, a new word¹, devised in the council of *Nice*; for it was in use before ᵘ, as *Athanasius* has proved from the same *Eusebius*: "The "bishops, he says, (that is, those assembled at *Nice*) did not invent these words "of themselves, but having a testimony from the Fathers, so they wrote; for "the ancient bishops near a hundred and thirty years before, both in the great "city of *Rome*, and in our city (*Alexandria*) reproved those that said that the Son "was a creature, and not *consubstantial* with the Father;" and this *Eusebius*, who was bishop of *Cæsarea*, knew, who first gave into the Arian heresy, but afterwards subscribed to the synod at *Nice*; for being confirmed, he wrote to his own people thus, "We find, says he, some sayings of the ancient and famous "bishops and writers, who use the word *consubstantial* in treating of the deity "of the Father and of the Son." And certain it is, that it is used by *Gregory* of *Neocæsarea* ʷ, who lived before the council of *Nice*, and by the synod at *Antioch* in their creed ˣ, held A. D. 272.

V. In the fifth century Arianism continued and prospered, having many abettors, as well as many who opposed it: other heresies also arose, and some in opposition to the Sonship of Christ.

1*st*, *Felicianus*, the Arian, argued against it thus, "If Christ was born of a vir- "gin, how can he be said to be co-eternal with God the Father?" To whom *Austin* replied, "The Son of God entered into the womb of the virgin, that "he might be again born, who had been already begotten before, he received "the whole man (or whole humanity) who had had already perfect deity from "the Father, not unlike was he to the begetter, when being everlasting he was "begotten from eternity, nor unlike to men when born of his mother ʸ."

2*dly*, *Faustus*, the Manichee, asserted, that according to the evangelists, Christ was not the Son of God, only the Son of *David*, until he was thirty years of age, and was baptized; to which *Austin* replied, "The catholic and apostolic "faith is, that our Lord and Saviour Jesus Christ, is the Son of God, accord- "ing to deity, and the Son of *David*, according to the flesh; which we so "prove

---

t Theodoret, ibid. c. 13.    ᵘ In Theodoret ibid. c. 8.    ᵛ In ibid. c. 12.
ʷ In Annuntiat. S. Mariæ sermo, 2. p. 25. & in S. Theophan. p. 36. & expos. fidei, p. 101.
ˣ Apud Forbes. instruct. Hist. Theolog. l. 1. c. 4. p. 10.    ʸ Aug. contr. Felician. c. 11.

" prove from the evangelic and apoftolic writings, as that no man can contra-
" dict our proofs, unlefs he contradicts their exprefs words ʸ."

3*dly*, The Prifcillianifts afferted that Chrift is called the only begotten Son of God, becaufe he only was born of a virgin; to which *Leo Magnus* makes anfwer, " Let them take which they will, their tenets tend to great impiety,
" whether they mean, that the Lord Chrift had his beginning from his mother,
" or deny him to be the only begotten of God the Father; fince he was born
" of his mother, who was God the Word, and none is begotten of the Father
" but the Word ᶻ."

The writers in this century are many, who have plainly and ftrongly afferted the eternal generation and Sonfhip of Chrift; as *Auguftine*, *Chryfoftom*, *Proclus* archbifhop of *Conftantinople*, *Leo Magnus*, *Theodoret*, *Cyril* of *Alexandria*, *Paulinus*, *Victor*, *Maximus Taurinenfis* ᵃ, &c. it may be abundantly fufficient only to mention the following formulas or confeffions of faith.

1. Of *Auguftine*, bifhop of *Hippo*, or of *Sennadius*, prefbyter of *Marfeilles* in *France*, to whom it is fometimes afcribed; " We believe there is one God, the
" Father, Son and holy Spirit; the Father becaufe he has a Son, the Son be-
" caufe he has a Father, the holy Spirit becaufe he is from the Father and the
" Son (proceding and co-eternal with the Father and the Son,)—the eternal
" Father, becaufe he has an eternal Son, of whom he is the eternal Father; the
" eternal Son, becaufe he is co-eternal with the Father and the holy Spirit; the
" eternal holy Spirit, becaufe he is co-eternal with the Father and the Son ᵇ."

2. Of *Flavianus*, bifhop of *Conftantinople*, which he delivered in conc. *Conftantinop.* A. D. 448. approved of by the fynod at *Chalcedon*, A. D. 451. " Our
" Lord Jefus Chrift, the only begotten Son of God, perfect God and perfect
" man, of a reafonable foul and body; *begotten* indeed *of the Father*, without
" beginning and *before the world*, according to deity, but in the end, in the laft
" days, the fame was born of the virgin *Mary* for our falvation, according to
" humanity; confubftantial with the Father, according to deity, confubftantial
" with his mother according to humanity; for of two natures we confefs that
" Chrift is after the incarnation in one fubfiftence, in one perfon; we confefs one
" Chrift, one Son, one Lord ᶜ."

3. Of the council at *Chalcedon*, confifting of fix hundred and thirty Fathers;
" Following the holy fathers, fay they, we all harmonioufly teach and confefs
" our Lord Jefus Chrift: that he is perfect in deity and perfect in humanity,
" truly God and truly man, of a rational foul and body; co-effential with the Father according to the deity, and co-effential with us according to the humanity,
" in

---
ʸ Ibid. contr. Fauftum, l. 23. c. 1—5.   ᶻ Leo Magn. Ep. 93. c. 3.
ᵃ Vid. Magdeburg. centuriat. cent. 5. p. 75, &c.   ᵇ Eccles. Dogm. c. 1. Appendix. tom. 3. Aug. operum.   ᶜ Apud Forbes. Inftruct. Hift. Theolog. l. 2, c. 10. p. 88.

"in all things like unto us, excepting sin, but *begotten of the Father before the world*, according to the deity; and in the last days, for us and our salvation, was of the virgin *Mary* the mother of our Lord, according to the humanity ᵈ, &c."

VI. In the sixth century were a sort of hereticks called Bo-o-nosians, who held that Christ was not the proper but adoptive Son; against whom *Justinian* bishop of *Vale* in *Spain* wrote ᵉ; and Arianism spread and prevailed under the Gothic kings in several parts. *Fulgentius* speaks of the tenets of the Arians in this time, that the Word or Son of God was not of the same substance with the Father ᶠ. This author wrote an answer to ten objections of theirs: to the first, concerning diversity of words and names used, he replies, "When Father and Son are named, in these two names a diversity of words is acknowledged, but neither by those two different words the nature of both is signified, for the diversity of those names does not divide the natures, but shews the truth of the generation, as from one true Father, we know that one true Son exists." To the second objection, concerning the ineffability of generation, he observes, "because the generation of the Son is unspeakable, it is not unknowable, nor does it follow, because it cannot be declared, that it cannot be known ᵍ."

*Chilpericus*, king of the *Franks*, endeavoured to revive the Sabellian heresy, but was opposed by *Gregory Furnensis* ʰ: besides *Fulgentius* and *Gregory*, there were others in this age who asserted and defended the eternal generation and Sonship of Christ, as *Fortunatus*, *Cassiodorus*, *Gregorius Magnus*, and others ⁱ; and even by a synod consisting of Gothic bishops ᵏ, in number sixty three. In the same century the famous *Boetius* declares his faith in God the Father, in God the Son, and in God the holy Ghost; that the Father has a Son begotten of his substance, and co-eternal with him, whose generation no human mind can conceive of ˡ

VII. In the seventh century, towards the beginning of it, rose up that vile impostor *Mahomet*, as bitter an enemy to the true, proper and eternal Sonship of Christ, as ever was, for which he gave the following brutish and stupid reasons; "because God did not need a Son, because if he had a Son, they might not agree, and so the government of the world be disturbed ᵐ." Reasons which require no answer. Not to take notice of the several councils at *Toletum*,

held

---

ᵈ Apud ibid. c. 12. p. 92. ᵉ Isidor. Orig. l. 8. c. 5. vid eund. de Script. eccl. c. 20. & Chronicum Goth. p. 276. ᶠ Ad hominum l. 3. c. 1. ᵍ Contr. object. Arian. p. 38, 39. ʰ Vid. Magdeburg. centur. cent. 6. p. 154. ⁱ Ibid. p. 53, 54. &c. ᵏ Ibid. p. 313. ˡ Confess. Fidei, p. 173.
ᵐ Altreg. Theolog. Hist. loc 3. p. 236. vid. Forbes. instruct. Hist. Theolog. l. 4 c. 6. p. 189, 190.

held in this century, in which the article of Chrift's eternal Sonfhip was afferted and maintained, I would obferve what is faid in a Roman fynod, confifting of a *hundred and twenty five* bifhops, in which *Agatho* the Roman pontiff prefided; "We believe, fay they, in God the Father almighty, maker of heaven and "earth, and of all things vifible and invifible; and in his only begotten Son, "who was begotten of him before all worlds ᵐ ".

VIII. In the eighth century, the notion that Chrift, though the true, proper, and natural Son of God according to the divine nature, yet according to the human nature was only the Son of God by adoption and grace, an adoptive Son, was propagated by *Elipandus* and *Felix*, Spanifh bifhops, but condemned by the council at *Frankfort*, called by *Charles* the great ⁿ; and the eternal Sonfhip and generation of Chrift was afferted and maintained by *Damafcene*, *Bede*, *Albinus*, and others °.

IX. In the ninth, tenth and eleventh centuries, the controverfies were chiefly about Image-worfhip, Tranfubftantiation, &c. yet in thefe and the following centuries, we have teftimonies from various writers to the truth of Chrift's proper and eternal Sonfhip by generation; it would be too numerous to produce them all; it will be fufficient to fay, it was not oppofed by any, but plainly and ftrongly affirmed by *Rabanus*, *Macerus*, and *Haymo* in cent. 9. by *Theophilaӕ*, in cent. 10. by *Anfelm*, in cent. 11. by *Peter Lombard* and *Bernard*, in cent. 12. by *Thomas Aquinas* and *Albertus Magnus*, in cent 13. but in thefe and the following centuries, till the Reformation, Satan had other work to do than to ftir up men to oppofe the Trinity, or any of the divine perfons in it, having enough to do to fupport the hierarchy of *Rome*, and the peculiar tenets of Popery, againft the witneffes who rofe up at different times to oppofe them, and to endeavour to carry the pride and tyranny of the bifhop of *Rome* to the higheft pitch poffible.

X. When the Reformation began in the fixteenth century, and fpread throughout many nations in *Europe*, great evangelical light broke forth among the Reformers; and Satan fearing his kingdom would greatly fuffer hereby, went to his old game again, which he had played with fo much fuccefs in the firft ages of chriftianity, namely, to ftir up an oppofition to the doctrine of the Trinity, and the perfon of Chrift; which was firft begun by *Servetus* in *Helvetia*, who

---

ᵐ Apud Forbes. ibid. l. 5. c. 3. p. 227.   ⁿ Ibid. l. 6. c. 1. p. 292, &c.
° Magdeburg. centur. cent. 8. c. 4. p. 51, 52. &c.

ETERNAL SONSHIP OF CHRIST, &c.    561

who afterwards came to *Geneva* and there ended his life ᵐ. *Blandrata*, infected with his principles, went into *Poland*, and there artfully spread his poison in the reformed churches, assisted by others, and which at length issued in a division in those churches; when *Faustus Socinus*, who had imbibed some bad notions from the papers of his uncle *Lælius* about the Trinity, came into *Poland*, and joined the Antitrinitarians there, and strengthened their cause, and where the notions of him and his followers took root and flourished much: and from thence have been transplanted into other countries. Those men, who were men of keen parts and abilities, saw clearly that could they demolish the article of Christ's Sonship by eternal generation, it would be all over with the doctrine of the Trinity; and therefore set themselves with all their might against it ⁿ. *Socinus* himself says ᵒ of it, not only that it is error and a meer human invention, and which he represents as if it was held to be *more animantium*; but that it is most absurd, most unworthy of God, and contrary to his absolute perfection and unchangeable eternity ᵖ; and asserts, that Christ is not called the only begotten Son of God, because generated of the substance of God; and that there is no other, nor ever existed any other only begotten Son of God, besides that man, Jesus of *Nazareth*: and expresly says, it clearly appears, that the human nature of Christ is the person of the Son of God; and elsewhere ᑫ makes the same objection to Sonship by generation as *Mahomet* did, for he says, " Those who accommodate the Word *brought forth* in *Prov.* viii. 24. to the Son, " are not, according to the judgment of the Homoousians, to be reckoned very " distant from the blasphemy of the Turks, who when they hear that the Chris- " tians say, God has a Son, ask, Who is his wife?" And in this article concerning the Sonship of Christ, and also with respect to the doctrine of the Trinity, the Remonstrants ʳ, in the seventeenth century and onwards, seem to agree with them; but the contrary has been maintained by all sound divines and evangelical churches, from the Reformation to the present time, as appears by their writings and harmony of confessions: so that upon the whole it is clear,

---

ᵐ Servetus has these blasphemous words concerning eternal generation, " debuisseat dicere quod pater " ce'ebat uxorem quandam spiritua!em, vel quod solus ipse masculo-fœmineus, aut hermaphroditus, " simul erat pater & mater, &c nam ratio vocabuli non patitur ut quis dicatur sine matre pater." Servetus de Trinit. error Septen. l. 1. A. D. 1531. And again, " Si Logos filius erat natus ex " patre sine matre, dic mihi quomodo peperit eum, per ventrem an per latus." Ibid. l. 2. p. 52. apud Hornbeck Socin consolat. tom. 1. p. 17. Servetus would not own Christ to be the eternal Son of God, only the Son of the eternal God. Socinus apud Hornbeck Ibid. p. 20.
ⁿ Vid. Racov. Catech. c. 1. qu. 17—20. Wolzogen de essentia & natura Dei, c. 9 p. 25, &c.
ᵒ Christ.Relig.Institut. inter opera ejus, vol. 1 p.655.    ᵖ Quod regni Polon. c.4. f.2. p. 698,699.
ᑫ Respons. ad Vujekum, c. 7. p. 607. vol. 2.    ʳ Vid. Peltii Herman Remonstr. & Socin. artic. 4. paragr. 1. 4. p. 15, 19.

Vol. II.                    4 C                    that

that the church of God has been in the poffeffion of this doctrine of the eternal generation and Sonfhip of Chrift, from the beginning of chriftianity to the prefent age, almoft *eighteen hundred years*; nor has there been any one man who profeffed to hold the doctrine of the Trinity, or of the three diftinct divine perfons in the unity of the divine effence, that ever oppofed it, till the latter end of the *feventeenth* century: if any fuch perfon in this courfe of time can be named, let him be named: none but the followers of *Simon Magus, Cerinthus, Ebion, Carpocrates,* the Gnofticks, *&c.* in the two firft centuries, and then by the Sabellians, Samofatenians, Arians, Photinians, Mahometans, Socinians, and more lately by the Remonftrants, fuch as are Antitrinitarians. The only two perfons I have met with who have profeffed to hold the doctrine of the Trinity, as it has been commonly received, that have publicly expreffed their doubts or diffatisfaction about the phrafe *eternal generation,* I mean fuch as are of any note or character, for as for the trifling tribe of ignorant writers and fcribblers, who know not what they fay nor whereof they affirm, I make no account of them; I fay, I have met with only two of this fort. The one is *Roell,* a Dutch Profeffor at *Franeker,* who lived at the latter end of the laft century; this man profeffed to believe that there are three diftinct divine perfons, the Father, Son, and Spirit, and that thefe three are one; that the fecond perfon in the Trinity was begotten by the Father from all eternity, and that this is the firft and chief reafon that he is called a Son; nor did he object to the ufe of the phrafe *eternal generation,* nor did he difufe it, but explained it to another fenfe than that in which it was commonly taken, that is, that it only fignified the co-exiftence of the fecond perfon with the firft, and communion of nature with him. But as the fame may be faid of the firft and third perfons, the phrafe of generation fo underftood might be faid of them as well as of the fecond; he therefore was obliged to have recourfe to the oeconomy of falvation, and the manifeftation of the three perfons in it [s]. On the whole, he was oppofed by the very learned *Vitringa* [t], and his opinion was profcribed and condemned by almoft all the fynods of the Dutch churches, and he was forbid by the authority of his fupreme magiftrate to propagate it; and moft of the fynods have decreed, that the candidates for the miniftry fhall be examined about this opinion, before they are admitted into the miniftry [u]. The other perfon, who has objected to the eternal generation of the Son of God, is Dr *Thomas Ridgley,* Profeffor of Divinity in *London,* towards the beginning of the prefent century [w]: who ftrongly afferts, and contends for the doctrine of a Trinity of divine diftinct perfons in

---

[s] Vid. Roell. Differt. de generatione filii, &c. p. 4, 5, 31, 40.
[t] Difputatio Theolog. & Epilog. Difputat. de generatione filii.
[u] Maftrict. Theolog. l, 2 c 26. f. 17. p. 257.  [w] See his body of divinity, p. 121, &c.

in the Godhead, and yet ſtrangely adopts the Socinian notion of Sonſhip by office, and makes the eternal Sonſhip of Chriſt to be what he calls his mediatorial Sonſhip. There is indeed a third perſon of great fame among us, Dr *Iſaac Watts*, who has expreſſed his diſſatisfaction with the doctrine of the eternal generation of the Son of God, but then he is not to be reckoned a Trinitarian, being ſo manifeſtly in the Sabellian ſcheme, as appears by his *Diſſertations* publiſhed in 1725. inſomuch that the celebrated *Fred. Adolphus Lampe*, who publiſhed his *Theological Diſputations*. concerning the holy Spirit, two or three years after, ſpares not to reckon him among the groſſer Sabellians: his words are [x], "Nupe-
"rius novum ſyſtema Socinianum de Trinitate Anglice J. Wats edidit, additis
"quibuſdam diſſertationibus eam illuſtrantibus, quarum quinta ex profeſſo de
"ſpiritu S. agit. Exiſtimat quidem ſect. 2. p. 126. eatenus ſe a Socino, Schlictingio,
"Crellio eſſe diſtinguatum, quod virtutem in Deo non accidentalem, ſed eſ-
"ſentialem, ſeu ſubſtantialem pro ſpiritu S. habeat: hoc tamen ita facit, ut non
"cenſeat hanc notionem conſtanter ubique obtinere: nam ſæpius cum craſſiori-
"bus Sabellianis ſpiritum S. eſſe Deum ipſum, p. 130. ſ. 49. defendit."

Upon the whole, ſetting aſide the ſaid perſons, the teſtimonies for and againſt the eternal generation and Sonſhip of Chriſt ſtand thus:

| For ETERNAL GENERATION, &c. | AGAINST IT. |
|---|---|
| Ignatius, Polycarp, Juſtin Martyr, Irenæus, Athenagoras, Theophilus of *Antioch*, Clemens of *Alexandria*, Tertullian, Origen, Cyprian, Gregory of *Neocæſaria*, Dionyſius of *Alexandria*, the *three hundred and eighteen* Nicene Fathers; Athanaſius, Alexander biſhop of *Alexandria*, Epiphanius, Hilary, Fauſtinus, Gregory of *Nazianzum*, Baſil, Gregory of *Nyſſa*, Ambroſe, Jerom, Ruffinus, Cyril of *Jeruſalem*, beſides the *many hundreds* of biſhops and preſbyters aſſembled at different times and in different places, as, at *Syrmium*, *Antioch*, *Ariminum*, *Seleucia*, and *Conſtantinople*, and elſewhere; Auguſtine, Chryſoſtom, Leo Magnus, Theodoret, Cyril of *Alexandria*, Pau- | Simon Magus, Cerinthus, and Ebion, and their reſpective followers; Carpocrates and the Gnoſticks, Valentinus, Theodotus the currier, Artemon, and others their aſſociates; Beryllus of *Boſtra*, Praxeus, Hermogenes, Noetius and Sabellius, the Samoſatenians, Arians, Aetians, Eunomians and Photinians, the Priſcillianiſts and Bonotians; Mahomet and his followers; the Socinians and Remonſtrants; and all Antitrinitarians. |

linus,

---

[x] Lampe diſp. 2. de ſpiritu, ſ. c. 3. ſ. 13. p. 14.

linus, Flavianus, Victor, Maximus Taurienfis, *six hundred and thirty fathers* in the council at *Chalcedon*; Fulgentius, GregoryTurnafis, Fortunatus, Cassiodorus, Gregorius Magnus, the *many* bishops in the several councils at *Toletum*, the Roman synod of a *hundred and twenty-five* under Agatho, Damascene, Beda, Albinus, and the fathers in the council of *Franckford*, with many others in later times, and all the found divines and evangelic churches since the reformation.

Now since it appears that all the found and orthodox writers have unanimously declared for the eternal generation and Sonship of Christ in all ages, and that those only of an unsound mind and judgment, and corrupt in other things as well as this, and many of them men of impure lives and vile principles, have declared against it, such must be guilty of great temerity and rashness to join in an opposition with the one against the other; and to oppose a doctrine the church of God has always held, and especially being what the scriptures abundantly bear testimony unto, and is a matter of such moment and importance, being a fundamental doctrine of the christian religion, and indeed what distinguishes it from all other religions, from those of Pagans, Jews and Mahometans, who all believe in God, and generally in *one* God, but none of them believe in the Son of God: that is peculiar to the christian religion.

# A DISSERTATION

CONCERNING

## The RISE and PROGRESS of POPERY.

WHAT is generally meant and understood by Popery, is well known. As for the name it matters not from whence and from whom it is, nor when it began to be in use, nor in what sense the word *papa* is used in heathen and ecclesiastical writers. By the latter it was given to christian bishops in common; as to *Cyprian, Athanasius, Austin, Epiphanius*, and others; until the bishops of *Rome* assumed it as peculiar to themselves: but it is not the name, but the thing we are inquiring after; and as things are before they have a name, so Popery was in being before it bore this name. It did not begin at *Rome*, nor was it always confined there; nor did it cease at the Reformation in the reformed churches; some of its unholy relics continued with them, and still do, and even in *Geneva* itself. It is commonly believed by Protestants, that the Pope of *Rome* is Antichrist; and the Roman church, its hierarchy, doctrines and practices, Antichristian; and by Protestant writers and interpreters, for the most part, it is supposed that the same Antichrist is meant in 2 *Thess.* ii. 3—10, to whom the description agrees; as, *the man of sin, the son of perdition, who exalts himself above all that is called God, or is worshipped; sitting in the temple of God, shewing himself to be God.* Now this same man of sin, was then in being in the apostles time, though not arrived to his manhood; to deny this, would be just such good sense as to deny that an infant exists because it is not grown up to man's estate. Antichrist was not then revealed, but was to be revealed in his proper time, when that which hindered his being revealed was taken away, even the Roman empire: he was in being, though he lay hid and concealed till an apportunity offered to shew himself. The mystery of iniquity, which is one of the names of mystical *Babylon*, or the Antichristian whore of *Rome*, Rev. xvii. 5. began to work already, when the apostle wrote the above prophecy, and gave the above description of Antichrist; and so the apostle

*John*

## 566 A DISSERTATION CONCERNING THE

*John* says, that *the spirit of antichrist*, which *should come*, even now already *is it in the world*, 1 *John* iv. 3. Antichrist was not only in embryo in the times of the apostles, but was arrived to some bigness, so as to be active and operative. Now Popery may be considered in a twofold respect; both as an hierarchy, an usurped jurisdiction, and tyrannical domination over others; and as a system of antichristian doctrines and practices: and in both views it will appear, that what is now so called, had a very early beginning.

I. Popery may be considered as an antichristian hierarchy, a tyrannical jurisdiction over other churches, gradually obtained by usurpation; and though such an affectation of pre-eminence and dominion was forbidden, and condemned by Christ, *Matt.* xx. 26, 27. and chap. xxiii. 8, 11. and by his apostles, and even by *Peter*, whom the pope of *Rome* claims as his predecessor, 2 *Cor.* i. 24. 1 *Pet.* v. 3. yet this Diotrephesian spirit, or love of pre-eminence, appeared even in the apostolic age, 3 *John* ix. and though the office of bishop or overseer, and of presbyter or elder, and of pastor, is one and the same, and equal, according to the scripture-account, *Acts* xx. 27. and there were but two officers in the church, bishops and deacons, *Phil* i. 1. yet we soon hear of the superiority of bishops to presbyters, and of the subjection of presbyters to bishops, as well as of deacons to both, and of the people to them all; as appears from the epistles of *Ignatius*, in the second century; and in the third and following, we read of a great variety of offices, together with others since added, which make the present antichristian hierarchy; as will be observed hereafter.

The bishops of *Rome* very early discovered a domineering spirit over other bishops and churches; they grasped at power and exercised it, though they met with rebuffs in it. In the second century there was a controversy about keeping Easter. The Asian churches observed it on the 14th day of the new moon, let it fall on what day of the week it might; but the church of *Rome*, with other churches, observed it on the Lord's day following. *Victor*, then bishop of *Rome*, being a fierce and blustering bishop, threatened at least to excommunicate, if he did not excommunicate, the said churches, for not observing Easter at the same time that he did. *Eusebius* says [a], that he attempted to do it; from which *Irenæus* [b] of *France*, endeavoured to dissuade him, though he was of the same mind with him, with respect to the observance of Easter; but *Socrates* the historian says [c], he did send them an excommunication; which was an instance of tyrannical jurisdiction exercised over other churches. In the middle of the third century there was a dispute about rebaptizing hereticks who repented and came over to the church: the African churches and bishops, as *Cyprian* and others

[a] Eccl. Hist. l. 5. c. 24.  [b] Apud ibid.  [c] Socrat. Eccl. Hist. l. 5. c. 22.

others, were for rebaptizing them, and did; but *Stephen*, bishop of *Rome*, violently opposed the baptism of them, and cut off all the churches in *Africa* for the practice of it; which is another instance of the power the bishop of *Rome* thus early usurped over other churches: though indeed it was highly resented by the eastern churches [d], and displays his imperious and imposing temper, as if he wanted to make himself a bishop of bishops [e].

In the beginning of the third century, in *Tertullian*'s time, the bishop of *Rome* had the titles of *Pontifex Maximus*, and of *Episcopus Episcoporum* [f]. *Julius* I. in the fourth century, took upon him to reprove some eastern bishops for deposing others, and ordered the restitution of them; though they despised his reproofs, and even deposed him for first communing with *Athanasius* and others [g]. *Platina* says [h], that he reproved them for calling a council at *Antioch*, without the leave of the bishop of *Rome*; which he urged, could not be done without his authority, seeing the church of *Rome* had the pre-eminence over the rest of the churches: but the same author says, they confuted his claim with a sneer. *Adolphus Lampe*, in his Ecclesiastical History [i], observes, that it is thought that *Mark*, sitting in the Roman chair, A. D. 335. first arrogated to himself the title of universal bishop: and indeed, if the letters of *Athanasius* and the Egyptian bishops to him [k], and his to them, are genuine, they both gave the title to him, and he took it to himself; their letter to him runs thus, "To the reverend *Mark*, pope of the holy Roman and apostolic See, and of the universal church." And his to them begins thus, "To the venerable brethren *Athanasius*, and all the bishops in *Egypt*, *Mark*, the bishop of the holy Roman and apostolic See, and of the universal church." And in the former, the See of *Rome* is called the *mother* and *head* of all churches.

Though historians generally agree, that the title of universal bishop was given by *Phocas* to *Boniface* III. in the year 606. at the beginning of the seventh century, yet an anonymous writer [l], in *an essay on scripture prophecy*, p. 104. published in 1724. quotes from *Sigonius De occid. Imper.* p. 106, and 314. two passages, shewing, that *Valentinian*, the third emperor of the west, in A. D. 445. and *Marcion*, emperor of the east, in A. D. 450. assigned something like an universal power to pope *Leo* I. which was more than a century and a half before the times of *Phocas*. The title of universal bishop might not be established by authority of the emperor until his time, yet pretensions were made to it, and it was claimed by the bishops of *Rome* before, and in some instances given. And

though.

[d] Vid. Cyprian Ep. 75.  [e] Concil. Carthag. inter opera Cyprian. p. 397.
[f] Tertullian de pudicitia, c. 1.  [g] Socrates, l. 2. c. 15. Sozomen, l. 3. c. 8, 11.
[h] Vit. Pontific. p. 44, 45.  [i] L. 2. c. 5. f. 17.  [k] Athanasii opera.
[l] In the abstract of the history of popery, p. 1. margin.

568    A DISSERTATION CONCERNING THE

though pope *Gregory* I. in the sixth century, a little before the time of *Phocas*, condemned *John* of *Constantinople* as antichrist, for taking upon him the title of *Oecumenical* bishop, because it intrenched upon his own power and authority; yet this humble pope, who called himself *servus servorum*, asserted, that the apostolic see, meaning the see of *Rome*, was the head of all the churches; and vehemently inveighed against the emperor, for taking it to himself[l]. And it is certain that this pope claimed a jurisdiction over the churches in *Britain*, since he appointed his legate, *Augustine* the monk, metropolitan over the whole island [m]; who endeavoured to bring the British bishops and churches to a conformity to the Roman church, and the rites of it, and to acknowledge the pope's authority. This was before the time of pope *Boniface* the third, who obtained of the emperor the title of universal bishop.

The primacy of the church of *Rome* to other churches, with respect to rank and order, which made way for primacy of power, was very early asserted, claimed, and allowed. Several sayings of the antient writers much contributed to it: from the grandeur and magnificence of the city of *Rome*, being the metropolis of the empire, an argument was very early used to a superior regard to the church in it. *Irenæus*[n], who lived in the second century, observes, that " to this church (the Roman church) every church should convene (or join in " communion;) that is, those every where who are believers; *propter potentiorem* " *principalitatem*; in which always by them who are, every where is preserved " that tradition which is from the apostles." And *Cyprian*[o], in the middle of the third century, calls it the chair of *Peter*, and the principal church, from whence the sacerdotal unity arises. *Jerom*[p], in the fourth century, writing to pope *Damasus*, calls him *his blessedness*, and the chair of *Rome*, the chair of *Peter:* and *Optatus*[q], in the same century, says, the Roman church is the episcopal chair, first conferred on *Peter*, in which he sat the head of all the apostles, and the chair of *Peter:* and earlier in this century the council of *Nice* was held, the sixth canon of which gave equal power to the bishop of *Rome*, over the bishops of his province, as the bishop of *Alexandria* had by custom; and by the third canon of the council at *Constantinople*, A. D. 381, 382. the bishop of *Constantinople* had the prerogative of honour after the bishop of *Rome*, because *Constantinople* was *New Rome*[r]: and this was confirmed by *Justinian* the emperor, in the sixth century, who ordained, that the pope of *Rome* should have the first seat, and after him the archbishop of *Constantinople*. And what served to strengthen the primacy of the church of *Rome*, and increase its power, and which the bishops

of

---

[l] Vid. Magdeburg. Eccles Hist. cent. 6. p. 217.  
[m] Adv. Hæres. l. 3. c. 3.  
[n] Ep. 55 p. 119.  
[q] De Schism. Donatist. l. 2. p. 35, 37, 40.  
[m] Bed. Hist. Euseb.  
[p] Opera tom. 2. p. 44, 45.  
[r] Socrat. Eccl. Hist. l. 5. c. 8.

## RISE AND PROGRESS OF POPERY.

of it failed not to avail themselves of, was the bringing of causes in difference between other bishops and their churches to them, either to have their advice or to be decided by them: and indeed this was done by the order of *Constantine* himself, who enjoined, that the causes of contending bishops should be brought to the bishop of *Rome* and his collegues, and there decided [r]: and this was advised to by some eminent doctors of the church, particularly *Ambrose*, who calls the Roman church the head of the whole Roman world or empire [s]: and advised *Theophilus*, that what was committed to him by the synod at *Capua*, should be referred by him to the priest of the Roman church (the pontiff) [t]. And it is no wonder that *Leo* I. in the fifth century, should require such respect and obedience to himself, who claimed the apostolical and episcopal dignity of *Peter* [u]; and subjection to the see of *Rome*, as to the blessed apostle *Peter* [w]: yea, he required of *Theodosius* the emperor himself, that the writings of the bishop of *Constantinople* might be sent to him; testifying that he embraced the true doctrine, and condemned those that dissented from it [x]. In his epistle to the bishop of *Thessalonica* [y], he asserts his care of all the churches, and the see of *Rome* to be the apostolic see; and ordered him, that all matters of difference should be brought to him to decide, according to the pleasure of God. He ordered the African hereticks who repented, to send the account of their repentance and faith to him, that it might appear they were catholic [z]. He also assumed a power of calling general councils [a]: and termed *Peter*'s seat, or the see of *Rome*, universal [b]; and *Peter* the Præful of the see of *Rome*, and the primate of all bishops [c]. In the beginning of the fifth century, during the sixth council at *Carthage*, which lasted six years, the popes *Zozimus*, *Boniface* I. and *Cælestinus* I. strove with all their might and main to get some sort of primacy and monarchy over the other bishops, though they failed in their attempt [d].

The care of the church of Christ at first, with respect both to things temporal and spiritual, lay wholly and entirely in the hands of the apostles; but finding the temporal affairs of the church too burdensome to them, they directed it to choose a sort of officers called *Deacons*, to take care of them, *Acts* vi. 1—6. and so there were two offices, and two only, as before observed, in the primitive apostolic churches, *Phil.* i. 1. but they were soon increased, by distinguishing bishops and presbyters, making the latter to be a distinct office from and subservient to the former: and afterwards offices became numerous;

---

[r] Euseb. Eccl. Hist. l. 10. c. 5.    [s] Ep. l. 1. Ep. 4.    [t] Ibid. Ep 9.
[u] Serm. in Annivers. die Assump. p. 95.    [w] Ep. 89. ad episcop. Vienn. p. 159.
[x] Ep. 33. p. 118.    [y] Epist. 84.    [z] Ep 87. c. 3.    [a] Ep. 93. c. 17.
[b] Spanheim. Isagog. ad Hist. eccles. p. 221.    [c] In anniverf. die Assumpt. Serm. 2.
[d] Vid. Alsted. Chronolog. p. 360, 408.

and before the bishop of *Rome* had the title of universal bishop by authority; and were the same which now constitute the hierarchy of the church of *Rome*, very few excepted; for even in the third century the following orders are ascribed to *Caius* bishop of *Rome*, as of his appointment, and as degrees to a bishoprick; first a door-keeper, then a reader, then an exorcist, an acolyte, a subdeacon, a deacon, and a presbyter, and then a bishop [d]: nor is it improbable that such orders and offices obtained as early, since *Cyprian*, in the same century, makes mention of an acolyte often [e], and of readers; of *Aurelius* a reader, and of *Saturnus* a reader [f], and of *Optatus* a subdeacon, and of exorcists [g]: and *Cornelius* bishop of *Rome*, who lived about the same time *Cyprian* did, writing to *Fabius* bishop of *Antioch*, concerning *Novatus*, says, That in the catholic church were but one bishop, forty-four presbyters, seven deacons, and as many subdeacons, forty-two acolytes, exorcists and readers, with door-keepers, fifty-two [h]. All these are mentioned together, excepting acolytes, by *Epiphanius* in the fourth century [i]. And *Eusebius* [k] observes, that in the persecution under *Dioclesian*, the prisons were filled with bishops, presbyters, deacons, readers and exorcists: that in the council of *Nice* there were bishops, presbyters, deacons and acolytes. And *Jerom* [l], in the same century, speaks of a reader, an acolyte, and a psalm-finger: and likewise *Ambrose* [m], speaking of the qualifications for different offices, one, he says, is fit to read distinctly; another is more agreeable for singing psalms; another for exorcising evil spirits; and another to take the care of the vestry: all which, he says, the priest should look after, and what every one is fit for, appoint him to that office. *Sozomen* [n] speaks of an archdeacon in the church of *Alexandria*, whose office it was to read the holy Bible; and *Optatus* calls *Cæcilianus* an archdeacon [o]: and in *Persia*, *Sozomen* says [p], *Simeon* was archbishop of *Seleucia* and *Ctesiphon*, famous cities in it; and there were patriarchs appointed over provinces by the synod at *Constantinople*, as *Socrates* relates [q]; and both he [r] and *Sozomen* [s] make mention of *Peter*, an arch-presbyter of *Alexandria*, and of *Timothy* an archdeacon there, in the fifth century; so that long before Popery arrived to its height, there was much the same popish hierarchy as now: that of *Cardinals* seems to be the only exception, yet there were of the name, though not of the same office and dignity.

In the fourth century, monkery, celibacy and virginity came much into vogue; the monastic life was much commended in this age by *Basil* and his father,

[d] Platinæ vit. Pontif. p. 34.
[e] Ep. 47. p. 90. Ep. 55. p. 114.
[f] Ep. 24. p. 50. & Ep 76. p. 202.
[g] Ep. 33. p. 55.
[h] Apud Euseb. Eccl. Hist. l.6. c.43.
[i] Compend. de fide prope finem.
[k] Eccl. Hist. l.8. c.6.
[l] Ad Nepotian. fol. 5. D. tom. 1.
[m] De officiis l. 1. c. 44.
[n] Eccl. Hist. l. 7. c. 19.
[o] Contra Parmen. l. 1. p. 18.
[p] Eccl. Hist. l. 2. c. 9.
[q] Eccl. Hist. l. 5. c. 8.
[r] Ibid. l.6. c. 9. & l. 7. c. 7.
[s] Eccl. Hist. l. 8. c. 12.

father, as may be seen in his works. The first of these Monks, Anchorites and Eremites, is said to be one *Paul* of *Thebes*, as *Jerom* relates [t]; and their disciples, in less than half an age, were so multiplied, that the deserts of *Egypt* and *Arabia* were full of them. These indeed were men of more strict and religious lives than those of later ages, who go by the name of monks. Even before the time of *Constantine*, and in it, there were societies of virgins, professing perpetual virginity, which he had a great regard unto [u]; and such *Helena* found at or near *Jerusalem*, in whose company she took great pleasure, and ministered unto them [v]. *Arius* is said to infect with the poison of his doctrine seven hundred virgins professing virginity [x]. And *Ambrose* says, the virgins came to *Milan* from various parts, even from the furthest parts of *Mauritania*, to be consecrated and veiled [y] : so early were monasteries and nunneries set up, at least the foundation of such institutions were so early laid, and the forms, rules, rites and ceremonies of them prescribed, which now make so great a figure in Popery.

II. Popery may be considered as a system of antichristian doctrines and practices, some of the principal of which the apostle *Paul* has prophetically given notice of in a few words, 1 *Tim.* iv. 1—3. *Now the spirit speaketh expresly, that in the latter times some shall depart from the faith, giving heed to seducing spirits, and doctrines of devils; speaking lies in hypocrisy; having their conscience seared with a hot iron: forbidding to marry, and commanding to abstain from meats, which God hath created to be received with thanksgiving of them which believe and know the truth.* All which are notorious doctrines and practices of the Papists, and are here plainly pointed at; and which, with others, are a branch of the mystery of iniquity which began to work in the times of the apostles, and more manifestly appeared soon after their departure. Very remarkable are the words of *Hegesippus*, an antient historian [z] testifying, that " till the times of *Trajan* (A.D. " 100.) the church continued a virgin pure and incorrupt ;—but after the sa- " cred company of the apostles ended their lives by various kinds of death, " then the conspiracy of impious error began to take place, through the deceit " of false teachers." For this branch of popery, or mystery of iniquity, takes its rise from the heresies of false teachers of the first ages, and from unguarded expressions and errors of those who have been called fathers of the church; and who, in other points, were counted sound and orthodox; and which, by degrees, grew up to that enormous mass of antichristian doctrines which are the

peculiars

---

t Ad Eustach. de virginitate fol. 50. K. & in vita Paul Eremitæ, fol. 81. K.
u Euseb. de vita Constantin. l. 4. c. 28.    v Socrat. Eccl. Hist. l. 1. c. 17.
x Epiphan. hæres. 69.    y De virginibus, l. 1. prope finem.
z Apud Euseb. Eccl. Hist. l 3 c. 32.

peculiars of popery: and, to begin with those the apostle foretold in the above quoted passage,

1. Worshipping of angels and praying to saints departed; which are meant by the *doctrines of devils*, or dæmons, as Mr *Mede* thinks, such as the heathens reckoned a sort of mediators between God and men; as the papists esteem angels to be mediators of intercession, though not of redemption; and therefore invoke them to intercede for them; and the papists are they who are meant in *Rev.* ix. 20. said to *worship devils, and idols of gold and silver,* &c. And this doctrine of worshipping dæmons or angels, was embraced by a few, even in the times of the apostles; for the apostle *Paul* warns the Colossians, that no *man beguiled them in a voluntary humility, and worshipping of angels,* Col. ii. 18. This was a tenet of *Simon Magus,* the father of heresies, who held, that the world was made by angels: and this is ascribed to him by *Tertullian*[a]. And *Theodoret* reckons it as the notion of *Carpocrates, Epiphanes, Prodicus,* and the *Caiani*[b]; and in his exposition of *Col.* ii. 18. he says, that this evil notion continued long in *Phrygia* and *Pisidia*: wherefore the synod which met at *Laodicea,* the metropolis of *Phrygia,* forbad by a law to pray to angels; and he says, that to his time might be seen among the people of those countries, and those that bordered upon them, the oratories of St *Michael*

In the latter end of the second century lived the hereticks Angelici, so called because they worshipped angels, as says *Isidore*[c]. *Origen,* who lived about the same time, and in the beginning of the third century, gives a form of prayer to angels: "Come, O angel, receive one in word converted from his former
" error, from the doctrine of devils, from iniquity, speaking highly; and receiv-
" ing him as a good physician, cherish and instruct him; he is a little one, he
" is born to day, an old man growing young again; and receive, retributing
" to him, the baptism of the second regeneration; and call to thee other com-
" panions of thy ministry, that all ye equally may instruct in the faith, who
" were sometimes deceived[d]." *Austin* in the fourth century, and beginning of the fifth, seems to favour the same: quoting *Phil.* iv. 6. he observes[e], requests are not to be understood " as made known to God, who knows them before
" they were made, but as made known by us to God through patience; or
" perhaps also, they are made known by angels, who are with God, that they
" might in some sort offer them to God; and consult concerning them, and
" that they might know what was to be fulfilled; he commanding, as they
" ought to know, and bring it to us, either openly or secretly;" for which he quotes, *Tobit* xii. 12. *The angel said to the man, When thou and Sarah prayest, I offer up your prayer in the sight of the love of God.*

Praying

[a] De præscrip. Hæref. c. 33.    [b] Divinar. Decret. Epitome p. 295.
[c] Origines l. 7. c. 5.    [d] Homil. 1. in Ezekiel fol. 133. 4.    [e] Epist. 121. c. 9.

Praying to saints was used as early; so *Origen* directs a prayer to *Job*, in this manner; "O blessed *Job*, living for ever with God, abiding in the presence of the king and lord; pray for us miserable ones, that also the terrible majesty of God may protect us in all tribulations and deliver us from all the oppressions of the wicked one, and number us with the just, and write us with them who are saved, and make us rest with them in his kingdom, where we may perpetually magnify him with the saints [f]." And elsewhere [g], "I think, says he, that all the fathers who died before us, fight with us, and help us by their prayers;" and which he confirms by a Doctor of the church senior to him. *Cyprian*, in the third century, hints the same, when he says [h], "If any of us go first from hence, through the celerity of the divine worthiness, let our love persevere with God for our brethren and sisters; and let not our prayer for the mercy of the father cease." So *Basil*, in the fourth century, in his homily on the forty martyrs, has these words; "Here is help prepared for christians, namely, the church of martyrs, the army of the triumphants, the chorus of those that praise God? often have ye used means, often have ye laboured to find one praying for you; there are forty sending forth one voice of prayer; *where two or three are met together,* &c. but where there are forty, who can doubt of the presence of God; he who is pressed with any trouble, let him flee to them; he that rejoices, let him recur to them; the one to be delivered from evils, the other to continue in prosperity." In the same century there are instances of *Nazianzen* praying to *Cyprian*, and to *Basil* dead [i], and particularly to the virgin *Mary* very early was prayer made, and her intercession implored. *Irenæus* [k], in the second century, calls the virgin *Mary* the advocate of the virgin *Eve*, which at best is an unguarded expression. *Athanasius*, in the fourth century, puts up a prayer to her in this manner [l], "Hear, O daughter of *David* and *Abraham*; incline thine ear to our prayers, and do not forget thy people and us, who are of the family and house of thy father;—unto thee we cry, remember us most holy virgin, who hast remained a virgin from the birth, and reward us for those speeches with great gifts from the riches of thy grace-gift thou art full of.—Hail full of grace, the Lord is with thee! intercede for us, dame, mistress, queen, and mother of God." And *Nazianzen* makes mention of one *Justina*, a virgin, in the times of *Cyprian*, who was delivered from a temptation by applying to the virgin *Mary* [m]. *Epiphanius* [n] speaks of some who made a God of her, and of some in *Arabia* who offered

cakes

[f] Tract. 2. in Job in fine. [g] Homil. 16. in Josuam fol. 168. 2.
[h] Epist. 57. p. 134. [i] Orat. 18. in fine & Orat. 20. in fine. [k] Adv. Hæres. l. 5. c. 19.
[l] De sanctissime Dei para prope finem. [m] Orat. 18. in laudem Cyprian.
[n] Contra Hæres. l. 3. hær. 78, 79.

cakes to her, and celebrated sacred things in her name: and in the fifth century, *Petrus Gnaphæus*, or the fuller, bishop of *Antioch*, ordered that the mother of God should be named in every prayer ⁿ.

2. Another tenet, and which is a popish one, the apostle *Paul* foretold would be broached in future time, is *forbidding to marry*, 1 *Tim.* iv. 3. so antichrist, as described by the prophet *Daniel*, is said *not to regard the desire of women*, Dan. xi. 37. This was a tenet of the antient hereticks; this branch of the mystery of iniquity soon began to operate among them, and was held by them; by the Ebionites, who, as *Epiphanius* says º, magnified virginity, and by the Saturnalians, who said, to marry and beget children was of the devil ᵖ; and that matrimony was a doctrine of the devil ᵠ; and by the Severians, who said, that a woman is the work of satan ʳ; and by the Marcionites, who condemned marriage as an evil and unchaste business ˢ; and from these sprung the Encretites, at the head of whom was *Tatian*, who, as those before, called marriages, corruptions and fornications ᵗ: and if the canons ascribed to the apostles are theirs, persons holding such a tenet were in their days, since the 51ˢᵗ canon runs thus; " If any bi-
" shop, presbyter, or deacon, or whole of the sacerdotal list, abstain from mar-
" riage, flesh and wine, not for exercise, but through abomination of them,
" forgetting that all things are very good, and that God made man male and fe-
" male; but blaspheming, accuses the workmanship of God, either let him be
" corrected (amended or set right;) or be deposed, and cast out of the church;
" and so if a layman." The notion of celibacy, and in disfavour of marriage, began to obtain early among those who were counted orthodox. *Dionysius*, bishop of *Athens*, supposed to be the same as in *Acts* xvii. 34. is said to write an epistle to the Gnossians, still extant ᵘ, in which he admonishes *Pinytus*, their bishop, not to impose as necessary the yoke of chastity or continence upon the brethren; but to consider the infirmity which is in most men; which supposes that such a yoke was attempted to be laid. *Athenagoras*, in the second century, seems to speak too highly of celibacy; " you will find many of us, says he ʷ,
" of both sexes, who are become old and are unmarried, in hope of having more
" communion with God." And a little after, he speaks severely against second marriages, condemning them as adultery, and as a transgression of the law of God. In the third century, not only second marriages were spoken against by *Tertullian, Origen*, and *Cyprian*, but marriage itself was slightly spoken of, and
continence

---
ⁿ Theodori Lactor. Hist. Eccl. l. 2. p. 566.   º Contr. Hæres hær. 30.
ᵖ Ibid. l. 1. hær. 23. Irenæus adv. hær. l. 1. c. 22.   ᵠ Theodoret Hæret. Fab. fab. 4.
ʳ Epiphan. hær. 45. vid. Origen. in Rom. l. 10. fol. 216. 2.
ˢ Tertullian adv. Marcion. l. 1. c. 29, 30 & de præscript. hæret. c. 33.
ᵗ Irenæus l. 1. c. 31. Clement. Stromat. l. 3. p. 460, 465. Euseb. Eccl. hist. l. 1. c. 29. Epiphan. contr. hæref. l 1. hær. 46.   ᵘ Apud Euseb. Eccl. hist. l. 4. c. 23.
ʷ Legat. pro christian. p. 37.

continence, celibacy and virginity, were highly extolled. *Tertullian* says [x], "he preferred continence and virginity to marriage, though not forbid, but gave the preference to a fuller holiness." *Origen* calls virginity the work of perfection [y]; and *Cyprian* commends chastity (or the single life) as a state of angelic quality [z], and "virginity, he says [a], equals itself to angels; yea, if ye diligently examine it, it exceeds, while it strives with the flesh, it carries off a victory against nature, which angels have not:" and again [b], "though marriage is good and instituted by God, yet continence is better, and virginity more excellent, which neither necessity nor command compel to, but the choice of perfection persuades to it." I have observed already how the monastic life, celibacy and virginity, were in great vogue in the fourth century; in the former part of which, the council of *Nice* was held, in which it was moved by some bishops, that those who were married before they were in holy orders, should not cohabit with their wives; upon which *Paphnutius*, a confessor, rose up and vehemently opposed it, as putting an heavy burden upon them; alledging, that all had not such strict continence, that marriage was honourable, and that to make such a rule might be an occasion of scandal to them and to their wives; and that it was sufficient to observe the *antient tradition* of the church, that those who came into holy orders unmarried, should not marry afterwards; but that those who were married before, should not be separated from their wives; to which the synod assented [c]: but then it should be observed, that it had been an *antient tradition* that men in holy orders should not marry, if not married before they came into them. *Athanasius*, in the same century, says [d] many things in praise of virginity and continence, "O virginity, never failing opulence: O virginity, a never fading crown. O virginity, the temple of God and the dwelling-place of the holy Spirit. O virginity, a precious pearl, to many inconspicuous, and found by a few only. O continence, hated by many, but known and respected by thy worthy ones: O continence, which makes death and hell to flee, and which is possessed by immortality; O continence, the joy of the prophets, and the boast of the apostles: O continence, the life of angels, and the crown of saints; blessed is he that retaineth thee." *Jerom* has many things in his writings, too numerous to transcribe, in favour of virginity and celibacy, and to the discouragement of marriage. And *Austin* [e], though he in some places speaks well of marriage, yet he was of the mind, that virgins devoted to holiness have more merit with God than believers who are married; opposing *Jovinian*, who denied it. It is easy to observe, how much these

---

* Adv. Marcion. l. 5. c. 15.     y In Roman l. 10.     z De singular cleric. p. 532.
a De bono pudicitiæ. p. 419.     b De nativitate Christ. p. 448.
c Socrat. Eccl. Hist. l. 1. c. 11. Sozomen. ibid. l. 1. c. 23.     d De virginitate in fine.
e De peccat. merit. l. 3. c. 7.

these notions got ground, and monkery obtained, and was established in the fifth and sixth centuries before the man of sin was at his heighth.

3. Another popish tenet, foretold by the apostle *Paul* as a part of the apostasy which would hereafter come on, is *abstaining from meats*, 1 Tim. iv. 3. and observing fasts, such as the *Quadragesima* or *Lent*, &c. and which quickly took place: the abovementioned antient hereticks, the Saturnalians, Ebionites, Gnostics, Marcionites, and Encratites, who were against marriage, were also for abstinence from meats; as appears from *Irenæus, Clemens Alexandrinus, Tertullian, Origen, Eusebius, Epiphanius,* and *Theodoret,* in the places before referred to. The Gnosticks observed the fourth and fifth days of the week as fast days; and who knew, as *Clemens* of *Alexandria* says [f], the enigmatical meaning of them, the one being called the day of *Mercury*; and the other the day of *Venus*; and the Montanists are said to be the first that instituted laws concerning fasting, and who laid the foundation for many antichristian practices. *Quadragesima,* or *Lent,* and fasting on Wednesdays and Fridays, very early obtained in the church. The former was differently observed by the antients. *Irenæus,* in the second century, says [g], there was a dispute about Easter day, and of the manner of the fast itself, that is, which was before it; some thought they must fast one day, others two, others more, some forty hours, reckoning a night and day for a day, and this difference was not in this present age, but long before. *Socrates* relates [h], that the fast before Easter was differently kept; they at *Rome* fasted three weeks before it, excepting the sabbath, (saturday) and the Lord's day; and they in *Illyria* and in all *Greece* and in *Alexandria,* fasted six weeks before it; and that they called Quadragesima. Others began the fast seven weeks before Easter, and fasted three weeks only, and but five days in a week, nevertheless they called this Quadragesima; but, says the historian, to me it seems wonderful that they should disagree about the number of days, and yet call it by the same name: and to the same purpose *Sozomen* [i] says, "that Quadragesima, in which the people "fast, some count it six weeks, as the Illyrians and the western nations, all *Ly-* "*bia* and *Egypt,* with *Palestine*; some seven, as at *Constantinople,* and in all the "provinces round about unto *Phænicia*; some, out of these six or seven weeks, "fast three weeks by intervals; others only three weeks together before the "feast; some only two, as the Montanists." And *Socrates* the historian relates [k], that "the antients were not only found to differ about the number of days on "which they fasted, but about the food also they abstained from; some abstained "from animals entirely, others of animals only eat fish, some with fishes eat "fowl also, because they are of the water, according to *Moses*; some abstained
"from

[f] Stromat. l 7. p. 744.  [g] Apud Euseb. Eccl. Hist. l. 5. c. 24.
[h] Eccl Hist. l. 5. c. 22.  [i] Eccl. hist. l. 7. c. 19.  [k] Eccl. hist. l. 5. c. 22.

"from fruits of trees, and from eggs; some eat-bread only, and others not
"that." And *Epiphanius* observes [l], that the customs of the church were various, "some abstained from all flesh, beasts, fowls and fishes, and from eggs
"and cheese; some from beasts only, but eat fowls and the rest; some abstained
"from fowls and used eggs and fishes; others did not eat eggs; and others fishes
"only; some abstained from fishes, but eat cheese; others did not make use of
"cheese; others, moreover, abstained from bread; and others abstained from the
"hard fruits of trees, and from nuts, and from things boiled." Wednesdays and
Fridays were kept as fast-days in *Tertullian*'s time, by the catholics, whom he calls
Psychici [m], he being himself then a Montanist. And *Origen* [n] speaks of those
days, and of Lent, as solemn fasts in his time. The canons, commonly called
the *canons of the apostles*, were, according to bishop *Beveridge* [o], collected before
the end of the third century, and in them is one which runs thus, can. 60. "If
"any bishop, or presbyter, or deacon, or reader, or singer, does not fast on
"the holy Quadragesima of Easter, nor on the fourth day (of the week), nor on
"the preparation (to the sabbath, Saturday, which preparation was on Friday),
"except he is hindered through bodily weakness, let him be deposed; if a lay-
"man, let him be separated." In the fourth century, *Jerom* speaks of keeping
Lent as an apostolical tradition; "We fast one Quadragesima, according to the
"tradition of the apostles, in the whole year, at the time agreeable to us; they
"(the Montanists) make three Quadragesimas in a year, as if three Saviours suf-
"fered [p]." And in another place [q], he says, "The Lord himself, the true *Jonah*,
"being sent to preach the gospel, fasted forty days, and leaving us an inheritance
"of fasting, prepared our souls for the eating of his body under this number."
And elsewhere [r] he observes, "should any say, if it is not lawful to observe days
"and months and times and years, we must be guilty of a like crime in observ-
"ing the fourth day of the week, the preparation, and the Lord's day, and the
"fast of Quadragesima, and the feast of Easter, and the joy of Pentecost."
To which he makes answer. *Austin* likewise not only mentions the fast of
forty days, but thus reasons for it [s]: "The Quadragesima of fasts has indeed au-
"thority both in the antient books (the old testament,) from the fastings of *Moses*
"and *Elias*; and out of the gospel, because the Lord fasted so many days; shew-
"ing that the gospel does not dissent from the law and the prophets." And a
little after, "In what part of the year could the observation of the Quadrage-
"sima be fixed more fitly, than near and contiguous to the passion of the Lord?"
*Ambrose*, in the same century, has these words, "It is good at all times to fast,
"but

[l] Compend. de fide prope finem.  [m] De Jejun. c.2.14.  [n] Homil. 10. in Levit. fol. 81.4.
[o] In ibid. l. 1. c. 2. f. 7.  [p] Epist. ad Marcellam, adv. Montanist. tom. 2. fol. 44. B.
[q] Comment. in Jonam. fol. 57. M. tom. 6.  [r] Comment. in Gala: 4. fol 79. A. tom. 9.
[s] Ep. 86. & Ep. 119. c. 15.

"but it is better to faft with Chrift in Quadragefima (or Lent); for this Quadra-
"gefima the Lord has confecrated to us by his own fafting." And in another
place, "The Lord has fo ordained, that as in his paffion, and the faft of Quadra-
"gefima, we fhould forrow; fo in his refurrection, and in the feaft of Quinqua-
"gefima, (or Pentecoft,) we fhould rejoice [t]."

4. Popifh feftivals were obferved very early, long before the Pope of *Rome*
arrived to the height of his ambition. The feaft of Eafter was kept in the fecond
century, as the controverfy between *Anicetus* and *Polycarp*, and between *Victor*
and the Afiatic churches, fhews; yea in the fifth century, if *Polycrates* [u] is to
be credited, who fays, that "*Philip* the apoftle who died at *Hierapolis*, and *John*
"at *Ephefus*, *Polycarp* bifhop of *Smyrna*, *Thrafeas* of *Eumenia*, *Sagaris*, who
"died at *Laodicea*, *Papyrius* and *Melito*, all kept Eafter on the 14th day of the
"month; and the bifhops of *Rome*, before *Victor*, as well as he, kept it on the
"Lord's day following; fo *Anicetus*, *Pius*, *Hyginus*, *Telefphorus*, *Xyftus* and
"*Soter*." And fo did *Irenæus* in *France*; and thus it continued to be obferved
by the order of *Conftantine* [w]. The vigils of the paffover, or Eafter-eve, were
very early obferved; *Eufebius* [x] makes mention thereof as in the times of *Narciffus*,
patriarch of *Jerufa'em*, in the fecond century; and *Tertullian* [y] fpeaks of the
whole night preceding Eafter-day, as very folemn; and *Auftin*, in the fourth
century, mentions Eafter-eve [z] as folemn likewife. Pentecoft was obferved as
early as Eafter, and is fpoken of along with it by *Tertullian* [a], by *Origen* [b], and by
*Jerom* [c]; and *Ambrofe* fays [d], "Let us rejoice on this holy day as at Eafter; on
"both days there is the fame and the like folemnity; at Eafter all the Gentiles
"ufed to be baptized, and at Pentecoft the apoftles were baptized," that is,
with the holy Ghoft.

Chriftmas-day, or Chrift's birth-day, was celebrated in the fecond century, on
the 8th of the calends of *January*; as appears from the pafchal epiftle of *Theophilus* [e]. In the times of *Dioclefian*, and before the council at *Nice*, *Anthimas*,
bifhop of *Nicomedia*, with fome thoufands, were burnt, by fire being fet to the
place where they were affembled to keep the feaft of Chrift's birth day [f]. *Bafil*,
in the fourth century, has a fermon upon it, in which he calls it *Theophania*, the
appearance of God, and fays, "Let us celebrate the folemnities of a faved world,
"the birth day of mankind." *Ambrofe* has feveral fermons upon it; and in one
of them, ferm. 10. fays, "the vulgar ufed to call the Lord's birth-day the new
"fun: and fo *Chryfoftom* in the fifth century.

The

---

t Serm. 31. & ferm. 60 tom. 5.  u Apud Eufeb. Eccl. Hift. l. 5. c. 4.
w Socrat. Eccl. Hift l. 5. c. 22.  x Eccl. Hift. l. 6. c. 9. fee c. 34.
y Ad uxor. l. 2. c. 4.  z Ep. 19. c. 2.  a Coron. mil. c. 3.
b Contr. Celf. l. 8. p. 392.  c Comment. in Gal. 4. fol. 79. A.
d Serm. 60. p. 82. tom. 5.  e Vid. Magdeburg. Centuriat. cent. 2. p. 89, 90.
f Nicephor. l. 7. c. 6. apud Selden of the birth-day of our Saviour, L 4. p. 33.

The feaſt of the Annunciation of the virgin *Mary* was obſerved by the antients. *Gregory* of *Neocæſarea*, called *Thaumaturgus*, in the third century, has three ſermons on the annunciation, and calls it a feſtival. It is mentioned by [g] *Athanaſius* in the fourth century, concerning which he ſays, "This is one of the feaſts of the Lord, and is quite venerable; ſo that according to the order of things which are preached in the goſpel of Chriſt, it ought to be accounted an holy day, ſince in it we treat concerning the deſcent of the Son of God from heaven." Feaſts kept in memory of the martyrs, we read of ſtill more early. *Origen*, in the latter end of the ſecond century, ſays [h], "We do memory to the ſaints, our parents and friends, who die in the faith;—we celebrate the religious with the prieſts, calling together the faithful with the clergy, inviting the needy and the poor, the fatherleſs and the widow, filling them with food, that our feſtivals may be done to the memory of reſt to the deceaſed, whoſe memory we celebrate." So *Tertullian*, in the beginning of the third century, affirms [i], "We make oblations for the dead, and for their anniverſary birth-days." And *Cyprian*, in the middle of it, ſays of ſome dead [k], "The days on which they depart are regiſtered by us, that we may celebrate their memories among the memories of the martyrs." And even in a ſynod [l] in his time, notice is taken of ſacrifices and offerings made for perſons after death." In the fourth century it was uſual in all churches to obſerve them. *Euſebius* [m] relates, that by the order of *Conſtantine*, governors of provinces, and thoſe under them, not only obſerved the Lord's day, but honoured the feaſt-days of the martyrs; alſo the eccleſiaſtical feſtivities. *Sozomen* reports [n], that the Alexandrians kept with great pomp a feaſt on the day that *Peter* their biſhop was martyred; and *Theodoret* [o], that the church at *Antioch* kept an annual feaſt to the honour of the martyrs *Juventinus* and *Maximinus*. *Ambroſe* has a ſermon for the ſaints throughout the year, and makes mention of the feaſts of the apoſtles *Peter* and *Paul* [p]; and in one place he ſays [q], "We forget the birth-days of the dead, but the day on which they die we renew with great ſolemnity;" and again, "Whoſe life we know not, their deaths we celebrate." And *Jerom* obſerves [r], that according to the variety of countries, different times are appointed in honour of the martyrs.

In the fourth century the relicks of the martyrs came much in vogue. *Sozomen* [s] makes mention of the relicks of many ſaints and martyrs being found, and removed, and laid up with great honour and veneration. And ſo *Ambroſe* [t], of the bodies of St *Gervaſius* and *Proteſius*, in a letter to his ſiſter *Marcellina*, in which

---

[g] De ſanctiſſima Dei para, p 810.    [h] Tract. 3. in Job fol 39. 3.    [i] De Coron. mil. c. 3.
[k] Ep. 37. p. 32.    [l] Concil. Carthag. cit. in Epiſt. 66.    [m] De vita Conſtantin l. 4. c. 23.
[n] Eccl. Hiſt. l. 2. c. 17.    [o] Eccl. Hiſt. l. 3. c. 15.    [p] Serm. 1. p. 129. tom. 5.
[q] De fide Reſurrect. p. 322, 327.    [r] Comment. in Gal. 4. fol. 79. A.
[s] Eccl. Hiſt. l. 2. 13. & 3. 14. & 59. & 7. 30.    [t] Epiſt. l. 7. ep 54.

which he gives an account of the finding and tranflation of them, and miracles done; and concludes, "Let us lay up the holy relicks, and carry them into "temples worthy of them, and celebrate the whole day with true devotion." In the fixth century, part of the wood of the crofs on which Chrift was crucified was found, and the relicks of the martyr *Sergius*, as *Evagrius* relates ᵗ. And in the fourth and following centuries, temples were dedicated to the faints, and images placed in them, with wax candles and lamps burning.

5. The popifh notions of a *Limbus patrum*, of purgatory, and praying for the dead, were embraced long before the pope of *Rome* was declared an univerfal bifhop. *Clemens* of *Alexandria*, in the fecond century, had a notion, that before Chrift came none were faved, but thofe that lived pioufly were in hell; and Chrift, when he came, went thither, and preached to them, and fo did his apoftles; and thereby they were converted and faved ᵘ; and of the place of the faints after death, *Tertullian* feems to have fuch a notion, that they were not in heavenly blifs; "the bofom of *Abraham*, he fays ʷ, is not celeftial, yet higher than hell; "and in the mean while affords refrefhment to the fouls of the righteous, until "the confummation of all things at the refurrection." And a little after he fays, "The bofom of *Abraham* is fome temporal receptacle of believing fouls." Purgatory was the opinion of *Origen* in the third century; he was the firft, as *Theophilus Gale* fays ˣ, that introduced purgatory from the Platonic fchool at *Alexandria* into the church of God, and gave a great advance to the whole fyftem of papifm or antichriftianifm. "I think, fays he ʸ, the faints, when they depart out of "this life, remain in fome place the divine fcripture calls paradife; and as in "fome place of learning, an *auditorium*, if I may fo fay, or a fchool of fouls, in "which they may be taught of all thofe things they have feen on earth." And in fome places he gives plain hints of purgatory; "it is certain, fays he ᶻ, there "remains a fire, which is prepared for finners, and we fhall come to that fire, "in which the fire will prove every one's work, what it is; and as I think we "muft all come to the fire, even if any one is a *Paul* or a *Peter*, yet he muft come "to the fire; but fuch fhall hear, *though thou poffeth through the fire, the flame* "*shall not burn thee*; but if any one, like me, is a finner, he fhall come indeed "to the fire, as *Peter* and *Paul*, but he fhall not fo pafs through as *Peter* and "*Paul*." In another place he fays ᵃ, "Whofe fin is fuch that it is neither for- "given in the prefent world, nor in that to come; he paffes on in his unclean- "nefs one and another week, and at the beginning of the third week he is purg- "ed from his uncleannefs." And in another work of his ᵇ, he has thefe words,
"To

---

ᵗ Eccl. Hift. l.4. c. 26, 28.    ᵘ Stromat. l.6. p. 637, 638.    ʷ Adv. Marcion, l.4. c.34.
ˣ Court of the Gentiles, part 3. B. 2. ch. 1. p. 134, 135, 221.    De principiis, l. 2. prope finem.    ᶻ Homil. 3. in Pf. 36. fol. 45. C.    ᵃ Homil. 8. in Levit. fol. 75. C.
ᵇ Contr. Celfum, l. 5. p. 241.

"To every one of these who have need of punishment by this fire, and together
also of healing, it burns, but does not burn them out, who have no matter
to be consumed by fire; but it burns and burns them out, who build on a
building of actions, words and thoughts, figuratively called *wood, hay,* and
*stubble.*" And he has various hints of this kind in other parts of his writings.
*Lactantius,* in the fourth century, says [b], "When God shall judge the righteous,
he shall also try them by fire: them whose sins, either in weight or in number,
have prevailed, they shall be touched by the fire, and shall be burnt; but
those whose righteousness and virtue are in full maturity, they shall not perceive the fire." And a little after, "Let no one think, that souls are immediately judged; after death they are all detained in one common prison, until
the time comes, that the great judge shall make trial of the merits of men."
*Jerom* expresses his faith in this point, thus [c]; "As we believe the eternal tor-
ments of the devil, and of all deniers and ungodly persons; so we believe a
moderate sentence of the judge, mixed with clemency, on sinners and ungodly persons, and yet christians, whose works are to be proved and purged
by fire." *Epiphanius,* in the same century, delivers the faith of christians in
this manner [d], "We believe that Christ came to give pardon to those who of
old knew him, and did not stray from his deity, though for errors were detained in hell; to them who were then in the world, by repentance; to them
that were in hell, by mercy and salvation." And he was of opinion, that
prayers made for the dead profited them, though they did not cut off all fault [e]
And of the same opinion was *Austin* [f], who says, "It is not to be denied, that
the souls of the dead are relieved by the piety of the living; since for them
the sacrifice of the mediator is offered, or alms are made in the church; but
these are profitable to them, who when they lived merited, that they might
be profitable to them afterwards." More of this may be read in another tract [g]
of his. Elsewhere he says [h], "In the old saints the holy Spirit was not so, as
he is now in believers; because when they went out of the world, they were
in hell, and it is incongruous that he who goes from hence, having the Spirit
of God, should be held in hell." And he seems in one place [i], to grant a purgatory; "That some such thing is done after this life, is not incredible; and
whether it is so, may be enquired; that some believers are either found or hid
by a certain purgatory-fire, how much the more or less they have loved perishing goods, so much the slower or sooner they are saved." *Gregory Nyssene.* says
of children dying in infancy [k], "What shall we think of such, who so die? shall
"the

---
[b] De divino præmio, l. 7. c. 21.     [c] Comment in Esaiam, l. 18 in fine.
[d] Contr. Hæres l. 1. hær. 46.    [e] Ibid. l. 3. hær. 75.    [f] Enchirid. ad Laurent. c 110.
[g] De cura pro mortuis.    [h] Quæstiones vet. & nov. Test. qu. 123.    [i] Enchirid. c. 69.
De iis qui præmature abrup. p 754. vol. 2.

"the soul see the judge? shall it be presented with others before the tribunal?
"shall it undergo the judgment of those who have lived? shall it receive a re-
"ward according to merit? or be purged with fire according to the words of
"the gospel? or be refreshed with the dew of blessing?" *Boetius*, in the sixth
century, is express for purgatory; his words are, "Are there no punishments
"after you leave the body dead? The answer is, yea and great ones truly; some
"are exercised, I think, with a severe punishment, and others with a mild pur-
"gatory [k]." *Gregory* I. defended the opinion of purgatory in the same century.

6. The popish notion of transubstantiation had its rise from the old hereticks, and was cherished and strengthened by the unguarded expressions and erroneous sentiments of the ancient fathers, even before the man of sin arrived to his manhood. *Mark*, the heretick, in the second century, would have it thought that he changed the wine into blood by invocation upon it [l], just as a popish priest would be thought by pronouncing some words to change the bread into the body, and the wine into the blood of Christ. *Irenæus* [m], in the same century, has an expression which has too favourable an aspect on this very absurd notion; "when
"the cup mixt, and the bread broken, perceive the word of God, they become the
"eucharist of the blood and body of Christ." In the third century, the phrases of offering the sacrifice of Christ, and of sanctifying the cup by the priest, were used; as by *Tertullian* [n], who calls the administration of the supper, offering the sacrifice; and by *Cyprian* [o], who speaks of the Lord's sacrifice being celebrated by a lawful sanctification, and of the priest's sanctifying the cup; and says, that
"the priest officiates in the room of Christ, and imitates that which Christ did,
"and then offers up a true and full sacrifice in the church to God the Father."
In the fourth century several unguarded expressions were used, as by *Athanasius* [p], that there was nothing of the flesh and blood of Christ to be found in the world, but what was daily spiritually made by the hands of priests upon the altar; and by *Nazianzen* [q], who speaks of some defiling the altars with blood, which have their name from the most pure and *unbloody sacrifice:* and *Ambrose* speaks often of celebrating mass and offering the sacrifice; and he composed some prayers preparatory to it, and he produces examples to prove, that "not that in which
"nature has formed, but which the blessing hath consecrated, and the great-
"er is the force of blessing than of nature, because nature itself is *changed* by
"the blessing." And after many instances of the miracles in *Egypt*, he observes [r], that, "if human blessing could do so much, what shall we say of the divine con-
"secration itself, where the words of the Lord the Saviour operate?" And a

little

[k] De Consolat. Philosoph. l. 4. p. 101.    [l] Irenæus adv. Hæres. l. 1. c. 9. Epiphan. contr. hæref. l. 1. hær. 34.    [m] Adv. Hæref. l. 5. c. 2.    [n] De cultu fœmin. l. 2. c. 11.    [o] Epist. 63. 148. 149.    [p] De imagine Christi. c. 7.    [q] Orat. 4. p. 126.    [r] De initiandis, c. 9.

little after, he has thefe words "*this is my body*; before the bleffing of the hea-
"venly words the fpecies is named, after the confecration, the body of Chrift
"is fignified, he calls it his *own blood*. Before the confecration another thing
"is faid, after the confecration it is called *blood*." *Cyril* of *Jerufalem* fays [t],
"The bread and the wine of the eucharift, before the holy invocation of the
"Trinity, are mere bread and wine; but when the invocation is made, the bread
"becomes the body of Chrift, and the wine the blood of Chrift." *Gregory Nyffen*
fays [‡], "The bread is made the body of Chrift by facrification; the bread a little
"before was common bread, but when the myftery has made it holy, it is *made*
"and called the body of Chrift; fo the myftical oil; fo the wine, though of
"fmall worth before the bleffing, after the fanctification of the Spirit, both of
"them work differently." And elfewhere [t], he fays, "I rightly believe that
"the bread fanctified by the word of God, μετατοιεῖσθαι, is *tranfmuted* into the
"body of God the Word; for bread was that body, potentially it was fanctified
"by the indwelling of the Word, which tabernacled in the flefh; thence therefore
"the bread tranfmuted in that body, paffes into a divine power, by the fame
"now alfo became equal.—The bread is immediately tranfmuted by the Word
"into the body, as it is faid by the Word, *This is my body*." *Chryfoftom*, in the
fifth century, feems to ftrengthen the doctrine of tranfubftantiation, when he
fays [u], "Do you fee the bread? do you fee the wine? do they go as the reft of
"the food into the privy? God forbid, that thou fhouldft fo think; for as if
"wax put to the fire is affimilated to it, nothing of the fubftance remains;
"fo likewife here think that the myfteries are confumed in the fubftance of the
"body." In the fixth century, *Gregory* I. fays, it appears that they called the Lord's
fupper a *viaticum*; and even in the fourth century, it ufed to be given to dying
perfons as fuch. *Honoratus*, prieft of *Verceil*, gave it to St *Ambrofe*, who as
foon as he received it died, carrying with him the good *viaticum*, as *Paulinus*
in his life relates. And *Ambrofe* himfelf fays [w], that in his time, travellers and
failors ufed to carry it with them. Yea, even in the third century, it ufed to be
fent to thofe who were hindered by ficknefs from partaking of it; there is even
an inftance of its being fent by a boy, and put into the mouth of a dying man,
upon which he expired [x].

The firft inftance of corruption in baptifm, as to the form of it, and alfo as
to the mode of it, was made by *Mark*, the heretick, and his followers; who
made a mixture of oil and water, and poured it on the head [y]. And the next inftance is in *Novatus*, who received baptifm on a fick bed by perfufion (as the
*Clinici* alfo did), if he might be faid to receive it, as *Cornelius*, the then bifhop of
Rome

---

[x] Cateches. myftagog. 1. f. 4.  
[t] Catechet orat. c 37 p. 536. vol. 2.  
[x] Eufeb. Eccl. Hift. l. 6. c. 44.  
[t] In baptifm. Chrifti. vol. 2 p 802.  
[u] De Eucharistia.  
[y] Irenæus adv. Hæref. l. 1. c. 18.  
[w] De obitu fatyr. fratris.

Rome obferves [\*]; and when he recovered, and got to be made a prefbyter, all the clergy and many of the people, judged it was not lawful, that fuch an one, who was baptized in that manner, fhould be admitted among the clergy; nor could fuch an one be a prefbyter, according to the 10th canon of the council of *Neocæfarea*. An innovation with refpect to the fubjects began to be made in the third century, in the African churches, and prevailed much in the fourth, through the zeal of *Auftin* in favour of original fin, and for the falvation of infants, which he thought could not be faved without it. This ufe of chrifm, exorcifm, figning with the fign of the crofs, and other corruptions early introduced, have been obferved in fome former treatifes of mine [♦]. Thus we fee that the principal things of which the popifh hierarchy confifts, and the chief principles and practices which are now reckoned popifh ones, were held and maintained before the popes of *Rome* arrived to the full power they had long been aiming at; and which together make up what we call POPERY.

## THE COROLLARY

FROM all this is, That fince it can be no objection to the doctrine of invocation of angels and faints departed, being called a popifh doctrine; nor to the prohibition of marriage, and abftaining from meats, and keeping divers fafts and feftivals, being called parts of popery; nor to the doctrines of purgatory and tranfubftantiation being popifh ones, though they were feverally broached and embraced ages before the pope of *Rome* was declared univerfal Bifhop; it can be no objection to INFANT-BAPTISM being called a part and branch of popery, though it was introduced into the churches in the *third* and *fourth* centuries, and fo before the Roman antichrift arrived to his higheft pitch of grandeur; it being a tenet held by the Papifts, as founded upon the tradition of the church; and being no more agreeable to the word of God, than the other above tenets held by them are. Truth indeed is moft ancient; but error follows clofely at its heels, and is nearly as antient; fo that high pretenfions to antiquity in matters of faith and worfhip, are no otherwife to be regarded, but as they have the concurrent evidence and teftimony of the facred fcriptures; they only can be trufted to with fafety.

[\*] Apud Eufeb. ut fupra, c. 43.
[♦] The argument from apoftolical tradition, &c. and Infant-baptifm a part and pillar of Popery.

DYING

# DYING THOUGHTS:

CONSISTING OF

## A Few UNFINISHED HINTS,

Written by Dr GILL,

A little before his DECEASE.

THE use our Lord makes of the doctrine of death, is, *Matt.* xxiv. 44. *Therefore be ye also ready, for in such hour as ye think not, the Son of man cometh*: Either to judgment, or by death: and happy they, who, with the wise virgins, are ready to go in to the marriage-chamber, and partake of the marriage-supper, *Matt.* xxv. 10. and it is one great business of the gospel ministry, under the influence of the Spirit and grace of God, *to make ready a people prepared for the Lord*, Luke i. 17. that is, the elect of God, whom he has reserved for himself. But the great question is, wherein lies this readiness and preparation for death and eternity? and this may be considered,

FIRST, *Negatively*, what it is not. Many and fatal are the mistakes of persons about it; some placing it in one thing, and some in another.

(1.) Some think it is a *well-spent life*; and that if a man can look back on such a life, he is ready for death, come when it may. But let us consider what this well-spent life is. The life of the apostle *Paul* was undoubtedly a life as wellspent, as, perhaps, any that can be mentioned among men. Before conversion, his life was irreproachable; as to external morality, he lived in all good conscience before men; after conversion, his life was devoted to the service of Christ and his gospel; his gladness and ambition were, to spend and be spent, wherever he came, for the good of immortal souls; he travelled much, endured great hardships, and laboured more than the rest of the apostles; which he imputes not to his own goodness, industry and power, but to the grace of God. And when the time of his departure was at hand, as it was when he wrote his epistle to the Philippians, being then a prisoner at *Rome*; what did he seek after, or judge to be his readiness for another world? not his well-spent life: no; he desired to be *found in* CHRIST, *not having his own righteousness*, in which must be included his well-spent life, and which indeed was the main of it; but *the righteousness which is of God by faith*, even the righteousness of Christ. He *forgot* the things which were *behind*; his labours, services and sufferings for Christ, all his attainments and usefulness; and *pressed forward*, not in a view of his well-spent life, but having his eye on the *mark*, Christ and his righteousness, *for the prize of the high calling of God* in him, Phil. iii. 9—13, 14. The life of a common believer is a well-spent life, in comparison of others; he lives by faith on Christ, and gives him the glory of his salvation; and, from a principle of love to him, walks in all his commandments and ordinances, and is very desirous of living a life of holiness, and of spiritual and heavenly-mindedness, and does so live in some measure. But when the believer comes to look back on his past life of faith and holiness, what *deficiencies* and *imperfections* in his faith! what unbelief in him, at such and such a time will he observe! what tarnishes in his life and walk! and how few the minutes were in which he was spiritual and heavenly-minded! and how frequently and long was such a frame interrupted with carnal and sensual lusts! The saint, before his conversion, is as other men, being born in sin, and living in it: after conversion, prone to backsliding; even in all things he offends, and sins in his most solemn and religious services. He must therefore betray great ignorance of himself, who flatters himself, or suffers himself to be flattered, with a reflection on a well-spent life, as his readiness and preparation for death and another world.

(2.) Others imagine, because they have *done no injury* to any man's person and property, nay, have *done justice* between man and man, and have *paid* every man his own, they are ready for death come when it may. These are all very good things, and ought to be done; for it is written, *owe no man any thing*: but then they are no other than what such a man would chuse to have done to himself, and which he ought to do to others; and are no other than what honour, conscience, and the laws of God and man oblige to; and where is the *merit* of all this? And what obligation does this lay upon God? As *Elihu* argues, Job xxxv. 7, 8. *If thou be righteous, what givest thou him? or what receiveth he of thine hand? Thy wickedness may hurt a man, as thou art,* by injuring his person or property; *and thy righteousness may profit the Son of man,* by fair trade and paying just debts; but what profit is this to God? And, perhaps, after all, such a man has never thought about the payment of his debts to God, and how THEY must be paid, when he owes ten thousand talents, and has nothing to pay, nor to make a composition with. How can he think of appearing

before

## A FEW UNFINISHED HINTS.

before his great creditor, with such a charge and load of debts upon him? may he not justly fear, that he will order him to prison, there to lie, until the uttermost farthing is paid? The great concern should be, to know whether Christ is his surety, and has paid his debts for him, cancelled the bond, and blotted out the hand-writing against him, and so his account with God stands clear and fair. This is the best preparation for death and eternity.

(3.) Others think, that by *giving alms to the poor*, they get a readiness for death. *To do good and to communicate*, to do acts of beneficence from a right principle, are sacrifices with which God is well pleased; but these may be done only to be seen of men, and get applause from men; and such have their reward in this world, but not in another. A man may give all his goods to the poor, and yet not have charity, or true grace, and so be unfit to die. And very preposterous and monstrously absurd it is, in some persons, who choose to give little away in their lifetime, and leave large estates for charitable uses after their death, as if what was to be done *after* death could be a *preparation* for it: than which nothing can be more ridiculous.

(4.) Some place readiness for death in the *mercy of God*; imploring that in their last moments: and yet they cannot be sure they shall have time even to say, " Lord have mercy on us." There is mercy with God, and it is a ground of hope; but then it must be applied for by such who are sensible of their sins, confess them, forsake them, and turn to the Lord; such find mercy. And besides, mercy is only had through Christ. God, out of Christ, is a consuming fire; a sinner should go to God through Christ for mercy, saying, as the publican did, *God be merciful*, or propitious, *to me a sinner*; that is, through the propitiatory sacrifice of his Son, *Luke* xviii. 13.

(5.) Others flatter themselves that they have *made their peace with God*, and so are prepared for death whenever it comes. And yet these persons, perhaps, never saw the flaming sword of justice brandished against sin, nor the heavens opened, and wrath of God revealed from thence against all ungodliness of men; nor never heard the vollies of curses from a righteous law, which pronounces every man *cursed*, that continues not in all things written in it do them; and were never truly acquainted with what is required to be done in order to make peace, as satisfying justice by fulfilling the law, through obeying its precepts and bearing its penalty, with their own inability to do these things: they imagine, that their own humiliation, repentance, and imperfect obedience, are to make peace for them. They should know, that *Christ* ONLY *is the peace-maker*; and their concern should be to know that *he* HAS *made peace* for them by the blood of his cross, and to lay hold upon him as such, *Isai.* xxvii. 5.

(6.) Others make their readiness for death to lie in a little negative holiness, and thank God, as the Pharisee did, that they are not as other men are; *not guilty* of such gross and flagitious crimes as some are; they have not been guilty of *murder, adultery, theft,* and such like sins as others have. But this is a very slender preparation for death; publicans and harlots, repenting and believing, go into the kingdom of heaven before such.

(7.) Others, with greater plausibility, please themselves with a *profession of religion* they have made and held. They have constantly attended on hearing the word, have submitted to baptism, sat down at the Lord's table, and observed every duty of religion. But all this a man may do, and not be ready. He may have *a form of godliness,* without the *power* of it. Some who have heard Christ preach, or his ministers, have eat and drank in his presence, will be bid to depart from him, as not known by him. In short,

(8.) *Not any external righteousness whatever* makes a man ready for death and eternity. For by it he is not justified before God, and by it he is not saved. Except he has *a* BETTER *righteousness,* he will never enter into the kingdom of heaven. And it should be our concern, with the apostle, to be *found in Christ,* and in *his* righteousness, and not in our *own,* which will leave us short of heaven and happiness.

SECONDLY, *Positively,* what that is, which constitutes a readiness and preparation for death; that which is certain, constant, and abiding, let a man's frames and circumstances be what they may; lies in the following things·

(1.) In *regeneration.* Without this, a man cannot see, nor enter into, the kingdom of heaven. It is by *the washing of regeneration* God saves men; and the life with which a man is then quickened, is connected with eternal life. The grace then implanted is *a well of living water, springing up* into a life that never dies. As soon as a man is born again, he is prepared for death, be his regeneration sooner or later, and from that moment always continues so.

(2.) In *sanctification,* or a work of grace and holiness, which takes place immediately upon regeneration; and without which no man shall see the Lord; but where this is begun, it shall be carried on, and be performed, until the day of Christ; and so furnishes us with a readiness for that day. This is that oil of grace, which the wise virgins had in the vessels of their hearts, besides lamps of profession; and so were ready when the bridegroom came.

(3.) The *righteousness of Christ* imputed, is a constant readiness for death and eternity. The church is said to *make herself ready*; which was done, by putting on *the fine linen clean and white,* the righteousness of Christ, which made her ready to meet him. Were it possible for a man to get into heaven, the marriage-chamber, without the nuptial robe, as it is not; he would be turned out, as unready and unfit, with, *friend, how camest thou in hither, not having a wedding*

*ding garment?* And he *speechless*, having nothing to alledge as a plea for his being there. Now such as are found in Christ, and cloathed with his righteousness, will be found, at death, neither *naked* nor *speechless*, but shall have a ready and an abundant entrance into Christ's kingdom and glory.

(4.) A *being washed in the blood of Christ*, and so clear from all guilt and charge of it, and condemnation by it, is a sure and lasting readiness for death. Christ's blood is a fountain opened to wash in; and it has such virtue in it, as to cleanse from *all sin whatever*, and leaves *none* behind; so that a person once washed or purged by it, is clear from it, and when death comes, shall immediately inherit the kingdom of God: which none shall, but those who are washed, sanctified, and justified.

(5.) Spiritual *knowledge of Christ*, and true *faith* in him, have eternal life connected with them inseparably; though not always clear, and unbeclouded, and in lively exercise, yet the principle itself always abides, and is never lost; and such who know in whom they have believed, are faithfully kept by him, to whom they have committed themselves, against the day of death and judgment.

There is another sort of readiness which is not always the same, and lies in the *frame* and posture of the soul, and which a saint is desirous of having when death comes, both for his own comfort and the glory of God; though he knows that his safety does not lie in it, and he wishes to be found in the lively exercise of faith, and hope, and love, and patience, and resignation to the will of God: to be awake, and not in a slumbering frame; but watching and on his guard against the enemy, and expecting his Lord's coming; to be frequently meditating on death, and making it familiar to himself, and so become free from the fear and dread of it; and to be in such a disposition of mind, as to be desirous of death, and willing to depart; and rather choosing it, and longing for it; saying, *why are his chariot-wheels so long in coming?* And to be so fearless of death, as to triumph over it, and say, *Death, where is thy sting! Grave, where is thy victory!* Or however, he wishes to be in a waiting posture when death comes, waiting for the hope of righteousness by faith, and looking for his Lord's coming, with his loins girt and his lamp burning; and *blessed indeed are those servants whom, when their Lord comes, he shall find so doing*, Luke xii. 35—37, 43.

II. There are several things which may serve to reconcile men to death, though it is so disagreeable to nature; as, 1. The necessity of death to free them from sin and sorrow, without which they will not be free. Whilst they are in this tabernacle they are burdened with sin, and groan under their burden; nor will they be eased till the tabernacle is dissolved, or pulled down by death. Whilst they are in this land, the Canaanites are in it, their inbred sins and corruptions,

ruptions, and these are *thorns in their sides, and pricks in their eyes;* and will continue such. But, when they have got through death into the better and heavenly country, there will be no pricking briar, nor grieving thorn, throughout the land. 2. Death is no other to saints, than going to their father's and Christ's father's house; where are many mansions provided, and where they shall enjoy the kingdom it is their father's good pleasure to give, and where they shall have his presence for evermore. 3. It is in order to be with Christ, which is infinitely preferable to being in this world, and where they shall be for ever with him and behold his glory. 4. Which, though of lesser consideration than the former, yet it has something in it to reconcile to death, that that will introduce them into the presence and company of pious relations and friends that are gone before, and died in Christ; so *David* took some satisfaction in this, that though his child was dead, and should not return to him, yet he should go to that, 2 *Sam.* xii. 23. 5. Death is the time of the Lord's in-gathering of his people to himself; then it is he comes into his garden, and gathers his lilies, and this and the other flower, to put into his bosom. Heaven is his garner, into which he gathers his wheat; and this is done at death. Now it is, that he *makes up his jewels,* his full number of them, one by one, and will lose none. 6. The death of the saints is precious in the sight of God, *Psal.* cxv. 16. and if it is precious to him, they should not shrink at it themselves.

*Thirdly,* Death is very terrible to nature, and to natural men. The philosopher calls it, *the most terrible of all terribles* [a]. And the wise man, when he suggests what is most grievous, distressing, and intolerable, says, " What is *more* " *bitter than death?*" Eccl. vii. 26. To Christless sinners, death is the king of terrors; and even some gracious persons *are, all their lifetime, through fear of death, subject to bondage*; but as formidable as it is, there are some things which may serve to fortify us against the fears of death: as, 1. That the *sting* of death is *taken away* by Christ; which is sin: and a very venomous sting it is; and death, thus armed, is to be feared. But, when its sting is taken out, it is not to be dreaded: any insect with a sting we are naturally afraid of, but if its sting is drawn, we have no fear of it, though it flies and buzzes about us; the believer may sing and say, *Death where is thy sting?* and be fearless of it. 2. It is a blessing and privilege to a believer, it is reckoned among his privileges, 1Cor. iii. 22. *they are blessed that die in the Lord;* and are more happy than the saints alive, because free from sin and sorrow, see *Rev.* xiv. 13. *Eccl.* iv. 2.
3. Death

[a] των φοβερων φοβερωτατον ὁ θανατος. Aristot. Ethic. l. 3. c. 9. and no wonder he should call it so, since he adds, according to his opinion, *it is the end of all things: and to one that is dead, there is neither good nor evil.* Such a notion of death, as being an extinction, must be terrible.

3. Death is but once, and foon over; the bitternefs of it is quickly paft, and will never be repeated; *it is appointed to men* ONCE *to die,* and no more. 4. The confideration of the refurrection from the dead, may yield comfort in the view of death; as it did to *Job,* ch. xix. 26, 27 the body, though a vile body as laid in the grave, *will be raifed, and fafhioned like to the* GLORIOUS *body of Chrift*. It will be raifed in *incorruption : this corruptible fhall put on incorruption*. It will be raifed in *glory,* like Chrift; it will be raifed in *power,* and be *durable,* and always remain in a ftate of immortality. It will be raifed a *fpiritual* body, and fo more fit for fpiritual fervices than ever, 1 *Cor.* xv. 42, 43. fo that the faints will be no loofers, but gainers, by death; and need not fear it. 5. Be it that death is an *enemy,* as it is contrary to nature; it is the *laft* enemy that fhall be deftroyed; and, when that is conquered, the victory will be compleat over every enemy, fin, fatan, the world, death and the grave, 1 *Cor.* xv. 26, 55, 57. - *Thanks, therefore, to God, who giveth us the victory through our Lord Jefus Chrift.*

F I N I S.

*Just Published*,

A

SCRIPTURAL CHECK

TO

SOCINIANISM:

OR,

The FIRST CHAPTER of S. JOHN's GOSPEL,

With Dr GILL's COMMENTARY on it.

To which is prefixed, by another Hand,

A PREFACE,

Recommended to the serious Consideration of the

Rev. Dr PRIESTLY.

---

JESUS CHRIST the true GOD and Eternal Life, 1 John v. 20.
Denying the only LORD GOD and our LORD JESUS CHRIST, Jude 4.

---

PRINTED FOR GEORGE KEITH, IN GRACECHURCH-STREET.

*N. B.* This is intended as a SPECIMEN of a NEW EDITION of the Author's COMMENTARY on the WHOLE BIBLE; containing a Double Version of the Sacred Text, the first by itself, the other with the several Translations and Paraphrases of the Original Versions, and large Explanations Critical, Historical, Doctrinal, and Practical; which hath been long desired, and is now ready for Publication, with his last Corrections and Improvements.

Lightning Source UK Ltd.
Milton Keynes UK
UKOW05f1824291116
288855UK00010B/145/P